organizational
behavior

key concepts, skills & best practices

third edition

organizational behavior

key concepts, skills & best practices

Angelo Kinicki

Robert Kreitner

*Both of
Arizona State University*

McGraw-Hill Irwin

Boston   Burr Ridge, IL   Dubuque, IA   Madison, WI   New York   San Francisco   St. Louis
Bangkok   Bogotá   Caracas   Kuala Lumpur   Lisbon   London   Madrid   Mexico City
Milan   Montreal   New Delhi   Santiago   Seoul   Singapore   Sydney   Taipei   Toronto

McGraw-Hill
Irwin

ORGANIZATIONAL BEHAVIOR: KEY CONCEPTS, SKILLS & BEST PRACTICES
Published by McGraw-Hill/Irwin, a business unit of The McGraw-Hill Companies, Inc., 1221 Avenue of the
Americas, New York, NY, 10020. Copyright © 2008 by The McGraw-Hill Companies, Inc. All rights
reserved. No part of this publication may be reproduced or distributed in any form or by any means, or
stored in a database or retrieval system, without the prior written consent of The McGraw-Hill Companies,
Inc., including, but not limited to, in any network or other electronic storage or transmission, or broadcast
for distance learning.

Some ancillaries, including electronic and print components, may not be available to customers outside the
United States.

Printed in China

This book is printed on acid-free paper.

4 5 6 7 8 9 0 SDB/SDB 0 9 8

ISBN: 978-0-07-340496-7
MHID: 0-07-340496-9

Editorial director: *John E. Biernat*
Executive editor: *John Weimeister*
Senior developmental editor: *Christine Scheid*
Associate marketing manager: *Margaret A. Beamer*
Media producer: *Benjamin Curless*
Project manager: *Dana M. Pauley*
Production supervisor: *Gina Hangos*
Lead designer: *Mathew Baldwin*
Senior photo research coordinator: *Jeremy Cheshareck*
Photo researcher: *Jennifer Blankenship*
Senior media project manager: *Susan Lombardi*
Typeface: *10.5/12 Times Roman*
Compositor: *International Typesetting and Composition*
Printer: *Shen Zhen Donnelley Printing Co., Ltd.*

Library of Congress Cataloging-in-Publication Data

Kinicki, Angelo.
   Organizational behavior : key concepts, skills & best practices / Angelo Kinicki,
Robert Kreitner.—3rd ed.
     p. cm.
   Includes index.
   ISBN-13: 978-0-07-340496-7 (alk. paper)
   ISBN-10: 0-07-340496-9 (alk. paper)
   1. Organizational behavior. I. Kreitner, Robert. II. Title.
HD58.7.K5265 2008
658.3—dc22   2006033184

www.mhhe.com

With love to my parents, Madeline and Henry Kinicki.

———A.K.

With love to Margaret, the other half of the dancing bears.

———B.K.

Angelo Kinicki (pictured on the right) is a Professor of Management and Dean's Council of 100 Distinguished Scholar at the W. P. Carey School of Business at Arizona State University. He also was awarded the Weatherup/Overby Chair in Leadership in 2005. He has held his current position since 1982 when he received his doctorate in organizational behavior from Kent State University.

Angelo is recognized for both his teaching and research. As a teacher,

(1991–1992), and Undergraduate Teaching Excellence Award (1987–1988). He also was selected into *Who's Who of American Colleges and Universities* and *Beta Gamma Sigma*. Angelo is an active researcher. He has published more than 80 articles in a variety of leading academic and professional journals and has coauthored six college textbooks (15 counting revisions). His textbooks have used by hundreds of universities around the world. Angelo's experience as a

the *Academy of Management Journal* for period of 1996–1999.

Angelo also is an active international consultant who works with top management teams to create organizational change aimed at increasing organizational effectiveness and profitability. He has worked with many *Fortune* 500 firms as well as numerous entrepreneurial organizations in diverse industries. His expertise includes facilitating strategic/operational planning sessions, diagnosing the causes of organizational and work-unit problems, implementing performance management systems, designing and implementing performance appraisal systems, developing and administering surveys to assess employee attitudes, and leading management/executive education programs. He developed a 360-degree leadership feedback instrument called the Performance Management Leadership Survey (PMLS) that is used by companies throughout the United States and Europe.

One of Angelo's strengths is his ability to teach students at all levels within a university. He uses an interactive environment to enhance undergraduates' understanding about management and organizational behavior. He focuses MBAs on applying management concepts to solve complex problems; PhD students learn the art and science of conducting scholarly research.

Angelo has been the recipient of several awards, including the John W Teets Outstanding Graduate Teacher Award (2004–2005), Graduate Teaching Excellence Award (1998–1999), Continuing Education Teaching Excellence Award

researcher also resulted in his selection to serve on the editorial review boards for the *Academy of Management Journal,* the *Journal of Vocational Behavior,* and the *Journal of Management*. He received the All-Time Best Reviewer Award from

Angelo and his wife, Joyce, have enjoyed living in the beautiful Arizona desert for 25 years but are natives of Cleveland, Ohio. They enjoy traveling, golfing, and hiking.

Robert Kreitner, PhD, is a professor emeritus of management at Arizona State University. Prior to joining ASU in 1975, Bob taught at Western Illinois University. He also has taught organizational behavior at Thunderbird. Bob is a popular speaker who has addressed a diverse array of audiences worldwide on management topics. He is a member of ASU's W. P. Carey School of Business Faculty Hall of Fame. Bob has authored articles for journals such as *Organizational Dynamics, Business Horizons,* and *Journal of Business Ethics.* He also is the coauthor (with Fred Luthans) of the award-winning book *Organizational Behavior Modification and Beyond: An Operant and Social Learning Approach,* and the author of *Management,* 10th edition, a best-selling introductory management text.

Among his consulting and executive development clients have been American Express, SABRE Computer Services, Honeywell, Motorola, Amdahl, the Hopi Indian Tribe, State Farm Insurance, Goodyear Aerospace, Doubletree Hotels, Bank One–Arizona, Nazarene School of Large Church Management, US Steel, Ford, Caterpillar, and Allied-Signal. In 1981–82 he served as chairman of the Academy of Management's Management Education and Development Division.

On the personal side, Bob was born in Buffalo, New York. After a four-year enlistment in the US Coast Guard, including service on the icebreaker *Eastwind* in Antarctica, Bob attended the University of Nebraska–Omaha on a football scholarship. Bob also holds an MBA from the University of Nebraska–Omaha and a PhD from the University of Nebraska–Lincoln. While working on his PhD in business at Nebraska, he spent six months teaching management courses for the University in Micronesia. In 1996, Bob taught two courses in Albania's first-ever MBA program (funded by the US Agency for International Development and administered by the University of Nebraska–Lincoln). He taught a summer leadership program in Switzerland from 1995 to 1998. Bob and his wife, Margaret, live in Phoenix and enjoy travel, hiking, woodcarving, and fishing.

preface

In our many years of teaching organizational behavior and management to undergraduate and graduate students in various countries, we *never* had a student say, "I want a longer, more expensive textbook with more chapters." We got the message! Indeed, there is a desire for shorter and less expensive textbooks in today's fast-paced world where overload and tight budgets are a way of life. Within the field of organizational behavior, so-called "essentials" texts have attempted to satisfy this need. Too often, however, brevity has been achieved at the expense of up-to-date examples, artful layout, and learning enhancements. We believe "brief" does not have to mean outdated and boring.

A New Standard

Kinicki and Kreitner's *Organizational Behavior: Key Concepts, Skills & Best Practices,* 3rd edition, represents a new standard in OB essentials textbooks. The following guiding philosophy inspired our quest for this new standard: "Create a short, up-to-date, practical, user-friendly, interesting, and engaging introduction to the field of organizational behavior."

Thus, in this book, you will find lean and efficient coverage of topics recommended by the accreditation organizations AACSB International and ACBSP conveyed with pedagogical features found in full-length OB textbooks. Among those pedagogical enhancements are current, real-life chapter-opening vignettes, a rich array of contemporary in-text examples, a strong skills emphasis including Skills & Best Practices boxes throughout the text, at least one interactive exercise integrated into each chapter, an appealing four-color presentation, interesting captioned photos, poignant cartoons, instructive chapter summaries, and chapter-closing Ethical Dilemma exercises.

Efficient and Flexible Structure

The 16 chapters in this text (including the ethics module following Chapter 1) are readily adaptable to traditional 15-week semesters, 10-week terms, summer and inter-sessions, management development seminars, and distance learning programs via the Internet. Following

up-front coverage of important topics—including ethics, international OB, and managing diversity—the topical flow of this text goes from micro (individuals) to macro (groups, teams, and organizations). Mixing and matching chapters (and topics within each chapter) in various combinations is not only possible but strongly encouraged to create optimum teaching/learning experiences.

A Solid Base of Fresh and Relevant Source Material

Wise grocery shoppers gauge the freshness of essential purchases such as bread and milk by checking the sell by dates. So, too, OB textbooks need to be checked for freshness to ensure the reader's time is well spent on up-to-date and relevant theory, research, and practical examples. By our count, **you will find 494 chapter endnotes dated 2006, indicating a thorough updating of this new edition.** Additionally, 14 of the chapter-opening vignettes and 19 of the in-text Skills & Best Practices boxes are from timely 2006 material.

A Rich Array of OB Research Insights

To enhance the instructional value of our coverage of major topics, we systematically cite "hard" evidence from five different categories. Worthwhile evidence was obtained by drawing upon the following *priority* of research methodologies:

- *Meta-analyses.* A **meta-analysis** is a statistical pooling technique that permits behavioral scientists to draw general conclusions about certain variables from many different studies. It typically encompasses a vast number of subjects, often reaching the thousands. Meta-analyses are instructive because they focus on general patterns of research evidence, not fragmented bits and pieces or isolated studies.

- *Field studies.* In OB, a **field study** probes individual or group processes in an organizational setting. Because field studies involve real-life situations, their results often have immediate and practical relevance for managers.

- *Laboratory studies.* In a **laboratory study,** variables are manipulated and measured in contrived situations. College students are commonly used as subjects. The highly controlled nature of laboratory studies enhances research precision. But generalizing the results to organizational management requires caution.

- *Sample surveys.* In a **sample survey,** samples of people from specified populations respond to questionnaires. The researchers then draw conclusions about the relevant population. Generalizability of the results depends on the quality of the sampling and questioning techniques.

- *Case studies.* A **case study** is an in-depth analysis of a single individual, group, or organization. Because of their limited scope, case studies yield realistic but not very generalizable results.

meta-analysis

Pools the results of many studies through statistical procedure.

field study

Examination of variables in real-life settings.

laboratory study

Manipulation and measurement of variables in contrived situations.

sample survey

Questionnaire responses from a sample of people.

case study

In-depth study of a single person, group, or organization.

Emphasis on Ethics in the Third Edition

We have continued (and updated) two features from the second edition—a comprehensive module on Ethics following Chapter 1 and an Ethical Dilemma exercise at the end of every chapter—to set a proper moral tone for managing people at work. The 16 Ethical Dilemma exercises raise contemporary ethical issues, ask tough questions, and have corresponding interpretations on our Web site at www.mhhe.com/kinickiob3e. An instructive Group Exercise, "Investigating the Difference in Moral Reasoning between Men and Women," follows the Ethics module.

ethics learning module

Fines and Jail Time Await Unethical Contractors and U.S. Officials

Do you think Robert Stein and Philip Bloom should serve jail time? Explain.

FOR DISCUSSION

In January 2004, Robert Stein, a senior U.S. contracting official in Iraq, sent an unusual email to American businessman Philip Bloom. Mr. Stein wrote that he had arranged for a new set of lucrative rebuilding contracts to be awarded to Mr. Bloom, but wanted the businessman to send his bid on the letterhead of a fake company to avoid attracting attention in Baghdad. A few days later, Mr. Bloom replied that he would "bring with me the dummies . . . I have five dummies per bid." The contracts were awarded a short time later.

The emails illustrate how closely U.S. officials on active duty, like Mr. Stein, were willing to work with Mr. Bloom to help him defraud the government through a massive bid-rigging scheme in southern Iraq. They were released . . . as part of a guilty plea from Mr. Bloom, who admitted to steering $2 million in cash and other bribes to government officials in exchange for $8.6 million in Iraqi construction and demolition contracts. Mr. Bloom—who also admitted to providing the officials with jewelry, first-class plane tickets and sexual favors from women he employed at a villa in Baghdad—faces as long as 40 years in prison and nearly $8 million in penalties.

The plea to charges of conspiracy, bribery and money laundering is the latest to emerge from an investigation into alleged corruption by American officials in Hillah, a restive southern city. Mr. Stein, a former civilian occupation official charged with overseeing $82 million in rebuilding funds there, pleaded guilty on Feb. 2 [2006] to conspiracy, bribery and using stolen government money to purchase an array of high-powered rifles and grenade launchers.

Lt. Col. Michael Wheeler and Lt. Col. Debra Harrison, who both worked in Hillah, were arrested late last year [2005] and charged with similar offenses; both are free on bond. Lt. Col. Wheeler's attorney didn't return a call; Lt. Col. Harrison declined to comment. Three other military officials are mentioned in the court papers, and law enforcement authorities say more arrests are likely. "There was no oversight anywhere near them at the time and they did not believe they would be caught," says Special Inspector General for Iraq Reconstruction Stuart Bowen, whose investigators uncovered the ring. "They considered it a free-fraud zone."[1]

Ethical considerations are not always as clear-cut as the case of Robert Stein and Philip Bloom. For example, a recent study of 170 medical experts who created the generally accepted bible for diagnosing mental illness found that 56 percent had undisclosed ties to drugmakers.[2] Do you think that these links to pharmaceutical companies might

ethical dilemma

You Mean Cheating Is Wrong?

College students are disturbed by recent corporate scandals: Some 84% believe the U.S. is having a business crisis, and 77% think CEOs should be held personally responsible for it.

But when the same students are asked about their own ethics, it's another story. Some 59% admit cheating on a test (66% of men, 54% of women). And only 19% say they would report a classmate who cheated (23% of men, but 15% of women—even though recent whistle-blowers have been women).

The survey of 1,100 students on 27 U.S. campuses was conducted by Students in Free Enterprise (SIFE), a non-profit that teams up with corporations to teach students

How Should We Interpret This Hypocritical Double Standard?

1. Don't worry, most students know the difference between school and real life. They'll do the right thing when it really counts. Explain your rationale.

2. Whether in the classroom or on the job, pressure for results is the problem. People tend to take shortcuts and bend the rules when they're pressured. Explain.

3. A cheater today is a cheater tomorrow. Explain.

4. College professors need to do a better job with ethics education. How?

A Structural Change

Reviewer and user feedback prompted us to switch the order of Chapters 9 and 10 from the 2nd edition. The chapter on groups and teams now precedes the chapter on decision making to provide a better context and smoother flow.

Active Learning

Engaging Pedagogy

We have a love and a passion for teaching organizational behavior in the classroom and via textbooks because it deals with the intriguing realities of working in modern organizations. Puzzling questions, insights, and surprises hide around every corner. Seeking useful insights about how and why people behave as they do in the workplace is a provocative, interesting, and oftentimes fun activity. After all, to know more about organizational behavior is to know more about both ourselves and life in general. We have designed this text to facilitate *active* learning by relying on the following learning enhancements:

Chapter-Opening Vignettes—

For some real-world context, these brief cases use topics that are timely and relevant to actual life situations. The text's Web site also features interpretations for each case.

HOME DEPOT IS CHANGING ITS ORGANIZATIONAL CULTURE

Military analogies are commonplace at Home Depot, Inc. these days. Five years after his December, 2000, arrival, Chief Executive Robert L. Nardelli is putting his stamp on what was long a decentralized, entrepreneurial business under founders Bernie Marcus and Arthur Blank. And if his company starts to look and feel like an

launched in 2002, almost half—528—are junior military officers. More than 100 of them now run Home Depots....

Importing ideas, people, and platitudes from the military is a key part of Nardelli's sweeping move to reshape Home Depot, the world's third-largest retailer, into a more centralized

you have 2,100 colonels running things," explains Craig R. Johnson, president of Customer Growth Partners Inc., a retail consulting firm....

Even as other companies seek to stoke creativity and break down hierarchies, Nardelli is trying to build a disciplined corps, one predisposed to following orders, operating in high-pressure environments, and executing with high standards....

Although he has yet to win all the hearts and minds of his employees, and probably never will, Nardelli's feisty spirit is rekindling stellar financial performance. Riding a housing and home-improvement boom, Home Depot sales have soared, from $46 billion in 2000, the year Nardelli took over, to $81.5 billion in 2005, an average annual growth rate of 12%, according to results announced on Feb. 21....

The high stakes of Home Depot's services gambit is one of the main reasons Nardelli has pushed his cultural makeover so hard in the five years since he has been at the helm. But not all have embraced him, or his plans. *BusinessWeek* spoke with 11 former executives, a majority of whom requested anonymity lest the company sue them for violating

Home Depot is attempting to change its organizational culture. What are some of the challenges it will face?

army, that's the point. Nardelli loves to hire soldiers. In fact, he seems to love almost everything about the armed services. The military, to a large extent, has become the management model for his entire enterprise. Of the 1,142 people hired into Home Depot's store leadership program, a two-year training regimen for future store managers

organization. That may be an untrendy idea in management circles, but Nardelli couldn't care less. It's a critical element of his strategy to rein in an unwieldy 2,048-store chain and prepare for its next leg of growth. "The kind of discipline and maturity that you get out of the military is something that can be very, very useful in an organization where basically

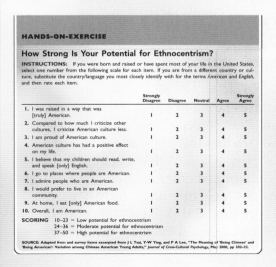

HANDS-ON-EXERCISE

How Strong Is Your Potential for Ethnocentrism?

INSTRUCTIONS: If you were born and raised or have spent most of your life in the United States, select one number from the following scale for each item. If you are from a different country or culture, substitute the country/language you most closely identify with for the terms *American* and *English*, and then rate each item.

	Strongly Disagree	Disagree	Neutral	Agree	Strongly Agree
1. I was raised in a way that was [truly] American.	1	2	3	4	5
2. Compared to how much I criticize other cultures, I criticize American culture less.	1	2	3	4	5
3. I am proud of American culture.	1	2	3	4	5
4. American culture has had a positive effect on my life.	1	2	3	4	5
5. I believe that my children should read, write, and speak [only] English.	1	2	3	4	5
6. I go to places where people are American.	1	2	3	4	5
7. I admire people who are American.	1	2	3	4	5
8. I would prefer to live in an American community.	1	2	3	4	5
9. At home, I eat [only] American food.	1	2	3	4	5
10. Overall, I am American.	1	2	3	4	5

SCORING   10–23 = Low potential for ethnocentrism
24–36 = Moderate potential for ethnocentrism
37–50 = High potential for ethnocentrism

SOURCE: Adapted from and survey items excerpted from J L Tsai, Y-W Ying, and P A Lee, "The Meaning of 'Being Chinese' and 'Being American': Variation among Chinese American Young Adults," *Journal of Cross-Cultural Psychology*, May 2000, pp 302–32.

Hands-On Exercises—

These 16 exercises are included to help readers personalize and expand upon key concepts as they are presented in the text. These exercises encourage active and thoughtful interaction rather than passive reading.

Active Learning

Skills & Best Practices Boxes—

These additional readings and practical application items are designed to sharpen users' skills by either recommending how to apply a concept, theory, or model, or by giving an exemplary corporate application. Students will benefit from real-world experiences and direct skill-building opportunities.

It is the manager who determines whether our social institutions serve us well or whether they squander our talents and resources."[12]

Extending our managerial thrust, let us take a closer look at the skills managers need to perform and the future direction of management.

A Skills Profile for Managers

Observational studies by Mintzberg and others have found the typical manager's day to be a fragmented collection of brief episodes.[13] Interruptions are commonplace, while large blocks of time for planning and reflective thinking are not. In one particu-

Test Your Knowledge
Management's Historical Figures

A Dynamic New Active Learning Feature for the Third Edition—

New to this edition are 68 Web-based readings and exercises keyed to relevant textual material with OLC (Online Learning Center) logos in the margin. Both student-initiated and instructor-assigned access to these enrichment materials will make reading this book an active and robust learning process, rather than the usual passive activity. These Web resources fall into four categories: Test your Knowledge (supplemental readings and quizzes), Self-Assessment Exercises (for greater self-awareness), Group Exercises (for team building), and Manager's Hot Seat Video Applications (for realistic on-the-job experience and skill building). All this material can be easily accessed via the OLC at www.mhhe.com/kinickiob3e—just look for the *Group and Video Resource Manual* link.

Active Learning

Up-to-Date Real-World Examples—
Nothing brings material to life better than in-text examples featuring real companies, people, and situations. These examples, including organizations such as Southwest Airlines, DaimlerChrysler, Seagate Technology, Baptist Health Care, US Marine Crop., Procter & Gamble, and General Electric, permeate the text.

chapter summary

- *Discuss the layers and functions of organizational culture.* The three layers of organizational culture are observable artifacts, espoused values, and basic underlying assumptions. Each layer varies in terms of outward visibility and resistance to change. Four functions of organization culture are organizational identity, collective commitment, social system stability, and sense-making device.

- *Discuss the three general types of organizational culture and their associated normative beliefs.* The three general types of organizational culture are constructive, passive–defensive, and aggressive–defensive. Each type is grounded in different normative beliefs. Normative beliefs represent an individual's thoughts and beliefs about how members of a particular group or organization are expected to approach their work and interact with others. A constructive culture is associated with the beliefs of achievement, self-actualizing, humanistic-encouraging, and affiliative. Passive–defensive organizations tend to endorse the beliefs of approval, conventional, dependent, and avoidance. Aggressive–defensive cultures tend to endorse the beliefs of oppositional, power, competitive, and perfectionistic.

- *Summarize the methods used by organizations to embed their cultures.* Embedding a culture amounts to teaching employees about the organization's preferred values, beliefs, expectations, and behaviors. This is accomplished by using one or more of the following 11 mechanisms: (a) formal statements of organizational philosophy, mission, vision, values, and materials used for recruiting, selection, and socialization; (b) the design of physical space, work environments, and buildings; (c) slogans, language, acronyms, and sayings; (d) deliberate role modeling, training programs; teaching, and coaching by managers and supervisors; (e) explicit rewards, status symbols, and promotion criteria; (f) stories, legends, and myths about key people and events; (g) the organizational activities, processes, or outcomes that leaders pay attention to, measure, and control; (h) leader reactions to critical incidents and organizational crises; (i) the workflow and organizational structure; (j) organizational systems and procedures; and (k) organizational goals and associated criteria used for recruitment, selection, development, promotion, layoffs, and retirement of people.

- *Describe the three phases in Feldman's model of organizational socialization.* The three phases of Feldman's model are anticipatory socialization, encounter, and change and acquisition. Anticipatory socialization begins before an individual actually joins the organization. The encounter phase begins when the employment contract has been signed. Phase 3 involves the period in which employees master important tasks and resolve any role conflicts.

- *Discuss the various socialization tactics used to socialize employees.* There are six key socialization tactics. They are collective versus individual, formal versus informal, sequential versus random, fixed versus variable, serial versus disjunctive, and investiture versus divestiture (see Table 2–2). Each tactic provides organizations with two opposing options for socializing employees.

- *Explain the four types of development networks derived from a developmental network model of mentoring.* The four development networks are receptive, traditional, entrepreneurial, and opportunistic. A receptive network is composed of a few weak ties from one social system. A traditional network contains a few strong ties between an employee and developers that all come from one social system. An entrepreneurial network is made up of strong ties among developers from several social systems, and an opportunistic network is associated with having weak ties with multiple developers from different social systems.

Chapter Summaries—
This section includes responses to the learning objectives in each chapter, making it a handy review tool for all users.

Active Learning

discussion questions

1. In the context of the chapter-opening vignette, how much does family history affect one's self-esteem and emotional intelligence? Explain.
2. How is someone you know with low self-efficacy, relative to a specified task, "programming themselves for failure"? What could be done to help that individual develop high self-efficacy?
3. What importance do you attach to self-talk in self-management? Explain.
4. On scales of low = 1 to high = 10, how would you rate yourself on the Big Five personality dimensions? Is your personality profile suitable for your present (or chosen) line of work? Explain.
5. Which of the four key components of emotional intelligence is (or are) your strong suit? Which is (or are) your weakest? What are the everyday implications of your EI profile?

Discussion Questions—
Focused and challenging, these questions help facilitate classroom discussion or review material.

Ethical Dilemmas—
These 16 exercises raise contemporary ethical issues, ask tough questions, and have corresponding interpretations on the Online Learning Center at www.mhhe.com/kinickiob3e.

ethical dilemma

You Mean Cheating Is Wrong?

College students are disturbed by recent corporate scandals: Some 84% believe the U.S. is having a business crisis, and 77% think CEOs should be held personally responsible for it.

But when the same students are asked about their own ethics, it's another story. Some 59% admit cheating on a test (66% of men, 54% of women). And only 19% say they would report a classmate who cheated (23% of men, but 15% of women—even though recent whistle-blowers have been women).

The survey of 1,100 students on 27 U.S. campuses was conducted by Students in Free Enterprise (SIFE), a nonprofit that teams up with corporations to teach students ethical business practices. "There's a lack of understanding about ethics and how ethics are applied in real life," says Alvin Rohrs, SIFE'S CEO. "We have to get young people to stop and think about ethics and the decisions

How Should We Interpret This Hypocritical Double Standard?

1. Don't worry, most students know the difference between school and real life. They'll do the right thing when it really counts. Explain your rationale.
2. Whether in the classroom or on the job, pressure for results is the problem. People tend to take shortcuts and bend the rules when they're pressured. Explain.
3. A cheater today is a cheater tomorrow. Explain.
4. College professors need to do a better job with ethics education. How?
5. Both students and managers need to be held personally accountable for their unethical behavior. How?
6. Invent other interpretations or options. Discuss.

Instructor supplements

Organizational Behavior 3e gives you all the support material you need for an enriched classroom experience.

Instructor's Resource Guide

The Instructor's Manual is a creative guide to understanding organizational behavior. It combines traditional elements of instructor's manuals with newer features such as teaching tips throughout the lecture outline, additional discussion ideas for the Opening Vignettes, note pages for the PPT slides, a matrix from the Group & Video Resource Manual on how to incorporate Test Your Knowledge features, Self-Assessment Exercises, Group Exercises, and Manager Hot Seat Video Applications, answers to Discussion Questions and End of Chapter material, and much more. Each element will assist the instructor and students in maximizing the ideas, issues, concepts, and important organizational behavior approaches included in each chapter. We'd like to thank Mindy West of Northern Arizona University for helping us update our Instructor's Guide.

Computerized Test Bank

We've aligned our Test Bank with new AACSB guidelines, tagging each question according to its knowledge and skills areas. Categories include Global, Ethics and Social Responsibility, Legal and other External Environment, Communication, Diversity, Group Dynamics, Individual Dynamics, Production, and IT. Previous designations aligning questions with Learning Objectives, boxes, and features still exist as well, with over 1,200 questions from which to choose. Our thanks to Eileen Hogan of Kutztown University for her help in developing our new Test Bank.

Instructor's CD-ROM

ISBN: 9780073296579; MHID: 0073296570

All of the above-mentioned materials, including PowerPoint slides, can be located on the Instructor's CD-ROM. This CD-ROM allows professors to easily create their own custom presentation. They can pull from resources on the CD, like the Instructor's Manual, the Test Bank, and PowerPoint, or from their own files. Additional downloads of figures and tables from the text are available for use.

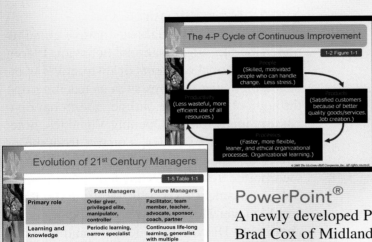

PowerPoint®

A newly developed PowerPoint presentation created by Brad Cox of Midlands Tech allows for new functionality and variety in the classroom. With the inclusion of video usage suggestions and links to additional information, instructors have the availability to tailor their presentations to their class needs.

Videos on DVD

ISBN: 9780073283128; MHID: 0073283126

If you're looking for a way to bring real-life experience into the classroom, an all-new video collection delivered on DVD is available. Segments such as "Pike Place Fish Market," "Johnson & Johnson: Creating a Global Learning Organization," or "Wal-Mart's Public Image Campaign" demonstrate current OB topics, but also help students apply them to everyday organizations.

The Manager's Hot Seat Videos Online
www.mhhe.com/MHS
In today's workplace, managers are confronted daily with issues like ethics, diversity, working in teams, and the virtual workplace. The manager's Hot Seat videos allow students to watch as 15 real managers apply their years of experience to confront these issues. Students assume the role of the manager as they watch the video and answer multiple-choice questions that pop up, forcing them to make decisions on the spot. They learn from the manager's mistakes and successes, and then write a report critiquing the manager's approach by defending their reasoning. Reports can be e-mailed or printed out for credit. These video segments are powerful tool for your course that truly immerses your students in the learning experience. **The Manager's Hot Seat online is just an additional $10 when packaged with this text.**

Group and Video Resource Manual: An Instructor's Guide to an Active Classroom
in print ISBN: 9780073044347; MHID: 0073044342 or online at www.mhhe.com/mobmanual

Prepared by Amanda Johnson and Angelo Kinicki, this manual created for instructors contains everything needed to successfully integrate activities into the classroom. It includes a menu of items to use as teaching tools in class. All of our self-assessment exercises, Test Your Knowledge quizzes, group exercises, and Manager's Hot Seat exercises are located in this one manual along with teaching notes and PowerPoint slides to use in class. Group exercises include everything you would need to use the exercise in class—handouts, figures, and more.

This manual is organized into 25 topics including ethics, decision making, change, and leadership for easy inclusion in your lecture. A matrix is included at the front of the manual that references each resource by topic. Students access all of the exercises and self-assessments on their textbook's Web site. The Manager's Hot Seat exercises are located online at www.mhhe.com/MHS.

Instructor supplements

Online Learning Center
www.mhhe.com/kinickiob3e
More and more students are studying online. That's why we offer an Online Learning Center (OLC) that follows *Organizational Behavior* chapter by chapter. It doesn't require any building or maintenance on your part. It's ready to go the moment you and your students type in the URL.

As your students study, they can refer to the OLC Web site for such benefits as:

- Internet-based activities
- Self-grading quizzes
- Learning objectives
- Chapter summaries
- Additional video

A secured Instructor Resource Center stores your essential course materials to save you prep time before class. The Instructor's Manual, PowerPoint, and sample syllabi are now just a couple of clicks away. You will also find useful packaging information and Video notes.

Grateful Appreciation

Our sincere thanks and gratitude go to our editor, John Weimeister, and his first-rate team at McGraw-Hill/Irwin who encouraged and facilitated our pursuit of "something better." Key contributors include Christine Scheid, Senior Developmental Editor; Meg Beamer, Marketing Manager; and Dana Pauley, Project Manager. We would also like to thank Mindy West of Northern Arizona University for her work on the Instructor's Guide, Eileen Hogan of Kutztown University for her help revising and updating the Test Bank, and Brad Cox of Midlands Tech for developing the PowerPoint presentation slides.

We'd also like to give a special thank you to those colleagues who gave their comments and suggestions over the years to help us create all three editions. They are:

Abe Bakhshesy
University of Utah

Jodi Barnes-Nelson
NC State–Raleigh

Joy Benson
University of Illinois–Springfield

Linda Boozer
Suny AG & Tech College–Morrisville

Emilio Bruna
University of Texas at El Paso

Mark Butler
San Diego State University

Holly Buttner
University of North Carolina–Greensboro

John Byrne
St. Ambrose University

Diane Caggiano
Fitchburg State College

Dave Carmichel
Oklahoma City University

Xiao-Ping Chen
University of Washington

Jack Chirch
Hampton University

Bongsoon Cho
SUNY–Buffalo

Savannah Clay
Central Piedmont Community College

Ray Coye
DePaul University

Denise Daniels
Seattle Pacific University

W. Gibb Dyer, Jr.
Brigham Young University

Mark Fichman
Carnegie Mellon University

David A. Foote
Middle Tennessee State University

Lucy Ford
Rutgers University

Thomas Gainey
State University of West Georgia

Jacqueline Gilbert
Middle Tennessee State University

Leonard Glick
Northeastern University

Barbara Hassell
IUPUI–Indianapolis

Hoyt Hayes
Columbia College–Columbia

Kim Hester
Arkansas State University

Chad Higgins
University of Washington

Kristine Hoover
Bowling Green State University

David Jalajas
Long Island University

Andrew Johnson
Bellevue Community College

Dong Jung
San Diego State University

Jordan Kaplan
Long Island University

John Keeling
Old Dominion University

Claire Killian
University of Wisconsin–River Falls

Karen Markel
Oakland University

Tom McDermott
Pittsburgh Technical Institute

Edward Miles
Georgia State University

Linda Morable
Richland College

Jay Nathan
St. John's University

Regina Oneil
Suffolk University

Joseph Petrick
Wright State University

Dave Phillips
Purdue University–Westville

Amy Randel
Wake Forest University

Clint Relyea
Arkansas State University

Patricia Rice
Finger Lakes Community College

Janet Romaine
St. Anselm College

Paula Silva
University of New Mexico

Randi Sims
Nova University

Peggy Takahashi
University of San Francisco

Jennie Carter Thomas
Belmont University

Brian Usilaner
University of Maryland–University College

Matthew Valle
Elon University

Andrew Ward
Emory University

John Washbush
University of Wisconsin

John Watt
University of Central Arkansas

Ken Weidner
St. Josephs University

Scott Williams
Wright State University

Lynn Wilson
Saint Leo University

Finally, we would like to thank our wives, Joyce and Margaret. Their love, support, and managerial experience are instrumental to *everything* we do. They lift our tired spirits when needed and encourage and coach us at every turn.

This project has been a fun challenge from start to finish. Not only did we enjoy reading and learning more about the latest developments within the field of organizational behavior, but completion of this edition has deepened our twenty-five-year friendship. We hope you enjoy this textbook. Best wishes for success and happiness!

Angelo & Bob

brief contents

Part One
Managing People in a Global Economy   1

Chapter One
Needed: People-Centered Managers and Workplaces   2
Ethics Learning Module   24

Chapter Two
Organizational Culture, Socialization, and Mentoring   38

Chapter Three
Developing Global Managers   62

Part Two
Managing Individuals   87

Chapter Four
Understanding Social Perception and Managing Diversity   88

Chapter Five
Appreciating Individual Differences: Self-Concept, Personality, Emotions   116

Chapter Six
Motivation I: Needs, Job Design, Intrinsic Motivation, and Satisfaction   144

Chapter Seven
Motivation II: Equity, Expectancy, and Goal Setting   172

Chapter Eight
Improving Performance with Feedback, Rewards, and Positive Reinforcement   198

Part Three
Managing Social Processes and Making Decisions   221

Chapter Nine
Effective Groups and Teamwork   222

Chapter Ten
Making Decisions   246

Chapter Eleven
Managing Conflict and Negotiating   272

Part Four
Managing Organizational Processes   295

Chapter Twelve
Communicating in the Internet Age   296

Chapter Thirteen
Influence, Power, and Politics: An Organizational

Survival Kit   324

Chapter Fourteen
Leadership   344

Part Five
Managing Evolving Organizations   373

Chapter Fifteen
Designing Effective Organizations   374

Chapter Sixteen
Managing Change and Organizational Learning   396

Endnotes   422
Credits   456
Glossary   457
Index   461

contents

Part One
Managing People in a Global Economy   1

Chapter One
Needed: People-Centered Managers and Workplaces   2

Why America's Number 1 Steelmaker Won't Rust   3

Managers Get Results with and through Others   6

   A Skills Profile for Managers   7

SKILLS & BEST PRACTICES: The Effective Manager's Skill Profile   7

   21st-Century Managers   8

The Field of Organizational Behavior: Past and Present   8

   The Human Relations Movement   9

   The Total Quality Management Movement   11

SKILLS & BEST PRACTICES: Southwest Airlines Hires with High-Quality Service in Mind   12

   The Contingency Approach to Management   13

New Directions in OB   14

   The Age of Human and Social Capital   14

   The Emerging Area of Positive Organizational Behavior (POB)   16

SKILLS & BEST PRACTICES: IBM Takes the Ethical High Road to Build Human and Social Capital   17

   The Internet and E-Business Revolution   18

SKILLS & BEST PRACTICES: Practical E-Leadership Lessons from a "Virtual CEO"   20

Key Terms   21

Chapter Summary   21

Discussion Questions   22

Ethical Dilemma   22

Ethics Learning Module: Fines and Jail Time Await Unethical Contractors and U.S. Officials   24

A Model of Ethical Behavior   25

   Internal Organizational Influences   26

   External Organizational Influences   27

   Neutralizing/Enhancing Factors   28

A Decision Tree for Ethical Decisions   29

Do Moral Orientations Vary by Gender?   30

HANDS-ON EXERCISE: How Ethical Are These Behaviors?   31

General Moral Principles   32

How to Improve the Organization's Ethical Climate   33

Group Exercise: Investigating the Difference in Moral Reasoning between Men and Women   35

Discussion Questions   36

Chapter Two
Organizational Culture, Socialization, and Mentoring   38

Home Depot Is Changing Its Organizational Culture   39

Organizational Culture: Definition and Context   41

Dynamics of Organizational Culture   42

   Layers of Organizational Culture   42

   Four Functions of Organizational Culture   44

SKILLS & BEST PRACTICES: Williams-Sonoma's Espoused Values Focus on Employees, Customers, Shareholders, Ethical Behavior, and the Environment   44

   Types of Organizational Culture   46

   Outcomes Associated with Organizational Culture   48

   How Cultures Are Embedded in Organizations   49

SKILLS & BEST PRACTICES: How Do Managers Develop Stories That Have Impact?   50

The Organizational Socialization Process   51

A Three-Phase Model of Organizational Socialization   51

SKILLS & BEST PRACTICES: Sedona Center Relies on Current Employees for Anticipatory Socialization   53

Practical Application of Socialization Research   54

Embedding Organizational Culture through Mentoring   56

Functions of Mentoring   57

Developmental Networks Underlying Mentoring   57

Personal and Organizational Implications   58

SKILLS & BEST PRACTICES: Building an Effective Mentoring Network   59

Key Terms   59

Chapter Summary   60

Discussion Questions   60

Ethical Dilemma   61

Chapter Three
Developing Global Managers   62

A Team of Foreign Trainers in Afghanistan   63

Developing a Global Mind-Set   66

A Model of Societal and Organizational Cultures   66

Ethnocentrism: Removing a Cultural Roadblock in the Global Economy   68

HANDS-ON EXERCISE: How Strong Is Your Potential for Ethnocentrism?   69

Becoming a Global Manager   69

SKILLS & BEST PRACTICES: Geekcorps Volunteers Gain Valuable International Experience   70

The Hofstede Study: How Well Do US Management Theories Apply in Other Countries?   70

Becoming Cross-Culturally Competent   70

Cultural Paradoxes Require Cultural Intelligence   71

Nine Basic Cultural Dimensions from the GLOBE Project   71

Individualism versus Collectivism: A Closer Look   74

High-Context and Low-Context Cultures   75

Cultural Perceptions of Time   76

SKILLS & BEST PRACTICES: Breaking through the Context Barrier in Culturally Diverse US Workplaces   76

Leadership Lessons from the GLOBE Project   77

Preparing for a Foreign Assignment   78

A Poor Track Record for American Expatriates   79

Some Good News: North American Women on Foreign Assignments   79

Avoiding OB Trouble Spots in the Foreign Assignment Cycle   80

SKILLS & BEST PRACTICES: KeY Cross-Cultural Competencies   80

Key Terms   84

Chapter Summary   84

Discussion Questions   84

Ethical Dilemma   85

Part Two
Managing Individuals   87

Chapter Four
Understanding Social Perception and Managing Diversity   88

Perceptions and Attributions Influence Communication Problems between Chinese and American Politicians   89

A Social Information Processing Model of Perception   91

Stage 1: Selective Attention/Comprehension   92

Stage 2: Encoding and Simplification   93

Stage 3: Storage and Retention   94

Stage 4: Retrieval and Response   96

Managerial Implications   96

SKILLS & BEST PRACTICES: Avoid Four Behavioral Tendencies That Are Negatively Perceived When Trying to Sell or Pitch an Idea   97

SKILLS & BEST PRACTICES: Characteristics of Effective Web Page Design   98

Causal Attributions   98

Kelley's Model of Attribution   99

Attributional Tendencies   100

Defining and Managing Diversity   101

Layers of Diversity   102

Affirmative Action and Managing Diversity   103

Increasing Diversity in the Workforce   105

HANDS-ON EXERCISE: What Are the Strategies for Breaking the Glass Ceiling?   106

SKILLS & BEST PRACTICES: Ernst & Young Implements Program to Keep Women on the Path to Partnership   109

Organizational Practices Used to Effectively Manage Diversity   110

Barriers and Challenges to Managing Diversity   110

Ann Morrison Identifies Specific Diversity Initiatives   111

Key Terms   113

Chapter Summary   113

Discussion Questions   114

Ethical Dilemma   114

Chapter Five
Appreciating Individual Differences: Self-Concept, Personality, Emotions   116

Clear Priorities Guide Xerox's Sophie Vandebroek   117

From Self-Concept to Self-Management   119

Self-Esteem   120

Self-Efficacy ("I can do that.")   121

SKILLS & BEST PRACTICES: How to Build Self-Esteem in Yourself and Others   121

Self-Monitoring   125

HANDS-ON EXERCISE: How Good Are You at Self-Monitoring?   126

Self-Management: A Social Learning Model   127

Personality Dynamics 131

The Big Five Personality
Dimensions 131

**SKILLS & BEST PRACTICES: Turn
Common Complaints into a
Business Plan 133**

Locus of Control: Self or
Environment? 133

**SKILLS & BEST PRACTICES:
How Lucky People Make Their Own
Luck 134**

Attitudes 135

Intelligence and Cognitive
Abilities 136

OB Gets Emotional 137

Positive and Negative Emotions 138

Good (and Bad) Moods Are
Contagious 138

Emotional Labor (It has *not* been a
pleasure serving you!) 139

Emotional Intelligence 140

**SKILLS & BEST PRACTICES:
Developing Emotional
Intelligence 140**

Key Terms 141

Chapter Summary 142

Discussion Questions 142

Ethical Dilemma 143

**Chapter Six
Motivation I: Needs, Job
Design, Intrinsic Motivation,
and Satisfaction 144**

ARUP Laboratories, IBM, Versant, Inc.,
and Great River Health Systems Use
Positive Work Environments to Motivate
Employees 145

The Fundamentals of Employee
Motivation 147

A Job Performance Model of
Motivation 147

Need Theories of Motivation 149

Motivating Employees through Job
Design 150

The Mechanistic Approach 151

Motivational Approaches 151

**SKILLS & BEST PRACTICES: Steps
for Applying the Job Characteristics
Model 155**

Biological and Perceptual-Motor
Approaches 156

Cultivating Intrinsic Motivation 157

The Foundation of Intrinsic
Motivation 157

A Model of Intrinsic Motivation 158

**HANDS-ON EXERCISE: Are You
Intrinsically Motivated at Work? 160**

Research and Managerial
Implications 161

Job Satisfaction and Work–Family
Relationships 161

**HANDS-ON EXERCISE: How
Satisfied Are You with Your Present
Job? 162**

The Causes of Job Satisfaction 162

**SKILLS & BEST PRACTICES:
Lockheed Martin Uses Surveys to
Assess Employees' Job
Satisfaction and Improve Employee
Engagement 163**

Major Correlates and Consequences of
Job Satisfaction 164

**SKILLS & BEST PRACTICES:
McDonald's Creative Approach for
Reducing Absenteeism 166**

Work versus Family Life
Conflict 167

Key Terms 170

Chapter Summary 170

Discussion Questions 171

Ethical Dilemma 171

**Chapter Seven
Motivation II: Equity,
Expectancy, and Goal
Setting 172**

Pay for Performance Programs Are Being
Applied to Teachers across the United
States 173

Adams's Equity Theory of
Motivation 175

The Individual–Organization
Exchange Relationship 175

Negative and Positive Inequity 176

Dynamics of Perceived Inequity 176

Expanding the Concept of Equity:
Organizational Justice 178

**SKILLS & BEST PRACTICES:
Susan Lyne Gives Back Part of Her
Bonus to Restore Equity 178**

Practical Lessons from Equity
Theory 179

**HANDS-ON EXERCISE: Measuring
Perceived Fair Interpersonal
Treatment 180**

Expectancy Theory of Motivation 181

Vroom's Expectancy Theory 181

Research on Expectancy Theory and
Managerial Implications 183

Motivation through Goal Setting 185

**SKILLS & BEST PRACTICES:
Jamba Juice Company Links
Performance and Rewards 185**

Goals: Definition and
Background 186

How Does Goal Setting Work? 186

Insights from Goal-Setting
Research 187

Practical Application of Goal
Setting 190

Putting Motivational Theories
to Work 192

**SKILLS & BEST PRACTICES:
Managerial Actions for Enhancing
Goal Commitment 192**

Key Terms 194

Chapter Summary 195

Discussion Questions 196

Ethical Dilemma 196

**Chapter Eight
Improving Performance with
Feedback, Rewards, and
Positive Reinforcement 198**

Keeping Score at UMB Bank 199

Providing Effective Feedback 201

Two Functions of Feedback 202

Three Sources of Feedback:
Others, Task, and Self 203

The Recipient's Perspective of
Feedback 203

**HANDS-ON EXERCISE: Measuring
Your Desire for Performance
Feedback 204**

Behavioral Outcomes of
Feedback 204

Nontraditional Upward Feedback and
360-Degree Feedback 205

**SKILLS & BEST PRACTICES: Good
Advice on Feedback and Executive
Coaches from Jack and Suzy
Welch 205**

Why Feedback Often Fails 207

**SKILLS & BEST PRACTICES: How
to Make Sure Feedback Gets
Results 207**

Organizational Reward Systems 208

Types of Rewards   208

Distribution Criteria   209

Desired Outcomes   210

SKILLS & BEST PRACTICES: Gainsharing at Whole Foods   210

Pay for Performance   210

Why Rewards Often Fail to Motivate   211

Positive Reinforcement   212

Thorndike's Law of Effect   212

Skinner's Operant Conditioning Model   212

Contingent Consequences   213

Schedules of Reinforcement   214

Shaping Behavior with Positive Reinforcement   217

SKILLS & BEST PRACTICES: How to Effectively Shape Job Behavior   217

Key Terms   218

Chapter Summary   218

Discussion Questions   218

Ethical Dilemma   219

Part Three
Managing Social Processes and Making Decisions   221

Chapter Nine
Effective Groups and Teamwork   222

Is Teamwork the R$_x$ for Hospitals?   223

Fundamentals of Group Behavior   225

Formal and Informal Groups   226

Functions of Formal Groups   226

The Group Development Process   227

Group Member Roles   229

Norms   231

Teams, Trust, and Teamwork   232

A Team Is More Than Just a Group   232

Developing Teamwork Competencies   233

SKILLS & BEST PRACTICES: How Strong Are Your Teamwork Competencies?   233

Team Building   234

Trust: A Key Ingredient of Teamwork   234

Self-Managed Teams   236

HANDS-ON EXERCISE: How Autonomous Is Your Work Group?   237

Virtual Teams   238

SKILLS & BEST PRACTICES: Cross-Functional Teams Bring Innovation to Life   238

Threats to Group and Team Effectiveness   240

Groupthink   240

Social Loafing   241

SKILLS & BEST PRACTICES: How to Prevent Groupthink   241

Key Terms   242

Chapter Summary   242

Discussion Questions   243

Ethical Dilemma   243

Chapter Ten
Making Decisions   246

Analytics Is Used to Improve Decision Making   247

Models of Decision Making   249

The Rational Model   249

SKILLS & BEST PRACTICES: Michael Dell and Kevin Rollins Make Decisions Collaboratively   250

Simon's Normative Model   251

Dynamics of Decision Making   252

Improving Decision Making through Effective Knowledge Management   252

General Decision-Making Styles   254

Escalation of Commitment   256

HANDS-ON EXERCISE: What Is Your Decision-Making Style?   257

Creativity   259

SKILLS & BEST PRACTICES: Recommendations to Reduce Escalation of Commitment   259

SKILLS & BEST PRACTICES: Avoid These Creativity/Innovation Killers   260

Group Decision Making   261

Group Involvement in Decision Making   261

HANDS-ON EXERCISE: Assessing Participation in Group Decision Making   262

Advantages and Disadvantages of Group-Aided Decision Making   263

Participative Management   264

Group Problem-Solving Techniques   265

Key Terms   268

Chapter Summary   268

Discussion Questions   269

Ethical Dilemma   269

Chapter Eleven
Managing Conflict and Negotiating   272

Microsoft Gets Caught Up in the Culture Wars   273

A Modern View of Conflict   275

A Conflict Continuum   275

Functional versus Dysfunctional Conflict   276

Antecedents of Conflict   277

Why People Avoid Conflict   277

Desired Outcomes of Conflict   278

Major Forms of Conflict   278

Personality Conflicts   278

HANDS-ON EXERCISE: Workplace Incivility: Are You Part of the Problem?   280

Intergroup Conflict   280

SKILLS & BEST PRACTICES: How to Deal with Personality Conflicts   281

Cross-Cultural Conflict   282

SKILLS & BEST PRACTICES: How to Build Cross-Cultural Relationships   284

Managing Conflict   284

Programming Functional Conflict   284

SKILLS & BEST PRACTICES: How Toro Mows Down Bad Ideas   286

Alternative Styles for Handling Dysfunctional Conflict   287

Third-Party Interventions: Alternative Dispute Resolution   288

Negotiating   289

   Two Basic Types of Negotiation   289

   Added-Value Negotiation   290

**SKILLS & BEST PRACTICES:
Seven Steps to Negotiating Your
Salary   290**

   Applying What You Have Learned:
How to Negotiate Your Pay and
Benefits   291

Key Terms   291

Chapter Summary   292

Discussion Questions   292

Ethical Dilemma   293

Part Four

Managing Organizational Processes   295

**Chapter Twelve
Communicating in the
Internet Age   296**

Boeing Company Joins the
Blogosphere   297

Basic Dimensions of the Communication
Process   299

   A Perceptual Process Model of
Communication   300

   Barriers to Effective
Communication   303

Interpersonal Communication   305

**HANDS-ON EXERCISE: What Is
Your Business Etiquette?   306**

   Assertiveness, Aggressiveness, and
Nonassertiveness   307

   Sources of Nonverbal
Communication   307

**SKILLS & BEST PRACTICES:
Advice to Improve Nonverbal
Communication Skills   309**

   Active Listening   309

   Women and Men Communicate
Differently   311

Communication in the Computerized
Information Age   313

   Internet/Intranet/Extranet   314

   Electronic Mail   316

   Handheld Devices   317

**SKILLS & BEST PRACTICES:
Managing Your E-Mail   317**

   Blogs   318

**SKILLS & BEST PRACTICES: Fast-
Food Chains Use iPods to Train
Employees   318**

   Videoconferencing   319

   Group Support Systems   319

   Teleworking   320

Key Terms   321

Chapter Summary   321

Discussion Questions   322

Ethical Dilemma   322

**Chapter Thirteen
Influence, Power, and
Politics: An Organizational
Survival Kit   324**

How Ursula Burns Gets Results at
Xerox   325

Influencing and Persuading Others   327

   Nine Generic Influence Tactics   327

   Three Influence Outcomes   328

   Practical Research Insights   328

   How to Do a Better Job of Influencing
and Persuading Others   329

**SKILLS & BEST PRACTICES: A
Second Chance Can Tap the Power
of Reciprocity   329**

Social Power and Empowerment   330

   Five Bases of Power   331

**SKILLS & BEST PRACTICES: How
to "Get Elected Boss" after Being
Promoted to Management   331**

**HANDS-ON EXERCISE: How Much
Power Do You Have?   332**

   Practical Lessons from Research   333

   Employee Empowerment   333

   Making Empowerment Work   334

**SKILLS & BEST PRACTICES:
Hitting the Right Note with
Empowerment   334**

Organizational Politics and Impression
Management   335

   Definition and Domain of
Organizational Politics   335

   Impression Management   338

   Keeping Organizational Politics in
Check   340

**SKILLS & BEST PRACTICES:
How to Keep Organizational
Politics within Reasonable
Bounds   340**

Key Terms   341

Chapter Summary   341

Discussion Questions   342

Ethical Dilemma   342

**Chapter Fourteen
Leadership   344**

A New Leader Is Righting the Ship at
Citigroup   345

What Does Leadership Involve?   347

   Trait and Behavioral Theories of
Leadership   348

   Trait Theory   348

   Behavioral Styles Theory   351

**SKILLS & BEST PRACTICES: Peter
Drucker's Tips for Improving
Leadership Effectiveness   352**

Situational Theories   352

   Fiedler's Contingency Model   352

   Path–Goal Theory   354

   Hersey and Blanchard's Situational
Leadership Theory   357

The Full-Range Model of Leadership:
From Laissez-Faire to Transformational
Leadership   358

   How Does Transformational Leadership
Transform Followers?   360

   Research and Managerial
Implications   361

**SKILLS & BEST PRACTICES:
Recommendations for Creating
World-Class Leadership
Development Programs   362**

Additional Perspectives on
Leadership   362

   The Leader–Member Exchange Model of
Leadership   362

HANDS-ON EXERCISE:
Assessing Your Leader–Member
Exchange 364

　Shared Leadership 365

　Servant-Leadership 365

　Level 5 Leadership 367

Key Terms 369

Chapter Summary 370

Discussion Questions 371

Ethical Dilemma 371

Part Five
Managing Evolving Organizations 373

Chapter Fifteen
Designing Effective
Organizations 374

The Two Faces of Wal-Mart 375

Organizations: Definition and
Dimensions 377

　What Is an Organization? 377

　Organization Charts 378

Organizational Metaphors 379

　Needed: Open-System Thinking 380

　Organizations as Military/Mechanical
　Bureaucracies 380

　Organizations as Biological
　Systems 381

SKILLS & BEST PRACTICES:
Closed-System Thinking Has Both
Hurt and Helped Apple's CEO
Steve Jobs 381

　Organizations as Cognitive
　Systems 383

Striving for Organizational
Effectiveness 383

　Generic Effectiveness Criteria 383

　Mixing Effectiveness Criteria: Practical
　Guidelines 386

SKILLS & BEST PRACTICES:
Creativity and Innovation Pay Off
on the Bottom Line 386

The Contingency Approach to Designing
Organizations 387

　Mechanistic versus Organic
　Organizations 387

SKILLS & BEST PRACTICES:
W L Gore's Organic "Bubble-Up"
Structure Enhances
Innovation 387

HANDS-ON EXERCISE:
Mechanistic or Organic? 388

　New-Style versus Old-Style
　Organizations 390

　Virtual Organizations 391

SKILLS & BEST PRACTICES: How
to Manage Geographically
Dispersed Employees 392

Key Terms 392

Chapter Summary 393

Discussion Questions 393

Ethical Dilemma 393

Chapter Sixteen
Managing Change and Organizational Learning 396

Intel Is Undergoing Major Organizational
Change 397

Forces of Change 399

　External Forces 399

　Internal Forces 401

Models of Planned Change 401

　Lewin's Change Model 402

　A Systems Model of Change 403

　Kotter's Eight Steps for Leading
　Organizational Change 405

　Creating Change through Organization
　Development 407

Understanding and Managing Resistance
to Change 409

　Why People Resist Change in the
　Workplace 410

　Alternative Strategies for Overcoming
　Resistance to Change 411

HANDS-ON EXERCISE: Does Your
Commitment to a Change Initiative
Predict Your Behavioral Support for
the Change? 412

Creating a Learning Organization 414

　Defining Organizational Learning and a
　Learning Organization 414

　Building an Organization's Learning
　Capability 415

　Leadership Is the Foundation of a
　Learning Organization 418

　Unlearning the Organization 419

Key Terms 419

Chapter Summary 419

Discussion Questions 420

Ethical Dilemma 421

Endnotes 422

Credits 456

Glossary 457

Index 461

part
One

Managing People in a Global Economy

One   Needed: People-Centered Managers and Workplaces
          Ethics Learning Module

Two   Organizational Culture, Socialization, and Mentoring

Three Developing Global Managers

chapter One

Needed: People-Centered Managers and Workplaces

LEARNING OBJECTIVES

After reading the material in this chapter, you should be able to:

- Identify at least four of Pfeffer's people-centered practices, and define the term *management*.

- Contrast McGregor's Theory X and Theory Y assumptions about employees.

- Explain the managerial significance of Deming's 85–15 rule, and identify the four principles of total quality management (TQM).

- Contrast human and social capital, and identify five measurable outcomes when building human capital.

- Explain the impact of the positive psychology movement on the field of organizational behavior (OB).

- Define the term *e-business*, and explain at least three practical lessons about effective e-leadership in a virtual organization.

BusinessWeek

It was about 2 p.m. on Mar. 9 [2006] when three Nucor Corp. electricians got the call from their colleagues at the Hickman (Ark.) plant. It was bad news: Hickman's electrical grid had failed. For a minimill steelmaker like Nucor, which melts scrap steel from autos, dishwashers, mobile homes, and the like in an electric arc furnace to make new steel, there's little that could be worse. The trio immediately dropped what they were doing and headed out to the plant. Malcolm McDonald, an electrician from the Decatur (Ala.) mill, was in Indiana visiting another facility. He drove down, arriving at 9 o'clock that night. Les Hart and Bryson Trumble, from Nucor's facility in Hertford Country, N.C., boarded a plane that landed in Memphis at 11 p.m. Then they drove two hours to the troubled plant.

No supervisor had asked them to make the trip, and no one had to. They went on their own. Camping out in the electrical substation with the Hickman staff, the team worked 20-hour shifts to get the plant up and running again in three days instead of the anticipated full week. There wasn't any direct financial incentive for them to blow their weekends, no extra money in their next

Nucor Corp. excels at rewarding and empowering its employees.

paycheck, but for the company their contribution was huge. Hickman went on to post a first-quarter record for tons of steel shipped. . . .

In an industry as Rust Belt as they come, Nucor has nurtured one of the most dynamic and engaged workforces around. The 11,300 nonunion employees at the Charlotte (N.C.) company don't see themselves as worker bees waiting for instructions from above. Nucor's flattened hierarchy and emphasis on pushing power to the front line lead its employees to adopt the mindset of owner-operators. It's a profitable formula: Nucor's 387% return to shareholders over the past five years handily beats almost all other companies in the Standard & Poor's 500-stock index, including New Economy icons Amazon.com, Starbucks, and eBay. . . .

Nucor gained renown in the late 1980s for its radical pay practices, which base the vast majority of most workers' income on their performance. An upstart nipping at the heels of the integrated steel giants, Nucor had a close-knit culture that was the natural outgrowth of its underdog identity. Legendary leader F. Kenneth Iverson's radical insight: that employees, even hourly clock-punchers, will make an extraordinary effort if you reward them richly, treat them with respect, and give them real power.

Nucor is an upstart no more, and the untold story of how it has clung to that core philosophy even as it has grown into the largest steel company in the U.S. is in many ways as compelling as the celebrated tale of its brash youth. Iverson retired in 1999. Under CEO Daniel R. DiMicco, a 23-year veteran, Nucor has snapped up 13 plants over the past five years while managing to instill its unique culture in all of the facilities it has bought, an achievement that makes him a more than worthy successor to Iverson. . . .

At Nucor the art of motivation is about an unblinking focus on the people on the front line of the business. It's about talking to them, listening to them, taking a risk on their ideas, and accepting the occasional failure. It's a culture built in part with symbolic gestures. Every year, for example, every single employee's name goes on the cover of the annual report. And, like Iverson before him, DiMicco flies commercial, manages without an executive parking space, and really does make the coffee in the office when he takes the last cup. Although he has an Ivy League pedigree, including degrees from Brown University and the University of Pennsylvania, DiMicco retains the plain-talking style of a guy raised in a middle-class family in Mt. Kisco, N.Y. Only 65 people—yes, 65—work alongside him at headquarters. . . .

At a time when many observers are busy hammering the final nail into the coffin of American heavy manufacturing, Nucor's business model is well worth considering. It raises the question of whether troubled companies such as General Motors and Ford—not to mention nonmanufacturers such as Delta Airlines or Verizon Communications—could energize their workers by adopting some version of this plan. But Nucor's path is hard to follow. It requires managers to abandon the command-and-control model that has dominated American business for the better part of a century, trust their people, and do a much better job of sharing corporate wealth.[1]

FOR DISCUSSION

Which of Nucor's employee-friendly practices do you think has the greatest motivational impact? Explain. For an interpretation of this case and additional comments, visit our Online Learning Center (OLC):

www.mhhe.com/kinickiob3e

HOW IMPORTANT ARE PEOPLE to organizational success? For a quick answer, we go to Gary Kelly, the former accountant who is the CEO of Southwest Airlines. "'My top priority is, as it always has been at Southwest, our people,' Kelly says. 'If our employees love working at Southwest Airlines, everything else will fall into place.'"[2] Considering that Kelly has nearly 32,000 fellow employees at Southwest Airlines, he certainly has a full plate.[3]

A longer research-based answer comes from Stanford's Jeffrey Pfeffer: "There is a substantial and rapidly expanding body of evidence, some of it quite methodologically sophisticated, that speaks to the strong connection between how firms manage their people and the economic results achieved."[4] His review of research from the United States and Germany showed *people-centered practices* strongly associated with higher profits and lower employee turnover. Seven people-centered practices in successful companies are:

1. Job security (to eliminate fear of layoffs).
2. Careful hiring (emphasizing a good fit with the company culture).
3. Power to the people (via decentralization and self-managed teams).
4. Generous pay for performance.
5. Lots of training.
6. Less emphasis on status (to build a "we" feeling).
7. Trust building (through the sharing of critical information).[5]

Importantly, these factors are a *package* deal, meaning they need to be installed in a coordinated and systematic manner—not in bits and pieces.

Sadly, too many managers act counter to their declarations that people are their most important asset. Pfeffer blames a number of modern management trends and practices. For example, undue emphasis on short-term profit precludes long-term efforts to nurture human resources. Also, excessive layoffs, when managers view people as a cost rather than an asset, erode trust, commitment, and loyalty.[6] *Only 12% of today's organizations, according to Pfeffer, have the systematic approaches and persistence to qualify as true people-centered organizations, thus giving them a competitive advantage.*[7] No surprise, then, that "a recent Gallup Poll shows 71% of U.S. workers consider themselves 'disengaged' clock-watchers who can't wait to go home."[8]

To us, an 88% shortfall in the quest for people-centered organizations represents a tragic loss, both to society and to the global economy. We all need to accept the challenge to do better.[9] *Fortune* magazine's annual list of "The 100 Best Companies to Work For" shows what is being done at progressive organizations that put people first. For example, Northwestern Mutual, the Milwaukee life insurance firm with 4,382 employees, "hasn't laid off a single person in 145 years."[10] Importantly, as documented in a recent study, companies making *Fortune*'s "100 Best" list tend to outperform the competition.[11]

The mission of this book is to help increase the number of people-centered managers and organizations around the world. Our jumping-off point is the 4-P model of strategic results in Figure 1–1. The 4-P model emphasizes the larger strategic context for managing people. Of course, other factors such as planning, technology, and finances also require good management. Further, the 4-P model stresses the importance of day-to-day *continuous improvement* in all aspects of organizational endeavor to cope with more demanding customers and stiffer competition.

In this chapter, we discuss the manager's job, define and examine organizational behavior and its evolution, and explore new directions.

Test Your Knowledge

Levels of Strategy

FIGURE 1–1   Strategic Results: The 4-P Cycle of Continuous Improvement

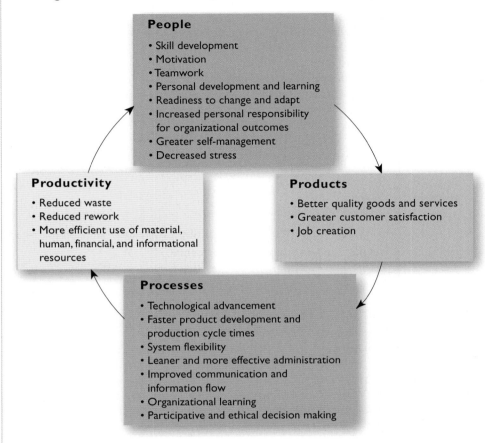

People
- Skill development
- Motivation
- Teamwork
- Personal development and learning
- Readiness to change and adapt
- Increased personal responsibility for organizational outcomes
- Greater self-management
- Decreased stress

Productivity
- Reduced waste
- Reduced rework
- More efficient use of material, human, financial, and informational resources

Products
- Better quality goods and services
- Greater customer satisfaction
- Job creation

Processes
- Technological advancement
- Faster product development and production cycle times
- System flexibility
- Leaner and more effective administration
- Improved communication and information flow
- Organizational learning
- Participative and ethical decision making

Managers Get Results with and through Others

management

Process of working with and through others to achieve organizational objectives efficiently and ethically.

For better or for worse, managers touch our lives in many ways. Schools, hospitals, government agencies, and large and small businesses all require systematic management. Formally defined, **management** is the process of working with and through others to achieve organizational objectives in an efficient and ethical manner. From the standpoint of organizational behavior, the central feature of this definition is "working with and through others." Managers play a constantly evolving role. Today's successful managers are no longer the I've-got-everything-under-control order givers of yesteryear. Rather, they need to creatively envision and actively sell bold new directions in an ethical and sensitive manner. Effective managers are team players empowered by the willing and active support of others who are driven by conflicting self-interests. Each of us has a huge stake in how well managers carry out their evolving role. Henry Mintzberg, a respected management scholar, observed: "No job is more vital to our society than that of the manager.

It is the manager who determines whether our social institutions serve us well or whether they squander our talents and resources."[12]

Extending our managerial thrust, let us take a closer look at the skills managers need to perform and the future direction of management.

Test Your Knowledge
Management's Historical Figures

A Skills Profile for Managers

Observational studies by Mintzberg and others have found the typical manager's day to be a fragmented collection of brief episodes.[13] Interruptions are commonplace, while large blocks of time for planning and reflective thinking are not. In one particular study, four top-level managers spent 63% of their time on activities lasting less than nine minutes each. Only 5% of the managers' time was devoted to activities lasting more than an hour.[14] But what specific skills do effective managers perform during their hectic and fragmented workdays?

Many attempts have been made over the years to paint a realistic picture of what managers do.[15] Diverse and confusing lists of managerial functions and roles have been suggested. Fortunately, a stream of research over the past 25 years by Clark Wilson and others has given us a practical and statistically validated profile of managerial *skills*[16] (see Skills & Best Practices). Wilson's managerial skills profile focuses on 11 observable categories of managerial behavior. This is very much in tune with today's emphasis on managerial competency.[17] Wilson's unique skills-assessment technique goes beyond the usual self-report approach with its natural bias. In addition to surveying a given manager about his or her 11 skills, the Wilson approach also asks those who report directly to the manager to answer questions about their boss's skills. According to Wilson and his colleagues, the result is an assessment of skill *mastery,* not simply skill awareness.[18] The logic behind Wilson's approach is both simple and compelling. Who better to assess a manager's skills than the people who experience those behaviors on a day-to-day basis—those who report directly to the manager?

The Wilson managerial skills research yields three useful lessons:

1. Dealing effectively with people is what management is all about. The 11 skills constitute a goal creation/commitment/feedback/reward/ accomplishment cycle with human interaction at every turn.

2. Managers with high skills mastery tend to have better subunit performance and employee morale than managers with low skills mastery.[19]

3. *Effective* female and male managers *do not* have significantly different skill profiles,[20] contrary to claims in the popular business press in recent years.[21]

The Effective Manager's Skill Profile

1. *Clarifies goals and objectives* for everyone involved.

2. *Encourages participation,* upward communication, and suggestions.

3. *Plans and organizes* for an orderly work flow.

4. Has *technical and administrative expertise* to answer organization-related questions.

5. *Facilitates work* through team building, training, coaching, and support.

6. *Provides feedback* honestly and constructively.

7. *Keeps things moving* by relying on schedules, deadlines, and helpful reminders.

8. *Controls details* without being overbearing.

9. Applies reasonable *pressure for goal accomplishment.*

10. *Empowers and delegates* key duties to others while maintaining goal clarity and commitment.

11. *Recognizes good performance* with rewards and positive reinforcement.

SOURCE: Adapted from material in F Shipper, "A Study of the Psychometric Properties of the Managerial Skill Scales of the Survey of Management Practices," *Educational and Psychological Measurement,* June 1995, pp 468–79; and C L Wilson, *How and Why Effective Managers Balance Their Skills: Technical, Teambuilding, Drive* (Columbia, Maryland: Rockatech Multimedia Publishing, 2003).

TABLE 1–1 | Evolution of the 21st-Century Manager

	Past Managers	Future Managers
Primary role	Order giver, privileged elite, manipulator, controller	Facilitator, team member, teacher, advocate, sponsor, coach, partner
Learning and knowledge	Periodic learning, narrow specialist	Continuous life-long learning, generalist with multiple specialties
Compensation criteria	Time, effort, rank	Skills, results
Cultural orientation	Monocultural, monolingual	Multicultural, multilingual
Primary source of influence	Formal authority	Knowledge (technical and interpersonal)
View of people	Potential problem	Primary resource
Primary communication Pattern	Vertical	Multidirectional
Decision-making style	Limited input for individual decisions	Broad-based input for joint decisions
Ethical considerations	Afterthought	Forethought
Nature of interpersonal relationships	Competitive (win–lose)	Cooperative (win–win)
Handling of power and key information	Hoard and restrict access	Share and broaden access
Approach to change	Resist	Facilitate

21st-Century Managers

Today's workplace is indeed undergoing immense and permanent changes.[22] Organizations have been "reengineered" for greater speed, efficiency, and flexibility.[23] Teams are pushing aside the individual as the primary building block of organizations.[24] Command-and-control management is giving way to participative management and empowerment.[25] Ego-centered leaders are being replaced by customer-centered leaders. Employees increasingly are being viewed as internal customers. All this creates a mandate for a new kind of manager in the 21st century.[26] Table 1–1 contrasts the characteristics of past and future managers. As the balance of this book will demonstrate, the managerial shift in Table 1–1 is not just a good idea, it is an absolute necessity in the new workplace.

The Field of Organizational Behavior: Past and Present

organizational behavior (OB)

Interdisciplinary field dedicated to better understanding and managing people at work.

Organizational behavior, commonly referred to as OB, is an interdisciplinary field dedicated to better understanding and managing people at work. By definition, organizational behavior is both research and application oriented. Three basic levels of analysis in OB are individual, group, and organizational. OB draws upon a diverse array of disciplines, including psychology, management, sociology, organization theory, social psychology, statistics, anthropology, general systems theory, economics, information technology, political science, vocational counseling, human stress management, psychometrics, ergonomics, decision theory, and ethics. This rich heritage has spawned many competing perspectives and theories about human work behavior. In fact, one researcher identified 73 established OB theories.[27]

Organizational behavior is an academic designation. With the exception of teaching/research positions, OB is not an everyday job category such as accounting, marketing, or finance. Students of OB typically do not get jobs in organizational behavior, per se. This reality in no way demeans OB or lessens its importance in effective organizational management. OB is a *horizontal* discipline that cuts across virtually every job category, business function, and professional specialty. Anyone who plans to make a living in a large or small, public or private, organization needs to study organizational behavior. Both managers and nonmanagers alike need a solid grounding in OB.

A historical perspective of the study of people at work helps in studying organizational behavior. According to a management history expert, this is important because

> Historical perspective is the study of a subject in light of its earliest phases and subsequent evolution. Historical perspective differs from history in that the object of historical perspective is to sharpen one's vision of the present, not the past.[28]

In other words, we can better understand where the field of OB is today and where it appears to be headed by appreciating where it has been. Let us examine three significant landmarks in the evolution of understanding and managing people:

1. The human relations movement.
2. The total quality management movement.
3. The contingency approach to management.

The Human Relations Movement

A unique combination of factors during the 1930s fostered the human relations movement. First, following legalization of union–management collective bargaining in the United States in 1935, management began looking for new ways of handling employees. Second, behavioral scientists conducting on-the-job research started calling for more attention to the "human" factor. Managers who had lost the battle to keep unions out of their factories heeded the call for better human relations and improved working conditions. One such study, conducted at Western Electric's Chicago-area Hawthorne plant, was a prime stimulus for the human relations movement. Ironically, many of the Hawthorne findings have turned out to be more myth than fact.

The Hawthorne Legacy   Interviews conducted decades later with three subjects of the Hawthorne studies and reanalysis of the original data with modern statistical techniques do not support initial conclusions about the positive effect of supportive supervision. Specifically, money, fear of unemployment during the Great Depression, managerial discipline, and high-quality raw materials—not supportive supervision—turned out to be responsible for high output in the relay assembly test room experiments.[29] Nonetheless, the human relations movement gathered momentum through the 1950s, as academics and managers alike made stirring claims about the powerful effect that individual needs, supportive supervision, and group dynamics apparently had on job performance.

These relay assembly test room employees in the classic Hawthorne Western Electric studies turned in record performance. Why? No one knows for certain, and debate continues to this day. Supportive supervision was long believed to be the key factor. Whatever the reason, Hawthorne gave the budding human relations movement needed research credibility.

The Writings of Mayo and Follett

Essential to the human relations movement were the writings of Elton Mayo and Mary Parker Follett. Australian-born Mayo, who headed the Harvard researchers at Hawthorne, advised managers to attend to employees' emotional needs in his 1933 classic, *The Human Problems of an Industrial Civilization.* Follett was a true pioneer, not only as a female management consultant in the male-dominated industrial world of the 1920s, but also as a writer who saw employees as complex bundles of attitudes, beliefs, and needs. Mary Parker Follett was way ahead of her time in telling managers to motivate job performance instead of merely demanding it, a "pull" rather than "push" strategy. She also built a logical bridge between political democracy and a cooperative spirit in the workplace.[30]

McGregor's Theory Y   In 1960, Douglas McGregor wrote a book entitled *The Human Side of Enterprise,* which has become an important philosophical base for the modern view of people at work.[31] Drawing upon his experience as a management consultant, McGregor formulated two sharply contrasting sets of assumptions about human nature (see Table 1–2). His Theory X assumptions were pessimistic and negative and, according to McGregor's interpretation, typical of how managers traditionally perceived employees. To help managers break with this negative tradition, McGregor formulated his **Theory Y,** a modern and positive set of assumptions about people. McGregor believed managers could accomplish more through others by viewing them as self-energized, committed, responsible, and creative beings.

A survey of 10,227 employees from many industries across the United States challenges managers to do a better job of acting on McGregor's Theory Y assumptions. From the employees' perspective, Theory X management practices are the major barrier to productivity improvement and employee well-being. The researcher concluded:

Theory Y

McGregor's modern and positive assumptions about employees being responsible and creative.

The most noteworthy finding from our survey is that an overwhelming number of American workers—some 97%—desire work conditions known to facilitate high productivity. Workers uniformly reported—regardless of the type of organization, age, gender, pay schedule, or level in the organizational hierarchy—that they needed and wanted in their own workplaces the conditions for collaboration, commitment, and creativity research has demonstrated as necessary for both productivity and health. Just as noteworthy, however, is the finding that the actual conditions of work supplied by management are those conditions that research has identified as *competence suppressors*—procedures, policies, and practices that prevent or punish expressions of competence and most characterize unproductive organizations.[32]

New Assumptions about Human Nature   Unfortunately, unsophisticated behavioral research methods caused the human relationists to embrace some naive and misleading conclusions. For example, human relationists believed in the axiom, "A satisfied employee is a hardworking employee." Subsequent research, as discussed later in this book, shows the satisfaction–performance linkage to be more complex than originally thought.

McGregor's Theory X and Theory Y | **TABLE 1–2**

Outdated (Theory X) Assumptions about People at Work	Modern (Theory Y) Assumptions about People at Work
1. Most people dislike work; they avoid it when they can.	1. Work is a natural activity, like play or rest.
2. Most people must be coerced and threatened with punishment before they will work. People require close direction when they are working.	2. People are capable of self-direction and self-control if they are committed to objectives.
3. Most people actually prefer to be directed. They tend to avoid responsibility and exhibit little ambition. They are interested only in security.	3. People generally become committed to organizational objectives if they are rewarded for doing so.
	4. The typical employee can learn to accept and seek responsibility.
	5. The typical member of the general population has imagination, ingenuity, and creativity.

SOURCE: Adapted from D McGregor, *The Human Side of Enterprise* (New York: McGraw-Hill, 1960), Ch 4.

Despite its shortcomings, the human relations movement opened the door to more progressive thinking about human nature. Rather than continuing to view employees as passive economic beings, managers began to see them as active social beings and took steps to create more humane work environments.[33]

The Total Quality Management Movement

In 1980, NBC aired a television documentary titled *If Japan Can . . . Why Can't We?* It was a wake-up call for North American companies to dramatically improve product quality or continue losing market share to Japanese electronics and automobile companies. A full-fledged movement ensued during the 1980s and 1990s. Much was written, said, and done about improving the quality of both goods and services.[34] Thanks to the concept of *total quality management (TQM),* the quality of much of what we buy today is significantly better than in the past. The underlying principles of TQM are more important than ever given the growth of both e-business on the Internet and the overall service economy. According to one business writer:

> A company stuck in the industrial-age mentality is very likely to get squashed because "zero-defect" quality has become an ante to compete, not a differentiator. Even "zero-time" operations that address customers' expectations for immediate response and gratification are becoming common in today's digital age.[35]

In a survey of 1,797 managers from 36 countries by the American Management Association, "customer service" and "quality" ranked as the corporate world's top two concerns.[36] TQM principles have profound practical implications for managing people today.[37]

Group Exercise

Exploring Total Quality Management

total quality management (TQM)

An organizational culture dedicated to training, continuous improvement, and customer satisfaction.

What Is TQM? Experts on the subject offered this definition of **total quality management:**

TQM means that the organization's culture is defined by and supports the constant attainment of customer satisfaction through an integrated system of tools, techniques, and training. This involves the continuous improvement of organizational processes, resulting in high-quality products and services.[38]

Quality consultant Richard J Schonberger sums up TQM as "continuous, customer-centered, employee-driven improvement."[39] TQM is necessarily employee driven because product/service quality cannot be continuously improved without the active learning and participation of *every* employee. Thus, in successful quality improvement programs, TQM principles are embedded in the organization's culture and hiring is very selective (see Skills & Best Practices).

The Deming Legacy TQM is firmly established today thanks in large part to the pioneering work of W Edwards Deming.[40] Ironically, the mathematician credited with Japan's post–World War II quality revolution rarely talked in terms of quality. He instead preferred to discuss "good management" during the hard-hitting seminars he delivered right up until his death at age 93 in 1993.[41] Although Deming's passion was the statistical measurement and reduction of variations in industrial processes, he had much to say about how employees should be treated. Regarding the human side of quality improvement, Deming called for the following:

- Formal training in statistical process control techniques and teamwork.
- Helpful leadership, rather than order giving and punishment.
- Elimination of fear so employees will feel free to ask questions.
- Emphasis on continuous process improvements rather than on numerical quotas.
- Teamwork.
- Elimination of barriers to good workmanship.[42]

One of Deming's most enduring lessons for managers is his 85–15 rule.[43] Specifically, when things go wrong, there is roughly an 85% chance the *system* (including management, machinery, and rules) is at fault. Only about 15% of the time is the individual employee at fault. Unfortunately, as Deming observed, the typical manager spends most of his or her time

Southwest Airlines Hires with High-Quality Service in Mind

You don't just get interviewed when you apply for a job at Southwest Airlines. You get auditioned—and it starts the moment you call for an application.

Given that ultrafriendly service is critical to the $7.6 billion carrier's success, it's little wonder that HR [Human Resource] managers don't wait until the interview to start screening. When a candidate calls for an application, managers jot down anything memorable about the conversation, good or bad. The same is true when the company flies recruits out for interviews. They receive special tickets, which alert gate agents, flight attendants, and others to pay special attention: Are they friendly to others or griping about service and slurping cocktails at 8 a.m.? If what the employees observe seems promising—or not—they're likely to pass it on to HR.

Even when recruits aren't on the spot, they're on the spot. During group interviews of flight attendants, applicants take turns giving three-minute speeches about themselves in front of as many as 50 others. The catch? Managers are watching the audience as closely as the speaker. Candidates who pay attention pass the test; those who seem bored or distracted get bounced. "We want to see how they interact with people when they think they're not being evaluated," says Southwest recruiter Michael Burkhardt. The screening method not only keeps turnover low (about 5.5 percent annually) but keeps customers happy. Every year since 1987, the carrier has received the lowest number of passenger complaints in the industry.

SOURCE: M V Copeland, "The Job Audition," *Business 2.0*, April 2006, p 85.

wrongly blaming and punishing individuals for system failures. Statistical analysis is required to uncover system failures.

Principles of TQM   Despite variations in the language and scope of TQM programs, it is possible to identify four common TQM principles:

1. Do it right the first time to eliminate costly rework.
2. Listen to and learn from customers and employees.
3. Make continuous improvement an everyday matter.
4. Build teamwork, trust, and mutual respect.[44]

Deming's influence is clearly evident in this list. Once again, as with the human relations movement, we see people as the key factor in organizational success. DaimlerChrysler drives that point home for high-end customers who plunk down $190,000 for a new Mercedes-Benz CL65 AMG:

> Every CL65 sold this year will ease onto its owner's cobbled drive boasting an aluminum V-12 bi-turbo engine, signed on its carbon-fiber face by the exacting craftsman who assembled it by hand.[45]

For both producers and consumers of high-quality goods and services, quality is indeed a matter of *personal* importance.

In summary, TQM advocates have made a valuable contribution to the field of OB by providing a *practical* context for managing people. When people are managed according to TQM principles, everyone is more likely to get the employment opportunities and high-quality goods and services they demand. As you will see many times in later chapters, this book is anchored to Deming's philosophy and TQM principles.

The Contingency Approach to Management

Scholars have wrestled for many years with the problem of how best to apply the diverse and growing collection of management tools and techniques. Their answer is the contingency approach. The **contingency approach** calls for using management concepts and techniques in a situationally appropriate manner, instead of trying to rely on "one best way."

The contingency approach encourages managers to view organizational behavior within a situational context. According to this modern perspective, evolving situations, not hard-and-fast rules, determine when and where various management techniques are appropriate. Harvard's Clayton Christensen put it this way: "Many of the widely accepted principles of good management are only situationally appropriate."[46] For example, as will be discussed in Chapter 14, contingency researchers have determined that there is no single best style of leadership. Organizational behavior specialists embrace the contingency approach because it helps them realistically interrelate individuals, groups, and organizations. Moreover, the contingency approach sends a clear message to managers in today's global economy: Carefully read the situation and then apply lessons learned from published research studies,[47] observing role models, self-study and training, and personal experience in situationally appropriate ways.

contingency approach

Using management tools and techniques in a situationally appropriate manner; avoiding the one-best-way mentality.

Manager's Hot Seat Application

Project Management: Steering the Committee

New Directions in OB

The field of OB is a dynamic work in progress—not static and in final form. As such, OB is being redirected and reshaped by various forces both inside and outside the discipline, including new concepts, models, and technology. In this section, we explore three general new directions for OB: human and social capital, *positive* organizational behavior, and impacts of the Internet revolution.

The Age of Human and Social Capital

Management is a lot like juggling. Everything is constantly in motion, with several things up in the air at any given time. Strategically speaking, managers juggle human, financial, material, informational, and technological resources. Each is vital to success in its own way. But jugglers remind us that some objects are rubber and some are glass. Dropped rubber objects bounce; dropped glass objects break. As more and more managers have come to realize, we cannot afford to drop the people factor (referred to in Figure 1–2 as human and social capital).

FIGURE 1–2
The Strategic Importance and Dimensions of Human and Social Capital

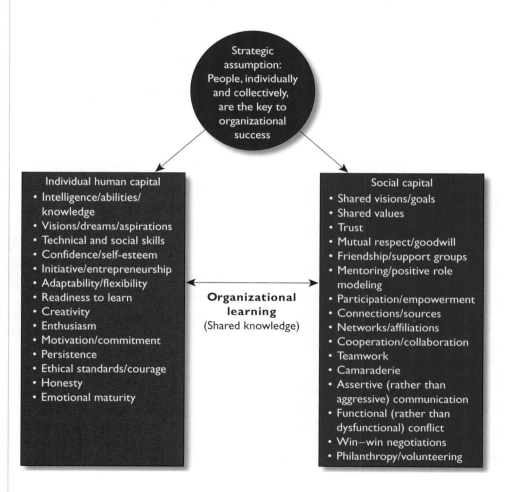

What Is Human Capital? (Hint: Think BIG)   A team of human resource management authors recently offered this perspective:

> We're living in a time when a new economic paradigm—characterized by speed, innovation, short cycle times, quality, and customer satisfaction—is highlighting the importance of intangible assets, such as brand recognition, knowledge, innovation, and particularly human capital.[48]

Human capital is the productive potential of an individual's knowledge and actions.[49] *Potential* is the operative word in this intentionally broad definition. When you are hungry, money in your pocket is good because it has the potential to buy a meal. Likewise, a present or future employee with the right combination of knowledge, skills, and motivation to excel represents human capital with the potential to give the organization a competitive advantage. Computer chip maker Intel, for example, is a high-tech company whose future depends on innovative engineering. It takes years of math and science studies to make world-class engineers. Not wanting to leave the future supply of engineers to chance, Intel annually spends millions of dollars funding education at all levels. The company encourages youngsters to study math and science and sponsors science competitions with generous scholarships for the winners.[50] Additionally, Intel encourages its employees to volunteer at local schools by giving the schools $200 for every 20 hours contributed.[51] Will all of the students end up working for Intel? No. That's not the point. The point is much bigger—namely, to build the *world's* human capital.

human capital

The productive potential of one's knowledge and actions.

Within the context of individual organizations, researchers have identified and defined five important human capital *outcomes* (see Table 1–3). These definitions are a necessary first step toward eventually measuring an organization's attempts to build its human capital.[52] Measurement, of course, is the key to accountability.

Five Human Capital Outcomes Defined   **TABLE 1–3**

	Definition
Leadership/managerial practices	The effectiveness of managers' and leaders' ability to optimize the organization's human capital through communication, performance feedback, efforts to instill confidence, and demonstration of key organizational values
Workforce optimization	The organization's success in optimizing the performance of its workforce by means of developing and sustaining talent (skills, competencies, abilities, etc.) and guiding and managing its application on the job
Learning capacity	The organization's overall ability to learn, change, and continually improve
Knowledge accessibility	The extent of the organization's "collaborativeness" and its current efforts and ability to share knowledge and ideas across the organization
Talent engagement	The organization's ability to retain, engage, and optimize the value of its talent

SOURCE: L Bassi and D McMurrer, "Developing Measurement Systems for Managing in the Knowledge Era," *Organizational Dynamics*, no. 2, 2005, Table 2, p 190.

social capital

The productive potential of strong, trusting, and cooperative relationships.

Test Your Knowledge

Training Methods

What Is Social Capital?   Our focus now shifts from the individual to social units (e.g., friends, family, company, group or club, nation). Think *relationships*. **Social capital** is productive potential resulting from strong relationships, goodwill, trust, and cooperative effort.[53] Again, the word *potential* is key. According to experts on the subject: "It's true: the social capital that used to be a given in organizations is now rare and endangered. But the social capital we can build will allow us to capitalize on the volatile, virtual possibilities of today's business environment."[54] Relationships do matter. In a recent general survey, 77% of the women and 63% of the men rated "Good relationship with boss" extremely important. Other factors—including good equipment, resources, easy commute, and flexible hours—received lower ratings.[55]

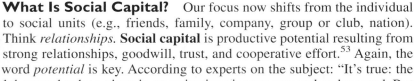

How to Build Human and Social Capital
Making the leap from concept to practice within this broad domain appears to be a daunting task. But we have a handy shortcut to jump-start your imagination. *Fortune* magazine, as mentioned earlier, publishes its annual list of "The 100 Best Companies to Work For" every January. Reading the brief side comments about the 100 selected companies is time well spent because they are both interesting and inspiring (as well as being a great resource for job hunters). These model companies are good at building human and/or social capital. Another area to watch is the *social entrepreneurship* movement that challenges students and businesspeople to create businesses with a dual bottom line. Laura D'Andrea Tyson, Dean of London Business School, explains:

Target has been recognized for its financial performance and strength. It has been honored as one of America's most admired companies, one of the best companies for both working mothers and Latinos, one of the best corporate citizens, and a leader in its commitment to the education and training of its people. To what extent do you think its positive work environment affects its financial success?

> At the broadest level, a social entrepreneur is one driven by a social mission, a desire to find innovative ways to solve problems that are not being or cannot be addressed by either the market or the public sector. . . . Well-documented cases of grassroots entrepreneurial activities to tackle such diverse social problems as child abuse, disability, illiteracy, and environmental degradation give life to it. . . . Such businesses have a dual or "blended" bottom line that encompasses both a financial rate of return and a social rate of return.[56]

This promising initiative meshes nicely with the areas of corporate social responsibility and business ethics (see Skills & Best Practices). Meanwhile, relative to the field of OB, many of the ideas discussed in this book relate directly or indirectly to building human and social capital (e.g., managing diversity, self-efficacy, self-management, emotional intelligence, goal setting, positive reinforcement, group problem-solving, group development, building trust, teamwork, managing conflict, communicating, empowerment, leadership, and organizational learning).

The Emerging Area of Positive Organizational Behavior (POB)

OB draws heavily on the field of psychology. So major shifts and trends in psychology eventually ripple through to OB. One such shift being felt in OB is the positive psychology movement. This exciting new direction promises to broaden the scope and practical relevance of OB.

Thanks to college courses leading to a teaching license, paid for by her old employer, Susan Luerich will teach high school science following her recent retirement from IBM. Hundreds of other IBM employees are interested in the program, which the company believes is the first of its kind.

IBM Takes the Ethical High Road to Build Human and Social Capital

Research Triangle Park, N.C.—After more than three decades at IBM, Larry Leise and Susan Luerich could be planning a leisurely retirement. Instead, the married couple are headed back to college, with plans to start new careers in retirement as high school science teachers.

"Seeing the proverbial light bulb come on (in a student), there is no better feeling," said Luerich, 54. "It's a way to give back."

And their bosses at IBM Corp. are only too happy to help.

Luerich and Leise, 58, are among the first batch of IBM employees taking the company up on its offer to pay for the college classes needed to leave Big Blue behind for a math or science classroom, where a shortage of qualified teachers concerns a company that thrives on high-tech innovation.

SOURCE: Excerpted from N Gott, "IBM Helps Workers Move into Science, Math Class," *The Arizona Republic,* **April 8, 2006, p D6.**

The Positive Psychology Movement   Something curious happened to the field of psychology during the last half of the 20th century. It took a distinctly negative turn. Theory and research became preoccupied with mental and behavioral pathologies; in other words, what was *wrong* with people! Following the traditional medical model, most researchers and practicing psychologists devoted their attention to diagnosing what was wrong with people and trying to make them better. At the turn of the 21st century, bits and pieces of an alternative perspective advocated by pioneering psychologists such as Abraham Maslow and Carl Rogers were pulled together under the label of positive psychology. This approach recommended focusing on human strengths and potential as a way to possibly *prevent* mental and behavioral problems and improve the general quality of life. A pair of positive psychologists described their new multilevel approach as follows:

> The field of positive psychology at the subjective level is about valued subjective experiences: well-being, contentment, and satisfaction (in the past); hope and optimism (for the future); and flow and happiness (in the present). At the individual level, it is about positive individual traits: the capacity for love and vocation,

courage, interpersonal skill, aesthetic sensibility, perseverance, forgiveness, originality, future mindedness, spirituality, high talent, and wisdom. At the group level, it is about the civic virtues and the institutions that move individuals toward better citizenship: responsibility, nurturance, altruism, civility, moderation, tolerance, and work ethic.[57]

This is an extremely broad agenda for understanding and improving the human condition. However, we foresee a productive marriage between the concepts of human and social capital and the positive psychology movement, as it evolves into POB.[58]

Positive Organizational Behavior: Definition and Key Dimensions

University of Nebraska OB scholar Fred Luthans defines **positive organizational behavior (POB)** as "the study and application of positively oriented human resource strengths and psychological capacities that can be measured, developed, and effectively managed for performance improvement in today's workplace."[59] His emphasis on study and measurement (meaning a coherent body of theory and research evidence) clearly sets POB apart from the quick-and-easy self-improvement books commonly found on best-seller lists. Also, POB focuses positive psychology more narrowly on the workplace.[60] Luthans created the CHOSE acronym to identify five key dimensions of POB (see Table 1–4). Progressive managers already know the value of a positive workplace atmosphere, as evidenced by the following situations: At Plante & Moran, the 1,356-employee accounting firm in Southfield, Michigan, the "goal is a 'jerk-free' workforce . . . , where the staff is encouraged to live by the Golden Rule and abide by the credo 'Speak up! If it's not right, we'll change it.'"[61] Meanwhile, Intuit creates a positive work climate for its 6,516 employees in Mountain View, California, in a somewhat different way: "These brainiacs know how to party. The inventors of Quicken, TurboTax, and other financial tools are legendary for their Friday afternoon socials, summer cookouts, and beach parties at the end of tax season."[62]

positive organizational behavior (POB)

The study and improvement of employees' positive attributes and capabilities.

E-business

Running the *entire* business via the Internet.

The Internet and E-Business Revolution

Experts on the subject draw an important distinction between *e-commerce* (buying and selling goods and services over the Internet) and **e-business,** using the Internet to facilitate *every* aspect of running a business.[63] Says one industry observer: "Strip away the highfalutin talk, and at bottom, the Internet is a tool that dramatically lowers the cost of communication. That means it can radically alter any industry or activity that depends heavily on the flow of information."[64] Relevant information includes everything from customer needs and product design specifications to prices, schedules, finances, employee performance data, and corporate strategy. Intel has taken this broad view of the Internet to heart. This builder of human capital, as discussed earlier, is striving to become what it calls an e-corporation, one that relies primarily on the Internet to not only buy and sell things, but to facilitate

© 2002 Ted Goff

"So what's the problem with morale now?"

Luthans' CHOSE Model of Key POB Dimensions (with cross-references to related topics in this textbook)

TABLE 1–4

Confidence/self-efficacy: One's belief (confidence) in being able to successfully execute a specific task in a given context. (See Chapter 5.)

Hope: One who sets goals, figures out how to achieve them (identify pathways) and is self-motivated to accomplish them, that is, willpower and "waypower." (See Chapters 5 and 7.)

Optimism: Positive outcome expectancy and/or a positive causal attribution, but is still emotional and linked with happiness, perseverance, and success. (See Chapters 4, 5, 7, and 16.)

Subjective well-being: Beyond happiness emotion, how people cognitively process and evaluate their lives, the satisfaction with their lives. (See Chapters 4, 5, and 6.)

Emotional intelligence: Capacity for recognizing and managing one's own and others' emotions—self-awareness, self-motivation, being empathetic, and having social skills. (See Chapters 5, 9, 11, 12, 13, and 14.)

SOURCE: From *The Academy of Management Executive: The Thinking Manager's Source* by F. Luthans. Copyright © 2002 by Academy of Management. Reproduced with permission of Academy of Management via Copyright Clearance Center.

all business functions, exchange knowledge among its employees, and build partnerships with outsiders as well. Intel is on the right track according to this survey finding: "[F]irms that embraced the Internet averaged a 13.4% jump in productivity . . . compared with 4.9% for those that did not."[65]

E-business has significant implications for OB because it eventually will seep into every corner of life both on and off the job. Thanks to the Internet, we are able to make quicker and better decisions because of speedy access to vital information. The Internet also allows us to seemingly defy the laws of physics by being in more than one place at a time. For example, consider the futuristic situation at Hackensack University Medical Center in New Jersey:

> Doctors can tap an interval Web site to examine X-rays from a PC anywhere. Patients can use 37-inch plasma TVs in their rooms to surf the Net for information about their medical conditions. There's even a life-size robot, Mr Rounder, that doctors can control from their laptops at home. They direct the digital doc, complete with white lab coat and stethoscope, into hospital rooms and use two-way video to discuss patients' conditions.[66]

In short, organizational life will never be the same because of e-mail, e-learning,[67] e-management, e-leadership (see Skills & Best Practices), virtual teams, and virtual organizations. You will learn more about virtual teams and virtual organizations in later chapters.

Practical E-Leadership Lessons from a "Virtual CEO"

Background: Stephen McDonnell is the founder and CEO of Applegate Farms. The Bridgewater, New Jersey, company specializes in natural and organic meat products and employs 54 people. Customers include Whole Foods, Wild Oats, and Trader Joe's. For 17 years, McDonnell has managed Applegate Farms remotely from his family farm in Bucks County, Pennsylvania. In a typical week, he spends four days at home and one day at the office. Every employee has access to 120 online databases that capture every significant detail of the business. Here are the lessons he has learned about e-leadership, e-management, and virtual organizations:

1. **Visibility:** Make sure you and your management team see all key business data. Assign responsibility for monitoring the data for accuracy and for needed action. Build weekly and monthly meetings around data points as a forum to discuss problems rather than micromanaging on the spot.

2. **Replication:** Hire and train management people who look at data and information the way you do. Be relentless about instilling the precise way you want every number, invoice, quote, e-mail, meeting, and discussion handled. These are your core operating principles.

3. **Consciousness:** Create a public forum for issues of the day and week to be posted—not just for the CEO's benefit but to expose all personnel to issues that affect the business. This data can give great insight into hidden stressors in the system.

4. **Weekly Meetings:** Route issues into key weekly meetings with the core management team. Jumping on issues instantly can inhibit the self-reliance the system needs to develop. Unless it's a true crisis, don't micromanage the situation by voice or e-mail. If you do, the team will always look to you for a solution rather than looking within.

5. **Park the Ego:** Be comfortable when the organization no longer needs its hand held on a tactical level. This is a sign that you've built a strong system and have the right team in place. It doesn't mean they don't need you—it means they need you looking ahead.

SOURCE: Background material adapted from and list excerpted from D Fenn, "The Remote Control CEO," *Inc.,* October 2005, pp 96–101, 144, 146.

Stephen McDonnell, founder and CEO of Applegate Farms, manages his organic foods company of more than 50 people by working at home four days a week, where he can also spend time with his daughters. Computer technology has made it possible for McDonnell to put into practice his philosophy that in order to succeed, a manager should give employees complete access to relevant information and the freedom and responsibility to use it—and then get out of the way.

key terms

contingency approach   13

e-business   18

human capital   15

management   6

organizational behavior (OB)   8

positive organizational
   behavior (POB)   18

social capital   16

Theory Y   10

total quality management
   (TQM)   12

chapter summary

- *Identify at least four of Pfeffer's people-centered practices, and define the term* management. Pfeffer's seven people-centered practices are job security, careful hiring, power to the people, generous pay for performance, lots of training, less emphasis on status, and trust building. *Management* is the process of working with and through others to achieve organizational objectives in an efficient and ethical manner.

- *Contrast McGregor's Theory X and Theory Y assumptions about employees.* Theory X employees, according to traditional thinking, dislike work, require close supervision, and are primarily interested in security. According to the modern Theory Y view, employees are capable of self-direction, of seeking responsibility, and of being creative.

- *Explain the managerial significance of Deming's 85–15 rule, and identify the four principles of total quality management (TQM).* Deming claimed that about 85% of organizational failures are due to system breakdowns involving factors such as management, machinery, or work rules. He believed the workers themselves are responsible for failures only about 15% of the time. Consequently, Deming criticized the standard practice of blaming and punishing individuals for what are typically *system* failures beyond their immediate control. The four principles of TQM are (a) do it right the first time to eliminate costly rework; (b) listen to and learn from customers and employees; (c) make continuous improvement an everyday matter; and (d) build teamwork, trust, and mutual respect.

- *Contrast human and social capital, and identify five measurable outcomes when building human capital.* Human capital involves *individual* characteristics and abilities; social capital involves *social* relationships. Human capital is the productive potential of an individual's knowledge and actions. Social capital is productive potential resulting from strong relationships, goodwill, trust, and cooperative effort. Five measurable outcomes of programs to build human capital are (a) leadership/managerial practices; (b) workforce optimization; (c) learning capacity; (d) knowledge accessibility; and (e) talent engagement.

- *Explain the impact of the positive psychology movement on the field of OB.* Reversing psychology's long-standing preoccupation with what is wrong with people, positive psychology instead focuses on identifying and building human strengths and potential. Accordingly, Luthans recommends positive organizational behavior (POB) and identifies its basic elements with the CHOSE model. This acronym stands for Confidence/self-efficacy, Hope, Optimism, Subjective well-being, and Emotional intelligence.

- *Define the term* e-business, *and explain at least three practical lessons about effective e-leadership in a virtual organization.* E-business involves using the Internet to more effectively and efficiently manage *every* aspect of a business. The "virtual CEO" of Applegate Farms learned five useful lessons about e-leadership: *visibility* (all managers need access to essential and accurate performance data and periodic meetings to discuss key data), *replication* (core operating principles based on data need to be instilled during hiring and training), *consciousness* (prevent buildup of stress in the system by posting issues online in a public forum), *weekly meetings* (weekly management meetings foster day-to-day self-reliance and prevent micromanaging), and *park the ego* (once you've built a strong team, let it run; look ahead).

discussion questions

1. Which of Pfeffer's seven people-centered practices are evident in the chapter-opening vignette on Nucor Corp.? Explain.

2. In your opinion, what are the three or four most important strategic results in Figure 1–1? Why?

3. What is your personal experience with Theory X and Theory Y managers (see Table 1–2)? Which did you prefer? Why?

4. What are you doing to build human and social capital?

5. As the field of positive organizational behavior (POB) evolves, what potential impacts on the practice of management do you foresee?

ethical dilemma

You Mean Cheating Is Wrong?

College students are disturbed by recent corporate scandals: Some 84% believe the U.S. is having a business crisis, and 77% think CEOs should be held personally responsible for it.

But when the same students are asked about their own ethics, it's another story. Some 59% admit cheating on a test (66% of men, 54% of women). And only 19% say they would report a classmate who cheated (23% of men, but 15% of women—even though recent whistle-blowers have been women).

The survey of 1,100 students on 27 U.S. campuses was conducted by Students in Free Enterprise (SIFE), a non-profit that teams up with corporations to teach students ethical business practices. "There's a lack of understanding about ethics and how ethics are applied in real life," says Alvin Rohrs, SIFE'S CEO. "We have to get young people to stop and think about ethics and the decisions they're making." Otherwise, today's students may be tomorrow's criminals.[68]

How Should We Interpret This Hypocritical Double Standard?

1. Don't worry, most students know the difference between school and real life. They'll do the right thing when it really counts. Explain your rationale.

2. Whether in the classroom or on the job, pressure for results is the problem. People tend to take shortcuts and bend the rules when they're pressured. Explain.

3. A cheater today is a cheater tomorrow. Explain.

4. College professors need to do a better job with ethics education. How?

5. Both students and managers need to be held personally accountable for their unethical behavior. How?

6. Invent other interpretations or options. Discuss.

For an interpretation of this situation, visit our Web site, www.mhhe.com/kinickiob3e.

If you're looking for additional study materials, be sure to check out the Online Learning Center at

www.mhhe.com/kinickiob3e

for more information and interactivities that correspond to this chapter.

ethics learning module

Fines and Jail Time Await Unethical Contractors and U.S. Officials

FOR DISCUSSION

Do you think Robert Stein and Philip Bloom should serve jail time? Explain.

In January 2004, Robert Stein, a senior U.S. contracting official in Iraq, sent an unusual email to American businessman Philip Bloom. Mr. Stein wrote that he had arranged for a new set of lucrative rebuilding contracts to be awarded to Mr. Bloom, but wanted the businessman to send his bid on the letterhead of a fake company to avoid attracting attention in Baghdad. A few days later, Mr. Bloom replied that he would "bring with me the dummies . . . I have five dummies per bid." The contracts were awarded a short time later.

The emails illustrate how closely U.S. officials on active duty, like Mr. Stein, were willing to work with Mr. Bloom to help him defraud the government through a massive bid-rigging scheme in southern Iraq. They were released . . . as part of a guilty plea from Mr. Bloom, who admitted to steering $2 million in cash and other bribes to government officials in exchange for $8.6 million in Iraqi construction and demolition contracts. Mr. Bloom—who also admitted to providing the officials with jewelry, first-class plane tickets and sexual favors from women he employed at a villa in Baghdad—faces as long as 40 years in prison and nearly $8 million in penalties.

The plea to charges of conspiracy, bribery and money laundering is the latest to emerge from an investigation into alleged corruption by American officials in Hillah, a restive southern city. Mr. Stein, a former civilian occupation official charged with overseeing $82 million in rebuilding funds there, pleaded guilty on Feb. 2 [2006] to conspiracy, bribery and using stolen government money to purchase an array of high-powered rifles and grenade launchers.

Lt. Col. Michael Wheeler and Lt. Col. Debra Harrison, who both worked in Hillah, were arrested late last year [2005] and charged with similar offenses; both are free on bond. Lt. Col. Wheeler's attorney didn't return a call; Lt. Col. Harrison declined to comment. Three other military officials are mentioned in the court papers, and law enforcement authorities say more arrests are likely. "There was no oversight anywhere near them at the time and they did not believe they would be caught," says Special Inspector General for Iraq Reconstruction Stuart Bowen, whose investigators uncovered the ring. "They considered it a free-fraud zone."[1]

Ethical considerations are not always as clear-cut as the case of Robert Stein and Philip Bloom. For example, a recent study of 170 medical experts who created the generally accepted bible for diagnosing mental illness found that 56 percent had undisclosed ties to drugmakers.[2] Do you think that these links to pharmaceutical companies might create a conflict of interest for the medical experts? Is it possible that these medical experts' opinions might be swayed by the connections they have with various companies? One can argue both sides of this issue. The problem when discussing ethics is that there is no universal standard of ethical behavior.[3]

US industries lose about $600 billion a year from unethical and criminal behavior. Another nationwide survey revealed that over 50% of the respondents felt some pressure to compromise their organization's ethical standards.[4] Unethical behavior is a relevant issue for all employees. It occurs from the bottom to the top of the organization. For example, a recent study of 2,099 employees revealed that more than 33% had seen a co-worker engage in unethical or illegal behavior.[5] The problem also occurs in school settings. A recent study of 50,000 undergraduate students at 69 schools demonstrated that 26% of business majors cheated on exams while 54% indicated that they had cheated on written assignments.[6] As you will learn, there are a variety of individual and organizational characteristics that contribute to unethical behavior. OB is an excellent vantage point for better understanding and improving workplace ethics. If OB can provide insights about managing human work behavior, then it can teach us something about avoiding *misbehavior*.

Lucrative rebuilding contracts in Iraq appear to have tempted some business executives and government officials to act unethically in bidding for the work being done there.

Ethics involves the study of moral issues and choices. It is concerned with right versus wrong, good versus bad, and the many shades of gray in supposedly black-and-white issues. Moral implications spring from virtually every decision, both on and off the job. Managers are challenged to have more imagination and the courage to do the right thing.

To enhance your understanding about ethics and organizational behavior, we discuss (1) a conceptual framework of ethical behavior, (2) a decision tree for diagnosing ethical decisions, (3) whether moral orientations vary by gender, (4) general moral principles for managers, and (5) how to improve an organization's ethical climate.

ethics

Study of moral issues and choices.

A Model of Ethical Behavior

Ethical and unethical conduct is the product of a complex combination of influences (see Figure A–1 on page 27). At the center of the model in Figure A–1 is the individual decision maker. He or she has a unique combination of personality characteristics, values, and moral principles, leaning toward or away from ethical behavior. Personal experience with being rewarded or reinforced for certain behaviors and punished for others also shapes the individual's tendency to act ethically or unethically. Finally, gender plays an important role in explaining ethical behavior. Men and women have different moral orientations toward organizational behavior.[7] This issue is discussed later in this section.

Bernard Ebbers, former CEO of WorldCom, was convicted in an $11 billion accounting fraud at the company he ran. What accounts for such massive wrong-doing? Do actions like Ebbers's encourage poor ethical choices by others?

Next, Figure A–1 illustrates two major sources of influence on one's role expectations. People assume many roles in life, including those of employee or manager. One's expectations for how those roles should be played are shaped by a combination of internal and external organizational factors. Let us now examine how various internal and external organizational influences impact ethical behavior and how these effects are neutralized or enhanced by characteristics possessed by an organization's top management team.

Internal Organizational Influences

Figure A–1 shows six key internal organizational influences on ethical behavior.[8] Corporate ethical codes of conduct and organizational culture, discussed in Chapter 2, clearly contribute to reducing the frequency of unethical behavior. Consider the example of Rudder Finn, the world's largest privately owned public relations agency.

> Rudder Finn established an ethics committee early on in its history because the founders maintain that public relations professionals have a special obligation to believe in what they are doing. David Finn, co-founder and CEO, chairs every ethics committee meeting to demonstrate how seriously he takes this issue. In part, these meetings perform the function of a training program in that all members of staff are invited to participate in an open forum, during which actual ethical problems are freely discussed and an outside adviser provides objectivity. "Employees have to trust that if they go to a line manager to discuss a delicate situation or seek advice, they can do so without fear of repercussions," says Finn.[9]

This example also illustrates the importance of top management support in creating an ethical work environment.

A number of studies have uncovered a positive relationship between organizational size and unethical behavior: Larger firms are more likely to behave illegally. Interestingly, research also reveals that managers are more likely to behave unethically in decentralized organizations. Unethical behavior is suspected to occur in this context because lower-level managers want to "look good" for the corporate office. In support of this conclusion, many studies have found a tendency among middle- and lower-level managers to act unethically in the face of perceived pressure for results.[10] By fostering a pressure-cooker atmosphere for results, managers can unwittingly set the stage for unethical shortcuts by employees who seek to please and be loyal to the company. Consider what happened at Qwest under the leadership of the company's former CEO Joe Nacchio.

> "The market was collapsing," recounts Nik Nesbitt, a former Qwest senior vice president. "[There were] unreachable demands: 'We need to sell this many millions of dollars in hosting services in the next 90 days,' when the lead time to sell hosting services was 180 days. You'd ask questions, and it was just, 'Don't ask questions. Just go and do it, and if you don't do it, you're not part of the team.'"
>
> Managers were terrified they wouldn't match Nacchio's expectations. . . . Down through the hierarchy, Qwest managers believed they had to make their numbers in any way possible. "[Managers would say] 'What can I do? My arm is being twisted. I just gotta do what the boss says,'" recalls Nesbitt.[11]

A Model of Ethical Behavior in the Workplace   FIGURE A–1

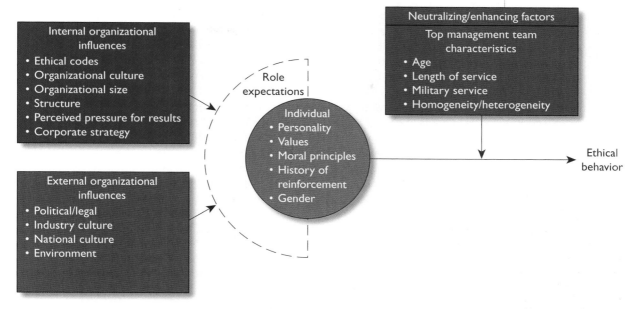

SOURCE: Based in part on A J Daboub, A M A Rasheed, R L Priem, and D A Gray, "Top Management Team Characteristics and Corporate Illegal Activity," *Academy of Management Review*, January 1995, pp 138–70.

Nacchio ultimately lost his job, being forced out by Qwest's board of directors while in the midst of a multibillion-dollar accounting scandal. This example also reinforces that individuals are more likely to behave ethically/unethically when they have incentives to do so. Managers are encouraged to examine their reward systems to ensure that the preferred types of behaviors are being reinforced.

External Organizational Influences

Figure A–1 identifies four key external influences on role expectations and ethical behavior. The political/legal system clearly impacts ethical behavior. As previously mentioned, the United States is currently experiencing an increase in the extent to which its political/legal system is demanding and monitoring corporate ethical behavior. In contrast, other countries such as China do not put as much emphasis on monitoring unethical and potentially illegal actions. Consider the case of counterfeiting. The World Customs Organization estimates counterfeiting cost companies $512 billion in lost revenue in 2004. China is the largest contributor to counterfeiting in the world, accounting for

CEO Paulette Cole wants to make ethical behavior part of the corporate strategy of ABC Carpet and Home, a trendy Manhattan department store with nearly $80 million in sales. Jewelry made by Ugandan women with AIDS and other products whose proceeds go to foster schools in Central America are being sold there as Cole begins a new business plan. "Knowing that your investment in a product actually has a positive effect on somebody's life makes the design in your hands more important," she says. "My goal is for the store to be 100 percent responsible design."

nearly two-thirds of all the fake goods worldwide.[12] Past research also uncovered a tendency for firms in certain industries to commit more illegal acts. Researchers partially explained this finding by speculating that an industry's culture, defined as shared norms, values, and beliefs among firms, predisposes managers to act unethically.

Moreover, Figure A–1 shows that national culture affects ethical behavior (national cultures are discussed in Chapter 3). This conclusion was supported in a multination study (including the United States, Great Britain, France, Germany, Spain, Switzerland, India, China, and Australia) of management ethics. Managers from each country were asked to judge the ethicality of the 12 behaviors listed in the Hands-On Exercise on page 31. Results revealed significant differences across the 10 nations.[13] That is, managers did not agree about the ethicality of the 12 behaviors. What is your attitude toward these behaviors? (You can find out by completing the Hands-On Exercise.) Finally, the external environment influences ethical behavior. For example, unethical behavior is more likely to occur in environments that are characterized by less generosity and when industry profitability is declining.

Neutralizing/Enhancing Factors

In their search for understanding the causes of ethical behavior, OB researchers uncovered several factors that may weaken or strengthen the relationship between the internal and external influencers shown in Figure A–1 and ethical behavior. These factors all revolve around characteristics possessed by an organization's top management team (TMT): A TMT consists of the CEO and his or her direct reports.[14] The relationship between ethical influencers and ethical behavior is weaker with increasing average age and increasing tenure among the TMT. This result suggests that an older and more experienced group of leaders is less likely to allow unethical behavior to occur. Further, the ethical influencers are less likely to lead to unethical behavior as the number of TMT members with military experience increases and when the TMT possesses heterogenous characteristics (e.g., diverse in terms of gender, age, race, religion, etc.). This conclusion has two important implications.

First, it appears that prior military experience favorably influences the ethical behavior of executives. While OB researchers are uncertain about the cause of this relationship, it may be due to the military's practice of indoctrinating recruits to endorse the values of duty, discipline, and honor. Regardless of the cause, military experience within a TMT is positively related to ethical behavior. Organizations thus should consider the merits of including

Although China is the largest contributor to counterfeit business around the world, officials like these in Zhejiang Province have been increasing their efforts to confiscate fake products. These officials found 460,000 fake Sony batteries and 30,000 fake Sony earphones. Would you buy a designer knockoff if the price was right?

military experience as one of its selection criteria when hiring or promoting managers. Second, organizations are encouraged to increase the diversity of its TMT if they want to reduce the chances of unethical decision making. Chapter 4 thoroughly discusses how employee diversity can increase creativity, innovation, group problem solving, and productivity.

A Decision Tree for Ethical Decisions

Ethical decision making frequently involves trade-offs. This section presents a decision tree that managers can use to help navigate through the ethical trade-offs.

The decision tree shown in Figure A–2 can be applied to any type of decision or action that an individual manager or corporation is contemplating.[15] Looking at the tree, the first question to ask is whether or not the proposed action is legal. If the action is illegal, do not do it. If the action is legal, then consider the impact of the action on shareholder value. A decision maximizes shareholder value when it results in a more favorable financial position (e.g., increased profits) for an organization. Whether or not an action maximizes shareholder value, the decision tree shows that managers still need to consider the ethical implications of the decision or action. For example, if an action maximizes shareholder value, the next question to consider is whether or not the action is ethical. The answer to this question is based on considering the positive effect of the action on an organization's other key constituents

Test Your Knowledge

Ethics

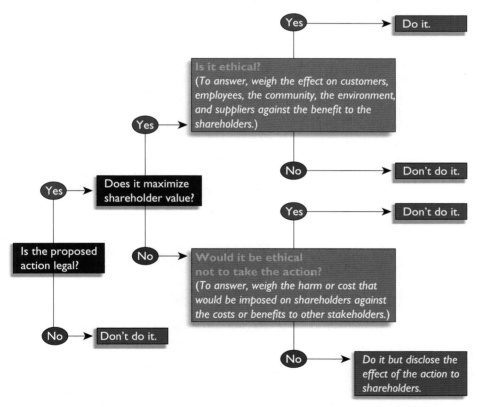

FIGURE A–2
An Ethical Decision Tree

(i.e., customers, employees, the community, the environment, and suppliers) against the benefit to the shareholders. According to the decision tree framework, managers should make the decision to engage in an action if the benefits to the shareholders exceed the benefits to the other key constituents. Managers should not engage in the action if the other key constituents benefit more from the action than shareholders.

Figure A–2 illustrates that managers use a slightly different perspective when their initial conclusion is that an action does not maximize shareholder value. In this case, the question becomes "Would it be ethical not to take action?" This question necessitates that a manager consider the *harm or cost* of an action to shareholders against the *costs or benefits* to other key constituents. If the costs to shareholders from a managerial decision exceed the costs or benefits to other constituents, the manager or company should not engage in the action. Conversely, the manager or company should take action when the perceived costs or benefits to the other constituents are greater than the costs to shareholders. Let us apply this decision tree to the example of whether or not a company should decrease its contributions to retiree health-care benefits while simultaneously raising retirees' contributions. IBM, for example, made the decision to follow this practice.

Is it legal for a company to decrease its contribution to retiree health-care benefits while simultaneously raising retirees' contributions? The answer is yes.[16] Does an organization maximize shareholder value by decreasing its retiree health-care expenses? Again, the answer is yes. We now have to consider the overall benefits to shareholders against the overall benefits to other key constituents. The answer to this question is more complex than it appears and is contingent on an organization's corporate values. Consider the following two examples. In company one, the organization is losing money and it needs cash in order to invest in new product development. Management believes that new products will fuel the company's economic growth and ultimate survival. This company's statement of corporate values also reveals that the organization values profits and shareholder return more than employee loyalty. In this case, the company should make the decision to increase retirees' health-care contributions. Company two, in contrast, is profitable and has been experiencing increased market share with its products. This company's statement of corporate values also indicates that employees are the most important constituent it has, even more than shareholders. Southwest Airlines is a good example of a company with these corporate values. In this case, the company should not make the decision to decrease its contribution to retirees' benefits.

It is important to keep in mind that the decision tree cannot provide a quick formula that managers and organizations can use to assess every ethical question. It does, however, provide a framework for considering the trade-offs between managerial and corporate actions and managerial and corporate ethics. Try using this decision tree the next time you are faced with an ethical question or problem.

Group Exercise

Applying the Ethical Decision-Making Tree

Manager's Hot Seat Application

Ethics: Let's Make a Fourth Quarter Deal

Do Moral Orientations Vary by Gender?

It is interesting to note that two women, Sherron Watkins and Maureen Castaneda, played key roles as whistle-blowers (i.e., when an employee informs others about corporate wrongdoing) in the Enron fiasco. "Watkins, Enron's vice president of corporate development, wrote the prescient memo to Enron's chief executive that warned him the company was in deep financial trouble. Castaneda, Enron's director of foreign exchange, is the one who told authorities that Enron was still shredding documents after its officials were ordered to preserve every piece of paper."[17] Does this suggest that women are more likely to be whistle-blowers because they have different moral principles than men?[18]

HANDS-ON EXERCISE

How Ethical Are These Behaviors?

INSTRUCTIONS Evaluate the extent to which you believe the following behaviors are ethical. Circle your responses on the rating scales provided. Compute your average score and compare it to the norms.

	Very Unethical	Unethical	Neither Ethical nor Unethical	Ethical	Very Ethical
Accepting gifts/favors in exchange for preferential treatment	1	(2)	3	4	5
Giving gifts/favors in exchange for preferential treatment	1	(2)	3	4	5
Divulging confidential information	1	(2)	3	4	5
Calling in sick to take a day off	1	2	(3)	4	5
Using the organization's materials and supplies for personal use	(1)	(2)	3	4	5
Doing personal business on work time	1	(2)	3	4	5
Taking extra personal time (breaks, etc.)	1	2	(3)	4	5
Using organizational services for personal use	1	2	(3)	4	5
Passing blame for errors to an innocent co-worker	(1)	2	3	4	5
Claiming credit for someone else's work	(1)	2	3	4	5
Not reporting others' violations of organizational policies	1	(2)	3	4	5
Concealing one's errors	1	(2)	3	4	5

Average score = 2.0

Norms (average scores by country)
- United States = 1.49
- Great Britain = 1.70
- Australia = 1.44
- France = 1.66
- China = 1.46
- Average of all 10 countries = 1.67

SOURCE: The survey behaviors were taken from T Jackson, "Cultural Values and Management Ethics: A 10-Nation Study," *Human Relations*, October 2001, pp 1287–88.

A study of 300 self-described whistle-blowers revealed that gender was not related to employees' reporting wrongdoing.[19] Still, other research suggests that men and women view moral problems and situations differently. Carol Gilligan, a well-known psychologist, proposed one underlying cause of these gender differences. Her research revealed that men and women differed in terms of how they perceived moral problems. Males perceived moral problems in terms of a **justice perspective**, whereas women relied

justice perspective

Based on the ideal of reciprocal rights and driven by rules and regulations.

At great risk to her career, Enron executive Sherron Watkins reported financial misconduct as a whistle-blower. Would you have the courage to do so?

care perspective

Involves compassion and an ideal of attention and response to need.

on a **care perspective.** The two perspectives are described as follows:

> A justice perspective draws attention to problems of inequality and oppression and holds up an ideal of reciprocal rights and equal respect for individuals. A care perspective draws attention to problems of detachment or abandonment and holds up an ideal of attention and response to need. Two moral injunctions, not to treat others unfairly and not to turn away from someone in need, capture these different concerns.[20]

This description underscores the point that men are expected to view moral problems in terms of rights, whereas women are predicted to conceptualize moral problems as an issue of care involving empathy and compassion.

A meta-analysis of 113 studies tested these ideas by examining whether or not the justice and care orientations varied by gender. Results did not support the expectation that the care perspective was used predominantly by females and the justice orientation predominantly by males.[21] The authors concluded that "although distinct moral orientations may exist, these orientations are not strongly associated with gender."[22] This conclusion suggests that future research is needed to identify the source of moral reasoning differences between men and women. Which moral perspective do you prefer: justice or care?

General Moral Principles

Management consultant and writer Kent Hodgson has helpfully taken managers a step closer to ethical decisions by identifying seven general moral principles (see Table A–1). Hodgson calls them "the magnificent seven" to emphasize their timeless and worldwide relevance. Both the justice and care perspectives are clearly evident in the magnificent seven, which are more detailed and, hence, more practical. Importantly, according to Hodgson, there are no absolute ethical answers for decision makers. The goal for managers should be to rely on moral principles so their decisions are *principled, appropriate,* and *defensible.*[23]

Valero Energy, which was voted the third best company to work for by *Fortune* in 2005, and Timberland, voted the 41st best place to work, are good examples of companies trying to follow this recommendation. Valero employees pull together to help others. "After hurricanes Katrina and Rita hit, Valero dispatched semis filled with supplies, set up temporary housing for employees, fed volunteers—and donated $1 million to the Red Cross." Timberland also relies on principled decisions. "Helping to save the world is a big goal at this boot and outdoor gear label. Employees who buy a hybrid car get a $3,000 credit, and the company pays for up to 40 hours per year of volunteer work in the community."[24]

The Magnificent Seven: General Moral Principles for Managers | TABLE A–1

1. *Dignity of human life: The lives of people are to be respected.* Human beings, by the fact of their existence, have value and dignity. We may not act in ways that directly intend to harm or kill an innocent person. Human beings have a right to live; we have an obligation to respect that right to life. Human life is to be preserved and treated as sacred.

2. *Autonomy: All persons are intrinsically valuable and have the right to self-determination.* We should act in ways that demonstrate each person's worth, dignity, and right to free choice. We have a right to act in ways that assert our own worth and legitimate needs. We should not use others as mere "things" or only as means to an end. Each person has an equal right to basic human liberty, compatible with a similar liberty for others.

3. *Honesty: The truth should be told to those who have a right to know it.* Honesty is also known as integrity, truth telling, and honor. One should speak and act so as to reflect the reality of the situation. Speaking and acting should mirror the way things really are. There are times when others have the right to hear the truth from us; there are times when they do not.

4. *Loyalty: Promises, contracts, and commitments should be honored.* Loyalty includes fidelity, promise keeping, keeping the public trust, good citizenship, excellence in quality of work, reliability, commitment, and honoring just laws, rules, and policies.

5. *Fairness: People should be treated justly.* One has the right to be treated fairly, impartially, and equitably. One has the obligation to treat others fairly and justly. All have the right to the necessities of life—especially those in deep need and the helpless. Justice includes equal, impartial, unbiased treatment. Fairness tolerates diversity and accepts differences in people and their ideas.

6. *Humaneness.* There are two parts: (1) *Our actions ought to accomplish good,* and (2) *we should avoid doing evil.* We should do good to others and to ourselves. We should have concern for the well-being of others; usually, we show this concern in the form of compassion, giving, kindness, serving, and caring.

7. *The common good: Actions should accomplish the "greatest good for the greatest number" of people.* One should act and speak in ways that benefit the welfare of the largest number of people, while trying to protect the rights of individuals.

SOURCE: From *A Rock and a Hard Place: How to Make Ethical Business Decisions When the Choices Are Tough,* by Kent Hodgson, 1992, American Management Association. Reprinted with permission of the author.

How to Improve the Organization's Ethical Climate

A team of management researchers recommended the following actions for improving on-the-job ethics:[25]

- *Behave ethically yourself.* Managers are potent role models whose habits and actual behavior send clear signals about the importance of ethical conduct. Ethical behavior is a top-to-bottom proposition. Part of Enron's legal and ethical problems were most likely associated with Jeff Skilling and Ken Lay, who violated this recommendation. Consider the following example.

Skilling testified that he'd invested $180,000 in a tiny Internet startup called Photofete, run by a girlfriend, which counted Enron as by far its biggest customer. While company policy dictated that corporate officers were required to report such potential conflicts of interest in writing, Skilling never did. As it turned out, Lay invested in the same firm—some $120,000. ("Skilling really put the pressure on," Lay's stepson advised him in an e-mail.) What's more, Lay failed to report the conflict. On the stand, he reluctantly acknowledged that he'd "probably" violated Enron's ethics code.[26]

- *Screen potential employees.* Surprisingly, employers are generally lax when it comes to checking references, credentials, transcripts, and other information on applicant résumés. More diligent action in this area can screen out those given to fraud and misrepresentation. Integrity testing is fairly valid but is no panacea.[27]

- *Develop and communicate a meaningful code of ethics.* Codes of ethics can have a positive impact if they satisfy these four criteria:

  1. They are distributed to every employee.[28]
  2. They are firmly supported by top management.
  3. They refer to *specific* practices and ethical dilemmas likely to be encountered by target employees (e.g., salespersons paying kickbacks, purchasing agents receiving payoffs, laboratory scientists doctoring data, or accountants "cooking the books").
  4. They are evenly enforced with rewards for compliance and strict penalties for noncompliance.

- *Provide ethics training.* Employees can be trained to identify and deal with ethical issues during orientation and through seminar, video, and Internet training sessions.[29]

- *Reinforce ethical behavior.* Behavior that is reinforced tends to be repeated, whereas behavior that is not reinforced tends to disappear. Ethical conduct too often is punished or ignored while unethical behavior is rewarded.

- *Create positions, units, and other structural mechanisms to deal with ethics.* Ethics needs to be an everyday affair, not a one-time announcement of a new ethical code that gets filed away and forgotten. Computer Associates (CA) International Inc., for example, is adhering to this recommendation more or less due to an agreement reached with the US Justice Department. "To avoid criminal trial over alleged accounting fraud, CA accepted a deferred prosecution agreement in late 2004 that required it to set aside $225 million for shareholders and impose a variety of reforms, including hiring an internal cop to prevent future chicanery."[30]

group exercise

Investigating the Difference in Moral Reasoning between Men and Women

Objectives

1. To determine if men and women resolve moral/ethical problems differently.
2. To determine if males and females use justice and care perspectives, respectively, to solve moral/ethical problems.
3. To improve your understanding about the moral reasoning used by men and women.

Introduction

Men and women view moral problems and situations dissimilarly. This is one reason men and women solve identical moral or ethical problems differently. Some researchers believe that men rely on a justice perspective to solve moral problems whereas women are expected to use a care perspective. This exercise presents two scenarios that possess a moral/ethical issue. You will be asked to solve each problem and to discuss the logic behind your decision. The exercise provides you with the opportunity to hear the thought processes used by men and women to solve moral/ethical problems.

Instructions

Your instructor will divide the class into groups of four to six. (An interesting option is to use gender-based groups.) Each group member should first read the scenario alone and then make a decision about what to do. Once this is done, use the space provided to outline the rationale for your decision for this scenario. Next, read the second scenario and follow the same procedure: Make a decision and explain your rationale. Once all group members have completed their analyses for both scenarios, meet as a group to discuss the results. One at a time, each group member should present his or her final decision and the associated reasoning for the first scenario. Someone should keep a running tally of the decisions so that a summary can be turned in to the professor at the end of your discussion. Follow the same procedure for the second scenario.[31]

Scenario 1

You are the manager of a local toy store. The hottest Christmas toy of the year is the new "Peter Panda" stuffed animal. The toy is in great demand and almost impossible to find. You have received your one and only shipment of 12, and they are all promised to people who previously stopped in to place a deposit and reserve one. A woman comes by the store and pleads with you, saying that her six-year-old daughter is in the hospital very ill, and that "Peter Panda" is the one toy she has her heart set on. Would you sell her one, knowing that you will have to break your promise and refund the deposit to one of the other customers? (There is no way you will be able to get an extra toy in time.)

Your Decision: _____

	Would Sell	Would Not Sell	Unsure
Men			
Women			

Rationale for your decision:

Scenario 2

You sell corporate financial products, such as pension plans and group health insurance. You are currently negotiating with Paul Scott, treasurer of a *Fortune* 500 firm, for a sale that could be in the millions of dollars. You feel you are in a strong position to make the sale, but two competitors are also negotiating with Scott, and it could go either way. You have become friendly with Scott, and over lunch one day he confided in you that he has recently been under treatment for manic depression. It so happens that in your office there is a staff psychologist who does employee counseling. The thought has occurred to you that such a trained professional might be able to coach you on how to act with and relate to a personality such as Scott's, so as to persuade and influence him most effectively. Would you consult the psychologist?

Your Decision: _____

	Would Consult	Would Not Consult	Unsure
Men			
Women			

Rationale for your decision:

Questions for Discussion

1. Did males and females make different decisions in response to both scenarios? (Comparative norms can be found in Note 32.)
2. What was the moral reasoning used by women and men to solve the two scenarios?[33]
3. To what extent did males and females use justice and care perspectives, respectively?
4. What useful lessons did you learn from this exercise?

discussion questions

1. How many ethical breakdowns can you identify in the opening vignette about reconstruction fraud in Iraq? Explain. How could this situation have been prevented?
2. Why do you think there is an increase in the number of indictments against executives in the United States?
3. If you were a professor at a university, what would you do to discourage students from cheating on assignments and exams? Explain your recommendations.

chapter two

Organizational Culture, Socialization, and Mentoring

HOME DEPOT IS CHANGING ITS ORGANIZATIONAL CULTURE

Military analogies are commonplace at Home Depot Inc. these days. Five years after his December, 2000, arrival, Chief Executive Robert L. Nardelli is putting his stamp on what was long a decentralized, entrepreneurial business under founders Bernie Marcus and Arthur Blank. And if his company starts to look and feel like an

launched in 2002, almost half—528—are junior military officers. More than 100 of them now run Home Depots....

Importing ideas, people, and platitudes from the military is a key part of Nardelli's sweeping move to reshape Home Depot, the world's third-largest retailer, into a more centralized

you have 2,100 colonels running things," explains Craig R. Johnson, president of Customer Growth Partners Inc., a retail consulting firm....

Even as other companies seek to stoke creativity and break down hierarchies, Nardelli is trying to build a disciplined corps, one predisposed to following orders, operating in high-pressure environments, and executing with high standards....

Although he has yet to win all the hearts and minds of his employees, and probably never will, Nardelli's feisty spirit is rekindling stellar financial performance. Riding a housing and home-improvement boom, Home Depot sales have soared, from $46 billion in 2000, the year Nardelli took over, to $81.5 billion in 2005, an average annual growth rate of 12%, according to results announced on Feb. 21....

Home Depot is attempting to change its organizational culture. What are some of the challenges it will face?

army, that's the point. Nardelli loves to hire soldiers. In fact, he seems to love almost everything about the armed services. The military, to a large extent, has become the management model for his entire enterprise. Of the 1,142 people hired into Home Depot's store leadership program, a two-year training regimen for future store managers

organization. That may be an untrendy idea in management circles, but Nardelli couldn't care less. It's a critical element of his strategy to rein in an unwieldy 2,048-store chain and prepare for its next leg of growth. "The kind of discipline and maturity that you get out of the military is something that can be very, very useful in an organization where basically

The high stakes of Home Depot's services gambit is one of the main reasons Nardelli has pushed his cultural makeover so hard in the five years since he has been at the helm. But not all have embraced him, or his plans. *BusinessWeek* spoke with 11 former executives, a majority of whom requested anonymity lest the company sue them for violating nondisclosure agreements. Some describe a demoralized staff and say a "culture of fear" is causing customer service to wane. Nardelli's own big-time pay package, $28.5 million for the year ended Jan. 30, 2005, rubs many workers the wrong way. His guaranteed bonus, the only locked-in payout at the company, rose to $5.8 million in 2004, from $4.5 million in 2003, at a time when Home Depot's stock price finished below its yearend price in 2000, when Nardelli took over.

Before he arrived, managers ran Home Depot's stores on "tribal knowledge," based on years of experience about what sold and what didn't. Now they click nervously through BlackBerrys at the end of each week, hoping they "made plan," a combination of sales and profit targets. The once-heavy ranks of full-time Home Depot store staff have been replaced with part-timers to drive down labor costs. Underperforming executives are routinely culled from the ranks. Since 2001, 98% of Home Depot's 170 top executives are new to their positions and, at headquarters in Atlanta, 56% of job changes involved bringing new managers in from outside the company. Says one former executive: "Every single week you shuddered when you looked at e-mail because another officer was gone."

As a manager, Nardelli is relentless, demanding, and determined to prove wrong every critic of Home Depot. He treats Saturdays and Sundays as ordinary working days and often expects those around him to do the same. . . .

Still, it's hard even for Nardelli critics, including ones he has fired, not to admire his unstinting determination to follow his makeover plan in the face of scores of naysayers. They describe being "in awe" of his command of minute details. But some of them question whether the manufacturing business model that worked for him at GE Transportation and GE Power Systems—squeezing efficiencies out of the core business while buying up new businesses—can work in a retail environment where taking care of customers is paramount. "Bob has brought a lot of operational efficiencies that Home Depot needed," says Steve Mahurin, chief merchandising officer at True Value Co. and a former senior vice-president for merchandising at Home Depot. "But he failed to keep the orange-blooded, entrepreneurial spirit alive. Home Depot is now a factory."[1]

How would you describe the organizational culture at Home Depot? Explain. For an interpretation of this case and additional comments, visit our Online Learning Center at

www.mhhe.com/kinickiob3e

FOR DISCUSSION

THE OPENING CASE HIGHLIGHTS the role of organizational culture in contributing to organizational effectiveness. Home Depot's culture, which highly values discipline, meeting goals, and execution, significantly contributes to the organization's success. The case also highlights that an organization's culture is strongly influenced by the values and attitudes of top management, particularly the CEO.

This chapter will help you better understand how managers can use organizational culture as a competitive advantage. After defining and discussing the context of organizational culture, we examine (1) the dynamics of organizational culture, (2) the organization socialization process, and (3) the embedding of organizational culture through mentoring.

Organizational Culture: Definition and Context

Organizational culture is "the set of shared, taken-for-granted implicit assumptions that a group holds and that determines how it perceives, thinks about, and reacts to its various environments."[2] This definition highlights three important characteristics of organizational culture. First, organizational culture is passed on to new employees through the process of socialization, a topic discussed later in this chapter. Second, organizational culture influences our behavior at work. Finally, organizational culture operates at different levels.

organizational culture

Shared values and beliefs that underlie a company's identity.

Figure 2–1 provides a conceptual framework for reviewing the widespread impact organizational culture has on organizational behavior.[3] It also shows the linkage between this chapter—culture, socialization, and mentoring—and other key topics in

A Conceptual Framework for Understanding Organizational Culture   FIGURE 2-1

Antecedents	Organizational culture	Organizational structure and practices	Group and social processes	Collective attitudes and behavior	Organizational outcomes
• Founder's values • Industry and business environment • National culture (Ch. 3) • Senior leaders' vision and behavior (Ch. 14)	• Observable artifacts ↓ ↑ • Espoused values ↓ ↑ • Basic assumptions	• Reward systems (Ch. 8) • Organization design (Ch. 15)	• Socialization • Mentoring • Group dynamics (Ch. 9) • Decision making (Ch. 10) • Communication (Ch. 12) • Influence and empowerment (Ch. 13) • Leadership (Ch. 14)	• Work attitudes (Ch. 6) • Motivation (Chs. 6,7)	• Effectiveness (Ch. 15) • Resistance to change (Ch. 16)

SOURCE: Adapted in part from C Ostroff, A Kinicki, and M Tamkins, "Organizational Culture and Climate," in *Handbook of Psychology*, Vol 12, eds W C Burman, D R ligen, and R J Klimoski (New York: Wiley and Sons, 2003), pp 565–93.

this book. Figure 2–1 reveals organizational culture is shaped by four key components: the founders' values, the industry and business environment, the national culture, and the senior leaders' vision and behavior. In turn, organizational culture influences the type of organizational structure adopted by a company and a host of practices, policies, and procedures implemented in pursuit of organizational goals. These organizational characteristics then affect a variety of group and social processes. This sequence ultimately affects employees' attitudes and behavior and a variety of organizational outcomes. All told, Figure 2–1 reveals that organizational culture is a contextual variable influencing individual, group, and organizational behavior.

Dynamics of Organizational Culture

To provide a better understanding of how organizational culture is formed and used by employees, this section begins by discussing the layers of organizational culture. It then reviews the four functions of organizational culture, types of organizational culture, outcomes associated with organizational culture, and how cultures are embedded within organizations.

Layers of Organizational Culture

Figure 2–1 shows the three fundamental layers of organizational culture. Each level varies in terms of outward visibility and resistance to change, and each level influences another level.[4]

Observable Artifacts At the more visible level, culture represents observable artifacts. Artifacts consist of the physical manifestation of an organization's culture. Organizational examples include acronyms, manner of dress, awards, myths and stories told about the organization, published lists of values, observable rituals and ceremonies, special parking spaces, decorations, and so on. This level also includes visible behaviors exhibited by people and groups. Artifacts are easier to change than the less visible aspects of organizational culture. JCPenney Co., for example, is trying to revamp a culture based on tradition and hierarchy to one that is less formal and flexible by using the following artifacts: "emphasizing the use of first names among colleagues and their superiors; selling the company's art collection—including work by Andy Warhol—and replacing it with employee photos; re-emphasizing business-casual attire during the week, and allowing jeans on Fridays; and allowing employees access to all parts of the headquarters' campus, including the executive suite and its elevator."[5]

values

Enduring belief in a mode of conduct or end-state.

espoused values

The stated values and norms that are preferred by an organization.

Espoused Values Values possess five key components. "**Values** (1) are concepts or beliefs, (2) pertain to desirable end-states or behaviors, (3) transcend situations, (4) guide selection or evaluation of behavior and events, and (5) are ordered by relative importance."[6] It is important to distinguish between values that are espoused versus those that are enacted.

Espoused values represent the explicitly stated values and norms that are preferred by an organization. They are generally established by the founder of a new or small company and by the top management team in a larger organization. Consider, for example, the espoused values of Williams-Sonoma, Inc. (see Skills & Best Practices on page 44). Because espoused values constitute aspirations that are explicitly communicated to employees, managers hope that espoused values will directly influence employee behavior. Unfortunately, aspirations do not automatically produce the desired behaviors because people do not always "walk the talk."

Enacted values, on the other hand, represent the values and norms that actually are exhibited or converted into employee behavior. They represent the values that employees ascribe to an organization based on their observations of what occurs on a daily basis. The following two examples are excellent representations of the difference between espoused and enacted values.

enacted values

The values and norms that are exhibited by employees.

> A major international corporation hung signs in its hallways proclaiming that "trust" was one of its driving principles. Yet that same company searched employees' belongings each time they entered or exited the building. In another case, a multinational corporation that claimed to be committed to work/life values drew up an excellent plan to help managers incorporate work/life balance into the business. The company gathered its top 80 officers to review the plan—but scheduled the meetings on a weekend.[7]

The first company espoused that it valued trust and then behaved in an untrusting manner by checking employees' belongings. The second company similarly created a mismatch between espoused and enacted values by promoting work/life balance while simultaneously asking managers to attend weekend meetings.

It is important for managers to reduce gaps between espoused and enacted values because they can significantly influence employee attitudes and organizational performance. For example, a study of 312 British rail drivers revealed that employees were more cynical about safety when they believed that senior managers' behavior was inconsistent with the stated values regarding safety.[8] Managers can use a "cultural fit assessment" survey to determine the match between espoused and enacted values. Guidant Corp., an Indianapolis, Indiana–based medical device manufacturer, for instance, implemented its "Vital Signs" survey to assess employees' opinions about the organizational culture, work activities, and total compensation. Results of the survey were used to improve the work environment and to align the organization's espoused and enacted values.[9]

Basic Assumptions Basic underlying assumptions are unobservable and represent the core of organizational culture.

An observable artifact of the culture at the offices of Bloomberg, the financial news and information company in New York, is the office itself, a glass-walled structure that has been compared to a beehive cut open. There are no private offices and no cubicles in a space intended to express the company's energy and sense of style. And, says CEO Lex Fenwick, a big benefit is the information the view from his office affords him. "I know quicker than any piece of damn software when we have a problem," he says. "I can see it right in front of me when it happens. . . . What does it allow me to do? Get on someone to fix it in seconds. The communication this setup affords is staggering."

Williams-Sonoma's Espoused Values Focus on Employees, Customers, Shareholders, Ethical Behavior, and the Environment

People First We believe the potential of our company has no limit and is driven by our associates and their imagination. We are committed to an environment that attracts, motivates and recognizes high performance.

Customers We are here to please our customers—without them nothing else matters.

Quality We must take pride in everything we do. From our people, to our products and in our relationships with business partners and our community, quality is our signature.

Shareholders We must provide a superior return to our shareholders. It's everyone's job.

Ethical Sourcing Williams-Sonoma, Inc., and all of its brands are committed to maintaining the highest level of integrity and honesty throughout all aspects of our business, and strive to ensure that our business associates, including agents, vendors and suppliers, share our commitment to socially responsible employment conditions.

Environmental Paper Procurement Policy Williams-Sonoma, Inc., is committed to environmental stewardship, and more specifically, to sound paper procurement practices that ensure the sustainability of forests and other natural resources.

Recycling The launch of Williams-Sonoma, Inc.'s, "Recycle 100" brings our companywide "Greening Our Home" initiative to our customers' homes. 50% of American households recycle their paper products. Our customers recycle 60%, but, in sharing their environmental concern, we're making 100% recycling the goal for this innovative new program.

SOURCE: Excerpted from "Corporate Values," www.williams-sonomainc.com/car/car_valu.cfm, accessed May 10, 2006.

They constitute organizational values that have become so taken for granted over time that they become assumptions that guide organizational behavior. They thus are highly resistant to change. When basic assumptions are widely held among employees, people will find behavior based on an inconsistent value inconceivable. Google, for example, is noted for its innovative culture. Employees at Google would be shocked to see management act in ways that did not value creativity and innovation.[10]

Four Functions of Organizational Culture

As illustrated in Figure 2–2, an organization's culture fulfills four functions.[11] To help bring these four functions to life, let us consider how each of them has taken shape at Southwest Airlines.[12] Southwest is a particularly instructive example because it has grown to become the fourth-largest US airline since its inception in 1971 and has achieved 33 consecutive years of profitability. *Fortune* has ranked Southwest in the top five of the Best Companies to Work For in America from 1997–2000; Southwest has chosen not to participate in this ranking process since 2000. Southwest also was ranked as the third most admired company in the United States by *Fortune* in 2006, partly due to its strong and distinctive culture.

1. *Give members an organizational identity.* Southwest Airlines is known as a fun place to work that values employee satisfaction and customer loyalty over corporate profits. Herb Kelleher, executive chairman, commented on this issue.

   > Who comes first? The employees, customers, or shareholders? That's never been an issue to me. The employees come first. If they're happy, satisfied, dedicated, and energetic, they'll take real good care of the customers. When the customers are happy, they come back. And that makes the shareholders happy.[13]

   The company also has a catastrophe fund based on voluntary contributions for distribution to employees who are experiencing serious personal difficulties. Southwest's people-focused identity is reinforced by the fact that it is an employer of choice. For example, Southwest received 260,109 résumés and hired 2,766 new employees in 2005. The company also was noted as an employer of choice among college students by *Fortune*.

2. *Facilitate collective commitment.* The mission of Southwest Airlines "is dedication to the highest quality of Customer Service delivered with a sense of warmth, friendliness, individual pride, and Company Spirit."[14] Southwest's

Four Functions of Organizational Culture   FIGURE 2–2

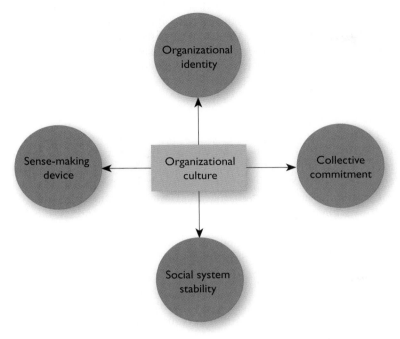

SOURCE: Adapted from discussion in L Smircich, "Concepts of Culture and Organizational Analysis," *Administrative Science Quarterly*, September 1983, pp 339–58. Reprinted with permission.

more than 31,000 employees are committed to this mission. The Department of Transportation's Air Travel Consumer Report reported Southwest was ranked number one in fewest customer complaints since 1987.

3. *Promote social system stability.* Social system stability reflects the extent to which the work environment is perceived as positive and reinforcing, and the extent to which conflict and change are effectively managed. Southwest is noted for its philosophy of having fun, having parties, and celebrating. For example, each city in which the firm operates is given a budget for parties. Southwest also uses a variety of performance-based awards and service awards to reinforce employees. The company's positive and enriching environment is supported by the lowest turnover rates in the airline industry and the employment of 1,100 married couples.

4. *Shape behavior by helping members make sense of their surroundings.* This function of culture helps employees understand why the organization does what it does and how it intends to accomplish its long-term goals. Keeping in mind that Southwest's leadership originally viewed ground transportation as their main competitor in 1971, employees come to understand why the airline's primary vision is to be the best primarily short-haul, low-fare,

Fun is the norm at Southwest Airlines. Executive Chairman Herb Kelleher noted, "The employees come first. If they're happy, satisfied, dedicated, and energetic, they'll take real good care of the customers." Do you agree with Herb's philosophy?

high-frequency, point-to-point carrier in the United States. Employees understand they must achieve exceptional performance, such as turning a plane in 20 minutes, because they must keep costs down in order to compete against Greyhound and the use of automobiles. In turn, the company reinforces the importance of outstanding customer service and high performance expectations by using performance-based awards and profit sharing. Employees own at least 10% of the company stock.

Types of Organizational Culture

Researchers have attempted to identify and measure various types of organizational culture in order to study the relationship between types of culture and organizational effectiveness. This pursuit was motivated by the possibility that certain cultures were more effective than others. Unfortunately, research has not uncovered a universal typology of cultural styles that everyone accepts.[15] Just the same, there is value in providing an example of various types of organizational culture. Table 2–1 is thus presented as an illustration rather than a definitive conclusion about the types of organizational culture that exist. Awareness of these types provides you with greater understanding about the manifestations of culture.

Table 2–1 shows that there are three general types of organizational culture—constructive, passive–defensive, and aggressive–defensive—and that each type is associated with a different set of normative beliefs.[16] **Normative beliefs** represent an individual's thoughts and beliefs about how members of a particular group or organization are expected to approach their work and interact with others. A *constructive culture* is one in which employees are encouraged to interact with others and to work on tasks and projects in ways that will assist them in satisfying their need to grow and develop. This type of culture endorses normative beliefs associated with achievement, self-actualizing, humanistic-encouraging, and affiliative. In contrast, a *passive–defensive culture* is characterized by an overriding belief that employees must interact with others in ways that do not threaten their own job security. This culture reinforces the normative beliefs associated with approval, conventional, dependent, and avoidance (see Table 2–1). Mitsubishi is a good example of a company with a passive–defensive culture. According to *BusinessWeek* reporters:

> This was a company whose managers were so reluctant to relay bad news to higher-ups that they squelched complaints about quality defects for decades to avoid costly product recalls. Many Daimler [DaimlerChrysler spent $2.4 billion to obtain a 37% stake in Mitsubishi] critics also say its culture contributed to the failed turnaround: The push was always on for results, and few wanted to alert Stuttgart to major problems. Later, to help U.S. sales, Mitsubishi resorted to an ultragenerous financing campaign—no money down and no payments for a year. The result was almost half a billion in bad loans.[17]

Finally, companies with an *aggressive–defensive culture* encourage employees to approach tasks in forceful ways in order to protect their status and job security. This type of culture is more characteristic of normative beliefs reflecting oppositional, power, competitive, and perfectionistic. ExxonMobil is a prime example. The company is known to relentlessly pursue efficiency, consistency, and discipline, which, in turn, has produced one of the best-run energy firms in the world. For example, "As Royal Dutch Shell struggles to replace the oil and gas it pumps out of the ground and watches its production sag, Exxon has replaced more than it has produced for the last 12 years. Since 2004, its stock has outperformed BP's and Chevron's."[18]

normative beliefs

Thoughts and beliefs about expected behavior and modes of conduct.

Group Exercise

Exploring Organizational Culture

Self-Assessment Exercise

Corporate Culture Preference Scale

General Types of Culture	Normative Beliefs	Organizational Characteristics
Constructive	Achievement	Organizations that do things well and value members who set and accomplish their own goals. Members are expected to set challenging but realistic goals, establish plans to reach these goals, and pursue them with enthusiasm. (Pursuing a standard of excellence)
Constructive	Self-actualizing	Organizations that value creativity, quality over quantity, and both task accomplishment and individual growth. Members are encouraged to gain enjoyment from their work, develop themselves, and take on new and interesting activities. (Thinking in unique and independent ways)
Constructive	Humanistic-encouraging	Organizations that are managed in a participative and person-centered way. Members are expected to be supportive, constructive, and open to influence in their dealings with one another. (Helping others to grow and develop)
Constructive	Affiliative	Organizations that place a high priority on constructive interpersonal relationships. Members are expected to be friendly, open, and sensitive to the satisfaction of their work group. (Dealing with others in a friendly way)
Passive–defensive	Approval	Organizations in which conflicts are avoided and interpersonal relationships are pleasant—at least superficially. Members feel that they should agree with, gain the approval of, and be liked by others. ("Going along" with others)
Passive–defensive	Conventional	Organizations that are conservative, traditional, and bureaucratically controlled. Members are expected to conform, follow the rules, and make a good impression. (Always following policies and practices)
Passive–defensive	Dependent	Organizations that are hierarchically controlled and nonparticipative. Centralized decision making in such organizations leads members to do only what they are told and to clear all decisions with superiors. (Pleasing those in positions of authority)
Passive–defensive	Avoidance	Organizations that fail to reward success but nevertheless punish mistakes. This negative reward system leads members to shift responsibilities to others and avoid any possibility of being blamed for a mistake. (Waiting for others to act first)
Aggressive–defensive	Oppositional	Organizations in which confrontation and negativism are rewarded. Members gain status and influence by being critical and thus are reinforced to oppose the ideas of others. (Pointing out flaws)
Aggressive–defensive	Power	Nonparticipative organizations structured on the basis of the authority inherent in members' positions. Members believe they will be rewarded for taking charge, controlling subordinates and, at the same time, being responsive to the demands of superiors. (Building up one's power base)
Aggressive–defensive	Competitive	Winning is valued and members are rewarded for outperforming one another. Members operate in a "win–lose" framework and believe they must work against (rather than with) their peers to be noticed. (Turning the job into a contest)
Aggressive–defensive	Perfectionistic	Organizations in which perfectionism, persistence, and hard work are valued. Members feel they must avoid any mistake, keep track of everything, and work long hours to attain narrowly defined objectives. (Doing things perfectly)

SOURCE: Adapted from R A Cooke and J L Szumal, "Measuring Normative Beliefs and Shared Behavioral Expectations in Organizations: The Reliability and Validity of the Organizational Culture Inventory," *Psychological Reports*, 1993, Vol. 72, pp 1299–1330.

Although an organization may predominately represent one cultural type, it can manifest normative beliefs and characteristics from the others. Research demonstrates that organizations can have functional subcultures, hierarchical subcultures based on one's level in the organization, geographical subcultures, occupational subcultures based on one's title or position, social subcultures derived from social activities such as a bowling or golf league and a reading club, and countercultures.[19] It is important for managers to be aware of the possibility that conflict between subgroups that form subcultures can undermine an organization's overall performance.

Outcomes Associated with Organizational Culture

Both managers and academic researchers believe that organizational culture can be a driver of employee attitudes and organizational effectiveness and performance. To test this possibility, various measures of organizational culture have been correlated with a variety of individual and organizational outcomes. So what have we learned? First, several studies demonstrated that organizational culture was significantly correlated with employee behavior and attitudes. For example, a constructive culture was positively related with job satisfaction, intentions to stay at the company, and innovation. It also was negatively associated with work avoidance. In contrast, passive–defensive and aggressive–defensive cultures were negatively correlated with job satisfaction and intentions to stay at the company.[20] These results suggest that employees seem to prefer organizations that encourage people to interact and work with others in ways that assist them in satisfying their needs to grow and develop. Second, results from several studies revealed that the congruence between an individual's values and the organization's values was significantly associated with organizational commitment, job satisfaction, intention to quit, performance, and turnover.[21]

Third, a summary of 10 quantitative studies showed that organizational culture did not predict an organization's financial performance.[22] This means that there is not one type of organizational culture that fuels financial performance. That said, however, a study of 207 companies from 22 industries for an 11-year period demonstrated that financial performance was higher among companies that had adaptive and flexible cultures.[23] Finally, studies of mergers indicated that they frequently failed due to incompatible cultures. Due to the increasing number of corporate mergers around the world, and the conclusion that 7 out of 10 mergers and acquisitions failed to meet their financial promise, managers within merged companies would be well advised to consider the role of organizational culture in creating a new organization.[24]

These research results underscore the significance of organizational culture. It is essential that managers consider the consistency between an organization's culture and the many different types of change initiatives that an organization pursues in trying to achieve its strategies and goals.[25] According to Mark Fields, Ford Motor Co.'s president of the Americas, "Culture

Farcus

by David Waisglass
Gordon Coulthart

www.farcus.com

© 1994 Farcus Cartoons   WAISGLASS/COULTHART

"I don't think this change in corporate culture is gonna pay-off."

eats strategy for breakfast. You can have the best plan in the world, and if the culture isn't going to let it happen, it's going to die on the vine."[26] As suggested by Fields, an organization's culture is not determined by fate. It is formed and shaped by everyone who works in an organization. We encourage managers to take an active role in creating and shaping the type of cultures they desire.

How Cultures Are Embedded in Organizations

An organization's initial culture is an outgrowth of the founder's philosophy and values. For example, an achievement culture is likely to develop if the founder is an achievement-oriented individual driven by success. Over time, the original culture is either embedded as is or it is modified to fit the current environmental situation. Edgar Schein, an OB scholar, notes that embedding a culture involves a teaching process. That is, organizational members teach each other about the organization's preferred values, beliefs, expectations, and behaviors. This is accomplished by using one or more of the following mechanisms:[27]

1. *Formal statements of organizational philosophy, mission, vision, values, and materials used for recruiting, selection, and socialization.* Sam Walton, the founder of Wal-Mart, established three basic beliefs or values that represent the core of the organization's culture. They are (1) respect for the individual, (2) service to our customer, and (3) striving for excellence. Further, Nucor Corp. attempts to emphasize the value it places on its people by including every employee's name on the cover of the annual report. This practice also reinforces the family-type culture the company wants to encourage.[28] Would you be attracted to work there?

2. *The design of physical space, work environments, and buildings.*

Training programs help preserve and embed the culture in an organization. Infosys Technologies, the rapidly growing software firm headquartered in Bangalore, India, hires about 40 new employees every day and trains them by the thousands at one of the world's largest corporate training centers, in Mysore. Here chairman and founder Narayana Murthy welcomes "freshers" via video.

3. *Slogans, language, acronyms, and sayings.* For example, Robert Mittelstaedt, Dean of the W.P. Carey School of Business at Arizona State University, promotes his vision of having one of the best business schools in the world through the slogan "Top-of-mind business school." Employees are encouraged to engage in activities that promote the quality and reputation of the school's academic programs.

4. *Deliberate role modeling, training programs, teaching, and coaching by managers and supervisors.* Boeing's CEO, Jim McNerney, leads by example. "He wins praise from co-workers for paying attention to the small things like remembering people's names, listening closely to their presentations, and not embarrassing underlings in public."[29]

5. *Explicit rewards, status symbols (e.g., titles), and promotion criteria.* Boeing is revising its reward system in order to reform its culture. "In the old days, no points were awarded for collaborating with other units or following ethics rules. Now pay and bonuses are directly linked to how well executives embrace a set of six leadership attributes such as 'Living Boeing Values.' That includes new criteria such as promoting integrity and avoiding abusive behavior."[30]

6. *Stories, legends, and myths about key people and events.* Southwest Airlines, for example, does an excellent job at telling stories to reinforce the company's commitment to customer service. One example involves a mechanic in Buffalo who used a snowmobile during a blizzard to drive seven miles in 20 feet of snow in order to get to the airport to free up a plane for takeoff.[31] The Skills & Best Practices contains recommendations for how managers can find stories with impact.

7. *The organizational activities, processes, or outcomes that leaders pay attention to, measure, and control.* Consider the behavior of Jamie Dimon, CEO of J.P. Morgan Chase.

> He has imposed rigorous pay-for-performance metrics and requires managers to present exhaustive monthly reviews, then grills them on the data for hours at a time. . . . To be sure he's getting the real story, Dimon button holes staffers in the elevators and calls suppliers out of the blue like a hyperactive gumshoe, collecting scraps of information he can throw back at executives. . . . He yanked Bank One's sponsorship of the Masters golf tournament because the country club hosting the event doesn't accept women members.[32]

8. *Leader reactions to critical incidents and organizational crises.*[33]

9. *The workflow and organizational structure.* Hierarchical structures are more likely to embed an orientation toward control and authority than a flatter organization.

10. *Organizational systems and procedures.* An organization can promote achievement and competition through the use of sales contests.[34]

II. *Organizational goals and the associated criteria used for recruitment, selection, development, promotion, layoffs, and retirement of people.* PepsiCo reinforces a high-performance culture by setting challenging goals.

The Organizational Socialization Process

Organizational socialization is defined as "the process by which a person learns the values, norms, and required behaviors which permit him to participate as a member of the organization."[35] As previously discussed, organizational socialization is a key mechanism used by organizations to embed their organizational cultures. In short, organizational socialization turns outsiders into fully functioning insiders by promoting and reinforcing the organization's core values and beliefs. This section introduces a three-phase model of organizational socialization and examines the practical application of socialization research.

> **organizational socialization**
>
> Process by which employees learn an organization's values, norms, and required behaviors.

A Three-Phase Model of Organizational Socialization

One's first year in a complex organization can be confusing. There is a constant swirl of new faces, strange jargon, conflicting expectations, and apparently unrelated events. Some organizations treat new members in a rather haphazard, sink-or-swim manner. More typically, though, the socialization process is characterized by a sequence of identifiable steps.

Organizational behavior researcher Daniel Feldman has proposed a three-phase model of organizational socialization that promotes deeper understanding of this important process. As illustrated in Figure 2–3, the three phases are (1) anticipatory socialization, (2) encounter, and (3) change and acquisition. Each phase has its associated perceptual and social processes. Feldman's model also specifies behavioral and affective outcomes that can be used to judge how well an individual has been socialized. The entire three-phase sequence may take from a few weeks to a year to complete, depending on individual differences and the complexity of the situation.

Phase 1: Anticipatory Socialization Anticipatory socialization occurs before an individual actually joins an organization. It is represented by the information people have learned about different careers, occupations, professions, and organizations. For example, anticipatory socialization partially explains the different perceptions you might have about working for the US government versus a high-technology company like Intel or Microsoft. Anticipatory socialization information comes from many sources. An organization's current employees are a powerful source of anticipatory socialization. Consider the case of Sedona Center, which includes Amara Creekside Resort, two shopping plazas, and three restaurants in Sedona, Arizona. The organization's 200 employees apparently like to tell others in the labor market about the company's employee-focused organizational culture (see Skills & Best Practices on page 53). In turn, job openings are filled with employees who better "fit" within Sedona Center's culture and ultimately are more

> **anticipatory socialization**
>
> Occurs before an individual joins an organization, and involves the information people learn about different careers, occupations, professions, and organizations.

FIGURE 2–3   A Model of Organizational Socialization

Outsider

Phases

Perceptual and Social Processes

1. Anticipatory socialization
Learning that occurs prior to
joining the organization

- Anticipating realities about the organization and
  the new job
- Anticipating organization's needs for one's skills
  and abilities
- Anticipating organization's sensitivity to one's
  needs and values

2. Encounter
Values, skills, and attitudes start to
shift as new recruit discovers what
the organization is truly like

- Managing lifestyle-versus-work conflicts
- Managing intergroup role conflicts
- Seeking role definition and clarity
- Becoming familiar with task and group dynamics

3. Change and acquisition
Recruit masters skills and roles
and adjusts to work group's
values and norms

- Competing role demands are resolved
- Critical tasks are mastered
- Group norms and values are internalized

Behavioral Outcomes

Socialized
insider

Affective Outcomes

- Performs role assignments
- Remains with organization
- Spontaneously innovates
  and cooperates

- Generally satisfied
- Internally motivated to work
- High job involvement

SOURCE: Adapted from material in D C Feldman, "The Multiple Socialization of Organization Members," *Academy of Management Review,*
April 1981, pp 309–18.

Boot camp, which is part of the encounter phase, is used by the
military to quickly and firmly instill values endorsed by the military.

satisfied and less likely to quit. The company's
turnover rate—13 to 18%—is less than half the
national average for this industry.[36]

Phase 2: Encounter This second phase begins
when the employment contract has been signed.
During the **encounter phase** employees come to
learn what the organization is really like. It is a time
for reconciling unmet expectations and making sense
of a new work environment. Many companies use a
combination of orientation and training programs to
socialize employees during the encounter phase.
Onboarding is one such technique. **Onboarding**
programs help employees to integrate, assimilate,
and transition to new jobs by making them familiar

with corporate policies, procedures, and culture and by clarifying work role expectations and responsibilities.[37] Bristol-Myers Squibb's onboarding program, for example, resulted in substantial improvement in the retention rate for managers. The program makes

> new executives the object of a laserlike focus during the first 30 to 60 days of their employment, providing guidelines, clarifying roles, setting up meetings with influential colleagues and fostering each newcomer's understanding of the company's cultural norms. Follow-up meetings are held during the executive's first year to check progress and resolve problems.[38]

encounter phase

Employees learn what the organization is really like and reconcile unmet expectations.

onboarding

Programs aimed at helping employees integrate, assimilate, and transition to new jobs.

change and acquisition

Requires employees to master tasks and roles and to adjust to work group values and norms.

Phase 3: Change and Acquisition   The **change and acquisition** phase requires employees to master important tasks and roles and to adjust to their work group's values and norms. Table 2–2 presents a list of socialization processes or tactics used by organizations to help employees through this adjustment process. Trilogy, for example, uses a variety of these tactics in its renowned socialization program. The three-month program takes place at the organization's corporate university, called Trilogy University.

Month One   When you arrive at Trilogy University, you are assigned to a section and to an instruction track. Your section, a group of about 20, is your social group for the duration of TU. . . . Tracks are designed to be microcosms of future work life at Trilogy. . . . The technical challenges in such exercises closely mimic real customer engagements, but the time frames are dramatically compressed. The assignments pile up week after week for the first month, each one successively more challenging than the last. During that time, you're being constantly measured and evaluated, as assignment grades and comments are entered into a database monitoring your progress. . . .

Month Two   Month two is TU project month. . . . In teams of three to five people, they have to come up with an idea, create a business model for it, build the product, and develop the marketing plan. In trying to launch bold new ideas in a hyperaccelerated time frame, they gain a deep appreciation of the need to set priorities, evaluate probabilities, and measure results. Mind you, these projects are not hypothetical—they're the real thing. . . .

Month Three   Month three at Trilogy University is all about finding your place and having a broader impact in the larger organization. A few students continue with their TU projects, but most move on to "graduation projects," which generally are assignments within various Trilogy business units. People leave TU on a rolling basis as they find sponsors out in the company who are willing to take them on.[39]

The change and acquisition phase at Trilogy is stressful, exhilarating, and critical for finding one's place within

TABLE 2–2   Socialization Tactics

Tactic	Description
Collective vs. individual	Collective socialization consists of grouping newcomers and exposing them to a common set of experiences rather than treating each newcomer individually and exposing him or her to more or less unique experiences.
Formal vs. informal	Formal socialization is the practice of segregating a newcomer from regular organization members during a defined socialization period versus not clearly distinguishing a newcomer from more experienced members. Army recruits must attend boot camp before they are allowed to work alongside established soldiers.
Sequential vs. random	Sequential socialization refers to a fixed progression of steps that culminate in the new role, compared to an ambiguous or dynamic progression. The socialization of doctors involves a lock-step sequence from medical school, to internship, to residency before they are allowed to practice on their own.
Fixed vs. variable	Fixed socialization provides a timetable for the assumption of the role, whereas a variable process does not. American university students typically spend one year apiece as freshmen, sophomores, juniors, and seniors.
Serial vs. disjunctive	A serial process is one in which the newcomer is socialized by an experienced member, whereas a disjunctive process does not use a role model.
Investiture vs. divestiture	Investiture refers to the affirmation of a newcomer's incoming global and specific role identities and attributes. Divestiture is the denial and stripping away of the newcomer's existing sense of self and the reconstruction of self in the organization's image. During police training, cadets are required to wear uniforms and maintain an immaculate appearance, they are addressed as "officer," and told they are no longer ordinary citizens but are representatives of the police force.

SOURCE: Descriptions were taken from B E Ashforth, *Role Transitions in Organizational Life: An Identity-Based Perspective* (Mahwah, NJ: Lawrence Erlbaum Associates, 2001), pp 149–83.

the organization. How would you like to work there? Returning to Table 2–2, can you identify the socialization tactics used by Trilogy?

Practical Application of Socialization Research

Past research suggests four practical guidelines for managing organizational socialization.

1. Managers should avoid a haphazard, sink-or-swim approach to organizational socialization because formalized socialization tactics positively affect new hires. Formalized orientation programs are more effective.[40]

Have You Been Adequately Socialized?

INSTRUCTIONS: Complete the following survey items by considering either your current job or one you held in the past. If you have never worked, identify a friend who is working and ask that individual to complete the questionnaire for his or her organization. Read each item and circle your response by using the rating scale shown below. Compute your total score by adding up your responses and compare it to the scoring norms.

	Strongly Disagree	Disagree	Neutral	Agree	Strongly Agree
1. I have been through a set of training experiences that are specifically designed to give newcomers a thorough knowledge of job-related skills.	1	2	3	(4)	5
2. This organization puts all newcomers through the same set of learning experiences.	1	(2)	3	4	5
3. I did not perform any of my normal job responsibilities until I was thoroughly familiar with departmental procedures and work methods.	1	(2)	3	4	5
4. There is a clear pattern in the way one role leads to another, or one job assignment leads to another, in this organization.	1	2	3	(4)	5
5. I can predict my future career path in this organization by observing other people's experiences.	1	2	(3)	4	5
6. Almost all of my colleagues have been supportive of me personally.	1	2	3	(4)	5
7. My colleagues have gone out of their way to help me adjust to this organization.	1	2	3	(4)	5
8. I received much guidance from experienced organizational members as to how I should perform my job.	1	2	3	(4)	5

Total Score ___0___ ___4___ ___3___ _20_ ___0___

SCORING NORMS

8–18 = Low socialization   19–29 = Moderate socialization   30–40 = High socialization

SOURCE: Adapted from survey items excerpted from **D Cable and C Parsons,** "Socialization Tactics and Person-Organization Fit," *Personnel Psychology,* Spring 2001, pp 1–23.

2. Managers play a key role during the encounter phase. Studies of newly hired accountants demonstrated that the frequency and type of information obtained during their first six months of employment significantly affected their job performance, their role clarity, and the extent to which they were socially integrated.[41] Managers need to help new hires integrate within the organizational culture. Consider the approach used by John Chambers, CEO of Cisco Systems. "He meets with groups of new hires to welcome them soon after they start, and at monthly breakfast meetings workers are encouraged to ask him tough questions.[42]

   Take a moment now to complete the Hands-On Exercise. It measures the extent to which you have been socialized into your current work organization. Have you been adequately socialized? If not, you may need to find a mentor. Mentoring is discussed in the next section.

3. The organization can benefit by training new employees to use proactive socialization behaviors. A study of 154 entry-level professionals showed that effectively using proactive socialization behaviors influenced the newcomers' general anxiety and stress during the first month of employment and their motivation and anxiety six months later.[43]

4. Managers should pay attention to the socialization of diverse employees. Research demonstrated that diverse employees, particularly those with disabilities, experienced different socialization activities than other newcomers. In turn, these different experiences affected their long-term success and job satisfaction.[44]

Embedding Organizational Culture through Mentoring

The modern word *mentor* derives from Mentor, the name of a wise and trusted counselor in Greek mythology. Terms typically used in connection with mentoring are *teacher, coach, sponsor,* and *peer.* **Mentoring** is defined as the process of forming and maintaining intensive and lasting developmental relationships between a variety of developers (i.e., people who provide career and psychosocial support) and a junior person (the protégé, if male; or protégée, if female).[45] Mentoring can serve to embed an organization's culture when developers and the protégé/protégée work in the same organization for two reasons. First, mentoring contributes to creating a sense of oneness by promoting the acceptance of the organization's core values throughout the organization. Second, the socialization aspect of mentoring also promotes a sense of membership.

mentoring

Process of forming and maintaining developmental relationships between a mentor and a junior person.

Not only is mentoring important as a tactic for embedding organizational culture, but research suggests it can significantly influence the protégé/protégée's future career. For example, mentored employees performed better on the job and experienced more rapid career advancement than nonmentored employees. Mentored employees also reported higher job and career satisfaction and working on more challenging job assignments.[46] With this information in mind, this section focuses on how people can use mentoring to their advantage. We discuss the functions of mentoring, the developmental networks underlying mentoring, and the personal and organizational implications of mentoring.

Functions of Mentoring

Test Your Knowledge

Mentoring

Kathy Kram, a Boston University researcher, conducted in-depth interviews with both members of 18 pairs of senior and junior managers. As a by-product of this study, Kram identified two general functions—career and psychosocial—of the mentoring process. Five *career functions* that enhanced career development were sponsorship, exposure-and-visibility, coaching, protection, and challenging assignments. Four *psychosocial functions* were role modeling, acceptance-and-confirmation, counseling, and friendship. The psychosocial functions clarified the participants' identities and enhanced their feelings of competence.[47]

Developmental Networks Underlying Mentoring

Historically, it was thought that mentoring was primarily provided by one person who was called a mentor. Today, however, the changing nature of technology, organizational structures, and marketplace dynamics requires that people seek career information and support from many sources. Mentoring is currently viewed as a process in which protégés and protégées seek developmental guidance from a network of people, who are referred to as developers. Lori McKee, a project manager with Chubb Group of Insurance Cos., is a good example of someone who used a network of people to advance her career. She started a book club at the company, and 19 Chubb Group women across the country meet via teleconference once a month to discuss career issues associated with books they have read. "As a result of her increased visibility at the company, the 31-year-old Ms. McKee says she has been offered bigger assignments, including one to help upgrade the company's financial systems worldwide. 'The way I got it was through these discussions and getting mentoring from other women in the group,' she says."[48] This example implies that the diversity and strength of a person's network of relationships is instrumental in obtaining the type of career assistance needed to manage his or her career. Figure 2–4 presents a developmental network typology based on integrating the diversity and strength of developmental relationships.[49]

The **diversity of developmental relationships** reflects the variety of people within the network an individual uses for developmental assistance. There are two subcomponents associated with network diversity: (1) the number of different people the person is networked with and (2) the various social systems from which the networked relationships stem (e.g., employer, school, family, community, professional associations, and religious affiliations). As shown in Figure 2–4, developmental relationship diversity ranges from low (few people or social systems) to high (multiple people or social systems). **Developmental relationship strength** reflects the quality of relationships among an individual and those involved in his or her developmental network. For example, strong ties are reflective of relationships based on frequent interactions, reciprocity, and positive affect. Weak ties, in contrast, are based more on superficial relationships. Together, the diversity and strength of developmental relationships results in four types of developmental networks (see Figure 2–4): receptive, traditional, entrepreneurial, and opportunistic.

A *receptive* developmental network is composed of a few weak ties from one social system such as an employer or a professional association. The single oval

diversity of developmental relationships

The variety of people in a network used for developmental assistance.

developmental relationship strength

The quality of relationships among people in a network.

FIGURE 2–4
Developmental
Networks
Associated
with
Mentoring

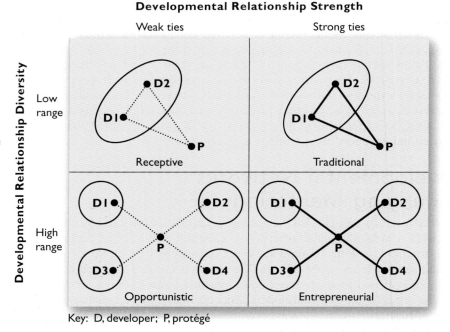

Developmental Relationship Strength

SOURCE: From *Academy of Management Review* by M Higgins and K Kram, "Reconceptualizing Mentoring at Work: A Developmental Network Perspective," April 2001, p 270. Copyright 2001 by Academy of Management. Reproduced with permission of Academy of Management via Copyright Clearance Center.

around D1 and D2 in Figure 2–4 is indicative of two developers who come from one social system. In contrast, a *traditional* network contains a few strong ties between an employee and developers that all come from one social system. An entrepreneurial network, which is the strongest type of developmental network, is made up of strong ties among several developers (D1–D4) who come from four different social systems. Finally, an opportunistic network is associated with having weak ties with multiple developers from different social systems.

Personal and Organizational Implications

There are three key personal implications to consider. First, job and career satisfaction are likely to be influenced by the consistency between an individual's career goals and the type of developmental network at his or her disposal. For example, people with an entrepreneurial developmental network are more likely to experience change in their careers and to benefit from personal learning than people with receptive, traditional, and opportunistic networks. If this sounds attractive to you, you should try to increase the diversity and strength of your developmental relationships. In contrast, lower levels of job satisfaction are expected when employees have receptive developmental networks and they desire to experience career advancement in multiple organizations. Receptive developmental networks, however, can be satisfying to someone who does not desire to be promoted up the career ladder. Second, a developer's willingness to provide career and psychosocial assistance is a function of the protégé/protégée's ability, potential, and the quality of the interpersonal relationship.[50] This implies that you must take ownership for enhancing your skills, abilities, and developmental networks if you desire to experience career advancement throughout your life (see Skills & Best Practices). Third, put effort into finding a mentor. A recent study of 4,559 leaders and 944 human resource professionals from 42 countries showed that 91% of those who used a mentor found the experience moderately or greatly beneficial to their career success.[51]

Research also supports the organizational benefits of mentoring. In addition to the obvious benefit of employee development, mentoring enhances the effectiveness of organizational communication. Specifically, mentoring increases the amount of vertical communication both up and down an organization, and it provides a mechanism for modifying or reinforcing organizational culture. As found at Blue Cross and Blue Shield of North Carolina, an effective mentoring program can also reduce employee turnover and increase productivity. Their program pairs employees with company leaders for one year.

Designed to identify high-potential employees, develop talent, enhance cross-functional relationships and create networking opportunities, the program consists of nine-month commitments on the part of the mentor and mentee. Employees who are accepted into the program (anyone can apply) are paired with a mentor who has completed rigorous training and is typically from a different department and/or division than the mentee. . . . Since the program's inauguration in 2000, turnover among mentees has averaged 46 percent lower than BCBSNC's general employee population. What's more, the BCBSNC's Corporate Leadership Council's formula for calculating the cost of turnover showed that this program, which costs less than $4,500 per year in out-of-pocket expense, generated a cost avoidance of more than $1.4 million. Additionally, 18 percent of mentees in 2001 and 25 percent in 2002 received outstanding performance ratings, compared to 10 percent for the general population for the same periods.[52]

Building an Effective Mentoring Network

1. Become the perfect protégé. It is important to invest ample time and energy to develop and maintain a network of developmental relationships. Trust and respect are needed among network members.

2. Engage in 360-degree networking. Share information and maintain good relationships with those above, below, and at the same status/responsibility level as yourself.

3. Commit to assessing, building, and adjusting the mentor network. Begin by assessing the competencies you want to build. Next, find mentors that can assist in building your desired competencies. Finally, change network members commensurate with changes in your experience and knowledge.

4. Develop diverse, synergistic connections. Find and develop relationships with multiple, diverse mentors. Pursue both formal and informal mentoring opportunities.

5. Realize that change is inevitable and that all good things come to an end. Most mentoring relationships last an average of five years. When a relationship ceases to be beneficial, end the mentoring relationship.

SOURCE: Derived from Suzanne C de Janasz, Sherry E Sullivan, and Vicki Whiting, "Mentor Networks and Career Success: Lessons for Turbulent Times," *Academy of Management Executive*, November 2003, pp 78–91.

key terms

anticipatory socialization   51
change and acquisition   53
developmental relationship
   strength   57
diversity of developmental
   relationships   57

enacted values   43
encounter phase   53
espoused values   42
mentoring   56
normative beliefs   46
onboarding   53

organizational culture   41
organizational socialization   51
values   42

chapter summary

- *Discuss the layers and functions of organizational culture.* The three layers of organizational culture are observable artifacts, espoused values, and basic underlying assumptions. Each layer varies in terms of outward visibility and resistance to change. Four functions of organizational culture are organizational identity, collective commitment, social system stability, and sense-making device.

- *Discuss the three general types of organizational culture and their associated normative beliefs.* The three general types of organizational culture are constructive, passive–defensive, and aggressive–defensive. Each type is grounded in different normative beliefs. Normative beliefs represent an individual's thoughts and beliefs about how members of a particular group or organization are expected to approach their work and interact with others. A constructive culture is associated with the beliefs of achievement, self-actualizing, humanistic-encouraging, and affiliative. Passive–defensive organizations tend to endorse the beliefs of approval, conventional, dependent, and avoidance. Aggressive–defensive cultures tend to endorse the beliefs of oppositional, power, competitive, and perfectionistic.

- *Summarize the methods used by organizations to embed their cultures.* Embedding a culture amounts to teaching employees about the organization's preferred values, beliefs, expectations, and behaviors. This is accomplished by using one or more of the following 11 mechanisms: (a) formal statements of organizational philosophy, mission, vision, values, and materials used for recruiting, selection, and socialization; (b) the design of physical space, work environments, and buildings; (c) slogans, language, acronyms, and sayings; (d) deliberate role modeling, training programs, teaching, and coaching by managers and supervisors; (e) explicit rewards, status symbols, and promotion criteria; (f) stories, legends, and myths about key people and events; (g) the organizational activities, processes, or outcomes that leaders pay attention to, measure, and control; (h) leader reactions to critical incidents and organizational crises; (i) the workflow and organizational structure; (j) organizational systems and procedures; and (k) organizational goals and associated criteria used for recruitment, selection, development, promotion, layoffs, and retirement of people.

- *Describe the three phases in Feldman's model of organizational socialization.* The three phases of Feldman's model are anticipatory socialization, encounter, and change and acquisition. Anticipatory socialization begins before an individual actually joins the organization. The encounter phase begins when the employment contract has been signed. Phase 3 involves the period in which employees master important tasks and resolve any role conflicts.

- *Discuss the various socialization tactics used to socialize employees.* There are six key socialization tactics. They are collective versus individual, formal versus informal, sequential versus random, fixed versus variable, serial versus disjunctive, and investiture versus divestiture (see Table 2–2). Each tactic provides organizations with two opposing options for socializing employees.

- *Explain the four types of development networks derived from a developmental network model of mentoring.* The four development networks are receptive, traditional, entrepreneurial, and opportunistic. A receptive network is composed of a few weak ties from one social system. A traditional network contains a few strong ties between an employee and developers that all come from one social system. An entrepreneurial network is made up of strong ties among developers from several social systems, and an opportunistic network is associated with having weak ties with multiple developers from different social systems.

discussion questions

1. How would you describe the type of organizational culture that exists at Home Depot? Be sure to provide examples about the extent to which Home Depot displayed the 12 types of normative beliefs shown in Table 2–1.
2. How would you respond to someone who made the following statement? "Organizational cultures are not important as far as managers are concerned."
3. Can you think of any organizational heroes who have influenced your work behavior? Describe them, and explain how they affected your behavior.
4. Why is socialization essential to organizational success?
5. Have you ever had a mentor? Explain how things turned out.

ethical dilemma

Arthur Andersen's Pursuit of Consulting Income Created Ethical Challenges in Its Auditing Operations[53]

Andersen realized long ago that no one was going to get rich doing just audits. So for partners to share in hundreds of thousands of dollars of firm profits each year, Andersen would have to boost its lucrative consulting business. That quest for revenue is how the firm lost sight of its obligation to cast a critical eye on its clients' accounting practices, some critics say. . . .

The problems with focusing on consulting are evident in Andersen's biggest accounting blowups. Consider Waste Management, Inc., which generated millions of dollars in consulting fees for Andersen. Last year, securities regulators alleged that Andersen bent the accounting rules so far the firm committed fraud. Time and again, starting in 1988 up through 1997, when Waste Management announced what at the time was the biggest financial restatement in US history, Andersen auditors knew the company was violating generally accepted accounting principles, the Securities and Exchange Commission said in a settled complaint filed in a Washington, DC, federal court.

Throughout the late 1990s, Andersen proposed hundreds of millions of dollars of accounting adjustments to rectify the situation, the SEC said in its suit. But when Waste Management refused to follow their recommendations, to the auditors' disappointment, they caved in. Those decisions were backed at the highest levels of Andersen's Chicago office, the SEC suit says.

Before taking over Waste Management's audit in 1991, Andersen partner Robert Allgyer had been in charge of coordinating the Chicago office's efforts to cross-sell nonaudit services to Andersen's audit clients. Indeed, for Andersen, nonaudit services were the only potential source of revenue growth from the trash hauler. That year, Waste Management had capped the amount of audit fees it would pay Andersen. The company, however, allowed Andersen to earn additional fees for "special work."

What Would You Have Done If You Were Auditing Waste Management's Financial Statements?

1. Vigorously challenge Waste Management employees to correct their accounting practices.

2. Go to your manager when you first realize Waste Management was not following generally accepted accounting principles and tell him or her that you will not work on this account until Waste Management changes its ways.

3. Complete the work as best you can because your efforts contribute to Andersen's financial goals.

4. Invent other options. Discuss.

For an interpretation of this situation, visit our Web site, www.mhhe.com/kinickiob3e.

If you're looking for additional study materials, be sure to check out the Online Learning Center at

www.mhhe.com/kinickiob3e

for more information and interactivities that correspond to this chapter.

chapter three

Developing Global Managers

LEARNING OBJECTIVES

After reading the material in this chapter, you should be able to:

- Define *ethnocentrism,* and explain what Hofstede concluded about applying American management theories in other countries.

- Identify and describe the nine cultural dimensions from the GLOBE project.

- Draw a distinction between individualistic cultures and collectivist cultures.

- Demonstrate your knowledge of these two distinctions: high-context versus low-context cultures and monochronic versus polychronic cultures.

- Explain what the GLOBE project has taught us about leadership.

- Identify an OB trouble spot for each stage of the foreign assignment cycle.

A TEAM OF FOREIGN TRAINERS IN AFGHANISTAN

The following is an account from Steve Coyle, a US citizen living in Malaysia and working for Malaysia-based Service-Winners International. Coyle and his training team provided supervisory and sales development training to employees of a mobile phone operator in Kabul . . . [in 2005].

Training in Afghanistan may not be for everyone, but for

trainers survived the Dec. 26, 2004, Asian tsunami on Penang Island, Malaysia. After that experience, training employees at Telecom Development Company Afghanistan in Kabul sounded doable.

The learning environment in Kabul was more diverse than usual. As trainers, we were aware of multiple dynamics within

We had Pashtuns, Hazaras, Uzbeks and Tajiks in our classroom. These ethnic lines are further sub-divided by religious sects. Our client had Sunni and Shia Muslim employees. Then, the learners were further sub-divided by clans. Besides the local ethnic and religious groups, each of our workshops contained a few ex-pats who came from Algeria, France, Canada and India.

There were other differences within the classroom—some learners had prejudices against those who fled the country to escape the wars. They were considered undeserving of good positions in the company, whereas those who fled considered themselves better educated and in possession of more valuable work experience than those who stayed behind.

There were age divisions. Our client's workforce consisted primarily of those in their late teens to early 20s since most of the middle-age population has been decimated by wars. Some older staff in a traditional society like Afghanistan had difficulty working for a supervisor in his or her late teens who was educated in Pakistan and spoke fluent English.

Telecom Development Company's Afghanistan employees.

our training team, it was an exhilarating experience. The team from our company consisted of myself, Dalwi Lee Wei Keat, a Malaysian of Chinese descent and Jude Louis, a Malaysian of Indian descent. The chance to train in Afghanistan presented itself right after two of our

the classroom. For example, some women felt uncomfortable sitting next to men. Also, taking a group photo is *de rigueur* in our home base of Malaysia, but in Afghanistan, it was a totally different story.

Afghanistan is comprised of multiple ethnic groups.

There was also a gender imbalance in the classroom; 80 percent of the learners were male. During the Taliban era, women were forbidden to work. As a result, women lack English-language and business skills.

Although the learners come from diverse backgrounds, it was refreshing to see that they considered themselves Afghans first. They were proud of their nation and genuinely wanted to better themselves both for their own good and the good of their nation.

The Afghan learners were like sponges. They were eager to learn as much as possible. They cornered you at breaks, lunch and after work to learn from you. The training coordinators advised us that running the sessions during the weekends was acceptable as this is the first "modern" training many of the learners had ever received. . . .

Per-capita income in Afghanistan is low, and life is tough. These conditions foster a scarcity mentality within the society that enters the classroom. For example, when we offered small tokens as prizes for best project work (a practice common in Southeast Asia), the learners were extremely keen to win. They perceived the value of the tokens far higher than other Asian learners we have trained. Competition sometimes got a bit out of control in the group work activities with some groups criticizing . . . [other groups] to win a token. They thrived on recognition from the trainers and wanted us to say which group was better.

The learning environment is fairly traditional. Afghans expect to be called on by the "teachers." As trainers, we are taught that adults are responsible for their own learning, but in Afghanistan the learners complained if we didn't call on or volunteer those who weren't participating. They wanted the whole group to be involved. We also found that generally the wallflowers, although stressed when called upon, liked the opportunity to be forced to participate.

In some sessions, learners would take our handbooks home to study; this would enable them to answer our future questions and ask their own questions. . . .

There are, of course, safety and health concerns when teaching in a politically unstable environment. Security is a topic that each individual must weigh. Our team never felt threatened at any time. There were a lot of uniformed people carrying machine guns in Kabul, but we never heard any gunfire. . . .

Modern hospital facilities are difficult to find in Kabul. I recommend only those who are physically fit and willing to push their bodies to extremes travel to Afghanistan. Even physically fit bodies will likely eventually experience diarrhea or altitude sickness (Kabul has an altitude of 5,900 feet) at one time or another.

Training in Afghanistan is not for everyone. It was the most difficult international project my team has been involved in, yet it was also the most rewarding. Afghanistan has huge training needs for those who are mentally and physically ready to answer.[1]

FOR DISCUSSION

Could you get the job done in this difficult cross-cultural situation? Why or why not? For an interpretation of this case and additional comments, visit our Online Learning Center at

www.mhhe.com/kinickiob3e

WE HEAR A LOT about the global economy these days. On one level, it all seems so grand, so vague, and so distant. But, on another level, it is here, it is now, and it is *very* personal. For example, consider this scenario:

> Liz awakens to a new workday in her San Diego home as her made-in-China alarm clock buzzes. She flips on a Japanese lamp with a bulb made by Philips, a Dutch company. After showering and applying French makeup, she puts on an outfit sewn in Singapore and slips into her favorite hand-crafted Italian shoes. A quick check of the weather on her assembled-in-Mexico television accompanies a hurried breakfast of juice from Brazilian oranges, an apple from New Zealand, a chunk of Danish cheese, and toast smeared with British marmalade. As she stops her German Mercedes SUV (made in Alabama) to fill up on gasoline refined from Venezuelan crude oil, her cell phone made by Finland's Nokia rings and she chats with her best friend thanks to equipment from Canada's Nortel Networks. Down the road, Liz parks outside the offices of her employer, Qualcomm, the wireless technology firm that "has employees originating from more than 100 countries who altogether speak over 50 languages."[2]

Yes, welcome to the global economy! And *you* are a big part of it—just check the labels on the products you buy and the clothes on your back. As *USA Today* pointed out during a recent year-end shopping season: "More than 80% of the toys, bikes and Christmas ornaments sold in the USA come from China. About 90% of all sporting goods and 95% of shoes are foreign-made."[3] Goods, money, and talent are crossing international borders at an accelerating pace. For better or for worse, even more economic globalization lies ahead. Those worried about having their jobs "offshored" to lower-cost foreign countries can take some comfort in this perspective from *BusinessWeek:* "there's still plenty of demand in the US for people who combine technical skills with industry-specific knowledge and people skills."[4] From an OB standpoint, continued globalization means an exponential increase in both cross-cultural interactions and the demand for managers who are comfortable and effective working with people from other countries and cultures.

Even managers and employees who are intent on never leaving the United States cannot escape the global economy and its increased cross-cultural interactions. For example, "roughly half the people who work at the 2,400 Marriott hotels in the USA were born outside this country. Employees speak 47 different languages."[5] Globalization of the auto industry is equally stunning: "Forecaster CSM Worldwide says foreign-owned plants in the US will turn out almost 6 million cars and trucks by 2009, a 20% boost over this year's [2006] expected 5 million."[6]

Competition for both businesses and those seeking good-paying jobs in the global economy promises to be very tough. The purpose of this chapter is to help you move toward meeting the challenge.

Courtesy of Vahan Shirvanian.

Developing a Global Mind-Set

Managing in a global economy is as much about patterns of thinking and behavior as it is about trade agreements, goods and services, and currency exchange rates. Extended periods in a single dominant culture ingrain assumptions about how things are and should be. Today's managers, whether they work at home for a foreign-owned company or actually work in a foreign country, need to develop a global mind-set (involving open-mindedness, adaptability, and a strong desire to learn).[7]

This section encourages a global mind-set by defining societal culture and contrasting it with organizational culture, discussing ethnocentrism, exploring ways to become a global manager, and examining the applicability of American management theories in other cultures.

A Model of Societal and Organizational Cultures

societal culture

Socially derived, taken-for-granted assumptions about how to think and act.

Societal culture involves "shared meanings" that generally remain below the threshold of conscious awareness because they involve *taken-for-granted assumptions* about how one should perceive, think, act, and feel.[8] Cultural anthropologist Edward T Hall put it this way:

> Since much of culture operates outside our awareness, frequently we don't even know what we know. We pick . . . [expectations and assumptions] up in the cradle. We unconsciously learn what to notice and what not to notice, how to divide time and space, how to walk and talk and use our bodies, how to behave as men or women, how to relate to other people, how to handle responsibility, whether experience is seen as whole or fragmented. This applies to all people. The Chinese or the Japanese or the Arabs are as unaware of their assumptions as we are of our own. We each assume that they're part of human nature. What we think of as "mind" is really internalized culture.[9]

Peeling the Cultural Onion   Culture is difficult to grasp because it is multi-layered. International management experts Fons Trompenaars (from the Netherlands) and Charles Hampden-Turner (from Britain) offer this instructive analogy in their landmark book, *Riding the Waves of Culture:*

> Culture comes in layers, like an onion. To understand it you have to unpeel it layer by layer.
>   On the outer layer are the products of culture, like the soaring skyscrapers of Manhattan, pillars of private power, with congested public streets between them. These are expressions of deeper values and norms in a society that are not directly visible (values such as upward mobility, "the more-the-better," status, material success). The layers of values and norms are deeper within the "onion," and are more difficult to identify.[10]

Thus, the September 11, 2001, destruction of the New York World Trade Center towers by terrorists was as much an attack on American cultural values as it was on lives and property. That deepened the hurt and made the anger more profound for Americans and their friends around the world. In both life and business, culture is a serious matter.

Merging Societal and Organizational Cultures   As illustrated in Figure 3–1, culture influences organizational behavior in two ways. Employees bring

Cultural Influences on Organizational Behavior | FIGURE 3–1

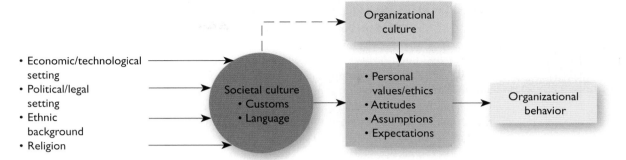

their societal culture to work with them in the form of customs and language. Organizational culture, a by-product of societal culture, in turn affects the individual's values, ethics, attitudes, assumptions, and expectations.[11] The term *societal culture* is used here instead of national culture because the boundaries of many modern nation-states were not drawn along cultural lines. The former Soviet Union, for example, included 15 republics and more than 100 ethnic nationalities, many with their own distinct language.[12] Meanwhile, English-speaking Canadians in Vancouver are culturally closer to Americans in Seattle than to their French-speaking compatriots in Quebec. Societal culture is shaped by the various environmental factors listed in the left-hand side of Figure 3–1.

Once inside the organization's sphere of influence, the individual is further affected by the *organization's* culture. Mixing of societal and organizational cultures can produce interesting dynamics in multinational companies. For example, with French and American employees working side by side at General Electric's medical imaging production facility in Waukesha, Wisconsin, unit head Claude Benchimol witnessed some culture shock:

> The French are surprised the American parking lots empty out as early as 5 PM; the Americans are surprised the French don't start work at 8 AM. Benchimol feels the French are more talkative and candid. Americans have more of a sense of hierarchy and are less likely to criticize. But they may be growing closer to the French. Says Benchimol: "It's taken a year to get across the idea that we are all entitled to say what we don't like to become more productive and work better."[13]

Same company, same company culture, yet GE's French and American co-workers have different attitudes about time, hierarchy, and communication. They are the products of different societal cultures.[14]

When managing people at work, the individual's societal culture, the organizational culture, and any interaction between the two need to be taken into consideration.[15] For example, American workers' cultural orientation toward quality improvement differs significantly from the Japanese cultural pattern:

> Unlike Japanese workers, Americans aren't interested in making small step-by-step improvements to increase quality. They want to achieve the breakthrough, the impossible dream. The way to motivate them: Ask for the big leap, rather than for tiny steps.[16]

Ethnocentrism: Removing a Cultural Roadblock in the Global Economy

ethnocentrism

Belief that one's native country, culture, language, and behavior are superior.

Manager's Hot Seat Application

Cultural Differences: Let's Break a Deal

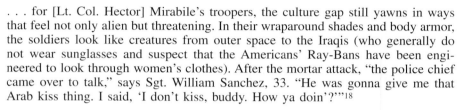

Ethnocentrism, the belief that one's native country, culture, language, and modes of behavior are superior to all others, has its roots in the dawn of civilization. First identified as a behavioral science concept in 1906, involving the tendency of groups to reject outsiders,[17] the term *ethnocentrism* generally has a more encompassing (national or societal) meaning today. Worldwide evidence of ethnocentrism is plentiful. For example, consider these awkward cross-cultural circumstances reported from the war in Iraq in 2003:

> . . . for [Lt. Col. Hector] Mirabile's troopers, the culture gap still yawns in ways that feel not only alien but threatening. In their wraparound shades and body armor, the soldiers look like creatures from outer space to the Iraqis (who generally do not wear sunglasses and suspect that the Americans' Ray-Bans have been engineered to look through women's clothes). After the mortar attack, "the police chief came over to talk," says Sgt. William Sanchez, 33. "He was gonna give me that Arab kiss thing. I said, 'I don't kiss, buddy. How ya doin'?'"[18]

Ethnocentrism led to deadly "ethnic cleansing" in Bosnia and Kosovo and genocide in the African nations of Rwanda, Burundi, and Sudan.

Less dramatic, but still troublesome, is ethnocentrism within managerial and organizational contexts. Experts on the subject framed the problem this way:

Prominent Americans such as George Clooney (left) and Chris Rock have spoken publicly to draw the world's attention to the devastating genocide in Darfur. Non-Arab Muslims in the war-torn African nation are in rebellion against the mostly Arab central government and its militia. By 2006, as many as 180,000 had died and about 2 million were homeless.

> [Ethnocentric managers have] a preference for putting home-country people in key positions everywhere in the world and rewarding them more handsomely for work, along with a tendency to feel that this group is more intelligent, more capable, or more reliable. . . . Ethnocentrism is often not attributable to prejudice as much as to inexperience or lack of knowledge about foreign persons and situations. This is not too surprising, since most executives know far more about employees in their home environments. As one executive put it, "At least I understand why our own managers make mistakes. With our foreigners, I never know. The foreign managers may be better. But if I can't trust a person, should I hire him or her just to prove we're multinational?"[19]

Research Insight Research suggests ethnocentrism is bad for business. A survey of 918 companies with home offices in the United States (272 companies), Japan (309), and Europe (337) found ethnocentric staffing and human resource policies to be associated with increased personnel problems. Those problems included recruiting difficulties, high turnover rates, and lawsuits over personnel policies. Among the three regional samples, Japanese companies had the most ethnocentric human resource practices and the most international human resource problems.[20]

Dealing with Ethnocentrism in Ourselves and Others Current and future managers can effectively deal with ethnocentrism through education,

How Strong Is Your Potential for Ethnocentrism?

INSTRUCTIONS: If you were born and raised or have spent most of your life in the United States, select one number from the following scale for each item. If you are from a different country or culture, substitute the country/language you most closely identify with for the terms *American* and *English*, and then rate each item.

	Strongly Disagree	Disagree	Neutral	Agree	Strongly Agree
1. I was raised in a way that was [truly] American.	1	2	3	4	5
2. Compared to how much I criticize other cultures, I criticize American culture less.	1	2	3	4	5
3. I am proud of American culture.	1	2	3	4	5
4. American culture has had a positive effect on my life.	1	2	3	4	5
5. I believe that my children should read, write, and speak [only] English.	1	2	3	4	5
6. I go to places where people are American.	1	2	3	4	5
7. I admire people who are American.	1	2	3	4	5
8. I would prefer to live in an American community.	1	2	3	4	5
9. At home, I eat [only] American food.	1	2	3	4	5
10. Overall, I am American.	1	2	3	4	5

SCORING 10–23 = Low potential for ethnocentrism
24–36 = Moderate potential for ethnocentrism
37–50 = High potential for ethnocentrism

SOURCE: Adapted from and survey items excerpted from J L Tsai, Y-W Ying, and P A Lee, "The Meaning of 'Being Chinese' and 'Being American': Variation among Chinese American Young Adults," *Journal of Cross-Cultural Psychology,* May 2000, pp 302–32.

greater cross-cultural awareness, international experience, and a conscious effort to value cultural diversity.[21] (Take a moment to complete the Hands-On Exercise.) Results of the Hands-On Exercise need to be interpreted cautiously because this version has not been scientifically validated; thus, it is for instructional and discussion purposes only.

Becoming a Global Manager

On any given day in today's global economy, a manager can interact with colleagues from several different countries or cultures. For instance, at PolyGram, the British music company, the top 33 managers are from 15 different countries.[22] If they are to be effective, present and future managers in such multicultural situations need to develop a global mind-set and cross-cultural skills (see Skills & Best Practices). Developing skilled managers who move comfortably from culture to culture takes time. Consider, for example, this comment by the head of Gillette, who wants twice

Geekcorps Volunteers Gain Valuable International Experience

Matt Berg spent his first few postcollege years like any other geek: coding software under the glow of fluorescent lights. But today the 28-year-old rigs makeshift radio towers near the sands of Tombouctou. As a volunteer for U.S.-based Geekcorps, he's part of an IT-savvy army that's bringing technology infrastructure to developing nations around the world. "I have always been interested in how technology can make people's lives better," he says.

Since it was launched in 2000, . . . Geekcorps has become a sort of Peace Corps for young tech workers. A division of the International Executive Service Corps, the nonprofit has deployed more than 80 volunteers to develop software in Vietnam, assemble computer networks in Romania, and help the Lebanese IT industry increase international exports. Volunteers typically take four-month sabbaticals from their jobs, and Geekcorps provides housing, airfare, and a stipend for meals and incidental expenses.

SOURCE: Excerpted from D Kushner, "A Peace Corps for the Tech Set," *Business 2.0,* **March 2006; http://money.cnn.com/magazines/business2/business2_archive/2006/03/01/8370556/index.htm**

as many global managers on the payroll. "We could try to hire the best and the brightest, but it's the experience with Gillette that we need. About half of our [expatriates] are now on their fourth country—that kind of experience. It takes 10 years to make the kind of Gillette manager I'm talking about."[23]

Importantly, these global skills will help managers in culturally diverse countries such as the United States and Canada do a more effective job on a day-to-day basis.

The Hofstede Study: How Well Do US Management Theories Apply in Other Countries?

The short answer to this important question: *not very well.* This answer derives from a landmark study conducted nearly 30 years ago by Dutch researcher Geert Hofstede. His unique cross-cultural comparison of 116,000 IBM employees from 53 countries worldwide focused on four cultural dimensions:

- *Power distance.* How much inequality does someone expect in social situations?[24]
- *Individualism-collectivism.* How loosely or closely is the person socially bonded?
- *Masculinity-femininity.* Does the person embrace stereotypically competitive, performance-oriented masculine traits or nurturing, relationship-oriented feminine traits?

Test Your Knowledge

Hofstede's Model of National Culture

- *Uncertainty avoidance.* How strongly does the person desire highly structured situations?

The US sample ranked relatively low on power distance, very high on individualism, moderately high on masculinity, and low on uncertainty avoidance.[25]

The high degree of variation among cultures led Hofstede to two major conclusions: (1) Management theories and practices need to be adapted to local cultures. This is particularly true for made-in-America management theories (e.g., Maslow's need hierarchy) and Japanese team management practices. *There is no one best way to manage across cultures.*[26] (2) Cultural arrogance is a luxury individuals, companies, and nations can no longer afford in a global economy.

Becoming Cross-Culturally Competent

Cultural anthropologists believe interesting and valuable lessons can be learned by comparing one culture with another. Many dimensions have been suggested over the years to help contrast and compare the world's rich variety of cultures. Five cultural perspectives, especially relevant to present and aspiring global managers, discussed in this section are basic cultural dimensions, individualism versus collectivism, high-context and low-context cultures, monochronic and polychronic time orientation, and cross-cultural leadership. Separately or together these cultural distinctions can become huge stumbling blocks when doing business across cultures. But first we need to think about cultural stereotyping and the need for *cultural intelligence.*

Cultural Paradoxes Require Cultural Intelligence

An important qualification needs to be offered at this juncture. All of the cultural differences in this chapter and elsewhere need to be viewed as *tendencies* and *patterns* rather than as absolutes. As soon as one falls into the trap of assuming *all* Italians are this, and *all* Koreans will do that, and so on, potentially instructive generalizations become mindless stereotypes. A pair of professors with extensive foreign work experience advises, "As teachers, researchers, and managers in cross-cultural contexts, we need to recognize that our original characterizations of other cultures are best guesses that we need to modify as we gain more experience."[27] Consequently, they contend, we will be better prepared to deal with inevitable *cultural paradoxes.* By paradox, they mean there are always exceptions to the rule: individuals who do not fit the expected cultural pattern. A good example is the head of Canon. "By Japanese CEO standards, Canon, Inc.'s Fujio Mitarai is something of an anomaly. For starters, he's fast and decisive—a far cry from the consensus builders who typically run Japan, Inc."[28] One also encounters lots of cultural paradoxes in large and culturally diverse nations such as the United States and Brazil. This is where the need for cultural intelligence arises.

Cultural intelligence, the ability to accurately interpret ambiguous cross-cultural situations, is an important skill in today's diverse workplaces. Two OB scholars explain:

> A person with high cultural intelligence can somehow tease out of a person's or group's behavior those features that would be true of all people and all groups, those peculiar to this person or this group, and those that are neither universal nor idiosyncratic. The vast realm that lies between those poles is culture.[29]

Those interested in developing their cultural intelligence need to first develop their *emotional intelligence,* discussed in detail in Chapter 5, and then practice in ambiguous cross-cultural situations. Of course, as in all human interaction, there is no adequate substitute for really getting to know, listen to, and care about others.

> **cultural intelligence**
>
> **The ability to interpret ambiguous cross-cultural situations accurately.**

Jackie Fouse is CFO of Alcon, one of the world's biggest producers of eye-care products. Before taking the number 2 job at the $4.4 billion global manufacturer, she had spent nine years working abroad, adding subtle skills like cultural sensitivity to her management expertise. Of her global experience at Nestlé and Swissair, Fouse, who is fluent in French and German, says, "Everything else being equal—educational background, years of experience—that was the thing more than any other that set me apart from other people."

Nine Basic Cultural Dimensions from the GLOBE Project

Project GLOBE (Global Leadership and Organizational Behavior Effectiveness) is the brainchild of University of Pennsylvania professor Robert J House.[30] It is a massive and ongoing attempt to "develop an empirically based theory to describe, understand, and predict the impact of specific cultural variables on leadership and

Genevieve Bell, an anthropologist employed by Intel Research, has been researching how people use technology in Asia and the Pacific to learn more about values and habits in emerging markets. Much of what Bell has learned challenges Western assumptions regarding technology and its use across the globe. Countries like Japan have little "private" space in homes and therefore younger occupants are attracted to text-messaging. The South Korean electronics company LG Electronics has introduced a mobile phone with an embedded compass to allow Muslim users to locate the direction of Mecca using Global Positioning System technology. All of these considerations can make it difficult for one company like Intel to market one product globally. Pictured here is one of the many mobile phone chargers that can be found across China.

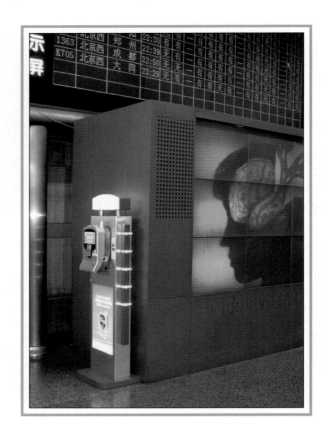

organizational processes and the effectiveness of these processes."[31] GLOBE has evolved into a network of more than 160 scholars from 62 societies since the project was launched in Calgary, Canada, in 1994. Most of the researchers are native to the particular cultures they study, thus greatly enhancing the credibility of the project. During the first two phases of the GLOBE project, a list of nine basic cultural dimensions was developed and statistically validated. Translated questionnaires based on the nine dimensions were administered to thousands of managers in the banking, food, and telecommunications industries around the world to build a database. Results are being published on a regular basis.[32] Much work and many years are needed if the project's goal, as stated above, is to be achieved. In the meantime, we have been given a comprehensive, valid, and up-to-date tool for better understanding cross-cultural similarities and differences.

The nine cultural dimensions from the GLOBE project are:

- *Power distance:* How much unequal distribution of power should there be in organizations and society?
- *Uncertainty avoidance:* How much should people rely on social norms and rules to avoid uncertainty and limit unpredictability?
- *Institutional collectivism:* How much should leaders encourage and reward loyalty to the social unit, as opposed to the pursuit of individual goals?
- *In-group collectivism:* How much pride and loyalty should individuals have for their family or organization?

- *Gender egalitarianism:* How much effort should be put into minimizing gender discrimination and role inequalities?
- *Assertiveness:* How confrontational and dominant should individuals be in social relationships?
- *Future orientation:* How much should people delay gratification by planning and saving for the future?
- *Performance orientation:* How much should individuals be rewarded for improvement and excellence?
- *Humane orientation:* How much should society encourage and reward people for being kind, fair, friendly, and generous?[33]

Notice how the two forms of collectivism, along with the dimensions of power distance and uncertainty avoidance, correspond to the similarly labeled variables in Hofstede's classic study, discussed earlier.

Bringing the GLOBE Cultural Dimensions to Life A fun and worthwhile exercise is to reflect on your own cultural roots, family traditions, and belief system and develop a personal cultural profile, using as many of the GLOBE dimensions as possible. As a case in point, which of the GLOBE cultural dimensions relates to the following biographical sketch?

> Christopher Jones, 24, [is] a UCLA grad who's a musician, playing with his rock band at clubs in Los Angeles.
>
> Like many his age, he has no money for rainy-day savings, let alone the long term.
>
> "At this point, my attitude of life is 'carpe diem.' If I have some money, take a trip, something like that," Jones said.
>
> "I understand that being a young person and saving money is the right thing to do. But finding happiness is more important to me than having a little money down the line."[34]

If you said "future orientation," you're right! Indeed, like too many Americans (of all ages), Christopher Jones scores low on future orientation and thus has inadequate savings for the future.

Country Profiles and Practical Implications How do different countries score on the GLOBE cultural dimensions? Data from 18,000 managers yielded the profiles in Table 3–1. A quick overview shows a great deal of cultural diversity around the world. But thanks to the nine GLOBE dimensions, we have more precise understanding of *how* cultures vary. Closer study reveals telling cultural *patterns,* or cultural fingerprints for nations. The US managerial sample, for instance, scored high on assertiveness and performance orientation. Accordingly, Americans are widely perceived as pushy and hardworking. Switzerland's high scores on uncertainty avoidance and future orientation help explain its centuries of political neutrality and world-renowned banking industry. Singapore is known as a great place to do business because it is clean and safe and its people are well educated and hardworking. This is no surprise, considering Singapore's high scores on institutional collectivism, future orientation, and performance orientation. In contrast, Russia's low scores on future orientation and performance orientation could foreshadow a slower than hoped for transition from a centrally planned economy to free enterprise capitalism. These illustrations bring us to an important practical lesson: *Knowing the cultural tendencies of foreign business partners and competitors can give you a strategic competitive advantage.*

TABLE 3–1   Countries Ranking Highest and Lowest on the
GLOBE Cultural Dimensions

Dimension	Highest	Lowest
Power distance	Morocco, Argentina, Thailand, Spain, Russia	Denmark, Netherlands, South Africa—black sample, Israel, Costa Rica
Uncertainty avoidance	Switzerland, Sweden, German—former West, Denmark, Austria	Russia, Hungary, Bolivia, Greece, Venezuela
Institutional collectivism	Sweden, South Korea, Japan, Singapore, Denmark	Greece, Hungary, Germany—former East, Argentina, Italy
In-group collectivism	Iran, India, Morocco, China, Egypt	Denmark, Sweden, New Zealand, Netherlands, Finland
Gender egalitarianism	Hungary, Poland, Slovenia, Denmark, Sweden	South Korea, Egypt, Morocco, India, China
Assertiveness	Germany—former East, Austria, Greece, US, Spain	Sweden, New Zealand, Switzerland, Japan, Kuwait
Future orientation	Singapore, Switzerland, Netherlands, Canada—English speaking, Denmark	Russia, Argentina, Poland, Italy, Kuwait
Performance orientation	Singapore, Hong Kong, New Zealand, Taiwan, US	Russia, Argentina, Greece, Venezuela, Italy
Humane orientation	Philippines, Ireland, Malaysia, Egypt, Indonesia	Germany—former West, Spain, France, Singapore, Brazil

SOURCE: Adapted from M Javidan and R J House, "Cultural Acumen for the Global Manager: Lessons from Project GLOBE," *Organizational Dynamics*, Spring 2001, pp 289–305.

Individualism versus Collectivism: A Closer Look

Have you ever been torn between what you personally wanted and what the group, organization, or society expected of you? If so, you have firsthand experience with a fundamental and important cultural distinction in both the Hofstede and GLOBE studies: individualism versus collectivism. Awareness of this distinction, as we will soon see, can spell the difference between success and failure in cross-cultural business dealings.

individualistic culture

Primary emphasis on personal freedom and choice.

collectivist culture

Personal goals less important than community goals and interests.

Individualistic cultures, characterized as "I" and "me" cultures, give priority to individual freedom and choice. **Collectivist cultures,** oppositely called "we" and "us" cultures, rank shared goals higher than individual desires and goals. People in collectivist cultures are expected to subordinate their own wishes and goals to those of the relevant social unit. A worldwide survey of 30,000 managers by Trompenaars and Hampden-Turner, who prefer the term *communitarianism* to collectivism, found the highest degree of individualism in Israel, Romania, Nigeria, Canada, and the United States. Countries ranking lowest in individualism—thus qualifying as collectivist cultures—were Egypt, Nepal, Mexico, India, and Japan. Brazil, China, and France also ended up toward the collectivist end of the scale.[35]

Consider this feet-on-the-ground comparison between the United States and Mexico:

"There is a very clear criticism of American life, at least in Mexico, as being overly individualistic, as being selfish," says Jennifer Hirsch, associate professor of sociomedical sciences at Columbia University. "My experience of life in rural Mexico is that it's a society that takes much more pleasure from human connection."[36]

A Business Success Factor Of course, one can expect to encounter both individualists and collectivists in culturally diverse countries such as the United States.[37] For example, imagine the frustration of Dave Murphy, a Boston-based mutual fund salesperson, when he recently tried to get Navajo Indians in Arizona interested in saving money for their retirement. After several fruitless meetings with groups of Navajo employees, he was given this cultural insight by a local official: "If you come to this environment, you have to understand that money is different. It's there to be spent. If you have some, you help your family."[38] To traditional Navajos, enculturated as collectivists, saving money is an unworthy act of selfishness. Subsequently, the sales pitch was tailored to emphasize the *family* benefits of individual retirement savings plans.

Allegiance to Whom? The Navajo example brings up an important point about collectivist cultures. Specifically, which unit of society predominates? For the Navajos, family is the key reference group. But, as Trompenaars and Hampden-Turner observe, important differences exist among collectivist (or communitarian) cultures:

> For each single society, it is necessary to determine the group with which individuals have the closest identification. They could be keen to identify with their trade union, their family, their corporation, their religion, their profession, their nation, or the state apparatus. The French tend to identify with *la France, la famille, le cadre;* the Japanese with the corporation; the former eastern bloc with the Communist Party; and Ireland with the Roman Catholic Church. Communitarian goals may be good or bad for industry depending on the community concerned, its attitude and relevance to business development.[39]

High-Context and Low-Context Cultures

People from **high-context cultures**—including China, Korea, Japan, Vietnam, Mexico, and Arab cultures—rely heavily on situational cues for meaning when perceiving and communicating with others.[40] Nonverbal cues such as one's official position, status, or family connections convey messages more powerfully than do spoken words. Thus, we come to better understand the ritual of exchanging *and reading* business cards in Japan.

high-context cultures

Primary meaning derived from nonverbal situational cues.

Japanese culture is relatively high context. One's business card, listing employer and official position, conveys vital silent messages about one's status to members of Japan's homogeneous society. Also, people from high-context cultures who are not especially talkative during a first encounter with a stranger are not necessarily being unfriendly; they are simply taking time to collect "contextual" information.

Reading the Fine Print in Low-Context Cultures In **low-context cultures,** written and spoken words carry the burden of shared meanings. Low-context cultures include those found in Germany, Switzerland, Scandinavia, North America, and Great Britain. True to form, Germany has precise written rules for even the smallest details of

low-context cultures

Primary meaning derived from written and spoken words.

daily life. In *high*-context cultures, agreements tend to be made on the basis of someone's word or a handshake, after a rather prolonged get-acquainted and trust-building period. Low-context Americans and Canadians, who have cultural roots in Northern Europe, see the handshake as a signal to get a signature on a detailed, lawyer-approved, iron-clad contract.

Avoiding Cultural Collisions   Misunderstanding and miscommunication often are problems in international business dealings when the parties are from high- versus low-context cultures. A Mexican business professor made this instructive observation:

> Over the years, I have noticed that across cultures there are different opinions on what is expected from a business report. US managers, for instance, take a pragmatic, get-to-the-point approach, and expect reports to be concise and action-oriented. They don't have time to read long explanations: "Just the facts, ma'am."
>
> Latin American managers will usually provide long explanations that go beyond the simple facts. . . .
>
> I have a friend who is the Latin America representative for a United States firm and has been asked by his boss to provide regular reports on sales activities. His reports are long, including detailed explanations on the context in which the events he is reporting on occur and the possible interpretations that they might have. His boss regularly answers these reports with very brief messages, telling him to "cut the crap and get to the point!"[41]

Awkward situations such as this can be avoided when those on both sides of the context divide make good-faith attempts to understand and accommodate their counterparts (see Skills & Best Practices).

Cultural Perceptions of Time

In North American and Northern European cultures, time seems to be a simple matter. It is linear, relentlessly marching forward, never backward, in standardized chunks. To the American who received a watch for his or her third birthday, time is like money. It is spent, saved, or wasted.[42] Americans are taught to show up 10 minutes early for appointments. When working across cultures, however, time becomes a very complex matter. For example, consider this recent clipping from the business press:

> The impact of China's global shopping spree is being felt even in tiny Poca, W.Va., population 1,024. At Kanawha Scales & Systems, Chinese orders for the company's sophisticated coal-loading machines have grown to about one-third of the company's roughly $50 million in annual revenue.
>
> "The last three or four years, it's increased substantially. A lot," says Jim Bradbury, president of KSS.
>
> Bradbury, 61, made his first trip to China in 1986, spending a month in Beijing in a fruitless quest for an order. Six years later, the company

SKILLS & BEST PRACTICES

Breaking through the Context Barrier in Culturally Diverse US Workplaces

- People on both sides of the context barrier must be trained to make adjustments.

- A new employee should be greeted by a group consisting of his or her boss, the secretary, several colleagues who have similar duties, and an individual located near the newcomer.

- Background information is essential when explaining anything. Include the history and personalities involved.

- Do not assume the newcomer is self-reliant. Give explicit instructions not only about objectives, but also about the process involved.

- High-context workers from abroad need to learn to ask questions outside their department and function.

- Foreign workers must make an effort to become more self-reliant.

SOURCE: Excerpted from R Drew, "Working with Foreigners," *Management Review*, September 1999, p 6.

finally landed its first deal, a $3 million contract to install coal load-out systems at a Chinese coal mine.[43]

The need for patience in this cross-cultural business deal can be explained in part by the distinction between **monochronic time** and **polychronic time:**

> The former is revealed in the ordered, precise, schedule-driven use of public time that typifies and even caricatures efficient Northern Europeans and North Americans. The latter is seen in the multiple and cyclical activities and concurrent involvement with different people in Mediterranean, Latin American, and especially Arab cultures.[44]

monochronic time

Preference for doing one thing at a time because time is limited, precisely segmented, and schedule driven.

polychronic time

Preference for doing more than one thing at a time because time is flexible and multidimensional.

A Matter of Degree   Monochronic and polychronic are relative rather than absolute concepts. Generally, the more things a person tends to do at once, the more polychronic that person is.[45] Thanks to computers and advanced telecommunications systems, highly polychronic managers can engage in "multitasking."[46] For instance, it is possible to talk on the telephone, read and respond to e-mail messages, print a report, check a cell phone message, *and* eat a stale sandwich all at the same time. Unfortunately, this extreme polychronic behavior too often is not as efficient as hoped and can be very stressful.[47] Monochronic people prefer to do one thing at a time. What is your attitude toward time?

Practical Implications   Low-context cultures, such as that of the United States, tend to run on monochronic time while high-context cultures, such as that of Mexico, tend to run on polychronic time. People in polychronic cultures view time as flexible, fluid, and multidimensional. The Germans and Swiss have made an exact science of monochronic time. In fact, a radio-controlled watch made by a German company, Junghans, is "guaranteed to lose no more than one second in 1 million years."[48] Many a visitor has been a minute late for a Swiss train, only to see its taillights leaving the station. Time is more elastic in polychronic cultures. During the Islamic holy month of Ramadan in Middle Eastern nations, for example, the faithful fast during daylight hours, and the general pace of things markedly slows.[49] Managers need to reset their mental clocks when doing business across cultures.

Leadership Lessons from the GLOBE Project

In phase 2, the GLOBE researchers set out to discover which, if any, attributes of leadership were universally liked or disliked. They surveyed 17,000 middle managers working for 951 organizations across 62 countries. Their results, summarized in Table 3–2, have important implications for trainers and present and future global managers. Visionary and inspirational *charismatic leaders* who are good team builders generally do the best. On the other hand, *self-centered leaders* seen as loners or face-savers generally receive a poor reception worldwide. (See Chapter 14 for a comprehensive treatment of leadership.) Local and foreign managers who heed these results are still advised to use a contingency approach to leadership after using their cultural intelligence to read the local people and culture.[50] David Whitwam, the longtime CEO of appliance maker Whirlpool, recently framed the challenge this way:

> Leading a company today is different from the 1980s and '90s, especially in a global company. It requires a new set of competencies. Bureaucratic structures don't work anymore. You have to take the command-and-control types out of the

Test Your Knowledge

International Cultural Diversity

TABLE 3–2 | Leadership Attributes Universally Liked and Disliked across 62 Nations

Universally Positive Leader Attributes	Universally Negative Leader Attributes
Trustworthy	Loner
Just	Asocial
Honest	Noncooperative
Foresight	Irritable
Plans ahead	Nonexplicit
Encouraging	Egocentric
Positive	Ruthless
Dynamic	Dictatorial
Motive arouser	
Confidence builder	
Motivational	
Dependable	
Intelligent	
Decisive	
Effective bargainer	
Win–win problem solver	
Administrative skilled	
Communicative	
Informed	
Coordinator	
Team builder	
Excellence oriented	

SOURCE: Excerpted and adapted from P W Dorfman, P J Hanges, and F C Brodbeck, "Leadership and Cultural Variation: The Identification of Culturally Endorsed Leadership Profiles," in *Culture, Leadership, and Organizations: The GLOBE Study of 62 Societies*, eds R J House, P J Hanges, M Javidan, P W Dorfman, and V Gupta (Thousand Oaks, CA: Sage, 2004), Tables 21.2 and 21.3, pp 677–78.

system. You need to allow and encourage broad-based involvement in the company. Especially in consumer kinds of companies, we need a diverse workforce with diverse leadership. You need strong regional leadership that lives in the culture. We have a North American running the North American business, and a Latin American running the Latin American business.[51]

Preparing for a Foreign Assignment

As the reach of global companies continues to grow, many opportunities for living and working in foreign countries will arise. Imagine, for example, the opportunities for foreign duty and cross-cultural experiences at Siemens, the German electronics giant. "While Siemens' corporate headquarters is near Munich, nearly 80% of the firm's business is international. Worldwide the company has 470,000 employees, including 75,000 in the United States and 25,000 in China."[52] Siemens and other global players need a vibrant and growing cadre of employees who are willing and able to do business across cultures. Thus, the purpose of this final section is to help you prepare yourself and others to work successfully in foreign countries.

A Poor Track Record for American Expatriates

As we use the term here, **expatriate** refers to anyone living and/or working outside their home country. Hence, they are said to be *expatriated* when transferred to another country and *repatriated* when transferred back home. US expatriate managers usually are characterized as culturally inept and prone to failure on international assignments. Sadly, research supports this view. A pair of international management experts offered this assessment:

expatriate
Anyone living or working in a foreign country.

> Over the past decade, we have studied the management of expatriates at about 750 US, European, and Japanese companies. We asked both the expatriates themselves and the executives who sent them abroad to evaluate their experiences. In addition, we looked at what happened after expatriates returned home. . . .
>
> Overall, the results of our research were alarming. We found that between 10% and 20% of all US managers sent abroad returned early because of job dissatisfaction or difficulties in adjusting to a foreign country. Of those who stayed for the duration, nearly one-third did not perform up to the expectations of their superiors. And perhaps most problematic, one-fourth of those who completed an assignment left their company, often to join a competitor, within one year after repatriation. That's a turnover rate double that of managers who did not go abroad.[53]

A more recent study of why expatriate employees returned home early found the situation to be slowly improving. Still, *personal and family adjustment problems* (36.6%) and *homesickness* (31%) were found to be major stumbling blocks for American managers working in foreign countries.[54] A survey asking 72 human resource managers at multinational corporations to identify the most important success factor in a foreign assignment provided this insight: "Nearly 35% said cultural adaptability: patience, flexibility, and tolerance for others' beliefs."[55]

US multinational companies clearly need to do a better job of preparing employees and their families for foreign assignments, particularly in light of the high costs involved:

> The tab for sending an executive who earns $160,000 in the US, plus a spouse and two children, to India for two years is about $900,000, says Jacqui Hauser, vice president of consulting services for Cendant Mobility, a relocation-services firm in Danbury, Conn. This includes housing and cost-of-living allowances, foreign- and hardship-pay premiums, tax-assistance, education and car allowances and paid transportation home each year for the entire family.[56]

Some Good News: North American Women on Foreign Assignments

Historically, a woman from the United States or Canada on a foreign assignment was a rarity. Things are changing, albeit slowly. A review of research evidence and anecdotal accounts uncovered these insights:

- The proportion of corporate women from North America on foreign assignments grew from about 3% in the early 1980s to between 11% and 15% in the late 1990s.

- Self-disqualification and management's assumption that women would not be welcome in foreign cultures—not foreign prejudice, itself—are the primary barriers for potential female expatriates.
- Expatriate North American women are viewed first and foremost by their hosts as being foreigners, and only secondarily as being female.
- North American women have a very high success rate on foreign assignments.[57]

Considering the rapidly growing demand for global managers, self-disqualification and management's prejudicial policies are counterproductive. Our advice to women who have their heart set on a foreign assignment: "Go for it!"

Avoiding OB Trouble Spots in the Foreign Assignment Cycle

Finding the right person (often along with a supportive and adventurous family) for a foreign position is a complex, time-consuming, and costly process.[58] For our purposes, it is sufficient to narrow the focus to common OB trouble spots in the foreign assignment cycle. As illustrated in Figure 3–2, the first and last stages of the cycle occur at home. The middle two stages occur in the foreign or host country. Each stage hides an OB-related trouble spot that needs to be anticipated and neutralized. [59] Otherwise, the bill for another failed foreign assignment will grow.

Avoiding Unrealistic Expectations with Cross-Cultural Training Realistic job previews (RJPs) have proven effective at bringing people's unrealistic expectations about a pending job assignment down to earth by providing a realistic balance of good and bad news. People with realistic expectations tend to quit less often and be more satisfied than those with unrealistic expectations. RJPs are a must for future expatriates. In addition, cross-cultural training is required.

Cross-cultural training is any type of structured experience designed to help departing employees adjust to

Key Cross-Cultural Competencies

Cross-Cultural Competency Cluster	Knowledge or Skill Required
Building relationships	Ability to gain access to and maintain relationships with members of host culture
Valuing people of different cultures	Empathy for difference; sensitivity to diversity
Listening and observation	Knows cultural history and reasons for certain cultural actions and customs
Coping with ambiguity	Recognizes and interprets implicit behavior, especially nonverbal cues
Translating complex information	Knowledge of local language, symbols or other forms of verbal language, and written language
Taking action and initiative	Understands intended and potentially unintended consequences of actions
Managing others	Ability to manage details of a job including maintaining cohesion in a group
Adaptability and flexibility	Views change from multiple perspectives
Managing stress	Understands own and other's mood, emotions, and personality

SOURCE: Excerpted from Y Yamazaki and D C Kayes, "An Experiential Approach to Cross-Cultural Learning: A Review and Integration of Competencies for Successful Expatriate Adaptation," *Academy of Management Learning and Education*, December 2004, Table 2, p 372.

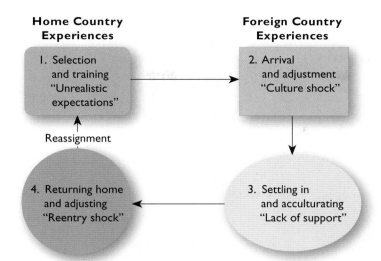

FIGURE 3–2
The Foreign Assignment Cycle (with OB Trouble Spots)

a foreign culture. The trend is toward more such training. Although costly, companies believe cross-cultural training is less expensive than failed foreign assignments. Programs vary widely in type and also in rigor.[60] Of course, the greater the difficulty, the greater the time and expense:

cross-cultural training
Structured experiences to help people adjust to a new culture/country.

- *Easiest.* Predeparture training is limited to informational materials, including books, lectures, films, videos, and Internet searches.

- *Moderately difficult.* Experiential training is conducted through case studies, role playing, assimilators (simulated intercultural incidents), and introductory language instruction.

Group Exercise
Applying Hofstede's Cultural Values

- *Most difficult.* Departing employees are given some combination of the preceding methods plus comprehensive language instruction and field experience in the target culture. As an example of the latter, PepsiCo Inc. transfers "about 25 young foreign managers a year to the US for one-year assignments in bottling plants."[61]

Which approach is the best? Research to date does not offer a final answer. One study involving US employees in South Korea led the researcher to recommend a *combination* of informational and experiential predeparture training.[62] As a general rule of thumb, the more rigorous the cross-cultural training, the better. The nine competencies detailed in Skills & Best Practices should be the core of any comprehensive cross-cultural training program.

Our personal experience with teaching OB to foreign students both in the United States and abroad reminds us that there really is no substitute for an intimate knowledge of the local language and culture.[63] Who would you say will likely have the advantage in the future world of business, given these recent figures? According to the US Department of Education, 24,000 American children are studying Chinese, while 200 million Chinese students are studying English.[64]

Avoiding Culture Shock   Have you ever been in a totally unfamiliar situation and felt disoriented and perhaps a bit frightened? If so, you already know something about culture shock. According to anthropologists, **culture shock** involves anxiety and doubt caused by an overload of unfamiliar expectations and social cues.[65] For example, consider

culture shock
Anxiety and doubt caused by an overload of new expectations and cues.

Despite classes like Christine Wang's, in which first-graders in Maryland learn basic Chinese, managers in the United States are likely to lag behind those in China in their ability to understand and appreciate someone else's language and culture. Many experts worry that lack of foreign language skills goes hand-in-hand with a general lack of global awareness in the United States.

the experience of US Secretary of Labor Elaine Chao as a young immigrant unable to speak English:

> Chao sailed with her mother, Ruth, and two siblings in 1961 to the USA to join her father, Chinese student James Chao, when she was 8. He had come to New York three years earlier while the rest of the family waited in Taiwan until he had saved enough money to send for them. Her parents had three children in the USA; Chao is the oldest of six girls.
>
> It was a culture shock. One afternoon in October, Chao and her sisters opened the door to find other children dressed in ghost and goblin costumes, holding out bags. Believing they were being robbed, they gave the trick-or-treaters their meager weekly provisions of food, including cereal and bread.[66]

College freshmen often experience a variation of culture shock. An expatriate manager, or family member, may be thrown off balance by an avalanche of strange sights, sounds, and behaviors. Among them may be unreadable road signs, strange-tasting food, inability to use your left hand for social activities (in Islamic countries, the left hand is the toilet hand), or failure to get a laugh with your sure-fire joke. For the expatriate manager trying to concentrate on the fine details of a business negotiation, culture shock is more than an embarrassing inconvenience. It is a disaster! Like the confused college freshman who quits and goes home, culture-shocked employees often panic and go home early.

The best defense against culture shock is comprehensive cross-cultural training, including intensive language study. Once again, the only way to pick up subtle—yet important—social cues is via the local language. Quantum, the Milpitas, California, maker of computer hard-disk drives has close ties to its manufacturing partner in Japan, Matsushita-Kotobuki Electronics (MKE):

> MKE is constantly proposing changes in design that make new disk drives easier to manufacture. When the product is ready for production, 8 to 10 Quantum engineers descend on MKE's plant in western Japan for at least a month. To smooth teamwork, Quantum is offering courses in Japanese language and culture, down to mastering etiquette at a tea ceremony.[67]

This type of program reduces culture shock by taking the anxiety-producing mystery out of an unfamiliar culture.

Support During the Foreign Assignment   Especially during the first six months, when everything is so new to the expatriate, a support system needs to be in place.[68] *Host-country sponsors*, assigned to individual managers or families, are recommended because they serve as "cultural seeing-eye dogs." In a foreign country, where even the smallest errand can turn into an utterly exhausting production, sponsors can get things done quickly because they know the cultural and geographical territory. Honda's Ohio employees, for example, enjoyed the help of family sponsors when training in Japan:

Honda smoothed the way with Japanese wives who once lived in the US. They handled emergencies such as when Diana Jett's daughter Ashley needed stitches in her chin. When Task Force Senior Manager Kim Smalley's daughter, desperate to fit in at elementary school, had to have a precisely shaped bag for her harmonica, a Japanese volunteer stayed up late to make it.[69]

Another way to support expatriates during the transition phase of a new foreign assignment is to maintain an active dialog with established *mentors from back home*. This can be accomplished via e-mail, telephone, and, when possible, an occasional face-to-face meeting.[70]

Avoiding Reentry Shock   Strange as it may seem, many otherwise successful expatriate managers encounter their first major difficulty only after their foreign assignment is over. Why? Returning to one's native culture is taken for granted because it seems so routine and ordinary. But having adjusted to another country's way of doing things for an extended period of time can put one's own culture and surroundings in a strange new light. Three areas for potential reentry shock are work, social activities, and general environment (e.g., politics, climate, transportation, food). Ira Caplan's return to New York City exemplifies reentry shock:

During the past 12 years, living mostly in Japan, he and his wife had spent their vacations cruising the Nile or trekking in Nepal. They hadn't seen much of the US. . . .

They are getting an eyeful now. . . .

Prices astonish him. The obsession with crime unnerves him. What unsettles Mr Caplan more, though, is how much of himself he has left behind.

In a syndrome of return no less stressful than that of departure, he feels displaced, disregarded, and diminished. . . .

In an Italian restaurant, crowded at lunchtime, the waiter sets a bowl of linguine in front of him. Mr Caplan stares at it. "In Asia, we have smaller portions and smaller people," he says.

Asia is on his mind. He has spent years cultivating an expertise in a region of huge importance. So what? This is New York.[71]

Work-related adjustments were found to be a major problem for samples of repatriated Finnish, Japanese, and American employees.[72] Upon being repatriated, a 12-year veteran of one US company said: "Our organizational culture was turned upside down. We now have a different strategic focus, different 'tools' to get the job done, and different buzzwords to make it happen. I had to learn a whole new corporate 'language.'"[73] Reentry shock can be reduced through employee career counseling and home-country mentors. Simply being forewarned about the problem of reentry shock is a big step toward effectively dealing with it.[74]

Overall, the key to a successful foreign assignment is making it a well-integrated link in a career chain rather than treating it as an isolated adventure.

key terms

collectivist culture 74

cross-cultural training 81

cultural intelligence 71

culture shock 81

ethnocentrism 68

expatriate 79

high-context cultures 75

individualistic culture 74

low-context cultures 75

monochronic time 77

polychronic time 77

societal culture 66

chapter summary

- *Define ethnocentrism, and explain what Hofstede concluded about applying American management theories in other countries.* Ethnocentrism is a prejudicial belief that one's native country, culture, language, behavior, and traditions are better than all others. Due to the wide variations in key dimensions Hofstede found among cultures, he warned against directly applying American-made management theories to other cultures without adapting them first. He said there is no one best way to manage across cultures.

- *Identify and describe the nine cultural dimensions from the GLOBE project.* (1) *Power distance*—How equally should power be distributed? (2) *Uncertainty avoidance*—How much should social norms and rules reduce uncertainty and unpredictability? (3) *Institutional collectivism*—How much should loyalty to the social unit override individual interests? (4) *In-group collectivism*—How strong should one's loyalty be to family or organization? (5) *Gender egalitarianism*—How much should gender discrimination and role inequalities be minimized? (6) *Assertiveness*—How confrontational and dominant should one be in social relationships? (7) *Future orientation*—How much should one delay gratification by planning and saving for the future? (8) *Performance orientation*—How much should individuals be rewarded for improvement and excellence? (9) *Humane orientation*—How much should individuals be rewarded for being kind, fair, friendly, and generous?

- *Draw a distinction between individualistic cultures and collectivist cultures.* People in individualistic cultures think primarily in terms of "I" and "me" and place a high value on freedom and personal choice. Collectivist cultures teach people to be "we" and "us" oriented and to subordinate

- *Demonstrate your knowledge of these two distinctions: high-context versus low-context cultures and monochronic versus polychronic cultures.* People in high-context cultures (such as China, Japan, and Mexico) derive great meaning from situational cues, above and beyond written and spoken words. Low-context cultures (including Germany, the United States, and Canada) derive key information from precise and brief written and spoken messages. In monochronic cultures (e.g., the United States), time is precise and rigidly measured. Polychronic cultures, such as those found in Latin America and the Middle East, view time as multidimensional, fluid, and flexible. Monochronic people prefer to do one thing at a time, while polychronic people like to tackle multiple tasks at the same time.

- *Explain what the GLOBE project has taught us about leadership.* Across 62 cultures, they identified leader attributes that are universally liked and universally disliked. The universally liked leader attributes—including trustworthy, dynamic, motive arouser, decisive, and intelligent—are associated with the charismatic/transformational leadership style that is widely applicable. Universally disliked leader attributes—such as noncooperative, irritable, egocentric, and dictatorial—should be avoided in all cultures.

- *Identify an OB trouble spot for each stage of the foreign assignment cycle.* The four stages of the foreign assignment cycle (and OB trouble spots) are (a) selection and training (unrealistic expectations), (b) arrival and adjustment (culture shock), (c) settling in and acculturating (lack of support), and (d) returning home and adjusting (reentry shock).

discussion questions

1. How many of the cultural dimensions discussed in this chapter can you identify in the chapter-opening vignette? Explain.

2. How would you describe the prevailing culture in your country to a stranger from another land, in terms of the nine GLOBE project dimensions?

3. Why are people from high-context cultures such as China and Japan likely to be misunderstood by low-context Westerners?

4. How strong is your desire for a foreign assignment? Why? If it is strong, where would you like to work? Why? How prepared are you for a foreign assignment? What do you need to do to be better prepared?

5. What is your personal experience with culture shock? Which of the OB trouble spots in Figure 3–2 do you believe is the greatest threat to expatriate employee success? Explain.

ethical dilemma

3M Tries to Make a Difference in Russia

Russian managers aren't inclined . . . to reward people for improved performance. They spurn making investments for the future in favor of realizing immediate gains. They avoid establishing consistent business practices that can reduce uncertainty. Add in the country's high political risk and level of corruption, and it's no wonder that many multinationals have all but given up on Russia. . . .

The Russian business environment can be corrupt and dangerous; bribes and protection money are facts of life. But unlike many international companies, which try to distance themselves from such practices by simply banning them, 3M Russia actively promotes not only ethical behavior but also the personal security of its employees. . . .

3M Russia also strives to differentiate itself from competitors by being an ethical leader. For example, it holds training courses in business ethics for its customers.[75]

Should 3M Export Its American Ethical Standards to Russia?

1. If 3M doesn't like the way things are done in Russia, it shouldn't do business there. Explain your rationale.

2. 3M should do business in Russia but not meddle in Russian culture. "When in Russia, do things the Russian way." Explain your rationale.

3. 3M has a basic moral responsibility to improve the ethical climate in foreign countries where it does business. Explain your rationale.

4. 3M should find a practical middle ground between the American and Russian ways of doing business. How should that happen?

5. Invent other options. Discuss.

For an interpretation of this situation, visit our Web site, www.mhhe.kinickiob3e.

If you're looking for additional study materials, be sure to check out the Online Learning Center at
www.mhhe.com/kinickiob3e
for more information and interactivities that correspond to this chapter.

part
two

Managing
Individuals

Four   Understanding Social Perception and Managing Diversity

Five   Appreciating Individual Differences: Self-Concept, Personality, Emotions

Six   Motivation I: Needs, Job Design, Intrinsic Motivation, and Satisfaction

Seven   Motivation II: Equity, Expectancy, and Goal Setting

Eight   Improving Performance with Feedback, Rewards, and Positive Reinforcement

Understanding Social Perception and Managing Diversity

LEARNING OBJECTIVES

After reading the material in this chapter, you should be able to:

- Describe *perception* in terms of the social information processing model.

- Identify and briefly explain six managerial implications of social perception.

- Explain, according to Kelley's model, how external and internal causal attributions are formulated.

- Demonstrate your familiarity with the demographic trends that are creating an increasingly diverse workforce.

- Identify the barriers and challenges to managing diversity.

- Discuss the organizational practices used to manage diversity identified by Ann Morrison.

PERCEPTIONS AND ATTRIBUTIONS INFLUENCE COMMUNICATION PROBLEMS BETWEEN CHINESE AND AMERICAN POLITICIANS

Why do China and America have such difficulty communicating?

Sure, the two nations are half a world apart, geographically, historically, and politically. But the cause of their at times cacophonous discourse could lie in something less obvious: the strikingly

China's president Hu Jintao on a recent history-making visit to the United States.

different academic training of their political leaders.

The majority of American senators and congressmen were schooled as lawyers. But each of China's senior leaders—all nine members of the Politburo's Standing Committee—was trained as an engineer: President Hu in hydropower, Premier Wen Jiabao in geological structure, for instance. Perhaps

the difficulties between China and the U.S. lie less with dissimilar languages, cultures, and histories, and more with the divergent ways of thinking between lawyers and engineers.

This is no small difference. Engineers strive for "better," while lawyers prepare for the

worst. Failing to appreciate the implications of these different approaches (and the relating styles they engender) can lead to missed signals.

Such miscommunication occurred when a U.S. plane accidentally bombed the Chinese embassy in Belgrade, Yugoslavia, in 1999. When the Chinese government bused students from

college campuses across Beijing to the U.S. Embassy to protest, American politicians assumed that Chinese leaders orchestrated the demonstrations to whip up nationalistic fervor. (To lawyers, the evidence was prima facie.) In truth, the Chinese leaders—the engineers—worried that if protesting students were allowed to march through the city, their ranks would swell with workers and ordinary citizens, creating an even larger, less manageable problem. So busing them contained, rather than exacerbated, the volatile situation.

Another dichotomy: More than 90% of Chinese, including professionals often critical of their government, saw the bombing as deliberate. But most Americans believed the bombing had been, as U.S. officials claimed, an accident due to the use of "old maps."

Why such disparity? The Chinese have an idealized picture of the U.S. as so technologically advanced that it would have been impossible for it to make such a stupid mistake. Americans, on the other hand, are quite used to their government's stupid mistakes.

More worrisome, most Americans perceive China as an economic predator concerned solely about its own welfare. Beijing does not deny its policies benefit its own people, as any legitimate government's would. But it asserts that in a global economy, China's stability and development are essential for world peace and prosperity. Disturb the former, it warns, and you disrupt the latter. Given that consequence, it's time the lawyers and engineers began communicating better.[1]

FOR DISCUSSION

Why do people from China and the United States have different perceptions of the same events? Explain. For an interpretation of this case and additional comments, visit our Online Learning Center at

www.mhhe.com/kinickiob3e

HOW IMPORTANT IS THE perception process? As highlighted in the chapter-opening vignette, perception can be the source of communication distortion and conflict between people from different cultures. Our perceptions and feelings are influenced by information we receive from newspapers, magazines, television, radio, family, and friends. You see, we all use information stored in our memories to interpret the world around us, and our interpretations, in turn, influence how we respond and interact with others. As human beings, we constantly strive to make sense of our surroundings. The resulting knowledge influences our behavior and helps us navigate our way through life. Think of the perceptual process that occurs when meeting someone for the first time. Your attention is drawn to the individual's physical appearance, mannerisms, actions, and reactions to what you say and do. You ultimately arrive at conclusions based on your perceptions of this social interaction. The brown-haired, green-eyed individual turns out to be friendly and fond of outdoor activities. You further conclude that you like this person and then ask him or her to go to a concert, calling the person by the name you stored in memory.

The reciprocal process of perception, interpretation, and behavioral response also applies at work. Consider the experience of Lisa Bromiley Meier after losing her job at Enron. She told a reporter from *BusinessWeek* that "she endured six months of potential employers asking her the same question: 'So, were you corrupt or were you stupid?'"[2] Interviewers apparently assumed or perceived that Lisa was either a crook or stupid because she worked for Enron. They could not have been more wrong. Today, Lisa is the CFO of Flotek Industries, Inc., a maker of chemicals and drilling tools for the oil industry.

Managing diversity is a sensitive, potentially volatile, and sometimes uncomfortable issue. Yet managers are required to deal with it in the name of organizational survival. Accordingly, the purpose of this chapter is to enhance your understanding of the perceptual process and how it influences the manner in which managers manage diversity. We begin by focusing on a social information processing model of perception and then discuss the perceptual outcome of causal attributions. Next, we define diversity and describe the organizational practices used to manage diversity effectively.

A Social Information Processing Model of Perception

Perception is a cognitive process that enables us to interpret and understand our surroundings. Recognition of objects is one of this process's major functions.[3] For example, both people and animals recognize familiar objects in their environments. You would recognize a picture of your best friend; dogs and cats can recognize their food dishes or a favorite toy. Reading involves recognition of visual patterns representing letters in the alphabet. People must recognize objects to meaningfully interact with their environment. But since OB's principal focus is on people, the following discussion emphasizes *social* perception rather than object perception.

> **perception**
>
> **Process of interpreting one's environment.**

Social perception involves a four-stage information processing sequence (hence, the label "social information processing"). Figure 4–1 illustrates a basic social information processing model. Three of the stages in this model—selective attention/comprehension, encoding and simplification, and storage and retention—describe

FIGURE 4–1   Social Perception: A Social Information Processing Model

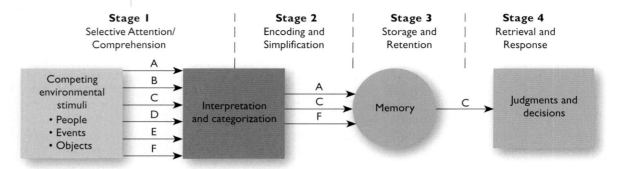

SOURCE: R Kreitner and A Kinicki, *Organizational Behavior* 7th ed (Burr Ridge, IL: McGraw-Hill), p 207.

how specific social information is observed and stored in memory. The fourth and final stage, retrieval and response, involves turning mental representations into real-world judgments and decisions.

Keep the following everyday example in mind as we look at the four stages of social perception. Suppose you were thinking of taking a course in, say, personal finance. Three professors teach the same course, using different types of instruction and testing procedures. Through personal experience, you have come to prefer good professors who rely on the case method of instruction and essay tests. According to social perception theory, you would likely arrive at a decision regarding which professor to take following the steps outlined in the following sections.

Stage 1: Selective Attention/Comprehension

People are constantly bombarded by physical and social stimuli in the environment. Because they do not have the mental capacity to fully comprehend all this information, they selectively perceive subsets of environmental stimuli. This is where attention plays a role. **Attention** is the process of becoming consciously aware of something or someone. Attention can be focused on information either from the environment or from memory. Regarding the latter situation, if you sometimes find yourself thinking about totally unrelated events or people while reading a textbook, your memory is the focus of your attention. Research has shown that people tend to pay attention to salient stimuli.

attention

Being consciously aware of something or someone.

Salient Stimuli   Something is *salient* when it stands out from its context. For example, a 250-pound man would certainly be salient in a women's aerobics class but not at a meeting of the National Football League Players' Association. One's needs and goals often dictate which stimuli are salient. For a driver whose gas gauge is on empty, an Exxon or Shell sign is more salient than a McDonald's or Burger King sign. The reverse would be true for a hungry driver with a full gas tank. Moreover, research shows that people have a tendency to pay more attention to negative than positive information. This leads to a negativity bias.[4] This bias helps explain the gawking factor that slows traffic to a crawl following a car accident.

cognitive categories

Mental depositories for storing information.

schema

Mental picture of an event or object.

Back to Our Example You begin your search for the "right" personal finance professor by asking friends who have taken classes from the three professors. You also may interview the various professors who teach the class to gather still more relevant information. Returning to Figure 4–1, all the information you obtain represents competing environmental stimuli labeled A through F. Because you are concerned about the method of instruction (e.g., line A in Figure 4–1), testing procedures (e.g., line C), and past grade distributions (e.g., line F), information in those areas is particularly salient to you. Figure 4–1 shows that these three salient pieces of information thus are perceived, and you then progress to the second stage of information processing. Meanwhile, competing stimuli represented by lines B, D, and E in Figure 4–1 fail to get your attention and are discarded from further consideration.

Denis Hennequin, a Parisian and president of McDonald's operations in Europe, discovered the power of stereotypes when his family in France learned he would be working for the American fast-food chain, a job that entails overseeing more than 6,000 restaurants in 41 countries. "My grandmother thought I was selling French fries on the Boulevard Saint-Michel," he said.

Stage 2: Encoding and Simplification

Observed information is not stored in memory in its original form. Encoding is required; raw information is interpreted or translated into mental representations. To accomplish this, perceivers assign pieces of information to **cognitive categories.** "By *category* we mean a number of objects that are considered equivalent. Categories are generally designated by names, e.g., *dog, animal.*"[5] People, events, and objects are interpreted and evaluated by comparing their characteristics with information contained in schemata (or schema in singular form).

Schema According to social information processing theory, a **schema** represents a person's mental picture or summary of a particular event or type of stimulus. For example, picture your image of a sports car. Does it contain a smaller vehicle with two doors? Is it red? If you answered yes, you would tend to classify all small, two-door, fire-engine-red vehicles as sports cars because this type of car possesses characteristics that are consistent with your "sports car schema."

Group Exercise

Win, Lose or Schema

Stereotypes Are Used During Encoding People use stereotypes during encoding in order to organize and simplify social information.[6] "A **stereotype** is an individual's set of beliefs about the characteristics or attributes of a group."[7] Stereotypes are not always negative. For example, the belief that engineers are good at math is certainly part of a stereotype. Stereotypes may or may not be accurate. Engineers may in fact be better at math than the general population. In general, stereotypic characteristics are used to differentiate a particular group of people from other groups.

stereotype

Beliefs about the characteristics of a group.

Unfortunately, stereotypes can lead to poor decisions; can create barriers for women, older individuals, people of color, and people with disabilities; and can undermine loyalty and job satisfaction. For example, a study of 427 members of the National Association of Black Accountants revealed that 59% believed that they received biased performance evaluations because of their race, and 63% felt no obligation to remain with their current employer.[8] It thus is not surprising that the turnover rate for African-American executives is 40% higher than for their white counterparts.[9] Another sample of 238 males and females of different ethnicity and

Group Exercise

Do Stereotypes Unconsciously Influence the Perception Process?

color revealed that women of color were harassed more often than male and female Caucasians and males of color.[10]

Stereotyping is a four-step process. It begins by categorizing people into groups according to various criteria, such as gender, age, race, and occupation. Next, we infer that all people within a particular category possess the same traits or characteristics (e.g., all women are nurturing, older people have more job-related accidents, all African-Americans are good athletes, all professors are absentminded). Then, we form expectations of others and interpret their behavior according to our stereotypes. Finally, stereotypes are maintained by (1) overestimating the frequency of stereotypic behaviors exhibited by others, (2) incorrectly explaining expected and unexpected behaviors, and (3) differentiating minority individuals from oneself. Although these steps are self-reinforcing, there are ways to break the chain of stereotyping.

Research shows that the use of stereotypes is influenced by the amount and type of information available to an individual and his or her motivation to accurately process information.[11] People are less apt to use stereotypes to judge others when they encounter salient information that is highly inconsistent with a stereotype. For instance, you are unlikely to assign stereotypic "professor" traits to a new professor you have this semester if he or she rides a Harley-Davidson, wears leather pants to class, and has a pierced nose. People also are less likely to rely on stereotypes when they are motivated to avoid using them. That is, accurate information processing requires mental effort. Stereotyping is generally viewed as a less effortful strategy of information processing.

Encoding Outcomes We use the encoding process to interpret and evaluate our environment. Interestingly, this process can result in differing interpretations and evaluations of the same person or event. Table 4–1 describes five common perceptual errors that influence our judgments about others. Because these perceptual errors often distort the evaluation of job applicants and of employee performance, managers need to guard against them.

Back to Our Example Having collected relevant information about the three personal finance professors and their approaches, you compare this information with other details contained in schemata. This leads you to form an impression and evaluation of what it would be like to take a course from each professor. In turn, the relevant information contained on paths A, C, and F in Figure 4–1 are passed along to the third stage of information processing.

Stage 3: Storage and Retention

This phase involves storage of information in long-term memory. Long-term memory is like an apartment complex consisting of separate units connected to one another. Although different people live in each apartment, they sometimes interact. In addition, large apartment complexes have different wings (such as A, B, and C). Long-term memory similarly consists of separate but related categories. Like the individual apartments inhabited by unique residents, the connected categories contain different types of information. Information also passes among these categories. Finally, long-term memory is made up of three compartments (or wings) containing categories of information about events, semantic materials, and people.[12]

Test Your Knowledge

Potential Errors in the Rating Process

Commonly Found Perceptual Errors | TABLE 4–1

Perceptual Error	Description	Example
Halo	A rater forms an overall impression about an object and then uses that impression to bias ratings about the object.	Rating a professor high on the teaching dimensions of ability to motivate students, knowledge, and communication because we like him or her.
Leniency	A personal characteristic that leads an individual to consistently evaluate other people or objects in an extremely positive fashion.	Rating a professor high on all dimensions of performance regardless of his or her actual performance. The rater who hates to say negative things about others.
Central tendency	The tendency to avoid all extreme judgments and rate people and objects as average or neutral.	Rating a professor average on all dimensions of performance regardless of his or her actual performance.
Recency effects	The tendency to remember recent information. If the recent information is negative, the person or object is evaluated negatively.	Although a professor has given good lectures for 12 to 15 weeks, he or she is evaluated negatively because lectures over the last 3 weeks were done poorly.
Contrast effects	The tendency to evaluate people or objects by comparing them with characteristics of recently observed people or objects.	Rating a good professor as average because you compared his or her performance with three of the best professors you have ever had in college. You are currently taking courses from the three excellent professors.

Event Memory This compartment is composed of categories containing information about both specific and general events. These memories describe appropriate sequences of events in well-known situations, such as going to a restaurant, going on a job interview, going to a food store, or going to a movie.

Semantic Memory Semantic memory refers to general knowledge about the world. In so doing, it functions as a mental dictionary of concepts. Each concept contains a definition (e.g., a good leader) and associated traits (outgoing), emotional states (happy), physical characteristics (tall), and behaviors (works hard). Just as there are schemata for general events, concepts in semantic memory are stored as schemata. Given our previous discussion of international OB in Chapter 3, it should come as no surprise that there are cultural differences in the type of information stored in semantic memory.

Person Memory Categories within this compartment contain information about a single individual (your supervisor) or groups of people (managers).

Back to Our Example   As the time draws near for you to decide which personal finance professor to take, your schemata of them are stored in the three categories of long-term memory. These schemata are available for immediate comparison and/or retrieval.

Stage 4: Retrieval and Response

People retrieve information from memory when they make judgments and decisions. Our ultimate judgments and decisions are either based on the process of drawing on, interpreting, and integrating categorical information stored in long-term memory or on retrieving a summary judgment that was already made.

Concluding our example, it is registration day and you have to choose which professor to take for personal finance. After retrieving from memory your schemata-based impressions of the three professors, you select a good one who uses the case method and gives essay tests (line C in Figure 4–1). In contrast, you may choose your preferred professor by simply recalling the decision you made two weeks ago.

Managerial Implications

Social cognition is the window through which we all observe, interpret, and prepare our responses to people and events. A wide variety of managerial activities, organizational processes, and quality-of-life issues are thus affected by perception. Consider, for example, the following implications.

Hiring   Interviewers make hiring decisions based on their impression of how an applicant fits the perceived requirements of a job. Inaccurate impressions in either direction produce poor hiring decisions. Moreover, interviewers with racist or sexist schemata can undermine the accuracy and legality of hiring decisions. Those invalid schemata need to be confronted and improved through coaching and training.[13] Failure to do so can lead to poor hiring decisions. For example, a study of 46 male and 66 female financial institution managers revealed that their hiring decisions were biased by the physical attractiveness of applicants. More attractive men and women were hired over less attractive applicants with equal qualifications.[14] On the positive side, however, a study demonstrated that interviewer training can reduce the use of invalid schema. Training improved interviewers' ability to obtain high-quality, job-related information and to stay focused on the interview task. Trained interviewers provided more balanced judgments about applicants than did nontrained interviewers.[15]

Performance Appraisal   Faulty schemata about what constitutes good versus poor performance can lead to inaccurate performance appraisals, which erode work motivation, commitment, and loyalty. For example, a study of 166 production employees indicated that they had greater trust in management when they

"Let me guess.
You're a salesperson, right?"

© 2002 Ted Goff

perceived that the performance appraisal process provided accurate evaluations of their performance.[16] Therefore, it is important for managers to accurately identify the behavioral characteristics and results indicative of good performance at the beginning of a performance review cycle. These characteristics then can serve as the benchmarks for evaluating employee performance. The importance of using objective rather than subjective measures of employee performance was highlighted in a meta-analysis involving 50 studies and 8,341 individuals. Results revealed that objective and subjective measures of employee performance were only moderately related. The researchers concluded that objective and subjective measures of performance are not interchangeable.[17] Managers are thus advised to use more objectively based measures of performance as much as possible because subjective indicators are prone to bias and inaccuracy. In those cases where the job does not possess objective measures of performance, however, managers should still use subjective evaluations. Furthermore, because memory for specific instances of employee performance deteriorates over time, managers need a mechanism for accurately recalling employee behavior. Research reveals that individuals can be trained to be more accurate raters of performance.[18]

Leadership   Research demonstrates that employees' evaluations of leader effectiveness are influenced strongly by their schemata of good and poor leaders. A leader will have a difficult time influencing employees when he or she exhibits behaviors contained in employees' schemata of poor leaders. A team of researchers investigated the behaviors contained in our schemata of good and poor leaders. Good leaders were perceived as exhibiting the following behaviors: (1) assigning specific tasks to group members, (2) telling others that they had done well, (3) setting specific goals for the group, (4) letting other group members make decisions, (5) trying to get the group to work as a team, and (6) maintaining definite standards of performance. In contrast, poor leaders were perceived to exhibit these behaviors: (1) telling others that they had performed poorly, (2) insisting on having their own way, (3) doing things without explaining themselves, (4) expressing worry over the group members' suggestions, (5) frequently changing plans, and (6) letting the details of the task become overwhelming.[19]

Communication and Interpersonal Influence   Managers must remember that social perception is a screening process that can distort communication, both coming and going. Because people interpret oral and written communications by using schemata developed through past experiences, your ability to influence others is affected by information contained in others' schemata regarding age, gender, ethnicity, appearance, speech, mannerisms, personality, and other

Avoid Four Behavioral Tendencies That Are Negatively Perceived When Trying to Sell or Pitch an Idea

1. **Being a pushover.** This tendency involves giving up on an idea rather than defending it. Be prepared to defend your ideas with facts, figures, and passion. Do not simply drop an idea because someone questions it.

2. **Being a robot.** This tendency involves a communication style and approach that is too formulaic. When answering questions about your ideas, do not use canned answers. Rather, first try to understand the other individual's point of view or source of confusion/resistance. You then can provide an answer that specifically responds to the person's concerns.

3. **Being a used-car salesman.** This tendency involves being pushy, close-minded, and argumentative. Remember, you can catch more bees with honey than with vinegar.

4. **Being a charity case.** This tendency is characterized by desperation and pleading.

Perception colors our interpretation of management behaviors. An employee whose manager multitasks while talking to her is likely to believe that their conversation—and therefore the employee's work and even the employee herself—are not very important.

personal characteristics. It is important to keep this in mind when trying to influence others or when trying to sell your ideas. The Skills & Best Practices box on page 97 identifies four behavioral tendencies that are negatively perceived by others when trying to pitch or sell them an idea. Avoiding these tendencies can help you to achieve greater acceptance of your ideas or opinions.

Characteristics of Effective Web Page Design

- Individuals read Web pages in an "F" pattern. They're more inclined to read longer sentences at the top of a page and less and less as they scroll down. That makes the first two words of a sentence very important. . . .

- Surfers connect well with images of people looking directly at them. It helps if the person in the photo is attractive, but not too good looking. . . .

- Images in the middle of a page can present an obstacle course.

- People respond to pictures that provide useful information, not just decoration.

SOURCE: Excerpted from E C Baig, "Survey Offers a 'Sneak Peek' into Net Surfers' Brains," *USA Today*, March 27, 2006, p 4B.

Physical and Psychological Well-Being   The negativity bias can lead to both physical and psychological problems. Specifically, research shows that perceptions of fear, harm, and anxiety are associated with the onset of illnesses such as asthma and depression.[20] We should all attempt to avoid the tendency of giving negative thoughts too much attention. Try to let negative thoughts roll off yourself just like water off a duck.

Designing Web Pages   Researchers have recently begun to explore what catches viewers' attention on Web pages by using sophisticated eye-tracking equipment. This research can help organizations to spend their money wisely when designing Web pages. Kara Pernice Coyne, director of a research project studying Web page design, praised the Web pages of JetBlue Airways and Sears while noting problems with the one used by Agree Systems.[21] The accompanying Skills & Best Practices feature shows four characteristics of effective Web page design.

Causal Attributions

Attribution theory is based on the premise that people attempt to infer causes for observed behavior. Rightly or wrongly, we constantly formulate cause-and-effect explanations for our own and others' behavior. Attributional statements such as the following are common: "Joe drinks too much because he has no willpower; but I need a couple of drinks after work because I'm under a lot of pressure." Formally defined, **causal attributions** are suspected or inferred causes of behavior. Even though our causal attributions tend to be self-serving and are often invalid, it is important to understand how people formulate attributions because they profoundly affect organizational behavior. For

causal attributions

Suspected or inferred causes of behavior.

Performance Charts Showing Low and High Consensus, Distinctiveness, and Consistency Information   FIGURE 4–2

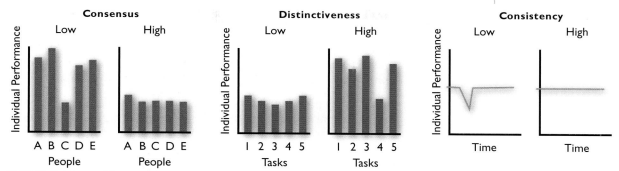

SOURCE: K A Brown, "Explaining Group Poor Performance: An Attributional Analysis," *Academy of Management Review,* January 1984, p 56. Copyright © 2001 by Academy of Management. Reproduced with permission of Academy of Management via Copyright Clearance Center.

example, a supervisor who attributes an employee's poor performance to a lack of effort might reprimand that individual. However, training might be deemed necessary if the supervisor attributes the poor performance to a lack of ability.

Generally speaking, people formulate causal attributions by considering the events preceding an observed behavior. This section introduces Harold Kelley's model of attribution and two important attributional tendencies.

Kelley's Model of Attribution

Current models of attribution, such as Kelley's, are based on the pioneering work of the late Fritz Heider. Heider, the founder of attribution theory, proposed that behavior can be attributed either to **internal factors** within a person (such as ability) or to **external factors** within the environment (such as a difficult task). Building on Heider's work, Kelley attempted to pinpoint major antecedents of internal and external attributions. Kelley hypothesized that people make causal attributions after gathering information about three dimensions of behavior: consensus, distinctiveness, and consistency.[22] These dimensions vary independently, thus forming various combinations and leading to differing attributions.

internal factors

Personal characteristics that cause behavior.

external factors

Environmental characteristics that cause behavior.

Figure 4–2 presents performance charts showing low versus high consensus, distinctiveness, and consistency. These charts are now used to help develop a working knowledge of all three dimensions in Kelley's model.

- *Consensus* involves a comparison of an individual's behavior with that of his or her peers. There is high consensus when one acts like the rest of the group and low consensus when one acts differently. As shown in Figure 4–2, high consensus is indicated when persons A, B, C, D, and E obtain similar levels of individual performance. In contrast, person C's performance is low in consensus because it significantly varies from the performance of persons A, B, D, and E.

- *Distinctiveness* is determined by comparing a person's behavior on one task with his or her behavior on other tasks. High distinctiveness means the individual has performed the task in question in a significantly different manner than he or she has performed other tasks. Low distinctiveness means stable performance or quality from one task to another. Figure 4–2 reveals that the employee's performance on task 4 is highly distinctive because it significantly varies from his or her performance on tasks 1, 2, 3, and 5.

- *Consistency* is determined by judging if the individual's performance on a given task is consistent over time. High consistency implies that a person performs a certain task the same, time after time. Unstable performance of a given task over time would mean low consistency. The downward spike in performance depicted in the consistency graph of Figure 4–2 represents low consistency. In this case, the employee's performance on a given task varied over time.

It is important to remember that consensus relates to other *people,* distinctiveness relates to other *tasks,* and consistency relates to *time.* The question now is: How does information about these three dimensions of behavior lead to internal or external attributions?

Kelley hypothesized that people attribute behavior to *external* causes (environmental factors) when they perceive high consensus, high distinctiveness, and low consistency. *Internal* attributions (personal factors) tend to be made when observed behavior is characterized by low consensus, low distinctiveness, and high consistency. So, for example, when all employees are performing poorly (high consensus), when the poor performance occurs on only one of several tasks (high distinctiveness), and the poor performance occurs during only one time period (low consistency), a supervisor will probably attribute an employee's poor performance to an external source such as peer pressure or an overly difficult task. In contrast, performance will be attributed to an employee's personal characteristics (an internal attribution) when only the individual in question is performing poorly (low consensus), when the inferior performance is found across several tasks (low distinctiveness), and when the low performance has persisted over time (high consistency). Many studies supported this predicted pattern of attributions.[23]

Attributional Tendencies

Researchers have uncovered two attributional tendencies that distort one's interpretation of observed behavior—*fundamental attribution bias* and *self-serving bias.*

fundamental attribution bias

Ignoring environmental factors that affect behavior.

Fundamental Attribution Bias   The **fundamental attribution bias** reflects one's tendency to attribute another person's behavior to his or her personal characteristics, as opposed to situational factors. This bias causes perceivers to ignore important environmental forces that often significantly affect behavior. For example, a study of 1,420 employees of a large utility company demonstrated that supervisors tended to make more internal attributions about worker accidents than did the workers. Interestingly, research also shows that people from Westernized cultures tend to exhibit the fundamental attribution bias more than individuals from East Asia.[24]

self-serving bias

Taking more personal responsibility for success than failure.

Self-Serving Bias   The **self-serving bias** represents one's tendency to take more personal responsibility for success than for failure. The self-serving bias suggests employees will attribute their success to internal factors (high ability or hard work) and their failures to uncontrollable external factors (tough job, bad luck, unproductive co-workers, or an unsympathetic boss). Ken Lay, former CEO of Enron, provides a good example of this bias.

Lay told jurors there had been "a real conspiracy" against Enron. He asserted that one newspaper in particular, *The Wall Street Journal,* "was on a witch hunt" aimed at the company and its onetime chief financial officer, Andrew S. Fastow. While also blaming Fastow, who has pled guilty to fraud and testified for the government, Lay zeroed in on articles the newspaper published in the fall of 2001 that he said "kicked off a run on the bank" that doomed the company. . . . He also lashed out at short sellers, investors who bet that the company's shares would fall.[25]

This example illustrates how Lay blamed everyone beside himself for Enron's financial demise.

Managerial Application and Implications   Attribution models can be used to explain how managers handle poorly performing employees. One study revealed that managers gave employees more immediate, frequent, and negative feedback when they attributed their performance to low effort. This reaction was even more pronounced when the manager's success was dependent on an employee's performance. A second study indicated that managers tended to transfer employees whose poor performance was attributed to a lack of ability. These same managers also decided to take no immediate action when poor performance was attributed to external factors beyond an individual's control.[26]

The preceding situations have several important implications for managers. First, managers tend to disproportionately attribute behavior to *internal* causes.[27] This can result in inaccurate evaluations of performance, leading to reduced employee motivation. No one likes to be blamed because of factors they perceive to be beyond their control. Further, because managers' responses to employee performance vary according to their attributions, attributional biases may lead to inappropriate managerial actions, including promotions, transfers, layoffs, and so forth. This can dampen motivation and performance. Attributional training sessions for managers are in order. Basic attributional processes can be explained, and managers can be taught to detect and avoid attributional biases. Finally, an employee's attributions for his or her own performance have dramatic effects on subsequent motivation, performance, and personal attitudes such as self-esteem. For instance, people tend to give up, develop lower expectations for future success, and experience decreased self-esteem when they attribute failure to a lack of ability. In contrast, employees are more likely to display high performance and job satisfaction when they attribute success to internal factors such as ability and effort.[28] Fortunately, attributional realignment can improve both motivation and performance. The goal of attributional realignment is to shift failure attributions away from ability and towards attributions of low effort or some other external cause (e.g., lack of resources).

Defining and Managing Diversity

Diversity represents the multitude of individual differences and similarities that exist among people. This definition underscores a key issue about managing diversity. There are many different dimensions or components of diversity. This implies that diversity pertains to everybody. It is not an issue of age, race, or gender. It is not an issue of being heterosexual, gay, or lesbian or of being Catholic, Jewish, Protestant, or Muslim. Diversity also does not pit white males against all other groups of people. Diversity pertains to the host of individual differences that make all of us unique and different from others.

diversity

The host of individual differences that make people different from and similar to each other.

Self-Assessment Exercise

Appreciating and Valuing Diversity

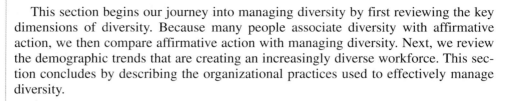

This section begins our journey into managing diversity by first reviewing the key dimensions of diversity. Because many people associate diversity with affirmative action, we then compare affirmative action with managing diversity. Next, we review the demographic trends that are creating an increasingly diverse workforce. This section concludes by describing the organizational practices used to effectively manage diversity.

Layers of Diversity

Like seashells on a beach, people come in a variety of shapes, sizes, and colors. This variety represents the essence of diversity. Lee Gardenswartz and Anita Rowe, a team of diversity experts, identified four layers of diversity to help distinguish the important ways in which people differ (see Figure 4–3). Taken together, these layers define your personal identity and influence how each of us sees the world.[29]

FIGURE 4–3
The Four Layers of Diversity

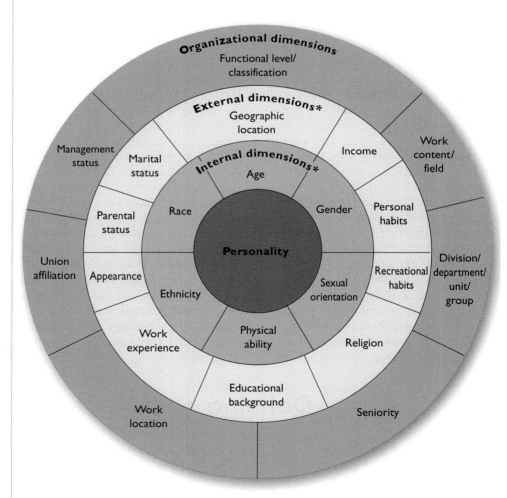

*Internal Dimensions and External Dimensions are adapted from Loden and Rosener, *Workforce America!* (Homewood, IL: Business One Irwin, 1991).

SOURCE: From L Gardenswartz and A Rowe, *Diverse Teams at Work: Capitalizing on the Power of Diversity*, 1994, 2003, p 33. Published by the Society for Human Resource Management. Reprinted with permission.

Figure 4–3 shows that personality is at the center of the diversity wheel. Personality is at the center because it represents a stable set of characteristics that is responsible for a person's identity: The dimensions of personality are discussed later in Chapter 5. The next layer of diversity consists of a set of internal dimensions that are referred to as the primary dimensions of diversity. These dimensions, for the most part, are not within our control, but strongly influence our attitudes and expectations and assumptions about others, which, in turn, influence our behavior. Take the encounter experienced by an African-American woman in middle management while vacationing at a resort:

> While she was sitting by the pool, "a large 50-ish white male approached me and demanded that I get him extra towels. I said, 'Excuse me?' He then said, 'Oh, you don't work here,' with no shred of embarrassment or apology in his voice."[30]

Stereotypes regarding one or more of the primary dimensions of diversity most likely influenced this man's behavior toward the woman.

Figure 4–3 reveals that the next layer of diversity is composed of external influences, which are referred to as secondary dimensions of diversity. They represent individual differences that we have a greater ability to influence or control. Examples include where you grew up and live today, your religious affiliation, whether you are married and have children, and your work experiences. These dimensions also exert a significant influence on our perceptions, behavior, and attitudes. The final layer of diversity includes organizational dimensions such as seniority, job title and function, and work location.

Affirmative Action and Managing Diversity

Effectively managing diversity requires organizations to adopt a new way of thinking about differences among people. Rather than pitting one group against another, managing diversity entails recognition of the unique contribution every employee can make. As found at Designer Blinds, a 170-employee company located in Omaha, Nebraska, with a turnover rate of 167%, effectively managing diversity can lower turnover and increase productivity and quality.

> Top managers began by viewing recruiting and retention strategically and quantitatively. An entirely new approach to hiring was launched. One aspect was networking with representatives of various cultures, including the local Sudanese community, which had not been well represented in the workforce. Company supervisors and coworkers studied the culture and embraced it. The firm also identified Hispanics as the fastest-growing group in the area and made a sincere effort to welcome members of the community and to provide English-as-a-second-language classes.
>
> The diversification of the workplace has produced good results for several years, especially the last two. Employee efficiency and productivity is skyrocketing, quality is a benchmark for the industry, and turnover has plunged from stratospheric highs to 8 percent a year.[31]

The management philosophies used at Designer Blinds earned the company the Optimas Award for excellence in people management and are much different from

Achieving diversity remains a challenge for many organizations, including the New York City Fire Department, which despite efforts to recruit more blacks, Hispanics, Asian-Americans, and women, remains predominantly white and male. Fewer women and minorities apply than white men, and fewer still complete the five steps needed to reach the final hiring pool. One Brooklyn councilwoman applauded the department's diversity recruiting efforts but noted that "women have not necessarily been embraced once they've gotten on the force, notwithstanding their own intestinal fortitude."

Test Your Knowledge

Comparing Affirmative Action, Valuing Diversity, and Managing Diversity

the management philosophies associated with affirmative action. This section highlights the differences between affirmative action and managing diversity.

Affirmative Action   **Affirmative action** represents "voluntary and mandatory efforts undertaken by federal, state, and local governments; private employers; and schools to combat discrimination and to promote equal opportunity in education and employment for all."[32] Affirmative action is proactive. That is, the goal of affirmative action is to eliminate discrimination and to create equal opportunity for everyone. According to a variety of Equal Employment Opportunity laws, it is illegal to discriminate on the basis of race, color, religion, gender, national origin, age, religious affiliation, and physical abilities. Affirmative action, however, does not legitimize quotas. Quotas are illegal. They can only be imposed by judges who conclude that a company has engaged in discriminatory practices. It also is important to note that under no circumstances does affirmative action require companies to hire unqualified people.

> **affirmative action**
>
> **Voluntary and involuntary efforts to achieve equality of opportunity for everyone.**

Although affirmative action created tremendous opportunities for women and minorities, it does not foster the type of thinking that is needed to effectively manage diversity. For example, affirmative action is resisted more by white males than women and minorities because it is perceived as involving preferential hiring and treatment based on group membership. Affirmative action plans are more successful when employees view them as fair and equitable.[33]

Affirmative action programs also were found to negatively affect the women and minorities expected to benefit from them. Research demonstrated that women and minorities, supposedly hired on the basis of affirmative action, felt negatively stigmatized as unqualified or incompetent. They also experienced lower job satisfaction and more stress than employees supposedly selected on the basis of merit.[34]

> **managing diversity**
>
> **Creating organizational changes that enable all people to perform up to their maximum potential.**

Managing Diversity   **Managing diversity** enables people to perform up to their maximum potential. It focuses on changing an organization's culture and infrastructure such that people provide the highest productivity possible. Consider whether or not Alarm One, Inc., a home security systems company in Fresno, California, was effectively managing diversity in its attempt to motivate the sales force. In company-sponsored meetings, "sales teams were encouraged to compete, and the losers were made fun of, forced to eat baby food, required to wear diapers and spanked with a rival company's yard signs." Janet Orlando, one of these sales employees, was spanked three times. She ultimately sued the company for sexual harassment and was awarded $1.7 million by a jury.[35] We find it amazing that any manager would consider using such practices to motivate today's workforce. In contrast to the example of Alarm One, let us consider the methods used to effectively manage diversity.

Ann Morrison, a diversity expert, conducted a study of 16 organizations that successfully managed diversity. Her results uncovered three key strategies for success: education, enforcement, and exposure. She describes them as follows:

> The education component of the strategy has two thrusts: one is to prepare nontraditional managers for increasingly responsible posts, and the other is to help traditional managers overcome their prejudice in thinking about and interacting with people who are of a different sex or ethnicity. The second component of the strategy, enforcement, puts teeth in diversity goals and encourages behavior change. The third component, exposure to people with different backgrounds and

characteristics, adds a more personal approach to diversity by helping managers get to know and respect others who are different.[36]

In summary, both consultants and academics believe that organizations should strive to manage diversity rather than only valuing it or simply using affirmative action.

Increasing Diversity in the Workforce

This section explores four demographic trends that are creating an increasingly diverse workforce: (1) women are encountering a glass ceiling, (2) racial groups are encountering a glass ceiling and perceived discrimination, (3) there is a mismatch between workers' educational attainment and occupational requirements, and (4) the workforce is aging.

Women Are Encountering a Glass Ceiling   In spite of the fact that women constituted 46% of the labor force in 1996 and are expected to represent 48% by 2010, they continue to encounter the glass ceiling. The **glass ceiling** represents an invisible barrier that separates

> **glass ceiling**
>
> **Invisible barrier blocking women and minorities from top management positions.**

women and minorities from advancing into top management positions. Women, therefore, find themselves stuck in lower level jobs, ones that do not have profit-and-loss responsibility, and those with less visibility and influence. In general, these positions result in a lack of power because the job holder does not have control over others, resources, or technology. The end result is that women face legitimate power deficits while trying to climb the corporate ladder.[37]

There are a variety of statistics that support the existence of a glass ceiling. As of December 2004, women were still underpaid relative to men: Women received 80% of men's earnings.[38] Even when women are paid the same as men, they may suffer in other areas of job opportunities. For example, a study of 69 male and female executives from a large multinational financial services corporation revealed

no differences in base salary or bonus. However, the women in this sample received fewer stock options than the male executives, even after controlling for level of education, performance, and job function, and reported less satisfaction with future career opportunities.[39] A follow-up study of 13,503 female managers and 17,493 male managers from the same organization demonstrated that women at higher levels in the managerial hierarchy received fewer promotions than males at comparable positions.[40] Would you be motivated if you were a woman working in this organization?

Women still have not broken into the highest echelon of corporate America to a significant extent. For example, there were only 11 and 21 female CEOs in the *Fortune* 500 and *Fortune* 1000 as of 2006, respectively. Women also accounted for only 15.7% of corporate-officer positions and 5.2% of top earners at *Fortune* 500 companies in 2002.[41] Further, the majority of women in top jobs are working in staff rather than line positions. In general, roles associated with line jobs contain more power and influence than staff positions.

Carolyn Kepcher, Trump's right-hand woman on *The Apprentice*, told the women in one episode that she "wanted to see less sexuality and more 'smarts.'" Not long after the show was over, some of these same women posed rather scantily clad for a magazine. Do you think it was in their best interest to do this? Do you still "take them seriously" as effective and successful businesswomen?

HANDS-ON EXERCISE

What Are the Strategies for Breaking the Glass Ceiling?

INSTRUCTIONS: Read the 13 career strategies shown below that may be used to break the glass ceiling. Next, rank order each strategy in terms of its importance for contributing to the advancement of a woman to a senior management position. Rank the strategies from 1 (most important) to 13 (least important). Once this is completed, compute the gap between your rankings and those provided by the women executives who participated in this research. Their rankings are presented in Endnote 42 at the back of the book. In computing the gaps, use the absolute value of the gap. (Absolute values are always positive, so just ignore the sign of your gap.) Finally, compute your total gap score. The larger the gap, the greater the difference in opinion between you and the women executives. What does your total gap score indicate about your recommended strategies?

Strategy	My Rating	Survey Rating	Gap | Your Rating − Survey Rating |
1. Develop leadership outside office	_____	_____	_____
2. Gain line management experience	_____	_____	_____
3. Network with influential colleagues	_____	_____	_____
4. Change companies	_____	_____	_____
5. Be able to relocate	_____	_____	_____
6. Seek difficult or high-visibility assignments	_____	_____	_____
7. Upgrade educational credentials	_____	_____	_____
8. Consistently exceed performance expectations	_____	_____	_____
9. Move from one functional area to another	_____	_____	_____
10. Initiate discussion regarding career aspirations	_____	_____	_____
11. Have an influential mentor	_____	_____	_____
12. Develop style that men are comfortable with	_____	_____	_____
13. Gain international experience	_____	_____	_____

SOURCE: Strategies and data were taken from B R Ragins, B Townsend, and M Mattis, "Gender Gap in the Executive Suite: CEOs and Female Executives Report on Breaking the Glass Ceiling," *The Academy of Management Executive,* February 1998, pp 28–42.

How can women overcome the glass ceiling? A team of researchers attempted to answer this question by surveying 461 executive women who held titles of vice president or higher in *Fortune* 1000 companies. Respondents were asked to evaluate the extent to which they used 13 different career strategies to break through the glass ceiling. The 13 strategies are shown in the Hands-On Exercise. Before discussing the results from this study, we would like you to complete the Hands-On Exercise.

Findings indicated that the top nine strategies were central to the advancement of these female executives. Within this set, however, four strategies were identified as critical toward breaking the glass ceiling: consistently exceeding performance expectations, developing a style with which male managers are comfortable, seeking out difficult or challenging assignments, and having influential mentors.[43]

Racial Groups Are Encountering a Glass Ceiling and Perceived Discrimination

Historically, the United States has been a black-and-white country. The percentage change in US population between 2000 and 2050 by race reveals that this pattern no longer exists. Asians and Hispanics are expected to have the largest growth in population between 2000 and 2050. The Asian population will triple to 33 million by 2050, and the Hispanics will increase their ranks by 118% to 102.6 million. Hispanics will account for 25% of the population in 2050. All told, the so-called minority groups will constitute 49.9% of the population in 2050 according to the Census Bureau.[44]

Unfortunately, three additional trends suggest that current-day minority groups are experiencing their own glass ceiling. First, minorities are advancing even less in the managerial and professional ranks than women. For example, blacks and Hispanics held 11.3% and 10.9%, respectively, of all managerial and professional jobs in 2001; women held 46.6% of these positions. Second, the number of race-based charges of discrimination that were deemed to show reasonable cause by the US Equal Employment Opportunity Commission increased from 294 in 1995 to 1,161 in 2005. Companies paid a total of $76.5 million to resolve these claims outside of litigation in 2005.[45] Third, minorities also tend to earn less than whites. Median household income in 2004 was $30,442, $33,884, and $49,061 for African-Americans, Hispanics, and whites, respectively. Interestingly, Asians had the highest median income—$57,196.[46] Finally, a number of studies showed that minorities experience more perceived discrimination than whites.[47]

Mismatch between Educational Attainment and Occupational Requirements

Approximately 27% of the labor force has a college degree.[48] Unfortunately, many of these people are working in jobs for which they are overqualified. This creates underemployment. **Underemployment** exists when a job requires less than a person's full potential as determined by his or her formal education, training, or skills. Underemployment is associated with higher arrest rates and the likelihood of becoming an unmarried parent for young adults. It also is negatively correlated with job satisfaction, work commitment, job involvement, internal work motivation, life satisfaction, and psychological well-being. Underemployment also is related to higher absenteeism and turnover.[49] On a positive note, however, underemployment is one of the reasons more new college graduates are starting businesses of their own. Moreover, research reveals that over time a college graduate's income ranges from 50% to 100% higher than that obtained by a high-school graduate. For example, the median income in the United States was $25,360 and $42,404 for employees with a high-school diploma and a bachelor's degree, respectively, in 2004.[50] It pays to graduate from college!

underemployment
The result of taking a job that requires less education, training, or skills than possessed by a worker.

There is another important educational mismatch. The national high-school dropout rate was about 10% in 2004, and more than 20% of the adult US population read at or below a fifth-grade level. Further, it is estimated that 90 million adults are functionally illiterate, and this costs corporate America an estimated $60 billion a year in lost productivity.[51] Literacy is defined as "an individual's ability to read, write, and speak in English, compute and solve problems at levels of proficiency necessary to function on the job and in society, to achieve one's goals, and develop one's knowledge and potential."[52] These statistics are worrisome because 70% of on-the-job reading materials are written for ninth-grade to college levels.

The Aging Workforce

America's population and workforce are getting older. Between 1995 and 2020, the number of individuals in the United States

Manager's Hot Seat Applications

Office Romance: Groping for Answers

Diversity: Mediating Morality

Personal Disclosure: Confession

Coincidence Diversity in Hiring: Candidate Conundrum

over age 65 will increase by 60%, the 45- to 64-year-old population by 34%, and those between ages 18 and 44 by 4%.[53] Life expectancy is increasing as well. The number of people living into their 80s is increasing rapidly, and this group disproportionately suffers from chronic illness. The United States is not the only country with an aging population. Japan, Eastern Europe, and former Soviet republics, for example, are expected to encounter significant economic and political problems due to an aging population.[54]

Managerial Implications of Demographic Diversity   Regardless of gender, race, or age, all organizations need employees who possess the skills and abilities needed to successfully complete their jobs. To attract the best workers, companies need to adopt policies and procedures that meet the needs of all employees. Programs such as day care, elder care, flexible work schedules, and benefits such as paternal leaves, less rigid relocation policies, concierge services, and mentoring programs are likely to become more popular.[55] Pfizer, for example, offers on-site child care at four locations and elder care.[56] That said, however, special effort is needed to eliminate the glass ceiling that has impacted women and minorities. Ernst & Young, for instance, followed this recommendation after recognizing that the turnover rate among female employees was higher than male peers and that there were very few female partners: The cost of turnover averaged 150% of a departing employee's annual salary. The seven-step program, which is outlined in Skills & Best Practices on page 109, resulted in significantly reducing the turnover of female employees throughout the organization and tripling the percentage of women partners.[57]

Given the projected increase in the number of Hispanics entering the workforce over the next 20 years, managers should consider progressive methods to recruit, retain, and integrate this segment of the population into their organizations. Consider the examples set by Kmart, the University of North Carolina Health Care System at Chapel Hill, PricewaterhouseCoopers, Chevron, and PepsiCo:

> K-mart recruits at colleges and universities that have large numbers of Hispanic students. The company also advertises in Hispanic publications and uses online Hispanic job boards. It also has translated employment and benefit information into Spanish. The University of North Carolina Health Care System at Chapel Hill, NC, has brought in Spanish interpreters at its new-employee orientations and printed part of its job application information in Spanish. . . . PricewaterhouseCoopers . . . set up employee support and socialization groups where Hispanic managers act as leaders to Hispanic employees, and the company provides scholarships for Hispanic accounting students. Chevron sponsors a Hispanic employee network . . . Pepsi works with national Hispanic organizations to help with recruiting and is planning a leadership forum for some Hispanic executives. The program will give the executives access to the CEO and other company leaders.[58]

Mismatches between the amount of education needed to perform current jobs and the amount of education possessed by members of the workforce are growing. This trend creates two potential problems for organizations. First, there will be a shortage of qualified people in technical fields. To combat this issue, both Lockheed Martin and Agilent Technologies offer some type of paid apprenticeship or internship to attract high-school students interested in the sciences.[59] Second, underemployment among college graduates threatens to erode job satisfaction and work motivation. As well-educated workers begin to look for jobs commensurate with their qualifications and expectations, absenteeism and turnover likely will increase. This problem underscores the need for job redesign (see the discussion in Chapter 6). In addition, organizations will need to consider interventions, such as realistic job previews and positive reinforcement programs, to reduce absenteeism and turnover. On-the-job remedial skills and literacy training will be necessary to help the growing number of dropouts and illiterates cope with job demands.[60]

There are two general recommendations for helping organizations effectively adapt to an aging workforce. The first involves the need to help employees deal with personal issues associated with elder care. Elder care is a critical issue for employees that have aging parents, and failing to deal with it can drive up an employer's costs. For example, MetLife estimates that a lack of elder care costs organizations at least $11 billion a year in lost productivity and increased absenteeism, workday interruptions, and turnover.[61] Second, employers need to make a concerted effort to keep older workers engaged and committed and their skills current. The following seven initiatives can help accomplish this objective.[62]

1. Provide challenging work assignments that make a difference to the firm.

2. Give the employee considerable autonomy and latitude in completing a task.

3. Provide equal access to training and learning opportunities when it comes to new technology.

4. Provide frequent recognition for skills, experience, and wisdom gained over the years.

5. Provide mentoring opportunities whereby older workers can pass on accumulated knowledge to younger employees.

6. Ensure that older workers receive sensitive, high-quality supervision.

7. Design a work environment that is both stimulating and fun.

Ernst & Young Implements Program to Keep Women on the Path to Partnership

Process Steps	Supportive Tactics
1. Focus	Pilot projects targeted five office locations for improvement on specific issues. For example, Minneapolis focused on mentoring and New Jersey on flexible work arrangements.
2. Committed leadership	E&Y's chairman convened a diversity task force of partners and created an Office of Retention.
3. New roles	Certain individuals are targeted as "career watchers" and are given assignment and projects aimed at improving their leadership skills.
4. Policy changes	All employees were equipped for telework, and it was made policy that flexible work schedules would not affect anyone's opportunity for advancement.
5. Peer networking	Professional women's networks were established in 41 offices, and a three-day women's leadership conference is offered every 18 months.
6. Learning resources	All employees are encouraged to use the company's Achievement Flexibility Web site to learn about flexible work arrangements.
7. Accountability	An annual employee survey is used to assess the extent to which managers foster an inclusive, flexible work environment. Managers are also rated on metrics associated with the number of women on key accounts, in key leadership jobs, and in the partner pipeline.

SOURCE: Excerpted and adapted from S A Hewlett and C Buck Luce, "Off-Ramps and On-Ramps: Keeping Talented Women on the Road to Success," *Harvard Business Review*, March 2005, p 51.

Organizational Practices Used to Effectively Manage Diversity

Many organizations throughout the United States are unsure of what it takes to effectively manage diversity. In addition, the sensitive and potentially volatile nature of managing diversity has led to significant barriers when trying to move forward with diversity initiatives. This section reviews the barriers to managing diversity and discusses a framework for categorizing organizational diversity initiatives developed by Ann Morrison.

Barriers and Challenges to Managing Diversity

Organizations encounter a variety of barriers when attempting to implement diversity initiatives. It thus is important for present and future managers to consider these barriers before rolling out a diversity program. The following is a list of the most common barriers to implementing successful diversity programs.[63]

1. *Inaccurate stereotypes and prejudice.* This barrier manifests itself in the belief that differences are viewed as weaknesses. In turn, this promotes the view that diversity hiring will mean sacrificing competence and quality.

2. *Ethnocentrism.* The ethnocentrism barrier represents the feeling that one's cultural rules and norms are superior or more appropriate than the rules and norms of another culture.

3. *Poor career planning.* This barrier is associated with the lack of opportunities for diverse employees to get the type of work assignments that qualify them for senior management positions.

4. *An unsupportive and hostile working environment for diverse employees.* Diverse employees are frequently excluded from social events and the friendly camaraderie that takes place in most offices.

5. *Lack of political savvy on the part of diverse employees.* Diverse employees may not get promoted because they do not know how to "play the game" of getting along and getting ahead in an organization. Research reveals that women and people of color are excluded from organizational networks.[64]

6. *Difficulty in balancing career and family issues.* Women still assume the majority of the responsibilities associated with raising children. This makes it harder for women to work evenings and weekends or to frequently travel once they have children. Even without children in the picture, household chores take more of a woman's time than a man's time.

7. *Fears of reverse discrimination.* Some employees believe that managing diversity is a smoke screen for reverse discrimination. This belief leads to very strong resistance because people feel that one person's gain is another's loss.

8. *Diversity is not seen as an organizational priority.* This leads to subtle resistance that shows up in the form of complaints and negative attitudes. Employees may complain about the time, energy, and resources devoted to diversity that could have been spent doing "real work."

9. *The need to revamp the organization's performance appraisal and reward system.* Performance appraisals and reward systems must reinforce the need to

effectively manage diversity. This means that success will be based on a new set of criteria. Employees are likely to resist changes that adversely affect their promotions and financial rewards.

10. *Resistance to change.* Effectively managing diversity entails significant organizational and personal change. As discussed in Chapter 16, people resist change for many different reasons.

Ann Morrison Identifies Specific Diversity Initiatives

Ann Morrison conducted a landmark study of the diversity practices used by 16 organizations that successfully managed diversity. Her results uncovered 52 different practices, 20 of which were used by the majority of the companies sampled. She classified the 52 practices into three main types: accountability, development, and recruitment.[65] The top 10 practices associated with each type are shown in Table 4–2. They are discussed next in order of relative importance.

Accountability Practices **Accountability practices** relate to managers' responsibility to treat diverse employees fairly. Table 4–2 reveals that companies predominantly accomplish this objective by creating administrative procedures aimed at integrating diverse employees

accountability practices
Focus on treating diverse employees fairly.

Common Diversity Practices | TABLE 4–2

Accountability Practices	Development Practices	Recruitment Practices
1. Top management's personal intervention	1. Diversity training programs	1. Targeted recruitment of nonmanagers
2. Internal advocacy groups	2. Networks and support groups	2. Key outside hires
3. Emphasis on EEO statistics, profiles	3. Development programs for all high-potential managers	3. Extensive public exposure on diversity (AA)
4. Inclusion of diversity in performance evaluation goals, ratings	4. Informal networking activities	4. Corporate image as liberal, progressive, or benevolent
5. Inclusion of diversity in promotion decisions, criteria	5. Job rotation	5. Partnerships with educational institutions
6. Inclusion of diversity in management succession planning	6. Formal mentoring program	6. Recruitment incentives such as cash supplements
7. Work and family policies	7. Informal mentoring program	7. Internships (such as INROADS)
8. Policies against racism, sexism	8. Entry development programs for all high-potential new hires	8. Publications or PR products that highlight diversity
9. Internal audit or attitude survey	9. Internal training (such as personal safety or language)	9. Targeted recruitment of managers
10. Active AA/EEO committee, office	10. Recognition events, awards	10. Partnership with nontraditional groups

SOURCE: Abstracted from Tables A.10, A.11, and A.12 in A M Morrison, *The New Leaders: Guidelines on Leadership Diversity in America* (San Francisco: Jossey-Bass, 1992).

into the management ranks (practice numbers 3, 4, 5, 6, 8, 9, and 10). In contrast, work and family policies, practice 7, focuses on creating an environment that fosters employee commitment and productivity. Progress Energy, an energy company that serves the Carolinas and Florida, uses a variety of accountability practices in its attempt to manage diversity.

> The chairman of the diversity council is also the chairman and CEO of the company, William Cavanaugh III. The council meets once a quarter and subcouncils throughout the company meet monthly. In addition, every manager in the company is accountable for the way diversity is both perceived and practiced within his or her organization. Every year employees fill out a written questionnaire that evaluates employee satisfaction with the work environment. If a particular group provides negative feedback regarding issues (including diversity), the company follows up and addresses the issues.[66]

Development Practices   The use of development practices to manage diversity is relatively new compared with the historical use of accountability and recruitment practices. **Development practices** focus on preparing diverse employees for greater responsibility and advancement. These activities are needed because most nontraditional employees have not been exposed to the type of activities and job assignments that develop effective leadership and social networks. Table 4–2 indicates that diversity training programs, networks and support groups, and mentoring programs are among the most frequently used developmental practices. Consider the networking practices used by Xerox and Fannie Mae.

development practices

Focus on preparing diverse employees for greater responsibility and advancement.

> Many years ago when Xerox was trying to ensure more participation from blacks in its workforce, a caucus established among black employees had the blessing of then-CEO David Kearns, who encouraged black employees to get together periodically to talk about their challenges in moving through the organization and to get help from other managers. After that, there arose a women's caucus, an Hispanic caucus, and so on. Fannie Mae has taken the idea of employee caucus groups a step further. It has 14 Employee Networking Groups for African-Americans, Hispanics, Native Americans, Catholics, Christians, Muslims, older workers, gays, lesbians, veterans, and so forth. The groups serve as social and networking hubs, and they foster workplace communication about diversity issues among all employees, including senior managers.[67]

Recruitment Practices   **Recruitment practices** focus on attracting job applicants at all levels who are willing to accept challenging work assignments. This focus is critical because people learn the leadership skills needed for advancement by successfully accomplishing increasingly challenging and responsible work assignments. As shown in Table 4–2, targeted recruitment of nonmanagers (practice 1) and managers (practice 9) are commonly used to identify and recruit women and people of color.

recruitment practices

Attempts to attract qualified, diverse employees at all levels.

key terms

accountability practices   111

affirmative action   104

attention   92

causal attributions   98

cognitive categories   92

development practices   112

diversity   101

external factors   99

fundamental attribution bias   100

glass ceiling   105

internal factors   99

managing diversity   104

perception   91

recruitment practices   112

schema   92

self-serving bias   100

stereotype   93

underemployment   107

chapter summary

- *Describe perception in terms of the social information processing model.* Perception is a mental and cognitive process that enables us to interpret and understand our surroundings. Social perception, also known as social cognition and social information processing, is a four-stage process. The four stages are selective attention/comprehension, encoding and simplification, storage and retention, and retrieval and response. During social cognition, salient stimuli are matched with schemata, assigned to cognitive categories, and stored in long-term memory for events, semantic materials, or people.

- *Identify and briefly explain six managerial implications of social perception.* Social perception affects hiring decisions, performance appraisals, leadership perceptions, communication, and interpersonal influence, physical and psychological well-being, and the design of Web pages. Inaccurate schemata or racist and sexist schemata may be used to evaluate job applicants. Similarly, faulty schemata about what constitutes good versus poor performance can lead to inaccurate performance appraisals. Invalid schemata need to be identified and replaced with appropriate schemata through coaching and training. Further, managers are advised to use objective rather than subjective measures of performance. With respect to leadership, a leader will have a difficult time influencing employees when he or she exhibits behaviors contained in employees' schemata of poor leaders. Because people interpret oral and written communications by using schemata developed through past experiences, an individual's ability to influence others is affected by information contained in others' schemata regarding age, gender, ethnicity, appearance, speech, mannerisms, personality, and other personal characteristics.

- Research also shows a connection between negative thinking and one's physical and psychological health. We should

all attempt to avoid the tendency of giving negative thoughts too much attention. Finally, the extent to which a Web page garners interests and generates sales is partly a function of perceptual processes. Organizations are encouraged to consider the characteristics of effective Web page design.

- *Explain, according to Kelley's model, how external and internal causal attributions are formulated.* Attribution theory attempts to describe how people infer causes for observed behavior. According to Kelley's model of causal attribution, external attributions tend to be made when consensus and distinctiveness are high and consistency is low. Internal (personal responsibility) attributions tend to be made when consensus and distinctiveness are low and consistency is high.

- *Demonstrate your familiarity with the demographic trends that are creating an increasingly diverse workforce.* There are four key demographic trends: (a) women are encountering a glass ceiling, (b) racial groups are encountering a glass ceiling and perceived discrimination, (c) a mismatch exists between workers' educational attainment and occupational requirements, and (d) the workforce is aging.

- *Identify the barriers and challenges to managing diversity.* There are 10 barriers to successfully implementing diversity initiatives: (a) inaccurate stereotypes and prejudice, (b) ethnocentrism, (c) poor career planning, (d) an unsupportive and hostile working environment for diverse employees, (e) lack of political savvy on the part of diverse employees, (f) difficulty in balancing career and family issues, (g) fears of reverse discrimination, (h) diversity is not seen as an organizational priority, (i) the need to revamp the organization's performance appraisal and reward system, and (j) resistance to change.

- *Discuss the organizational practices used to manage diversity identified by Ann Morrison.* Ann Morrison's study of diversity practices identified three main types or categories of activities. Accountability practices relate to a manager's responsibility to treat diverse employees fairly. Development practices focus on preparing diverse employees for greater responsibility and advancement. Recruitment practices emphasize attracting job applicants at all levels who are willing to accept challenging work assignments. Table 4–3 presents a list of activities that are used to accomplish each main type.

discussion questions

1. In the context of the chapter-opening vignette, to what extent did the Chinese and Americans display the fundamental attribution bias and the self-serving bias? Explain.
2. Why is it important for managers to have a working knowledge of perception and attribution?
3. How would you formulate an attribution, according to Kelley's model, for the behavior of a classmate who starts arguing in class with your professor?
4. Does diversity suggest that managers should follow the rule, "Do unto others as you would have them do unto you"?
5. How can Ann Morrison's diversity initiatives be helpful in overcoming the barriers and challenges to managing diversity?

ethical dilemma

Enron Employees Try to Alter the Perceptions of Wall Street Analysts[68]

Some current and former employees of Enron's retail-energy unit say the company asked them to pose as busy electricity and natural-gas sales representatives one day in 1998 so the unit could impress Wall Street analysts visiting its Houston headquarters.

Enron rushed 75 employees of Enron Energy Services—including secretaries and actual sales representatives—to an empty trading floor and told them to act as if they were trying to sell energy contracts to businesses over the phone, the current and former employees say.

"When we went down to the sixth floor, I remember we had to take the stairs so the analysts wouldn't see us," said Kim Garcia, who at the time was an administrative assistant for Enron Energy Services and was laid off in December.

"We brought some of our personal stuff, like pictures, to make it look like the area was lived in," Ms Garcia said in an interview. "There were a bunch of trading desks on the sixth floor, but the desks were totally empty. Some of the computers didn't even work, so we worked off of our laptops. When the analysts arrived, we had to make believe we were on the phone buying and selling electricity and natural gas. The whole thing took like 10 minutes."

Penny Marksberry—who also worked as an Enron Energy Services administrative assistant in 1998 and was laid off in December—and two employees who still work at the unit also say they were told to act as if they were trying to sell contracts.

"They actually brought in computers and phones and they told us to act like we were typing or talking on the phone when the analysts were walking through," Ms Marksberry said. "They told us it was very important for us to make a good impression and if the analysts saw that the operation was disorganized, they wouldn't give the company a good rating."

What Would You Do If You Were Asked to Act Busy in Front of the Analysts?

1. Follow the company's instructions by going to the sixth floor and acting busy in front of the analysts.

2. Explain to your manager that this behavior is inconsistent with your personal values and that you will not participate.

3. Go to the sixth floor in support of the company's request, but do not act busy or bring personal artifacts to create a false impression.

4. Invent other options. Discuss.

For an interpretation of this situation, visit our Web site, www.mhhe.com/kinickiob3e.

chapter
five

Appreciating Individual Differences: Self-Concept, Personality, Emotions

LEARNING OBJECTIVES

After reading the material in this chapter, you should be able to:

- Distinguish between self-esteem and self-efficacy.

- Contrast high and low self-monitoring individuals, and describe resulting problems each may have.

- Explain the social learning model of self-management.

- Identify and describe the Big Five personality dimensions, specify which one is correlated most strongly with job performance, and describe the proactive personality.

- Explain the difference between an internal and external locus of control.

- Explain the concepts of emotional contagion and emotional labor, and identify the four key components of emotional intelligence.

When Sophie Vandebroek was appointed head of Xerox Corp.'s Canadian research and development operations in 1999, she didn't move to its headquarters in Mississauga, Ontario. Instead, for a year and a half she would get in her car Monday morning at her Penfield (N.Y.) home, drive the 2 hours and 42 minutes it took to get there, and work until 11:00 at night. After a quesadilla dinner and a night's rest at the nearby Holiday Inn, she would work until 4 on Tuesday afternoon, then head home. Wednesdays were spent in Xerox research facilities in Webster, N.Y., near her home. Thursday and Friday was another round-trip to Mississauga.

This was no one-time exercise in extreme commuting for Vandebroek, who has lived in the same home for the past 14 years. She has traveled by plane to jobs in Stamford and Hartford, Conn. When she was pregnant with her second child, she worked seven hours away, living in an apartment during the week while her toddler daughter, Elena, was home with her husband, Bart, an engineer.

But Vandebroek would be the first to disabuse anyone of the idea that she's a kind of superwoman. To some degree, she's simply done what she had to do. Ten years ago her husband died of a severe asthma attack while they were camping in the Adirondack Mountains, leaving Vandebroek to raise their

Sophie Vandebroek has stayed on the fast track at Xerox, but on her own terms.

three children an ocean away from family in Europe. [She was born in Belgium.] Since then, she's made her life work not by trying to do it all, but by focusing on what's most important.

An ability to prioritize is part of why Vandebroek, 44, is such a successful executive. On Jan. 1 the 14-year Xerox veteran became chief technology officer, overseeing

its 600 researchers and engineers and directing the $760 million plus the copier maker spends each year on R&D. "Sophie is one in a million on a level of skill, knowledge, and intellect," says Bernard S. Meyerson, CTO for IBM Systems and Technology Group and a friend of Vandebroek's since the early 1990s, when they worked together in IBM's Thomas J. Watson Research Center. "But she maintains her modesty."

These days, the commute is a relaxing 12 minutes from her door to Xerox' Webster campus, but Vandebroek's latest job will be a big challenge.... Optimism seems a prerequisite for a job where taking the wrong path can easily cost millions. So is a lot of hard work. Vandebroek's typical workday, when she's in Webster, starts at 6:40 a.m., making breakfast for Elena, 17, Arno, 15, and Jonas, 13. At 7:15 they're on the school bus, and she's working out on her rowing machine while listening to the BBC news on satellite radio. At the office, the day is usually packed with meetings, many with participants piped in from one of the four other research centers she oversees around the world. On a January day,

Vandebroek, dressed in a stylish pants suit with a silk scarf and high-heeled suede boots, rushed from one meeting to the next, often stepping aside to clear the e-mail from her BlackBerry or sip from her ever-present 1-liter bottle of lime seltzer. She tries to be home by 6:30 to dine with her kids. Then she spends most nights reading printouts of e-mails she couldn't get to earlier in the day.

A master of efficiency, Vandebroek had to teach herself not to be all business at work. In her early days as a manager she was so focused on getting the job done that she assumed everyone would buy her arguments on logic alone. An executive coach assigned to her as part of Xerox' talent-development program advised her to open up, talk about herself. Vandebroek laughs remembering the surprise of her staff when she opened a Monday morning meeting with a discussion of her weekend ski trip. Soon she was coordinating Thursday evening team outings for chicken wings and beer. The only rule: No talk about work. "It's about the human fabric of the organization," she says, "taking the time to listen to [employees'] concerns."

Still, for years many at Xerox didn't even know she was a widow. After her husband's death, Vandebroek plowed herself into work. In speeches, she often quotes a Chinese proverb that has guided her: "In crisis there is opportunity." Beyond the good that her focus on work has done for her career, Vandebroek sees ways in which her family has grown stronger since the tragedy. They are a close bunch, and she describes her children as "compassionate," a rare trait in any teenager.[1]

What personal characteristics and traits have helped Sophie Vandebroek succeed in the business world? Explain. For an interpretation of this case and additional comments, visit our Online Learning Center at

www.mhhe.com/kinickiob3e

FOR DISCUSSION

THANKS TO A VAST array of individual differences, modern organizations have a rich and interesting human texture. On the other hand, individual differences make the manager's job endlessly challenging. In fact, according to research, "variability among workers is substantial at all levels but increases dramatically with job complexity. In life insurance sales, for example, variability in performance is around six times as great as in routine clerical jobs."[2]

Growing workforce diversity (nearly one out of every seven workers in the US is foreign born)[3] compels managers to view individual differences in a fresh new way. Rather than limiting diversity, as in the past, today's managers need to better understand and accommodate employee diversity and individual differences.[4]

This chapter explores the following important dimensions of individual differences: (1) self-concept and self-management, (2) personality traits, (3) attitudes, (4) mental abilities, and (5) emotions. Figure 5–1 is a conceptual model showing the relationship between self-concept (how you view yourself), personality (how you appear to others), and key forms of self-expression. Considered as an integrated package, these factors provide a foundation for better understanding yourself and others as unique and special individuals

From Self-Concept to Self-Management

Self is the core of one's conscious existence. Awareness of self is referred to as one's self-concept. Individualistic North American cultures have been called self-centered. Not surprisingly, when people ages 16 to 70 were asked in a recent survey what they would do differently if they could live life over again, 48% chose the response category "Get in touch with self."[5] To know more about self-concept is to understand more about life in general.[6] Sociologist Viktor Gecas defines **self-concept** as "the concept the individual has of himself as a physical, social, and spiritual or moral being."[7] In other words, because you have a self-concept, you recognize yourself as a distinct human being. A self-concept would be impossible without the capacity to think. This brings us to the role of cognitions. **Cognitions** represent "any knowledge, opinion, or belief about the environment, about oneself, or about one's

self-concept

Person's self-perception as a physical, social, spiritual being.

cognitions

A person's knowledge, opinions, or beliefs.

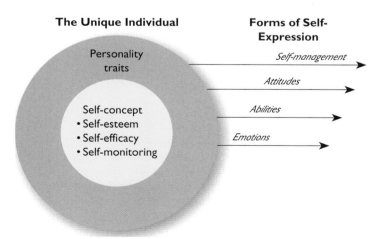

The Unique Individual

Personality traits

Self-concept
• Self-esteem
• Self-efficacy
• Self-monitoring

Forms of Self-Expression

Self-management

Attitudes

Abilities

Emotions

FIGURE 5–1
An OB Model for Studying Individual Differences

Terri Kelly, CEO of W L Gore & Associates, understands the importance of self-awareness in managers. In fact, in a company famous for its lack of hierarchy, Kelly has an acute perception about her own role. "The idea of me as CEO managing the company is a misperception," she says. "My goal is to provide the overall direction. I spend a lot of time making sure we have the right people in the right roles."

behavior."[8] Among many different types of cognitions, those involving anticipation, planning, goal setting, evaluating, and setting personal standards are particularly relevant to OB. Cognitively based topics covered in this book include social perception, behavioral self-management, modern motivation theories, and decision-making styles.

Importantly, ideas of self and self-concept vary from one historical era to another, from one socio-economic group to another, and from culture to culture.[9] How well one detects and adjusts to different cultural notions of self can spell the difference between success and failure in international dealings. For example, Japanese–US communication and understanding often are hindered by significantly different degrees of self-disclosure. With a comparatively large public self, Americans pride themselves in being open, honest, candid, and to the point. Meanwhile, Japanese, who culturally discourage self-disclosure, typically view Americans as blunt, prying, and insensitive to formalities. For their part, Americans tend to see Japanese as distant, cold, and evasive.[10] One culture is not right and the other wrong. They are just different, and a key difference involves culturally rooted conceptions of self and self-disclosure.

Keeping this cultural qualification in mind, let us explore three topics invariably mentioned when behavioral scientists discuss self-concept. They are self-esteem, self-efficacy, and self-monitoring. A social learning model of self-management is presented as a practical capstone for this section. Each of these areas deserves a closer look by those who want to better understand and effectively manage people at work. Terri Kelly, CEO of W L Gore & Associates, the maker of Gore-Tex fabrics popular among outdoor enthusiasts, recently told *Fast Company* magazine, "Leaders have to be very self-aware. They have to understand their flaws, their own behavior, and the impact they have on others."[11]

Self-Esteem

self-esteem

One's overall self-evaluation.

Self-esteem is a belief about one's own self-worth based on an overall self-evaluation.[12] Self-esteem is measured by having survey respondents indicate their agreement or disagreement with both positive and negative statements. A positive statement on one general self-esteem survey is: "I feel I am a person of worth, the equal of other people."[13] Among the negative items is: "I feel I do not have much to be proud of."[14] Those who agree with the positive statements and disagree with the negative statements have high self-esteem. They see themselves as worthwhile, capable, and acceptable. People with low self-esteem view themselves in negative terms. They do not feel good about themselves and are hampered by self-doubts.[15]

A Cross-Cultural Perspective   What are the cross-cultural implications for self-esteem, a concept that has been called uniquely Western? In a survey of 13,118 students from 31 countries worldwide, a moderate positive correlation was found between self-esteem and life satisfaction. But the relationship was stronger in individualistic cultures (e.g., United States, Canada, New Zealand, Netherlands) than in collectivist cultures (e.g., Korea, Kenya, Japan). The researchers concluded that individualistic cultures socialize people to focus more on themselves, while people in collectivist cultures "are socialized to fit into the community and to do their duty. Thus, how a collectivist feels about him- or herself is less relevant to . . . life satisfaction."[16] Global managers need to remember to deemphasize self-esteem when doing business in collectivist ("we") cultures, as opposed to emphasizing it in individualistic ("me") cultures.[17]

Can General Self-Esteem Be Improved?
The short answer is *yes* (see Skills & Best Practices). More detailed answers come from research. In one study, youth-league baseball coaches who were trained in supportive teaching techniques had a positive effect on the self-esteem of young boys. A control group of untrained coaches had no such positive effect.[18] Another study led to this conclusion: "Low self-esteem can be raised more by having the person think of *desirable* characteristics *possessed* rather than of undesirable characteristics from which he or she is free."[19] Yet another comprehensive study threw cold water on the popular view that high self-esteem is the key to better performance. The conclusion:

> . . . self-esteem and school or job performance are correlated. But long overdue scientific scrutiny points out the foolishness of supposing that people's opinion of themselves can be the *cause* of achievement. Rather, high-esteem is the *result* of good performance.[20]

This is where self-efficacy comes to the forefront.

Self-Efficacy ("I can do that.")

Have you noticed how those who are confident about their ability tend to succeed, while those who are preoccupied with failing tend to fail? Perhaps that explains the comparative golfing performance of your authors! One consistently stays in the

How to Build Self-Esteem in Yourself and Others

What nurtures and sustains self-esteem in grown-ups is not how others deal with us but how we ourselves operate in the face of life's challenges—the choices we make and the actions we take.

This leads us to the six pillars of self-esteem.

1. *Live consciously:* Be actively and fully engaged in what you do and with whom you interact.

2. *Be self-accepting:* Don't be overly judgmental or critical of your thoughts and actions.

3. *Take personal responsibility:* Take full responsibility for your decisions and actions in life's journey.

4. *Be self-assertive:* Be authentic and willing to defend your beliefs when interacting with others, rather than bending to their will to be accepted or liked.

5. *Live purposefully:* Have clear near-term and long-term goals and realistic plans for achieving them to create a sense of control over your life.

6. *Have personal integrity:* Be true to your word and your values.

Between self-esteem and the practices that support it, there is reciprocal causation. This means that the behaviors that generate good self-esteem are also expressions of good self-esteem.

SOURCE: Excerpted and adapted from Nathaniel Branden, *Self-Esteem at Work: How Confident People Make Powerful Companies* (San Francisco: Jossey-Bass, 1998), pp 33–36.

fairways and hits the greens. The other spends the day thrashing through the under-brush, wading in water hazards, and blasting out of sand traps. At the heart of this performance mismatch is a specific dimension of self-esteem called self-efficacy. **Self-efficacy** is a person's belief about his or her chances of successfully accomplishing a specific task. According to one OB writer, "Self-efficacy arises from the gradual acquisition of complex cognitive, social, linguistic, and/or physical skills through experience."[21]

self-efficacy

Belief in one's ability to do a task.

Helpful nudges in the right direction from parents, role models, and mentors are central to the development of high self-efficacy. Consider, for example, how former US Army Green Beret Earl Woods used his tough-love style to build his son Tiger's self-efficacy on the golf links:

Long after Tiger Woods is finished playing golf, people will study Earl Woods. They will want to hear the stories of exactly how he raised this generation's most popular athlete. . . .

"I tried to break him down mentally, tried to intimidate him verbally, by saying. 'Water on the right, OB [out of bounds] on the left,' just before his downswing," Earl Woods once told the Associated Press. "He would look at me with the most evil look, but he wasn't permitted to say anything. . . . One day I did all my tricks, and he looked at me and smiled. At the end of the round, I told him, 'Tiger, you've completed the training.' And I made him a promise. 'You'll never run into another person as mentally tough as you.' He hasn't. And he won't."[22]

The relationship between self-efficacy and performance is a cyclical one. Efficacy → performance cycles can spiral upward toward success or downward toward failure.[23] Researchers have documented a strong linkage between high self-efficacy expecta-tions and success in widely varied physical and mental tasks, anxiety reduction, addiction control, pain tolerance, illness recovery, and avoidance of seasickness in naval cadets.[24] Oppositely, those with low self-efficacy expectations tend to have low success rates. Chronically low self-efficacy is associated with a condition called **learned helplessness,** the severely debilitating belief that one has no control over one's environment.[25] Although self-efficacy sounds like some sort of mental magic, it operates in a very straightforward man-ner, as a model will show.

learned helplessness

Debilitating lack of faith in one's ability to control the situation.

Mechanisms of Self-Efficacy   A basic model of self-efficacy is displayed in Figure 5–2. It draws upon the work of Stanford psychologist Albert Bandura.[26] Let us explore this model with a simple illustrative task. Imagine you have been told to prepare and deliver a 10-minute talk to an OB class of 50 students on the workings of the self-efficacy model in Figure 5–2. Your self-efficacy calculation would involve cognitive appraisal of the interaction between your perceived capability and situa-tional opportunities and obstacles.

As you begin to prepare for your presentation, the four sources of self-efficacy beliefs would come into play. Because prior experience is the most potent source, according to Bandura, it is listed first and connected to self-efficacy beliefs with a solid line.[27] Past success in public speaking would boost your self-efficacy. But bad experiences with delivering speeches would foster low self-efficacy. Regarding behav-ior models as a source of self-efficacy beliefs, you would be influenced by the suc-cess or failure of your classmates in delivering similar talks. Their successes would tend to bolster you (or perhaps their failure would if you were very competitive and

Self-Efficacy Beliefs Pave the Way for Success or Failure | FIGURE 5–2

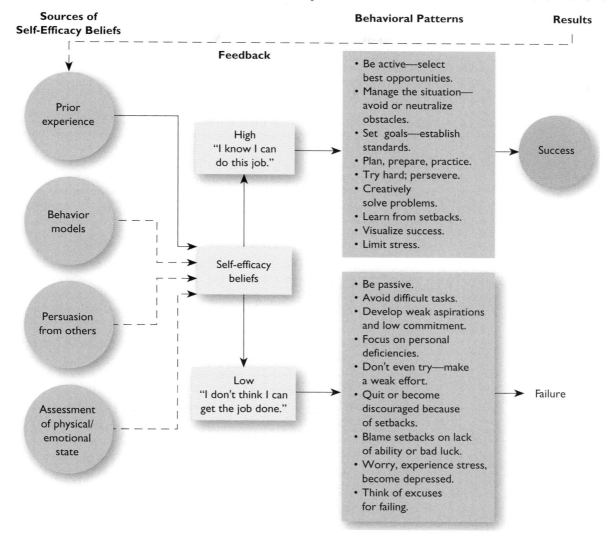

SOURCES: Adapted from discussion in A Bandura, "Regulation of Cognitive Processes through Perceived Self-Efficacy," *Developmental Psychology,* September 1989, pp 729–35; and R Wood and A Bandura, "Social Cognitive Theory of Organizational Management," *Academy of Management Review,* July 1989, pp 361–84.

had high self-esteem). Likewise, any supportive persuasion from your classmates that you will do a good job would enhance your self-efficacy. Physical and emotional factors also might affect your self-confidence. A sudden case of laryngitis or a bout of stage fright could cause your self-efficacy expectations to plunge. Your cognitive evaluation of the situation then would yield a self-efficacy belief—ranging from high to low expectations for success. Importantly, self-efficacy beliefs are not merely boastful statements based on bravado; they are deep convictions supported by experience.

Moving to the *behavioral patterns* portion of Figure 5–2, we see how self-efficacy beliefs are acted out. In short, if you have high self-efficacy about giving your 10-minute speech you will work harder, more creatively, and longer when preparing for your talk than will your low-self-efficacy classmates. The results would then take shape accordingly. People program themselves for success or failure by enacting their self-efficacy expectations. Positive or negative results subsequently become feedback for one's base of personal experience. Bob Schmonsees, a software entrepreneur, is an inspiring example of the success pathway through Figure 5–2:

> A contender in mixed-doubles tennis and a former football star, Mr Schmonsees was standing near a ski lift when an out-of-control skier rammed him. His legs were paralyzed. He would spend the rest of his life in a wheelchair.
>
> Fortunately, he discovered a formula for his different world: Figure out the new rules for any activity, then take as many small steps as necessary to master those rules. After learning the physics of a tennis swing on wheels and the geometry of playing a second bounce (standard rules), he became the world's top wheelchair player over age 40.[28]

Managerial Implications   On-the-job research evidence encourages managers to nurture self-efficacy, both in themselves and in others. In fact, a meta-analysis encompassing 21,616 subjects found a significant positive correlation between self-efficacy and job performance.[29] Self-efficacy requires constructive action in each of the following managerial areas:

1. *Recruiting/selection/job assignments.* Interview questions can be designed to probe job applicants' general self-efficacy as a basis for determining orientation and training needs. Pencil-and-paper tests for self-efficacy are not in an advanced stage of development and validation. Care needs to be taken not to hire solely on the basis of self-efficacy because studies have detected below-average self-esteem and self-efficacy among women and protected minorities.[30]

2. *Job design.* Complex, challenging, and autonomous jobs tend to enhance perceived self-efficacy.[31] Boring, tedious jobs generally do the opposite.

3. *Training and development.* Employees' self-efficacy expectations for key tasks can be improved through guided experiences, mentoring, and role modeling.[32]

4. *Self-management.* Systematic self-management training involves enhancement of self-efficacy expectations.[33]

5. *Goal setting and quality improvement.* Goal difficulty needs to match the individual's perceived self-efficacy.[34] As self-efficacy and performance improve, goals and quality standards can be made more challenging.

6. *Creativity.* Supportive managerial actions can enhance the strong linkage between self-efficacy beliefs and workplace creativity.[35]

7. *Coaching.* Those with low self-efficacy and employees victimized by learned helplessness need lots of constructive pointers and positive feedback.[36]

8. *Leadership.* Needed leadership talent surfaces when top management gives high self-efficacy managers a chance to prove themselves under pressure.

9. *Rewards.* Small successes need to be rewarded as stepping-stones to a stronger self-image and greater achievements.

Self-Monitoring

Consider these contrasting scenarios:

1. You are rushing to an important meeting when a co-worker pulls you aside and starts to discuss a personal problem. You want to break off the conversation, so you glance at your watch. He keeps talking. You say, "I'm late for a big meeting." He continues. You turn and start to walk away. The person keeps talking as if he never received any of your verbal and nonverbal signals that the conversation was over.

2. Same situation. Only this time, when you glance at your watch, the person immediately says, "I know, you've got to go. Sorry. We'll talk later."

In the first all-too-familiar scenario, you are talking to a "low self-monitor." The second scenario involves a "high self-monitor." But more is involved here than an irritating situation. A significant and measurable individual difference in self-expression behavior, called self-monitoring, is highlighted. **Self-monitoring** is the extent to which a person observes their own self-expressive behavior and adapts it to the demands of the situation.[37] Experts on the subject offer this explanation:

> **self-monitoring**
>
> Observing one's own behavior and adapting it to the situation.

> Individuals high in self-monitoring are thought to regulate their expressive self-presentation for the sake of desired public appearances, and thus be highly responsive to social and interpersonal cues of situationally appropriate performances. Individuals low in self-monitoring are thought to lack either the ability or the motivation to so regulate their expressive self-presentations. Their expressive behaviors, instead, are thought to functionally reflect their own enduring and momentary inner states, including their attitudes, traits, and feelings.[38]

In organizational life, both high and low self-monitors are subject to criticism. High self-monitors are sometimes called *chameleons,* who readily adapt their self-presentation to their surroundings. Low self-monitors, on the other hand, often are criticized for being on their own planet and insensitive to others. Importantly, within an OB context, self-monitoring is like any other individual difference—not a matter of right or wrong or good versus bad, but rather a source of diversity that needs to be adequately understood by present and future managers.

A Matter of Degree   Self-monitoring is not an either-or proposition. It is a matter of degree; a matter of being relatively high or low in terms of related patterns of self-expression. The Hands-On Exercise is a self-assessment of your self-monitoring tendencies. It can help you better understand your*self.* Take a short break from your reading to complete the 10-item survey. Does your score surprise you in any way? Are you unhappy with the way you present yourself to others? What are the ethical implications of your score (particularly with regard to items 9 and 10)?

Research Insights and Practical Recommendations   According to field research, there is a positive relationship between high self-monitoring and career success. Among 139 MBA graduates who were tracked for five years, high self-monitors enjoyed more internal and external promotions than did their low self-monitoring classmates.[39] Another study of 147 managers and professionals found that high self-monitors had a better record of acquiring a mentor (someone to act as a personal career coach and professional sponsor).[40] These results mesh

How Good Are You at Self-Monitoring?

INSTRUCTIONS: In an honest self-appraisal, mark each of the following statements as true (T) or false (F), and then consult the scoring key.

_____ **1.** I guess I put on a show to impress or entertain others.

_____ **2.** In a group of people I am rarely the center of attention.

_____ **3.** In different situations and with different people, I often act like very different persons.

_____ **4.** I would not change my opinions (or the way I do things) in order to please someone or win their favor.

_____ **5.** I have considered being an entertainer.

_____ **6.** I have trouble changing my behavior to suit different people and different situations.

_____ **7.** At a party I let others keep the jokes and stories going.

_____ **8.** I feel a bit awkward in public and do not show up quite as well as I should.

_____ **9.** I can look anyone in the eye and tell a lie with a straight face (if for a right end).

_____ **10.** I may deceive people by being friendly when I really dislike them.

SCORING KEY Score one point for each of the following answers:

1. T; 2. F; 3. T; 4. F; 5. T; 6. F; 7. F; 8. F; 9. T; 10. T

Score: _____

1–3 = Low self-monitoring
4–5 = Moderately low self-monitoring
6–7 = Moderately high self-monitoring
8–10 = High self-monitoring

SOURCE: Excerpted and adapted from M Snyder and S Gangestad, "On the Nature of Self-Monitoring: Matters of Assessment, Matters of Validity," *Journal of Personality and Social Psychology*, July 1986, p 137.

well with an earlier study that found managerial success (in terms of speed of promotions) tied to political savvy (knowing how to socialize, network, and engage in organizational politics).[41]

The foregoing evidence and practical experience lead us to make these practical recommendations:

For high, moderate, and low self-monitors: Become more consciously aware of your self-image and how it affects others (the Hands-On Exercise is a good start).

For high self-monitors: Don't overdo it by turning from a successful chameleon into someone who is widely perceived as insincere, dishonest, phoney, and untrustworthy. You cannot be everything to everyone.

For low self-monitors: You can bend without breaking, so try to be a bit more accommodating while being true to your basic beliefs. Don't wear out your welcome when communicating. Practice reading and adjusting to nonverbal cues in various public situations. If your conversation partner is bored or distracted, stop—because he or she is not really listening.

Self-Management: A Social Learning Model

Albert Bandura, the Stanford psychologist introduced earlier, extended his self-efficacy concept into a comprehensive model of human learning. According to Bandura's *social learning theory*, an individual acquires new behavior through the interplay of environmental cues and consequences and cognitive processes.[42] When you consciously control this learning process yourself, you are engaging in self-management. Bandura explains:

> [A] distinguishing feature of social learning theory is the prominent role it assigns to self-regulatory capacities. By arranging environmental inducements, generating cognitive supports, and producing consequences for their own actions people are able to exercise some measure of control over their own behavior.[43]

In other words, to the extent that you can control your environment and your cognitive representations of your environment, you are the master of your own behavior. The practical model displayed in Figure 5–3 is derived from social learning theory. The two-headed arrows reflect dynamic interaction among all factors in the model. Each of the four major components of this self-management model requires

A Social Learning Model of Self-Management   FIGURE 5–3

Person
(Psychological self)
- Symbolic coding (visual/verbal)
- Rehearsal (mental/actual)
- Self-talk

Behavior
- Behavior changes needed for self-improvement

Situational cues
- Reminders and attention focusers
- Self-observation data
- Avoidance of negative cues
- Seeking of positive cues
- Personal goal setting
- Self-contracts

Consequences
- Self-reinforcement/self-punishment
- Building activities into the task that are *naturally rewarding* (e.g., activities that increase one's sense of competence, self-control, and purpose)
- Reinforcement from relevant others

TABLE 5–1   Covey's Eight Habits: An Agenda for Managerial Self-Improvement

1. *Be proactive.* Choose the right means and ends in life, and take personal responsibility for your actions. Make timely decisions and make positive progress.

2. *Begin with the end in mind.* When all is said and done, how do you want to be remembered? Be goal oriented.

3. *Put first things first.* Establish firm priorities that will help you accomplish your mission in life. Strike a balance between your daily work and your potential for future accomplishments.

4. *Think win/win.* Cooperatively seek creative and mutually beneficial solutions to problems and conflicts.

5. *Seek first to understand, then to be understood.* Strive hard to become a better listener.

6. *Synergize.* Because the whole is greater than the sum of its parts, you need to generate teamwork among individuals with unique abilities and potential. Value interpersonal differences.

7. *Sharpen the saw.* "This is the habit of self-renewal, which has four elements. The first is mental, which includes reading, visualizing, planning, and writing. The second is spiritual, which means value clarification and commitment, study, and meditation. Third is social/emotional, which involves service, empathy, synergy, and intrinsic security. Finally, the physical element includes exercise, nutrition, and stress management."

8. *"Find your voice and inspire others to find theirs."* Take your life to a higher level by seeking fulfillment, doing things passionately, and making a significant contribution.

SOURCES: Adapted from discussion in S R Covey, *The 7 Habits of Highly Effective People* (New York: Simon & Schuster, 1989). Excerpt in No. 7 from "Q & A with Stephen Covey," *Training,* December 1992, p 38. Eighth habit quoted and adapted from C Lee, "Stephen Covey Talks About the 8th Habit: Effective Is No Longer Enough," *Training,* February 2005, pp 17–19 (emphasis added).

a closer look. Since the focal point of this model is *behavior change,* let us begin by discussing the behavior component in the center of the triangle.[44]

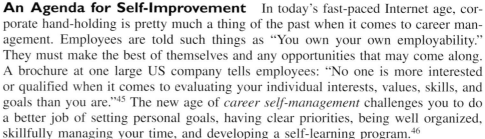

Self-Assessment Exercise

Assessing Your Flexibility

An Agenda for Self-Improvement   In today's fast-paced Internet age, corporate hand-holding is pretty much a thing of the past when it comes to career management. Employees are told such things as "You own your own employability." They must make the best of themselves and any opportunities that may come along. A brochure at one large US company tells employees: "No one is more interested or qualified when it comes to evaluating your individual interests, values, skills, and goals than you are."[45] The new age of *career self-management* challenges you to do a better job of setting personal goals, having clear priorities, being well organized, skillfully managing your time, and developing a self-learning program.[46]

Fortunately, Stephen R Covey, in his best-selling books *The 7 Habits of Highly Effective People* and *The 8th Habit,* has given managers a helpful agenda for improving themselves (see Table 5–1). Covey refers to the eight habits, practiced by truly successful people, as "principle-centered, character-based."[47] The first step for putting the model in Figure 5–3 to work is to pick one or more of the eight habits that are personal trouble spots and translate them to specific behaviors. For example, "think win/win" might remind a conflict-prone manager to practice cooperative teamwork behaviors with co-workers. Habit number five might prompt another manager to stop interrupting others during conversations. Next, a supportive environment is needed for the target behavior.

Managing Situational Cues   When people try to give up a nagging habit such as smoking, the cards are stacked against them. Many people (friends who smoke) and situations (after dinner, when under stress at work, or when relaxing) serve as subtle yet powerful cues telling the individual to light up. If the behavior is to be changed, the cues need to be rearranged so as to trigger the alternative behavior. Six techniques for managing situational cues are listed in the left column of Figure 5–3.

Reminders and attention focusers do just that. For example, many students and managers cue themselves about deadlines and appointments with Post-it™ notes stuck all over their work areas, refrigerators, and dashboards. Self-observation data, when compared against a goal or standard, can be a potent cue for improvement. Those who keep a weight chart near their bathroom scale will attest to the value of this tactic. Successful self-management calls for avoiding negative cues while seeking positive cues. Managers in Northwestern Mutual Life Insurance Company's new business department appreciate the value of avoiding negative cues: "On Wednesdays, the department shuts off all incoming calls, allowing workers to speed processing of new policies. On those days, the unit averages 23% more policies than on other days."[48]

Goals, as repeatedly mentioned in this text, are the touchstone of good management. So it is with challenging yet attainable personal goals and effective self-management. Personal finance expert Jean Chatzky offers this perspective:

> For setting goals, you get a substantial payoff. For working toward them, you get a greater one. Nearly half—48%—of Americans who are steadily working toward their goals or have already achieved them say they are very happy with their lives overall. A little over 30% of those who have just started to achieve their goals say they are very happy—and only 18% of those who haven't identified goals or taken the first step toward them say they're very happy. People who have at least started to achieve their goals are much more likely to feel useful, content and confident.[49]

Goals simultaneously provide a target and a measuring stick of progress. Finally, a self-contract is an "if-then" agreement with oneself. For example, if you can define all the key terms in this chapter, treat yourself to something special.

Arranging Cognitive Supports   Referring to the *person* portion of the self-management model in Figure 5–3, three cognitive supports for behavior change are symbolic coding, rehearsal, and self-talk. These amount to psychological, as opposed to environmental, cues. Yet, according to Bandura, they prompt appropriate behavior in the same manner. Each requires brief explanation:

- *Symbolic coding.* From a social learning theory perspective, the human brain stores information in visual and verbal codes. For example, a sales manager could use the visual picture of a man chopping down a huge tree to remember Woodman, the name of a promising new client. In contrast, people commonly rely on acronyms to recall names, rules for behavior, and other information. An acronym (or verbal code) that is often heard in managerial circles is the KISS principle, standing for "Keep It Simple, Stupid."

- *Rehearsal.* While it is true that practice often makes perfect, mental rehearsal of challenging tasks also can increase one's chances of success. Importantly, experts draw a clear distinction between systematic visualization of how one should proceed and daydreaming about success:

  > The big difference between daydreaming and visualizing is that "visualizing is much more specific and detailed," says Philadelphia consultant Judith Schuster. "A daydream typically has gaps in it—we jump immediately to where we want to wind up. In visualization, we use building blocks and, step-by-step, construct the result we want."[50]

This sort of visualization has been recommended for use in managerial planning.[51]

Managers stand to learn a great deal about mental rehearsal and visualization from successful athletes. Kim Woodring, Wittenberg University's two-time All-American volleyball player, is a good example. She effectively combines visualization and self-talk:

> "I'm always positive," she says. "Even if I'm losing. I talk positively to myself. I go on with the next play and don't worry about the last one. When I visualize, I always see the perfect pass, perfect hit, perfect set, perfect kill, perfect result."[52]

Job-finding seminars are very popular on college campuses today because they typically involve mental and actual rehearsal of tough job interviews. This sort of manufactured experience can build the confidence and self-efficacy necessary for real-world success.[53]

- *Self-talk.* According to an expert on the subject, "**self-talk** is the set of evaluating thoughts that you give yourself about facts and events that happen to you."[54] Personal experience tells us that self-talk tends to be a self-fulfilling prophecy. Negative self-talk tends to pave the way for failure, whereas positive self-talk often facilitates success. Replacing negative self-talk ("I'll never get a raise") with positive self-talk ("I deserve a raise and I'm going to get it") is fundamental to better self-management. One business writer, while urging salespeople to be their own cheerleaders, offered this advice for handling difficult situations:

self-talk
Evaluating thoughts about oneself.

  > Tell yourself there's a positive side to everything and train yourself to focus on it. At first your new self-talk will seem forced and unnatural, but stick with it. Use mental imagery to help you concentrate on the benefits of what you think is a bad situation. If you don't like cold calling, for example, think of how good you'll feel when you're finished, knowing you have a whole list of new selling opportunities. Forming a new habit isn't easy, but the effort will pay off.[55]

Self-Reinforcement The completion of self-contracts and other personal achievements calls for self-reinforcement. According to Bandura, three criteria must be satisfied before self-reinforcement can occur:

1. The individual must have *control over desired reinforcers.*
2. Reinforcers must be *self-administered on a conditional basis.* Failure to meet the performance requirement must lead to self-denial.
3. *Performance standards must be adopted* to establish the quantity and quality of target behavior required for self-reinforcement.[56]

In view of the following realities, self-reinforcement strategies need to be resourceful and creative:

> Self-granted rewards can lead to self-improvement. But as failed dieters and smokers can attest, there are short-run as well as long-run influences on self-reinforcement. For the overeater, the immediate gratification of eating has more influence than the promise of a new wardrobe. The same sort of dilemma plagues procrastinators. Consequently, one needs to weave a powerful web of cues, cognitive supports, and internal and external consequences to win the tug-of-war with status-quo payoffs. Primarily because it is so easy to avoid, self-punishment tends to be ineffectual. As with managing the behavior of others, positive instead of negative consequences are recommended for effective self-management.[57]

In addition, it helps to solicit positive reinforcement for self-improvement from supportive friends, co-workers, and relatives.

Personality Dynamics

Individuals have their own way of thinking and acting, their own unique style or *personality*. **Personality** is defined as the combination of stable physical and mental characteristics that give the individual his or her identity. These characteristics or traits—including how one looks, thinks, acts, and feels—are the product of interacting genetic and environmental influences.[58] In this section, we introduce the Big Five personality dimensions and discuss key personality dynamics including locus of control, attitudes, intelligence, and mental abilities.

> **personality**
>
> **Stable physical and mental characteristics responsible for a person's identity.**

The Big Five Personality Dimensions

Long and confusing lists of personality dimensions have been distilled in recent years to the Big Five.[59] They are extraversion, agreeableness, conscientiousness, emotional stability, and openness to experience (see Table 5–2 for descriptions). Standardized personality tests determine how positively or negatively a person scores on each of the Big Five. For example, someone scoring negatively on extraversion would be an introverted person prone to shy and withdrawn behavior.[60] Someone scoring negatively on emotional stability would be nervous, tense, angry, and worried. A person's scores on the Big Five reveal a personality profile as unique as his or her fingerprints.

Self-Assessment Exercise

Assessing How Personality Type Impacts Your Goal Setting Skills

The Big Five Personality Dimensions   **TABLE 5–2**

Personality Dimension	Characteristics of a Person Scoring Positively on the Dimension
1. Extraversion	Outgoing, talkative, sociable, assertive
2. Agreeableness	Trusting, good-natured, cooperative, softhearted
3. Conscientiousness	Dependable, responsible, achievement oriented, persistent
4. Emotional stability	Relaxed, secure, unworried
5. Openness to experience	Intellectual, imaginative, curious, broad-minded

SOURCE: Adapted from M R Barrick and M K Mount, "Autonomy as a Moderator of the Relationships between the Big Five Personality Dimensions and Job Performance," *Journal of Applied Psychology*, February 1993, pp 111–18.

But one important question lingers: Are personality models ethnocentric and unique to the culture in which they were developed? At least as far as the Big Five model goes, cross-cultural research evidence points in the direction of "no." Specifically, the Big Five personality structure held up very well in a study of women and men from Russia, Canada, Hong Kong, Poland, Germany, and Finland.[61] However, as emphasized by a recent study of 27,965 adults from 36 different cultures, this does *not* mean there is a global personality profile. Some geographic clustering of the Big Five dimensions was observed. For example, the results "showed a clear contrast of European and American cultures with Asian and African cultures. The former were higher in extraversion and openness to experience and lower in agreeableness."[62] This is useful diversity information for expatriate employees and tourists.

Personality and Job Performance   Those interested in OB want to know the connection between the Big Five and job performance. Ideally, Big Five personality dimensions that correlate positively and strongly with job performance would be helpful in the selection, training, and appraisal of employees. A meta-analysis of 117 studies involving 23,994 subjects from many professions offers guidance.[63] Among the Big Five, *conscientiousness* had the strongest positive correlation with job performance and training performance. According to the researchers, "those individuals who exhibit traits associated with a strong sense of purpose, obligation, and persistence generally perform better than those who do not."[64] So it comes as no surprise that British researchers recently found that people scoring *low* on conscientiousness tended to have significantly more accidents both on and off the job.[65]

After starting and managing a number of billion-dollar firms, some of which he has sold, Robert Louis Johnson is opening a bank. The Urban Trust Bank will offer mortgages, investment opportunities, and student loans mainly to African-Americans and other minorities. Johnson is a prime example of a proactive personality, having let few things stand in the way of becoming the first African-American billionaire, the owner of the first black-owned business to go public on the New York Stock Exchange, and the first African-American to be the sole owner of a professional sports team.

Another expected finding: Extraversion (an outgoing personality) was associated with success for managers and salespeople. Also, extraversion was a stronger predictor of job performance than agreeableness, across all professions. The researchers concluded, "It appears that being courteous, trusting, straightforward, and softhearted has a smaller impact on job performance than being talkative, active, and assertive."[66] Not surprisingly, in a recent study, a strong linkage between conscientiousness and performance was found among those with polished social skills.[67] As an added bonus for extraverts, a recent positive psychology study led to this conclusion: "All you have to do is act extraverted and you can get a happiness boost."[68] So the next time you are on the job go initiate a conversation with someone and be more productive *and* happier!

The Proactive Personality   As suggested by the above discussion, someone who scores high on the Big Five dimension of conscientiousness is probably a *better* and *safer* worker. Thomas S Bateman and J Michael Crant took this important linkage an additional step by formulating the concept of the proactive personality. They define and characterize the **proactive personality** in these terms: "someone who is relatively unconstrained by situational forces and who effects environmental change. Proactive people identify opportunities and act

proactive personality

Action-oriented person who shows initiative and perseveres to change things.

on them, show initiative, take action, and persevere until meaningful change occurs."[69] In short, people with proactive personalities are "hardwired" to change the status quo. In a review of relevant studies, Crant found the proactive personality to be positively associated with individual, team, and organizational success.[70]

Successful entrepreneurs exemplify the proactive personality.[71] Take the dynamic duo in Skills & Best Practices, for example.

People with proactive personalities truly are valuable *human capital,* as defined in Chapter 1. Those wanting to get ahead would do well to cultivate the initiative, drive, and perseverance of someone with a proactive personality.

There Is No "Ideal Employee" Personality

A word of caution is in order here. The Big Five personality dimensions of conscientiousness and extraversion and the proactive personality are generally desirable in the workplace, but they are not panaceas. Given the complexity of today's work environments, the diversity of today's workforce, and recent research evidence,[72] the quest for an ideal employee personality profile is sheer folly. Just as one shoe does not fit all people, one personality profile does not fit all job situations. Good management involves taking the time to get to know *each* employee's *unique combination* of personality traits, abilities, and potential and then creating a productive and satisfying person-job fit.

Locus of Control: Self or Environment?

Individuals vary in terms of how much personal responsibility they take for their behavior and its consequences. Julian Rotter, a personality researcher, identified a dimension of personality he labeled *locus of control* to explain these differences. He proposed that people tend to attribute the causes of their behavior primarily to either themselves or environmental factors.[73] This personality trait produces distinctly different behavior patterns.

People who believe they control the events and consequences that affect their lives are said to possess an **internal locus of control.** For example, such a person tends to attribute positive outcomes, such as getting a passing grade on an exam, to her or his own abilities. Similarly, an "internal" tends to blame negative events, such as failing an exam, on personal shortcomings—not studying hard enough, perhaps. Many entrepreneurs eventually succeed because their *internal* locus of control helps them overcome setbacks and disappointments. They see themselves as masters of their own fate and not as simply lucky (see Skills & Best Practices on page 134).

SKILLS & BEST PRACTICES

Turn Common Complaints into a Business Plan

You know that feature your customers are always asking for? If your employer won't deliver it, maybe you should. That's what Jeff Gallino and Cliff LaCoursiere did. Back in 2001 the two worked for ThinkEngine Networks, a Boston-based telecom equipment company. Gallino handled relationships with software partners, while LaCoursiere ran sales. The two kept hearing customers ask for a way to digitally sift through recorded calls and analyze them.

Gallino and LaCoursiere brought the idea to their employer, but they received a halfhearted response. So the duo wrote a business plan during off-duty hours and left ThinkEngine Networks in 2002. They funded their new firm, CallMiner, for a year with money saved from their salaries.

Gallino wrote the first version of their software, which builds an overall picture of what's being said through speech recognition, pattern mining, and signal analysis. The product attracted angel investment and a venture round, including cash from In-Q-Tel, the CIA's venture fund. Today, CallMiner's applications are used by airline, energy, and cable companies to categorize call-center calls, while government agencies are evaluating the technology's ability to automate intelligence gathering.

SOURCE: E Schonfeld, "5 Ways to Start a Company (Without Quitting Your Day Job)," *Business 2.0,* May 2006, p 44. Copyright © 2006 Time Inc. All rights reserved.

---

internal locus of control

Attributing outcomes to one's own actions.

How Lucky People Make Their Own Luck

In an environment marked by rising tensions and diminished expectations, most of us could use a little luck—at our companies, in our careers, with our investments. Richard Wiseman thinks that he can help you find some.

Wiseman, 37, is head of a psychology research department at the University of Hertfordshire in England. For the past eight years, he and his colleagues at the university's Perrott-Warrick Research Unit have studied what makes some people lucky and others not. After conducting thousands of interviews and hundreds of experiments, Wiseman now claims that he's cracked the code. Luck isn't due to kismet, karma, or coincidence, he says. Instead, lucky folks—without even knowing it—think and behave in ways that create good fortune in their lives. In his new book, *The Luck Factor: Changing Your Luck, Changing Your Life: The Four Essential Principles* (Miramax, 2003), Wiseman reveals four approaches to life that turn certain people into luck magnets. . . .

1. **Maximize Chance Opportunities** Lucky people are skilled at creating, noticing, and acting upon chance opportunities. They do this in various ways, which include building and maintaining a strong network, adopting a relaxed attitude to life, and being open to new experiences.

2. **Listen to Your Lucky Hunches** Lucky people make effective decisions by listening to their intuition and gut feelings. They also take steps to actively boost their intuitive abilities—for example, by meditating and clearing their mind of other thoughts.

3. **Expect Good Fortune** Lucky people are certain that the future will be bright. Over time, that expectation becomes a self-fulfilling prophecy because it helps lucky people persist in the face of failure and positively shapes their interactions with other people.

4. **Turn Bad Luck Into Good** Lucky people employ various psychological techniques to cope with, and even thrive upon, the ill fortune that comes their way. For example, they spontaneously imagine how things could have been worse, they don't dwell on the ill fortune, and they take control of the situation.

SOURCE: Excerpted from D H Pink, "How To Make Your Own Luck," *Fast Company*, July 2003, pp 78–82. Reprinted with permission.

On the other side of this personality dimension are those who believe their performance is the product of circumstances beyond their immediate control. These individuals are said to possess an **external locus of control** and tend to attribute outcomes to environmental causes, such as luck or fate. Unlike someone with an internal locus of control, an "external" would attribute a passing grade on an exam to something external (an easy test or a good day) and attribute a failing grade to an unfair test or problems at home.

Research Lessons Researchers have found important behavioral differences between internals and externals:

- Internals display greater work motivation.
- Internals have stronger expectations that effort leads to performance.
- Internals exhibit higher performance on tasks involving learning or problem solving, when performance leads to valued rewards.
- There is a stronger relationship between job satisfaction and performance for internals than for externals.
- Internals obtain higher salaries and greater salary increases than externals.
- Externals tend to be more anxious than internals.[74]

Tempering an Internal Locus of Control with Humility Do you have an internal locus of control? Odds are high that you do, judging from the "typical" OB student we have worked with over the years. Good thing, because it should pay off in the workplace with opportunities, raises, and promotions. But before you declare yourself Grade A executive material, here is one more thing to toss into your tool kit: a touch of humility. **Humility** is "a realistic assessment of one's own contribution and the recognition of the contribution of others, along with luck and good fortune that made one's own success possible."[75] Humility has been called the silent virtue. How many truly humble people brag about being humble? Two OB experts recently offered this instructive perspective:

> Humble individuals have a down-to-earth perspective of themselves and of the events and relationships in their lives. Humility involves a capability to evaluate success, failure, work, and life without exaggeration. Furthermore, humility enables leaders to distinguish the delicate line between such characteristics as healthy

self-confidence, self-esteem, and self-assessment, and those of over-confidence, narcissism, and stubbornness. Humility is the mid-point between the two negative extremes of arrogance and lack of self-esteem. This depiction allows one to see that a person can be humble and competitive or humble and ambitious at the same time, which contradicts common—but mistaken—views about humility.[76]

> **external locus of control**
> **Attributing outcomes to circumstances beyond one's control.**

> **humility**
> **Considering the contributions of others and good fortune when gauging one's success.**

Cuban-born, Carlos Gutierrez, US secretary of commerce and former CEO of Kellogg Company, learned about humility from his father:

> He taught me that you have to keep your perspective and have a sense of humility. As he used to say, "Tell me what you brag about, and I'll tell you what you lack."[77]

> **Self-Assessment Exercise**
>
> Assessing Your Empathy Skills

Attitudes

Hardly a day goes by without the popular media reporting the results of another attitude survey. The idea is to take the pulse of public opinion. What do we think about candidate X, the war on drugs, gun control, or abortion? In the workplace, meanwhile, managers conduct attitude surveys to monitor such things as job and pay satisfaction. All this attention to attitudes is based on the assumption that attitudes somehow influence behavior such as voting for someone, working hard, or quitting one's job.

Attitudes versus Values   An **attitude** is defined as "a learned predisposition to respond in a consistently favorable or unfavorable manner with respect to a given object."[78] Attitudes affect behavior at a different level than do values. While values represent global beliefs that influence behavior across *all* situations, attitudes relate only to behavior directed toward *specific* objects, persons, or situations. Values and attitudes generally, but not always, are in harmony. A manager who strongly values helpful behavior may have a negative attitude toward helping an unethical co-worker.

Today someone called me pompous, overpaid, and out of touch. I think it's beginning to happen for me."

HARVARD BUSINESS REVIEW

Copyright © Leo Collum 2006.

How Stable Are Attitudes?   In one landmark study, researchers found the *job* attitudes of 5,000 middle-aged male employees to be very stable over a five-year period. Positive job attitudes remained positive; negative ones remained negative. Even those who changed jobs or occupations tended to maintain their prior job attitudes.[79] More recent research

> **attitude**
> **Learned predisposition toward a given object.**

suggests the foregoing study may have overstated the stability of attitudes because it was restricted to a middle-aged sample. This time, researchers asked: What happens to attitudes over the entire span of adulthood? *General* attitudes were found to be more susceptible to change during early and late adulthood than during middle adulthood. Three factors accounted for middle-age attitude stability: (1) greater personal certainty, (2) perceived abundance of knowledge, and (3) a need for strong attitudes. Thus, the conventional notion that general attitudes become less likely to change as the person ages was rejected. Elderly people, along with young adults, can and do change their general attitudes because they are more open and less self-assured.[80]

Some evidence suggests that attitudes toward work can vary between generations. Many people at or nearing retirement age, like Kathy Swartout, shown here with her husband, Mark, and their dog, are discovering that they crave the intangible benefits of working, such as the chance to learn new things, socialize with others, and feel appreciated. Swartout spent eight months sailing, gardening, and practicing yoga after retirement. Then she returned to a full-time job that she plans to cut back soon to three days a week. "Working part time balances financial security with family and all the other fun things I want to do," she says.

intelligence

Capacity for constructive thinking, reasoning, problem solving.

Intelligence and Cognitive Abilities

Although experts do not agree on a specific definition, **intelligence** represents an individual's capacity for constructive thinking, reasoning, and problem solving.[81] Historically, intelligence was believed to be an innate capacity, passed genetically from one generation to the next. Research since has shown, however, that intelligence (like personality) also is a function of environmental influences.[82] Organic factors have more recently been added to the formula as a result of mounting evidence of the connection between alcohol and drug abuse by pregnant women and intellectual development problems in their children.[83]

Researchers have produced some interesting findings about abilities and intelligence in recent years. A unique five-year study documented the tendency of people to "gravitate into jobs commensurate with their abilities."[84] This prompts the vision of the labor market acting as a giant sorting or sifting machine, with employees tumbling into various ability bins. Meanwhile, a steady and significant rise in average intelligence among those in developed countries has been observed over the last 70 years. Why? Experts at an American Psychological Association conference concluded, "Some combination of better schooling, improved socioeconomic status, healthier nutrition, and a more technologically complex society might account for the gains in IQ scores."[85] So if you think you're smarter than your parents and your teachers, you're probably right!

Two Types of Abilities   Human intelligence has been studied predominantly through the empirical approach. By examining the relationships between measures of mental abilities and behavior, researchers have statistically isolated major components of intelligence. Using this empirical procedure, pioneering psychologist Charles Spearman proposed in 1927 that all cognitive performance is determined by two types of abilities. The first can be characterized as a general mental ability needed for *all* cognitive tasks. The second is unique to the task at hand. For example, an individual's ability to complete crossword puzzles is a function of his or her broad mental abilities as well as the specific ability to perceive patterns in partially completed words.

Seven Major Mental Abilities   Through the years, much research has been devoted to developing and expanding Spearman's ideas on the relationship between cognitive abilities and intelligence.[86] One research psychologist listed 120 distinct mental abilities. Table 5–3 contains definitions of the seven most frequently cited mental abilities. Of the seven abilities, personnel selection researchers have found verbal ability, numerical ability, spatial ability, and inductive reasoning to be valid predictors of job performance for both minority and majority applicants. Also, according to a recent comprehensive research review, standard intelligence (IQ) tests do a good job of predicting both academic achievement and job performance.[87] This contradicts the popular notion that different cognitive abilities are needed for school and work. Plainly stated: "smarts" are "smarts."

Mental Abilities | **TABLE 5–3**

Ability	Description
1. Verbal comprehension	The ability to understand what words mean and to readily comprehend what is read.
2. Word fluency	The ability to produce isolated words that fulfill specific symbolic or structural requirements (such as all words that begin with the letter b and have two vowels).
3. Numerical	The ability to make quick and accurate arithmetic computations such as adding and subtracting.
4. Spatial	Being able to perceive spatial patterns and to visualize how geometric shapes would look if transformed in shape or position.
5. Memory	Having good rote memory for paired words, symbols, lists of numbers, or other associated items.
6. Perceptual speed	The ability to perceive figures, identify similarities and differences, and carry out tasks involving visual perception.
7. Inductive reasoning	The ability to reason from specifics to general conclusions.

SOURCE: Adapted from M D Dunnette, "Aptitudes, Abilities, and Skills," in *Handbook of Industrial and Organizational Psychology*, ed M D Dunnette (Skokie, IL: Rand McNally, 1976), pp 478–83.

OB Gets Emotional

In the ideal world of management theory, employees pursue organizational goals in a logical and rational manner. Emotional behavior seldom is factored into the equation. Yet day-to-day organizational life shows us how prevalent and powerful emotions can be. Anger and jealousy, both potent emotions, often push aside logic and rationality in the workplace. Managers use fear and other emotions to both motivate and intimidate. For example, consider Selina Y Lo, the head of marketing at Alteon WebSystems in San Jose, California:

> A 15-year veteran of the networking business, she has honed her in-your-face style at three startups, earning a reputation as one of the smartest, toughest managers in the industry. Lo's temper and intensity are legendary: During a product meeting last fall, recalls Alteon software engineer John Taylor, she sprang up yelling from her chair, banged her fist on the table, and shoved a finger in his face after Taylor said he couldn't add a feature she had asked for. Taylor quickly relented. "I've left a few dead bodies behind me," Lo crows.[88]

Less noisy, but still emotion laden, is Intel's former CEO Andy Grove's use of Grove's Law to keep a competitive edge in the global computer chip market. According to Grove's Law, "Only the paranoid survive."[89] A combination of curiosity and fear is said to drive Barry Diller, one of the media world's legendary dealmakers. Says Diller, "I and my friends succeeded because we were scared to death of failing."[90] These admired corporate leaders would not have achieved what they have without the ability to be logical and rational decision makers *and* be emotionally

Talk about baptism by fire. Just 10 months after being named CEO of American Express, Kenneth I. Chenault addressed 5,000 of his co-workers in an emotional meeting to begin the healing process following the September 11, 2001, terrorist attacks. The tragedy claimed the lives of 11 AmEx employees and closed the firm's New York headquarters for eight months of repairs. Chenault, seen here presiding over AmEx's May 13, 2002, headquarters homecoming celebration, reportedly handled the post-9/11 meeting with great skill and compassion.

charged. Too much emotion, however, could have spelled career and organizational disaster for either one of them.

In this final section, our examination of individual differences turns to defining emotions, reviewing a typology of 10 positive and negative emotions, and discussing the topics of emotional contagion, emotional labor, and emotional intelligence.

Positive and Negative Emotions

Richard S Lazarus, a leading authority on the subject, defines **emotions** as "complex, patterned, organismic reactions to how we think we are doing in our lifelong efforts to survive and flourish and to achieve what we wish for ourselves."[91] The word *organismic* is appropriate because emotions involve the *whole* person—biological, psychological, and social. Importantly, psychologists draw a distinction between *felt* and *displayed* emotions.[92] For example, you might feel angry (felt emotion) at a rude co-worker but not make a nasty remark in return (displayed emotion). Emotions play roles in both causing and adapting to stress and its associated biological and psychological problems. The destructive effect of emotional behavior on social relationships is all too obvious in daily life.

Lazarus's definition of emotions centers on a person's goals. Accordingly, his distinction between positive and negative emotions is goal oriented. Some emotions are triggered by frustration and failure when pursuing one's goals. Lazarus calls these *negative* emotions. They are said to be goal incongruent. For example, which of the six negative emotions in Figure 5–4 are you likely to experience if you fail the final exam in a required course? Failing the exam would be incongruent with your goal of graduating on time. On the other hand, which of the four *positive* emotions in Figure 5–4 would you probably experience if you graduated on time and with honors? The emotions you would experience in this situation are positive because they are congruent (or consistent) with an important lifetime goal. The individual's goals, it is important to note, may or may not be socially acceptable. Thus, a positive emotion, such as love/affection, may be undesirable if associated with sexual harassment. Oppositely, slight pangs of guilt, anxiety, and envy can motivate extra effort. On balance, the constructive or destructive nature of a particular emotion must be judged in terms of both its intensity and the person's relevant goal.

Good (and Bad) Moods Are Contagious

Have you ever had someone's bad mood sour your mood? That person could have been a parent, supervisor, co-worker, friend, or someone serving you in a store or restaurant. Appropriately, researchers call this *emotional contagion*. We, quite literally, can catch another person's good or bad mood or displayed emotions. This effect was documented in a recent study of 131 bank tellers (92% female) and 220 exit interviews with their customers. Tellers who expressed positive emotions tended to have more

emotions

Complex human reactions to personal achievements and setbacks that may be felt and displayed.

Positive and Negative Emotions | FIGURE 5–4

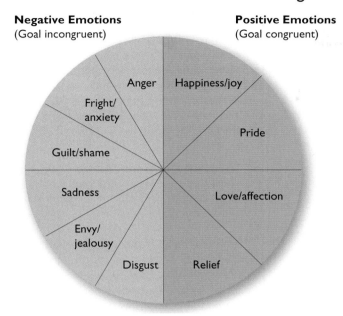

Negative Emotions
(Goal incongruent)

Positive Emotions
(Goal congruent)

Anger
Happiness/joy
Fright/anxiety
Pride
Guilt/shame
Love/affection
Sadness
Envy/jealousy
Disgust
Relief

SOURCE: Adapted from discussion in R S Lazarus, *Emotion and Adaptation* (New York: Oxford University Press, 1991), Chs 6, 7.

satisfied customers.[93] Two field studies with nurses and accountants as subjects found a strong linkage between the work group's collective mood and the individual's mood.[94] Both foul moods and good moods turned out to be contagious. Perhaps more managers should follow the lead of Lorin Maazel, director of the New York Philharmonic Orchestra:

> I have noticed in my long career that if I am really tired or I have a flu coming on that it's felt. Everybody gets into that mode, and pretty soon, they're playing as sluggishly as I'm conducting. I have learned to come to rehearsal fresh, energetic, projecting enthusiasm and go-go-go. It's got to be irresistible. If I don't think I'm up to it, I take a cold shower. That's my job—to energize people. If they grind it out and couldn't care less, then they wind up hating you and themselves because it's not why they practiced all of their lives. Emotion is what it's all about. Music making without emotion and passion is nothing.[95]

Emotional Labor (It has *not* been a pleasure serving you!)

Although they did not have the benefit of a catchy label or a body of sophisticated research, generations of managers have known about the power of emotional contagion in the marketplace. "Smile, look happy for the customers," employees are told over and over. But what if the employee is having a rotten day? What if they have to mask their true feelings and emotions? What if they have to fake it?

Developing Emotional Intelligence

Personal Competence: These capabilities determine how we manage ourselves.

Self-Awareness
- *Emotional self-awareness:* Reading one's own emotions and recognizing their impact; using "gut sense" to guide decisions.
- *Accurate self-assessment:* Knowing one's strengths and limits.
- *Self-confidence:* A sound sense of one's self-worth and capabilities.

Self-Management
- *Emotional self-control:* Keeping disruptive emotions and impulses under control.
- *Transparency:* Displaying honesty and integrity; trustworthiness.
- *Adaptability:* Flexibility in adapting to changing situations or overcoming obstacles.
- *Achievement:* The drive to improve performance to meet inner standards of excellence.
- *Initiative:* Readiness to act and seize opportunities.
- *Optimism:* Seeing the upside in events.

Social Competence: These capabilities determine how we manage relationships.

Social Awareness
- *Empathy:* Sensing others' emotions, understanding their perspective, and taking active interest in their concerns.
- *Organizational awareness:* Reading the currents, decision networks, and politics at the organizational level.
- *Service:* Recognizing and meeting follower, client, or customer needs.

Relationship Management
- *Inspirational leadership:* Guiding and motivating with a compelling vision.
- *Influence:* Wielding a range of tactics for persuasion.
- *Developing others:* Bolstering others' abilities through feedback and guidance.
- *Change catalyst:* Initiating, managing, and leading in a new direction.
- *Conflict management:* Resolving disagreements.
- *Building bonds:* Cultivating and maintaining a web of relationships.
- *Teamwork and collaboration:* Cooperation and team building.

SOURCE: Reprinted by permission of Harvard Business School Press. D Goleman, R Boyatzis, and A McKee, *Primal Leadership: Realizing the Power of Emotional Intelligence* (Boston: Harvard Business School Press, 2002), p 39. Copyright © 2002 by the Harvard Business School Publishing Corporation; all rights reserved.

Researchers have begun studying the dynamics of what they call *emotional labor.* A pair of authors, one from Australia, the other from the United States, recently summarized the research lessons to date:

> Emotional labor can be particularly detrimental to the employee performing the labor and can take its toll both psychologically and physically. Employees . . . may bottle up feelings of frustration, resentment, and anger, which are not appropriate to express. These feelings result, in part, from the constant requirement to monitor one's negative emotions and express positive ones. If not given a healthy expressive outlet, this emotional repression can lead to a syndrome of emotional exhaustion and burnout.[96]

Interestingly, a pair of laboratory studies with US college students as subjects found no gender difference in *felt* emotions. But the women were more emotionally *expressive* than the men.[97] This stream of research on emotional labor has major practical implications for productivity and job satisfaction, as well as for workplace anger, aggression, and violence. Clearly, managers need to be attuned to (and responsive to) the emotional states and needs of their people. This requires emotional intelligence.

Emotional Intelligence

In 1995, Daniel Goleman, a psychologist turned journalist, created a stir in education and management circles with the publication of his book *Emotional Intelligence.* Hence, an obscure topic among positive psychologists became mainstream. According to Goleman, traditional models of intelligence (IQ) are too narrow, failing to consider interpersonal competence. Goleman's broader agenda includes "abilities such as being able to motivate oneself and persist in the face of frustrations; to control impulse and delay gratification; to regulate one's moods and keep distress from swamping the ability to think; to empathize and to hope."[98] Thus, **emotional intelligence** is the ability to manage oneself and one's relationships in mature and constructive ways. Referred to by some as EI and others as EQ, emotional intelligence is said to have four key components: self-awareness, self-management, social awareness, and relationship management.[99] The first two constitute *personal competence;* the second two feed into *social competence* (see Skills & Best Practices).

These emotional intelligence skills need to be well polished in today's pressure-packed workplaces:

> Unanticipated hot spots often flare up during important meetings. Show patience, career experts say. Take deep breaths, compose your thoughts, restate the question—and use humor to defuse tension. If you avoid blurting out the first thing that comes to mind, "people will see your demeanor as cool and professional," observes [executive and author] David F D'Alessandro. . . .
>
> Most people don't do well with the unexpected because they lack a script, notes Dr. [Dory] Hollander. The workplace psychologist recommends acting classes for her clients.
>
> A year of lessons helped one female client advance into the executive ranks at a big technology company. The woman used to perform poorly when colleagues tossed out unforseen questions after presentations. "She looked like she was in pain," Dr. Hollander recalls.
>
> Today, the former middle manager acts confident and appears to enjoy herself even when she lands on the hot seat. "It really is theater," her coach concludes.[100]

> **emotional intelligence**
>
> Ability to manage oneself and interact with others in mature and constructive ways.

Self-assessment instruments supposedly measuring emotional intelligence have appeared in the popular management literature. Sample questions include: "I believe I can stay on top of tough situations,"[101] and "I am able to admit my own mistakes."[102] Recent research, however, casts serious doubt on the reliability and validity of such instruments.[103] Even Goleman concedes, "It's very tough to measure our own emotional intelligence, because most of us don't have a very clear sense of how we come across to other people. . . ."[104] Honest feedback from others is necessary. Still, the area of emotional intelligence is useful for teachers and organizational trainers because, unlike IQ, social problem solving and the ability to control one's emotions can be taught and learned. Scores on emotional intelligence tests definitely should *not* be used for making hiring and promotion decisions until valid measuring tools are developed.

Self-Assessment Exercise

Assessing Your Emotional Intelligence

key terms

attitude 135
cognitions 119
emotional intelligence 141
emotions 138
external locus of control 135
humility 135

intelligence 136
internal locus of control 133
learned helplessness 122
personality 131
proactive personality 132
self-concept 119

self-efficacy 122
self-esteem 120
self-monitoring 125
self-talk 130

chapter summary

- *Distinguish between self-esteem and self-efficacy.* Self-esteem is an overall evaluation of oneself, one's perceived self-worth. Self-efficacy is the belief in one's ability to successfully perform a task.

- *Contrast high and low self-monitoring individuals, and describe resulting problems each may have.* A high self-monitor strives to make a good public impression by closely monitoring his or her behavior and adapting it to the situation. Very high self-monitoring can create a "chameleon" who is seen as insincere and dishonest. Low self-monitors do the opposite by acting out their momentary feelings, regardless of their surroundings. Very low self-monitoring can lead to a one-way communicator who seems to ignore verbal and nonverbal cues from others.

- *Explain the social learning model of self-management.* Behavior results from interaction among four components: (a) situational cues, (b) the person's psychological self, (c) the person's behavior, and (d) consequences. Behavior, such as Covey's eight habits of highly effective people, can be developed by relying on supportive cognitive processes such as mental rehearsal and self-talk. Carefully arranged cues and consequences also help in the self-improvement process.

- *Identify and describe the Big Five personality dimensions, specify which one is correlated most strongly with job performance, and describe the proactive personality.* The Big Five personality dimensions are extraversion (social and talkative), agreeableness (trusting and cooperative), conscientiousness (responsible and persistent), emotional stability (relaxed and unworried), and openness to experience (intellectual and curious). Conscientiousness is the best predictor of job performance. A person with a proactive personality shows initiative, takes action, and perseveres until a desired change occurs.

- *Explain the difference between an internal and external locus of control.* People with an *internal* locus of control, such as entrepreneurs, believe they are masters of their own fate. Those with an *external* locus of control attribute their behavior and its results to situational forces.

- *Explain the concepts of emotional contagion and emotional labor, and identify the four key components of emotional intelligence.* Emotions are indeed contagious, with good and bad moods "infecting" others. Emotional labor occurs when people need to repress their emotional reactions when serving others. Resentment, frustration, and even anger can result when "putting on a happy face" for customers and others. Four key components of emotional intelligence are self-awareness and self-management (for personal competence) and social awareness and relationship management (for social competence).

discussion questions

1. In the context of the chapter-opening vignette, do you have what it takes to become a high-level executive? Explain.
2. How is someone you know with low self-efficacy, relative to a specified task, "programming themselves for failure"? What could be done to help that individual develop high self-efficacy?
3. What importance do you attach to self-talk in self-management? Explain.
4. On scales of low = 1 to high = 10, how would you rate yourself on the Big Five personality dimensions? Is your personality profile suitable for your present (or chosen) line of work? Explain.
5. Which of the four key components of emotional intelligence is (or are) your strong suit? Which is (or are) your weakest? What are the everyday implications of your EI profile?

ethical dilemma

Hot Heads!

Situation

You are the human resources vice president at a leading overnight express company. After lunch today, one of your top trainers excitedly plopped down in your office and said "Read this short section I marked in a *Business 2.0* article." You took it and read the following:

> Thrown any good lamps lately? Of course, you're probably too professional and well-bred to show anger at work. Just be aware: Being restrained may not be doing your career any good.
>
> For some years, Larissa Tiedens, an assistant professor of organizational behavior at Stanford Business School, has been studying the effects of anger in the workplace. Her research has revealed that employers have a bias toward promoting employees who get mad now and again. "I don't think we're cognizant of this," Tiedens says. "We make inferences about people all the time, and we don't always know where the information has come from."
>
> Tiedens began testing her hypothesis at a software firm in Palo Alto. She gave 24 of the employees a list of 10 or so emotions and asked them to rate how often their colleagues expressed each one. At the same time, the group managers filled out a questionnaire about how likely they would be to promote each of the employees. Those who were rated high on the anger scale were more likely to be on the promotion list. In a separate experiment, Tiedens had MBA students watch video clips of mock job interviews. In one tape the applicant shows visible signs of anger when discussing a presentation that went wrong, and in the other the candidate is fairly restrained. Most of the MBAs said they would have slotted the angry candidate for the higher-paying position.[105]

As you handed the reading back, you remarked, "Let me see if I get this. You want to teach our managers *how* to get angry, or get angry *more often?*" An ethical flag went up in your mind.

What Would You Do?

1. Kill the idea on the spot. Explain how.

2. Take an immediate cue from what you just read and angrily tell the trainer that some research shouldn't be taken so literally. How would you do that?

3. Make an appointment with the trainer to discuss and refine the concept to make it an acceptable part of your management training program. Explain how.

4. Without hurting the trainer's feelings or discouraging creativity, take a few minutes to review the ethical implications of what you just read.

5. Invent other options. Discuss.

For an interpretation of this situation, visit our Web site, www.mhhe.com/kinickiob3e.

chapter six

Motivation I: Needs, Job Design, Intrinsic Motivation, and Satisfaction

LEARNING OBJECTIVES

After reading the material in this chapter, you should be able to:

- Discuss the job performance model of motivation.

- Contrast Maslow's and McClelland's need theories.

- Describe the mechanistic, motivational, biological, and perceptual-motor approaches to job design.

- Review the four intrinsic rewards underlying intrinsic motivation, and discuss how managers can cultivate intrinsic motivation in others.

- Discuss the causes and consequences of job satisfaction.

- Describe the values model of work–family conflict.

U.S. industries lose nearly $300 billion a year—or $7,500 per worker—in employee absenteeism, diminished productivity, employee turnover and direct medical, legal and insurance fees related to workplace stress, according to the American Institute of Stress.

Employee wellness resources are an important way of maintaining employee motivation at IBM's TJ Watson Research Center in Yorktown Heights, NY.

Some organizations have responded to this and other business challenges, by creating workplaces that do more than just improve productivity; they aim to build a strong, vibrant organizational culture that supports the company itself. For instance, the Comporium Group, a South Carolina-based group of telecommunications com-panies, recently created a joint employee-management committee that evaluates ideas for new products and services in order to empower employees and reinforce their worth to the company. . . .

• Large for-profit: *ARUP Laboratories.* This Salt Lake City–based reference laboratory aims to create a balanced workplace by promoting the health and well-being of employees and their families. To do so, the lab offers a free, on-site health clinic that is open six days a week to provide services ranging from preventive to urgent care to employees and their families. The laboratory also aims to involve employees in a broad spectrum of company decisions through employee surveys, town hall meetings and "brown bag" lunches where executives answer other employees' questions. The bottom line? ARUP staff have increased their productivity, with an average of 598 tests per person per month in 2005, up from 530 tests per person per month in 2001.

• Large for-profit: *IBM—T.J. Watson Research Center.* Health and safety at IBM's Yorktown Heights, N.Y., research facility are a high priority. IBM maintains an extensive menu of employee wellness resources that includes online tools, classes on a variety of health-related topics and access to a workout center and other sports and recreation facilities. Other opportunities available to IBM employees at the worksite include health screenings, wellness evaluations, immunizations and lunch-and-learn presentations. The company's corporate commitment to the "whole employee" is also evident in the educational and training resources available through IBM's Global Campus Web site, which features thousands of online training options on topics ranging from nanoscience to business administration. The bottom line? Repeat measurements show a reduction in employee health risks and IBM's U.S. health insurance premiums from 1999–2005 were, on average, 4.7 percent lower than the national average and 6 to 15 percent lower than industry norms. . . .

- Small for-profit: *Versant Inc.* This marketing communications firm, based in Milwaukee, makes a commitment to enhancing employee growth and development to help each associate reach his or her potential. As such, Versant's culture allows all employees to make important decisions, contribute to the company's success and assume responsibility for results. Versant

encourages employees' continuous learning and development through coaching and mentoring, roundtable discussions, funded membership in trade organizations and on- and off-site education as a means of improving client solutions. The bottom line? Since 2001, Versant's productivity has increased 36 percent and fees billed per full-time worker have increased 31 percent.

- Not-for-profit: *Great River Health Systems.* This West Burlington, Iowa, health-care system's corporate culture is built upon a customer service philosophy dubbed EXCEL, or "being Enthusiastically friendly, X-ceeding expectations, showing Care and compassion, displaying Energetic teamwork, and through Leadership and professionalism." Building upon those values, Great River has developed programs that train employees to help new staff members transition

into the organization and that support cross-training to improve services and workplace relationships. The company also provides a number of services to help employees manage other life demands, such as adoption assistance, sick-child day care services in the pediatrics department and a lactation room for nursing mothers. The bottom line? Great River's turnover rate is 12.8 percent—compared with an average of 18 percent for hospitals in Iowa, and 17 percent for hospitals nationally.[1] . . .

FOR DISCUSSION

Which of the four companies profiled in the vignette would you most like to work for? Explain your rationale. For an interpretation of this case and additional comments, visit our Online Learning Center at

www.mhhe.com/kinickiob3e

EFFECTIVE EMPLOYEE MOTIVATION has long been one of management's most difficult and important duties. Success in this endeavor is becoming more challenging in light of organizational trends to downsize and reengineer and the demands associated with managing a diverse workforce. As revealed in the opening case, companies such as ARUP Laboratories, IBM, Versant, Inc., and Great River Health Systems consider employee motivation and satisfaction as critical for organizational success. The purpose of this chapter, as well as the next, is to provide you with a foundation for understanding the complexities of employee motivation.

After discussing the fundamentals of employee motivation, this chapter focuses on (1) an overview of job design methods used to motivate employees, (2) the process of enhancing intrinsic motivation, and (3) job satisfaction and work–family relationships. Coverage of employee motivation extends to Chapter 7.

The Fundamentals of Employee Motivation

The term *motivation* derives from the Latin word *movere,* meaning "to move." In the present context, **motivation** represents "those psychological processes that cause the arousal, direction, and persistence of voluntary actions that are goal directed."[2] Managers need to understand these psychological processes if they are to successfully guide employees toward accomplishing organizational objectives. This section thus provides a conceptual framework for understanding motivation and examines need theories of motivation.

> **motivation**
> **Psychological processes that arouse and direct goal-directed behavior.**

A Job Performance Model of Motivation

Terence Mitchell, a well-known OB researcher, proposed a broad conceptual model that explains how motivation influences job behaviors and performance. This model, which is shown in Figure 6–1, integrates elements from several of the theories we discuss in this book. It identifies the causes and consequences of motivation.[3]

Figure 6–1 shows that individual inputs and job context are the two key categories of factors that influence motivation. As discussed in Chapter 5, employees bring ability, job knowledge, dispositions and traits, emotions, moods, beliefs, and values to the work setting. The job context includes the physical environment, the tasks one completes, the organization's approach to recognition and rewards, the adequacy of supervisory support and coaching, and the organization's culture (recall our discussion in Chapter 2). These two categories of factors influence each other as well as the motivational processes of arousal, direction, and persistence. Consider how the job context within Wal-Mart's stores and its corporate headquarters influences the motivation of managers working in these different locations.

> **Group Exercise**
>
> What Motivates You?

Wal-Mart's strategy depends on standardization of store operations coupled with economies of scale in merchandising, marketing, and distribution. To ensure standardization, Wal-Mart sets the span of control for store managers at the "narrow" end of the scale. Although they nominally control their stores, Wal-Mart site managers have limited decision rights regarding hours of operation, merchandising displays, and pricing. By contrast, the span of control for managers at corporate headquarters who oversee merchandising and other core operations is set at "wide." They are responsible for implementing best practices and consolidating operations to

FIGURE 6–1 │ A Job Performance Model of Motivation

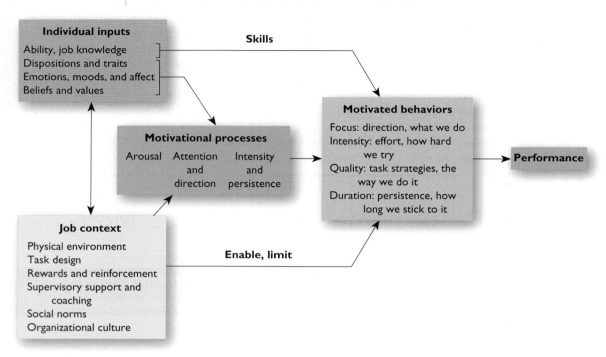

SOURCE: Adapted from T R Mitchell and D Daniels, "Motivation," in *Handbook of Psychology* (Vol 12), eds W C Borman, D R Ilgen, and R J Klimoski (Hoboken, NJ: John Wiley & Sons, Inc., 2003), p 226.

capture economies of scale. In addition to controlling purchasing, merchandising, and distribution, these managers even control the lighting and temperature at Wal-Mart's 3,500 stores by remote computer.[4]

Which location would you find more motivational? Both of us would prefer the corporate office because we value autonomy and the freedom to make decisions.

In support of the idea that job context influences employee motivation and performance, economics professors Sandra Black and Lisa Lynch estimated that 89% of the growth in multifactor productivity in the 1990s (i.e., the growth in productivity that goes beyond investments in new technology) was due to innovative workplace practices.[5] Examples include job rotation, which is discussed later in this chapter, tying compensation to performance (see Chapters 7 and 8), and employee empowerment (see Chapter 13).

Figure 6–1 further reveals that *motivated behaviors* are directly affected by an individual's ability and job knowledge (skills), motivation, and a combination of enabling and limiting job context factors. For instance, it would be difficult to persist on a project if you were working with defective raw materials or broken equipment. In contrast, motivated behaviors are likely to be enhanced when managers supply employees with adequate resources to get the job done and provide effective coaching. This coaching might entail furnishing employees with successful role models, showing employees how to complete complex tasks, and helping them maintain high self-efficacy and self-esteem (recall the discussion in Chapter 5). Performance is, in turn, influenced by motivated behavior.

Need Theories of Motivation

Need theories attempt to pinpoint internal factors that energize behavior. **Needs** are physiological or psychological deficiencies that arouse behavior. They can be strong or weak and are influenced by environmental factors. Human needs thus vary over time and place. Two popular need theories are discussed in this section: Maslow's need hierarchy theory and McClelland's need theory.

> **needs**
>
> **Physiological or psychological deficiencies that arouse behavior.**

Maslow's Need Hierarchy Theory   In 1943, psychologist Abraham Maslow published his now-famous need hierarchy theory of motivation. Although the theory was based on his clinical observation of a few neurotic individuals, it has subsequently been used to explain the entire spectrum of human behavior. Maslow proposed that motivation is a function of five basic needs—physiological, safety, love, esteem, and self-actualization.

Maslow said these five need categories are arranged in a prepotent hierarchy. In other words, he believed human needs generally emerge in a predictable stair-step fashion. Accordingly, when one's physiological needs are relatively satisfied, one's safety needs emerge, and so on up the need hierarchy, one step at a time. Once a need is satisfied it activates the next higher need in the hierarchy. This process continues until the need for self-actualization is activated.[6]

Although research does not clearly support this theory of motivation, there is one key managerial implication of Maslow's theory worth noting. That is, a satisfied need may lose its motivational potential. Therefore, managers are advised to motivate employees by devising programs or practices aimed at satisfying emerging or unmet needs. Many companies have responded to this recommendation by offering employees targeted benefits that meet their specific needs. Consider Robert W Baird & Co., an investment management firm located in Milwaukee, for example. For the third year in a row, Robert W Baird was ranked as one of *Fortune* magazine's 100 best companies to work for. They were ranked 31st in 2005. The company "encourages associates to find a balance between work, home and the community, and provides perks such as flexible work arrangement, tuition reimbursement, and online and classroom training through the firm's in-house Baird University."[7] The company also has a 37.5-hour work week and it varies employee health insurance contributions based on workers' income: "Lower-income workers pay 19% on average, higher-income workers pay 35%."[8] In conclusion, managers are more likely to fuel employee motivation by offering benefits and rewards that meet individual needs.

McClelland's Need Theory   David McClelland, a well-known psychologist, has been studying the relationship between needs and behavior since the late 1940s. Although he is most recognized for his research on the need for achievement, he also investigated the needs for affiliation and power. Let us consider each of these needs:

- The **need for achievement** is defined by the following desires:

  To accomplish something difficult. To master, manipulate, or organize physical objects, human beings, or ideas. To do this as rapidly and as independently as possible. To overcome obstacles and attain a high standard. To excel one's self. To rival and surpass others. To increase self-regard by the successful exercise of talent.[9]

> **need for achievement**
>
> **Desire to accomplish something difficult.**

As a child growing up in Japan, Junko Tabei was called weak and frail by other children. In 1975, Tabei led an all-woman expedition to the summit of Mount Everest. Twelve days after living through an avalanche, she became the first woman to ever reach the top.

Achievement-motivated people share three common characteristics: (1) a preference for working on tasks of moderate difficulty; (2) a preference for situations in which performance is due to their efforts rather than other factors, such as luck; and (3) they desire more feedback on their successes and failures than do low achievers. A review of research on the "entrepreneurial" personality showed that entrepreneurs were found to have a higher need for achievement than nonentrepreneurs.[10]

- People with a high **need for affiliation** prefer to spend more time maintaining social relationships, joining groups, and wanting to be loved. Individuals high in this need are not the most effective managers or leaders because they have a hard time making difficult decisions without worrying about being disliked.

- The **need for power** reflects an individual's desire to influence, coach, teach, or encourage others to achieve. People with a high need for power like to work and are concerned with discipline and self-respect. There is a positive and negative side to this need. The negative face of power is characterized by an "if I win, you lose" mentality. In contrast, people with a positive orientation to power focus on accomplishing group goals and helping employees obtain the feeling of competence. More is said about the two faces of power in Chapter 13. Because effective managers must positively influence others, McClelland proposes that top managers should have a high need for power coupled with a low need for affiliation. He also believes that individuals with high achievement motivation are *not* best suited for top management positions. Several studies support these propositions.[11]

There are three managerial implications associated with McClelland's need theory. First, given that adults can be trained to increase their achievement motivation, and achievement motivation is correlated with performance, organizations should consider the benefits of providing achievement training for employees.[12] Second, achievement, affiliation, and power needs can be considered during the selection process, for better placement. For example, a study revealed that people with a high need for achievement were more attracted to companies that had a pay-for-performance environment than were those with a low achievement motivation.[13] Finally, managers should create challenging task assignments or goals because the need for achievement is positively correlated with goal commitment, which, in turn, influences performance.[14]

need for affiliation

Desire to spend time in social relationships and activities.

need for power

Desire to influence, coach, teach, or encourage others to achieve.

Motivating Employees through Job Design

job design

Changing the content and/or process of a specific job to increase job satisfaction and performance.

Job design, also referred to as job redesign, "refers to any set of activities that involve the alteration of specific jobs or interdependent systems of jobs with the intent of improving the quality of employee job experience and their on-the-job productivity."[15] A team of researchers examined the various methods for conducting job design and integrated them into an interdisciplinary framework that contains four major approaches: mechanistic, motivational, biological, and perceptual-motor.[16] As you will learn, each approach to job design emphasizes different outcomes. This section discusses these four approaches to job design and focuses most heavily on the motivational methods.

The Mechanistic Approach

The mechanistic approach draws from research in industrial engineering and scientific management and is most heavily influenced by the work of Frederick Taylor. Taylor, a mechanical engineer, developed the principles of scientific management based on research and experimentation to determine the most efficient way to perform jobs. Because jobs are highly specialized and standardized when they are designed according to the principles of scientific management, this approach to job design targets efficiency, flexibility, and employee productivity.

Designing jobs according to the principles of scientific management has both positive and negative consequences. Positively, employee efficiency and productivity are increased. On the other hand, research reveals that simplified, repetitive jobs also lead to job dissatisfaction, poor mental health, higher levels of stress, and low sense of accomplishment and personal growth.[17] These negative consequences paved the way for several motivational approaches to job design.

Motivational Approaches

The motivational approaches to job design attempt to improve employees' affective and attitudinal reactions such as job satisfaction and intrinsic motivation as well as a host of behavioral outcomes such as absenteeism, turnover, and performance. We discuss three key motivational techniques: job enlargement, job enrichment, and a contingency approach called the job characteristics model.

"You seem to be bored and listless. How about a little 300 volt electric shock to perk you up?"

Copyright © Ted Goff. Reprinted with permission.

Job Enlargement   This technique was first used in the late 1940s in response to complaints about tedious and overspecialized jobs. **Job enlargement** involves putting more variety into a worker's job by combining specialized tasks of comparable difficulty. Some call this *horizontally loading* the job. Researchers recommend using job enlargement as part of a broader approach that uses multiple motivational methods because it does not have a significant and lasting positive effect on job performance by itself.[18]

Job Rotation   As with job enlargement, job rotation's purpose is to give employees greater variety in their work. **Job rotation** calls for moving employees from one specialized job to another. Rather than performing only one job, workers are trained and given the opportunity to perform two or more separate jobs on a rotating basis. By rotating employees from job to job, managers believe they can stimulate interest and motivation while providing employees with a broader perspective of the organization. Other proposed advantages of job rotation include increased worker flexibility and easier scheduling because employees are cross-trained to perform different jobs. General Electric, for example, experienced many of these benefits from its rotation program for human resource (HR) entry-level employees.

The goal of the program is to hire talented people who can become senior HR leaders in the company. . . . The program offers tremendous

job enlargement

Putting more variety into a job.

job rotation

Moving employees from one specialized job to another.

opportunities to participants, says Peters [Susan Peters is vice president for executive development]. "The big attraction is the variety they get in the first few years," she says. "They see different businesses and different functions. You might start in labor relations, and then go to compensation, then to staffing, then benefits."

About a decade ago, GE added a cross-functional rotation to the mix, and it has become a key component of the program's success. "You have to go on the audit staff or become a marketing person for one rotation," Peters says. "We've learned that the HR function has to have good connectivity with the business operations and it improves the credibility of the individual later on."[19]

Despite positive experiences from companies like GE, it is not possible to draw firm conclusions about the value of job rotation programs because they have not been adequately researched.

Job Enrichment   Job enrichment is the practical application of Frederick Herzberg's motivator–hygiene theory of job satisfaction. Herzberg's theory is based on a landmark study in which he interviewed 203 accountants and engineers.[20] These interviews sought to determine the factors responsible for job satisfaction and dissatisfaction. Herzberg found separate and distinct clusters of factors associated with job satisfaction and dissatisfaction. Job satisfaction was more frequently associated with achievement, recognition, characteristics of the work, responsibility, and advancement.

motivators

Job characteristics associated with job satisfaction.

These factors were all related to outcomes associated with the *content* of the task being performed. Herzberg labeled these factors **motivators** because each was associated with strong effort and good performance. He hypothesized that motivators cause a person to move from a state of no satisfaction to satisfaction (see Figure 6–2). Therefore, Herzberg's theory predicts managers can motivate individuals by incorporating "motivators" into an individual's job.

FIGURE 6–2
Herzberg's Motivator–Hygiene Model

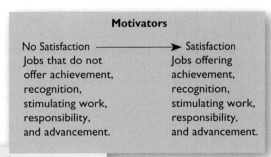

SOURCE: Adapted in part from D A Whitsett and E K Winslow, "An Analysis of Studies Critical of the Motivator–Hygiene Theory," *Personnel Psychology*, Winter 1967, pp 391–415.

Jesse Kiefer, a gumologist, is a good example of someone who is energized by the motivators contained in his job. Here is what he said to a reporter from *Fortune* about his job.

> Some days I don't blow any bubbles. Other days I have to blow a lot. It depends on what stage we are in the project. A piece of gum weighs just one to seven grams, but it's packed with a lot of different technology. It has to deliver a burst of flavor, a lot of sweetness, and a lot of tartness if it's a fruit gum. Our team figures out how to combine all those. For example, Trident Splash Strawberry with Lime—it's not easy to pick lime and strawberry flavors that complement each other. . . . When we work on the gum in its raw form, sometimes we use a hatchet to chop it up. I did my graduate work as a chemical engineer, and I started out working on detergent and soaps. But with gum there's just so many flavors! I find the job very stimulating.[21]

Jesse Kiefer (right) finds many rewards in his job as gumologist for Cadbury Schweppes, maker of Trident gum.

Herzberg found job *dissatisfaction* to be associated primarily with factors in the work *context* or environment. Specifically, company policy and administration, technical supervision, salary, interpersonal relations with one's supervisor, and working conditions were most frequently mentioned by employees expressing job dissatisfaction. Herzberg labeled this second cluster of factors **hygiene factors.** He further proposed that they were not motivational. At best, according to Herzberg's interpretation, an individual will experience no job dissatisfaction when he or she has no grievances about hygiene factors (refer to Figure 6–2).

hygiene factors

Job characteristics associated with job dissatisfaction.

The key to adequately understanding Herzberg's motivator–hygiene theory is recognizing that he believes that satisfaction is not the opposite of dissatisfaction. Herzberg concludes that "the opposite of job satisfaction is not job dissatisfaction, but rather no job satisfaction; and similarly, the opposite of job dissatisfaction is not job satisfaction, but no dissatisfaction."[22] Herzberg thus asserts that the dissatisfaction–satisfaction continuum contains a zero midpoint at which dissatisfaction and satisfaction are absent. Conceivably, an organization member who has good supervision, pay, and working conditions but a tedious and unchallenging task with little chance of advancement would be at the zero midpoint. That person would have no dissatisfaction (because of good hygiene factors) and no satisfaction (because of a lack of motivators).

Herzberg's theory generated a great deal of research and controversy. Although research does not support the two-factor aspect of his theory, it does support many of the theory's implications for job design.[23] Job enrichment is based on the application of Herzberg's ideas. Specifically, **job enrichment** entails modifying a job such that an employee has the opportunity to experience achievement, recognition, stimulating work, responsibility, and advancement. These characteristics are incorporated into a job through vertical loading. Rather than giving employees additional tasks of similar difficulty (horizontal loading), *vertical loading* consists of giving workers more responsibility. In other words, employees take on chores normally performed by their supervisors.

job enrichment

Building achievement, recognition, stimulating work, responsibility, and advancement into a job.

The Job Characteristics Model   Two OB researchers, J Richard Hackman and Greg Oldham, played a central role in developing the job characteristics approach. These researchers tried to determine how work can be structured so that employees are internally or intrinsically motivated. **Intrinsic motivation** occurs when an individual is "turned on to one's work because of the positive internal feelings that are generated by doing well, rather than being dependent on external factors (such as incentive pay or compliments from the boss) for the motivation to work effectively."[24] These positive feelings power a self-perpetuating cycle of motivation. As shown in Figure 6–3, internal work motivation is determined by three psychological states. In turn, these psychological states are fostered by the presence of five core job characteristics. As you can see in Figure 6–3, the object of this approach is to promote high intrinsic motivation by designing jobs that possess the five core job characteristics shown in Figure 6–3. Let us examine the core job characteristics.

intrinsic motivation

Motivation caused by positive internal feelings.

core job characteristics

Job characteristics found to various degrees in all jobs.

In general terms, **core job characteristics** are common characteristics found to a varying degree in all jobs. Three of the job characteristics shown in Figure 6–3 combine to determine experienced meaningfulness of work:

- *Skill variety.* The extent to which the job requires an individual to perform a variety of tasks that require him or her to use different skills and abilities.

- *Task identity.* The extent to which the job requires an individual to perform a whole or completely identifiable piece of work. In other words, task identity is high when a person works on a product or project from beginning to end and sees a tangible result.

FIGURE 6–3 | The Job Characteristics Model

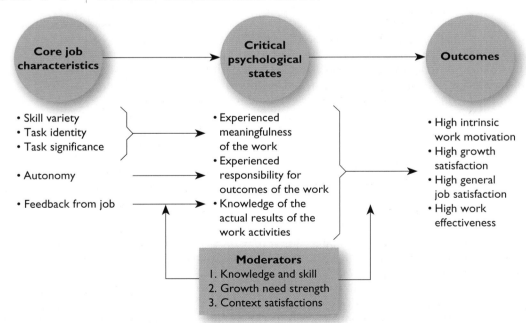

SOURCE: From J R Hackman and G R Oldham, *Work Redesign*, 1st Edition. Copyright © 1980. Adapted by permission of Pearson Education, Inc., Upper Saddle River, NJ.

- *Task significance.* The extent to which the job affects the lives of other people within or outside the organization.

Experienced responsibility is elicited by the job characteristic of autonomy, defined as follows:

- *Autonomy.* The extent to which the job enables an individual to experience freedom, independence, and discretion in both scheduling and determining the procedures used in completing the job.

Finally, knowledge of results is fostered by the job characteristic of feedback, defined as follows:

- *Feedback.* The extent to which an individual receives direct and clear information about how effectively he or she is performing the job.[25]

Hackman and Oldham recognized that everyone does not want a job containing high amounts of the five core job characteristics. They incorporated this conclusion into their model by identifying three attributes that affect how individuals respond to job enrichment. These attributes are concerned with the individual's knowledge and skill, growth need strength (representing the desire to grow and develop as an individual), and context satisfactions (see the box labeled Moderators in Figure 6–3). Context satisfactions represent the extent to which employees are satisfied with various aspects of their job, such as satisfaction with pay, co-workers, and supervision.

There are several practical implications associated with using the job characteristics model to enhance intrinsic motivation: Steps for applying this model are shown in Skills & Best Practices. Managers may want to use this model to increase employee job satisfaction. Research overwhelmingly demonstrates a moderately strong relationship between job characteristics and satisfaction.[26] Consistent with this finding, Northwest Community Hospital in Arlington Heights, Illinois, and Principal Financial Group in Des Moines, Iowa, attempted to enhance employees' satisfaction by designing more autonomy into employees' jobs. Both organizations allow employees to select from a variety of work schedules that meet their needs. At Principal Financial Group, for example, 69% of the workers use flexible hours, 20% use compressed workweeks, and the remainder spends some portion of time working from home.[27]

Moreover, research suggests that managers can enhance employees' intrinsic motivation, initiative, creativity, innovation, and commitment to their performance goals by increasing the core job characteristics.[28] Two separate meta-analyses also support the practice of using the job characteristics model to help managers reduce absenteeism and turnover.[29] On the negative side, however, job redesign appears to reduce the quantity of output just as often as it has a positive effect. Caution and situational appropriateness are advised. For example, one study demonstrated that job redesign works better in less complex organizations (small plants or companies).[30] Nonetheless, managers are likely to

---

Steps for Applying the Job Characteristics Model

1. Diagnose the work environment to determine the level of employee motivation and job satisfaction. Job design should be used when employee motivation ranges from low to moderately high. The diagnosis can be made using employee surveys.

2. Determine whether job redesign is appropriate for a given group of employees. Job redesign is most likely to work in a participative environment in which employees have the necessary knowledge and skills to perform the enriched tasks and their job satisfaction is average to high.

3. Determine how to best redesign the job. The focus of this effort is to increase those core job characteristics that are low. Employee input is essential during this step to determine the details of a redesign initiative.

SKILLS & BEST PRACTICES

find noticeable increases in the quality of performance after a job redesign program. Results from 21 experimental studies revealed that job redesign resulted in a median increase of 28% in the quality of performance.[31]

Job characteristics research also underscores an additional implication for companies undergoing reengineering. Reengineering potentially leads to negative work outcomes because it increases job characteristics beyond reasonable levels. This occurs for two reasons: (1) reengineering requires employees to use a wider variety of skills to perform their jobs, and (2) reengineering typically results in downsizing and short-term periods of understaffing.[32] The unfortunate catch is that understaffing was found to produce lower levels of group performance, and jobs with either overly low or high levels of job characteristics were associated with higher stress.[33] Managers are advised to carefully consider the level of perceived job characteristics when implementing reengineering initiatives.

Biological and Perceptual-Motor Approaches

The biological approach to job design benefits from the development of ergonomic office equipment, like the Kinesis ergonomic keyboard shown here.

The biological approach to job design is based on research from biomechanics, work physiology, and ergonomics and focuses on designing the work environment to reduce employees' physical strain, fatigue, and health complaints. An attempt is made to redesign jobs so that they eliminate or reduce the amount of repetitive motions from a worker's job. Intel, for example, has implemented the biological approach to job design.

At Intel, the most common types of workplace injuries are musculoskeletal disorders. That's one reason the company has stepped up efforts to prevent and treat repetitive-motion injuries. When employees change offices, Intel will tear down and rebuild their workstations if needed so that they are ergonomically customized. They've created an ergonomics-profile database for their Santa Clara, CA, facility which includes information on workers' heights, preferred chairs, mouse arrangement, ideal desk heights, and whether employees are left- or right-handed. A companywide database is under development.[34]

The perceptual-motor approach is derived from research that examines human factors engineering, perceptual and cognitive skills, and information processing. This approach to job design emphasizes the reliability of work outcomes by examining error rates, accidents, and workers' feedback about facilities and equipment.[35] IBM and Steelcase are jointly developing a new interactive office system, labeled BlueSpace, that is based on this method of job design. Its features include[36]

- *BlueScreen:* A touch screen that sits next to a user's computer monitor and puts users in control of their heat or cooling, ventilation, and light.
- *Everywhere Display:* A video projector that displays information on walls, floors, desktops, and other surfaces.
- *Monitor rail:* A moving rail that consists of a work surface that travels the length of a work space and a dual monitor arm that rotates to nearly a complete circle, letting users be positioned almost anywhere.

- *Threshold:* An L-shaped partial ceiling and wall on wheels that provides on-demand visual and territorial privacy to a user.

The frequency of using both the biological and perceptual-motor approaches to job redesign is increasing in light of the number of workers who experience injuries related to overexertion or repetitive motion. **Repetitive motion disorders (RMDs)** are "a family of muscular conditions that result from repeated motions performed in the course of normal work or daily activities. "RMDs include carpal tunnel syndrome, bursitis, tendonitis, epicondyliltis, ganglion cyst, tenosynovitis, and trigger finger. RMDs are caused by too many uninterrupted repetitions of an activity or motion, unnatural or awkward motions such as twisting the arm or wrist, overexertion, incorrect posture, or muscle fatigue."[37] Data from the US Department of Labor shows that RMDs result in the longest absences from work among the leading causes of absenteeism. The median time lost due to RMDs in 2005 was 23 days.[38] To combat this problem, the Occupational Safety and Health Administration (OSHA) implemented a new set of guidelines regarding ergonomic standards in the workplace due to this trend. The standards went into effect on October 14, 2001.

> **repetitive motion disorders (RMDs)**
>
> Muscular disorder caused by repeated motions.

Cultivating Intrinsic Motivation

The Gallup Organization has been studying employee engagement around the world for many years. It completed a study of employee engagement in the United States and 10 other countries. Sadly, results reveal that 31%, 52%, and 17% of the US workforce is actively engaged at work (i.e., loyal, productive, and satisfied), not engaged (i.e., not psychologically committed to their work role), and actively disengaged (i.e., disenchanted with their workplace) at work, respectively. Gallup estimates that the behavior and lower productivity of actively disengaged workers cost the US economy about $370 billion a year.[39] Results further reveal that the pattern of employee engagement is lower among the other 10 countries. These countries include Canada, Germany, Japan, Great Britain, Chile, France, Israel, Australia, New Zealand, and Singapore. Singapore, for instance, ranks among the lowest in the world in employee engagement, costing about $6 billion annually in lost productivity.[40]

Managers play a major role in the extent to which employees are engaged at work. Quite simply, employees tend to engage at work when they are intrinsically motivated. It thus is important to have an understanding of how managers can influence employees' intrinsic motivation.

We begin our exploration of intrinsic motivation by discussing the difference between intrinsic and extrinsic motivation and then presenting a model of intrinsic motivation. We conclude by reviewing the research and managerial implications pertaining to the model of intrinsic motivation.

The Foundation of Intrinsic Motivation

Intrinsic motivation was defined earlier as being driven by positive feelings associated with doing well on a task or job. Intrinsically motivated people are driven to act for the fun or challenge associated with a task rather than because of external rewards, pressures, or requests. Motivation comes from the psychological rewards

Group Exercise

What Rewards Motivate Student Achievement?

extrinsic motivation

Motivation caused by the desire to attain specific outcomes.

Are Olympic athletes like Sasha Cohen intrinsically or extrinsically motivated?

associated with doing well on a task that one enjoys. It is important to note that individual differences exist when it comes to intrinsic motivation. People are intrinsically motivated for some activities and not others, and everyone is not intrinsically motivated by the same tasks.[41] For example, while the authors of this book are intrinsically motivated to write, we do not jump for joy when asked to proofread hundreds of pages. In contrast, someone else may hate to write but love the task of finding typos in a document.

In contrast to completing tasks for the joy of doing them, **extrinsic motivation** drives people's behavior when they do things in order to attain a specific outcome. In other words, extrinsic motivation is fueled by a person's desire to avoid or achieve some type of consequence for his or her behavior.[42] For example, a student who completes homework because he or she wants to avoid the embarrassment of being called on in class without knowing the answer is extrinsically motivated because he or she is doing it to avoid the negative outcome of being embarrassed. Similarly, a student who does homework because he or she believes it will help him or her obtain a job also is extrinsically motivated because he or she is studying for its instrumental value rather than because of pure interest. As you can see, extrinsic motivation is related to the receipt of extrinsic rewards. *Extrinsic rewards* do not come from the work itself; they are given by others (e.g., teachers, managers, parents, friends, or customers). At work, they include things like salaries, bonuses, promotions, benefits, awards, and titles.

There has been an extensive amount of research on the topic of intrinsic motivation. The majority of this research relied on students performing tasks in laboratory experiments to determine whether or not the use of extrinsic rewards dampened their intrinsic motivation. Unfortunately, the overall pattern of results has created controversy and debate among researchers. Nonetheless, this conclusion does not detract from the value of focusing on the positive application of intrinsic motivation at work.

A Model of Intrinsic Motivation

Kenneth Thomas proposed the most recent model of intrinsic motivation. He developed his model by integrating research on empowerment, which is discussed in Chapter 13, with two previous models of intrinsic motivation.[43] Thomas specifically linked components of the job characteristics model of job design discussed in the last section with Edward Deci and Richard Ryan's cognitive evaluation theory. Deci and Ryan proposed people must satisfy their needs for autonomy and competence when completing a task for it to be intrinsically motivating.[44] Thomas's model is shown in Figure 6–4.

Figure 6–4 illustrates the four key intrinsic rewards underlying an individual's level of intrinsic motivation. Looking across the rows, rewards of meaningfulness and progress are derived from the purpose for completing various tasks, while the sense of choice and sense of competence come from the specific tasks one completes. Looking down the columns, the sense of choice and meaningfulness are related to the opportunity to use one's own judgment and to pursue a worthwhile purpose. In contrast, accomplishment rewards—a sense of competence and progress—are derived from the extent to which individuals feel competent in completing tasks and successful in attaining their original task purpose, respectively. Thomas believes intrinsic motivation is a direct result of the extent to which an individual experiences these four intrinsic rewards while working. Let us examine these intrinsic rewards in more detail.

FIGURE 6–4
A Model of Intrinsic Motivation

SOURCE: Reprinted with permission of the publisher. From *Intrinsic Motivation at Work: Building Energy and Commitment.* Copyright © 2000 by K Thomas. Berrett-Koehler Publishers, Inc., San Francisco, CA. All rights reserved, www.bkconnection.com.

Sense of Meaningfulness
"A **sense of meaningfulness** is the opportunity you feel to pursue a worthy task purpose. The feeling of meaningfulness is the feeling that you are on a path that is worth your time and energy—that you are on a valuable mission, that your purpose matters in the larger scheme of things."[45] This description reveals that it is not the task itself that drives intrinsic motivation, but rather the overall purpose for completing tasks. People have a desire to do meaningful work, work that makes a difference. This conclusion was supported by results from a national survey of employees. Results revealed that the primary contributor to workplace pride was that employees were doing work that mattered.[46]

sense of meaningfulness
The task purpose is important and meaningful.

Sense of Choice
"A **sense of choice** is the opportunity you feel to select task activities that make sense to you and to perform them in ways that seem appropriate. The feeling of choice is the feeling of being free to choose—of being able to use your own judgment and act out of your own understanding of the task."[47] Nordstrom's, for example, grants employees much latitude in determining how best to provide customer service. The company tells employees to use good judgment and to treat their job as if they were running their own business.[48]

sense of choice
The ability to use judgment and freedom when completing tasks.

Sense of Competence
"A **sense of competence** is the accomplishment you feel in skillfully performing task activities you have chosen. The feeling of competence involves the sense that you are doing good, high-quality work on a task."[49] A sense of competence also is related to the level of challenge associated with completing tasks. In general, people feel a greater sense of competence by completing challenging tasks.

sense of competence
Feelings of accomplishment associated with doing high-quality work.

Sense of Progress
"A **sense of progress** is the accomplishment you feel in achieving the task purpose. The feeling of progress involves the sense that the task is moving forward, that your activities are really accomplishing something."[50] A sense of progress promotes intrinsic motivation because it reinforces the feeling that one is wisely spending his or her time. A low sense of progress leads to discouragement. Over time, a low sense of progress can lower enthusiasm and lead to feelings of being stuck or helpless.

sense of progress
Feeling that one is accomplishing something important.

Are You Intrinsically Motivated at Work?

INSTRUCTIONS: The following survey was designed to assess the extent to which you are deriving intrinsic rewards from your current job: If you are not working, use a past job or your role as a student to complete the survey. There are no right or wrong answers to the statements. Circle your answer by using the rating scale provided. After evaluating each of the survey statements, complete the scoring guide.

	Strongly Disagree	Disagree	Neither Agree or Disagree	Agree	Strongly Agree
1. I am passionate about my work.	1	2	3	4	5
2. I can see how my work tasks contribute to my organization's corporate vision.	1	2	3	4	5
3. I have significant autonomy in determining how I do my job.	1	2	3	4	5
4. My supervisor/manager delegates important projects/tasks to me that significantly impact my department's overall success.	1	2	3	4	5
5. I have mastered the skills necessary for my job.	1	2	3	4	5
6. My supervisor/manager recognizes when I competently perform my job.	1	2	3	4	5
7. Throughout the year, my department celebrates its progress toward achieving its goals.	1	2	3	4	5
8. I regularly receive evidence/information about my progress toward achieving my overall performance goals.	1	2	3	4	5

SCORING KEY

Sense of meaningfulness (add items 1–2) _____

Sense of choice (add items 3–4) _____

Sense of competence (add items 5–6) _____

Sense of progress (add items 7–8) _____

Overall score (add all items) _____

ARBITRARY NORMS

For each intrinsic reward, a score of 2–4 indicates low intrinsic motivation, 5–7 represents moderate intrinsic motivation, and 8–10 indicates high intrinsic motivation. For the overall score, 8–19 is low, 20–30 is moderate, and 31–40 is high.

Research and Managerial Implications

Before discussing research and managerial implications, we would like you to complete the Hands-On Exercise entitled "Are You Intrinsically Motivated at Work?" It assesses the level of intrinsic motivation in your current or past job. How did you stack up? Does your job need a dose of intrinsic rewards? If it does, the following discussion outlines how you or your manager might attempt to increase your intrinsic motivation.

Thomas's model of intrinsic motivation has not been subjected to much research at this point in time. This is partly due to its newness in the field of organizational behavior and the fact that the model is based on integrating theories—the job characteristics model and cognitive evaluation theory—that have been supported by past research. This leads us to conclude that the basic formulation of the model appears to be on solid ground, and future research is needed to study the specific recommendations for leading others toward intrinsic motivation.[51] In the meantime, managers are encouraged to use a different set of managerial behaviors to increase each of the four intrinsic rewards. Let us consider these managerial behaviors.

Managers can foster a sense of *meaningfulness* by inspiring their employees and modeling desired behaviors. This can be done by helping employees to identify their passions at work and creating an exciting organizational vision that employees are motivated to pursue. This recommendation is very important in light of a recent study of employees from 336 different organizations. Results demonstrated that 66% of the respondents felt disengaged at work because they did not understand the organization's vision and business strategy.[52] Managers can lead for *choice* by empowering employees and delegating meaningful assignments and tasks. Managers can enhance a sense of *competence* by supporting and coaching their employees. Providing positive feedback and sincere recognition can also be coupled with the assignment of a challenging task to fuel the intrinsic reward of competence.[53] Finally, managers can increase employees' sense of *progress* by monitoring and rewarding them. On-the-spot incentives are a useful way to reward a broader-based group of employees. "If an employee's performance has been exceptional—such as filling in for a sick colleague, perhaps, or working nights or weekends or cutting costs for the company—the employer may reward the worker with a one-time bonus of $50, $100 or $500 shortly after the noteworthy actions."[54]

Job Satisfaction and Work–Family Relationships

An individual's work motivation is related to his or her job satisfaction and work–family relationships. Motivation is not independent of an employee's work environment or personal life. For example, your desire to study for your next OB test is jointly affected by how much you like the course and the state of your health at the time you are studying. It is very hard to study when you have a bad cold or the flu. Because of the dynamic relationships between motivation, job satisfaction, and work–family relationships, we conclude this chapter by discussing the causes and consequences of job satisfaction and work–family relationships. This information will increase your understanding about how to motivate others as well as yourself.

How Satisfied Are You with Your Present Job?

	Very Dissatisfied				Very Satisfied
1. The way I am noticed when I do a good job	1	2	3	4	5
2. The recognition I get for the work I do	1	2	3	4	5
3. The praise I get for doing a good job	1	2	3	4	5
4. How my pay compares with that for similar jobs in other companies	1	2	3	4	5
5. My pay and the amount of work I do	1	2	3	4	5
6. How my pay compares with that of other workers	1	2	3	4	5
7. The way my boss handles employees	1	2	3	4	5
8. The way my boss takes care of complaints brought to him/her by employees	1	2	3	4	5
9. The personal relationship between my boss and his/her employees	1	2	3	4	5

Total score for satisfaction with recognition (add questions 1–3), compensation (add questions 4–6), and supervision (add questions 7–9).

Comparative norms for each dimension of job satisfaction are: Total score of 3–6 = Low job satisfaction; 7–11 = Moderate satisfaction; 12 and above = High satisfaction.

SOURCE: Adapted from D J Weiss, R V Dawis, G W England, and L H Lofquist, Manual for the *Minnesota Satisfaction Questionnaire* (Minneapolis: Industrial Relations Center, University of Minnesota, 1967). Used with permission of Vocational Psychology Research, University of Minnesota.

The Causes of Job Satisfaction

job satisfaction

An affective or emotional response to one's job.

Job satisfaction is an affective or emotional response toward various facets of one's job. This definition means job satisfaction is not a unitary concept. Rather, a person can be relatively satisfied with one aspect of his or her job and dissatisfied with one or more other aspects. The Hands-On Exercise, for instance, assesses your satisfaction with recognition, compensation, and supervision. Please take a moment now to determine how satisfied you are with three aspects of your present or most recent job, and then use the norms to compare your score.[55] How do you feel about your job?

Research revealed that job satisfaction varied across countries. A study of 9,300 adults in 39 countries identified the percentage of workers who said they were "very satisfied with their jobs." The top five countries were Denmark (61%), India (urban middle- and upper-class only; 55%), Norway (54%), United States (50%), and Ireland (49%). Experts suggest that job satisfaction is highest in Denmark because labor and management have a great working relationship. The bottom five countries were Estonia (11%), China (11%), Czech Republic (10%), Ukraine (10%), and Hungary (9%). Why do Hungarian employees indicate the lowest job satisfaction? An average monthly salary of $302 and poor labor management relations are two possible causes.[56] OB researchers have identified other causes of job satisfaction and dissatisfaction.

Five predominant models of job satisfaction specify its causes. They are need fulfillment, discrepancy, value attainment, equity, and dispositional/genetic components. A brief review of these models will provide insight into the complexity of this seemingly simple concept.[57]

met expectations

The extent to which one receives what he or she expects from a job.

Need Fulfillment   These models propose that satisfaction is determined by the extent to which the characteristics of a job allow an individual to fulfill his or her needs. For example, a survey of 30 Massachusetts law firms revealed that 35% to 50% of law-firm associates left their employers within three years of starting because the firms did not accommodate family needs. This example illustrates that unmet needs can affect both satisfaction and turnover.[58] Although these models generated a great degree of controversy, it is generally accepted that need fulfillment is correlated with job satisfaction.[59]

Discrepancies   These models propose that satisfaction is a result of met expectations. **Met expectations** represent the difference between what an individual expects to receive from a job, such as good pay and promotional opportunities, and what he or she actually receives. When expectations are greater than what is received, a person will be dissatisfied. In contrast, this model predicts the individual will be satisfied when he or she attains outcomes above and beyond expectations. A meta-analysis of 31 studies that included 17,241 people demonstrated that met expectations were significantly related to job satisfaction.[60] Many companies use employee attitude or opinion surveys to assess employees' expectations and concerns (see Skills & Best Practices).

Value Attainment   The idea underlying **value attainment** is that satisfaction results from the perception that a job allows for fulfillment of an individual's important work values.[61] In general, research consistently supports the prediction that value fulfillment is positively related to job satisfaction.[62] Managers can thus enhance employee satisfaction by structuring the work environment and its associated rewards and recognition to reinforce employees' values.

Lockheed Martin Uses Surveys to Assess Employees' Job Satisfaction and Improve Employee Engagement

Bethesda, Md.-based Lockheed Martin (ranked 9 [in Fortune's 100 best companies to work for]) also uses surveys to help measure job retention efforts. The company conducts an all-employee survey biannually to assess satisfaction across 26 job attributes considered critical to recruitment, retention and performance. Survey results in 2001 showed a need for improvement in articulating the corporate mission for objectives and performance management. Lockheed's training organization played a key role in developing programs to meet those needs, including a new performance recognition system, performance management training, a formal mentoring program and training for coaching and mentoring. These carefully targeted programs worked. The results of the 2003 survey showed an 11 to 17 percent gain on all of Lockheed's targeted indices, including intention to remain and job engagement.

SOURCE: Excerpted from G Johnson, "And the Survey Says . . . ," *Training*, March 2004, p 28.

Equity   In this model, satisfaction is a function of how "fairly" an individual is treated at work. Satisfaction results from one's perception that work outcomes, relative to inputs, compare favorably with a significant other's outcomes/inputs. A meta-analysis involving 190 studies and 64,757 people supported this model. Employees' perceptions of being treated fairly at work were highly related to overall job satisfaction.[63] Managers thus are encouraged to monitor employees' fairness perceptions and to interact with employees in such a way that they feel equitably treated. Chapter 7 explores this promising model in more detail.

value attainment

The extent to which a job allows fulfillment of one's work values.

Dispositional/Genetic Components Have you ever noticed that some of your co-workers or friends appear to be satisfied across a variety of job circumstances, whereas others always seem dissatisfied? This model of satisfaction attempts to explain this pattern.[64] Specifically, the dispositional/genetic model is based on the belief that job satisfaction is partly a function of both personal traits and genetic factors. As such, this model implies that stable individual differences are just as important in explaining job satisfaction as are characteristics of the work environment. Although only a few studies have tested these propositions, results support a positive, significant relationship between personal traits and job satisfaction over time periods ranging from 2 to 50 years.[65] Genetic factors also were found to significantly predict life satisfaction, well-being, and general job satisfaction.[66] Overall, researchers estimate that 30% of an individual's job satisfaction is associated with dispositional and genetic components.[67]

Major Correlates and Consequences of Job Satisfaction

This area has significant managerial implications because thousands of studies have examined the relationship between job satisfaction and other organizational variables. Because it is impossible to examine them all, we will consider a subset of the more important variables from the standpoint of managerial relevance.

Table 6–1 summarizes the pattern of results. The relationship between job satisfaction and these other variables is either positive or negative. The strength of the relationship ranges from weak (very little relationship) to strong. Strong relationships imply that managers can significantly influence the variable of interest by increasing job satisfaction. Let us now consider several of the key correlates of job satisfaction.

TABLE 6–1 Correlates of Job Satisfaction

Variables Related with Satisfaction	Direction of Relationship	Strength of Relationship
Motivation	Positive	Moderate
Job involvement	Positive	Moderate
Organizational commitment	Positive	Moderate
Organizational citizenship behavior	Positive	Moderate
Absenteeism	Negative	Weak
Tardiness	Negative	Weak
Withdrawal cognitions	Negative	Strong
Turnover	Negative	Moderate
Heart disease	Negative	Moderate
Perceived stress	Negative	Strong
Pro-union voting	Negative	Moderate
Job performance	Positive	Moderate
Life satisfaction	Positive	Moderate
Mental health	Positive	Moderate

Motivation A recent meta-analysis of nine studies and 1,739 workers revealed a significant positive relationship between motivation and job satisfaction. Because satisfaction with supervision also was significantly correlated with motivation, managers are advised to consider how their behavior affects employee satisfaction.[68] Managers can potentially enhance employees' motivation through various attempts to increase job satisfaction.

Job Involvement Job involvement represents the extent to which an individual is personally involved with his or her work role. A meta-analysis involving 27,925 individuals from 87 different studies demonstrated that job involvement was moderately related with job satisfaction.[69] Managers are thus encouraged to foster satisfying work environments in order to fuel employees' job involvement.

Organizational Commitment Organizational commitment reflects the extent to which an individual identifies with an organization and is committed to its goals. A meta-analysis of 879 studies and 490,624 individuals uncovered a significant and moderate relationship between organizational commitment and satisfaction.[70] Managers are advised to increase job satisfaction in order to elicit higher levels of commitment. In turn, higher commitment can facilitate higher productivity.

Organizational Citizenship Behavior Organizational citizenship behaviors (OCBs) consist of employee behaviors that are beyond the call of duty. Examples include "such gestures as constructive statements about the department, expression of personal interest in the work of others, suggestions for improvement, training new people, respect for the spirit as well as the letter of housekeeping rules, care for organizational property, and punctuality and attendance well beyond standard or enforceable levels."[71] Managers certainly would like employees to exhibit these behaviors. A meta-analysis covering 7,100 people and 22 separate studies revealed a significant and moderately positive correlation between organizational citizenship behaviors and job satisfaction.[72] Moreover, additional research demonstrated that employees' citizenship behaviors were determined more by leadership and characteristics of the work environment than by an employee's personality.[73] It thus appears that managerial behavior significantly influences an employee's willingness to exhibit citizenship behaviors. This relationship is important to recognize because employees' OCBs were positively correlated with customer satisfaction, organizational commitment, and performance ratings.[74] Another recent study demonstrated a broader impact of OCBs on organizational effectiveness. Results revealed that the amount of OCBs exhibited by employees working in 28 regional restaurants was significantly associated with each restaurant's corporate profits one year later.[75] Because employees' perceptions of being treated fairly at work are related to their willingness to engage in OCBs, managers are encouraged to make and implement employee-related decisions in an equitable fashion. More is said about equity in Chapter 7.

> **organizational citizenship behaviors (OCBs)**
>
> **Employee behaviors that exceed work-role requirements.**

Absenteeism Absenteeism is not always what it appears to be, and it can be costly. For example, a 2004 study of 305 human resource executives throughout the US revealed that 35% of all absences are due to illness. The remaining 65% result from family issues (21%), personal needs (18%), entitlement mentality (14%), and

McDonald's Creative Approach for Reducing Absenteeism

To help reduce absenteeism and turnover—chronic problems for fast-food managers—McDonald's is testing an unusual program at some of its 1,250 British restaurants. Employees from the same immediate family can fill in for one another without clearing it with the boss, a new twist on job-sharing, according to Mercer Human Resources Consulting.

The so-called Family Contract is a response to surveys in which workers described juggling work and other duties as stressful. It permits family members—including same-sex partners—to sign on in pairs and take each other's shifts.

SOURCE: Excerpted from M Arndt, "The Family that Flips Together . . ." *BusinessWeek*, April 17, 2006, p 14.

stress (12%). While it is difficult to provide a precise estimate of the cost of absenteeism, findings from this study project it to be $660 per employee.[76] This would suggest that absenteeism costs $198,000 for a company with 300 employees. Imagine the costs for a company with 100,000 employees! Because of these costs, managers are constantly on the lookout for ways to reduce it: Read the accompanying Skills & Best Practices feature for a description of what McDonald's is doing. One recommendation has been to increase job satisfaction. If this is a valid recommendation, there should be a strong negative relationship (or negative correlation) between satisfaction and absenteeism. In other words, as satisfaction increases, absenteeism should decrease. A researcher tracked this prediction by synthesizing three separate meta-analyses containing a total of 74 studies. Results revealed a weak negative relationship between satisfaction and absenteeism.[77] It is unlikely, therefore, that managers will realize any significant decrease in absenteeism by increasing job satisfaction.

Withdrawal Cognitions   Although some people quit their jobs impulsively or in a fit of anger, most go through a process of thinking about whether or not they should quit. **Withdrawal cognitions** encapsulate this thought process by representing an individual's overall thoughts and feelings about quitting. What causes an individual to think about quitting his or her job? Job satisfaction is believed to be one of the most significant contributors. For example, a study of managers, salespersons, and auto mechanics from a national automotive retail store chain demonstrated that job dissatisfaction caused employees to begin the process of thinking about quitting. In turn, withdrawal cognitions had a greater impact on employee turnover than job satisfaction in this sample.[78] Results from this study imply that managers can indirectly help to reduce employee turnover by enhancing employee job satisfaction.

withdrawal cognitions

Overall thoughts and feelings about quitting a job

Turnover   Turnover is important to managers because it both disrupts organizational continuity and is very costly. Costs of turnover fall into two categories: separation costs and replacement costs.

> Separation costs may include severance pay, costs associated with an exit interview, out-placement fees, and possible litigation costs, particularly for involuntary separation. Replacement costs are the well-known costs of a hire, including sourcing expenses, HR processing costs for screening and assessing candidates, the time spent by hiring managers interviewing candidates, travel and relocation expenses, signing bonuses, if applicable, and orientation and training costs.[79]

Experts estimate that the cost of turnover for an hourly employee is roughly 30% of annual salary, whereas the cost can range up to 150% of yearly salary for professional employees.[80]

Although there are various things a manager can do to reduce employee turnover, many of them revolve around attempts to improve employees' job satisfaction. This trend is supported by results from a meta-analysis of 67 studies covering 24,556 people.

Job satisfaction obtained a moderate negative relationship with employee turnover.[81] Given the strength of this relationship, managers are advised to try to reduce employee turnover by increasing employee job satisfaction.

Perceived Stress   Stress can have very negative effects on organizational behavior and an individual's health. Stress is positively related to absenteeism, turnover, coronary heart disease, and viral infections. Based on a meta-analysis of seven studies covering 2,659 individuals, Table 6–1 reveals that perceived stress has a strong, negative relationship with job satisfaction.[82] It is hoped that managers would attempt to reduce the negative effects of stress by improving job satisfaction.

Job Performance   One of the biggest controversies within OB research centers on the relationship between job satisfaction and job performance. Although researchers have identified seven different ways in which these variables are related, the dominant beliefs are either that satisfaction causes performance or performance causes satisfaction.[83] A team of researchers recently attempted to resolve this controversy through a meta-analysis of data from 312 samples involving 54,417 individuals.[84] There were two key findings from this study. First, job satisfaction and performance are moderately related. This is an important finding because it supports the belief that employee job satisfaction is a key work attitude managers should consider when attempting to increase employees' job performance. Second, the relationship between job satisfaction and performance is much more complex than originally thought. It is not as simple as satisfaction causing performance or performance causing satisfaction. Rather, researchers now believe both variables indirectly influence each other through a host of individual differences and work-environment characteristics.[85] There is one additional consideration to keep in mind regarding the relationship between job satisfaction and job performance.

Researchers believe the relationship between satisfaction and performance is understated due to incomplete measures of individual-level performance. For example, if performance ratings used in past research did not reflect the actual interactions and interdependencies at work, inaccurate measures of performance served to lower the reported correlations between satisfaction and performance. Examining the relationship between *aggregate* measures of job satisfaction and organizational performance is one solution to correct this problem.[86] In support of these ideas, a team of researchers conducted a recent meta-analysis of 7,939 business units in 36 companies. Results uncovered significant positive relationships between business-unit-level employee satisfaction and business-unit outcomes of customer satisfaction, productivity, profit, employee turnover, and accidents.[87] It thus appears managers can positively affect a variety of important organizational outcomes, including performance, by increasing employee job satisfaction.

Work versus Family Life Conflict

A complex web of demographic and economic factors makes the balancing act between job and life very challenging for most of us. Demographically, there are more women in the workforce, more dual-income families, more single working parents, and an aging population that gives mid-career employees day care or elder care responsibilities, or both. On the economic front, years of downsizing and corporate cost-cutting have given employees heavier workloads. Meanwhile, an important trend was recently documented in a unique 25-year study of values in the United States: "employees have become less convinced that work should be an important part of one's life or that working hard makes one a better person."[88] Something has to give in this collision of trends. Too often family life suffers. Consider the case of Carol Bartz, former CEO of Autodesk.

> Over the holidays Bartz wrestled with whether it was time to leave. Fourteen years as CEO was a marathon stint in Silicon Valley. Her husband was retired, and her youngest child, Layne, would go to college soon. Before, Bartz could see her daughter between business trips; now she'd have to travel to see her. . . . Bartz, who's unabashed about her almost maternal love for Autodesk, "cried her eyes out" at the thought of leaving. She never felt she had to choose one "child" over the other, but as a working mom she had to strike a balance between her real and her metaphorical child every day.
>
> Consider this recent morning. She's in back-to-back meetings at a Starbucks near her home, dressed in jeans and an orange sweater, wearing no makeup. Earlier that morning Layne, who's anxiously awaiting responses from colleges, crawled into bed with her, something she hasn't done since she was a child. "She's more stressed than I've ever seen her," Bartz says. "I knew something was wrong and so I just hung." All the while, she knew the clock was ticking on a breakfast meeting she had scheduled. She comforted her daughter, threw on clothes, and raced out, already late. "The concept of balance is perfection," she says, miming a seesaw motion. "And that's crazy."[89]

Bartz ultimately resolved her work–life balance by resigning as CEO in May 2006 to become the company's executive chair.

In this section, we try to better understand work versus family life conflict by introducing a values-based model and discussing organizational responses to work–family issues.

A Values-Based Model of Work–Family Conflict   Pamela L Perrewé and Wayne A Hochwarter constructed the model in Figure 6–5. On the left, we see one's

FIGURE 6–5
A Values Model of Work–Family Conflict

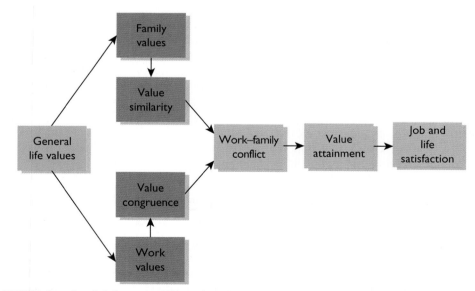

SOURCE: From Pamela L Perrewé and Wayne A Hochwarter, "Can We Really Have It All? The Attainment of Work and Family Values," *Current Directions in Psychological Science,* February 2001 Copyright © Association for Psychological Science. Reprinted with permission of Blackwell Publishing. © American Psychological Society.

general life values feeding into one's family-related values and work-related values. Family values involve enduring beliefs about the importance of family and who should play key family roles (e.g., child rearing, housekeeping, and income earning). Work values center on the relative importance of work and career goals in one's life. *Value similarity* relates to the degree of consensus among family members about family values. When a housewife launches a business venture despite her husband's desire to be the sole breadwinner, lack of family value similarity causes work–family conflict. *Value congruence,* on the other hand, involves the amount of value agreement between employee and employer. If, for example, refusing to go on a business trip to stay home for a child's birthday is viewed as disloyalty to the company, lack of value congruence can trigger work–family conflict.

In turn, "work–family conflict can take two distinct forms: work interference with family and family interference with work."[90] For example, suppose two managers in the same department have daughters playing on the same soccer team. One manager misses the big soccer game to attend a last-minute department meeting; the other manager skips the meeting to attend the game. Both may experience work–family conflict, but for different reasons.

The last two boxes in the model—value attainment and job and life satisfaction—are a package deal. Satisfaction tends to be higher for those who live according to their values and lower for those who do not. Overall, this model reflects much common sense. How does *your* life track through the model? Sadly, it is a painful trip for many these days.

Organizational Response to Work–Family Issues

Organizations have implemented a variety of "family-friendly" programs and services aimed at helping employees to balance the interplay between their work and personal lives. These programs included providing child-care services, flexible work schedules, cafeteria benefit plans, telecommuting, dry-cleaning services, concierge services, ATM at work, and stress reduction programs.[91] Although these programs are positively received by employees, experts now believe that such efforts are partially misguided because they focus on balancing work–family issues rather than integrating them. Balance is needed for opposites, and work and family are not opposites. Rather, our work and personal lives should be a well-integrated whole.[92] A team of researchers arrived at the following conclusion regarding the need to integrate versus balance work–life issues.

> Gendered assumptions and stereotypes based in the separation of [occupational and family] spheres constrain the choices of both women and men. Our vision of gender equity is to relax these social norms about separation so that men and women are free to experience these two parts of their lives as integrated rather than as separate domains that need to be "balanced." Integration would make it possible for both women and men to perform up to their capabilities and find satisfaction in both work and personal life, no matter how they allocate their time commitment between the two. To convey this goal, we speak of integrating work and personal life rather than balancing. This terminology expresses our belief in the need to diminish the separation between these two spheres of life in ways that will *change both,* rather than merely reallocating—or "balancing"—time between them as they currently exist.[93]

Some organizations have made great strides in meeting employees' family needs. At CMP Media in a New York City suburb, some employees, including Kimberly and Thomas LaSusa, bring their children to the child-care center on the building's first floor and take their lunch breaks with their kids. "There's a lot of stress having to find the right facility for your child," says Mrs. LaSusa, whose twins are two and have been cared for at the center since they were 10 weeks old. "But we didn't have to worry about it."

key terms

core job characteristics   154
extrinsic motivation   158
hygiene factors   153
intrinsic motivation   154
job design   150
job enlargement   151
job enrichment   153
job rotation   151
job satisfaction   162

met expectations   163
motivation   147
motivators   152
need for achievement   149
need for affiliation   150
need for power   150
needs   149
organizational citizenship
    behaviors (OCBs)   165

repetitive motion
    disorders (RMDs)   157
sense of choice   159
sense of competence   159
sense of meaningfulness   159
sense of progress   159
value attainment   163
withdrawal cognitions   166

chapter summary

- *Discuss the job performance model of motivation.* Individual inputs and job context variables are the two key categories of factors that influence motivation. In turn, motivation leads to motivated behaviors, which then affect performance.

- *Contrast Maslow's and McClelland's need theories.* Two well-known need theories of motivation are Maslow's need hierarchy and McClelland's need theory. Maslow's notion of a prepotent or stair-step hierarchy of five levels of needs has not stood up well under research. McClelland believes that motivation and performance vary according to the strength of an individual's need for achievement. High achievers prefer moderate risks and situations where they can control their own destiny. Top managers should have a high need for power coupled with a low need for affiliation.

- *Describe the mechanistic, motivational, biological, and perceptual-motor approaches to job design.* The mechanistic approach is based on industrial engineering and scientific management and focuses on increasing efficiency, flexibility, and employee productivity. Motivational approaches aim to improve employees' affective and attitudinal reactions and behavioral outcomes. Job enlargement, job enrichment, and a contingency approach called the job characteristics model are motivational approaches to job design. The biological approach focuses on designing the work environment to reduce employees' physical strain, effort, fatigue, and health complaints. The perceptual-motor approach emphasizes the reliability of work outcomes.

- *Review the four intrinsic rewards underlying intrinsic motivation, and discuss how managers can cultivate intrinsic motivation in others.* Intrinsic motivation is driven by the opportunity rewards of a sense of meaningfulness and a sense of choice, and the accomplishment rewards of a sense of competence and a sense of progress. Senses of meaningfulness and progress are driven by the purpose underlying task completion, whereas senses of choice and competence revolve around the tasks one performs at work. Managers specifically lead for meaningfulness, choice, competence, and progress by inspiring and modeling, empowering and delegating, supporting and coaching, and monitoring and rewarding, respectively.

- *Discuss the causes and consequences of job satisfaction.* Job satisfaction is an affective or emotional response toward various facets of one's job. Five models of job satisfaction specify its causes. They are need fulfillment, discrepancy, value attainment, equity, and trait/genetic components. Job satisfaction has been correlated with hundreds of consequences. Table 6–1 summarizes the pattern of results found for a subset of the more important variables.

- *Describe the values model of work–family conflict.* General life values determine one's values about family and work. Work–family conflict can occur when there is a lack of value similarity with family members. Likewise, work–family conflict can occur when one's own work values are not congruent with the company's values. When someone does not attain his or her values because of work–family conflicts, job or life satisfaction, or both, can suffer.

discussion questions

1. In the context of the chapter-opening case, to what extent did ARUP Laboratories, IBM, Versant, Inc., and Great River Health Systems apply the various theories of motivation discussed in this chapter? Explain.
2. Why should the average manager be well versed in the various motivation theories?
3. Which of the four types of job design is most likely to be used in the future? Explain your rationale.
4. To what extent is your behavior and performance as a student a function of intrinsic and extrinsic motivation? Explain.
5. What are the three most valuable lessons about employee motivation that you have learned from this chapter?

ethical dilemma

Should I Ignore the Cheating?

You are taking a college course. The tests and quizzes are online through the class Web site. The professor gives you a three-day window and you take the tests in your personal time. The professor has strict guidelines about cheating. At the beginning of the semester, he told all of you that the tests and quizzes will be timed so you will not have enough time to look the answers up in the book. You are in the computing commons taking one of the quizzes and notice a group of your classmates huddled around a computer. They are taking the quiz as well. One student is looking up the answers in the book, one is taking the quiz, and the other is recording the answers.

As a student, what would you do?

1. Immediately contact your professor about what is going on. It is unfair to the rest of your classmates if these three get away with cheating.

2. Form a similar test group of your own. The professor never specifically said you couldn't take the tests in groups.

3. Ignore the group's behavior and continue taking the test. You are sure these three will be caught eventually and at least you will know you *earned* your grade.

4. Invent other options. Discuss.

If you're looking for additional study materials, be sure to check out the Online Learning Center
at
www.mhhe.com/kinickiob3e
for more information and interactivities that correspond to this chapter.

Motivation II: Equity, Expectancy, and Goal Setting

LEARNING OBJECTIVES

After reading the material in this chapter, you should be able to:

- Discuss the role of perceived inequity in employee motivation.

- Describe the practical lessons derived from equity theory.

- Explain Vroom's expectancy theory.

- Describe the practical implications of expectancy theory.

- Identify five practical lessons to be learned from goal-setting research.

- Specify issues that should be addressed before implementing a motivational program.

A $2,600 bonus wasn't the only boost that Laurie Cunningham, a first-grade teacher, got from a new merit-pay plan at A.A. Nelson Elementary School in Lake Charles, La.

In addition to rewarding the 26-year-old teacher for improvements in student test scores, the school's compensation program also offered other important incentives: It matched

Ms. Cunningham with a more-experienced mentor and with a discussion group. As a result, she picked up class-room tips including a new word game, which she plays with students to help improve their vocabulary skills. "It gives you more specific infor-mation on what you should be doing," Ms. Cunningham says of the program.

Teachers unions continue to oppose many merit-pay proposals, maintaining they expose members to arbi-trary benchmarks set by school administrators. But many states and school dis-tricts are making headway in tying teacher pay to student achievement, ending the tradition of basing teachers' compensation almost entirely on seniority and academic degrees.

School districts in Florida and in Houston, Texas, have recently announced pay plans that closely link teacher pay and test scores. Denver, Colo., and districts in Minnesota have made test scores one of several criteria, along with performance assessments.

Merit-pay proponents have begun to defuse the

opposition, by getting teach-ers involved in planning the systems and offering incen-tives and support that go beyond test scores. "I would say there is a lot of momen-tum," says Allan Odden, a professor of educational administration at the University of Wisconsin, Madison, and a supporter of merit pay. . . .

Yesterday, the Teaching Commission, a group that studies educator training and improvement, released a report saying governors in 20 states have proposed changes in how teachers are paid, including the use of performance bonuses. The report says the increasing use of performance pay is a sign of progress. "We are seeing enough commitment to this idea that we have a chance to have it stick," says Louis Gerstner, the former International Business Machines Corp. chairman who formed the commission in 2003.

In Minnesota, school dis-tricts can become eligible for an extra $260-per-student in state aid if they sign up for the state's new "Q Comp" system, which requires dis-tricts to stop giving teachers automatic raises for senior-ity and instead base 60% of all pay increases on performance, as measured by test scores, classroom evaluations and other factors.

Districts hash out the details of their own pay plans, but they can't participate unless the teachers agree. So far, Minneapolis and eight other public school districts have signed up for the program, which was put in place last year; the state has received letters of intent from 134 others. Various plans offer bonuses ranging from as much as $600 per teacher for test-score gains to as much as $3,000 a year for veteran teachers who agree to be mentors. . . .

Teacher-union opposition has doomed some performance pay measures. In 2002, Cincinnati teachers voted against accepting their district's merit-pay proposal amid concerns about the objectivity of the evaluation system driving it. In the late 1990s, similar concerns in the Colonial School District, outside Philadelphia, led some teachers to donate their $500 checks to charities rather than cash them. The district eventually dropped the program.

"Whether these plans work depends on whether the work force buys into them," says Gayle Fallon, president of the Houston Federation of Teachers. "Nobody does passive-aggressive better than teachers."

The Teacher Advancement Program Foundation, a Los Angeles nonprofit working in the A.A. Nelson school and 105 others nationwide, introduces performance pay as part of a package of reforms, including on-site teacher training and extra pay for experienced teachers who coach younger colleagues. "We think that if you just do performance pay and don't provide teachers with the mechanisms to get better, it's not going to work," says Lewis Solmon, the foundation's president.[1]

FOR DISCUSSION

What are the pros and cons of basing teachers' rewards on student achievement scores? Explain. For an interpretation of this case and additional comments, visit our Online Learning Center at

www.mhhe.com/kinickiob3e

THE OPENING CASE ILLUSTRATES the application of theories of organizational behavior on teachers. As you will read in this chapter, the expectancy theory of motivation is based on the premise that motivation is a function of linking desired outcomes or results (e.g., student test scores) with rewards (e.g., teacher bonuses). You also will come to understand why the teacher union in Cincinnati was opposed to the incentive program implemented in 2002. This opposition could have been reduced or avoided had the school system followed the recommendations discussed at the end of this chapter. This chapter completes our discussion of motivation by exploring three cognitive theories of work motivation: equity, expectancy, and goal setting. Each theory is based on the premise that employees' cognitions are the key to understanding their motivation. To help you apply what you have learned about employee motivation, we conclude the chapter by highlighting the prerequisites of successful motivational programs.

Adams's Equity Theory of Motivation

Defined generally, **equity theory** is a model of motivation that explains how people strive for *fairness* and *justice* in social exchanges or give-and-take relationships. Equity theory is based on cognitive dissonance theory, developed by social psychologist Leon Festinger in the 1950s.[2]

> **equity theory**
>
> **Holds that motivation is a function of fairness in social exchanges.**

According to Festinger's theory, people are motivated to maintain consistency between their cognitive beliefs and their behavior. Perceived inconsistencies create cognitive dissonance (or psychological discomfort), which, in turn, motivates corrective action. For example, a cigarette smoker who sees a heavy-smoking relative die of lung cancer probably would be motivated to quit smoking if he or she attributes the death to smoking. Accordingly, when victimized by unfair social exchanges, our resulting cognitive dissonance prompts us to correct the situation. Corrective action may range from a slight change in attitude or behavior to stealing to the extreme case of trying to harm someone. For example, researchers have demonstrated that people attempt to "get even" for perceived injustices by using either direct (e.g., theft, sabotage, violence, or absenteeism) or indirect (e.g., intentionally working slowly, lower motivation, being less cooperative, or displaying less organizational citizenship behavior) retaliation.[3]

Psychologist J Stacy Adams pioneered application of the equity principle to the workplace. Central to understanding Adams's equity theory of motivation is an awareness of key components of the individual–organization exchange relationship. This relationship is pivotal in the formation of employees' perceptions of equity and inequity.

The Individual–Organization Exchange Relationship

Adams points out that two primary components are involved in the employee–employer exchange, *inputs* and *outcomes.* An employee's inputs, for which he or she expects a just return, include education/training, skills, creativity, seniority, age, personality traits, effort expended, and personal appearance. On the outcome side of the exchange, the organization provides such things as pay/bonuses, fringe benefits, challenging assignments, job security, promotions, status symbols, recognition, and participation in important decisions.[4] These outcomes vary widely, depending on one's organization and rank.

Negative and Positive Inequity

On the job, feelings of inequity revolve around a person's evaluation of whether he or she receives adequate rewards to compensate for his or her contributive inputs. People perform these evaluations by comparing the perceived fairness of their employment exchange to that of relevant others. This comparative process, which is based on an equity norm, was found to generalize across countries.[5] People tend to compare themselves to other individuals with whom they have close interpersonal ties—such as friends—and/or to similar others—such as people performing the same job or individuals of the same gender or educational level—rather than dissimilar others. For example, do you consider the average CEO in the US a relevant comparison person to yourself? If not, then you should not feel inequity because the average CEO of a Standard & Poor 500 company made $11.75 million in total compensation in 2005. This is approximately 185 times greater than the average employee's income.[6]

Three different equity relationships are illustrated in Figure 7–1: equity, negative inequity, and positive inequity. Assume the two people in each of the equity relationships in Figure 7–1 have equivalent backgrounds (equal education, seniority, and so forth) and perform identical tasks. Only their hourly pay rates differ. Equity exists for an individual when his or her ratio of perceived outcomes to inputs is equal to the ratio of outcomes to inputs for a relevant co-worker (see part A in Figure 7–1). Because equity is based on comparing *ratios* of outcomes to inputs, inequity will not necessarily be perceived just because someone else receives greater rewards. If the other person's additional outcomes are due to his or her greater inputs, a sense of equity may still exist. However, if the comparison person enjoys greater outcomes for similar inputs, **negative inequity** will be perceived (see part B in Figure 7–1). On the other hand, a person will experience **positive inequity** when his or her outcome to input ratio is greater than that of a relevant co-worker (see part C in Figure 7–1).

negative inequity

Comparison in which another person receives greater outcomes for similar inputs.

positive inequity

Comparison in which another person receives lesser outcomes for similar inputs.

Dynamics of Perceived Inequity

Managers can derive practical benefits from Adams's equity theory by recognizing that (1) people have varying sensitivities to perceived equity and inequity and (2) inequity can be reduced in a variety of ways.

Thresholds of Equity and Inequity   Have you ever noticed that some people become very upset over the slightest inequity whereas others are not bothered at all? Research has shown that people respond differently to the same level of inequity due to an individual difference called equity sensitivity. **Equity sensitivity** reflects an individual's "different preferences for, tolerances for, and reactions to the level of equity associated with any given situation."[7] Equity sensitivity spans a continuum ranging from benevolents to sensitives to entitled.

equity sensitivity

An individual's tolerance for negative and positive equity.

Benevolents are people who have a higher tolerance for negative inequity. They are altruistic in the sense that they prefer their outcome/input ratio to be lower than

Negative and Positive Inequity   **FIGURE 7–1**

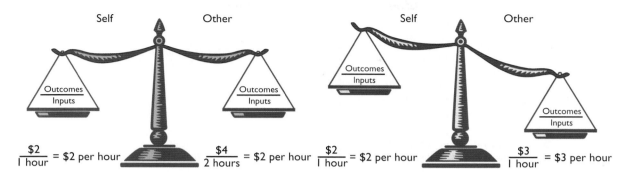

A. An Equitable Situation

$\dfrac{\$2}{1\ hour}$ = $2 per hour $\dfrac{\$4}{2\ hours}$ = $2 per hour

B. Negative Inequity

$\dfrac{\$2}{1\ hour}$ = $2 per hour $\dfrac{\$3}{1\ hour}$ = $3 per hour

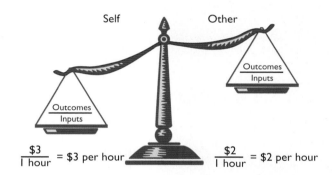

C. Positive Inequity

$\dfrac{\$3}{1\ hour}$ = $3 per hour $\dfrac{\$2}{1\ hour}$ = $2 per hour

ratios from comparison others. In contrast, equity *sensitives* are described as individuals who adhere to a strict norm of reciprocity and are quickly motivated to resolve both negative and positive inequity. Finally, *entitleds* have no tolerance for negative inequity. They actually expect to obtain greater output/input ratios than comparison others and become upset when this is not the case.[8]

Reducing Inequity   Equity ratios can be changed by attempting to alter one's outcomes or adjusting one's inputs. For example, negative inequity might be resolved by asking for a raise or a promotion (i.e., raising outputs) or by reducing inputs (i.e., working fewer hours or exerting less effort). It also is important to note that equity can be restored by altering one's equity ratios behaviorally and/or cognitively. A cognitive strategy entails psychologically distorting perceptions of one's own or one's comparison person's outcomes and inputs (e.g., conclude that comparison other has more experience or works harder).

The Skills & Best Practices feature on page 178 shows how Susan Lyne, CEO of Martha Stewart Living Omnimedia, Inc., attempted to correct for her positive inequity. In contrast to this positive managerial act, Hasso Platter, co-founder and former CEO of SAP, is potentially increasing negative inequity by announcing that the company "will pay $381 million to several hundred managers and key employees if they can double the company's market capitalization—from a $57 billion starting point—by the end of 2010. A third of that would go to the top seven executives."[9]

Susan Lyne Gives Back Part of Her Bonus to Restore Equity

Susan Lyne knows the power of a public statement. As chief executive of Martha Stewart Living Omnimedia, Inc., since late 2004, she has run the company through Stewart's jail term and much publicized comeback. With ad pages in the flagship magazine up 44% last year and a flurry of new deals sparking optimism for the brand, Lyne got a cash bonus of $625,500 last year. Instead of pocketing it, though, she asked the board to give $200,000 to a bonus pool for employees and convert the rest into restricted shares that won't fully vest until 2009.

Susan Lyne, CEO of Martha Stewart Living Omnimedia, Inc., put part of her bonus into a bonus pool for employees of the firm.

Lyne says she wanted to recognize the efforts of employees because her plan to boost the company's long-term health cut into annual bonuses. More important, she felt the gesture would be a potent symbol. "There was a period of time in the 1990s when the bigger your pay package, the more people respected you," says Lyne, who earned a $900,000 salary in 2005. "I think that has changed—dramatically. There's a very different sense of what makes a good leader of a public company."

SOURCE: Excerpted from D Brady, "Executive Pay: No Hair Shirts, but Still . . ." *BusinessWeek,* May 1,

Expanding the Concept of Equity: Organizational Justice

Beginning in the later 1970s, researchers began to expand the role of equity theory in explaining employee attitudes and behavior. This led to a domain of research called *organizational justice*. Organizational justice reflects the extent to which people perceive that they are treated fairly at work. This, in turn, led to the identification of three different components of organizational justice: distributive, procedural, and interactional.[10] **Distributive justice** reflects the perceived fairness of how resources and rewards are distributed or allocated. **Procedural justice** is defined as the perceived fairness of the process and procedures used to make allocation decisions. Research shows that positive perceptions of distributive and procedural justice are enhanced by giving employees a "voice" in decisions that affect them. Voice represents the extent to which employees who are affected by a decision can present relevant information about the decision to others. Voice is analogous to asking employees for their input into the decision-making process.

The last justice component, **interactional justice,** relates to the "quality of the interpersonal treatment people receive when procedures are implemented."[11] This form of justice does not pertain to the outcomes or procedures associated with decision making, but rather it focuses on whether or not people believe they are treated fairly when decisions are implemented. Fair interpersonal treatment necessitates that managers communicate truthfully and treat people with courtesy and respect. Consider the role of interactional justice in how a manager of information-management systems responded to being laid off by a New Jersey chemical company. The man gained access to the company's computer systems from home by using another executive's password and deleted critical inventory and personnel files. The sabotage ultimately caused $20 million in damage and postponed a public stock offering that had been in the works. Why would a former employee do something like this?

An anonymous note that he wrote to the company president sheds light on his motive. "I have been loyal to the company in good and bad times for over 30 years," he wrote. "I was expecting a member of top management to come down from his ivory tower to face us with the layoff announcement, rather than sending the kitchen supervisor with guards to escort us off the premises like criminals. You will pay for your senseless behavior."[12]

This employee's direct retaliation against the company was caused by the insensitive manner—interactional justice—in which employees were notified about the layoffs.

distributive justice

> The perceived fairness of how resources and rewards are distributed.

procedural justice

> The perceived fairness of the process and procedures used to make allocation decisions.

interactional justice

> Extent to which people feel fairly treated when procedures are implemented.

Practical Lessons from Equity Theory

Equity theory has at least nine important practical implications. First, equity theory provides managers with yet another explanation of how beliefs and attitudes affect job performance. According to this line of thinking, the best way to manage job behavior is to adequately understand underlying cognitive processes. Indeed, we are motivated powerfully to correct a situation when our ideas of fairness and justice are offended.

Second, research on equity theory emphasizes the need for managers to pay attention to employees' perceptions of what is fair and equitable. No matter how fair management thinks the organization's policies, procedures, and reward system are, each employee's *perception* of the equity of those factors is what counts. People respond positively when they perceive organizational and interpersonal justice and negatively when they do not. For example, employees were more likely to complete organizationally sponsored surveys when they felt a sense of procedural justice, and employees also reported greater insomnia when they experienced poor interactional justice.[13] Moreover, research demonstrates that employees' perceptions of distributive, procedural, and interactional justice are positively associated with job performance, job satisfaction, organizational commitment, and organizational citizenship behavior and negatively with intentions to quit.[14] Managers thus are encouraged to make hiring and promotion decisions on merit-based, job-related information. Moreover, because justice perceptions are influenced by the extent to which managers explain their decisions, managers are encouraged to explain the rationale behind their decisions.[15]

Third, managers benefit by allowing employees to participate in making decisions about important work outcomes. For example, employees were more satisfied with their performance appraisals and resultant outcomes when they had a "voice" during the appraisal review.[16] Fourth, employees should be given the opportunity to appeal decisions that affect their welfare. Being able to appeal a decision promotes the belief that management treats employees fairly.

Fifth, employees are more likely to accept and support organizational change when they believe it is implemented fairly and when it produces equitable outcomes.[17]

Sixth, managers can promote cooperation and teamwork among group members by treating them equitably. Research reveals that people are just as concerned with fairness in group settings as they are with their own personal interests.[18] Seventh, treating employees inequitably can lead to litigation and costly court settlements. Employees denied justice at work are more likely to file employee grievances, to seek arbitration, and to ultimately seek relief from the courts.[19] Eighth, employees' perceptions of justice are strongly influenced by the leadership behavior exhibited by their managers (leadership is discussed in Chapter 14).[20] It thus is important for managers to consider the justice-related implications of their decisions, actions, and public communications. Finally, managers should pay attention to the organization's climate for justice. For example, an organization's climate for justice was found to significantly influence employees' organizational citizenship behavior.[21]

Measuring Perceived Fair Interpersonal Treatment

INSTRUCTIONS: The following survey was designed to assess the extent to which you are treated fairly at your current job: If you are not working, use a past job or your role as a student to complete the survey. There is no right or wrong answer to the statements. Circle your answers by using the rating scale provided. After evaluating each of the survey statements, complete a total score and compare your total to the arbitrary norms.

	Strongly Disagree	Disagree	Neither	Agree	Strongly Agree
1. Employees are praised for good work.	1	2	3	4	5
2. Supervisors do not yell at employees.	1	2	3	4	5
3. Employees are trusted.	1	2	3	4	5
4. Employees' complaints are dealt with effectively.	1	2	3	4	5
5. Employees are treated with respect.	1	2	3	4	5
6. Employees' questions and problems are responded to quickly.	1	2	3	4	5
7. Employees are treated fairly.	1	2	3	4	5
8. Employees' hard work is appreciated.	1	2	3	4	5
9. Employees' suggestions are used.	1	2	3	4	5
10. Employees are told the truth.	1	2	3	4	5

Total score = _____

ARBITRARY NORMS

Very fair organization = 38–50
Moderately fair organization = 24–37
Unfair organization = 10–23

SOURCE: Adapted in part from M A Donovan, F Drasgow, and L J Munson, "The Perceptions of Fair Interpersonal Treatment Scale Development and Validation of a Measure of Interpersonal Treatment in the Workplace," *Journal of Applied Psychology,* October 1998, pp 683–92.

Researchers also believe that a climate of justice can significantly influence the type of customer service provided by employees. In turn, this level of service is likely to influence customers' perceptions of "fair service" and their subsequent loyalty and satisfaction.

Managers can attempt to follow these practical implications by monitoring equity and justice perceptions through informal conversations, interviews, or attitude surveys. For example, researchers have developed and validated a host of surveys that can be used for this purpose. Please take a moment now to complete the Hands-On Exercise. It contains part of a survey that was developed to measure employees' perceptions of fair interpersonal treatment. If you perceive your work organization as interpersonally unfair, you are probably dissatisfied and have contemplated quitting. In contrast, your organizational loyalty and attachment are likely greater if you believe you are treated fairly at work.

Expectancy Theory of Motivation

Expectancy theory holds that people are motivated to behave in ways that produce desired combinations of expected outcomes. Perception plays a central role in expectancy theory because it emphasizes cognitive ability to anticipate likely consequences of behavior. Embedded in expectancy theory is the principle of hedonism. Hedonistic people strive to maximize their pleasure and minimize their pain. Generally, expectancy theory can be used to predict behavior in any situation in which a choice between two or more alternatives must be made. For instance, it can be used to predict whether to quit or stay at a job; whether to exert substantial or minimal effort at a task; and whether to major in management, computer science, accounting, marketing, psychology, or communication.

> **expectancy theory**
> Holds that people are motivated to behave in ways that produce valued outcomes.

This section explores Victor Vroom's version of expectancy theory. Understanding the cognitive processes underlying this theory can help managers develop organizational policies and practices that enhance employee motivation.

Vroom's Expectancy Theory

Victor Vroom formulated a mathematical model of expectancy theory in his 1964 book *Work and Motivation.* Vroom's theory has been summarized as follows:

> The strength of a tendency to act in a certain way depends on the strength of an expectancy that the act will be followed by a given consequence (or outcome) and on the value or attractiveness of that consequence (or outcome) to the actor.[22]

Motivation, according to Vroom, boils down to the decision of how much effort to exert in a specific task situation. This choice is based on a two-stage sequence of expectations (effort → performance and performance → outcome). First, motivation is affected by an individual's expectation that a certain level of effort will produce the intended performance goal. For example, if you do not believe increasing the amount of time you spend studying will significantly raise your grade on an exam, you probably will not study any harder than usual. Motivation also is influenced by the employee's perceived chances of getting various outcomes as a result of accomplishing his or her performance goal. Finally, individuals are motivated to the extent that they value the outcomes received.

Vroom used a mathematical equation to integrate these concepts into a predictive model of motivational force or strength. For our purposes, however, it is sufficient to define and explain the three key concepts within Vroom's model—*expectancy, instrumentality,* and *valence.*

Expectancy   An **expectancy,** according to Vroom's terminology, represents an individual's belief that a particular degree of effort will be followed by a particular level of performance. In other words, it is an effort → performance expectation. Expectancies take the form of subjective probabilities. As you may recall from a course in statistics, probabilities range from zero to one. An expectancy of zero indicates effort has no anticipated impact on performance.

> **expectancy**
> Belief that effort leads to a specific level of performance.

For example, suppose you do not know how to type on a keyboard. No matter how much effort you exert, your perceived probability of typing 30 error-free words per minute likely would be zero. An expectancy of one suggests that performance is totally dependent on effort. If you decided to take a typing course as well as practice a couple of hours a day for a few weeks (high effort), you should be able to type 30 words per minute without any errors. In contrast, if you do not take a typing course and only practice an hour or two per week (low effort), there is a very low probability (say, a 20% chance) of being able to type 30 words per minute without any errors.

The following factors influence an employee's expectancy perceptions:

- Self-esteem.
- Self-efficacy.
- Previous success at the task.
- Help received from others.
- Information necessary to complete the task.
- Good materials and equipment to work with.[23]

instrumentality

A performance → outcome perception.

Instrumentality   An **instrumentality** is a performance → outcome perception. It represents a person's belief that a particular outcome is contingent on accomplishing a specific level of performance. Performance is instrumental when it leads to something else. For example, passing exams is instrumental to graduating from college.

Instrumentalities range from -1.0 to 1.0. An instrumentality of 1.0 indicates attainment of a particular outcome is totally dependent on task performance. An instrumentality of zero indicates there is no relationship between performance and receiving an outcome. For example, most companies link the number of vacation days to seniority, not job performance. Finally, an instrumentality of -1.0 reveals that high performance reduces the chance of obtaining an outcome while low performance increases the chance. For example, the more time you spend studying to get an A on an exam (high performance), the less time you will have for enjoying leisure activities. Similarly, as you lower the amount of time spent studying (low performance), you increase the amount of time that may be devoted to leisure activities.

The concept of instrumentality can be seen by considering the incentive programs used to pay the CEOs from General Electric, IBM, SBC Communications, Inc., and Apple.

> At General Electric Co., and at IBM . . . boards have performed radical surgery to better tie pay to performance. GE's Jeffrey R. Immelt could lose all 250,000 shares of stock GE awarded him last year unless he meets performance goals. And IBM's Samuel J. Palmisano will get options, but they'll be worthless until the stock rises by 10%. . . . At SBC Communications, Inc., 2003 operating income was down 25% and the stock lagged its peers. Yet CEO Edward E. Whitacre, Jr. earned $19.6 million, including a $5.7 million bonus and a $7.2 million stock grant—a 93% increase over 2002. . . . At Apple, Jobs's $74.8 million options-for-stock swap last March came after a three-year stretch in which the stock plummeted 80%, and then barely moved. What's more, Jobs will receive them in 2006, regardless of performance."[24]

The incentive programs at GE and IBM make performance instrumental for receiving stock options, but performance is not instrumental for receiving bonuses and stock options at SBC Communications and Apple.

valence

The value of a reward or outcome.

Valence   As Vroom used the term, **valence** refers to the positive or negative value people place on outcomes. Valence mirrors our personal preferences. For example, most employees have a positive valence for receiving additional money or recognition. In contrast, job stress and being laid off would likely be negatively valent for most individuals. In Vroom's expectancy model, *outcomes* refer to different consequences that are contingent on performance, such as pay, promotions, or recognition. An outcome's valence depends on an individual's needs and can be measured for research purposes with scales ranging from a negative value to a positive value. For example, an individual's valence toward more recognition can be assessed on a scale ranging from -2 (very undesirable) to 0 (neutral) to $+2$ (very desirable).

Vroom's Expectancy Theory in Action

Vroom's expectancy model of motivation can be used to analyze a real-life motivation program. Consider the following performance problem described by Frederick W Smith, founder and chief executive officer of Federal Express Corporation:

"My computer has the strangest virus. It bombards me with messages that say how wonderful you are and that you deserve a promotion."

Copyright © Ted Goff. Reprinted with permission.

> . . . we were having a helluva problem keeping things running on time. The airplanes would come in, and everything would get backed up. We tried every kind of control mechanism that you could think of, and none of them worked. Finally, it became obvious that the underlying problem was that it was in the interest of the employees at the cargo terminal—they were college kids, mostly—to run late, because it meant that they made more money. So what we did was give them all a minimum guarantee and say, "Look, if you get through before a certain time, just go home, and you will have beat the system." Well, it was unbelievable. I mean, in the space of about 45 days, the place was way ahead of schedule. And I don't even think it was a conscious thing on their part.[25]

How did Federal Express get its college-age cargo handlers to switch from low effort to high effort? According to Vroom's model, the student workers originally exerted low effort because they were paid on the basis of time, not output. It was in their best interest to work slowly and accumulate as many hours as possible. By offering to let the student workers *go home early if and when they completed their assigned duties*, Federal Express prompted high effort. This new arrangement created two positively valued outcomes: guaranteed pay plus the opportunity to leave early. The motivation to exert high effort became greater than the motivation to exert low effort.

Research on Expectancy Theory and Managerial Implications

Many researchers have tested expectancy theory. In support of the theory, a meta-analysis of 77 studies indicated that expectancy theory significantly predicted performance, effort, intentions, preferences, and choice.[26] Another summary of 16 studies revealed that expectancy theory correctly predicted occupational or organizational choice 63.4% of the time; this was significantly better than chance predictions.[27]

Nonetheless, expectancy theory has been criticized for a variety of reasons. For example, the theory is difficult to test, and the measures used to assess expectancy, instrumentality, and valence have questionable validity.[28] In the final analysis, however, expectancy theory has important practical implications for individual managers and organizations as a whole (see Table 7–1).

TABLE 7–1 | Managerial and Organizational Implications of Expectancy Theory

Implications for Managers	Implications for Organizations
Determine the outcomes employees value.	Reward people for desired performance, and do not keep pay decisions secret.
Identify good performance so appropriate behaviors can be rewarded.	Design challenging jobs.
Make sure employees can achieve targeted performance levels.	Tie some rewards to group accomplishments to build teamwork and encourage cooperation.
Link desired outcomes to targeted levels of performance.	Reward managers for creating, monitoring, and maintaining expectancies, instrumentalities, and outcomes that lead to high effort and goal attainment.
Make sure changes in outcomes are large enough to motivate high effort.	Monitor employee motivation through interviews or anonymous questionnaires.
Monitor the reward system for inequities.	Accommodate individual differences by building flexibility into the motivation program.

One way to link rewards to performance is to pay employees on the selling floor commissions on the products they sell. Sears has expanded its policy so that employees earn commissions in all departments of the store, not just in specialized areas like appliances or tools.

Managers are advised to enhance effort → performance expectancies by helping employees accomplish their performance goals. Managers can do this by providing support and coaching and by increasing employees' self-efficacy. It also is important for managers to influence employees' instrumentalities and to monitor valences for various rewards. This raises the issue of whether organizations should use monetary rewards as the primary method to reinforce performance. Although money is certainly a positively valent reward for most people, there are three issues to consider when deciding on the relative balance between monetary and nonmonetary rewards.

First, research shows that some workers value interesting work and recognition more than money.[29] Second, extrinsic rewards can lose their motivating properties over time and may undermine intrinsic motivation.[30] This conclusion, however, must be balanced by the fact that performance is related to the receipt of financial incentives. A recent meta-analysis of 39 studies involving 2,773 people showed that financial incentives were positively related to performance quantity but not to performance quality.[31] Third, monetary rewards must be large enough to generate motivation. For example, Robert Heneman, professor of management at Ohio State University, estimates that monetary awards must be at least 7% above employees' base pay to truly motivate people.[32] Although this percentage is well above the typical salary increase received by most employees, some organizations have designed their incentive systems with this recommendation in mind. Kimley-Horn & Associates, for instance, gives out annual bonuses that average 12% of base pay.[33]

In summary, there is no one best type of reward. Individual differences and need theories tell us that people are motivated by different rewards. Managers should therefore focus on linking employee performance to valued rewards regardless of the type of reward used to enhance motivation. Unfortunately, a recent survey of 265 US companies and an additional 1,100 workers revealed that managers are not doing an exceptional job at linking performance to rewards. Forty-eight percent of the respondents indicated that their managers failed to tie performance to pay raises.[34] There are four prerequisites to effectively linking performance and rewards:

1. Managers need to develop and communicate performance standards to employees. This is precisely what occurs at General Electric's health care business. Employees are told that 20% of their bonus is tied to positive ratings on a customer survey.[35]

2. Managers need valid and accurate performance ratings with which to compare employees. Inaccurate ratings create perceptions of inequity and thereby erode motivation.

3. Managers need to determine the relative mix of individual versus team contribution to performance and then reward accordingly. For example, pharmaceutical giant Pharmacia designed its reward system around its belief in creating an organizational culture that reinforced collaboration, customer focus, and speed. "The company's reward system reinforced this collaborative model by explicitly linking compensation to the actions of the group. Every member's compensation would be based on the time to bring the drug to market, the time for the drug to reach peak profitable share, and total sales. The system gave group members a strong incentive to talk openly with one another and to share information freely."[36]

4. Managers should use the performance ratings to differentially allocate rewards among employees. That is, it is critical that managers allocate significantly different amounts of rewards for various levels of performance. Jamba Juice Co. has taken this recommendation to heart (see the above Skills & Best Practices feature).

> ## Jamba Juice Company Links Performance and Rewards
>
> The 7,500-employee company bases its annual distribution of merit raises on established performance-ratings categories for employees. Performance is simply ranked as being outstanding, exceeding requirements, meeting requirements or falling below requirements. The higher the rating, the higher the raise.
>
> Those employees who rate below requirements do not receive a merit increase and are disqualified for any bonus opportunity as well. . . .
>
> Team members understand how they will be evaluated, and the company has made clear how their overall performance will correlate to their merit increase.
>
> **SOURCE:** Excerpted from S J Wells, "No Results, No Raise," *HR Magazine*, May 2005, p 79.

SKILLS & BEST PRACTICES

Motivation through Goal Setting

Regardless of the nature of their specific achievements, successful people tend to have one thing in common. Their lives are goal oriented. This is as true for politicians seeking votes as it is for world-class athletes. Within the context of employee motivation, this section explores the theory, research, and practice of goal setting.

Goals: Definition and Background

goal

What an individual is trying to accomplish.

Edwin Locke, a leading authority on goal setting, and his colleagues define a **goal** as "what an individual is trying to accomplish; it is the object or aim of an action."[37] The motivational effect of performance goals and goal-based reward plans has been recognized for a long time.

At the turn of the century, Frederick Taylor attempted to scientifically establish how much work of a specified quality an individual should be assigned each day. He proposed that bonuses be based on accomplishing those output standards. More recently, goal setting has been promoted through a widely used management technique called management by objectives (MBO).

management by objectives (MBO)

Management system incorporating participation in decision making, goal setting, and feedback.

Management by objectives is a management system that incorporates participation in decision making, goal setting, and objective feedback. A meta-analysis of MBO programs showed productivity gains in 68 of 70 different organizations. Specifically, results uncovered an average gain in productivity of 56% when top management commitment was high. The average gain was only 6% when commitment was low. A second meta-analysis of 18 studies further demonstrated that employees' job satisfaction was significantly related to top management's commitment to an MBO implementation.[38] These impressive results highlight the positive benefits of implementing MBO and setting goals. To further understand how MBO programs can increase both productivity and satisfaction, let us examine the process by which goal setting works.

How Does Goal Setting Work?

Despite abundant goal-setting research and practice, goal-setting theories are surprisingly scarce. An instructive model was formulated by Locke and his associates. According to Locke's model, goal setting has four motivational mechanisms.[39]

Goals Direct Attention   Goals direct one's attention and effort toward goal-relevant activities and away from goal-irrelevant activities. If, for example, you have a term project due in a few days, your thoughts and actions tend to revolve around completing that project. For example, Robert Ruffolo, CEO of drugmaker Wyeth, used the power of goals to direct the attention of the company's research and development operation. The company now sets goals for how many drug compounds must be produced by each scientist. Prior to instituting this goal-setting program, Wyeth averaged the development of only four drug compounds per year. Since establishing the research and development goals the company has averaged 12 per year with no increase in resources. Ruffolo increased this goal to 15 in 2006.[40]

Goals Regulate Effort   Not only do goals make us selectively perceptive, they also motivate us to act. The instructor's deadline for turning in your term project would prompt you to complete it, as opposed to going out with friends, watching television, or studying for another course. Generally, the level of effort expended is proportionate to the difficulty of the goal.

Goals Increase Persistence   Within the context of goal setting, persistence represents the effort expended on a task over an extended period of time: It takes effort to run 100 meters; it takes persistence to run a 26-mile marathon. Persistent people tend to see obstacles as challenges to be overcome rather than as reasons to fail.

A difficult goal that is important to an individual is a constant reminder to keep exerting effort in the appropriate direction. Annika Sorenstam is a great example of someone who persisted at her goal of being the best female golfer in the world. She has won 69 tournaments since starting on the LPGA tour in 1994.

She already has qualified for the LPGA and World Golf Halls of Fame, has won a career Grand Slam, shot the only round of 59 in women's pro golf and has won eight Player of the Year titles.[41]

Just like Tiger Woods, major titles and a single-season Grand Slam have become her new focus. "Nobody else has done it, so I think that says it all," she said. "But I like to set high goals, I like to motivate myself. If you believe it in your mind, I think you can do it."[42]

Goals Foster the Development and Application of Task Strategies and Action Plans

If you are here and your goal is out there somewhere, you face the problem of getting from here to there. For example, the person who has resolved to lose 20 pounds must develop a plan for getting from "here" (his or her present weight) to "there" (20 pounds lighter). Goals can help because they encourage people to develop strategies and action plans that enable them to achieve their goals. By virtue of setting a weight-reduction goal, the dieter may choose a strategy of exercising more, eating less, or some combination of the two.

Annika Sorenstam persisted in her goal of being the best female golfer in the world.

Insights from Goal-Setting Research

Research consistently has supported goal setting as a motivational technique. Setting performance goals increases individual, group, and organizational performance. Further, the positive effects of goal setting were found in six other countries or regions: Australia, Canada, the Caribbean, England, West Germany, and Japan. Goal setting works in different cultures. Reviews of the many goal-setting studies conducted over the past few decades have given managers five practical insights:

1. *Difficult goals lead to higher performance.* **Goal difficulty** reflects the amount of effort required to meet a goal. It is more difficult to sell nine cars a month than it is to sell three cars a month. A meta-analysis spanning 4,000 people and 65 separate studies revealed that goal difficulty was positively related to performance.[43]

    As illustrated in Figure 7–2, however, the positive relationship between goal difficulty and performance breaks down when goals are perceived to be impossible. Figure 7–2 reveals that performance goes up when employees are given hard goals as opposed to easy or moderate goals (section A). Performance then plateaus (section B) and drops (section C) as the difficulty of a goal goes from challenging to impossible.

    goal difficulty

    The amount of effort required to meet a goal.

2. *Specific, difficult goals lead to higher performance for simple rather than complex tasks.* **Goal specificity** pertains to the quantifiability of

    goal specificity

    Quantifiability of a goal.

FIGURE 7–2
Relationship between Goal Difficulty and Performance

A Performance of committed individuals with adequate ability
B Performance of committed individuals who are working at capacity
C Performance of individuals who lack commitment to high goals

SOURCE: From *A Theory of Goal Setting and Task Performance*, by Locke/Latham. Copyright © 1990 Pearson Education. Reprinted by permission of Pearson Education, Inc., Upper Saddle River, NJ.

a goal. For example, a goal of selling nine cars a month is more specific than telling a salesperson to do his or her best. In an early review of goal-setting research, 99 of 110 studies (90%) found that specific, hard goals led to better performance than did easy, medium, do-your-best, or no goals. This result was confirmed in a meta-analysis of 70 studies conducted between 1966 and 1984, involving 7,407 people.[44]

In contrast to these positive effects, several recent studies demonstrated that setting specific, difficult goals leads to poorer performance under certain circumstances. For example, a meta-analysis of 125 studies indicated that goal-setting effects were strongest for easy tasks and weakest for complex tasks.[45] There are two explanations for this finding. First, employees are not likely to put forth increased effort to achieve complex goals unless they "buy-in" or support them. Thus, it is important for managers to obtain employee buy-in to the goal-setting process. Second, novel and complex tasks can make employees anxious about succeeding, which in turn causes them to develop strategies in an unsystematic way and to fail to learn what strategies or actions are effective. This can further create pressure and performance anxiety. According to Locke and his colleagues, the antidote is to set specific challenging learning goals aimed at identifying the best way to accomplish the task or goal.[46] Specific, difficult goals thus impair performance on novel, complex tasks when employees do not have clear strategies for solving these types of problems. On a positive note, however, a study demonstrated that goal setting led to gradual improvements in performance on complex tasks when people were encouraged to explicitly solve the problem at hand.[47]

3. *Feedback enhances the effect of specific, difficult goals.* Feedback plays a key role in all of our lives. For example, consider the role of feedback in bowling. Imagine going to the bowling lanes only to find that someone had hung a sheet from the ceiling to the floor in front of the pins. How likely is it that you

would reach your goal score or typical bowling average? Not likely, given your inability to see the pins. Regardless of your goal, you would have to guess where to throw your second ball if you did not get a strike on your first shot. The same principles apply at work.

Feedback lets people know if they are headed toward their goals or if they are off course and need to redirect their efforts. Goals plus feedback is the recommended approach.[48] Goals inform people about performance standards and expectations so that they can channel their energies accordingly. In turn, feedback provides the information needed to adjust direction, effort, and strategies for goal accomplishment.

4. *Participative goals, assigned goals, and self-set goals are equally effective.* Both managers and researchers are interested in identifying the best way to set goals. Should goals be participatively set, assigned, or set by the employee him- or herself? A summary of goal-setting research indicated that no single approach was consistently more effective than others in increasing performance.[49]

Managers are advised to use a contingency approach by picking a method that seems best suited for the individual and situation at hand. For example, employees' preferences for participation should be considered. Some employees desire to participate in the process of setting goals, whereas others do not. Employees are also more likely to respond positively to the opportunity to participate in goal setting when they have greater task information, higher levels of experience and training, and greater levels of task involvement. Finally, a participative approach stimulates information exchange, which in turn results in the development of more effective task strategies and higher self-efficacy.[50]

5. *Goal commitment and monetary incentives affect goal-setting outcomes.* **Goal commitment** is the extent to which an individual is personally committed to achieving a goal. In general, an individual is expected to persist in attempts to accomplish a goal when he or she is committed to it. Researchers believe that goal commitment moderates the relationship between the difficulty of a goal and performance. That is, difficult goals lead to higher performance only when employees are committed to their goals. Conversely, difficult goals are hypothesized to lead to lower performance when people are not committed to their goals. A meta-analysis of 21 studies based on 2,360 people supported these predictions.[51] It also is important to note that people are more likely to commit to difficult goals when they have high self-efficacy about successfully accomplishing their goals. Managers thus are encouraged to consider employees' self-efficacy when setting goals.

> **goal commitment**
> Amount of commitment to achieving a goal.

Like goal setting, the use of monetary incentives to motivate employees is seldom questioned. Unfortunately, research uncovered some negative consequences when goal achievement is linked to individual incentives. Case studies, for example, reveal that pay should not be linked to goal achievement unless (a) performance goals are under the employees' control; (b) goals are quantitative and measurable; and (c) frequent, relatively large payments are made for performance achievement.[52] Goal-based incentive systems are more likely to produce undesirable effects if these three conditions are not satisfied.

Moreover, empirical studies demonstrated that goal-based bonus incentives produced higher commitment to easy goals and lower commitment to difficult goals. People were reluctant to commit to difficult goals that were tied to monetary incentives. People with high goal commitment also offered less help to their co-workers when they received goal-based bonus incentives to accomplish difficult individual goals. Individuals also neglected aspects of the job that were not covered in the performance goals.[53]

These findings underscore some of the dangers of using goal-based incentives, particularly for employees in complex, interdependent jobs requiring cooperation. Managers need to consider the advantages, disadvantages, and dilemmas of goal-based incentives prior to implementation.

Self-Assessment Exercise

Assessing How Personality Impacts Your Goal-Setting Skills

Practical Application of Goal Setting

There are three general steps to follow when implementing a goal-setting program. Serious deficiencies in one step cannot make up for strength in the other two. The three steps need to be implemented in a systematic fashion.

Step I: Set Goals Amazingly, this commonsense first step is not always followed. A recent survey of 1,900 managers revealed that nearly 46% of their project teams are not given specific, attainable goals. It thus should not be surprising to learn that only 33% of these managers indicated that their project teams complete their work on time and within budget.[54] Let us consider how managers can set goals with their employees or project teams.

Guitar Center is one of the fastest-growing retailers in the United States. At its 165 stores, service as a core value translates into a speific goal—salespeople are expected to answer the phone before the fourth ring. Company executives place calls periodically to make sure the goal is being met.

A number of sources can be used as input during this goal-setting stage. Time and motion studies are one source. Goals also may be based on the average past performance of job holders. Third, the employee and his or her manager may set the goal participatively, through give-and-take negotiation. Fourth, goals can be set by conducting external or internal benchmarking. Benchmarking is used when an organization wants to compare its performance or internal work processes to those of other organizations (external benchmarking) or to other internal units, branches, departments, or divisions within the organization (internal benchmarking). For example, a company might set a goal to surpass the customer service levels or profit of a benchmarked competitor. Finally, the overall strategy of a company (e.g., become the lowest-cost producer) may affect the goals set by employees at various levels in the organization.

In accordance with available research evidence, goals should be "SMART." SMART is an acronym that stands for specific, measurable, attainable, results oriented, and time bound. Table 7–2 contains a set of guidelines for writing SMART goals. There are two additional recommendations to consider when setting goals. First, for complex tasks, managers should train employees in problem-solving techniques and encourage them to develop a performance action plan. Action plans specify the strategies or tactics to be used in order to accomplish a goal.

Second, because of individual differences (recall our discussion in Chapter 5), it may be necessary to establish different goals for employees performing the same job. For example, a study of 103 undergraduate business students revealed that

Guidelines for Writing SMART Goals   TABLE 7–2

Specific	Goals should be stated in precise rather than vague terms. For example, a goal that provides for 20 hours of technical training for each employee is more specific than stating that a manager should send as many people as possible to training classes. Goals should be quantified when possible.
Measurable	A measurement device is needed to assess the extent to which a goal is accomplished. Goals thus need to be measurable. It also is critical to consider the quality aspect of the goal when establishing measurement criteria. For example, if the goal is to complete a managerial study of methods to increase productivity, one must consider how to measure the quality of this effort. Goals should not be set without considering the interplay between quantity and quality of output.
Attainable	Goals should be realistic, challenging, and attainable. Impossible goals reduce motivation because people do not like to fail. Remember, people have different levels of ability and skill.
Results oriented	Corporate goals should focus on desired end-results that support the organization's vision. In turn, an individual's goals should directly support the accomplishment of corporate goals. Activities support the achievement of goals and are outlined in action plans. To focus goals on desired end-results, goals should start with the word "to," followed by verbs such as complete, acquire, produce, increase, and decrease. Verbs such as develop, conduct, implement, or monitor imply activities and should not be used in a goal statement.
Time bound	Goals specify target dates for completion.

SOURCE: A J Kinicki, *Performance Management Systems* (Superstition Mt., AZ: Kinicki and Associates, Inc., 1992), pp 2–9. Reprinted with permission; all rights reserved.

individuals high in conscientiousness had higher motivation, had greater goal commitment, and obtained higher grades than students low in conscientiousness.[55] An individual's goal orientation is another important individual difference to consider when setting goals. Three types of goal orientations are a learning goal orientation, a performance-prove goal orientation, and a performance-avoid goal orientation. A team of researchers described the differences and implications for goal setting in the following way:

> People with a high learning goal orientation view skills as malleable. They make efforts not only to achieve current tasks but also to develop the ability to accomplish future tasks. People with a high performance-prove goal orientation tend to focus on performance and try to demonstrate their ability by looking better than others. People with a high performance-avoid goal orientation also focus on performance, but this focus is grounded in trying to avoid negative outcomes.[56]

Although some studies showed that people set higher goals, exerted more effort, had higher self-efficacy, and achieved higher performance when they possessed a learning goal orientation as opposed to either a performance-prove or

SKILLS & BEST PRACTICES

Managerial Actions for Enhancing Goal Commitment

1. Provide valued outcomes for goal accomplishment.

2. Raise employees' self-efficacy about meeting goals by (a) providing adequate training, (b) role modeling desired behaviors and actions, and (c) persuasively communicating confidence in the employees' ability to attain the goal.

3. Have employees make a public commitment to the goal.

4. Communicate an inspiring vision and explain how individual goals relate to accomplishing the vision.

5. Allow employees to participate in setting the goals.

6. Behave supportively rather than punitively.

7. Break a long-term goal (i.e., a yearly goal) into short-term subgoals.

8. Ensure that employees have the resources required to accomplish the goal.

SOURCE: These recommendations were derived from E A Locke and G P Latham, "Building a Practically Useful Theory of Goal Setting and Task Motivation," *American Psychologist*, September 2002, pp 705–17. Copyright © 2002 by the American Psychological Association. Adapted with permission.

performance-avoid goal orientation, other research demonstrated a more complex series of relationships.[57] The best we can conclude is that an individual's goal orientation influences the actions that he or she takes in the pursuit of accomplishing goals in specific situations.[58] In conclusion, managers are encouraged to consider individual differences when setting goals.

Step 2: Promote Goal Commitment Obtaining goal commitment is important because employees are more motivated to pursue goals they view as reasonable, obtainable, and fair. Goal commitment may be increased through a variety of methods. The Skills & Best Practices, for example, presents eight managerial actions that can be used to increase employees' goal commitment.

Step 3: Provide Support and Feedback Step 3 calls for providing employees with the necessary support elements or resources to get the job done. This includes ensuring that each employee has the necessary abilities, training, and information needed to achieve his or her goals. Unfortunately, a recent study suggests that organizations are deficient in this regard.[59] Training often is required to help employees achieve difficult goals. Moreover, managers should pay attention to employees' perceptions of effort → performance expectancies, self-efficacy, and valence of rewards. Finally, as we discuss in detail in Chapter 8, employees should be provided with timely, specific feedback (knowledge of results) on how they are doing.

Putting Motivational Theories to Work

Successfully designing and implementing motivational programs is not easy. Managers cannot simply take one of the theories discussed in this book and apply it word for word. Dynamics within organizations interfere with applying motivation theories in "pure" form. According to management scholar Terence Mitchell,

> There are situations and settings that make it exceptionally difficult for a motivational system to work. These circumstances may involve the kinds of jobs or people present, the technology, the presence of a union, and so on. The factors that hinder the application of motivational theory have not been articulated either frequently or systematically.[60]

Group Exercise

What Motivates You?

With Mitchell's cautionary statement in mind, this section uses Figure 6–1 (see page 148 in Chapter 6) to raise issues that need to be addressed before implementing a motivational program. Our intent is not to discuss all relevant considerations but rather to highlight a few important ones.

Assuming a motivational program is being considered to improve productivity, quality, or customer satisfaction, the first issue revolves around the difference between motivation and performance. As shown in Figure 6–1, motivation and performance are not one and the same. Motivation is only one of several factors that influence performance. For example, poor performance may be more a function of outdated or inefficient materials and machinery, not having goals to direct one's attention, a monotonous job, feelings of inequity, a negative work environment characterized by political behavior and conflict, poor supervisory support and coaching, or poor work flow. Motivation cannot make up for a deficient job context (see Figure 6–1). Managers, therefore, need to carefully consider the causes of poor performance and employee misbehavior. Employee surveys can be used to help determine the contextual causes of low motivation.[61]

Importantly, managers should not ignore the individual inputs identified in Figure 6–1. As discussed in this chapter as well as Chapters 5 and 6, individual differences are an important input that influence motivation and motivated behavior. Managers are advised to develop employees so that they have the ability and job knowledge to effectively perform their jobs. In addition, attempts should be made to nurture positive employee characteristics, such as self-esteem, self-efficacy, positive emotions, a learning goal orientation, and need for achievement.

Because motivation is goal directed, the process of developing and setting goals should be consistent with our previous discussion. Moreover, the method used to evaluate performance also needs to be considered. Without a valid performance appraisal system, it is difficult, if not impossible, to accurately distinguish good and poor performers. Managers need to keep in mind that both equity and expectancy theory suggest that employee motivation is squelched by inaccurate performance ratings. Consider the approach that General Electric, rated as the most admired company to work for by *Fortune* in 2005, takes in terms of developing and evaluating its employees.

> The company takes a lot of heat for getting rid of the bottom 10% of its employees every year, but that's only the end point of a process of constant appraisal. The fired ones are not surprised when the ax comes down. . . . Dan Mudd is the president and CEO of Fannie Mae; as president and CEO of GE Capital Japan from 1999 to mid-2005, he saw this dynamic from the inside. "GE, like anywhere else, has a little bit of politics, a little bit of personal stuff and all that," he says, "but compared with all the other organizations I know, it's minimized. It's upfront. You know what you have to do to succeed." Most companies, frankly, don't have the stomach to give frequent, rigorous evaluations—and to fire those who need to be fired.[62]

Finally, it is important for organizations to train their managers to properly assess people. While GE clearly adheres to this suggestion, a recent survey of 96 human resource professionals suggests that many companies do not. Sixty-one percent of the respondents concluded that managers were not properly trained to conduct performance evaluations.[63]

Consistent with expectancy theory, managers should make extrinsic rewards contingent on performance. In doing so, however, it is important to consider two issues. First, managers need to ensure that performance goals are directed to achieve the "right" end-results. For example, health insurers and medical groups wrestle over the relative focus on cost savings versus patient satisfaction. Consider the case of Oakland-based Kaiser Permanente:

> Telephone clerks at California's largest HMO received bonuses for keeping calls with patients brief and limiting the number of doctor visits they set up. . . . The

California Nurses Association, the union representing Kaiser's registered nurses, derided the program as deceitful and harmful to patients with serious medical problems.

"Patients don't understand they're talking to a high school graduate with no nursing background," [Jim] Anderson said.

The clerks, who generally have little to no medical training, answer phone calls from customers wanting to set up doctor appointments or asking simple medical questions.

Cash bonuses were paid to those who made appointments for fewer than 35% of callers and spent less than an average of three minutes, 45 seconds on the phone with each patient. Clerks were also encouraged to transfer fewer than 50% of the calls to registered nurses for further evaluation.[64]

Interestingly, incentives based on quality care and patient satisfaction are twice as common as cost-cutting incentives among heath insurers across the United States.[65] Second, the promise of increased rewards will not prompt higher effort and good performance unless those rewards are clearly tied to performance and they are large enough to gain employees' interest or attention.[66]

Moreover, equity theory tells us that motivation is influenced by employee perceptions about the fairness of reward allocations. Motivation is decreased when employees believe rewards are inequitably allocated. Rewards also need to be integrated appropriately into the appraisal system. If performance is measured at the individual level, individual achievements need to be rewarded. On the other hand, when performance is the result of group effort, rewards should be allocated to the group.[67]

Feedback also should be linked with performance. Feedback provides the information and direction needed to keep employees focused on relevant tasks, activities, and goals. Managers should strive to provide specific, timely, and accurate feedback to employees.

Finally, we end this chapter by noting that an organization's culture significantly influences employee motivation and behavior. A positive self-enhancing culture such as that at Nucor, for example, is more likely to engender higher motivation and commitment than a culture dominated by suspicion, fault finding, and blame.[68]

key terms

distributive justice   179

equity sensitivity   176

equity theory   175

expectancy   181

expectancy theory   181

goal   186

goal commitment   189

goal difficulty   187

goal specificity   187

instrumentality   182

interactional justice   179

management by objectives   186

negative inequity   176

positive inequity   176

procedural justice   179

valence   182

chapter summary

- *Discuss the role of perceived inequity in employee motivation.* Equity theory is a model of motivation that explains how people strive for fairness and justice in social exchanges. On the job, feelings of inequity revolve around a person's evaluation of whether he or she receives adequate rewards to compensate for his or her contributive inputs. People perform these evaluations by comparing the perceived fairness of their employment exchange with that of relevant others. Perceived inequity creates motivation to restore equity.

- *Describe the practical lessons derived from equity theory.* Equity theory has at least nine practical implications. First, because people are motivated to resolve perceptions of inequity, managers should not discount employees' feelings and perceptions when trying to motivate workers. Second, managers should pay attention to employees' *perceptions* of what is fair and equitable. It is the employee's view of reality that counts when trying to motivate someone, according to equity theory. Third, employees should be given a voice in decisions that affect them. Fourth, employees should be given the opportunity to appeal decisions that affect their welfare. Fifth, employees are more likely to accept and support organizational change when they believe it is implemented fairly and when it produces equitable outcomes. Sixth, managers can promote cooperation and teamwork among group members by treating them equitably. Seventh, treating employees inequitably can lead to litigation and costly court settlements. Eighth, managers need to pay attention to the organization's climate for justice because it influences employee attitudes and behavior. Finally, employees' perceptions of justice are strongly influenced by the leadership behavior exhibited by their managers.

- *Explain Vroom's expectancy theory.* Expectancy theory assumes motivation is determined by one's perceived chances of achieving valued outcomes. Vroom's expectancy model of motivation reveals how effort → performance expectancies and performance → outcome instrumentalities influence the degree of effort expended to achieve desired (positively valent) outcomes.

- *Describe the practical implications of expectancy theory.* Managers are advised to enhance effort → performance expectancies by helping employees accomplish their performance goals. With respect to instrumentalities and valences, managers should attempt to link employee performance and valued rewards. There are four prerequisites to linking performance and rewards: (a) Managers need to develop and communicate performance standards to employees, (b) managers need valid and accurate performance ratings, (c) managers need to determine the relative mix of individual versus team contribution to performance and then reward accordingly, and (d) managers should use performance ratings to differentially allocate rewards among employees.

- *Identify five practical lessons to be learned from goal-setting research.* Difficult goals lead to higher performance than easy or moderate goals: goals should not be impossible to achieve. Specific, difficult goals lead to higher performance for simple rather than complex tasks. Third, feedback enhances the effect of specific, difficult goals. Fourth, participative goals, assigned goals, and self-set goals are equally effective. Fifth, goal commitment and monetary incentives affect goal-setting outcomes.

- *Specify issues that should be addressed before implementing a motivational program.* Managers need to consider the variety of causes of poor performance and employee misbehavior. Undesirable employee performance and behavior may be due to a host of deficient individual inputs (e.g., ability, dispositions, emotions, and beliefs) or job context factors (e.g., materials and machinery, job characteristics, reward systems, supervisory support and coaching, and social norms). The method used to evaluate performance as well as the link between performance and rewards must be examined. Performance must be accurately evaluated and rewards should be equitably distributed. Managers should also recognize that employee motivation and behavior are influenced by organizational culture.

discussion questions

1. To what extent is the pay-for-performance systems for teachers discussed in the chapter-opening case consistent with the practical implications of expectancy theory? Explain.
2. Could a manager's attempt to treat his or her employees equally lead to perceptions of inequity? Explain.
3. If someone who reported to you at work had a low expectancy for successful performance, what could you do to increase this person's expectancy?
4. Goal-setting research suggests that people should be given difficult goals. How does this prescription mesh with expectancy theory? Explain.
5. How could a professor use equity, expectancy, and goal-setting theory to motivate students?

ethical dilemma

A High School Teacher Must Deal with Plagiarizing Students[69]

High school teacher Christine Pelton wasted no time after discovering that nearly a fifth of her biology students had plagiarized their semester projects from the Internet.

She had received her rural Kansas district's backing before when she accused students of cheating, and she expected it again this time after failing the 28 sophomores.

Her principal and superintendent agreed: It was plagiarism, and the students should get a zero for the assignment.

But after parents complained, the Piper School Board ordered her to go easier on the guilty. . . . The board ordered her to give the students partial credit and to decrease the project's value from 50% of the final course grade to 30%.

One of the complaining parents, Theresa Woolley, told the *Kansas City Star* that her daughter did not plagiarize but was not sure how much she needed to rewrite research material.

But Pelton said the course syllabus, which she required students to sign, warned of the consequences of cheating and plagiarism. . . .

What is worse, McCabe said [Donald McCabe is a professor of management at Rutgers University], is that tolerance of dishonesty disheartens other students, who have to compete with the cheaters to get into college.

"If they see teachers looking the other way, students feel compelled to participate even though it makes them uncomfortable," McCabe said.

What Would You Do If You Were Christine Pelton?

1. Resign your position in protest over the school board's lack of support. Explain your rationale.
2. Do what the school board ordered. Discuss the impact of this choice on the students who plagiarized and those who did not.
3. Ignore the school board's order and give the failing grades. Explain your rationale.
4. Invent other options. Discuss.

For an interpretation of this situation, visit our Web site, www.mhhe.com/kinickiob3e.

If you're looking for additional study materials, be sure to check out the Online Learning Center at

www.mhhe.com/kinickiob3e

for more information and interactivities that correspond to this chapter.

chapter Eight

Improving Performance with Feedback, Rewards, and Positive Reinforcement

LEARNING OBJECTIVES

After reading the material in this chapter, you should be able to:

- Specify the two basic functions of feedback and three sources of feedback.

- Define upward feedback and 360-degree feedback, and summarize the general tips for giving good feedback.

- Distinguish between extrinsic and intrinsic rewards, and give a job-related example of each.

- Summarize the research lessons about pay for performance, and explain why rewards often fail to motivate employees.

- State Thorndike's "law of effect" and explain Skinner's distinction between respondent and operant behavior.

- Demonstrate your knowledge of positive reinforcement, negative reinforcement, punishment, and extinction, and explain behavior shaping.

KEEPING SCORE AT UMB BANK

BusinessWeek

There are unusual early morning goings-on these days at community banks in the college town of Springfield, Mo. Before doors open at branches of **UMB Bank**, employees gather in a "sales huddle" and listen to managers dole out a mix of praise and exhortation. "It's all about pumping up the troops," says **Gil Trout**, who runs 25 branches in southeastern Missouri. The huddles seem to make a difference. Trout's branches upped their total retail customers so far this year to 3,800 from 3,500.

That may not seem like a lot in the grand scheme of things, but it's part of a sea change that has swept over **UMB Financial Corp.** The 92-year-old Kansas City-based bank, with branches in seven midwestern states, had become indolent early in the decade, so new management was brought in to shake things up. Key to this transformation project: electronic management scorecards. They help track the performance of a company,

set business-unit goals, stimulate new ideas, and motivate managers and employees to do better. The idea for using huddles came out of a discussion among Trout and his branch managers early this year. Under pressure to meet the quantitative benchmarks of the scorecards, they decided to try the face-to-face huddles,

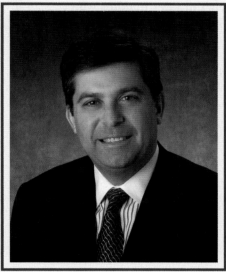

Peter deSilva, president of **UMB** Bank of Springfield, Missouri.

which had been developed earlier by the headquarters staff. "It's becoming part of our culture," says President Peter J. deSilva, who came to the bank from Fidelity Investments in Boston 22 months ago. "It's driving behavior, and

ultimately, behavior drives performance."

UMB is on the leading edge of one of the hottest trends in technology. CEOs are rapidly adopting electronic scorecards and similar programs to help them better understand and run their companies. Scorecards are sophisticated systems typically used by people at many levels in the company. Viewed through a Web browser, scorecards gather statistics from different databases about inventory, sales, and customer trends. "With these tools, CEOs are able to make better decisions on a more timely basis," says Forrester Research analyst Keith Gile. . . .

The most important move **UMB** made was tying compensation to scorecard results. In the past the bank paid people based primarily on seniority and cost-of-living adjustments. Now a substantial part of compensation for managers depends on how they perform against scorecard goals. The board of directors reviews results with top executives quarterly, and about 45 second-tier managers get reviewed monthly by the people above them. "If you don't review people and hold them accountable, you won't achieve anything," says deSilva. . . .

Experts say scorecards should include forward-looking stats instead of just historical data such as quarterly earnings. One example at UMB: the number of customer calls that commercial loan officers make in a month. "I urge my clients to make sure they're analyzing the right data," says John Potter, a principal at management consulting firm John Potter Global.

Once UMB has the scorecard process down cold, it plans to deploy a similar technology called dashboards. This Web tool has dials, like a car dashboard, that rise to yellow or red when something goes awry, such as sales falling behind expectations. At that point, UMB employees taking part in sales huddles won't have to find out from their bosses whether they've got something to cheer about. They'll already know.[1]

Looking ahead, what positives and negatives do you foresee for electronic scorecards and dashboards in the workplace? For an interpretation of this case and additional comments, visit our Online Learning Center at

www.mhhe.com/kinickiob3e

FOR DISCUSSION

PRODUCTIVITY AND QUALITY IMPROVEMENT EXPERTS tell us we need to work smarter, not harder. While it is true that a sound education and appropriate skill training are needed if one is to work smarter, the process does not end there. Today's employees need instructive and supportive feedback and desired rewards if they are to translate their knowledge into improved productivity and superior quality. This point was reinforced by a recent survey of 2,600 employees in the United States. Forty-two percent reported getting regular feedback on their job performance and only 29% said they were rewarded for good work. Worse yet, 29% claimed poor performers in their department were not managed appropriately.[2] Figure 8–1 illustrates a learning- and development-focused cycle in which feedback enhances ability, encourages effort, and acknowledges results. Rewards and reinforcement, in turn, motivate effort and compensate results.

This chapter concludes our coverage of individual behavior by discussing the effects of feedback, rewards, and positive reinforcement on behavior and by integrating those insights with what you have learned about perception, individual differences, and various motivational tools such as goal setting.[3]

Providing Effective Feedback

Numerous surveys tell us employees have a hearty appetite for feedback.[4] So also do achievement-oriented students. Following a difficult exam, for instance, students want to know two things: how they did and how their peers did. By letting students know how their work measures up to grading and competitive standards, an instructor's feedback permits the students to adjust their study habits so they can reach their goals. Likewise, managers in well-run organizations follow up goal setting with a feedback program to provide a

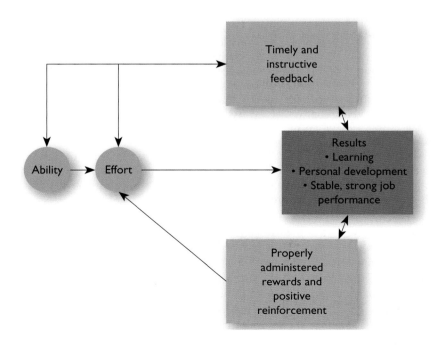

FIGURE 8–1

Bolstering the Job Performance Cycle with Feedback, Rewards, and Reinforcement

"I work best when someone is looking over my shoulder and telling me that I'm a screw-up."

SOURCE: *Harvard Business Review*, December 2005, p 97.
Copyright © 2005 Bob Vejtko. Reprinted with permission.

feedback

Objective information about performance.

rational basis for adjustment and improvement. For example, notice the importance Fred Smith, the founder and head of Federal Express, places on feedback when outlining his philosophy of leadership:

> When people walk in the door, they want to know: What do you expect out of me? What's in this deal for me? What do I have to do to get ahead? Where do I go in this organization to get justice if I'm not treated appropriately? They want to know how they're doing. They want some feedback. And they want to know that what they are doing is important.
>
> If you take the basic principles of leadership and answer those questions over and over again, you can be successful dealing with people.[5]

Feedback too often gets shortchanged. In fact, "poor or insufficient feedback" was the leading cause of deficient performance in a survey of US and European companies.[6]

As the term is used here, **feedback** is objective information about individual or collective performance shared with those in a position to improve the situation. Subjective assessments such as, "You're lazy" do not qualify as *objective* feedback. But hard data such as units sold, days absent, dollars saved, projects completed, customers satisfied, and quality rejects are all candidates for objective feedback programs. Management consultants Chip Bell and Ron Zemke offered this helpful perspective of feedback:

> Feedback is, quite simply, any information that answers those "How am I doing?" questions. *Good* feedback answers them truthfully and productively. It's information people can use either to confirm or correct their performance.
>
> Feedback comes in many forms and from a variety of sources. Some is easy to get and requires hardly any effort to understand. The charts and graphs tracking group and individual performance that are fixtures in many workplaces are an example of this variety. Performance feedback—the numerical type at least—is at the heart of most approaches to total quality management.
>
> Some feedback is less accessible. It's tucked away in the heads of customers and managers. But no matter how well-hidden the feedback, if people need it to keep their performance on track, we need to get it to them—preferably while it's still fresh enough to make an impact.[7]

Two Functions of Feedback

Experts say feedback serves two functions for those who receive it; one is *instructional* and the other *motivational*. Feedback instructs when it clarifies roles or teaches new behavior. For example, an assistant accountant might be advised to handle a certain entry as a capital item rather than as an expense item. On the other hand, feedback motivates when it serves as a reward or promises a reward.[8] Having the boss tell you that a grueling project you worked on earlier has just been completed can be a rewarding piece of news. As documented in one study, the motivational function of feedback can be significantly enhanced by pairing *specific,* challenging goals with *specific* feedback about results.[9] A recent laboratory study with college students divided into superior-subordinate pairs demonstrated not only the positive impact of helpful feedback on performance, but a dampening effect on perceived organizational politics as well.[10] As discussed in Chapter 13, organizational politics is often dysfunctional.

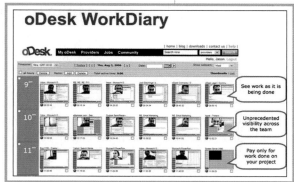

Three Sources of Feedback: Others, Task, and Self

It almost goes without saying that employees receive objective feedback from *others* such as peers, supervisors, lower-level employees, and outsiders. Perhaps less obvious is the fact that the *task* itself is a ready source of objective feedback.[11] Anyone who has spent hours on a "quick" Google search can appreciate the power of task-provided feedback. Similarly, skilled tasks such as computer programming or landing a jet airplane provide a steady stream of feedback about how well or poorly one is doing. A third source of feedback is *oneself,* but self-serving bias and other perceptual problems can contaminate this source. Those high in self-confidence tend to rely on personal feedback more than those with low self-confidence. Although circumstances vary, an employee can be bombarded by feedback from all three sources simultaneously. This is where the gatekeeping functions of perception and cognitive evaluation are needed to help sort things out.

The Recipient's Perspective of Feedback

The need for feedback is variable, across both individuals and situations[12] (see Hands-On Exercise). Feedback can be positive or negative. Generally, people tend to perceive and recall positive feedback more accurately than they do negative feedback.[13] But negative feedback (e.g., being told your performance is below average) can have a *positive* motivational effect. In fact, in one study, those who were told they were below average on a creativity test subsequently outperformed those who were led to believe their results were above average. The subjects apparently took the negative feedback as a challenge and set and pursued higher goals. Those receiving positive feedback apparently were less motivated to do better.[14] Nonetheless, feedback with a negative message or threatening content needs to be administered carefully to avoid creating insecurity and defensiveness.[15] Self-efficacy also can be damaged by negative feedback, as discovered in a pair of experiments with business students. The researchers concluded, "To facilitate the development of strong efficacy beliefs, managers should be careful about the provision of negative feedback. Destructive criticism by managers which attributes the cause of poor performance to internal factors reduces both the beliefs of self-efficacy and the self-set goals of recipients."[16]

Upon receiving feedback, people cognitively evaluate factors such as its accuracy, the credibility of the source, the fairness of the system (e.g., performance appraisal

A small California firm called oDesk connects companies that need to outsource specific tasks to outside workers skilled in programming, technical writing, and graphic design. Although these contract workers aren't employees and sign in from home, oDesk monitors their performance by means of Web cams, random screen shots of what they're working on, and logs showing mouse clicks and keystrokes per minute. It also developed a feedback system like eBay's through which workers and employers can rate each other.

Self-Assessment Exercise

Assessing Your Empathy Skills

Measuring Your Desire for Performance Feedback

INSTRUCTIONS: Circle one number indicating the strength of your agreement or disagreement with each statement. Total your responses, and compare your score with our arbitrary norms.

	Disagree				Agree
1. As long as I think that I have done something well, I am not too concerned about how other people think I have done.	5	4	3	2	1
2. How other people view my work is not as important as how I view my own work.	5	4	3	2	1
3. It is usually better not to put much faith in what others say about your work, regardless of whether it is complimentary or not.	5	4	3	2	1
4. If I have done something well, I know it without other people telling me so.	5	4	3	2	1
5. I usually have a clear idea of what I am trying to do and how well I am proceeding toward my goal.	5	4	3	2	1
6. I find that I am usually a pretty good judge of my own performance.	5	4	3	2	1
7. It is very important to me to know what people think of my work.	1	2	3	4	5
8. It is a good idea to get someone to check on your work before it's too late to make changes.	1	2	3	4	5
9. Even though I may think I have done a good job, I feel a lot more confident of it after someone else tells me so.	1	2	3	4	5
10. Since I cannot be objective about my own performance, it is best to listen to the feedback provided by others.	1	2	3	4	5

Total score = _____

ARBITRARY NORMS
10–23 = Low desire for feedback
24–36 = Moderate desire for feedback
37–50 = High desire for feedback

SOURCE: Excerpted and adapted from D M Herold, C K Parsons, and R B Rensvold, "Individual Differences in the Generation and Processing of Performance Feedback," *Educational and Psychological Measurement*, February 1996, Table 1, p 9. Copyright © 1996 by Sage Publications. Reprinted by permission of Sage Publications, Inc.

system), their performance-reward expectancies, and the reasonableness of the standards. Any feedback that fails to clear one or more of these cognitive hurdles will be rejected or downplayed. Personal experience largely dictates how these factors are weighed.

Behavioral Outcomes of Feedback

In Chapter 7, we discussed how goal setting gives behavior direction, increases expended effort, and fosters persistence. Because feedback is intimately related to the goal-setting process, it involves the same behavioral outcomes: direction, effort, and persistence. However, while the fourth outcome of goal setting involves formulating goal-attainment strategies, the fourth possible outcome of feedback is *resistance*. Feedback schemes that smack of manipulation or fail one or more of the perceptual and cognitive evaluation tests mentioned previously breed resistance.[17] Desirable work outcomes are more likely when feedback is part of a comprehensive *mentoring* or *coaching* process[18] (see Skills & Best Practices).

Nontraditional Upward Feedback and 360-Degree Feedback

Traditional top-down feedback programs have given way to some interesting variations in recent years. Two newer approaches, discussed in this section, are upward feedback and 360-degree feedback. Aside from breaking away from a strict superior-to-subordinate feedback loop, these newer approaches are different because they typically involve *multiple sources* of feedback.[19] Instead of getting feedback from one boss, often during an annual performance appraisal, more and more managers are getting structured feedback from superiors, lower-level employees, peers, and even outsiders such as customers. Nontraditional feedback is growing in popularity for at least six reasons:

1. Traditional performance appraisal systems have created widespread dissatisfaction. This was clearly evident in a recent survey of 96 human resource managers:

   > Sixty-one percent said managers have not been trained on how to properly assess people; 40 percent say the competencies managers are using to assess their employees do not accurately reflect the job and 28 percent report that managers play favorites.[20]

2. Team-based organization structures are replacing traditional hierarchies. This trend requires managers to have good interpersonal skills that are best evaluated by team members.

3. Multiple-rater systems are said to make feedback more valid than single-source feedback.[21]

4. Advanced computer network technology (the Internet and company intranets) greatly facilitates multiple-rater systems.[22]

5. Bottom-up feedback meshes nicely with the trend toward participative management and employee empowerment.

6. Co-workers and lower-level employees are said to know more about a manager's strengths and limitations than the boss.[23]

Good Advice on Feedback and Executive Coaches from Jack and Suzy Welch

Feedback

First and foremost, you need to actively mentor your people. Exude positive energy about life and the work that you are doing together, show optimism about the future, and care. Care passionately about each person's progress. Give your people feedback—not just at yearend and midyear performance reviews but after meetings, presentations, or visits to clients. Make every significant event a teaching moment. Discuss what you like about what they are doing and ways that they can improve. Your energy will energize those around you.

And there's no need for sugarcoating. Use total candor, which happens, incidentally, to be one of the defining characteristics of effective leaders.

Executive Coaches

Good executive coaches can provide a truly important service. . . . They can look you in the eye and tell you what no one else will, especially if you're the boss. You don't listen carefully enough. You're too much of a loner. You kiss up to the board but too often bully your people. You rely too much on the advice of one employee who really isn't very smart. Or any number of other unpleasant messages like that.

The challenge is for you to listen. Because at the end of the day, the ultimate value of executive coaching, done right, is only as big or small as your ability to hear it.

SOURCE: Excerpted from J and S Welch, "The Leadership Mindset," *BusinessWeek,* January 30, 2006, p 120; and J and S Welch, "How Healthy Is Your Company?" *BusinessWeek,* May 8, 2006, p 126. Jack Welch is the former CEO of General Electric and his wife, Suzy Welch, is the former editor of *Harvard Business Review.*

Together, these factors make a compelling case for looking at better ways to give and receive performance feedback.

upward feedback

Employees evaluate their boss.

Upward Feedback Upward feedback stands the traditional approach on its head by having lower-level employees provide feedback on a manager's style and performance. This type of feedback is generally anonymous. Most students are familiar with upward feedback programs from years of filling out anonymous teacher evaluation surveys. Early adopters of upward evaluations include AT&T, General Mills, Motorola, and Procter & Gamble.[24]

Managers often resist upward feedback programs because they believe it erodes their authority. Other critics say anonymous upward feedback can become little more than a personality contest or, worse, be manipulated by managers who make promises or threats. What does the research literature tell us about upward feedback?

Studies with diverse samples have given us these useful insights:

- The question of whether upward feedback should be *anonymous* was addressed by a study at a large US insurance company. All told, 183 employees rated the skills and effectiveness of 38 managers. Managers who received anonymous upward feedback received *lower* ratings and liked the process *less* than did those receiving feedback from identifiable employees. This finding confirmed the criticism that employees will tend to go easier on their boss when not protected by confidentiality.[25]

- A large-scale study at the US Naval Academy, where student leaders and followers live together day and night, discovered a positive impact of upward feedback on leader behavior.[26]

- In a field study of 238 corporate managers, upward feedback had a positive impact on the performance of low-to-moderate performers.[27]

360-degree feedback

Comparison of anonymous feedback from one's superior, subordinates, and peers with self-perceptions.

360-Degree Feedback Letting individuals compare their own perceived performance with behaviorally specific (and usually anonymous) performance information from their manager, subordinates, and peers is known as **360-degree feedback.** Even outsiders may be involved in what is sometimes called full-circle feedback. The idea is to let the individual know how their behavior affects others, with the goal of motivating change. Consider this manager's story, for example:

> Lydia Whitefield, vice president of corporate marketing at Avaya, has received dozens of performance reviews from dozens of bosses during her 10-year career in telecommunications. But the one review she never forgot, the one that pushed her to alter her management style, came from an employee.
>
> "He told me, 'You're angry a lot,'" says Ms. Whitefield. "I was stunned, because what he and other employees saw as anger, I saw as my passion." She subsequently learned to be more contained when discussing assignments with staff and to avoid reacting vehemently.
>
> "That feedback was a life-altering experience for me," says Ms. Whitefield, who currently supervises about 75 people. She believes in the need for appraisals by employees of their bosses. "They can sting, but they are always instructive," she says.[28]

In a 360-degree feedback program, a given manager will play different roles, including focal person, superior, subordinate, and peer. Of course, the focal person role is played only once. The other roles are played more than once for various other focal persons. As a barometer of popularity, the Society for Human Resource Management found 32% of the companies it surveyed in 2000 using 360-degree feedback.[29]

Because upward feedback is a part of 360-degree feedback programs, the evidence reviewed earlier applies here as well. As with upward feedback, peer- and self-evaluations, central to 360-degree feedback programs, also are a significant affront to tradition.[30] But advocates say co-workers and managers themselves are appropriate performance evaluators because they are closest to the action. Generally, research builds a stronger case for peer appraisals than for self-appraisals.[31] Self-serving bias, discussed in Chapter 4, is a problem.

Rigorous research evidence of 360-degree feedback programs is scarce. A two-year study of 48 managers given 360-degree feedback in a large US public utility company led to these somewhat promising results. According to the researchers, "The group as a whole developed its skills, but there was substantial variability among individuals in how much change occurred."[32] Thus, as with any feedback, individuals vary in their response to 360-degree feedback. This problem was addressed in a recent field study of 20 managers and 67 employees at a manufacturing company. In addition to receiving 360-degree feedback, the managers were coached to enhance their self-awareness and employ the self-management techniques we discussed in Chapter 5. According to the researchers, "this feedback-coaching resulted in improved manager and employee satisfaction, commitment, intentions to turnover, and at least indirectly, this firm's performance."[33]

Practical Recommendations   Research evidence on upward and 360-degree feedback leads us to *favor* anonymity and *discourage* use for pay and promotion decisions. Otherwise, managerial resistance and self-serving manipulation would prevail.[34] We enthusiastically endorse the use of upward and/or 360-degree feedback for management development and training purposes.

Why Feedback Often Fails

Experts on the subject cite the following six common trouble signs for organizational feedback systems:

1. Feedback is used to punish, embarrass, or put down employees.
2. Those receiving the feedback see it as irrelevant to their work.
3. Feedback information is provided too late to do any good.
4. People receiving feedback believe it relates to matters beyond their control.
5. Employees complain about wasting too much time collecting and recording feedback data.
6. Feedback recipients complain about feedback being too complex or difficult to understand.[35]

Managers can provide effective feedback by consciously avoiding these pitfalls and following the practical tips in Skills & Best Practices.

How to Make Sure Feedback Gets Results

- Relate feedback to existing performance goals and clear *expectations*.
- Give *specific* feedback tied to observable behavior or measurable results.
- Channel feedback toward *key result areas*.
- Give feedback as *soon* as possible.
- Give positive feedback for *improvement*, not just final results.
- Focus feedback on *performance*, not personalities.
- Base feedback on *accurate* and *credible* information.

SKILLS & BEST PRACTICES

FIGURE 8–2
Key Factors in
Organizational
Reward
Systems

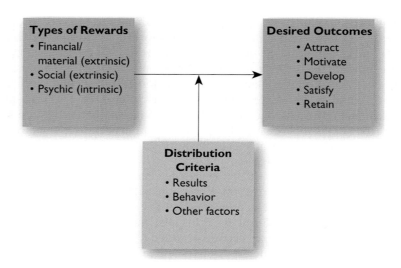

Organizational Reward Systems

Rewards are an ever-present and always controversial feature of organizational life.[36] Some employees see their job as the source of a paycheck and little else. Others derive great pleasure from their job and association with co-workers. Even volunteers who donate their time to charitable organizations, such as the Red Cross, walk away with rewards in the form of social recognition and pride of having given unselfishly of their time. Hence, the subject of organizational rewards includes, but goes far beyond, monetary compensation.[37] This section examines key components of organizational reward systems.

Despite the fact that reward systems vary widely, it is possible to identify and interrelate some common components. The model in Figure 8–2 focuses on three important components: (1) types of rewards, (2) distribution criteria, and (3) desired outcomes. Let us examine these components and then discuss pay for performance.

Types of Rewards

Including the usual paycheck, the variety and magnitude of organizational rewards boggles the mind—from subsidized day care to college tuition reimbursement to stock grants and options.[38] A US Bureau of Labor Statistics economist offered the following historical perspective of employee compensation:

> One of the more striking developments . . . over the past 75 years has been the growing complexity of employee compensation. Limited at the outbreak of World War I largely to straight-time pay for hours worked, compensation now includes a variety of employer-financed benefits, such as health and life insurance, retirement income, and paid time off. Although the details of each vary widely, these benefits are today standard components of the compensation package, and workers generally have come to expect them.[39]

Today, it is common for nonwage benefits to be 50% or more of total compensation.

In addition to the obvious pay and benefits, there are less obvious social and psychic rewards. Social rewards include praise and recognition from others both inside and outside the organization. Psychic rewards come from personal feelings of self-esteem, self-satisfaction, and accomplishment.

An alternative typology for organizational rewards is the distinction between extrinsic and intrinsic rewards. Financial, material, and social rewards qualify as **extrinsic rewards** because they come from the environment. Psychic rewards, however, are **intrinsic rewards** because they are self-granted. An employee who works to obtain extrinsic rewards, such as money or praise, is said to be extrinsically motivated. As we discussed in Chapter 6, one who derives pleasure from the task itself or experiences a sense of competence, pride, or self-determination is said to be intrinsically motivated.[40] The relative importance of extrinsic and intrinsic rewards is a matter of culture, personal tastes, and pressing circumstances. For example, consider this situation in hurricane-ravaged New Orleans in late 2005:

> **extrinsic rewards**
> Financial, material, or social rewards from the environment.
>
> **intrinsic rewards**
> Self-granted, psychic rewards.

> Many of BellSouth's 3,000 local workers lost their homes to Katrina. Some, such as manager Nancy Talbot Shebesta, were wiped out.
>
> Yet, here they are, slogging it out in the streets every day with the insistent goal of restoring phone service to a struggling city.
>
> Shebesta, a 32-year BellSouth veteran, has a ready explanation: "Providing phone service to people isn't just a business for us," she says. "It's a real point of pride."
>
> That feeling, she says, was what drove her to unfurl the BellSouth corporate flag—at half-staff—at the height of Katrina's fury. The image of BellSouth's flag flapping defiantly in the wind was captured by NBC and beamed around the world. It became a symbol of the city's resolve.[41]

Distribution Criteria

According to one expert on organizational reward systems, three general criteria for the distribution of rewards are as follows:

- *Performance: results.* Tangible outcomes such as individual, group, or organization performance; quantity and quality of performance.

- *Performance: actions and behaviors.* Such as teamwork, cooperation, risk taking, creativity.

- *Nonperformance considerations.* Customary or contractual, where the type of job, nature of the work, equity, tenure, level in hierarchy, etc., are rewarded.[42]

As illustrated in the following example, the trend today is toward *performance* criteria and away from nonperformance criteria:

> Del Wallick wears his pride under his sleeve. A handshake reveals his prized wristwatch, given to mark his 25th anniversary with Timken Co. "I only take it off to shower and sleep," he says.
>
> The hallways of Mr. Wallick's home in Canton, Ohio, are filled with an array of certificates marking the milestones in his 31-year career as a Timken steel-mill worker. Down in his rec room, a mantel clock that he and his wife picked out from a Timken gift catalog rests atop the family television.
>
> But these days, once-paternal companies like Timken are trying to move away from rewarding employees for long service. Many are reducing service-award programs—and a few are eliminating them entirely. Besides wanting to save money, these companies hope to tilt recognition more toward performance and away from years of loyal service.[43]

Group Exercise
What Rewards Motivate Student Achievement?

Test Your Knowledge
Appraisal Methods

For Urban Outfitters, the trendy clothing chain, everyone is expected to help with trend spotting, and they're well rewarded. Employees from managers to interns who bring back news of hot trends and styles to the buyers and design teams receive free concert tickets and evenings out, courtesy of the company. The chain won't give away exactly who it's spying on.

Gainsharing at Whole Foods

At $4.7 billion Whole Foods Market, when store department "teams" finish a four-week period under their payroll budget, the company doesn't keep the surplus. Rather, it gets handed down to the employees whose efficiency created the savings.

Here's how it works. Managers constantly track their payroll spending against their budget. Every four weeks they divide any surplus by the hours logged and add the result, or "gainshare," to workers' hourly wages. If the surplus is $2,000, on 1,200 hours, each employee gets an extra $1.67 per hour. The company claims the incentive not only pushes workers to step it up a notch but also aids in recruiting. Newcomers need a two-thirds vote from colleagues to be brought on permanently. As company spokeswoman Amy Schaefer notes, "It's a chance for team members to say, 'This person is not catching on, they're not productive,' because they're going to share their gainsharing with them."

SOURCE: From D Jacobson, "Gainsharing," *Business 2.0,* **April 2006, p 96. Copyright © 2006 Time Inc. All rights reserved.**

pay for performance

Monetary incentives tied to one's results or accomplishments.

We turn our attention to pay for performance after rounding out the reward system model in Figure 8–2.

Desired Outcomes

As listed in Figure 8–2, a good reward system should attract talented people and motivate and satisfy them once they have joined the organization.[44] Further, a good reward system should foster personal growth and development and keep talented people from leaving.

Pay for Performance

Pay for performance is the popular term for monetary incentives linking at least some portion of the paycheck directly to results or accomplishments. Many refer to it simply as *incentive pay,* while others call it *variable pay.*[45] The general idea behind pay-for-performance schemes—including but not limited to merit pay, bonuses, and profit sharing—is to give employees an incentive for working harder or smarter. Pay for performance is something extra, compensation above and beyond basic wages and salaries (see Skills & Best Practices). Proponents of incentive compensation say something extra is needed because hourly wages and fixed salaries do little more than motivate people to show up at work and put in the required hours.[46] The most basic form of pay for performance is the traditional piece-rate plan, whereby the employee is paid a specified amount of money for each unit of work. For example, 2,500 artisans at Longaberger's, in Frazeyburg, Ohio, are paid a fixed amount for each handcrafted wooden basket they weave. Together, they produce 40,000 of the prized maple baskets daily.[47] Sales commissions, whereby a salesperson receives a specified amount of money for each unit sold, are another long-standing example of pay for performance. Today's service economy is forcing management to creatively adapt and go beyond piece rate and sales commission plans to accommodate greater emphasis on product and service quality, interdependence, and teamwork.[48]

Current Practices   For an indication of current practices, see Table 8–1, which is based on a survey of 156 US executives. The lack of clear patterns in Table 8–1 is indicative of the still experimental nature of incentive compensation today. Much remains to be learned from research and practice.

Research Insights   According to available expert opinion and research results, pay for performance too often falls short of its goal of improved job performance. "Experts say that roughly half the incentive plans they see don't work, victims of poor design and administration."[49] In fact, one study documented how incentive pay had a *negative* effect on the performance of 150,000 managers from 500 financially distressed companies.[50] A meta-analysis of 39 studies found only a modest positive correlation between financial incentives and performance *quantity* and no impact on

The Use and Effectiveness of Modern Incentive Pay Plans **TABLE 8 – 1**

Plan Type	Presently Have	Rated Highly Effective
Annual bonus	74%	20%
Special one-time spot awards (after the fact)	42	38
Individual incentives	39	27
Long-term incentives (executive level)	32	44
Lump-sum merit pay	28	19
Competency-based pay	22	31
Profit-sharing (apart from retirement program)	22	43
Profit-sharing (as part of retirement program)	22	46
ESOP* stock plan	21	33
Suggestion/proposal programs	17	19
Team-based pay	15	29
Long-term incentives (below executive levels)	13	43
Skill-/knowledge-based pay	12	58
Group incentives (not team-based)	11	24
Pay for quality	9	29
Gainsharing	8	38
Special key-contributor programs (before the fact)	7	55

*Employee stock ownership plan.
SOURCE: Adapted from "Incentive Pay Plans: Which Ones Work . . . and Why," *HR Focus,* April 2001, p 3.

performance *quality.*[51] Other researchers have found only a weak statistical link between large executive bonuses paid out in good years and subsequent improvement in corporate profitability.[52] Also, in a survey of small business owners, more than half said their commission plans failed to motivate extra effort from their salespeople.[53] Linking teachers' merit pay to student performance, an exciting school reform idea, turned out to be a big disappointment: "The bottom line is that despite high hopes, none of the 13 districts studied was able to use teacher pay incentives to achieve significant, lasting gains in student performance."[54] Clearly, the pay-for-performance area is still very much up in the air.

Why Rewards Often Fail to Motivate

Despite huge investments of time and money for organizational reward systems, the desired motivational effect often is not achieved. A management consultant/writer recently offered these eight reasons:

1. Too much emphasis on monetary rewards.
2. Rewards lack an "appreciation effect."
3. Extensive benefits become entitlements.
4. Counterproductive behavior is rewarded. (For example, "a pizza delivery company focused its rewards on the on-time performance of its drivers, only to discover that it was inadvertently rewarding reckless driving."[55])

5. Too long a delay between performance and rewards.

6. Too many one-size-fits-all rewards.

7. Use of one-shot rewards with a short-lived motivational impact.

8. Continued use of demotivating practices such as layoffs, across-the-board raises and cuts, and excessive executive compensation.[56]

These stubborn problems have fostered a growing interest in more effective reward and compensation practices.[57]

Positive Reinforcement

Feedback and reward programs all too often are ineffective because they are administered in haphazard ways.[58] For example, consider these scenarios:

- A young programmer stops e-mailing creative suggestions to his boss because she never responds.
- The office politician gets a great promotion while her more skilled co-workers scratch their heads and gossip about the injustice.

law of effect

Behavior with favorable consequences is repeated; behavior with unfavorable consequences disappears.

In the first instance, a productive behavior faded away for lack of encouragement. In the second situation, unproductive behavior was unwittingly rewarded. Feedback and rewards need to be handled more precisely. Fortunately, the field of behavioral psychology can help. Thanks to the pioneering work of Edward L Thorndike, B F Skinner, and many others, a behavior modification technique called *positive reinforcement* helps managers achieve needed discipline and desired effect when providing feedback and granting rewards.[59]

Thorndike's Law of Effect

During the early 1900s, Edward L Thorndike observed in his psychology laboratory that a cat would behave randomly and wildly when placed in a small box with a secret trip lever that opened a door. However, once the cat accidentally tripped the lever and escaped, the animal would go straight to the lever when placed back in the box. Hence, Thorndike formulated his famous **law of effect,** which says *behavior with favorable consequences tends to be repeated, while behavior with unfavorable consequences tends to disappear.*[60] This was a dramatic departure from the prevailing notion a century ago that behavior was the product of inborn instincts.

respondent behavior

Skinner's term for unlearned stimulus–response reflexes.

operant behavior

Skinner's term for learned, consequence-shaped behavior.

Skinner's Operant Conditioning Model

Skinner refined Thorndike's conclusion that behavior is controlled by its consequences. Skinner's work became known as *behaviorism* because he dealt strictly with observable behavior.[61] As a behaviorist, Skinner believed it was pointless to explain behavior in terms of unobservable inner states such as needs, drives, attitudes, or thought processes.[62] He similarly put little stock in the idea of self-determination.

In his 1938 classic, *The Behavior of Organisms,* Skinner drew an important distinction between two types of behavior: respondent and operant behavior.[63] He labeled unlearned reflexes or stimulus–response (S–R) connections **respondent behavior.** This category of behavior was said to describe a very small proportion of adult human behavior. Examples of respondent behavior would include shedding tears while peeling onions and reflexively withdrawing one's hand from a hot stove.[64] Skinner attached the label **operant behavior** to behavior that is learned when one "operates on" the environment to produce desired consequences. Some call this the response–stimulus (R–S) model. Years of controlled experiments with pigeons in "Skinner boxes" helped Skinner develop a sophisticated technology of behavior control, or operant conditioning. For example, he taught pigeons how to pace figure eights and how to bowl by reinforcing the underweight (and thus hungry) birds with food whenever they more closely approximated target behaviors. Skinner's work has significant implications for OB because the vast majority of organizational behavior falls into the operant category.[65]

Renowned behavioral psychologist B F Skinner and your co-author Bob Kreitner met and posed for a snapshot at an Academy of Management meeting in Boston. As a behaviorist, Skinner preferred to deal with observable behavior and its antecedents and consequences in the environment rather than with inner states such as attitudes and cognitive processes. Professor Skinner was a fascinating man who left a permanent mark on modern psychology.

Contingent Consequences

Contingent consequences, according to Skinner's operant theory, control behavior in four ways: positive reinforcement, negative reinforcement, punishment, and extinction.[66] The term *contingent* means there is a systematic if-then linkage between the target behavior and the consequence. Remember Mom (and Pink Floyd) saying something to this effect: "If you don't finish your dinner, you don't get dessert" (see Figure 8–3)? To avoid the all-too-common mislabeling of these consequences, let us review some formal definitions.

Test Your Knowledge
Reinforcement Theory

Positive Reinforcement Strengthens Behavior Positive reinforcement is the process of strengthening a behavior by contingently presenting something pleasing. (Importantly, a behavior is strengthened when it increases in frequency and weakened when it decreases in frequency.) The watchwords for using positive reinforcement are "catch them doing something *right*!"[67] For example, good-performance awards are handed out by the thousands each year to employees at Baptist Health Care Hospital in Pensacola, Florida. A $15 gift certificate goes to anyone accumulating five of the awards.[68]

positive reinforcement

Making behavior occur more often by contingently presenting something positive.

Negative Reinforcement Also Strengthens Behavior Negative reinforcement is the process of strengthening a behavior by contingently withdrawing something displeasing. For example, an army sergeant who stops yelling when a recruit jumps out of bed has negatively reinforced that particular behavior. Similarly, the behavior of clamping our hands over our ears when watching a jumbo jet take off is negatively reinforced by relief from the noise. Negative reinforcement is often confused with punishment. But the two strategies have opposite effects on behavior. Negative reinforcement,

negative reinforcement

Making behavior occur more often by contingently withdrawing something negative.

FIGURE 8–3
Contingent
Consequences
in Operant
Conditioning

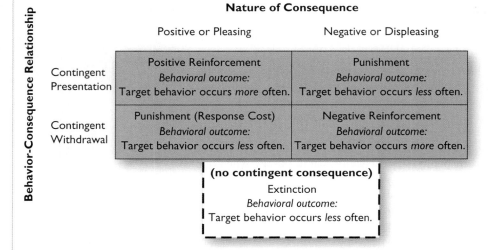

as the word *reinforcement* indicates, strengthens a behavior because it provides relief from an unpleasant situation.

punishment

Making behavior occur less often by contingently presenting something negative or withdrawing something positive.

Punishment Weakens Behavior **Punishment** is the process of weakening behavior through either the contingent presentation of something displeasing or the contingent withdrawal of something positive. A manager assigning a tardy employee to a dirty job exemplifies the first type of punishment. Docking a tardy employee's pay is an example of the second type of punishment, called "response cost" punishment.[69] Legal fines involve response cost punishment. Salespeople who must make up any cash register shortages out of their own pockets are being managed through response cost punishment. Ethical questions can and should be raised about this type of on-the-job punishment.[70]

extinction

Making behavior occur less often by ignoring or not reinforcing it.

Extinction Also Weakens Behavior **Extinction** is the weakening of a behavior by ignoring it or making sure it is not reinforced. Getting rid of a former boyfriend or girlfriend by refusing to return their phone calls is an extinction strategy. A good analogy for extinction is to imagine what would happen to your houseplants if you stopped watering them. Like a plant without water, a behavior without occasional reinforcement eventually dies. Although very different processes, both punishment and extinction have the same weakening effect on behavior.

Schedules of Reinforcement

As just discussed, contingent consequences are an important determinant of future behavior. The *timing* of behavioral consequences can be even more important. Based on years of tedious laboratory experiments with pigeons in highly controlled environments, Skinner and his colleagues discovered distinct patterns of responding for various schedules of reinforcement.[71] Although some of their conclusions can be generalized to negative reinforcement, punishment, and extinction, it is best to think only of positive reinforcement when discussing schedules.

Continuous Reinforcement As indicated in Table 8–2, every instance of a target behavior is reinforced when a **continuous reinforcement** (CRF) schedule is in effect. For instance, when your television set is operating properly, you are reinforced with a picture every time you turn it on (a CRF schedule). But, as with any CRF schedule of reinforcement, the behavior of turning on the television will undergo rapid extinction if the set breaks.

Intermittent Reinforcement Unlike CRF schedules, **intermittent reinforcement** involves reinforcement of some but not all instances of a target behavior. Four subcategories of intermittent schedules, described in Table 8–2, are fixed and variable ratio schedules and fixed and variable interval schedules. Reinforcement in *ratio* schedules is contingent on the number of responses emitted. *Interval* reinforcement is tied to the passage of time. Some common examples of the four types of intermittent reinforcement are as follows:

- *Fixed ratio*—piece-rate pay; bonuses tied to the sale of a fixed number of units.
- *Variable ratio*—slot machines that pay off after a variable number of lever pulls; lotteries that pay off after the purchase of a variable number of tickets.
- *Fixed interval*—hourly pay; annual salary paid on a regular basis.
- *Variable interval*—random supervisory praise and pats on the back for employees who have been doing a good job.

At Granite Construction in Watsonville, California, 20% of every manager's bonus depends on the person's "people skills." For most of its 80 years, a call from the boss's office meant bad news. "Employees were only contacted when something went wrong," says division manager Bruce McGowan, a 20-year veteran who oversees a staff of 700. Now the emphasis is on positive reinforcement.

Proper Scheduling Is Important The schedule of reinforcement can more powerfully influence behavior than the magnitude of reinforcement. Although this proposition grew out of experiments with pigeons, subsequent on-the-job research confirmed it. Consider, for example, a field study of 12 unionized beaver trappers employed by a lumber company to keep the large rodents from eating newly planted tree seedlings.[72]

The beaver trappers were randomly divided into two groups that alternated weekly between two different bonus plans. Under the first schedule, each trapper earned his regular $7 per hour wage plus $1 for each beaver caught. Technically, this bonus was paid on a CRF schedule. The second bonus plan involved the regular $7 per hour wage plus a one-in-four chance (as determined by rolling the dice) of receiving $4 for each beaver trapped. This second bonus plan qualified as a variable ratio (VR-4) schedule. In the long run, both incentive schemes averaged out to a $1-per-beaver bonus. Surprisingly, however, when the trappers were under the VR-4 schedule, they were 58% more productive than under the CRF schedule, despite the fact that the net amount of pay averaged out the same for the two groups during the 12-week trapping season.

> **continuous reinforcement**
> Reinforcing every instance of a behavior.
> **intermittent reinforcement**
> Reinforcing some but not all instances of behavior.

Work Organizations Typically Rely on the Weakest Schedule Generally, variable ratio and variable interval schedules of reinforcement produce the strongest behavior that is most resistant to extinction. As gamblers will attest, variable schedules hold the promise of reinforcement after the next target response. For

TABLE 8–2   Schedules of Reinforcement

Schedule	Description	Probable Effects on Responding
Continuous (CRF)	Reinforcer follows every response.	Steady high rate of performance as long as reinforcement continues to follow every response.
		High frequency of reinforcement may lead to early satiation.
		Behavior weakens rapidly (undergoes extinction) when reinforcers are withheld.
		Appropriate for newly emitted, unstable, or low-frequency responses.
Intermittent	Reinforcer does not follow every response.	Capable of producing high frequencies of responding.
		Low frequency of reinforcement precludes early satiation.
		Appropriate for stable or high-frequency responses.
Fixed ratio (FR)	A fixed number of responses must be emitted before reinforcement occurs.	A fixed ratio of 1:1 (reinforcement occurs after every response) is the same as a continuous schedule.
		Tends to produce a high rate of response, which is vigorous and steady.
Variable ratio (VR)	A varying or random number of responses must be emitted before reinforcement occurs.	Capable of producing a high rate of response, which is vigorous, steady, and resistant to extinction.
Fixed interval (FI)	The first response after a specific period of time has elapsed is reinforced.	Produces an uneven response pattern varying from a very slow, unenergetic response immediately following reinforcement to a very fast, vigorous response immediately preceding reinforcement.
Variable interval (VI)	The first response after varying or random periods of time have elapsed is reinforced.	Tends to produce a high rate of response, which is vigorous, steady, and resistant to extinction.

SOURCE: F Luthans and R Kreitner, *Organizational Behavior Modification and Beyond: An Operant and Social Learning Approach* (Glenview, IL: Scott, Foresman, 1985), p 58. Used with permission of the authors.

Test Your Knowledge

Reinforcing Performance

example, the following drama at a Laughlin, Nevada, gambling casino is one more illustration of the potency of variable ratio reinforcement:

> An elderly woman with a walker had lost her grip on the slot [machine] handle and had collapsed on the floor.
> "Help," she cried weakly.
> The woman at the machine next to her interrupted her play for a few seconds to try to help her to her feet, but all around her the army of slot players continued feeding coins to the machines.
> A security man arrived to soothe the woman and take her away.
> "Thank you," she told him appreciatively.
> "But don't forget my winnings."[73]

Organizations without at least some variable reinforcement are less likely to prompt this type of dedication to task. Despite the trend toward pay-for-performance, time-based pay schemes such as hourly wages and yearly salaries that rely on the weakest schedule of reinforcement (fixed interval) are still the rule in today's workplaces.

shaping

Reinforcing closer and closer approximations to a target behavior.

Shaping Behavior with Positive Reinforcement

Have you ever wondered how trainers at aquarium parks manage to get bottle-nosed dolphins to do flips, killer whales to carry people on their backs, and seals to juggle balls? The results are seemingly magical. Actually, a mundane learning process called shaping is responsible for the animals' antics.

Two-ton killer whales, for example, have a big appetite, and they find buckets of fish very reinforcing. So if the trainer wants to ride a killer whale, he or she reinforces very basic behaviors that will eventually lead to the whale being ridden. The killer whale is contingently reinforced with a few fish for coming near the trainer, then for being touched, then for putting its nose in a harness, then for being straddled, and eventually for swimming with the trainer on its back. In effect, the trainer systematically raises the behavioral requirement for reinforcement. Thus, **shaping** is defined as the process of reinforcing closer and closer approximations to a target behavior.

Shaping works very well with people, too, especially in training and quality programs involving continuous improvement. Praise, recognition, and instructive and credible feedback cost managers little more than moments of their time.[74] Yet, when used in conjunction with a behavior-shaping program, these consequences can efficiently foster significant improvements in job performance.[75] The key to successful behavior shaping lies in reducing a complex target behavior to easily learned steps and then faithfully (and patiently) reinforcing any improvement. For example, Continental Airlines used a cash bonus program to improve its on-time arrival record from one of the worst in the industry to one of the best. Employees originally were promised a $65 bonus each month Continental earned a top-five ranking. Now it takes a second- or third-place ranking to earn the $65 bonus and a $100 bonus awaits employees when they achieve a No. 1 ranking.[76] The airline handed out a total of $47 million in on-time bonuses in 2002.[77] (Skills & Best Practices lists practical tips on shaping.)

How to Effectively Shape Job Behavior

1. *Accommodate the process of behavioral change.* Behaviors change in gradual stages, not in broad, sweeping motions.

2. *Define new behavior patterns specifically.* State what you wish to accomplish in explicit terms and in small amounts that can be easily grasped.

3. *Give individuals feedback on their performance.* A once-a-year performance appraisal is not sufficient.

4. *Reinforce behavior as quickly as possible.*

5. *Use powerful reinforcement.* To be effective, rewards must be important to the employee—not to the manager.

6. *Use a continuous reinforcement schedule.* New behaviors should be reinforced every time they occur. This reinforcement should continue until these behaviors become habitual.

7. *Use a variable reinforcement schedule for maintenance.* Even after behavior has become habitual, it still needs to be rewarded, though not necessarily every time it occurs.

8. *Reward teamwork—not competition.* Group goals and group rewards are one way to encourage cooperation in situations in which jobs and performance are interdependent.

9. *Make all rewards contingent on performance.*

10. *Never take good performance for granted.* Even superior performance, if left unrewarded, will eventually deteriorate.

SOURCE: Adapted from A T Hollingsworth and D Tanquay Hoyer, "How Supervisors Can Shape Behavior," *Personnel Journal*, May 1985, pp 86, 88.

SKILLS & BEST PRACTICES

key terms

continuous reinforcement (CRF)   215
extinction   214
extrinsic rewards   209
feedback   202
intermittent reinforcement   215
intrinsic rewards   209

law of effect   212
negative reinforcement   213
operant behavior   212
pay for performance   210
positive reinforcement   213
punishment   214

respondent behavior   212
shaping   217
360-degree feedback   206
upward feedback   206

chapter summary

- *Specify the two basic functions of feedback and three sources of feedback.* Feedback, in the form of objective information about performance, both instructs and motivates. Individuals receive feedback from others, the task, and from themselves.

- *Define upward feedback and 360-degree feedback, and summarize the general tips for giving good feedback.* Lower-level employees provide upward feedback (usually anonymous) to their managers. A focal person receives 360-degree feedback from subordinates, the manager, peers, and selected others such as customers or suppliers. Good feedback is tied to performance *goals* and clear *expectations*, linked with *specific* behavior and/or results, reserved for *key result* areas, given as soon as possible, provided for *improvement* as well as for final results, focused on *performance* rather than on personalities, and based on *accurate* and *credible* information.

- *Distinguish between extrinsic and intrinsic rewards, and give a job-related example of each.* Extrinsic rewards, which are granted by others, include pay and benefits, recognition and praise, and favorable assignments and schedules. Intrinsic rewards are experienced internally or, in a sense, self-granted. Common intrinsic rewards include feelings of satisfaction, pride, and a sense of accomplishment.

- *Summarize the research lessons about pay for performance, and explain why rewards often fail to motivate employees.* Research on pay for performance has yielded mixed results, with no clear pattern of effectiveness. Reward systems can fail to motivate employees for these reasons:

overemphasis on money, no appreciation effect, benefits become entitlements, wrong behavior is rewarded, rewards are delayed too long, use of one-size-fits-all rewards, one-shot rewards with temporary effect, and demotivating practices such as layoffs.

- *State Thorndike's "law of effect," and explain Skinner's distinction between respondent and operant behavior.* According to Edward L Thorndike's law of effect, behavior with favorable consequences tends to be repeated, while behavior with unfavorable consequences tends to disappear. B F Skinner called unlearned stimulus–response reflexes *respondent behavior*. He applied the term *operant behavior* to all behavior learned through experience with environmental consequences.

- *Demonstrate your knowledge of positive reinforcement, negative reinforcement, punishment, and extinction, and explain behavior shaping.* Positive and negative reinforcement are consequence management strategies that strengthen behavior, whereas punishment and extinction weaken behavior. These strategies need to be defined objectively in terms of their actual impact on behavior frequency, not subjectively on the basis of intended impact. Behavior shaping occurs when closer and closer approximations of a target behavior are reinforced. In effect, the standard for reinforcement is made more difficult as the individual learns. The process begins with continuous reinforcement, which gives way to intermittent reinforcement when the target behavior becomes strong and habitual.

discussion questions

1. What is the motivational role of feedback in the chapter-opening vignette?

2. How has feedback instructed or motivated you lately?

3. How would you summarize the practical benefits and drawbacks of 360-degree feedback?

4. How would you respond to a manager who said, "Employees cannot be motivated with money"?

5. What real-life examples of positive reinforcement, negative reinforcement, both forms of punishment, and extinction can you draw from your recent experience? Were these strategies appropriately or inappropriately used?

ethical dilemma

You Have 20 Minutes to Surf the Web. Go.

It's getting harder than ever to wheedle a raise out of the boss. So maybe at this year's annual review you should ask for more Web browsing time instead. Several employers are turning to a software program from Websense in San Diego that puts workers on the clock for their personal Net use. Kozy Shack Enterprises, a Hicksville (N.Y.) maker of ready-to-eat pudding, uses the "quota time" feature in Websense Enterprise to give employees one hour each day to shop, chat, and otherwise browse.

Info-tech managers can choose what sites are available during that time and adjust access depending on job titles. "We have sales people who travel extensively, so we give them much more access to travel sites," says Kozy's IT director, Richard Lehan. At Bates County Memorial Hospital in Butler, Mo., staff get 20 minutes a day for personal Internet use; department managers get 40.

For some companies, that's just too Big Brother-esque. Employees at London-based high-end retailer Harvey Nichols sign an honor code stating that personal Web use will be limited to their lunch break or after hours. The chain uses Websense to block gambling, pornography, and other inappropriate sites, but it doesn't limit time. "We have quite a bit of trust in people in the company," says Lee Smith, technology business systems manager. And most tech outfits figure they can't be Web innovators while restricting its use. Says Microsoft spokesman Lou Gellos: "We expect all employees to exercise common sense and good judgment and shop on MSN shopping—and I say that kind of tongue in cheek."[78]

What Is Your Ethical Interpretation of This Situation?

1. There are no real ethical problems here because what an employee does on the company's time with the company's equipment is the company's business. Explain your ethical reasoning.

2. Employers either trust their employees or they don't. Any sort of monitoring of their Internet use says the employer doesn't trust them. Playing Big Brother only serves to erode loyalty and motivation. Explain the implications for hiring, along with your ethical reasoning.

3. Having employees sign an honor code about not abusing their Internet privileges is okay, but putting them on an electronic meter is going too far. Explain your ethical reasoning, and explore the practical implications.

4. Employers have a moral obligation to protect their employees from pornography, gambling, and other inappropriate Web sites with Internet blocks and filters. Explain.

5. Invent other options. Discuss.

For an interpretation of this situation, visit our Web site, www.mhhe.com/kinickiob3e.

If you're looking for additional study materials, be sure to check out the Online Learning Center at

www.mhhe.com/kinickiob3e

for more information and interactivities that correspond to this chapter.

part three

Managing Social Processes and Making Decisions

Nine Effective Groups and Teamwork

Ten Making Decisions

Eleven Managing Conflict and Negotiating

chapter
Nine

Effective Groups
and Teamwork

LEARNING OBJECTIVES

After reading the material in this chapter, you should be able to:

- Describe the five stages of Tuckman's theory of group development.

- Contrast roles and norms, and specify four reasons why norms are enforced in organizations.

- Explain how a work group becomes a team, and identify five teamwork competencies.

- List at least four things managers can do to build trust.

- Describe self-managed teams and virtual teams.

- Describe groupthink, and identify at least four of its symptoms

IS TEAMWORK THE R$_X$ FOR HOSPITALS?

Brain surgery isn't rocket science. But perhaps it should be. If medical staff worked together as a flight team does, they'd communicate more effectively, make fewer mistakes, and lose fewer lives.

That's the idea behind LifeWings, a one-year-old company that applies flight-tested safety lessons from the aviation industry to the world of medicine. Doctors,

98,000 patients die each year because of medical errors. LifeWings' president, Steve Harden, a former navy pilot and Top Gun instructor, spun the company out of a training program originally created for FedEx employees. "Human beings will eventually make errors," says Harden. "But you can equip them with communication behaviors that help detect

Harden says, "you notice it immediately, because it doesn't feel right." He also insists on regular briefings between teams, ensuring consistent care when patients are transferred between departments.

And if there's a problem, even the team's most junior members are trained to say something. That's tricky, since it means confronting medicine's doctor-as-deity culture. "It's sort of like giving permission to speak up," says Jennifer Baer, senior director of outcomes and performance improvement at the University of Texas Medical Branch at Galveston, who went through the six-month training last year with 627 other staffers. "Something as complicated as an OR procedure requires everyone being able to pick up on things that could lead to problems."

LifeWings applies training programs from the aviation industry to improve the performance of surgical teams in hospitals around the country. Pictured is Steve Harden, President, the principal architect of LifeWing's adaptation of aviation-based Hardwired Safety Tools^{sm} and practices of healthcare.

nurses, and technicians learn—from pilots and others with lives-on-the-line flying experience—how to perform under pressure as a team.

Crew resource management training, as it's known, caught hold in health care following a 1999 Institute of Medicine report that said

and correct those errors before they become serious."

Those behaviors start with checklists. LifeWings requires medical teams to create standardized lists of activities for every procedure to ensure, for example, that the right patient is being treated. "If there's a variation" from the checklist,

LifeWings has trained staff at more than 40 health-care organizations. Aside from a decline in the number of wrong surgeries (one hospital went from one every 60 days to one every 619, Harden says), the sessions tend to lift morale, leading to lower nurse turnover and increased efficiency. One hospital, says Harden, saved more than $100,000 a year after learning that sterile surgical kits were being opened but never used.

Of course, better communication can go just so far, observes Karlene Roberts, a University of California, Berkeley, business professor. Without support from employers and better med-school training, "we're going to be stuck with the same situation." Which is why Harden now insists on training a hospital's top brass first, to ensure the checklists and briefings become part of a permanent culture change. "This is not," he says, "a fire-and-forget program." That's pilot talk—but docs seem to get it.[1]

FOR DISCUSSION

According to your *personal* experience, what are the keys to effective teamwork? Explain. For an interpretation of this case and additional comments, visit our Online Learning Center at

www.mhhe.com/kinickiob3e

BOTH DAILY EXPERIENCE and research reveal the importance of social skills for individual and organizational success. An ongoing study by the Center for Creative Leadership (involving diverse samplings from Belgium, France, Germany, Italy, Spain, the United Kingdom, and the United States) found four stumbling blocks that tend to derail executives' careers. According to the researchers, "A derailed executive is one who, having reached the general manager level, finds that there is little chance of future advancement due to a misfit between job requirements and personal skills."[2] The four stumbling blocks, consistent across the cultures studied, are as follows:

1. Problems with interpersonal relationships.
2. Failure to meet business objectives.
3. Failure to build and lead a team.
4. Inability to change or adapt during a transition.[3]

Notice how both the first and third career stumbling blocks involve interpersonal skills—the ability to get along and work effectively with others. Managers with interpersonal problems typically were described as manipulative and insensitive. Interestingly, two-thirds of the derailed European managers studied had problems with interpersonal relationships. That same problem reportedly plagued one-third of the derailed US executives.[4] Management, as defined in Chapter 1, involves getting things done with and through others. The job is simply too big to do it alone.[5]

The purpose of this chapter is to shift the focus from individual behavior to collective behavior. We explore groups and teams, key features of modern life, and discuss how to make them effective while avoiding common pitfalls. Among the interesting variety of topics in this chapter are group development, trust, self-managed teams, virtual teams, and groupthink.

Fundamentals of Group Behavior

Drawing from the field of sociology,[6] we define a **group** as two or more freely interacting individuals who share collective norms and goals and have a common identity.[7] Organizational psychologist Edgar Schein shed additional light on this concept by drawing instructive distinctions between a group, a crowd, and an organization:

> **group**
> Two or more freely interacting people with shared norms and goals and a common identity.

> The size of a group is thus limited by the possibilities of mutual interaction and mutual awareness. Mere aggregates of people do not fit this definition because they do not interact and do not perceive themselves to be a group even if they are aware of each other as, for instance, a crowd on a street corner watching some event. A total department, a union, or a whole organization would not be a group in spite of thinking of themselves as "we," because they generally do not all interact and are not all aware of each other. However, work teams, committees, subparts of departments, cliques, and various other informal associations among organizational members would fit this definition of a group.[8]

Take a moment now to think of various groups of which you are a member. Does each of your "groups" satisfy the four criteria in our definition?

Formal and Informal Groups

formal group

> **Formed by the organization.**

informal group

> **Formed by friends.**

Individuals join groups, or are assigned to groups, to accomplish various purposes. If the group is formed by a manager to help the organization accomplish its goals, then it qualifies as a **formal group.** Formal groups typically wear such labels as work group, team, committee, or task force. An **informal group** exists when the members' overriding purpose of getting together is friendship.[9] Formal and informal groups often overlap, such as when a team of corporate auditors heads for the tennis courts after work. A recent survey of 1,385 office workers in the US found 71% had attended important events with co-workers, such as weddings and funerals.[10] Indeed, friendships forged on the job can be so strong as to outlive the job itself in an era of job hopping, reorganizations, and mass layoffs:

Teams serve many purposes at **Whole Foods Market**, where all employees belong to teams. Team members share equally in any savings they achieve for the company and vote on whether newcomers will be permanently hired. **Do you like this arrangement?**

> Many employees are finding that leaving their employer doesn't always mean saying goodbye: Membership in organized corporate "alumni" groups is increasingly in vogue.
>
> There are now alumni groups for hundreds of companies, including Hewlett-Packard, Ernst & Young and Texas Instruments. Yahoo alone lists more than 500 such ex-employee groups.
>
> Some groups are started by former employees, while others are formally sanctioned by employers as a way to stay in touch, creating a potential pool of boomerang workers that employers can draw from when hiring picks up.[11]

The desirability of overlapping formal and informal groups is problematic.[12] Some managers firmly believe personal friendship fosters productive teamwork on the job while others view workplace "bull sessions" as a serious threat to productivity. Both situations are common, and it is the manager's job to strike a workable balance, based on the maturity and goals of the people involved.

Functions of Formal Groups

Researchers point out that formal groups fulfill two basic functions: *organizational* and *individual*.[13] The various functions are listed in Table 9–1. Complex combinations of these functions can be found in formal groups at any given time.

For example, consider what Mazda's new American employees experienced when they spent a month working in Japan before the opening of the firm's Flat Rock, Michigan, plant:

> After a month of training in Mazda's factory methods, whipping their new Japanese buddies at softball and sampling local watering holes, the Americans were fired up. . . . [A maintenance manager] even faintly praised the Japanese practice of holding group calisthenics at the start of each working day: "I didn't think I'd like doing exercises every morning, but I kind of like it."[14]

While Mazda pursued the organizational functions it wanted—interdependent teamwork, creativity, coordination, problem solving, and training—the American workers benefited from the individual functions of formal groups. Among those benefits were

Formal Groups Fulfill Organizational and Individual Functions | **TABLE 9-1**

Organizational Functions	Individual Functions
1. Accomplish complex, interdependent tasks that are beyond the capabilities of individuals.	1. Satisfy the individual's need for affiliation.
2. Generate new or creative ideas and solutions.	2. Develop, enhance, and confirm the individual's self-esteem and sense of identity.
3. Coordinate interdepartmental efforts.	3. Give individuals an opportunity to test and share their perceptions of social reality.
4. Provide a problem-solving mechanism for complex problems requiring varied information and assessments.	4. Reduce the individual's anxieties and feelings of insecurity and powerlessness.
5. Implement complex decisions.	5. Provide a problem-solving mechanism for personal and interpersonal problems.
6. Socialize and train newcomers.	

SOURCE: Adapted from E H Schein, *Organizational Psychology*, 3rd ed (Englewood Cliffs. NJ: Prentice-Hall, 1980), pp 149–51.

affiliation with new friends, enhanced self-esteem, exposure to the Japanese social reality, and reduction of anxieties about working for a foreign-owned company. In short, Mazda created a workable blend of organizational and individual group functions by training its newly hired American employees in Japan.

The Group Development Process

Groups and teams in the workplace go through a maturation process, such as one would find in any life-cycle situation (e.g., humans, organizations, products). While there is general agreement among theorists that the group development process occurs in identifiable stages, they disagree about the exact number, sequence, length, and nature of those stages.[15] One oft-cited model is the one proposed in 1965 by educational psychologist Bruce W Tuckman. His original model involved only four stages (forming, storming, norming, and performing). The five-stage model in Figure 9–1 evolved when Tuckman and a doctoral student added "adjourning" in 1977.[16] A word of caution is in order. Somewhat akin to Maslow's need hierarchy theory, Tuckman's theory has been repeated and taught so often and for so long that many have come to view it as documented fact, not merely a theory. Even today, it is good to remember Tuckman's own caution that his group development model was derived more from group therapy sessions than from natural-life groups. Still, many in the OB field like Tuckman's five-stage model of group development because of its easy-to-remember labels and commonsense appeal.

Let us briefly examine each of the five stages in Tuckman's model. Notice in Figure 9–1 how individuals give up a measure of their independence when they join and participate in a group.[17] Also, the various stages are not necessarily of the same duration or intensity. For instance, the storming stage may be practically nonexistent or painfully long, depending on the goal clarity and the commitment and maturity of the members. You can make this process come to life by relating the various stages to your own experiences with work groups, committees, athletic teams, social or religious groups, or class project teams. Some group happenings that surprised you when they occurred may now make sense or strike you as inevitable when seen as part of a natural development process.

FIGURE 9–1   Tuckman's Five-Stage Theory of Group Development

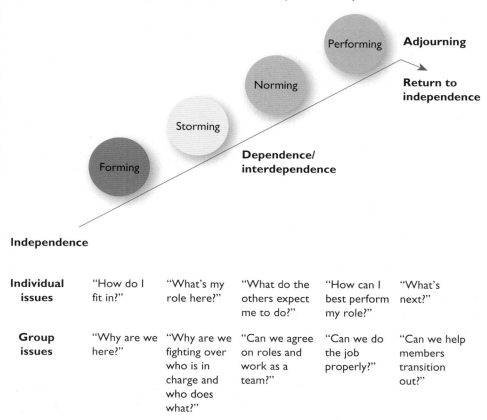

Individual issues	"How do I fit in?"	"What's my role here?"	"What do the others expect me to do?"	"How can I best perform my role?"	"What's next?"
Group issues	"Why are we here?"	"Why are we fighting over who is in charge and who does what?"	"Can we agree on roles and work as a team?"	"Can we do the job properly?"	"Can we help members transition out?"

Stage 1: Forming   During this "ice-breaking" stage, group members tend to be uncertain and anxious about such things as their roles, who is in charge, and the group's goals. Mutual trust is low, and there is a good deal of holding back to see who takes charge and how. In life-and-death situations, which are sometimes faced by surgical teams and airline cockpit crews, the period of uncertainty can be dangerous. According to the National Transportation Safety Board, "73% of commercial airline pilots' serious mistakes happen on crews' first day together."[18] If the formal leader (e.g., a supervisor) does not assert his or her authority, an emergent leader will eventually step in to fulfill the group's need for leadership and direction. Leaders typically mistake this honeymoon period as a mandate for permanent control. But later problems may force a leadership change.

Stage 2: Storming   This is a time of testing. Individuals test the leader's policies and assumptions as they try to determine how they fit into the power structure.[19] Subgroups take shape, and subtle forms of rebellion, such as procrastination, occur. Many groups stall in stage 2 because power politics erupts into open rebellion.

Stage 3: Norming   Groups that make it through stage 2 generally do so because a respected member, other than the leader, challenges the group to resolve its power struggles so something can be accomplished. Questions about authority and power are resolved through unemotional, matter-of-fact group discussion. A feeling of team spirit is experienced because members believe they have found their proper roles. **Group cohesiveness,** defined as the "we feeling" that binds members of a group together, is the principal by-product of stage 3.[20]

group cohesiveness

A "we feeling" binding group members together.

Stage 4: Performing Activity during this vital stage is focused on solving task problems. As members of a mature group, contributors get their work done without hampering others. There is a climate of open communication, strong cooperation, and lots of helping behavior. Conflicts and job boundary disputes are handled constructively and efficiently.[21] Cohesiveness and personal commitment to group goals help the group achieve more than could any one individual acting alone.

Stage 5: Adjourning The work is done; it is time to move on to other things. Having worked so hard to get along and get something done, many members feel a compelling sense of loss. The return to independence can be eased by rituals celebrating "the end" and "new beginnings." Parties, award ceremonies, graduations, or mock funerals can provide the needed punctuation at the end of a significant group project. Leaders need to emphasize valuable lessons learned in group dynamics to prepare everyone for future group and team efforts.

When the team responsible for redesigning the pages of *Fortune* magazine was ready to adjourn, the editors of the publication celebrated their achievement by announcing the new design and printing the team's photo on the editorial page. Team members are director Robert Newman (rear center) and, from the left, Kelly Peck, Robert Dominguez, Ann Decker, Samuel Velasco, and Linda Rubes.

Group Member Roles

Four centuries have passed since William Shakespeare had his character Jaques speak the following memorable lines in Act II of *As You Like It:* "All the world's a stage, And all the men and women merely players; They have their exits and their entrances; And one man in his time plays many parts. . . ." This intriguing notion of all people as actors in a universal play was not lost on 20th-century sociologists who developed a complex theory of human interaction based on roles. According to an OB scholar, "**roles** are sets of behaviors that persons expect of occupants of a position."[22] As described in Table 9–2, both task and maintenance roles need to be performed if a work group is to accomplish anything.[23]

roles

Expected behaviors for a given position.

task roles

Task-oriented group behavior.

maintenance roles

Relationship-building group behavior.

Task versus Maintenance Roles **Task roles** enable the work group to define, clarify, and pursue a common purpose. Meanwhile, **maintenance roles** foster supportive and constructive interpersonal relationships. In short, task roles keep the group *on track* while maintenance roles keep the group *together.* A project team member is performing a task function when he or she says at an update meeting, "What is the real issue here? We don't seem to be getting anywhere." Another individual who says, "Let's hear from those who oppose this plan," is performing a maintenance function. Importantly, each of the various task and maintenance roles may be played in varying combinations and sequences by either the group's leader or any of its members.

Group Exercise

Identifying Task and Maintenance Roles Within Groups

Checklist for Managers The task and maintenance roles listed in Table 9–2 can serve as a handy checklist for managers and group leaders who wish to ensure

TABLE 9–2 | Task and Maintenance Roles

Task Roles	Description
Initiator	Suggests new goals or ideas.
Information seeker/giver	Clarifies key issues.
Opinion seeker/giver	Clarifies pertinent values.
Elaborator	Promotes greater understanding through examples or exploration of implications.
Coordinator	Pulls together ideas and suggestions.
Orienter	Keeps group headed toward its stated goal(s).
Evaluator	Tests group's accomplishments with various criteria such as logic and practicality.
Energizer	Prods group to move along or to accomplish more.
Procedural technician	Performs routine duties (e.g., handing out materials or rearranging seats).
Recorder	Performs a "group memory" function by documenting discussion and outcomes.

Maintenance Roles	Description
Encourager	Fosters group solidarity by accepting and praising various points of view.
Harmonizer	Mediates conflict through reconciliation or humor.
Compromiser	Helps resolve conflict by meeting others "half way."
Gatekeeper	Encourages all group members to participate.
Standard setter	Evaluates the quality of group processes.
Commentator	Records and comments on group processes/dynamics.
Follower	Serves as a passive audience.

SOURCE: Adapted from discussion in K D Benne and P Sheats, "Functional Roles of Group Members," *Journal of Social Issues,* Spring 1948, pp 41–49.

proper group development. Roles that are not always performed when needed, such as those of coordinator, evaluator, and gatekeeper, can be performed in a timely manner by the formal leader or assigned to other members. The task roles of initiator, orienter, and energizer are especially important because they are *goal-directed* roles. Research studies on group goal setting confirm the motivational power of challenging goals. As with individual goal setting (in Chapter 7), difficult but achievable goals are associated with better group results.[24] Also in line with individual goal-setting theory and research, group goals are more effective if group members clearly understand them and are both individually and collectively committed to achieving them. Initiators, orienters, and energizers can be very helpful in this regard.

International managers need to be sensitive to cultural differences regarding the relative importance of task and maintenance roles. In Japan, for example, cultural tradition calls for more emphasis on maintenance roles, especially the roles of harmonizer and compromiser:

Courtesy requires that members not be conspicuous or disputatious in a meeting or classroom. If two or more members discover that their views differ—a fact that is tactfully taken to be unfortunate—they adjourn to find more information and to work toward a stance that all can accept. They do not press their personal opinions through strong arguments, neat logic, or rewards and threats. And they do not hesitate to shift their beliefs if doing so will preserve smooth interpersonal relations. (To lose is to win.)[25]

Norms

Norms are more encompassing than roles. While roles involve behavioral expectations for specific positions, norms help organizational members determine right from wrong and good from bad. According to one respected team of management consultants: "A **norm** is an attitude, opinion, feeling, or action—shared by two or more people—that guides their behavior."[26] Although norms are typically unwritten and seldom discussed openly, they have a powerful influence on group and organizational behavior.[27] PepsiCo Inc., for instance, has evolved a norm that equates corporate competitiveness with physical fitness. According to observers,

> Leanness and nimbleness are qualities that pervade the company. When Pepsi's brash young managers take a few minutes away from the office, they often head straight for the company's physical fitness center or for a jog around the museum-quality sculptures outside of PepsiCo's Purchase, New York, headquarters.[28]

norm

Shared attitudes, opinions, feelings, or actions that guide social behavior.

At PepsiCo and elsewhere, group members positively reinforce those who adhere to current norms with friendship and acceptance. On the other hand, nonconformists experience criticism and even **ostracism,** or rejection by group members. Anyone who has experienced the "silent treatment" from a group of friends knows what a potent social weapon ostracism can be.[29] Norms can be put into proper perspective by understanding how they develop and why they are enforced.

ostracism

Rejection by other group members.

How Norms Are Developed Experts say norms evolve in an informal manner as the group or organization determines what it takes to be effective. Generally speaking, norms develop in various combinations of the following four ways:

1. *Explicit statements by supervisors or co-workers.* For instance, a group leader might explicitly set norms about not drinking alcohol at lunch.

2. *Critical events in the group's history.* At times there is a critical event in the group's history that establishes an important precedent. (For example, a key recruit may have decided to work elsewhere because a group member said too many negative things about the organization. Hence, a norm against such "sour grapes" behavior might evolve.)

3. *Primacy.* The first behavior pattern that emerges in a group often sets group expectations. For example, this is how Paul Pressler set the norm for informality, creativity, and questioning when he took over as CEO of Gap Inc., the clothing retailer that owns the Old Navy and Banana Republic stores: "On his first day at work, speaking to 400 employees in Gap's first-floor auditorium, Pressler said, 'I've got a gazillion ideas, many of which are really stupid. But what the hell—you'll let me know!'"[30]

4. *Carryover behaviors from past situations.* Such carryover of individual behaviors from past situations can increase the predictability of group members' behaviors in new settings and facilitate task accomplishment. For instance, students and professors carry fairly constant sets of expectations from class to class.[31]

We would like you to take a few moments and think about the norms that are currently in effect in your classroom. List the norms on a sheet of paper. Do these norms help or hinder your ability to learn? Norms can affect performance either positively or negatively.

Why Norms Are Enforced   Norms tend to be enforced by group members when they

- Help the group or organization survive.
- Clarify or simplify behavioral expectations.
- Help individuals avoid embarrassing situations.
- Clarify the group's or organization's central values and/or unique identity.[32]

Teams, Trust, and Teamwork

The team approach to managing organizations is having diverse and substantial impacts on organizations and individuals. Teams promise to be a cornerstone of progressive management for the foreseeable future. General Electric's CEO, Jeffrey Immelt, offers this blunt overview: "You lead today by building teams and placing others first. It's not about you."[33] This means virtually all employees will need to polish their team skills. Southwest Airlines, a company that credits a strong team spirit for its success, puts team skills above all else. Case in point:

> Southwest rejected a top pilot from another airline who did stunt work for movie studios because he was rude to a receptionist. Southwest believes that technical skills are easier to acquire than a teamwork and service attitude.[34]

Fortunately, the trend toward teams has a receptive audience today. Both women and younger employees, according to research, thrive in team-oriented organizations.[35]

One negative reality in this otherwise positive picture involves a perception gap between upper management and nonmanagement. In a survey of 293,377 employees at 13 companies, 65% of upper managers agreed with the statement, "Teamwork and cooperation exist among departments."[36] Meanwhile, only 48% of the nonmanagers agreed. The resulting 17% perception gap challenges managers to "walk the talk" when it comes to teamwork.

In this section, we define the term *team,* look at teamwork competencies and team building, discuss trust as a key to real teamwork, and explore two evolving forms of teamwork—self-managed teams and virtual teams.

A Team Is More Than Just a Group

team

Small group with complementary skills who hold themselves mutually accountable for common purpose, goals, and approach.

Jon R Katzenbach and Douglas K Smith, management consultants at McKinsey & Company, say it is a mistake to use the terms *group* and *team* interchangeably. After studying many different kinds of teams—from athletic to corporate to military—they concluded that successful teams tend to take on a life of their own. Katzenbach and Smith define a **team** as "a small number of people with complementary skills who are committed to a common purpose, performance goals, and approach for which they hold themselves mutually accountable."[37]

Thus, a group becomes a team when the following criteria are met:

1. *Leadership* becomes a shared activity.
2. *Accountability* shifts from strictly individual to both individual and collective.
3. The group develops its own *purpose* or mission.
4. *Problem solving* becomes a way of life, not a part-time activity.
5. *Effectiveness* is measured by the group's collective outcomes and products.[38]

Relative to Tuckman's theory of group development covered earlier—forming, storming, norming, performing, and adjourning—teams are task groups that have matured to the *performing* stage. Because of conflicts over power and authority and unstable interpersonal relations, many work groups never qualify as a real team.[39] Katzenbach and Smith clarified the distinction this way: "The essence of a team is common commitment. Without it, groups perform as individuals; with it, they become a powerful unit of collective performance."[40]

When Katzenbach and Smith refer to "a small number of people" in their definition, they mean between 2 and 25 team members. They found effective teams to typically have fewer than 10 members. This conclusion was echoed in a survey of 400 workplace team members in the United States and Canada: "The average North American team consists of 10 members. Eight is the most common size."[41]

Developing Teamwork Competencies

Forming workplace teams and urging employees to be good team players are good starting points on the road to effective teams. But they are not enough today. Teamwork skills and competencies need to be role modeled and taught (see Skills & Best Practices). Notice the importance of group problem solving, mentoring, and conflict management skills, in addition to emotional intelligence. Teamwork competencies should be rewarded, too. For example, consider what has taken place at Internet equipment maker Cisco Systems:

[CEO John] Chambers took . . . steps to rein in Cisco's Wild West culture during 2002. Most pointedly, he made teamwork a critical part of top execs' bonus plans. He told them 30% of their bonuses for the 2003 fiscal year would depend on how well they collaborated with others. "It tends to formalize the discussion around how can I help you and how can you help me," says Sue Bostrom, head of Cisco's Internet consulting group.[42]

SKILLS & BEST PRACTICES

How Strong Are Your Teamwork Competencies?

Orients Team to Problem-Solving Situation
Assists the team in arriving at a common understanding of the situation or problem. Determines the important elements of a problem situation. Seeks out relevant data related to the situation or problem.

Organizes and Manages Team Performance
Helps team establish specific, challenging, and accepted team goals. Monitors, evaluates, and provides feedback on team performance. Identifies alternative strategies or reallocates resources to address feedback on team performance.

Promotes a Positive Team Environment
Assists in creating and reinforcing norms of tolerance, respect, and excellence. Recognizes and praises other team members' efforts. Helps and supports other team members. Models desirable team member behavior.

Facilitates and Manages Task Conflict
Encourages desirable and discourages undesirable team conflict. Recognizes the type and source of conflict confronting the team and implements an appropriate resolution strategy. Employs "win–win" negotiation strategies to resolve team conflicts.

Appropriately Promotes Perspective
Defends stated preferences, argues for a particular point of view, and withstands pressure to change position for another that is not supported by logical or knowledge-based arguments. Changes or modifies position if a defensible argument is made by another team member. Projects courtesy and friendliness to others while arguing position.

SOURCE: G Chen, L M Donahue, and R I Klimoski, "Training Undergraduates to Work in Organizational Teams," *Academy of Management Learning and Education*, March 2004, Appendix A, p 40. Copyright © 2004 by Academy of Management. Reproduced with permission of Academy of Management via Copyright Clearance Center.

Self-Assessment Exercise

Team Roles Preference Scale

Team Building

Team building is a catch-all term for a host of techniques aimed at improving the internal functioning of work groups. Whether conducted by company trainers or hired consultants (and done on-site or off-site), team-building workshops strive for greater cooperation, better communication, and less dysfunctional conflict. Rote memorization and lectures or discussions are discouraged by team builders who prefer *active* versus passive learning. Greater emphasis is placed on *how* work groups get the job done than on the task itself. Experiential learning techniques such as interpersonal trust exercises, conflict role-play sessions, and competitive games are common.[43] Some prefer off-site gatherings to get participants away from their work and out of their comfort zones. An exotic (and expensive) case in point is Seagate Technology:

> Plenty of companies try to motivate the troops, but few go as far as Seagate Technology. In February [2006] the $9.8 billion maker of computer storage hardware flew 200 staffers to New Zealand for its sixth annual Eco Seagate— an intense week of team-building topped off by an all-day race in which Seagaters had to kayak, hike, bike, swim, and rappel down a cliff. The tab? $9,000 per person. . . .
>
> This event, or social experiment, is [CEO Bill] Watkins' pet project. He dreamed up Eco Seagate as a way to break down barriers, boost confidence, and, yes, make staffers better team players. "Some of you will learn about teamwork because you have a great team," he . . . [said during his opening pep talk]. "Some of you will learn because your team is a disaster."[44]
>
> Seagate's chief financial officer, Charles Pope, originally a nonparticipant who doubted the program's worth, has since joined in and now sees Eco Seagate as an investment, not a vacation.
>
> *The Bottom Line:* Without clear goals, proper leadership, careful attention to details, and transfer of learning back to the job, both on-site and off-site team-building sessions can become an expensive disappointment (see Skills & Best Practices).[45]

Seagate's CEO Bill Watkins is an enthusiastic participant in the sometimes bizarre rituals managers experience during the company's annual week of team-building exercises. "You're going to think some of this is pretty dumb," he tells attendees. "Just get involved. Don't be too cool to participate." What do you think of this sort of "extreme" team building?

Trust: A Key Ingredient of Teamwork

These have not been good times for trust in the corporate world. Years of mergers, layoffs, bloated executive bonuses, and corporate criminal proceedings have left many of us justly cynical about trusting management. For example, consider these recent news clippings:

- "Calpine's directors voted to almost triple their salaries a week after the power generator, which is in Chapter 11 [bankruptcy], unveiled a cost-cutting plan that will eliminate 300 employees, or about 9% of its workforce."[46]

- "A court-approved [bankruptcy] plan to reward top United Airlines executives with $115 million in stock could be worth double or triple that sum, based on advance trading of new shares to be issued this week."[47]

Public opinion polls show the resulting damage: "In Harris Interactive's 2004 Annual Corporation Reputation Survey, 74% say corporate America's reputation is 'not good' or 'terrible.'"[48] While challenging readers of *Harvard Business Review* to do a better job of investing in social capital, experts offered this constructive advice:

> No one can manufacture trust or mandate it into existence. When someone says, "You can trust me," we usually don't, and rightly so. But leaders can make deliberate investments in trust. They can give people reasons to trust one another instead of reasons to watch their backs. They can refuse to reward successes that are built on untrusting behavior. And they can display trust and trustworthiness in their own actions, both personally and on behalf of the company.[49]

Three Dimensions of Trust Trust is defined as reciprocal faith in others' intentions and behavior.[50] Experts on the subject explain the reciprocal (give-and-take) aspect of trust as follows:

> When we see others acting in ways that imply that they trust us, we become more disposed to reciprocate by trusting in them more. Conversely, we come to distrust those whose actions appear to violate our trust or to distrust us.[51]

In short, we tend to give what we get: Trust begets trust; distrust begets distrust.

Trust is expressed in different ways. Three dimensions of trust are *overall trust* (expecting fair play, the truth, and empathy), *emotional trust* (having faith that someone will not misrepresent you to others or betray a confidence), and *reliableness* (believing that promises and appointments will be kept and commitments met).[52] These different dimensions contribute to a wide and complex range of trust, from very low to very high.

How to Build Trust Management professor/consultant Fernando Bartolomé offers the following six guidelines for building and maintaining trust:

1. *Communication.* Keep team members and employees informed by explaining policies and decisions and providing accurate feedback. Be candid about one's own problems and limitations. Tell the truth.[53]

2. *Support.* Be available and approachable. Provide help, advice, coaching, and support for team members' ideas.

3. *Respect.* Delegation, in the form of real decision-making authority, is the most important expression of managerial respect. Actively listening to the ideas of others is a close second. (Empowerment is not possible without trust.)[54]

SKILLS & BEST PRACTICES

How to Make Off-site Team Building Work: Advice from Event Planners

1. *Articulate your goals.* "You'd be amazed at how many can't tell us their goals for their off-site," says Howard Givner, president of Paint the Town Red, a New York events company. With an objective, it's easier to figure out whom to invite, what to do, and where to go.

2. *Make the location exotic.* "Wherever you go, you have to have the feeling that it's special," says Joy Pecchia of MSP Resources, a Minneapolis event planner. If you can go to Cancun, great, but if not, stay local and pick a hot restaurant or some other offbeat venue.

3. *Plan a signature moment.* And if you can tie it to the goal, that's ideal. "We put on an *Amazing Race*–type event for a publishing company's ad-sales staff where the participants created an ad," says Givner. "It's a critical part of their business, but something most of them had never done."

4. *Hangovers happen.* Eight a.m. breakfast meeting? Get real. People will party. Consider saving the really important stuff for the afternoon. If you must work mornings, Pecchia suggests evening activities like a night cruise where you can control the crowd more easily.

5. *Review your progress.* You want the ideas or lessons that come out of the off-site to live beyond those few days. So you have to continually gauge whether you're actually doing what you said you'd do when you get back to the office. Otherwise, what's the point?

SOURCE: Excerpted from R Underwood, "The Art of the Off-site," Fast Company, September 2005, p 30. Copyright © 2005 by Mansueto Ventures LLC. Reproduced with permission of Mansueto Ventures LLC via Copyright Clearance Center.

---

trust

Reciprocal faith in others' intentions and behavior.

"Day 24: Haven't gained their trust. Still can't get past secretary."

Copyright Scott Arthur Mesear. Reprinted with permission.

4. *Fairness.* Be quick to give credit and recognition to those who deserve it. Make sure all performance appraisals and evaluations are objective and impartial.

5. *Predictability.* Be consistent and predictable in your daily affairs. Keep both expressed and implied promises.

6. *Competence.* Enhance your credibility by demonstrating good business sense, technical ability, and professionalism.[55]

Trust needs to be earned; it cannot be demanded.

Self-Managed Teams

Have you ever thought you could do a better job than your boss? Well, if the trend toward self-managed work teams continues to grow as predicted, you just may get your chance. Entrepreneurs and artisans often boast of not having a supervisor. The same generally cannot be said for employees working in offices and factories. But things are changing. In fact, an estimated half of the employees at *Fortune* 500 companies are working on teams.[56] A growing share of those teams are self-managing. For example, "At a General Mills cereal plant in Lodi, California, teams . . . schedule, operate, and maintain machinery so effectively that the factory runs with no managers present during the night shift."[57] More typically, managers are present to serve as trainers and facilitators. Self-managed teams come in every conceivable format today, some more autonomous than others (see Hands-On Exercise).

self-managed teams

Groups of employees granted administrative oversight for their work.

Self-managed teams are defined as groups of workers who are given administrative oversight for their task domains. Administrative oversight involves delegated activities such as planning, scheduling, monitoring, and staffing. These are chores normally performed by managers. In short, employees in these unique work groups act as their own supervisor. Accountability is maintained *indirectly* by outside managers and leaders. According to a recent study of a company with 300 self-managed teams, 66 "team advisors" relied on these four indirect influence tactics:

- *Relating* (understanding the organization's power structure, building trust, showing concern for individual team members).
- *Scouting* (seeking outside information, diagnosing teamwork problems, facilitating group problem solving).
- *Persuading* (gathering outside support and resources, influencing team to be more effective and pursue organizational goals).
- *Empowering* (delegating decision-making authority, facilitating team decision-making process, coaching).[58]

Self-managed teams are variously referred to as semiautonomous work groups, autonomous work groups, and superteams.

Managerial Resistance   Something much more complex is involved than this apparently simple label suggests. The term *self-managed* does not mean simply turning workers loose to do their own thing. Indeed, an organization embracing

How Autonomous Is Your Work Group?

INSTRUCTIONS: Think of your current (or past) job and work group. Characterize the group's situation by selecting one number on the following scale for each statement. Add your responses for a total score:

Strongly Disagree						Strongly Agree
1	2	3	4	5	6	7

Work Method Autonomy

1. My work group decides how to get the job done. _____

2. My work group determines what procedures to use. _____

3. My work group is free to choose its own methods when carrying out its work. _____

Work Scheduling Autonomy

4. My work group controls the scheduling of its work. _____

5. My work group determines how its work is sequenced. _____

6. My work group decides when to do certain activities. _____

Work Criteria Autonomy

7. My work group is allowed to modify the normal way it is evaluated so some of our activities are emphasized and some deemphasized. _____

8. My work group is able to modify its objectives (what it is supposed to accomplish). _____

9. My work group has some control over what it is supposed to accomplish. _____

Total score = _____

NORMS

9–26 = Low autonomy
27–45 = Moderate autonomy
46–63 = High autonomy

SOURCE: Adapted from an individual autonomy scale in J A Breaugh, "The Work Autonomy Scales: Additional Validity Evidence," *Human Relations*, November 1989, pp 1033–56.

self-managed teams should be prepared to undergo revolutionary changes in management philosophy, structure, staffing and training practices, and reward systems. Moreover, the traditional notions of managerial authority and control are turned on their heads. Not surprisingly, many managers strongly resist giving up the reins of power to people they view as subordinates. They see self-managed teams as a threat to their job security.

Cross-Functionalism   A common feature of self-managed teams, particularly among those above the shop-floor or clerical level, is **cross-functionalism.**[59] In other words, specialists from different areas are put on the same team. Mark Stefik, a manager at the world-renowned Palo Alto Research Center in California, explains the wisdom of cross-functionalism:

cross-functionalism

Team made up of technical specialists from different areas.

> Something magical happens when you bring together a group of people from different disciplines with a common purpose. It's a middle zone, the breakthrough zone. The idea is to start a team on a problem—a hard problem, to keep people motivated. When there's an obstacle, instead of dodging it, bring in another point of view: an electrical engineer, a user interface expert, a sociologist, whatever spin on the market is needed. Give people new eyeglasses to cross-pollinate ideas.[60]

Cross-functionalism is seeping down into university programs to help students see the big picture and polish their team skills.[61] Also, the current drive for more

Manager's Hot Seat Application

Working in Teams: Cross-Functional Dysfunction

Cross-Functional Teams Bring Innovation Labs to Life

Innovation labs are a key part of a movement to overhaul old-style R&D. They are designed to comple- ment, and sometimes even replace, the intensive traditional system—which required that scien- tists or engineers toil away privately for years in the pursuit of patents, then hand their work over to product developers, who in turn dropped it onto designers' and marketers' laps for eventual shipment out to the public. . . .

Instead of assem- bly line, think swarm- ing beehive. *Teams* of people from different disciplines gather to focus on a problem. They brainstorm, tinker, and toy with different approaches— and generate answers that can be tested on customers and sped to the market. At times, it's true, inno- vation labs can seem like dot-com flashbacks, full of pretentious rhetoric, black-clad engineers, and inte- rior design clichés like cappuccino machines and foosball tables. But the fact is that the concept has been embraced by companies far removed from Silicon Valley. These organizations have discovered that innovation labs can be a powerful tool for big corpo- rations to cut through their own bureaucratic bloat.

SOURCE: Excerpted from J Weber, "'Mosh Pits' of Creativity," *BusinessWeek*, November 7, 2005, pp 98–100.

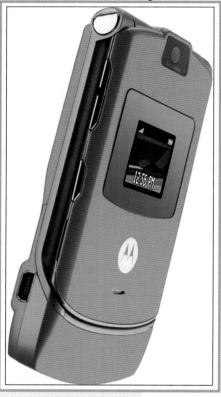

Members of Motorola's innovation lab are hard at work in downtown Chicago, 50 miles from head- quarters in an open-design lab intended to break down barriers and foster teamwork. It was here that the innovative Razr was developed, for example.

efficient research and development (R&D) and better and faster innovation leans heavily on cross-functional teams (see Skills & Best Practices).

Are Self-Managed Teams Effective? The Research Evidence Among companies with self-managed teams, the most commonly dele- gated tasks are work scheduling and dealing directly with outside customers. The least common team chores are hiring and firing.[62] Most of today's self-managed teams remain bunched at the shop-floor level in factory settings. Experts predict growth of the prac- tice in the managerial ranks and in service operations.[63]

Much of what we know about self- managed teams comes from testimonials and case studies. Fortunately, a body of higher quality field research is slowly devel- oping. A review of three meta-analyses cov- ering 70 individual studies concluded that self-managed teams had

- A positive effect on productivity.
- A positive effect on specific attitudes relating to self-management (e.g., respon- sibility and control).
- No significant effect on general attitudes (e.g., job satisfaction and organizational commitment).
- No significant effect on absenteeism or turnover.[64]

In a recent review of 28 studies, Dutch researchers found a positive relationship between self-managed teamwork and job satisfaction.[65] Although encouraging, these results do not qualify as a sweeping endorse- ment of self-managed teams. Nonetheless, experts say the trend toward self-managed work teams will continue upward in North America because of a strong cultural bias in favor of direct participation. Managers need to be prepared for the resulting shift in organizational administration.

Virtual Teams

Virtual teams are a product of modern times. They take their name from *virtual reality* computer simulations, where "it's almost like the real thing." Thanks to evolving information technologies such as the Internet, e-mail, videoconferencing, groupware, and fax machines, you can be a member of a work team without really being there.[66] Traditional team meetings are location specific. Team members are either physically present or absent. Virtual teams, in contrast, convene electronically with members reporting in from different locations, different organizations, and even different time zones. *BusinessWeek* recently offered this broad perspective:

> More and more, the creative class is becoming post-geographic. Location-independent. Office-agnostic. Demographers and futurists call this trend the rise of "the distributed workforce." Distributed workers are those who have no permanent office at their companies, preferring to work in home offices, cafes, airport lounges, high school stadium bleachers, client conference rooms, or some combination of what [author Richard] Florida calls the "no-collar workplace." They are people who do team projects over the Web and report to bosses who may be thousands of miles away. Currently, about 12% of the U.S. workforce qualifies as distributed, estimates . . . [one expert] who predicts that 40% of the workforce will be distributed by 2012. "We're at a tipping point."[67]

Because virtual teams are so new, there is no consensual definition. Our working definition of a **virtual team** is a physically dispersed task group that conducts its business through modern information technology.[68] Advocates say virtual teams are very flexible and efficient because they are driven by information and skills, not by time and location.[69] People with needed information and/or skills can be team members, regardless of where or when they actually do their work. For example, Volvo's new station wagon grew out of a global collaboration among designers in Sweden, Spain, and the United States:

virtual team

Information technology allows group members in different locations to conduct business.

> Using software called Alias, designers in Sweden and Detroit can change the curve of a fender or the shape of a headlight in real time. And if they want the big picture, they don 3-D goggles in special theaters that can project a full-size image of the car in two places at once. When Volvo's European designers put down their laser pens for the day, their counterparts in Irvine, Calif., pick up their pens and keep going. "We have almost 24-hour design," says [chief designer Peter] Horbury.[70]

On the negative side, lack of face-to-face interaction can weaken trust, communication, and accountability.

Research Insights As one might expect with a new and ill-defined area, research evidence to date is a bit spotty. Here is what we have learned so far from recent studies of computer-mediated groups:

- Virtual groups formed over the Internet follow a group development process similar to that for face-to-face groups.[71]
- Internet chat rooms create more work and yield poorer decisions than face-to-face meetings and telephone conferences.[72]
- Successful use of groupware (software that facilitates interaction among virtual group members) requires training and hands-on experience.[73]
- Inspirational leadership has a positive impact on creativity in electronic brainstorming groups.[74]

Practical Considerations Virtual teams may be in fashion, but they are not a cure-all. In fact, they may be a giant step backward for those not well versed in modern information technology and group dynamics.[75] Managers who rely on virtual teams agree on one point: *Meaningful face-to-face contact, especially during early phases of the group development process, is absolutely essential.* Virtual group members need "faces" in their minds to go with names and electronic messages.[76] Additionally, virtual teams cannot succeed without some old-fashioned factors such as top-management support, hands-on training, a clear mission and specific objectives, effective leadership, and schedules and deadlines.[77]

Threats to Group and Team Effectiveness

No matter how carefully managers staff and organize task groups and teams, group dynamics can still go haywire. Forehand knowledge of two major threats to group effectiveness—groupthink and social loafing—can help managers and team members alike take necessary preventive steps.

Groupthink

Systematic analysis of the decision-making processes underlying the war in Vietnam and other US foreign policy fiascoes prompted Yale University's Irving Janis to coin the term *groupthink*.[78] Modern managers can all too easily become victims of groupthink, just like professional politicians, if they passively ignore the danger.

groupthink

Janis's term for a cohesive in-group's unwillingness to realistically view alternatives.

Janis defines **groupthink** as "a mode of thinking that people engage in when they are deeply involved in a cohesive in-group, when members' strivings for unanimity override their motivation to realistically appraise alternative courses of action."[79] He adds, "Groupthink refers to a deterioration of mental efficiency, reality testing, and moral judgment that results from in-group pressures."[80] Members of groups victimized by groupthink tend to be friendly and tightly knit.

According to Janis's model, there are eight classic symptoms of groupthink. The greater the number of symptoms, the higher the probability of groupthink:

1. *Invulnerability.* An illusion that breeds excessive optimism and risk taking.
2. *Inherent morality.* A belief that encourages the group to ignore ethical implications.
3. *Rationalization.* Protects pet assumptions.
4. *Stereotyped views of opposition.* Cause group to underestimate opponents.
5. *Self-censorship.* Stifles critical debate.
6. *Illusion of unanimity.* Silence interpreted to mean consent.
7. *Peer pressure.* Loyalty of dissenters is questioned.
8. *Mindguards.* Self-appointed protectors against adverse information.[81]

These symptoms thrive in the sort of climate outlined in the following critique of corporate directors in the United States:

> Many directors simply don't rock the boat. "No one likes to be the skunk at the garden party," says [management consultant] Victor H Palmieri. . . . "One does not make friends and influence people in the boardroom or elsewhere by raising hard questions that create embarrassment or discomfort for management."[82]

In short, policy- and decision-making groups can become so cohesive that strong-willed executives are able to gain unanimous support for poor decisions.

Janis believes that prevention is better than cure when dealing with groupthink (see Skills & Best Practices for his preventive measures).[83]

Social Loafing

Is group performance less than, equal to, or greater than the sum of its parts? Can three people, working together, for example, accomplish less than, the same as, or more than they would working separately? An interesting study conducted more than a half century ago by a French agricultural engineer named Ringelmann found the answer to be "less than."[84] In a rope-pulling exercise, Ringelmann reportedly found that three people pulling together could achieve only two and a half times the average individual rate. Eight pullers achieved less than four times the individual rate. This tendency for individual effort to decline as group size increases has come to be called **social loafing.**[85] Let us briefly analyze this threat to group effectiveness and synergy with an eye toward avoiding it.

Social Loafing Theory and Research   Among the theoretical explanations for the social loafing effect are (1) equity of effort ("Everyone else is goofing off, so why shouldn't I?"), (2) loss of personal accountability ("I'm lost in the crowd, so who cares?"), (3) motivational loss due to the sharing of rewards ("Why should I work harder than the others when everyone gets the same reward?"), and (4) coordination loss as more people perform the task ("We're getting in each other's way.").

Laboratory studies refined these theories by identifying situational factors that moderated the social loafing effect. Social loafing occurred when

- The task was perceived to be unimportant, simple, or not interesting.[86]
- Group members thought their individual output was not identifiable.[87]
- Group members expected their co-workers to loaf.[88]

But social loafing did *not* occur when group members in two laboratory studies expected to be evaluated.[89] Also, research suggests that self-reliant "individualists" are more prone to social loafing than are group-oriented "collectivists." But individualists can be made more cooperative by keeping the group small and holding each member personally accountable for results.[90]

Practical Implications   These findings demonstrate that social loafing is not an inevitable part of group effort. Management can curb this threat to group effectiveness by making sure the task is challenging and perceived as important. Additionally, it is a good idea to hold group members personally accountable for identifiable portions of the group's task.[91] (Recall our discussion of the power of goal setting in Chapter 7.)

How to Prevent Groupthink

1. Each member of the group should be assigned the role of critical evaluator. This role involves actively voicing objections and doubts.

2. Top-level executives should not use policy committees to rubber-stamp decisions that have already been made.

3. Different groups with different leaders should explore the same policy questions.

4. Subgroup debates and outside experts should be used to introduce fresh perspectives.

5. Someone should be given the role of devil's advocate when discussing major alternatives. This person tries to uncover every conceivable negative factor.

6. Once a consensus has been reached, everyone should be encouraged to rethink their position to check for flaws.

SOURCE: Adapted from discussion in I L Janis, *Groupthink,* 2nd ed. (Boston: Houghton Mifflin, 1982), ch II.

social loafing

Decrease in individual effort as group size increases.

key terms

cross-functionalism 237	maintenance roles 229	task roles 229
formal group 226	norm 231	team 232
group 225	ostracism 231	team building 234
group cohesiveness 229	roles 229	trust 235
groupthink 240	self-managed teams 236	virtual team 239
informal group 226	social loafing 241	

chapter summary

- *Describe the five stages of Tuckman's theory of group development.* The five stages in Tuckman's theory are *forming* (the group comes together), *storming* (members test the limits and each other), *norming* (questions about authority and power are resolved as the group becomes more cohesive), *performing* (effective communication and cooperation help the group get things done), and *adjourning* (group members go their own way).

- *Contrast roles and norms, and specify four reasons why norms are enforced in organizations.* While roles are specific to the person's position, norms are shared attitudes that differentiate appropriate from inappropriate behavior in a variety of situations. Norms evolve informally and are enforced because they help the group or organization survive, clarify behavioral expectations, help people avoid embarrassing situations, and clarify the group's or organization's central values.

- *Explain how a work group becomes a team, and identify five teamwork competencies.* A team is a mature group where leadership is shared, accountability is both individual and collective, the members have developed their own purpose, problem solving is a way of life, and effectiveness is measured by collective outcomes. Five teamwork competencies are (1) orients team to problem-solving situations; (2) organizes and manages team performance; (3) promotes a positive team environment; (4) facilitates and manages task conflict; and (5) appropriately promotes perspective.

- *List at least four things managers can do to build trust.* Six recommended ways to build trust are through communication, support, respect (especially delegation), fairness, predictability, and competence.

- *Describe self-managed teams and virtual teams.* Self-managed teams are groups of workers who are given administrative oversight for various chores normally performed by managers—such as planning, scheduling, monitoring, and staffing. They are typically cross-functional, meaning they are staffed with a mix of specialists from different areas. Self-managed teams vary widely in the autonomy or freedom they enjoy. A virtual team is a physically dispersed task group that conducts its business through modern information technology such as the Internet. Periodic and meaningful face-to-face contact seems to be crucial for virtual team members, especially during the early stages of group development.

- *Describe groupthink, and identify at least four of its symptoms.* Groupthink plagues cohesive in-groups that shortchange moral judgment while putting too much emphasis on unanimity. Symptoms of groupthink include invulnerability, inherent morality, rationalization, stereotyped views of opposition, self-censorship, illusion of unanimity, peer pressure, and mindguards. Critical evaluators, outside expertise, and devil's advocates are among the preventive measures recommended by Irving Janis, who coined the term *groupthink*.

discussion questions

1. Relative to the chapter-opening vignette, how important is trust in the smooth functioning of a health-care team? Explain.
2. What is your opinion about managers being friends with the people they supervise (in other words, overlapping formal and informal groups)?
3. In your personal relationships, how do you come to trust someone? How fragile is that trust? Explain.

4. Are virtual teams likely to be a passing fad? Why or why not?
5. Have you ever witnessed groupthink or social loafing firsthand? Explain the circumstances and how things played out.

ethical dilemma

Group Dynamics Gone Wrong: The Fine Line between Workplace Romance and Sexual Harassment

The Legal Context (in the United States)

What exactly is sexual harassment? The Equal Employment Opportunity Commission (EEOC) says that unwelcome sexual advances, requests for sexual favors, and other verbal or physical conduct of a sexual nature constitute sexual harassment when submission to such conduct is made a condition of employment; when submission to or rejection of sexual advances is used as a basis for employment decisions; or when such conduct creates an intimidating, hostile, or offensive work environment. These EEOC guidelines interpreting Title VII of the Civil Rights Act of 1964 further state that employers are responsible for the actions of their supervisors and agents and that employers are responsible for the actions of other employees if the employer knows or should have known about the sexual harassment.[92]

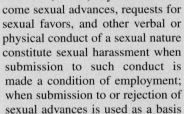

Manager's Hot Seat Application

Office Romance: Groping for Answers

Romance Blooms in the Workplace

For workplace sexual conduct to constitute prohibited sexual harassment, it generally must be unwelcome. If it's welcome, the conduct still may be inappropriate for the workplace, but usually it's not unlawful.

Here's a series of snapshots exposing the risks of dating, or attempts at dating, between a supervisor and a subordinate:

Take 1. Supervisor asks subordinate for a date. Subordinate says, "No." Supervisor asks again.

Problem: "No" means no.

Take 2. Supervisor asks subordinate for a date. Subordinate says, "I'm busy." Supervisor hears, "Ask me another time," so supervisor asks again.

Problem: Subordinate means "I'd rather die."

Take 3. Supervisor asks subordinate for a date. Subordinate says, "No." Supervisor does not ask again. However, supervisor later takes adverse action against subordinate for legitimate reasons.

Problem: Subordinate perceives adverse action to be retaliatory.

Take 4. Supervisor asks subordinate for a date. Subordinate says, "Yes." They love each other until they hate each other.

Problem: Subordinate claims that, although she participated in the affair, it was not welcome.

Take 5. Supervisor asks subordinate for a date. Subordinate says, "Yes." They date until they break up.

Problem: Subordinate claims that, while the affair was welcome, the supervisor is retaliating against him for ending it.

Take 6: Supervisor asks subordinate for a date. Subordinate says, "Yes." They fall in love and remain in love. There's no question that the relationship is entirely welcome.

Problem: No problem, so long as the consensual affair is isolated. But what if the supervisor is having more than one consensual affair? Or, what if more than one supervisor is having a consensual affair? Now, we have a problem.[93]

What Course of Action Would You Recommend?

1. As part of a comprehensive policy on sexual harassment, strictly enforce an organizationwide ban on dating between managers/supervisors and the employees who report directly to them. Monitor for compliance. Explain your rationale and discuss the practical implications.

2. Require all managers and supervisors to inform the human resources department about their romantic relationships with those who report directly to them. Monitor for sexual harassment. Explain your rationale.

3. Via the organization's culture, informally discourage managers and supervisors from dating people who report directly to them. Monitor for sexual harassment and take appropriate action on a case-by-case basis. Explain your rationale.

4. As a general rule, stay out of the personal affairs of employees. Communicate the organization's official policy on sexual harassment and intervene only when there is a formal charge of sexual harassment.

5. Invent other interpretations or options. Discuss.

For an interpretation of this situation, visit our Web site at www.mhhe.com/kinickiob3e.

If you're looking for additional study materials, be sure to check out the Online Learning Center at

www.mhhe.com/kinickiob3e

for more information and interactivities that correspond to this chapter.

Making Decisions

After reading the material in this chapter, you should be able to:

- Compare and contrast the rational model of decision making and Simon's normative model.

- Discuss knowledge management and techniques used by companies to increase knowledge sharing.

- Explain the model of decision-making styles and the stages of the creative process.

- Summarize the pros and cons of involving groups in the decision-making process.

- Explain how participative management affects performance.

- Contrast brainstorming, the nominal group technique, the Delphi technique, and computer-aided decision making.

ANALYTICS IS USED TO IMPROVE DECISION MAKING

Business today is awash in data and data crunchers, but only certain companies have transformed this technology from a supporting tool into a strategic weapon. Their ability to collect, analyze and act on data is the essence of their competitive advantage and the source of their superior performance.

double-digit profit gains for 20 straight quarters.

The core of the company's competitive capability is BudNer, a real-time network capable of gathering data on dozens of key performance indicators which the company's distributors report as they review shelves and product positioning in the

neighborhoods, allowing the company to design local promotions that match their markets to a tee.

Recently, Anheuser-Busch was the first to identify an important shift in customer purchasing preferences toward more healthy beverages, information the company harnessed to successfully capture the low-carb beer market.

Granted, organizations have been gathering massive amounts of data on customers buying habits and the efficiency of their operational processes for decades. But Anheuser-Busch is one of a new breed of data-driven companies that has taken analytics to a new level.

"Firms like Anheuser-Busch are outsmarting and outmaneuvering the competition because they have made information analysis and management a distinctive capability, one that is fundamental to their formula for doing business," observes Paul F. Nunes, an executive research fellow at the Accenture Institute for High Performance Business in Wellesley, Mass. . . .

Accenture has pinpointed the three approaches companies can choose from to join the ranks of analytics juggernauts.

Cemex S. A. uses analytics to reduce delivery time, an important consideration for its building-contractor customers.

A prime example is Anheuser-Busch Companies, Inc., brewer of many of the world's best-selling beers, based in St. Louis. It has made a science out of monitoring the metrics that allow it to understand when, where and why consumers buy beer—insights that have allowed the company to post

field. Analysts at corporate HQ regularly analyze and mine the data for decision support.

What's more, Anheuser-Busch combines the figures it gleans from its distributors, information systems with other key data, such as U.S. Census figures on the ethnic and economic makeup of

Put simply, organizations can, first, leverage analytics to add value to their offer in the form of service improvements, such as better or more timely delivery of goods and services; second, they can develop and deliver more personalized services to their customers; or third, they can expand their participation in the value chain.

Cemex S.A., a global supplier of cement and building solutions headquartered in Monterrey, Mexico, grew from a regional player to a world leader by using analytics to deliver its products to its customers on time and on their terms.

A deep understanding of its customers—which the company gained by meticulously gathering data about its customers' needs—allowed it to identify a crucial and unmet demand: quick delivery.

Ready-mix concrete is perishable and begins to set when a truck is loaded. Cemex found that, on average, it took three hours from the receipt of a contractor's order to the delivery of the concrete. These delays were costly to contractors, whose crews were at a standstill until the concrete arrived.

To complicate matters, Mexico, like other developing countries, is plagued by traffic congestion in its major cities, making it hard for a company to accurately plan deliveries.

Cemex determined that it could charge a premium to time-pressed contractors—as well as reduce costs by decreasing the amount of concrete that hardened en route—if they could reduce delivery times.

To accomplish this, Cemex again turned to analytics, this time to collect data and study the techniques and technologies used by couriers, delivery firms, police and paramedics.

Based on this research, Cemex devised a strategy to cut response times by equipping its concrete mixing trucks in Mexico with global-positioning satellite locators and Web-based vehicle dispatch technology. Using these systems to reconfigure its business processes allowed the company to deliver cement to its customers within a 20-minute window, boosting both productivity and customer loyalty.[1]

FOR DISCUSSION

Why don't more companies use analytics to make decisions? Explain. For an interpretation of this case and additional comments, visit our Online Learning Center at

www.mhhe.com/kinickiob3e

THOMAS STEWART, the editor of *Harvard Business Review,* recently concluded that "decisions are the essence of management."[2] The quality of a manager's decisions is important for two principal reasons. First, the quality of a manager's decisions directly affects his or her career opportunities, rewards, and job satisfaction. The second reason is highlighted in the chapter-opening vignette. Managerial decisions contribute to the success or failure of an organization.

The chapter-opening vignette highlights how successful companies such as Anheuser-Busch and Cemex S A use analytics to make decisions. **Analytics** involve a conscientious and explicit process of making decisions on the basis of the best available evidence. This process includes targeted approaches at collecting relevant information and data, studying or analyzing the information and data, and then making decisions on the basis of results. A recent study of 450 executives across 35 countries and 19 industries demonstrated that high-performance companies were five times more likely than low-performing companies to use analytics.[3]

Decision making entails identifying and choosing alternative solutions that lead to a desired state of affairs. The process begins with a problem and ends when a solution has been chosen. To gain an understanding of how managers can make better decisions, this chapter focuses on (1) models of decision making, (2) the dynamics of decision making, and (3) group decision making.

Models of Decision Making

There are two fundamental models of decision making: (1) the rational model and (2) Simon's normative model. Each is based on a different set of assumptions and offers unique insights into the decision-making process.

The Rational Model

The **rational model** proposes that managers use a rational, four-step sequence when making decisions: (1) identifying the problem, (2) generating alternative solutions, (3) selecting a solution, and (4) implementing and evaluating the solution. According to this model, managers are completely objective and possess complete information to make a decision. Despite criticism for being unrealistic, the rational model is instructive because it analytically breaks down the decision-making process and serves as a conceptual anchor for newer models.[4] Let us now consider each of these four steps.

Identifying the Problem A **problem** exists when the actual situation and the desired situation differ. For example, a problem exists when you have to pay rent at the end of the month and don't have enough money. Your problem is not that you have to pay rent. Your problem is obtaining the needed funds. Consider the situation faced by Baptist Health Care in Pensacola, Florida:

> [It] was the largest non-governmental employer in the Florida panhandle, with five hospitals, a nursing home, a mental health agency, and 5,500 employees. It was providing excellent care, but there were problems: low staff morale affected customer satisfaction and customer dissatisfaction was hurting market share. In 1995, flagship Baptist Hospital in Pensacola ranked close to the bottom in national surveys of patient satisfaction.[5]

analytics

A conscientious and explicit process of making decisions on the basis of the best available evidence.

decision making

Identifying and choosing solutions that lead to a desired end result.

Test Your Knowledge

The Vroom/Yetton/Jago Decision Model

rational model

Logical four-step approach to decision making.

problem

Gap between an actual and desired situation.

Michael Dell and Kevin Rollins Make Decisions Collaboratively

The following comments by Michael Dell and Kevin Rollins were obtained during an interview for the *Harvard Business Review*. The interview questions are shown in bold.

How do your decision-making styles differ?

Dell: We're pretty complementary. We've learned over time that each of us is right about 80% of the time, but if you put us together, our hit rate is much, much higher. We each think about a slightly different set of things, but there's a lot of overlap.
Rollins: We're both opinionated, but we also realize that listening to one another is a good thing. We have a lot of trust in each other's judgment.

You two have been a team for many years. Now Kevin is CEO and Michael is chairman—how does that relationship work?

Dell: We're very collaborative. We share all the issues and opportunities. It's not at all a typical hierarchy, and this transition was not at all a typical CEO-to-chairman transition. . . .

Ultimately, we make much better decisions because each of us comes up with ideas that aren't fully developed, we work through them together, and we end up with better decisions. For example, we both recognized the strategic importance of printers, but we debated the fine points between ourselves, and this led to a better decision process and rollout.
Rollins: From the beginning, Michael was enthusiastic about getting into printers, whereas I was a little risk averse. With regard to our storage partnership with EMC, our positions were reversed. So it's not as though one of us always plays the optimist and one the pessimist. In both cases, we each talked a lot about the issues and our concerns and got the other comfortable. Then we proceeded as a team.

SOURCE: Excerpted from T A Stewart and L O'Brien, "Execution without Excuses," *Harvard Business Review*, pp 107–8. Reprinted by permission of *Harvard Business Review*. Copyright © 2005 by the Harvard Business School Publishing Corporation; all rights reserved.

Baptist Health Care's problem was declining market share. The most immediate cause of this problem was customer dissatisfaction, which in turn was influenced by low staff morale.

Generating Solutions   After identifying a problem, the next logical step is generating alternative solutions. For repetitive and routine decisions such as deciding when to send customers a bill, alternatives are readily available through decision rules. For example, a company might routinely bill customers three days after shipping a product. This is not the case for novel and unstructured decisions. Because there are no simple procedures for dealing with novel problems, managers must creatively generate alternative solutions. Managers can use a number of techniques to stimulate creativity.

Selecting a Solution   Optimally, decision makers want to choose the alternative with the greatest value. Decision theorists refer to this as maximizing the expected utility of an outcome. This is no easy task. First, assigning values to alternatives is complicated and prone to error. Not only are values subjective, but they also vary according to the preferences of the decision maker. Research demonstrates that people vary in their preferences for safety or risk when making decisions. For example, a meta-analysis summarizing 150 studies revealed that males displayed more risk taking than females.[6] Michael Dell, chairman of Dell, and Kevin Rollins, Dell's CEO, attempt to overcome limitations associated with their personal preferences by extensively collaborating with each other when making decisions (see Skills & Best Practices). Their collaborative approach has been very successful. Further, evaluating alternatives assumes they can be judged according to some standards or criteria. This further assumes that (1) valid criteria exist, (2) each alternative can be compared against these criteria, and (3) the decision maker actually uses the criteria. As you know from making your own key life decisions, people frequently violate these assumptions. Finally, the ethics of the solution should be considered.

Implementing and Evaluating the Solution
Once a solution is chosen, it needs to be implemented. After a solution is implemented, the evaluation phase is used to assess its effectiveness. If the solution is effective, it should reduce the difference between the actual and desired states that created the problem. If the gap is not closed, the implementation was not successful, and one of the following is true: Either the problem was incorrectly identified, or the solution was inappropriate.

Summarizing the Rational Model The rational model is based on the premise that managers optimize when they make decisions. **Optimizing** involves solving problems by producing the best possible solution. As noted by Herbert Simon, a decision theorist who in 1978 earned the Nobel Prize for his work on decision making, "The assumptions of perfect rationality are contrary to fact. It is not a question of approximation; they do not even remotely describe the processes that human beings use for making decisions in complex situations."[7] Thus, the rational model is at best an instructional tool. Since decision makers do not follow these rational procedures, Simon proposed a normative model of decision making.

> **optimizing**
> Choosing the best possible solution.

Simon's Normative Model

This model attempts to identify the process that managers actually use when making decisions. The process is guided by a decision maker's bounded rationality. **Bounded rationality** represents the notion that decision makers are "bounded" or restricted by a variety of constraints when making decisions. These constraints include any personal or environmental characteristics that reduce rational decision making. Examples are the limited capacity of the human mind, problem complexity and uncertainty, amount and timeliness of information at hand, criticality of the decision, and time demands.[8]

> **bounded rationality**
> Constraints that restrict decision making.

As opposed to the rational model, Simon's normative model suggests that decision making is characterized by (1) limited information processing, (2) the use of judgmental heuristics, and (3) satisficing. Each of these characteristics is now explored.

Limited Information Processing Managers are limited by how much information they process because of bounded rationality. This results in the tendency to acquire manageable rather than optimal amounts of information. In turn, this practice makes it difficult for managers to identify all possible alternative solutions. In the long run, the constraints of bounded rationality cause decision makers to fail to evaluate all potential alternatives.

Judgmental heuristics can be powerful. Inspired by what he sees as a moral obligation, Bruce Karatz of KB Home, a building company, has vowed to rebuild some of the 200,000 homes destroyed by Hurricane Katrina even though no one is sure how many residents will return to New Orleans. "Nobody knows what demand will be," he says. "I just know we're doing the right thing."

Judgmental Heuristics **Judgmental heuristics** represent rules of thumb or shortcuts that people use to reduce information processing demands. Research also shows that we tend to use these heuristics when confronted with excessive amounts of choice or information, and we use them without conscious awareness.[9] The use of heuristics helps decision makers to reduce the uncertainty inherent within the decision-making process. Because these shortcuts represent knowledge gained from past experience, they can help decision makers evaluate current problems. But they also can lead to systematic errors that erode the quality of decisions. There are two

> **judgmental heuristics**
> Rules of thumb or shortcuts that people use to reduce information-processing demands.

common categories of heuristics that are important to consider: the availability heuristic and the representativeness heuristic.

availability heuristic

Tendency to base decisions on information readily available in memory.

The **availability heuristic** represents a decision maker's tendency to base decisions on information that is readily available in memory. Information is more accessible in memory when it involves an event that recently occurred, when it is salient (e.g., a plane crash), and when it evokes strong emotions (e.g., a high school student shooting other students). This heuristic is likely to cause people to overestimate the occurrence of unlikely events such as a plane crash or a high school shooting. This bias also is partially responsible for the recency effect discussed in Chapter 4. For example, a manager is more likely to give an employee a positive performance evaluation if the employee exhibited excellent performance over the last few months.

representativeness heuristic

Tendency to assess the likelihood of an event occurring based on impressions about similar occurrences.

The **representativeness heuristic** is used when people estimate the probability of an event occurring. It reflects the tendency to assess the likelihood of an event occurring based on one's impressions about similar occurrences. A manager, for example, may hire a graduate from a particular university because the past three people hired from this university turned out to be good performers. In this case, the "school attended" criterion is used to facilitate complex information processing associated with employment interviews. Unfortunately, this shortcut can result in a biased decision. Similarly, an individual may believe that he or she can master a new software package in a short period of time because he or she was able to learn how to use a different type of software. This estimate may or may not be accurate. For example, it may take the individual a much longer period of time to learn the new software because it requires the person to learn a new programming language.

satisficing

Choosing a solution that meets a minimum standard

Satisficing   People satisfice because they do not have the time, information, or ability to handle the complexity associated with following a rational process. This is not necessarily undesirable. **Satisficing** consists of choosing a solution that meets some minimum qualifications, one that is "good enough." Satisficing resolves problems by producing solutions that are satisfactory, as opposed to optimal. Finding a radio station to listen to in your car is a good example of satisficing. You cannot optimize because it is impossible to listen to all stations at the same time. You thus stop searching for a station when you find one playing a song you like or do not mind hearing.

Manager's Hot Seat Application

Office Romance: Groping for Answers

Dynamics of Decision Making

Decision making is part science and part art. Accordingly, this section examines four dynamics of decision making—knowledge management, decision-making styles, escalation of commitment, and creativity—that affect the "science" component. An understanding of these dynamics can help managers make better decisions.

Improving Decision Making through Effective Knowledge Management

Have you ever had to make a decision without complete information? If you have, then you know the quality of a decision is only as good as the information used to make the decision. The same is true for managerial decision making. In this case, however, managers frequently need information or knowledge possessed by people working in other parts of the organization. This realization has spawned a growing interest in the concept of knowledge management. **Knowledge management (KM)** is "the development of tools, processes, systems, structures, and cultures explicitly to improve the creation, sharing, and use of knowledge critical for decision making."[10] The effective use of KM helps organizations improve the quality of their decision making and correspondingly reduce costs and increase efficiency.[11] In contrast, ineffective use of knowledge management can be very costly. For example, experts estimate that *Fortune* 500 companies lose at least $31.5 billion a year by failing to share knowledge.[12]

> **knowledge management (KM)**
>
> Implementing systems and practices that increase the sharing of knowledge and information throughout an organization.

This section explores the fundamentals of KM so that you can use them to improve your decision making.

Knowledge Comes in Different Forms   There are two types of knowledge that impact the quality of decisions: tacit knowledge and explicit knowledge. **Tacit knowledge** "entails information that is difficult to express, formalize, or share. It . . . is unconsciously acquired from the experiences one has while immersed in an environment."[13] Many skills, for example, such as swinging a golf club or writing a speech, are difficult to describe in words because they involve tacit knowledge. Tacit knowledge is intuitive and is acquired by having considerable experience and expertise at some task or job. In contrast, **explicit knowledge** can easily be put into words and explained to others. This type of knowledge is shared verbally or in written documents or numerical reports. In summary, tacit knowledge represents private information that is difficult to share, whereas explicit knowledge is external or public and is more easily communicated. Although both types of knowledge affect decision making, experts suggest competitive advantages are created when tacit knowledge is shared among employees.[14] Let us now examine how companies foster this type of information sharing.

> **tacit knowledge**
>
> Information gained through experience that is difficult to express and formalize.
>
> **explicit knowledge**
>
> Information that can be easily put into words and shared with others.

Knowledge Sharing   Organizations increasingly rely on sophisticated KM software to share explicit knowledge. This software allows companies to amass large amounts of information that can be accessed quickly from around the world. These systems can also be used to obtain information and feedback from customers and other organizations. For example, Procter & Gamble uses scientific networks from outside the company to obtain information needed for new product development. The company now gets 35% of its new products from outside sources, enabling Procter & Gamble to increase its sales per R&D-person by 40%.[15] In contrast, tacit knowledge is shared most directly by observing, participating, or working with experts or coaches. Mentoring, which was discussed in Chapter 2, is another method for spreading tacit knowledge. Finally, informal networking, periodic meetings, and the design of office space can be used to facilitate KM. Alcoa, for example, designed its headquarters with the aim of increasing information sharing among its executives:

> Alcoa, the world's leading producer of aluminum, wanted to improve access between its senior executives. When designing their new headquarters they focused on open offices, family-style kitchens in the center of each floor, and plenty of open spaces. Previously, top executives would only interact with a couple of people in the elevator and those they had scheduled meetings with. Now, executives bump into each other more often and are more accessible for serendipitous conversations. This change in space has increased general accessibility as well as narrowed the gap between top executives and employees.[16]

It is important to remember that the best-laid plans for increasing KM are unlikely to succeed without the proper organizational culture. Effective KM requires a knowledge-sharing culture that both encourages and reinforces the spread of tacit knowledge. IBM Global Services has taken this recommendation to heart:

> IBM Global Services has incorporated knowledge creation, sharing, and reuse measurements into performance metrics. Performance metrics and incentives, particularly at the executive rank, have driven collaborative behavior into the day-to-day work practices of executive networks. Further, knowledge sharing has been incorporated into personal business commitments, which are required for certification and affect promotion decisions. This encourages employees at all levels to be collaborative with and accessible to each other.[17]

General Decision-Making Styles

This section focuses on how an individual's decision-making style affects his or her approach to decision making. A **decision-making style** reflects the combination of how an individual perceives and comprehends stimuli and the general manner in which he or she chooses to respond to such information.[18] A team of researchers developed a model of decision-making styles that is based on the idea that styles vary along two different dimensions: value orientation and tolerance for ambiguity.[19] *Value orientation* reflects the extent to which an individual focuses on either task and technical concerns or people and social concerns when making decisions. The second dimension pertains to a person's *tolerance for ambiguity*. This individual difference indicates the extent to which a person has a high need for structure or control in his or her life. When the dimensions of value orientation and tolerance for ambiguity are combined, they form four styles of decision making (see Figure 10–1): directive, analytical, conceptual, and behavioral.

decision-making style

A combination of how individuals perceive and respond to information.

Self-Assessment Exercise

Your Preferred Decision-Making Style

Directive   People with a directive style have a low tolerance for ambiguity and are oriented toward task and technical concerns when making decisions. They are efficient, logical, practical, and systematic in their approach to solving problems. People with this style are action oriented and decisive and like to focus on facts. In their pursuit of speed and results, however, these individuals tend to be autocratic,

FIGURE 10–1
Decision-Making Styles

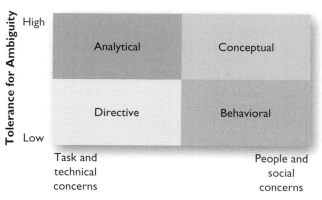

SOURCE: Based on discussion contained in A J Rowe and R O Mason, *Managing with Style: A Guide to Understanding, Assessing, and Improving Decision Making* (San Francisco: Jossey-Bass, 1987), pp 1–17.

Air-traffic controller
Paul Rinaldi uses a directive style to make quick
decisions at Dulles
International Airport.

exercise power and control, and focus on the short run. Interestingly, a directive style seems well-suited for an air-traffic controller. Here is what Paul Rinaldi had to say about his decision-making style to a reporter from *Fortune*.

> It's not so much analytical as it is making a decision quickly and sticking with it. You have to do that knowing that some of the decisions you're going to make are going to be wrong, but you're going to make that decision be right. You can't back out. You've constantly got to be taking into account the speed of the airplane, its characteristics, the climb rate, and how fast it's going to react to your instructions. You're taking all that in and processing it in a split second, hoping that it'll all work together. If it doesn't, then you go to plan B. . . . The percentage of us that make it to retirement is not real high. It takes a toll on you. We can't make mistakes.[20]

Analytical   This style has a much higher tolerance for ambiguity and is characterized by the tendency to overanalyze a situation. People with this style like to consider more information and alternatives than do directives. Analytic individuals are careful decision makers who take longer to make decisions but who also respond well to new or uncertain situations. They can often be autocratic.

Zhang Guangming is a good example of someone with an analytical style. "Zhang Guangming's car-buying synapses have been in overdrive for months. He has spent hours poring over Chinese car buff magazines, surfing Web sites to mine data on various models, and trekking out to a dozen dealerships across Beijing. Finally, Zhang settled on either a Volkswagen Bora or a Hyundai Sonata sedan. But with cutthroat competition forcing dealers to slash prices, he's not sure whether to buy now or wait."[21]

Conceptual   People with a conceptual style have a high tolerance for ambiguity and tend to focus on the people or social aspects of a work situation. They take a broad perspective to problem solving and like to consider many options and future possibilities. Conceptual types adopt a long-term perspective and rely on intuition and discussions with others to acquire information. They also are willing to take risks and are good at finding creative solutions to problems. General Peter Pace, US Marine Corps, vice chairman of the Joint Chiefs of Staff, possesses characteristics of a conceptual style of decision making. He described his approach to decision making as follows:

> When you have to make a decision about someone's future, or what kind of weapon system to invest in, or any other kind of businesslike decision, you should not let anybody rush you. On a battlefield, you don't have time to gather a lot of opinions. You have to assess the environment and make a decision based on your experience and training. You react instinctively. What I have learned is that if you're collaborative when you can be, it builds trust, so that when you have to decide right now, folks are more likely to trust your decision.[22]

On the downside, however, a conceptual style can foster an idealistic and indecisive approach to decision making.

Behavioral   People with this style work well with others and enjoy social interactions in which opinions are openly exchanged. Behavioral types are supportive, receptive to suggestions, show warmth, and prefer verbal to written information. Although they like to hold meetings, people with this style have a tendency to avoid conflict and to be too concerned about others. This can lead behavioral types to adopt a "wishy-washy" approach to decision making, to have a hard time saying no to others, and to have a hard time making difficult decisions.

Research and Practical Implications   Please take a moment now to complete the Hands-On Exercise. It assesses your decision-making style. How do your scores compare with the following norms: directive (75), analytical (90), conceptual (80), and behavioral (55)?[23] What do the differences between your scores and the survey norms suggest about your decision-making style?

Research shows that very few people have only one dominant decision-making style. Rather, most managers have characteristics that fall into two or three styles. Studies also show that decision-making styles vary across occupations, job level, and countries.[24] You can use knowledge of decision-making styles in three ways. First, knowledge of styles helps you to understand yourself. Awareness of your style assists you in identifying your strengths and weaknesses as a decision maker and facilitates the potential for self-improvement. Second, you can increase your ability to influence others by being aware of styles. For example, if you are dealing with an analytical person, you should provide as much information as possible to support your ideas. This same approach is more likely to frustrate a directive type. Finally, knowledge of styles gives you an awareness of how people can take the same information and yet arrive at different decisions by using a variety of decision-making strategies. It is important to conclude with the caveat that there is not a best decision-making style that applies in all situations. We should all strive to capitalize on the strengths of the various decision-making styles while trying to achieve a "state of clarity" when making decisions. According to a decision-making expert, "the clarity state is characterized by a balance of physical, mental and emotional systems. . . . it is actually a measurable physical and emotional state of being relaxed, positive and focused."[25]

Escalation of Commitment

escalation of commitment

Sticking to an ineffective course of action too long.

Escalation situations involve circumstances in which things have gone wrong but where the situation can possibly be turned around by investing additional time, money, or effort.[26] **Escalation of commitment**

What Is Your Decision-Making Style?

INSTRUCTIONS: This survey consists of 20 questions, each with four responses. You must consider each possible response for a question and then rank them according to how much you prefer each response. Because many of the questions are anchored to how individuals make decisions at work, you can feel free to use your student role as a frame of reference to answer the questions. For each question, use the space on the survey to rank the four responses with either a 1, 2, 4, or 8. Use the number 8 for the responses that are **most** like you, a 4 for those that are **moderately** like you, a 2 for those that are **slightly** like you, and a 1 for the responses that are **least** like you. For example, a question could be answered [8], [4], [2], [1]. Do not repeat any number when answering a question, and place the numbers in the boxes next to each of the answers. Once all of the responses for the 20 questions have been ranked, total the scores in each of the four columns. The total score for column one represents your directive style, column two your analytical style, column three your conceptual style, and column four your behavioral style.

1. My prime objective in life is to:	have a position with status	be the best in whatever I do	be recognized for my work	feel secure in my job
2. I enjoy work that:	is clear and well defined	is varied and challenging	lets me act independently	involves people
3. I expect people to be:	productive	capable	committed	responsive
4. My work lets me:	get things done	find workable approaches	apply new ideas	be truly satisfied
5. I communicate best by:	talking with others	putting things in writing	being open with others	having a group meeting
6. My planning focuses on:	current problems	how best to meet goals	future opportunities	needs of people in the organization
7. I prefer to solve problems by:	applying rules	using careful analysis	being creative	relying on my feelings
8. I prefer information:	that is simple and direct	that is complete	that is broad and informative	that is easily understood
9. When I'm not sure what to do:	I rely on my intuition	I search for alternatives	I try to find a compromise	I avoid making a decision
10. Whenever possible, I avoid:	long debates	incomplete work	technical problems	conflict with others
11. I am really good at:	remembering details	finding answers	seeing many options	working with people
12. When time is important, I:	decide and act quickly	apply proven approaches	look for what will work	refuse to be pressured
13. In social settings, I:	speak with many people	observe what others are doing	contribute to the conversation	want to be part of the discussion
14. I always remember:	people's names	places I have been	people's faces	people's personalities
15. I prefer jobs where I:	receive high rewards	have challenging assignments	can reach my personal goals	am accepted by the group
16. I work best with people who:	are energetic and ambitious	are very competent	are open minded	are polite and understanding
17. When I am under stress, I:	speak quickly	try to concentrate on the problem	become frustrated	worry about what I should do
18. Others consider me:	aggressive	disciplined	imaginative	supportive
19. My decisions are generally:	realistic and direct	systematic and logical	broad and flexible	sensitive to the other's needs
20. I dislike:	losing control	boring work	following rules	being rejected

Total score _____

SOURCE: © Dr. Alan J Rowe, Distinguished Emeritus Professor. Revised 12/18/98. Reprinted with permission.

Jason Fiber, president of Warner Music Group's new digital label Cordless Recordings, has a strategy for avoiding escalation of commitment. **"We advance money to artists for recording—not a terribly substantial amount, but enough that we think they can deliver some interesting material to us. In return, we ask for a two-year license and retain the rights for roughly five years. If we aren't able to generate the kind of interest we'd like, we give their masters back."**

refers to the tendency to stick to an ineffective course of action when it is unlikely that the bad situation can be reversed. Personal examples include investing more money into an old or broken car, waiting an extremely long time for a bus to take you somewhere that you could have walked just as easily, or trying to save a disruptive interpersonal relationship that has lasted 10 years. Case studies also indicate that escalation of commitment is partially responsible for some of the worst financial losses experienced by organizations.

OB researchers Jerry Ross and Barry Staw identified four reasons for escalation of commitment. They involve psychological and social determinants, organizational determinants, project characteristics, and contextual determinants.[27]

Psychological and Social Determinants   Ego defense and individual motivations are the key psychological contributors to escalation of commitment. Individuals "throw good money after bad" because they tend to (1) bias facts so that they support previous decisions, (2) take more risks when a decision is stated in negative terms (to recover losses) rather than positive ones (to achieve gains), and (3) get too ego-involved with the project. Because failure threatens an individual's self-esteem or ego, people tend to ignore negative signs and push forward.

Social pressures can make it difficult for a manager to reverse a course of action. For instance, peer pressure makes it difficult for an individual to drop a course of action when he or she publicly supported it in the past. Further, managers may continue to support bad decisions because they don't want their mistakes exposed to others.

Organizational Determinants   Breakdowns in communication, workplace politics, and organizational inertia cause organizations to maintain bad courses of action.

Project Characteristics   Project characteristics involve the objective features of a project. They have the greatest impact on escalation decisions. For example, because most projects do not reap benefits until some delayed time period, decision makers are motivated to stay with the project until the end.[28] Thus, there is a tendency to attribute setbacks to temporary causes that are correctable with additional expenditures. Moreover, escalation is related to whether the project has clearly defined goals and whether people receive clear feedback about performance. One study, for instance, revealed that escalation was fueled by ambiguous performance feedback and the lack of performance standards.[29]

Contextual Determinants   These causes of escalation are due to forces outside an organization's control. For instance, research showed that a manager's national culture influenced the amount of escalation in decision making. Samples of decision makers in Mexico and the United States revealed that Mexican managers exhibited more escalation than US managers.[30] External political forces also represent a contextual determinant.

Reducing Escalation of Commitment It is important to reduce escalation of commitment because it leads to poor decision making for both individuals and groups. Barry Staw and Jerry Ross, the researchers who originally identified the phenomenon of escalation, recommended several ways to reduce it (see Skills & Best Practices).

Creativity

In light of today's need for fast-paced decisions, an organization's ability to stimulate the creativity and innovation of its employees is becoming increasingly important.[31] Although many definitions have been proposed, **creativity** is defined here as the process of using intelligence, imagination, and skill to develop a new or novel product, object, process, or thought.[32] It can be as simple as locating a new place to hang your car keys or as complex as developing a pocket-size microcomputer. This definition highlights three broad types of creativity. One can create something new (creation), one can combine or synthesize things (synthesis), or one can improve or change things (modification).

Researchers are not absolutely certain how creativity takes place. Nonetheless, we do know that creativity involves "making remote associations" between unconnected events, ideas, information stored in memory (recall our discussion in Chapter 4), or physical objects. Consider how biologist Napoleone Ferrara's remote association led to the creation of a new type of cancer therapy that extends cancer patients' lives:

> Twenty years ago biologist Napoleone Ferrara discovered a mysterious protein in the pituitary gland of cows that seemed to make blood vessels grow. He foresaw a new weapon against cancer—block the protein and tumors may be unable to proliferate—but the finding was so obscure that even his boss was skeptical. Last month the drug that resulted from Ferrara's work began to look like a success: Genentech unveiled trial results that showed it extended colon cancer patients' lives by a median of five months, or 30%, one of the biggest advances in years.[33]

Dr. Ferrara obviously associated the characteristics of a cow protein with a solution for stopping the growth of cancerous tumors. Researchers, however, have identified five stages underlying the creative process: preparation, concentration, incubation, illumination, and verification. Let us consider these stages.

The *preparation* stage reflects the notion that creativity starts from a base of knowledge. Experts suggest that creativity involves a convergence between tacit or implied knowledge and explicit knowledge. During the *concentration* stage, an individual focuses on the problem at hand. Research shows that creative

creativity

Process of developing something new or unique.

"We need something to come after this part. Any ideas?"

Copyright © Ted Goff. Reprinted with permission.

ideas at work are often triggered by work-related problems, incongruities, or failures. This was precisely the case for aerospace engineer Walt Gillette when he was attempting to resolve aerodynamics problems for Boeing.

> Southwest Airlines Co. needed a small plane to break out of short hops and fly across the country. Gillette used an analytical method called computational fluid dynamics (CFD) to crack the toughest design problems, including figuring out how to sling powerful new engines on the wings of a small 737. "Every time we tried to put one of those big fat nacelles [engine enclosures] close to the wing, we got terrible aerodynamic interference between the nacelle and the wing," Gillette recalled. . . . Gillette and his team traveled the world, looked at every nacelle installation, studied them with CFD, and came up with a formula that changed aviation history. "We found five things, which remain trade secrets," he said in an interview, "five features that no one had used in such a combination. It let us shove a big nacelle really close to the wing."[34]

Interestingly, Japanese companies are noted for encouraging this stage as part of a quality improvement process more than American companies. For example, the average number of ideas per employee was 37.4 for Japanese workers versus .12 for US workers.[35]

Incubation is done unconsciously. During this stage, people engage in daily activities while their minds simultaneously mull over information and make remote associations. These associations ultimately are generated in the *illumination* stage. Finally, *verification* entails going through the entire process to verify, modify, or try out the new idea.

Let us examine the stages of creativity to determine why Japanese organizations propose and implement more ideas than do American companies. To address this issue, a creativity expert visited and extensively interviewed employees from five major Japanese companies. He observed that Japanese firms have created a management infrastructure that encourages and reinforces creativity. People were taught to identify problems (discontents) on their first day of employment. In turn, discontents were referred to as "golden eggs" to reinforce the notion that it is good to identify problems.

These organizations also promoted the stages of incubation, illumination, and verification through teamwork and incentives. For example, some companies posted the golden eggs on large wall posters in the work area; employees were then encouraged to interact with each other to execute the final three stages of the creative process. Employees eventually received monetary awards for any suggestions that passed all five phases of this process.[36] This research underscores the conclusion that creativity can be enhanced by effectively managing the creativity process and by fostering a positive and supportive work environment.[37] W L Gore & Associates, the maker of Gore-Tex fabrics and Glide dental floss, does this by relying on an organizational structure in which "there are no bosses, job titles, or organization charts, just sponsors, team members, and leaders."[38] See the Skills & Best Practices box "Avoid These

Creativity/Innovation Killers" for a list of work-environment factors found to kill creativity and innovation.

Group Decision Making

This section explores issues associated with group decision making. Specifically, we discuss (1) group involvement in decision making, (2) advantages and disadvantages of group-aided decision making, (3) participative management, and (4) group problem-solving techniques.

Group Involvement in Decision Making

Whether groups assemble in face-to-face meetings or rely on other technologically based methods to communicate, they can contribute to each stage of the decision-making process. In order to maximize the value of group-aided decision making, however, it is important to create an environment in which group members feel free to participate and express their opinions. A study sheds light on how managers can create such an environment.

A team of researchers conducted two studies to determine whether a group's innovativeness was related to *minority dissent,* defined as the extent to which group members feel comfortable disagreeing with other group members, and a group's level of participation in decision making. Results showed that the most innovative groups possessed high levels of both minority dissent and participation in decision making.[39] These findings encourage managers to seek divergent views from group members during decision making. They also support the practice of not seeking compliance from group members or punishing group members who disagree with a majority opinion. Take a moment now to complete the Hands-On Exercise (entitled "Assessing Participation in Group Decision Making"). It assesses the amount of minority dissent and participation in group decision making for a group project you have completed or are currently working on in school or on the job. Is your satisfaction with the group related to minority dissent and participation in decision making? If not, what might explain this surprising result?

The previously discussed study about minority dissent reinforces the notion that the quality of group decision making varies across groups. This, in turn, raises the issue of how to best assess a group's decision-making effectiveness. Although experts do not agree on the one "best" criterion, there is agreement that groups need to work through various aspects of decision making in order to be effective. One expert proposed that decision-making effectiveness in a group is dependent on successfully accomplishing the following:[40]

1. Developing a clear understanding of the decision situation.
2. Developing a clear understanding of the requirements for an effective choice.
3. Thoroughly and accurately assessing the positive qualities of alternative solutions.
4. Thoroughly and accurately assessing the negative qualities of alternative solutions.

To increase the probability of groups making high-quality decisions, managers, team leaders, and individual group members are encouraged to focus on satisfying these four requirements.[41]

Assessing Participation in Group Decision Making

INSTRUCTIONS: The following survey measures minority dissent, participation in group decision making, and satisfaction with a group. For each of the items, use the rating scale shown below to circle the answer that best represents your feelings based on a group project you were or currently are involved in. Next, use the scoring key to compute scores for the levels of minority dissent, participation in decision making, and satisfaction with the group.

1 = Strongly disagree
2 = Disagree
3 = Neither agree nor disagree
4 = Agree
5 = Strongly agree

1. Within my team, individuals disagree with one another.	1	2	3	4	5
2. Within my team, individuals do not go along with majority opinion.	1	2	3	4	5
3. Within my team, individuals voice their disagreement with the majority opinion.	1	2	3	4	5
4. Within my team, I am comfortable voicing my disagreement of the majority opinion.	1	2	3	4	5
5. Within my team, individuals do not immediately agree with one another.	1	2	3	4	5
6. As a team member, I have a real say in how work is carried out.	1	2	3	4	5
7. Within my team, most members have a chance to participate in decisions.	1	2	3	4	5
8. My team is designed so that everyone has the opportunity to participate in decisions.	1	2	3	4	5
9. I am satisfied with my group.	1	2	3	4	5
10. I would like to work with this group on another project.	1	2	3	4	5

SCORING KEY

Minority dissent (add scores for items 1, 2, 3, 4, 5): _____

Participation in decision making (add scores for items 6, 7, 8): _____

Satisfaction (add scores for items 9, 10): _____

ARBITRARY NORMS

Low minority dissent = 5–15

High minority dissent = 16–25

Low participation in decision making = 3–8

High participation in decision making = 9–15

Low satisfaction = 2–5

High satisfaction = 6–10

SOURCE: The items in the survey were developed from **C K W De Dreu and M A West, "Minority Dissent and Team Innovation: The Importance of Participation in Decision Making,"** *Journal of Applied Psychology*, December 2001, pp 119–201.

Advantages and Disadvantages of Group-Aided Decision Making **TABLE 10–1**

Advantages	Disadvantages
1. *Greater pool of knowledge.* A group can bring much more information and experience to bear on a decision or problem than can an individual acting alone.	1. *Social pressure.* Unwillingness to "rock the boat" and pressure to conform may combine to stifle the creativity of individual contributors.
2. *Different perspectives.* Individuals with varied experience and interests help the group see decision situations and problems from different angles.	2. *Domination by a vocal few.* Sometimes the quality of group action is reduced when the group gives in to those who talk the loudest and longest.
3. *Greater comprehension.* Those who personally experience the give-and-take of group discussion about alternative courses of action tend to understand the rationale behind the final decision.	3. *Logrolling.* Political wheeling and dealing can displace sound thinking when an individual's pet project or vested interest is at stake.
4. *Increased acceptance.* Those who play an active role in group decision making and problem solving tend to view the outcome as "ours" rather than "theirs."	4. *Goal displacement.* Sometimes secondary considerations such as winning an argument, making a point, or getting back at a rival displace the primary task of making a sound decision or solving a problem.
5. *Training ground.* Less experienced participants in group action learn how to cope with group dynamics by actually being involved.	5. *"Groupthink."* Sometimes cohesive "in-groups" let the desire for unanimity override sound judgment when generating and evaluating alternative courses of action. (Groupthink is discussed in Chapter 9.)

SOURCE: R Kreitner, *Management,* 10th ed (Boston: Houghton Mifflin, 2007), p 231. Used with permission.

Advantages and Disadvantages of Group-Aided Decision Making

Including groups in the decision-making process has both pros and cons (see Table 10–1). On the positive side, groups contain a greater pool of knowledge, provide more varied perspectives, create more comprehension of decisions, increase decision acceptance, and create a training ground for inexperienced employees. These advantages must be balanced, however, with the disadvantages listed in Table 10–1. In doing so, managers need to determine the extent to which the advantages and disadvantages apply to the decision situation. The following three guidelines may then be applied to help decide whether groups should be included in the decision-making process:

1. If additional information would increase the quality of the decision, managers should involve those people who can provide the needed information.

2. If acceptance is important, managers need to involve those individuals whose acceptance and commitment are important.

3. If people can be developed through their participation, managers may want to involve those whose development is most important.[42]

Group versus Individual Performance Before recommending that managers involve groups in decision making, it is important to examine whether groups perform better or worse than individuals. After reviewing 61 years of relevant research, a decision-making expert concluded that "Group performance was generally qualitatively and quantitatively superior to the performance of the average individual."[43] Although subsequent research of small-group decision making generally supported this conclusion, additional research suggests that managers should use a contingency approach when determining whether to include others in the decision-making process. Let us now consider these contingency recommendations.

Group
Exercise

Stranded in
the Desert:
An Exercise in
Decision Making

Practical Contingency Recommendations   If the decision occurs frequently, such as deciding on promotions or who qualifies for a loan, use groups because they tend to produce more consistent decisions than do individuals. Given time constraints, let the most competent individual, rather than a group, make the decision. In the face of environmental threats such as time pressure and the potentially serious effects of a decision, groups use less information and fewer communication channels. This increases the probability of a bad decision.[44] This conclusion underscores a general recommendation that managers should keep in mind: Because the quality of communication strongly affects a group's productivity, on complex tasks it is essential to devise mechanisms to enhance communication effectiveness.

Participative Management

An organization needs to maximize its workers' potential if it wants to successfully compete in the global economy. Participative management and employee empowerment, which is discussed in Chapter 13, are highly touted methods for meeting this productivity challenge. Confusion exists about the exact meaning of participative management (PM). One management expert clarified this situation by defining **participative management** as the process whereby employees play a direct role in (1) setting goals, (2) making decisions, (3) solving problems, and (4) making changes in the organization. Without question, participative management entails much more than simply asking employees for their ideas or opinions.

participative management

Involving employees in various forms of decision making.

Advocates of PM claim employee participation increases employee satisfaction, commitment, and performance. Consistent with both Maslow's need theory and the job characteristics model of job design (see Chapter 6), participative management is predicted to increase motivation because it helps employees fulfill three basic needs: (1) autonomy, (2) meaningfulness of work, and (3) interpersonal contact. Satisfaction of these needs enhances feelings of acceptance and commitment, security, challenge, and satisfaction. In turn, these positive feelings supposedly lead to increased innovation, satisfaction, and performance.[45]

Participative management does not work in all situations. The design of work, the level of trust between management and employees, and the employees' competence and readiness to participate represent three factors that influence the effectiveness of PM. With respect to the design of work, individual participation is counterproductive when employees are highly interdependent on each other, as on an assembly line. The problem with individual participation in this case is that interdependent employees generally do not have a broad understanding of the entire production process. Participative management also is less likely to succeed when employees do not trust management. Finally, PM is more effective when employees are competent, prepared, and interested in participating. Northwest Airlines is a good case in point. Employees responded very positively to the company's new employee suggestion system because they were motivated to help the airline reduce operating costs in order to save jobs. The suggestion system resulted in $6 million in annual savings from workers' ideas. "A flight attendant, for instance, noticed that too many coffeepots were being boarded on planes, so Northwest cut back and now saves $120,000 a year. A customer-service agent suggested that blanket folding and washing be done in-house, for savings of $205,000 annually. A manager in Minneapolis had an idea that resulted in an annual saving of $916,000 on maintenance on DC-10 thrust reversers."[46]

Group Problem-Solving Techniques

Using groups to make decisions generally requires that they reach a consensus. According to a decision-making expert, a **consensus** "is reached when all members can say they either agree with the decision or have had their 'day in court' and were unable to convince the others of their viewpoint. In the final analysis, everyone agrees to support the outcome."[47] This definition indicates that consensus does not require unanimous agreement because group members may still disagree with the final decision but are willing to work toward its success.

> **consensus**
>
> Presenting opinions and gaining agreement to support a decision.

Groups can experience roadblocks when trying to arrive at a consensus decision. For one, groups may not generate all relevant alternatives to a problem because an individual dominates or intimidates other group members. This is both overt and/or subtle. For instance, group members who possess power and authority, such as a CEO, can be intimidating, regardless of interpersonal style, simply by being present in the room. Moreover, shyness inhibits the generation of alternatives. Shy or socially anxious individuals may withhold their input for fear of embarrassment or lack of confidence. Satisficing is another hurdle to effective group decision making. As previously noted, groups satisfice due to limited time, information, or ability to handle large amounts of information.[48] A management expert offered the following "do's" and "don'ts" for successfully achieving consensus: Groups should use active listening skills, involve as many members as possible, seek out the reasons behind arguments, and dig for the facts. At the same time, groups should not horse trade

(I'll support you on this decision because you supported me on the last one), vote, or agree just to avoid "rocking the boat."[49] Voting is not encouraged because it can split the group into winners and losers.

Decision-making experts have developed three group problem-solving techniques—brainstorming, the nominal group technique, and the Delphi technique—to reduce the above roadblocks. Knowledge of these techniques can help current and future managers to more effectively use group-aided decision making. Further, the advent of computer-aided decision making enables managers to use these techniques to solve complex problems with large groups of people.

Brainstorming is a technique used to generate as many ideas as possible to solve a problem. You have probably engaged in brainstorming sessions for various class or work projects. Which of the seven rules for brainstorming do you think is most important?

Brainstorming   Brainstorming was developed by A F Osborn, an advertising executive, to increase creativity.[50] **Brainstorming** is used to help groups generate multiple ideas and alternatives for solving problems. This technique is effective because it helps reduce interference caused by critical and judgmental reactions to one's ideas from other group members.

> **brainstorming**
>
> Process to generate a quantity of ideas.

When brainstorming, a group is convened, and the problem at hand is reviewed. Individual members then are asked to silently generate ideas/alternatives for solving the problem. Silent idea generation is recommended over the practice of having group members randomly shout out their ideas because it leads to a greater number of unique ideas. Next, these ideas/alternatives are solicited and written on a board or flip chart. A recent study suggests that managers or team leaders may want to collect the brainstormed ideas anonymously. Results demonstrated that more controversial ideas and more nonredundant ideas were generated by anonymous than nonanonymous brainstorming groups.[51] Finally, a second session is used to critique and evaluate the alternatives. Managers are advised to follow the seven rules for brainstorming used by IDEO.[52]

1. *Defer judgment.* Don't criticize during the initial stage of idea generation. Phrases such as "we've never done it that way," "it won't work," "it's too expensive," and "our manager will never agree" should not be used.

2. *Build on the ideas of others.* Encourage participants to extend others' ideas by avoiding "buts" and using "ands."

3. *Encourage wild ideas.* Encourage out-of-the-box thinking. The wilder and more outrageous the ideas, the better.

4. *Go for quantity over quality.* Participants should try to generate and write down as many new ideas as possible. Focusing on quantity encourages people to think beyond their favorite ideas.

5. *Be visual.* Use different colored pens (e.g., red, purple, blue) to write on big sheets of flip chart paper, white boards, or poster board that are put on the wall.

6. *Stay focused on the topic.* A facilitator should be used to keep the discussion on target.

7. *One conversation at a time.* The ground rules are that no one interrupts another person, no dismissing of someone's ideas, no disrespect, and no rudeness.

Brainstorming is an effective technique for generating new ideas/alternatives. It is not appropriate for evaluating alternatives or selecting solutions.

nominal group technique (NGT)

Process to generate ideas and evaluate solutions.

The Nominal Group Technique   The **nominal group technique (NGT)** helps groups generate ideas and evaluate and select solutions. NGT is a structured group meeting that follows this format:[53] A group is convened to discuss a particular problem or issue. After the problem is understood, individuals silently generate ideas in writing. Each individual, in round-robin fashion, then offers one idea from his or her list. Ideas are recorded on a blackboard or flip chart; they are not discussed at this stage of the process. Once all ideas are elicited, the group discusses them. Anyone may criticize or defend any item. During this step, clarification is provided as well as general agreement or disagreement with the idea. The "30-second soap box" technique, which entails giving each participant a maximum of 30 seconds to argue for or against any of the ideas under consideration, can be used to facilitate this discussion. Finally, group members anonymously vote for their top choices with a weighted voting procedure (e.g., 1st choice = 3 points; 2nd choice = 2 points; 3rd choice = 1 point). Alternatively, group members can vote by placing colored dots next to their top choices. The group leader then adds the votes to determine the group's choice. Prior to making a final decision, the group may decide to discuss the top ranked items and conduct a second round of voting.

The nominal group technique reduces the roadblocks to group decision making by (1) separating brainstorming from evaluation, (2) promoting balanced participation among group members, and (3) incorporating mathematical voting techniques in order to reach consensus. NGT has been successfully used in many different decision-making situations, and has been found to generate more ideas than a standard brainstorming session.[54]

The Delphi Technique This problem-solving method was originally developed by the Rand Corporation for technological forecasting.[55] It now is used as a multipurpose planning tool. The **Delphi technique** is a group process that anonymously generates ideas or judgments from physically dispersed experts. Unlike the NGT, experts' ideas are obtained from questionnaires or via the Internet as opposed to face-to-face group discussions.

> **Delphi technique**
>
> **Process to generate ideas from physically dispersed experts.**

A manager begins the Delphi process by identifying the issue(s) he or she wants to investigate. For example, a manager might want to inquire about customer demand, customers' future preferences, or the effect of locating a plant in a certain region of the country. Next, participants are identified and a questionnaire is developed. The questionnaire is sent to participants and returned to the manager. In today's computer-networked environments, this often means that the questionnaires are e-mailed to participants. The manager then summarizes the responses and sends feedback to the participants. At this stage, participants are asked to (1) review the feedback, (2) prioritize the issues being considered, and (3) return the survey within a specified time period. This cycle repeats until the manager obtains the necessary information.

The Delphi technique is useful when face-to-face discussions are impractical, when disagreements and conflict are likely to impair communication, when certain individuals might severely dominate group discussion, and when groupthink is a probable outcome of the group process.[56]

Computer-Aided Decision Making The purpose of computer-aided decision making is to reduce consensus roadblocks while collecting more information in a shorter period of time. There are two types of computer-aided decision-making systems: chauffeur driven and group driven.[57] Chauffeur-driven systems ask participants to answer predetermined questions on electronic keypads or dials. Live television audiences on shows such as *Who Wants to Be a Millionaire* are frequently polled with this system. The computer system tabulates participants' responses in a matter of seconds.

Group-driven electronic meetings are conducted in one of two major ways. First, managers can use e-mail systems, which are discussed in Chapter 12, or the Internet to collect information or brainstorm about a decision that must be made. For example, Miami Children's Hospital uses a combination of the Internet and a conferencing software technology to make decisions about the design of its training programs. Here is what Loubna Noureddin, director of staff and community education, had to say about the organization's computer-aided decision making:

> "What I truly like about it is my connection to other hospitals," Noureddin says. "I'm able to understand what other hospitals are doing about specific things. I put my question out, and people can respond, and I can answer back." She explains, for instance, that using the system, she and her colleagues have received guidance from other corporate educators, and even subject matter experts, on how to best train workers in such fields as critical care. "You get many other hospitals logging into the system, and telling us what they do," she says.[58]

Noureddin claims that the system has saved the company time and money.

The second method of computer-aided, group-driven meetings are conducted in special facilities equipped with individual workstations that are networked to each other. Instead of talking, participants type their input, ideas, comments, reactions, or evaluations on their keyboards. The input simultaneously appears on a large projector screen at the front of the room, thereby enabling all participants to see all input. This computer-driven process reduces consensus roadblocks because input is anonymous, everyone gets a chance to contribute, and no one can dominate the process. Research demonstrated that computer-aided decision making produced greater quality and quantity of ideas than either traditional brainstorming or the nominal group technique for both small and large groups of people.[59]

Interestingly, however, another recent study suggests caution when determining what forms of computer-aided decision making to use. This meta-analysis of 52 studies compared the effectiveness of face-to-face decision-making groups with "chat" groups. Results revealed that the use of chat groups led to decreased group effectiveness and member satisfaction and increased time to complete tasks compared to face-to-face groups.[60] These findings underscore the need to use a contingency approach for selecting the best method of computer-aided decision making in a given situation.

key terms

analytics 249	decision-making style 254	optimizing 251
availability heuristic 252	Delphi technique 267	participative management 264
bounded rationality 251	escalation of commitment 256	problem 249
brainstorming 265	explicit knowledge 253	rational model 249
consensus 265	judgmental heuristics 251	representativeness heuristic 252
creativity 259	knowledge management (KM) 253	satisficing 252
decision making 249	nominal group technique (NGT) 266	tacit knowledge 253

chapter summary

- *Compare and contrast the rational model of decision making and Simon's normative model.* The rational decision-making model consists of identifying the problem, generating alternative solutions, evaluating and selecting a solution, and implementing and evaluating the solution. Research indicates that decision makers do not follow the series of steps outlined in the rational model.

  Simon's normative model is guided by a decision maker's bounded rationality. Bounded rationality means that decision makers are bounded or restricted by a variety of constraints when making decisions. The normative model suggests that decision making is characterized by (a) limited information processing, (b) the use of judgmental heuristics, and (c) satisficing.

- *Discuss knowledge management and techniques used by companies to increase knowledge sharing.* Knowledge management involves the implementation of systems and practices that increase the sharing of knowledge and information throughout an organization. There are two types of knowledge that impact the quality of decisions: tacit knowledge and explicit knowledge. Organizations use computer systems to share explicit knowledge. Tacit knowledge is shared by observing, participating, or working with experts or coaches. Mentoring, informal networking, meetings, and design of office space also influence knowledge sharing.

- *Explain the model of decision-making styles and the stages of the creative process.* The model of decision-making styles is based on the idea that styles vary along two different dimensions: value orientation and tolerance for ambiguity. When these two dimensions are combined, they form four styles of decision making: directive, analytical, conceptual, and behavioral. People with a directive style have a low tolerance for ambiguity and are oriented toward task and technical concerns. Analytics have a higher tolerance for ambiguity and are characterized by a tendency to overanalyze a situation. People with a conceptual style have a high threshold for ambiguity and tend to focus on people or social aspects of a work situation. The behavioral style is the most people oriented of the four styles.

Creativity is defined as the process of using intelligence, imagination, and skill to develop a new or novel product, object, process, or thought. There are five stages of the creative process: preparation, concentration, incubation, illumination, and verification.

- *Summarize the pros and cons of involving groups in the decision-making process.* There are both pros and cons to involving groups in the decision-making process (see Table 10–1). Although research shows that groups typically outperform the average individual, managers need to use a contingency approach when determining whether to include others in the decision-making process.

- *Explain how participative management affects performance.* Participative management reflects the extent to which employees participate in setting goals, making decisions, solving problems, and making changes in the organization. Participative management is expected to increase motivation because it helps employees fulfill three basic needs: (a) autonomy, (b) meaningfulness of work, and (c) interpersonal contact. Participative management does not work in all situations. The design of work and the level of trust between management and employees influence the effectiveness of participative management.

- *Contrast brainstorming, the nominal group technique, the Delphi technique, and computer-aided decision making.* Group problem-solving techniques facilitate better decision making within groups. Brainstorming is used to help groups generate multiple ideas and alternatives for solving problems. The nominal group technique assists groups both to generate ideas and to evaluate and select solutions. The Delphi technique is a group process that anonymously generates ideas or judgments from physically dispersed experts. The purpose of computer-aided decision making is to reduce consensus roadblocks while collecting more information in a shorter period of time.

discussion questions

1. Do analytics support more of a rational or normative model of decision making? Explain.
2. Do you think knowledge management will become more important in the future? Explain your rationale.
3. Why would decision-making styles be a source of interpersonal conflict?
4. Describe a situation in which you exhibited escalation of commitment. Why did you escalate a losing situation?
5. Given the intuitive appeal of participative management, why do you think it fails as often as it succeeds? Explain.

ethical dilemma

Should the Principal of Westwood High Allow an Exception to the Graduation Dress Code?[61]

This dilemma involves a situation faced by Helen Riddle, the principal of Mesa, Arizona's, Westwood High. "Westwood High has 225 Native American students, including 112 from the Salt River Pima-Maricopa Indian Community, most of which lies within the boundaries of the Mesa Unified School District." Districtwide, there are 452 Native American high school students, 149 of whom are from the Salt River Reservation. Here is the situation.

Native American students asked the principal for permission to wear eagle feathers during their graduation ceremony. While this may seem like a reasonable request given these students' customs and traditions, Westwood High had a rule stating that "students were only allowed to wear a traditional cap and gown for graduation with no other adornments or clothing, including military uniforms. The rules were based on past practice and tradition at schools, not School Board policy."

Advocates for the Native American students argued that students should be allowed to wear the eagle feathers because they represent a significant achievement in the lives of those individuals. In contrast, one school board member opposed the exception to the rule because "it would open the door for other students wanting to display symbols of their own culture or background."

What Would You Do If You Were the Principal of Westwood High?

1. Allow the Native American students to wear the eagle feathers now and in the future. This shows an appreciation for diversity.

2. Not allow the Native American students to wear the eagle feathers because it violates an existing rule. Allowing an exception opens the door for additional requests about changing the dress code. It would be difficult to defend one exception over another.

3. Allow the students to wear the eagle feathers only in this year's ceremony. Then form a committee to review the dress code requirements.

4. Invent other options. Discuss.

For an interpretation of this situation, visit our Web site, at www.mhhe.com/kinickiob3e

If you're looking for additional study materials, be sure to check out the Online Learning Center at

www.mhhe.com/kinickiob3e

for more information and interactivities that correspond to this chapter.

chapter
Eleven

Managing Conflict and Negotiating

LEARNING OBJECTIVES

After reading the material in this chapter, you should be able to:

- Define the term *conflict,* distinguish between functional and dysfunctional conflict, and identify three desired outcomes of conflict.

- Define *personality conflicts,* and explain how they should be managed.

- Discuss the role of in-group thinking in intergroup conflict, and explain what can be done to avoid cross-cultural conflict.

- Explain how managers can program functional conflict, and identify the five conflict-handling styles.

- Identify and describe at least four alternative dispute resolution (ADR) techniques.

- Draw a distinction between distributive and integrative negotiation, and explain the concept of added-value negotiation.

MICROSOFT GETS CAUGHT UP IN THE CULTURE WARS

Like many long-term Microsoft Corp. employees, Jeff Koertzen toyed with the idea of leaving the company. But the event that prompted the human resources manager to bolt for good was not a get-rich opportunity at a promising tech startup. Rather, it was the software giant's withdrawal of support for gay rights legislation in the state of Washington in mid-April

Jeff Koertzen resigned his job at Microsoft when the company withdrew support for gay rights legislation in its home state of Washington.

after criticism from a local evangelical preacher. "This stupid move affected my decision," says Koertzen, a gay, six-year Microsoft employee who submitted his resignation on May 4 [2005]. "I decided that now was time to go."

Plenty of co-workers shared his outrage. Idealistic techies who believed that Microsoft was more than just an ordinary profit-driven company, that it stood for a set of progressive values, were crestfallen. "One of the reasons I came to Microsoft is because of its very strong stance on human rights," complained Robert Scoble, on his popular employee blog, Scobleizer, a few days after the company's position became public. By May 10 an internal petition urging the company to support the anti-discrimination bill had 1,741 signatures—compared with 197 for a petition asking it to remain neutral.

All the pressure forced Chairman William H. Gates III and CEO Steven A. Ballmer to do something quite rare: backtrack. On May 6 the company announced that it would support the legislation when it comes up in the next session (it failed by one vote). The decision followed a dramatic period of soul-searching at Microsoft. Employees up and down the corporate hierarchy explored profound—and rarely examined—questions about the role of companies in contemporary America. "When should a public company take a position on a broader social issue, and when should it not?" Ballmer asked in a company-wide e-mail sent out on Apr. 22.

That's a question a lot more CEOs will likely be asking themselves. As the culture wars escalate, activists across the political spectrum are increasingly targeting Corporate America. Gay rights groups pressured Home Depot Inc. to add domestic partner benefits in September [2004]. But most of the outcry has been coming from the other camp. For instance, the American Family Assn. (AFA) in Tupelo, Miss., launched a letter-writing campaign against Kraft Foods Inc. on May 9 for supporting the Gay Olympics and is planning a boycott . . . against a yet-to-be identified larger company for courting gay customers. "Eventually corporations are going to learn—some the hard way—that these kinds of issues are divisive [and] that they'd be better served by just getting back to running the business," says AFA Chairman Donald E. Wildmon, the religious leader who has taken the most aggressive stance against companies that offend conservative values. . . .

CEOs are being caught by surprise in the cultural cross fire. Certainly, Microsoft did not anticipate a brouhaha when it withdrew its support from the Washington legislation, which would have prohibited discrimination on the basis of sexual orientation. "They told me they thought it wouldn't be a big deal," says state representative Ed Murray, who authored the bill.

That turned out to be a major miscalculation. After a local alternative newspaper revealed the company's decision, employees inundated Ballmer with hundreds of e-mails. Members of GLEAM, the gay, lesbian, bisexual, and transgender employees group at Microsoft, sent its own letter to Ballmer on Apr. 29, saying the decision "shook our trust in executive management, and has left us feeling abandoned, depressed, and embarrassed for Microsoft."

Ballmer, who was in Brussels [Belgium] trying to negotiate a settlement of the company's antitrust dispute with new European Union competition commissioner Neelie Kroes at the height of the controversy, had to devote hours to managing the crisis. He declined to speak to *BusinessWeek*. But company sources say he responded the way he always does when faced with thorny problems: by "wallowing," as he likes to put it, in the issue. The CEO dove into his e-mail box and spoke to several employees. "The amount of response to his first e-mail caused him to give it personal attention," says Greg Hullender, an engineer in the company's MSN Search group who has worked at Microsoft for 12 years and represented gay employees on Microsoft's Diversity Advisory Council.

The company's ultimate support for the anti-discrimination legislation won widespread praise from employees and gay rights groups. But it could come at a cost. Conservatives inside and outside of Microsoft have not given up the fight. Eric Boyd, a 28-year-old software tester at Microsoft who believes homosexuality is a sin, vows "the Christians here won't be quiet" next year when the bill resurfaces. And Reverend Ken Hutcherson, the local preacher who originally pressured Microsoft to drop its support for the legislation, plans to tap the broad network of likeminded religious conservatives to lean on the company. "We'll see what kind of pressure [Microsoft] can bear," he says.[1]

FOR DISCUSSION

To what extent should corporate managers get involved in general societal value conflicts? Explain. For an interpretation of this case and additional comments, visit our Online Learning Center at

www.mhhe.com/kinickiob3e

MAKE NO MISTAKE about it. Conflict is an unavoidable aspect of modern life. These major trends conspire to make *organizational* conflict inevitable:

- Constant change.
- Greater employee diversity.
- More teams (virtual and self-managed).
- Less face-to-face communication (more electronic interaction).
- A global economy with increased cross-cultural dealings.

Dean Tjosvold, from Canada's Simon Fraser University, notes that "Change begets conflict, conflict begets change"[2] and challenges us to do better with this sobering global perspective:

> Learning to manage conflict is a critical investment in improving how we, our families, and our organizations adapt and take advantage of change. Managing conflicts well does not insulate us from change, nor does it mean that we will always come out on top or get all that we want. However, effective conflict management helps us keep in touch with new developments and create solutions appropriate for new threats and opportunities.
>
> Much evidence shows we have often failed to manage our conflicts and respond to change effectively. High divorce rates, disheartening examples of sexual and physical abuse of children, the expensive failures of international joint ventures, and bloody ethnic violence have convinced many people that we do not have the abilities to cope with our complex interpersonal, organizational, and global conflicts.[3]

But respond we must. As outlined in this chapter, tools and solutions are available, if only we develop the ability and will to use them persistently. The choice is ours: Be active managers of conflict and effective negotiators, or be managed by conflict.[4]

A Modern View of Conflict

A comprehensive review of the conflict literature yielded this consensus definition: "**conflict** is a process in which one party perceives that its interests are being opposed or negatively affected by another party."[5] The word *perceives* reminds us that sources of conflict and issues can be real or imagined. The resulting conflict is the same. Conflict can escalate (strengthen) or deescalate (weaken) over time. "The conflict process unfolds in a context, and whenever conflict, escalated or not, occurs the disputants or third parties can attempt to manage it in some manner."[6] Consequently, current and future managers need to understand the dynamics of conflict and know how to handle it effectively (both as disputants and as third parties).

conflict

One party perceives its interests are being opposed or set back by another party.

A Conflict Continuum

Ideas about managing conflict underwent an interesting evolution during the 20th century. Initially, scientific management experts such as Frederick W Taylor believed all conflict ultimately threatened management's authority and thus had to be avoided or quickly resolved.[7] Later, human relationists recognized the inevitability of conflict and advised managers to learn to live with it. Emphasis remained on resolving conflict whenever possible, however. Beginning in the 1970s, OB specialists realized conflict had both positive and negative outcomes, depending on its nature and intensity. This perspective introduced the revolutionary idea that organizations could suffer from *too little* conflict.

Work groups, departments, or organizations experiencing too little conflict tend to be plagued by apathy, lack of creativity, indecision, and missed deadlines. Excessive conflict, on the other hand, can erode organizational performance because of political infighting, dissatisfaction, lack of teamwork, and turnover. Workplace aggression and violence can be manifestations of excessive conflict.[8] Appropriate types and levels of conflict energize people in constructive directions.[9]

Functional versus Dysfunctional Conflict

functional conflict

Serves organization's interests.

dysfunctional conflict

Threatens organization's interests.

The distinction between **functional conflict** and **dysfunctional conflict** pivots on whether the organization's interests are served. According to one conflict expert,

> Some [types of conflict] support the goals of the organization and improve performance; these are functional, constructive forms of conflict. They benefit or support the main purposes of the organization. Additionally, there are those types of conflict that hinder organizational performance; these are dysfunctional or destructive forms. They are undesirable and the manager should seek their eradication.[10]

Functional conflict is commonly referred to in management circles as constructive or cooperative conflict.[11]

Often, a simmering conflict can be defused in a functional manner or driven to dysfunctional proportions, depending on how it is handled. For example, consider these two very different outcomes at Southwest Airlines and Gateway, the computer maker with the familiar black-and-white cow shipping boxes:

Test Your Knowledge

Styles of Handling Conflict

> Recently tensions broke out between flight attendants and their schedulers (the ones with the sorry job of telling flight attendants they have to work on a day off). The flight attendants believed the schedulers were overworking them; the schedulers claimed the attendants were hostile and uncooperative. The solution was very, well, Southwest: Both sides had to switch jobs for a day and see how difficult the other side had it. For now, at least, the tactic has eased tensions.[12]

Meanwhile, trouble was brewing at Gateway, where sales were off sharply. Company founder Ted Waitt had retired one year earlier when his hand-picked successor, Jeff Weitzen, took over after being hired from AT&T. *Fortune* magazine followed the action:

> It all came to a head at Gateway's Jan. 17 [2001] board meeting. In a hostile and combative proceeding, insiders say, Waitt and the board interrogated Weitzen relentlessly. At one point, after Weitzen had finished talking about his plans to improve customer service, one board member snapped, "Why should we believe you?"
>
> After the meeting Weitzen was furious. Stewing all weekend, he confronted Waitt the following Monday. High-level insiders say they argued for hours behind locked doors over how and by whom Gateway should be run. Waitt told Weitzen that he wanted him to stay on as CEO while Waitt took a more active role as chairman. For Weitzen, this arrangement—effectively a demotion—was unacceptable. Weitzen delivered an ultimatum: Back off or he was quitting.
>
> Taking a day to think about it, Waitt decided he wasn't backing off.[13]

A few days later, Weitzen and most of his top-management team were gone and Waitt's brief retirement was over. No surprise, then, that Southwest Airlines is thriving today while Gateway continues to struggle.

Antecedents of Conflict

Certain situations produce more conflict than others. By knowing the antecedents of conflict, managers are better able to anticipate conflict and take steps to resolve it if it becomes dysfunctional. Among the situations that tend to produce either functional or dysfunctional conflict are

Layoff survivors typically complain about being overworked, thus paving the way for stress and conflict.

- Incompatible personalities or value systems.
- Overlapping or unclear job boundaries.
- Competition for limited resources.
- Interdepartment/intergroup competition.
- Inadequate communication.
- Interdependent tasks (e.g., one person cannot complete his or her assignment until others have completed their work).
- Organizational complexity (conflict tends to increase as the number of hierarchical layers and specialized tasks increase).
- Unreasonable or unclear policies, standards, or rules.
- Unreasonable deadlines or extreme time pressure.
- Collective decision making (the greater the number of people participating in a decision, the greater the potential for conflict).
- Decision making by consensus (dissenters may feel coerced).
- Unmet expectations (employees who have unrealistic expectations about job assignments, pay, or promotions are more prone to conflict).
- Unresolved or suppressed conflicts.[14]

Proactive managers carefully read these early warnings and take appropriate action. For example, group conflict sometimes can be reduced by making decisions on the basis of majority approval rather than striving for a consensus.

Why People Avoid Conflict

Are you uncomfortable in conflict situations? Do you go out of your way to avoid conflict? If so, you're not alone. Many of us avoid conflict for a variety of both good and bad reasons. Tim Ursiny, in his entertaining and instructive book, *The Coward's Guide to Conflict,* contends that we avoid conflict because we fear various combinations of the following things: "harm"; "rejection"; "loss of relationship"; "anger"; "being seen as selfish"; "saying the wrong thing"; "failing"; "hurting someone else"; "getting what you want"; and "intimacy."[15] This list is self-explanatory, except for the fear of "getting what you want." By this, Ursiny is referring to those who, for personal reasons, feel undeserving and/or fear the consequences of success (so they tend to sabotage themselves). For our present purposes, it is sufficient to become consciously aware of our fears and practice overcoming them. Reading, understanding, and acting upon the material in this chapter are steps in a positive direction.

Desired Outcomes of Conflict

Within organizations, conflict management is more than simply a quest for agreement. If progress is to be made and dysfunctional conflict minimized, a broader agenda is in order. Tjosvold's cooperative conflict model calls for three desired outcomes:

1. *Agreement.* But at what cost? Equitable and fair agreements are best. An agreement that leaves one party feeling exploited or defeated will tend to breed resentment and subsequent conflict.

2. *Stronger relationships.* Good agreements enable conflicting parties to build bridges of goodwill and trust for future use. Moreover, conflicting parties who trust each other are more likely to keep their end of the bargain.

3. *Learning.* Functional conflict can promote greater self-awareness and creative problem solving. Like the practice of management itself, successful conflict handling is learned primarily by doing. Knowledge of the concepts and techniques in this chapter is a necessary first step, but there is no substitute for hands-on practice. In a contentious world, there are plenty of opportunities to practice conflict management.[16]

Major Forms of Conflict

Certain antecedents of conflict deserve a closer look. This section explores the nature and organizational implications of three common forms of conflict: personality conflict, intergroup conflict, and cross-cultural conflict. Our discussion of each type of conflict includes some practical tips.

Pictured here is Joseph Tucci of EMC, a leading data storage company. His personality has been described as low key and unruffled, while prone to make decisions and take action quickly. Direct and easy to talk to, "He is not the imperial CEO," says his company's chief financial officer. These qualities help people trust and believe in him, and he has succeeded in leading more than one company out of a steep decline.

Personality Conflicts

As discussed in Chapter 5, your *personality* is the package of stable traits and characteristics creating your unique identity. According to experts on the subject:

> Each of us has a unique way of interacting with others. Whether we are seen as charming, irritating, fascinating, nondescript, approachable, or intimidating depends in part on our personality, or what others might describe as our style.[17]

Given the many possible combinations of personality traits, it is clear why personality conflicts are inevitable. We define a **personality conflict** as interpersonal opposition based on personal dislike and/or disagreement. This is an important topic, as evidenced by a recent survey of 173 managers in the US. When the managers were asked what makes them most uncomfortable, an overwhelming 73% said, "Building relationships with people I dislike." "Asking for a raise" (25%) and "speaking to large audiences" (24%) were the distant second and third responses.[18]

personality conflict

Interpersonal opposition driven by personal dislike or disagreement.

Workplace Incivility: The Seeds of Personality Conflict

Somewhat akin to physical pain, chronic personality conflicts often begin with seemingly insignificant irritations. For instance, consider this situation:

> The first thing Adam Weissman does when he arrives at his public relations job isn't to grab a cup of coffee or gab with his co-workers. Instead, the account executive with DBA Public Relations goes to his small office and turns on his iPod to listen to music through his speakers. . . .
>
> For Weissman, some days he listens to mellow music such as America's *Horse with No Name.* Other days it's ZZ Top. He says the portable music player that stores his 3,600 songs keeps him focused when he's not on the phone.
>
> Not all his co-workers are singing the same tune. When he recently asked them what they thought of his office pastime, his colleagues admitted that sometimes it's annoying when Weissman drums on his desk or sings along.[19]

Sadly, grim little scenarios such as this are all too common today, given the steady erosion of civility in the workplace.[20] Researchers say increased informality, pressure for results, and employee diversity have fostered an "anything goes" atmosphere in today's workplaces. They view incivility as a self-perpetuating vicious cycle that can end in violence[21] (see Hands-On Exercise). A new survey of 612 employees indicates the nature and extent of workplace incivility in the US:

- 35% heard *sexually offensive remarks* (up 4% from 2004 to 2005).
- 24% heard *ridicule about sexual orientation* (unchanged from 2002 to 2005).
- 29% heard *ethnic slurs* (unchanged from 2002 to 2005).
- 29% heard *racial slurs* (unchanged from 2002 to 2005).
- 22% heard *age-related ridicule* in 2005.[22]

Clearly, the need for diversity training and penalties for misconduct remains high.

Vicious cycles of incivility need to be avoided (or broken early) with an organizational culture that places a high value on respect for co-workers. This requires managers and leaders to act as caring and courteous role models. A positive spirit of cooperation, as opposed to one based on negativism and aggression, also helps. Some organizations have resorted to workplace etiquette training.[23] More specifically, constructive feedback and skillful positive reinforcement can keep a single irritating behavior from precipitating a full-blown personality conflict (or worse).

Dealing with Personality Conflicts   Personality conflicts are a potential minefield for managers. Let us frame the situation. Personality traits, by definition, are stable and resistant to change. Moreover, according to the American Psychiatric Association's *Diagnostic and Statistical Manual of Mental Disorders,* there are 410 psychological disorders that can and do show up in the workplace.[24] This brings up legal issues. Employees in the United States suffering from psychological disorders such as depression and mood-altering diseases such as alcoholism are protected from discrimination by the Americans with Disabilities Act.[25] (Other nations have similar laws.) Also, sexual harassment and other forms of discrimination can grow out of apparent personality conflicts.[26] Finally, personality conflicts can spawn workplace aggression and violence.[27]

Traditionally, managers dealt with personality conflicts by either ignoring them or transferring one party.[28] In view of the legal implications, just discussed, both of these options may be open invitations to discrimination lawsuits. Skills & Best Practices presents practical tips for both nonmanagers and managers who are involved in or affected by personality conflicts. Our later discussions of handling dysfunctional conflict and alternative dispute resolution techniques also apply.

Intergroup Conflict

Conflict among work groups, teams, and departments is a common threat to organizational competitiveness. For example, when Michael Volkema became CEO of Herman Miller in the mid-1990s, he found an inward-focused company with divisions fighting over budgets. He has since curbed intergroup conflict at the Michigan-based furniture maker by emphasizing collaboration and redirecting everyone's attention outward, to the customer.[29] Managers who understand the mechanics of intergroup conflict are better equipped to face this sort of challenge.

In-Group Thinking: The Seeds of Intergroup Conflict   As we discussed in Chapter 9, *cohesiveness*—a "we feeling" binding group members together—can be a good or bad thing. A certain amount of cohesiveness can turn a group of individuals into a smooth-running team. Too much cohesiveness, however, can breed groupthink because a desire to get along pushes aside critical thinking. The study of in-groups by small group researchers has revealed a whole package of changes associated with increased group cohesiveness. Specifically,

- Members of in-groups view themselves as a collection of unique individuals, while they stereotype members of other groups as being "all alike."

- In-group members see themselves positively and as morally correct, while they view members of other groups negatively and as immoral.

- In-groups view outsiders as a threat.

- In-group members exaggerate the differences between their group and other groups. This typically involves a distorted perception of reality.[30]

Avid sports fans who simply can't imagine how someone would support the opposing team exemplify one form of in-group thinking. Also, this pattern of behavior is a form of ethnocentrism, discussed as a cross-cultural barrier in Chapter 3. Reflect for a moment on evidence of in-group behavior in your life. Does your circle of friends make fun of others because of their race, gender, age, nationality, weight, sexual preference, or major in college?[31]

In-group thinking is one more fact of organizational life that virtually guarantees conflict. Managers cannot eliminate in-group thinking, but they certainly should not ignore it when handling intergroup conflicts.

How to Deal with Personality Conflicts

Tips for Employees Having a Personality Conflict	Tips for Third-Party Observers of a Personality Conflict	Tips for Managers Whose Employees Are Having a Personality Conflict
All employees need to be familiar with and *follow* company policies for diversity, antidiscrimination, and sexual harassment.		
• Communicate directly with the other person to resolve the perceived conflict (emphasize problem solving and common objectives, not personalities). • Avoid dragging co-workers into the conflict. • If dysfunctional conflict persists, seek help from direct supervisors or human resource specialists.	• Do not take sides in someone else's personality conflict. • Suggest the parties work things out themselves in a constructive and positive way. • If dysfunctional conflict persists, refer the problem to the parties' direct supervisors.	• Investigate and document conflict. • If appropriate, take corrective action (e.g., feedback or behavior modification). • If necessary, attempt informal dispute resolution. • Refer difficult conflicts to human resource specialists or hired counselors for formal resolution attempts and other interventions.

Research Lessons for Handling Intergroup Conflict   Sociologists have long recommended the contact hypothesis for reducing intergroup conflict. According to the *contact hypothesis,* the more the members of different groups interact, the less intergroup conflict they will experience. Those interested in improving race, international, and union-management relations typically encourage cross-group interaction. The hope is that *any* type of interaction, short of actual conflict, will reduce stereotyping and combat in-group thinking. But research has shown this approach to be naive and limited. For example, one study of 83 health center employees (83% female) at a Midwest US university probed the specific nature of intergroup relations and concluded:

> The number of *negative* relationships was significantly related to higher perceptions of intergroup conflict. Thus, it seems that negative relationships have a salience that overwhelms any possible positive effects from friendship links across groups.[32]

FIGURE 11–1 | Minimizing Intergroup Conflict: An Updated Contact Model

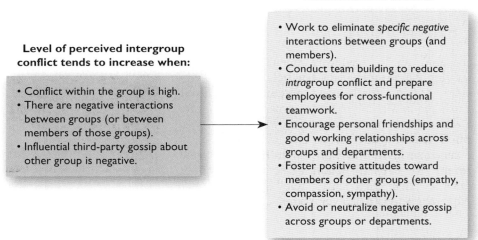

Recommended actions:

Level of perceived intergroup conflict tends to increase when:

- Conflict within the group is high.
- There are negative interactions between groups (or between members of those groups).
- Influential third-party gossip about other group is negative.

- Work to eliminate *specific negative* interactions between groups (and members).
- Conduct team building to reduce *intra*group conflict and prepare employees for cross-functional teamwork.
- Encourage personal friendships and good working relationships across groups and departments.
- Foster positive attitudes toward members of other groups (empathy, compassion, sympathy).
- Avoid or neutralize negative gossip across groups or departments.

SOURCE: Based on research evidence in G Labianca, D J Brass, and B Gray, "Social Networks and Perceptions of Intergroup Conflict: The Role of Negative Relationships and Third Parties," *Academy of Management Journal*, February 1998, pp 55–67; C D Batson et al., "Empathy and Attitudes: Can Feeling for a Member of a Stigmatized Group Improve Feelings toward the Group?" *Journal of Personality and Social Psychology*, January 1997, pp 105–18; and S C Wright et al., "The Extended Contact Effect: Knowledge of Cross-Group Friendships and Prejudice," *Journal of Personality and Social Psychology*, July 1997, pp 73–90.

Intergroup friendships are still desirable, as documented in many studies,[33] but they are readily overpowered by negative intergroup interactions. Thus, *priority number 1 for managers faced with intergroup conflict is to identify and root out specific negative linkages between (or among) groups.* A single personality conflict, for instance, may contaminate the entire intergroup experience. The same goes for an employee who voices negative opinions or spreads negative rumors about another group. Our updated contact model in Figure 11–1 is based on this and other recent research insights, such as the need to foster positive attitudes toward other groups.[34] Also, notice how conflict within the group and negative gossip from third parties are threats that need to be neutralized if intergroup conflict is to be minimized.

Cross-Cultural Conflict

Doing business with people from different cultures is commonplace in our global economy where cross-border mergers, joint ventures, outsourcing, and alliances are the order of the day.[35] Because of differing assumptions about how to think and act, the potential for cross-cultural conflict is both immediate and huge. Success or failure, when conducting business across cultures, often hinges on avoiding and minimizing actual or perceived conflict. For example, consider this cultural mismatch:

> Mexicans place great importance on saving face, so they tend to expect any conflicts that occur during negotiations to be downplayed or kept private. The prevailing attitude in the [United States], however, is that conflict should be dealt with directly and publicly to prevent hard feelings from developing on a personal level.[36]

This is not a matter of who is right and who is wrong; rather it is a matter of accommodating cultural differences for a successful business transaction. Awareness of the cross-cultural differences we discussed in Chapter 3 is an important first step. Beyond that, cross-cultural conflict can be moderated by using international consultants and building cross-cultural relationships.

Using International Consultants In response to broad demand, there is a growing army of management consultants specializing in cross-cultural relations. Competency and fees vary widely, of course. But a carefully selected cross-cultural consultant can be helpful, as this illustration shows:

> Last year, when electronics-maker Canon planned to set up a subsidiary in Dubai through its Netherlands division, it asked consultant Sahid Mirza of Glocom, based in Dubai, to find out how the two cultures would work together.
>
> Mirza sent out the test questionnaires and got a sizable response. "The findings were somewhat surprising," he recalls. "We found that, at the bedrock level, there were relatively few differences. Many of the Arab businessmen came from former British colonies and viewed business in much the same way as the Dutch."
>
> But at the level of behavior, there was a real conflict. "The Dutch are blunt and honest in expression, and such expression is very offensive to Arab sensibilities." Mirza offers the example of a Dutch executive who says something like, "We can't meet the deadline." Such a negative expression—true or not—would be gravely offensive to an Arab. As a result of Mirza's research, Canon did start the subsidiary in Dubai, but it trained both the Dutch and the Arab executives first.[37]

Consultants also can help untangle possible personality, value, and intergroup conflicts from conflicts rooted in differing national cultures. Note: Although we have discussed basic types of conflict separately, they typically are encountered in complex, messy bundles.

How to Build Cross-Cultural Relationships

Behavior	Rank
Be a good listener	1
Be sensitive to needs of others	2 ⎱ Tie
Be cooperative, rather than overly competitive	2 ⎰
Advocate inclusive (participative) leadership	3
Compromise rather than dominate	4
Build rapport through conversations	5
Be compassionate and understanding	6
Avoid conflict by emphasizing harmony	7
Nurture others (develop and mentor)	8

SOURCE: Adapted from R L Tung, "American Expatriates Abroad: From Neophytes to Cosmopolitans," *Journal of World Business*, Summer 1998, Table 6, p 136.

Building Relationships across Cultures Rosalie L Tung's study of 409 expatriates from US and Canadian multinational firms is very instructive.[38] Her survey sought to pinpoint success factors for the expatriates (14% female) who were working in 51 different countries worldwide. Nine specific ways to facilitate interaction with host-country nationals, as ranked from most useful to least useful by the respondents, are listed in Skills & Best Practices. Good listening skills topped the list, followed by sensitivity to others and cooperativeness rather than competitiveness. Interestingly, US managers often are culturally characterized as just the opposite: poor listeners, blunt to the point of insensitivity, and excessively competitive. Some managers need to add self-management to the list of ways to minimize cross-cultural conflict.

Managing Conflict

As we have seen, conflict has many faces and is a constant challenge for managers who are responsible for reaching organizational goals.[39] Our attention now turns to the active management of both functional and dysfunctional conflict. We discuss how to stimulate functional conflict, how to handle dysfunctional conflict, and how third parties can deal effectively with conflict.

Programming Functional Conflict

Sometimes committees and decision-making groups become so bogged down in details and procedures that nothing substantive is accomplished. Carefully monitored functional conflict can help get the creative juices flowing once again. Managers basically have two options. They can fan the fires of naturally occurring conflict—although this approach can be unreliable and slow. Alternatively, managers can resort to programmed conflict. Experts in the field define **programmed conflict** as "conflict that raises different opinions *regardless of the personal feelings of the managers.*"[40] The trick is to get contributors to either defend or criticize ideas based on relevant facts rather than on the basis of personal preference or political interests. This requires disciplined role playing and effective leadership. Two programmed conflict techniques with proven track records are devil's advocacy and the dialectic method. Let us explore these two ways of stimulating functional conflict.

programmed conflict

Encourages different opinions without protecting management's personal feelings.

Devil's Advocacy This technique gets its name from a traditional practice within the Roman Catholic Church. When someone's name came before the College of Cardinals for elevation to sainthood, it was absolutely essential to ensure that he or she had a spotless record. Consequently, one individual was assigned the role of

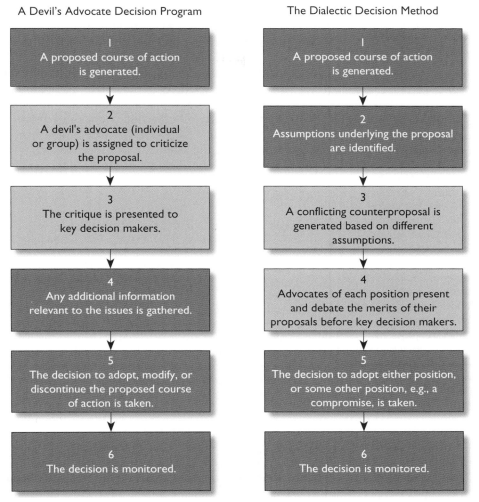

A Devil's Advocate Decision Program

I A proposed course of action is generated.
2 A devil's advocate (individual or group) is assigned to criticize the proposal.
3 The critique is presented to key decision makers.
4 Any additional information relevant to the issues is gathered.
5 The decision to adopt, modify, or discontinue the proposed course of action is taken.
6 The decision is monitored.

The Dialectic Decision Method

I A proposed course of action is generated.
2 Assumptions underlying the proposal are identified.
3 A conflicting counterproposal is generated based on different assumptions.
4 Advocates of each position present and debate the merits of their proposals before key decision makers.
5 The decision to adopt either position, or some other position, e.g., a compromise, is taken.
6 The decision is monitored.

FIGURE 11–2
Techniques for Stimulating Functional Conflict: Devil's Advocacy and the Dialectic Method

SOURCE: R A Cosier and C R Schwenk, "Agreement and Thinking Alike: Ingredients for Poor Decisions," *Academy of Management Executive: The Thinking Manager's Source,* February 1990, pp 72–73. Copyright 1990 by Academy of Management. Reproduced with permission of Academy of Management via Copyright Clearance Center.

devil's advocate to uncover and air all possible objections to the person's canonization. In accordance with this practice, **devil's advocacy** in today's organizations involves assigning someone the role of critic.[41] Recall from Chapter 9, Irving Janis recommended the devil's advocate role for preventing groupthink.

devil's advocacy
Assigning someone the role of critic.

In the left half of Figure 11–2, note how devil's advocacy alters the usual decision-making process in steps 2 and 3. This approach to programmed conflict is intended to generate critical thinking and reality testing.[42] It is a good idea to rotate the job of devil's advocate so no one person or group develops a strictly negative reputation. Moreover, periodic devil's advocacy role-playing is good training for developing analytical and communication skills and emotional intelligence (see Skills & Best Practices).

The Dialectic Method Like devil's advocacy, the dialectic method is a time-honored practice. This particular approach to programmed conflict traces back

How Toro Mows Down Bad Ideas

Toro, the $1.8 billion lawn-mower giant, knows how to curb the urge to merge. Anytime an M&A [merger and acquisition] pitch reaches the desk of CEO Mike Hoffman, he asks a due-diligence group to make the case to the company's board. But he also turns to the "contra team"—half a dozen vice presidents and directors—to deliver the voice of dissent. According to chairman Ken Melrose, . . . a few years ago the contras killed an eight-figure acquisition of a manufacturer that had pitched itself as a turnaround success. The contras' number crunching showed that its sector was facing a slump. The prospect's revenues have since tanked, while Toro has nearly doubled its sales. "Naysaying in corporate America isn't popular," Melrose says. "The contra team is a way to create negative views that are in the shareholders' best interest and the company's best interest."

SOURCE: Excerpted from P Kaihla, "Toro: The Contra Team," *Business 2.0*, April 2006, p 83.

to the dialectic school of philosophy in ancient Greece. Plato and his followers attempted to synthesize truths by exploring opposite positions (called *thesis* and *antithesis*). Court systems in the United States and elsewhere rely on directly opposing points of view for determining guilt or innocence. Accordingly, today's **dialectic method** calls for managers to foster a structured debate of opposing viewpoints prior to making a decision.[43] Steps 3 and 4 in the right half of Figure 11–2 set the dialectic approach apart from the normal decision-making process. Here is how Anheuser-Busch's corporate policy committee uses the dialectic method:

> When the policy committee . . . considers a major move—getting into or out of a business, or making a big capital expenditure—it sometimes assigns teams to make the case for each side of the question. There may be two teams or even three. Each is knowledgeable about the subject; each has access to the same information. Occasionally someone in favor of the project is chosen to lead the dissent, and an opponent to argue for it. Pat Stokes, who heads the company's beer empire, describes the result: "We end up with decisions and alternatives we hadn't thought of previously," sometimes representing a synthesis of the opposing views. "You become a lot more anticipatory, better able to see what might happen, because you have thought through the process."[44]

A major drawback of the dialectic method is that "winning the debate" may overshadow the issue at hand. Also, the dialectic method requires more skill training than does devil's advocacy. Regarding the comparative effectiveness of these two approaches to stimulating functional conflict, however, a laboratory study ended in a tie. Compared with groups that strived to reach a consensus, decision-making groups using either devil's advocacy or the dialectic method yielded equally higher quality decisions.[45] But, in a more recent laboratory study, groups using devil's advocacy produced more potential solutions and made better recommendations for a case problem than did groups using the dialectic method.[46]

dialectic method

Fostering a debate of opposing viewpoints to better understand an issue.

In light of this mixed evidence, managers have some latitude in using either devil's advocacy or the dialectic method for pumping creative life back into stalled deliberations. Personal preference and the role players' experience may well be the deciding factors in choosing one approach over the other. The important thing is to actively stimulate functional conflict when necessary, such as when the risk of blind conformity or groupthink is high. Joseph M Tucci, CEO of EMC, a leading data storage equipment company, fosters functional conflict by creating a supportive climate for dissent:

> Good leaders always leave room for debate and different opinions. . . .
> The team has to be in harmony. But before you move out, there needs to be a debate. Leadership is not a right. You have to earn it.

Five Conflict-Handling Styles | **FIGURE 11–3**

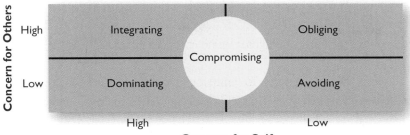

SOURCE: Reprinted by permission of Sage Publications Ltd from M A Rahim, "A Strategy for Managing Conflict in Complex Organizations," *Human Relations,* January 1985, p 84. Copyright © 1985 The Tavistock Institute.

> . . . [E]very company needs a healthy paranoia. It's the CEO's job to keep it on the edge, to put tension in the system. You have to do the right thing for the right circumstances.[47]

This meshes well with the results of a pair of laboratory studies that found a positive relationship between the degree of minority dissent and team innovation, *but only when participative decision making was used.*[48]

Alternative Styles for Handling Dysfunctional Conflict

People tend to handle negative conflict in patterned ways referred to as *styles.* Several conflict styles have been categorized over the years. According to conflict specialist Afzalur Rahim's model, five different conflict-handling styles can be plotted on a 2 × 2 grid. High to low concern for *self* is found on the horizontal axis of the grid while low to high concern for *others* forms the vertical axis (see Figure 11–3). Various combinations of these variables produce the five different conflict-handling styles: integrating, obliging, dominating, avoiding, and compromising.[49] There is no single best style; each has strengths and limitations and is subject to situational constraints.

Integrating (Problem Solving) In this style, interested parties confront the issue and cooperatively identify the problem, generate and weigh alternative solutions, and select a solution. Integrating is appropriate for complex issues plagued by misunderstanding. However, it is inappropriate for resolving conflicts rooted in opposing value systems. Its primary strength is its longer lasting impact because it deals with the underlying problem rather than merely with symptoms. The primary weakness of this style is that it is very time-consuming.

Nina Olson is the **IRS's** National Taxpayer Advocate, a job that sometimes places her in conflict with her bosses when she has to tell them about mistakes and violations within the agency. It's particularly difficult when she must inform her immediate supervisor that he's wrong. "It is really just a nutty position," she says. "You get to say to the boss, 'This is good, but . . .'" Ms. Olson and her boss meet once a month to discuss and resolve issues.

Obliging (Smoothing)   "An obliging person neglects his or her own concern to satisfy the concern of the other party."[50] This style, often called smoothing, involves playing down differences while emphasizing commonalities. Obliging may be an appropriate conflict-handling strategy when it is possible to eventually get something in return. But it is inappropriate for complex or worsening problems. Its primary strength is that it encourages cooperation. Its main weakness is that it's a temporary fix that fails to confront the underlying problem.

Dominating (Forcing)   High concern for self and low concern for others encourages "I win, you lose" tactics. The other party's needs are largely ignored. This style is often called forcing because it relies on formal authority to force compliance. Dominating is appropriate when an unpopular solution must be implemented, the issue is minor, or a deadline is near. It is inappropriate in an open and participative climate. Speed is its primary strength. The primary weakness of this domineering style is that it often breeds resentment.[51]

Avoiding   This tactic may involve either passive withdrawal from the problem or active suppression of the issue. Avoidance is appropriate for trivial issues or when the costs of confrontation outweigh the benefits of resolving the conflict. It is inappropriate for difficult and worsening problems. The main strength of this style is that it buys time in unfolding or ambiguous situations. The primary weakness is that the tactic provides a temporary fix that sidesteps the underlying problem.

Compromising   This is a give-and-take approach involving moderate concern for both self and others. Compromise is appropriate when parties have opposite goals or possess equal power. But compromise is inappropriate when overuse would lead to inconclusive action (e.g., failure to meet production deadlines). The primary strength of this tactic is that everyone gets something, but it's a temporary fix that can stifle creative problem solving.[52]

Group Exercise

Assessing the Effectiveness of Conflict-Handling Styles

Third-Party Interventions: Alternative Dispute Resolution

Disputes between employees, between employees and their employer, and between companies too often end up in lengthy and costly court battles. A more constructive, less expensive approach called alternative dispute resolution has enjoyed enthusiastic growth in recent years.[53] In fact, the widely imitated "People's Court"–type television shows operating outside the formal judicial system are part of this trend toward what one writer calls "do-it-yourself justice."[54] **Alternative dispute resolution (ADR),** according to a pair of Canadian labor lawyers, "uses faster, more user-friendly methods of dispute resolution, instead of traditional, adversarial approaches (such as unilateral decision making or litigation)."[55] The following ADR techniques represent a progression of steps third parties can take to resolve organizational conflicts.[56] They are ranked from easiest and least expensive to most difficult and costly. A growing number of organizations have formal ADR policies involving an established sequence of various combinations of these techniques:

alternative dispute resolution (ADR)

Avoiding costly lawsuits by resolving conflicts informally or through mediation or arbitration.

- *Facilitation.* A third party, usually a manager, informally urges disputing parties to deal directly with each other in a positive and constructive manner.

- *Conciliation.* A neutral third party informally acts as a communication conduit between disputing parties. This is appropriate when conflicting parties refuse to meet face to face. The immediate goal is to establish direct communication, with the broader aim of finding common ground and a constructive solution.

- *Peer review.* A panel of trustworthy co-workers, selected for their ability to remain objective, hears both sides of a dispute in an informal and confidential meeting. Any decision by the review panel may or may not be binding, depending on the company's ADR policy. Membership on the peer review panel often is rotated among employees.[57]

- *Ombudsman.* Someone who works for the organization, and is widely respected and trusted by his or her co-workers, hears grievances on a confidential basis and attempts to arrange a solution. This approach, more common in Europe than North America, permits someone to get help from above without relying on the formal hierarchy chain.

- *Mediation.* "The mediator—a trained, third-party neutral—actively guides the disputing parties in exploring innovative solutions to the conflict. Although some companies have in-house mediators who have received ADR training, most also use external mediators who have no ties to the company."[58] Unlike an arbitrator, a mediator does *not* render a decision. It is up to the disputants to reach a mutually acceptable decision.

- *Arbitration.* Disputing parties agree ahead of time to accept the decision of a neutral arbitrator in a formal courtlike setting, often complete with evidence and witnesses. Statements are confidential. Decisions are based on legal merits. Trained arbitrators, typically from outside agencies such as the American Arbitration Association, are versed in relevant laws and case precedents. Historically, employee participation in arbitration was voluntary. A 2001 US Supreme Court decision changed things. As part of the employment contract with nonunion workers, employers in the United States now have the legal right to insist upon *mandatory* arbitration in lieu of a court battle. A vigorous debate now rages over the fairness and quality of mandatory arbitration.[59]

Negotiating

Formally defined, **negotiation** is a give-and-take decision-making process involving interdependent parties with different preferences.[60] Common examples include labor-management negotiations over wages, hours, and working conditions and negotiations between supply chain specialists and vendors involving price, delivery schedules, and credit terms. Self-managed work teams with overlapping task boundaries also need to rely on negotiated agreements. Negotiating skills are more important than ever today.[61]

negotiation

Give-and-take process between conflicting interdependent parties.

Two Basic Types of Negotiation

Negotiation experts distinguish between two types of negotiation—*distributive* and *integrative.* Understanding the difference requires a change in traditional "fixed-pie" thinking:

> A *distributive* negotiation usually involves a single issue—a "fixed-pie"—in which one person gains at the expense of the other. For example, haggling over

Seven Steps to Negotiating Your Salary

1. **Know the going rate.** You probably won't get very far by telling your boss that competitors pay better than he does (unless one has made you an offer). But knowing your potential value can help steel you to ask for what you're really worth. . . .

2. **Don't fudge your past compensation.** Potential employers occasionally ask for a W-2, so be honest about what you're earning now.

3. **Present cold, hard proof of your value.** Remember, you're selling your boss on a hot productivity tool: you. So provide concrete, quantifiable examples of how you made previous bosses look good and saved them effort. . . .

4. **Let the other party name a figure first.** You don't want to show your hand. If pressed, suggest a salary range instead of a number. Career coach Lenore Mewton suggests upping what you think is a fair range by as much as 10 percent. "Notch it up a little without being unrealistic," she says. You can always come down later if you need to.

5. **Don't nickel-and-dime.** Set a fairly high target, but once the company has agreed on a number within a range that you deem acceptable, don't nitpick—you might seem not to be a person of your word. . . .

6. **Avoid extravagant extras.** This economic environment is no time to ask for expensive perks. "I'd be embarrassed to ask for first-class travel or a fancy office," says Andy Ellenthal, a senior vice president at PointRoll. . . . "It leaves the impression that you want to sit around on your butt all day."

7. **Seek incentives and practical perks.** In lieu of luxuries—or if you're stonewalled on a salary demand—request benefits that cost your employer little and suggest that they be contingent on how well you do your job.

SOURCE: B Brophy, "Bargaining for Bigger Bucks: A Step-by-Step Guide to Negotiating Your Salary," *Business 2.0,* May 2004, p 107. Copyright © 2004 Time Inc. All rights reserved.

the price of a rug in a bazaar is a distributive negotiation. In most conflicts, however, more than one issue is at stake, and each party values the issues differently. The outcomes available are no longer a fixed-pie divided among all parties. An agreement can be found that is better for both parties than what they would have reached through distributive negotiation. This is an *integrative* negotiation.

However, parties in a negotiation often don't find these beneficial trade-offs because each *assumes* its interests *directly* conflict with those of the other party. "What is good for the other side must be bad for us" is a common and unfortunate perspective that most people have. This is the mind-set we call the *mythical* "fixed-pie."[62]

Distributive negotiation involves traditional win–lose thinking. Integrative negotiation calls for a progressive win–win strategy.[63]

Added-Value Negotiation

One practical application of the integrative approach is **added-value negotiation (AVN).** During AVN, the negotiating parties cooperatively develop multiple deal packages while building a productive long-term relationship. AVN consists of these five steps:

1. *Clarify interests.* After each party identifies its tangible and intangible needs, the two parties meet to discuss their respective needs and find *common ground* for negotiation.

2. *Identify options.* A *marketplace of value* is created when the negotiating parties discuss desired elements of value (such as property, money, behavior, rights, and risk reduction).

3. *Design alternative deal packages.* While aiming for *multiple deals,* each party mixes and matches elements of value from both parties in workable combinations.

4. *Select a deal.* Each party analyzes deal packages proposed by the other party. Jointly, the parties discuss and select from feasible deal packages, with a spirit of *creative agreement.*

5. *Perfect the deal.* Together the parties discuss unresolved issues, develop a written agreement, and *build relationships* for future negotiations.[64]

Applying What You Have Learned: How to Negotiate Your Pay and Benefits

Fact: Women and other minorities too often come up short when it comes to negotiating fair compensation, in addition to being *under*-represented in top-management positions. *Harvard Business Review* recently offered this interpretation:

> Research has shown that both conscious and subconscious biases contribute to this problem. But we've discovered another, subtler source of inequality: Women often don't get what they want and deserve because they don't ask for it. In three separate studies, we found that men are more likely than women to negotiate for what they want. . . .
>
> Women are less likely than men to negotiate for themselves for several reasons. First, they often are socialized from an early age not to promote their own interests and to focus instead on the needs of others. . . . Women tend to assume that they will be recognized and rewarded for working hard and doing a good job. Unlike men, they haven't been taught that they can ask for more.
>
> Second, many companies' cultures penalize women when they do ask—further discouraging them from doing so.[65]

Consequently, women (and any other employees) who feel they are being shortchanged in pay and/or promotions need to polish their integrative negotiation skills (see Skills & Best Practices). Employers, meanwhile, need to cultivate a diversity ethic, grant rewards equitably, and foster a culture of dignity and fair play.

"Never, EVER purr during the negotiating process, Derwood!"

Copyright Scott Arthur Masear. Reprinted with permission.

added-value negotiation (AVN)

Cooperatively developing multiple-deal packages while building a long-term relationship.

key terms

added-value negotiation (AVN)   291
alternative dispute resolution
   (ADR)   288
conflict   275

devil's advocacy   285
dialectic method   286
dysfunctional conflict   276
functional conflict   276

negotiation   289
personality conflict   279
programmed conflict   284

chapter summary

- *Define the term conflict, distinguish between functional and dysfunctional conflict, and identify three desired outcomes of conflict.* Conflict is a process in which one party perceives that its interests are being opposed or negatively affected by another party. It is inevitable and not necessarily destructive. Too little conflict, as evidenced by apathy or lack of creativity, can be as great a problem as too much conflict. Functional conflict enhances organizational interests while dysfunctional conflict is counterproductive. Three desired conflict outcomes are agreement, stronger relationships, and learning.

- *Define personality conflicts, and explain how they should be managed.* Personality conflicts involve interpersonal opposition based on personal dislike and/or disagreement (or as an outgrowth of workplace incivility). Care needs to be taken with personality conflicts in the workplace because of the legal implications of diversity, discrimination, and sexual harassment. Managers should investigate and document personality conflicts, take corrective actions such as feedback or behavior modification if appropriate, or attempt informal dispute resolution. Difficult or persistent personality conflicts need to be referred to human resource specialists or counselors.

- *Discuss the role of in-group thinking in intergroup conflict, and explain what can be done to avoid cross-cultural conflict.* Members of in-groups tend to see themselves as unique individuals who are more moral than outsiders, whom they view as a threat and stereotypically as all alike. In-group thinking is associated with ethnocentric behavior. International consultants can prepare people from different cultures to work effectively together. Cross-cultural conflict can be minimized by having expatriates build strong cross-cultural relationships with their hosts (primarily by being good listeners, being sensitive to others, and being more cooperative than competitive).

- *Explain how managers can program functional conflict, and identify the five conflict-handling styles.* Functional conflict can be stimulated by permitting antecedents of conflict to persist or programming conflict during decision making with devil's advocates or the dialectic method. The five conflict-handling styles are integrating (problem solving), obliging (smoothing), dominating (forcing), avoiding, and compromising. There is no single best style.

- *Identify and describe at least four alternative dispute resolution (ADR) techniques.* Alternative dispute resolution (ADR) involves avoiding costly court battles with more informal and user-friendly techniques such as facilitation, conciliation, peer review, ombudsman, mediation, and arbitration.

- *Draw a distinction between distributive and integrative negotiation, and explain the concept of added-value negotiation.* Distributive negotiation involves fixed-pie and win–lose thinking. Integrative negotiation is a win–win approach to better results for both parties. The five steps in added-value negotiation are as follows: Step 1, clarify interests; Step 2, identify options; Step 3, design alternative deal packages; Step 4, select a deal; and Step 5, perfect the deal. Elements of value, multiple deals, and creative agreement are central to this approach.

discussion questions

1. Relative to the chapter-opening vignette, how could Microsoft's Ballmer have better handled the controversy? Explain.
2. What examples of functional and dysfunctional conflict have you observed in organizations lately? What were the outcomes? What caused the dysfunctional conflict?
3. Which of the five conflict-handling styles is your strongest? Your weakest? How can you improve your ability to handle conflict?
4. Which of the six ADR techniques appeals the most to you? Why?
5. How could added-value negotiation make your life a bit easier? Explain in terms of a specific problem, conflict, or deadlock.

ethical dilemma

A Matter of Style at German Software Giant SAP

While [co-founder and chairman Hasso] Plattner believes in obtaining consensus among his lieutenants, he doesn't care how much he irritates people along the way. In fact, his confrontational style is deliberate. "He creates stressful situations. He fuels the discussions with provocative statements. Sometimes he's rigid, even rude. But it's about getting people engaged so they can be creative," says Wolfgang Kemna, [former] CEO of SAP America, a 13-year SAP veteran. Co-CEO Henning Kagermann, whom Plattner elevated to work alongside him in 1998, is his counterweight in the organization—calm and efficient.[66]

Is Plattner's Heavy-handed Management Style an Ethical Issue?

I. No, not if he effectively stimulates creativity and functional conflict. Explain.

2. Yes, his abrasive personality will intimidate some co-workers and possibly even promote blind obedience or groupthink. Explain.

3. Yes, his intimidating management style could create a hostile work environment where sexual harassment might thrive. Explain.

4. Maybe. It depends upon the circumstances and individuals involved. Explain.

5. Not in this situation, because his tough ways are counterbalanced by his CEO's calm style. Explain.

6. Invent other options. Discuss.

For an interpretation of this situation, visit our Web site, www.mhhe.com/kinickiob3e.

part four

Managing Organizational Processes

Twelve Communicating in the Internet Age

Thirteen Influence, Power, and Politics (An Organizational Survival Kit)

Fourteen Leadership

chapter
twelve

Communicating in the Internet Age

LEARNING OBJECTIVES

After reading the material in this chapter, you should be able to:

- Describe the perceptual process model of communication.

- Describe the process, personal, physical, and semantic barriers to effective communication.

- Contrast the communication styles of assertiveness, aggressiveness, and nonassertiveness.

- Discuss the primary sources of nonverbal communication.

- Review the five dominant listening styles and 10 keys to effective listening.

- Explain the information technology of Internet/intranet/extranet, e-mail, handheld devices, blogs, videoconferencing, and group support systems, and explain the related use of teleworking.

BOEING COMPANY JOINS THE BLOGOSPHERE

Defense contractors and aerospace companies aren't known for their openness. After all, this is an industry built on security clearances and classified government projects. But today Boeing Co. is embracing a kind of management *glasnost* that would have been unthinkable a few years ago.

The evidence? Boeing's use of blogs. The Chicago aerospace giant—no

stranger to recent and well-publicized ethical and political scandals—is among a small but growing group of large nontech companies such as Walt Disney, General Motors, and McDonald's that are embracing the power of blogging. That means Boeing has learned to cede some control and expose itself to stinging criticism in exchange for a potentially

more constructive dialogue with the public, customers, and employees. "Companies are nervous about creating external blogs because they fear the negative comments," says Charlene Li, an analyst at Forrester Research Inc. "But negative comments do exist. A company is better off knowing about them."

Boeing's early results suggest that the rewards outweigh the risks. The company's two public blogs give Boeing a direct link to the public, something the 91-year-old company has never had before. And executives are starting to use internal blogs to get conversations going and allow employees to raise issues anonymously. "I've always been a big believer in open and honest dialogue

that gets the issues on the table," says James F. Albaugh, the chief executive of Boeing Integrated Defense Systems (IDS). He championed using blogs at the defense unit's meeting of 1,000 executives in February. "I was a little concerned and I had no idea how it would turn out, but I'm sold on it."

Heavy Flak

Boeing's entry into the blogosphere got off to a rocky start. Eighteen months ago, Randy Baseler, vice-president for marketing at Boeing Commercial Air-planes, started a Web log to talk about the company's view of the commercial airplane world. Almost immediately, he was blasted by the blogerati for not allowing comments, considered to be a key component of blogging. And he was dinged for the perception that his posts gave more of a marketing spin than an inside perspective. In one e-mail, an outside reader wrote: "Take down your blog. You embarrass us, everyone who reads it, and you make the world a dumber place."

Instead of backing down, Baseler responded. As the blog evolved, he found his voice. He began to offer insights into the industry that would be hard to find elsewhere, such as a post about emerging airplane markets in Latin America, called "Latin Rhythm." His explanation of the differences between Boeing's and Airbus' strategy, particularly an ongoing controversy about how they handle seat width, has been light on emotion and heavy on facts. The site drew 30,000 visitors in April, a new high for a blog that started with low expectations. . . .

Boeing's latest experiments have focused inward. In February, Boeing's senior IDS leaders set up blog kiosks at the annual strategy meeting in Los Angeles for the company's top 1,000 defense executives. During a series of briefings, managers went over new company policies and the division's top strategic and business priorities for the year. While Albaugh and his team discussed hot topics such as ethical compliance rules and a new management compensation plan, executives responded at the kiosks located outside the conference room. "As each exec talked, they would talk about comments from the blog," says DL Byron, a blogging consultant to Boeing.

In the end, the blog helped air questions about the unit's strategy and made sure everyone understood the human resources and diversity policies. It also let Albaugh understand what his top people knew or didn't know. For instance, he asked how many executives were actively using the division's Vision Support Plan software that helps managers track how their units are doing. About 30% said they weren't. Thanks to the blog, Albaugh can now try to create converts.[1]

FOR DISCUSSION

To what extent are blogs helping Boeing to provide good customer service? Explain. For an interpretation of this case and additional comments, visit our Online Learning Center at

www.mhhe.com/kinickiob3e

MANAGEMENT IS COMMUNICATION. Every managerial function and activity involves some form of direct or indirect communication. Whether planning and organizing or directing and leading, managers find themselves communicating with and through others. Managerial decisions and organizational policies are ineffective unless they are understood by those responsible for enacting them. Consider, for example, how the communication process within Adecco SA, the world's largest temporary help company, negatively affected the company's stock price:

> Eight days ago, the Swiss-based concern announced it wouldn't be able to release its year-end results on schedule in February and warned of "material weaknesses with internal controls" at its North American staffing business. But Adecco officials refused to elaborate on the terse statement, citing legal constraints. At the time, they wouldn't even confirm the identity of an independent counsel that Adecco's board has appointed to conduct its own investigation.
>
> The company's bunker mentalilty stirred anxiety among investors, who quickly dumped Adecco shares. Within a few hours, the company lost 35% of its market capitalization.[2]

Ineffective communication clearly contributed to the drop in Adecco's share price. Effective communication also is critical for employee motivation and job satisfaction. For example, a recent polling of 336 organizations revealed that 66% of the respondents did not know or understand their organization's mission and business strategy, which subsequently led them to feel disengaged at work. The apparent lack of communication in these organizations is a problem because employee disengagement is associated with lower productivity and product quality, and higher labor costs and turnover.[3]

Moreover, the chapter-opening vignette highlights how organizational communication has been dramatically affected by the introduction and explosive use of computers and information technology. Who would have guessed that companies would use blogs to communicate with customers and to obtain input during internal strategic planning meetings? Managers like James Albaugh and Randy Baseler need more than good interpersonal skills to effectively communicate in today's workplace. They also need to understand the pros and cons of different types of communication media and information technology. More is said about the pros and cons of blogging later in this chapter.

This chapter will help you to better understand how managers can both improve their communication skills and design more effective communication programs. We discuss (1) basic dimensions of the communication processes, focusing on a perceptual process model and barriers to effective communication; (2) interpersonal communication; and (3) communicating in the computerized information age.

Basic Dimensions of the Communication Process

Communication is defined as "the exchange of information between a sender and a receiver, and the inference (perception) of meaning between the individuals involved."[4] Analysis of this exchange reveals that communication is a two-way process consisting of consecutively linked elements (see Figure 12–1). Managers who understand this process can analyze their own communication patterns as well as design communication programs that fit organizational needs. This section

communication

Interpersonal exchange of information and understanding.

FIGURE 12–1
A Perceptual
Model of
Communication

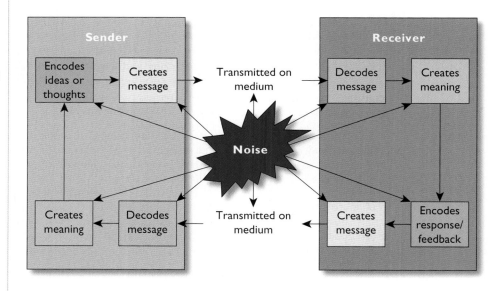

reviews a perceptual process model of communication and discusses the barriers to effective communication.

A Perceptual Process Model of Communication

As we all know, communicating is not that simple or clear-cut. Communication is fraught with miscommunication. In recognition of this, researchers have begun to examine communication as a form of social information processing (recall the discussion in Chapter 4) in which receivers interpret messages by cognitively processing information. This view led to development of a perceptual model of communication that depicts communication as a process in which receivers create meaning in their own minds. Let us briefly examine the elements of the perceptual process model shown in Figure 12–1.

Sender   The sender is an individual, group, or organization that desires or attempts to communicate with a particular receiver. Receivers may be individuals, groups, or organizations.

Encoding   Communication begins when a sender encodes an idea or thought. Encoding translates mental thoughts into a code or language that can be understood by others. Managers typically encode using words, numbers, gestures, nonverbal cues such as facial expressions, or pictures. Moreover, different methods of encoding can be used to portray similar ideas.

The Message   The output of encoding is a message. There are two important points to keep in mind about messages. First, they contain more than meets the eye. Messages may contain hidden agendas as well as trigger affective or emotional reactions. Second, messages need to match the medium used to transmit them. How would you evaluate the match between the message of letting someone know they

have been laid off and the communication medium used in the following example?

> Six months ago [January 2002], Tower Snow was chairman of Brobeck, Phleger & Harrison, one of the nation's premier law firms. Late Friday, as he got off a United Airlines flight in San Francisco, a gate agent handed him an envelope. Inside: notice that Brobeck had fired him.[5]

How would you feel if this happened to you? Surely there is a better way to let someone know he or she is being fired. This example illustrates how thoughtless managers can be when they do not carefully consider the interplay between a message and the medium used to convey it.

Selecting a Medium   Managers can communicate through a variety of media. Potential media include face-to-face conversations, telephone calls, electronic mail or e-mail, voice mail, videoconferencing, written memos or letters, photographs or drawings, meetings, bulletin boards, computer output, and charts or graphs. Choosing the appropriate media depends on many factors, including the nature of the message, its intended purpose, the type of audience, proximity to the audience, time horizon for disseminating the message, personal preferences, and the complexity of the problem/situation at hand.

All media have advantages and disadvantages and should be used in different situations. Face-to-face conversations, for example, are useful for communicating about sensitive or important issues that require feedback and intensive interaction. In contrast, telephones are convenient, fast, and private, but lack nonverbal information. Although writing memos or letters is time-consuming, it is a good medium when it is difficult to meet with the other person, when formality and a written record are important, and when face-to-face interaction is not necessary to enhance understanding. Electronic communication, which is discussed later in this chapter, can be used to communicate with a large number of dispersed people and is potentially a very fast medium when recipients of messages regularly check their e-mail.[6] Thomas Swidarski used the benefits of e-mail on the first day of his appointment as president and CEO of Diebold.

> He sent an e-mail to Diebold's 14,500 employees inviting comments and outlining his priorities, including building customer loyalty by speeding the flow of products through the supply chain, and "providing quality products and outstanding service." He told them that leading Diebold "does not rest with one person—it rests with each and every one of us." He received more than 1,000 responses.[7]

Decoding   Decoding is the receiver's version of encoding. Decoding consists of translating verbal, oral, or visual aspects of a message into a form that can be interpreted. Receivers rely on social information processing to determine the meaning of a message during decoding. Decoding is a key contributor to misunderstanding in interracial and intercultural communication because decoding by the receiver is subject to social values and cultural values that may not be understood by the sender.

Creating Meaning   The perceptual model of communication is based on the belief that a receiver creates the meaning of a message in his or her head. A receiver's interpretation of a message can thus differ from that intended by the sender. In turn, receivers act according to their own interpretations, not the communicator's.

Feedback   The receiver's response to a message is the crux of the feedback loop. At this point in the communication process, the receiver becomes a sender. Specifically, the receiver encodes a response and then transmits it to the original sender. This new message is then decoded and interpreted. As a case in point, consider how H Lee Scott Jr., CEO of Wal-Mart, responded to an e-mail message he received from an employee asking why "the largest company on the planet cannot offer some type of medical retirement benefits?" According to a reporter from the *New York Times* who had copies of the correspondence, "Scott first says that the cost of such benefits would leave Wal-Mart at a competitive disadvantage, but then, clearly annoyed, he suggests that the store manager is disloyal and should consider quitting."[8] Scott's feedback to a legitimate question was defensive and sarcastic. How do you think the employee decoded and interpreted this message? Do you think he or she was sorry for asking the question in the first place? Further, what impact might this e-mail message have on other employees who read it? As you can see from this example, feedback is used as a comprehension check. It gives senders an idea of how accurately their message is understood.

noise

Interference with the transmission and understanding of a message.

Noise   Noise represents anything that interferes with the transmission and understanding of a message. It affects all linkages of the communication process. Sue Weidemann, director of research for a consulting company, investigated the impact of noise at a large law firm. Her results indicated that "the average number of times that people were interrupted by noise, visual distractions and chatty visitors prairie-dogging over a cube wall was 16 a day—or 21 a day including work-related distractions." She concluded that it takes 2.9 minutes to recover concentration after these disruptions, "meaning people spend more than an hour a day trying to refocus. And that doesn't even count the time drain of the distraction itself."[9] Noise includes factors such as a speech impairment, poor telephone connections, illegible handwriting, inaccurate statistics in a memo or report, poor hearing and eyesight, environmental noises, people talking or whistling, and physical distance between sender and receiver. Managers can improve communication by reducing noise.[10]

Barriers to Effective Communication

Communication noise is a barrier to effective communication because it interferes with the accurate transmission and reception of a message. Management awareness of these barriers is a good starting point to improve the communication process. There are four key barriers to effective communication: (1) process barriers, (2) personal barriers, (3) physical barriers, and (4) semantic barriers.

Process Barriers   Every element of the perceptual model of communication shown in Figure 12–1 is a potential process barrier. Consider the following examples:

Test Your Knowledge

Barriers to Effective Communication

1. *Sender barrier.* A customer gets incorrect information from a customer service agent because he or she was recently hired and lacks experience.

2. *Encoding barrier.* An employee for whom English is a second language has difficulty explaining why a delivery was late.

3. *Message barrier.* An employee misses a meeting for which he or she never received a confirmation memo.

4. *Medium barrier.* A salesperson gives up trying to make a sales call when the potential customer fails to return three previous phone calls.

5. *Decoding barrier.* An employee can not complete an exit-interview survey (i.e., a survey that is completed when an employee quits a job) because it is not written in his or her own language.[11]

6. *Receiver barrier.* A student who is talking to his or her friend during a lecture asks the professor the same question that was just answered.

7. *Feedback barrier.* The nonverbal head nodding of an interviewer leads an interviewee to think that he or she is doing a great job answering questions.

Barriers in any of these process elements can distort the transfer of meaning. Reducing these barriers is essential but difficult given the current diversity of the workforce.

Personal Barriers   There are many personal barriers to communication. We highlight eight of the more common ones. The first is our *ability to effectively communicate.* As highlighted throughout this chapter, people possess varying levels of communication skills. The *way people process and interpret information* is a second barrier. Chapter 4 highlighted the fact that people use different frames of reference and experiences to interpret the world around them. We also learned that people selectively attend to various stimuli. All told, these differences affect both what we say and what we think we hear. Third, the *level of interpersonal trust between people* can either be a barrier or enabler of effective communication. Communication is more likely to be distorted when people do not trust each other. *Stereotypes and prejudices* are a fourth barrier. They can powerfully distort what we perceive about others. Our *egos* are a fifth barrier. Egos can cause political battles, turf wars, and pursuit of power, credit, and resources. Egos influence how people treat each other as well as our receptiveness to being influenced by others. *Poor listening skills* are a sixth barrier.[12]

Howard Schultz, CEO of Starbucks, has some definite ideas about interpersonal communication, which both starts and fills his day. He likes to keep it personal. "In the early morning I focus on Europe. I'll call Greece or Spain or whatever, either at home or on the drive into work, to talk about challenges . . . or to congratulate them. These personal conversations are very important. . . . I'm not a big e-mailer, though; it's a crutch that hinders person-to-person communication."

Carl Rogers, a renowned psychologist, identified the seventh and eighth barriers that interfere with interpersonal communication.[13] The seventh barrier is a *natural tendency to evaluate or judge a sender's message.* To highlight the natural tendency to evaluate, consider how you might respond to the statement, "I like the book you are reading." What would you say? Your likely response is to approve or disapprove the statement. You may say, "I agree," or alternatively, "I disagree, the book is boring." The point is that we all tend to evaluate messages from our own point of view or frame of reference. The tendency to evaluate messages is greatest when one has strong feelings or emotions about the issue being discussed. An *inability to listen with understanding* is the eighth personal barrier to effective communication. Listening with understanding occurs when a receiver can "see the expressed idea and attitude from the other person's point of view, to sense how it feels to him, to achieve his frame of reference in regard to the thing he is talking about."[14] Listening with understanding reduces defensiveness and improves accuracy in perceiving a message.

Physical Barriers   The distance between employees can interfere with effective communication. It is hard to understand someone who is speaking to you from 20 yards away. Time zone differences between the East and West Coasts also represent physical barriers. Work and office noise are additional barriers. The quality of telephone lines or crashed computers represent physical barriers that impact our ability to communicate with information technology.

In spite of the general acceptance of physical barriers, they can be reduced. For example, employees on the East Coast can agree to call their West Coast peers prior to leaving for lunch. Distracting or inhibiting walls also can be torn down. It is important that managers attempt to manage this barrier by choosing a medium that optimally reduces the physical barrier at hand.

Semantic Barriers   *Semantics* is the study of words. Semantic barriers show up as encoding and decoding errors because these phases of communication involve transmitting and receiving words and symbols. These barriers are partially fueled by the use of jargon and acronyms.[15] Semantic barriers also are related to the choice of words we use when communicating. Consider the case of using profanity at work.

Ann Garcia had to thread the needle. On the one hand, the No. 1 executive at her former company hated the use of profanity, seeing it as a sign of not having learned

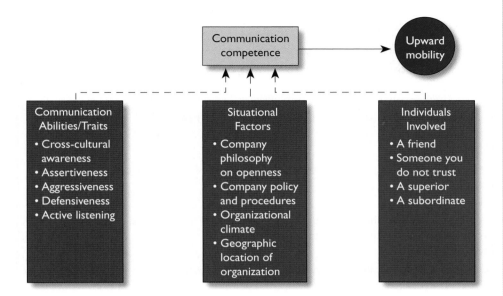

FIGURE 12–2
Communication
Competence
Affects
Upward
Mobility

to communicate effectively. On the other hand, the No. 2 executive appreciated a potty mouth now and then because it indicated passion. He "felt that if you weren't swearing, you probably didn't care enough," says Ms. Garcia.

As it happened, there weren't clashes over profanity so much as careful navigation of the office's language protocol. "When groups reported to the executive who was pro-profanity," it was acceptable, says Ms. Garcia. "With units who reported to the other one, things were very buttoned up."[16]

It also is important to note that the use of profanity is offensive to some people, and its use can create emotional responses that interfere with effective communication.

Choosing our words more carefully is the easiest way to reduce semantic barriers. This barrier can also be decreased by attentiveness to mixed messages and cultural diversity. Mixed messages occur when a person's words imply one message while his or her actions or nonverbal cues suggest something different. Obviously, understanding is enhanced when a person's actions and nonverbal cues match the verbal message.

Interpersonal Communication

The quality of interpersonal communication within an organization is very important. People with good communication skills helped groups to make more innovative decisions and were promoted more frequently than individuals with less developed abilities.[17] Although there is no universally accepted definition of **communication competence,** it is a performance-based index of an individual's abilities to effectively use communication behaviors in a given context.[18] Business etiquette, for example, is one component of communication competence. At this time we would like you to complete the business etiquette test in the Hands-On Exercise. How did you score?

communication competence

Ability to effectively use communication behaviors in a given context.

What Is Your Business Etiquette?

INSTRUCTIONS: Business etiquette is one component of communication competence. Test your business etiquette by answering the following questions. After circling your response for each item, calculate your score by reviewing the correct answers listed in note 19 in the Endnotes section of the book. Next, use the norms at the end of the test to interpret your results.

1. The following is an example of a proper introduction: "Ms Boss, I'd like you to meet our client, Mr Smith."
   True   False

2. If someone forgets to introduce you, you shouldn't introduce yourself, you should just let the conversation continue.
   True   False

3. If you forget someone's name, you should keep talking and hope no one will notice. This way you don't embarrass yourself or the person you are talking to.
   True   False

4. When shaking hands, a man should wait for a woman to extend her hand.
   True   False

5. Who goes through a revolving door first?
   a. Host   *b.* Visitor

6. It is all right to hold private conversations, either in person or on a cell phone in office bathrooms, elevators, and other public spaces.
   True   False

7. When two US businesspeople are talking to one another, the space between them should be approximately
   a. 1.5 feet   *b.* 3 feet   *c.* 7 feet

8. Business casual attire requires socks for men and hose for women.
   True   False

9. To signal that you do not want a glass of wine, you should turn your wine glass upside down.
   True   False

10. If a call is disconnected, it's the caller's responsibility to redial.
    True   False

11. When using a speakerphone, you should tell the caller if there is anyone else in the room.
    True   False

12. You should change your voicemail message if you are going to be out of the office.
    True   False

ARBITRARY NORMS

Low business etiquette (0–4 correct): Consider buying an etiquette book or hiring a coach to help you polish your professional image.

Moderate business etiquette (5–8 correct): Look for a role model or mentor, and look for ways you can improve your business etiquette.

High business etiquette (9–12 correct): Good for you. You should continue to practice good etiquette and look for ways to maintain your professional image.

SOURCE: This test was adapted from material contained in M Brody, "Test Your Etiquette," *Training & Development*, February 2002, pp 64–66. Copyright © February 2002 from *Training & Development* by M Brody. Reprinted with permission of American Society for Training & Development.

Communication competence is determined by three components: communication abilities and traits, situational factors, and the individuals involved in the interaction (see Figure 12–2 on page 305). Cross-cultural awareness, for instance, is an important communication ability/trait. Individuals involved in an interaction also affect communication competence. People are likely to withhold information and react emotionally or defensively when interacting with someone they dislike or do not trust. You can improve your communication competence through five communication styles/abilities/traits under your control: assertiveness, aggressiveness, nonassertiveness, nonverbal communication, and active listening. We conclude this section by discussing gender differences in communication.

Self-Assessment Exercise

What Is Your Communication Under Stress?

Assertiveness, Aggressiveness, and Nonassertiveness

The saying "You can attract more flies with honey than with vinegar" captures the difference between using an assertive communication style and an aggressive style. Research studies indicate that assertiveness is more effective than aggressiveness in both work-related and consumer contexts.[20] An **assertive style** is expressive and self-enhancing and is based on the "ethical notion that it is not right or good to violate our own or others' basic human rights, such as the right to self-expression or the right to be treated with dignity and respect."[21] In contrast, an **aggressive style** is expressive and self-enhancing and strives to take unfair advantage of others. A **nonassertive style** is characterized by timid and self-denying behavior. Nonassertiveness is ineffective because it gives the other person an unfair advantage.

assertive style

Expressive and self-enhancing, but does not take advantage of others.

aggressive style

Expressive and self-enhancing, but takes unfair advantage of others.

nonassertive style

Timid and self-denying behavior.

Managers may improve their communication competence by trying to be more assertive and less aggressive or nonassertive. This can be achieved by using the appropriate nonverbal and verbal behaviors listed in Table 12–1. For instance, managers should attempt to use the nonverbal behaviors of good eye contact, a strong, steady, and audible voice, and selective interruptions. They should avoid nonverbal behaviors such as glaring or little eye contact, threatening gestures, slumped posture, and a weak or whiny voice. Appropriate verbal behaviors include direct and unambiguous language and the use of "I" messages instead of "you" statements. For example, when you say, "Mike, I was disappointed with your report because it contained typographical errors," rather than "Mike, your report was poorly done," you reduce defensiveness. "I" statements describe your feelings about someone's performance or behavior instead of laying blame on the person.

Group Exercise

Nonverbal Communication: A Twist on Charades

Sources of Nonverbal Communication

Nonverbal communication is "Any message, sent or received independent of the written or spoken word . . . [It] includes such factors as use of time and space, distance between persons when conversing, use of color, dress, walking behavior, standing, positioning, seating arrangement, office locations and furnishings."[22]

Experts estimate that 65% to 90% of every conversation is partially interpreted through nonverbal communication.[23] It thus is important to ensure that your nonverbal signals are consistent with your intended verbal messages. Because of the prevalence of nonverbal communication

nonverbal communication

Messages sent outside of the written or spoken word.

TABLE 12-1 Communication Styles

Communication Style	Description	Nonverbal Behavior Pattern	Verbal Behavior Pattern
Assertive	Pushing hard without attacking; permits others to influence outcome; expressive and self-enhancing without intruding on others	Good eye contact Comfortable but firm posture Strong, steady, and audible voice Facial expressions matched to message Appropriately serious tone Selective interruptions to ensure understanding	Direct and unambiguous language No attributions or evaluations of others' behavior Use of "I" statements and cooperative "we" statements
Aggressive	Taking advantage of others; expressive and self-enhancing at others' expense	Glaring eye contact Moving or leaning too close Threatening gestures (pointed finger; clenched fist) Loud voice Frequent interruptions	Swear words and abusive language Attributions and evaluations of others' behavior Sexist or racist terms Explicit threats or put-downs
Nonassertive	Encouraging others to take advantage of us; inhibited; self-denying	Little eye contact Downward glances Slumped posture Constantly shifting weight Wringing hands Weak or whiny voice	Qualifiers ("maybe"; "kind of") Fillers ("uh," "you know," "well") Negaters ("It's not really that important"; "I'm not sure")

SOURCE: Adapted in part from J A Waters, "Managerial Assertiveness," *Business Horizons*, September/October 1982, pp 24–29.

and its significant effect on organizational behavior (including, but not limited to, perceptions of others, hiring decisions, work attitudes, turnover, and the acceptance of one's ideas in a presentation), it is important that managers become consciously aware of the sources of nonverbal communication.

Body Movements and Gestures   Body movements, such as leaning forward or backward, and gestures, such as pointing, provide additional nonverbal information that can either enhance or detract from the communication process. Open body positions, such as leaning backward, communicate *immediacy*, a term used to represent openness, warmth, closeness, and availability for communication. *Defensiveness* is communicated by gestures such as folding arms, crossing hands, and crossing one's legs. Although it is both easy and fun to interpret body movements and gestures, it is important to remember that body-language analysis is subjective, easily misinterpreted, and highly dependent on the context and cross-cultural differences.[24] Thus, managers need to be careful when trying to interpret body movements. Inaccurate interpretations can create additional "noise" in the communication process.

Touch   Touching is another powerful nonverbal cue. People tend to touch those they like. A meta-analysis of gender differences in touching indicated that women do more touching during conversations than men.[25] Touching conveys an impression of warmth and caring and can be used to create a personal bond between people. Be careful about touching people from diverse cultures, however, as norms for touching vary significantly around the world.[26]

Facial Expressions   Facial expressions convey a wealth of information. Smiling, for instance, typically represents warmth, happiness, or friendship, whereas frowning conveys dissatisfaction or anger. Do you think these interpretations apply to different cross-cultural groups? A summary of relevant research revealed that the association between facial expressions and emotions varies across cultures.[27] A smile, for example, does not convey the same emotion in different countries. Therefore, managers need to be careful in interpreting facial expressions among diverse groups of employees.

Eye Contact   Eye contact is a strong nonverbal cue that varies across cultures. Westerners are taught at an early age to look at their parents when spoken to. In contrast, Asians are taught to avoid eye contact with a parent or superior in order to show obedience and subservience.[28] Once again, managers should be sensitive to different orientations toward maintaining eye contact with diverse employees.

Practical Tips   It is important to have good nonverbal communication skills in light of the fact that they are related to the development of positive interpersonal relationships. The Skills & Best Practices offers insights into improving your nonverbal communication skills. Practice these tips by turning the sound off while watching television and then trying to interpret emotions and interactions. Honest feedback from your friends about your nonverbal communication style also may help.

Advice to Improve Nonverbal Communication Skills

Positive nonverbal actions include the following:

- Maintain eye contact.
- Nod your head to convey that you are listening or that you agree.
- Smile and show interest.
- Lean forward to show the speaker you are interested.
- Use a tone of voice that matches your message.

Negative nonverbal behaviors include the following:

- Avoiding eye contact and looking away from the speaker.
- Closing your eyes or tensing your facial muscles.
- Excessive yawning.
- Using body language that conveys indecisiveness or lack of confidence (e.g., slumped shoulders, head down, flat tones, inaudible voice).
- Speaking too fast or too slow.

Manager's Hot Seat Application

Listening Skills: Yeah, Whatever

Active Listening

Some communication experts contend that listening is the keystone communication skill for employees involved in sales, customer service, or management. In support of this conclusion, listening effectiveness was positively associated with customer satisfaction and negatively associated with employee intentions to quit. Poor communication between employees and management also was cited as a primary cause of employee discontent and turnover.[29] Listening skills are particularly important for all of us because we spend a great deal of time listening to others.

Listening involves much more than hearing a message. Hearing is merely the physical component of listening. **Listening** is the process of

listening

Actively decoding and interpreting verbal messages.

actively decoding and interpreting verbal messages. Listening requires cognitive attention and information processing; hearing does not. With these distinctions in mind, we examine listening styles and offer some practical advice for becoming a more effective listener.

Listening Styles   Communication experts believe that people listen with a preferred listening style. While people may lean toward one dominant listening style, we tend to use a combination of two or three. There are five dominant listening styles: appreciative, empathetic, comprehensive, discerning, and evaluative.[30] Let us consider each style.

An *appreciative* listener listens in a relaxed manner, preferring to listen for pleasure, entertainment, or inspiration. He or she tends to tune out speakers who provide no amusement or humor in their communications. *Empathetic* listeners interpret messages by focusing on the emotions and body language being displayed by the speaker as well as the presentation media. They also tend to listen without judging. A *comprehensive* listener makes sense of a message by first organizing specific thoughts and actions and then integrates this information by focusing on relationships among ideas. These listeners prefer logical presentations without interruptions. *Discerning* listeners attempt to understand the main message and determine important points. They like to take notes and prefer logical presentations. Finally, *evaluative* listeners listen analytically and continually formulate arguments and challenges to what is being said. They tend to accept or reject messages based on personal beliefs, ask a lot of questions, and can become interruptive.

You can improve your listening skills by first becoming aware of the effectiveness of the different listening styles you use in various situations. This awareness can then help you to modify your style to fit a specific situation. For example, if you are listening to a presidential debate, you may want to focus on using a comprehensive and discerning style. In contrast, an evaluative style may be more appropriate if you are listening to a sales presentation.[31]

Becoming a More Effective Listener   Effective listening is a learned skill that requires effort and motivation. That's right, it takes energy and desire to really listen to others. Unfortunately, it may seem like there are no rewards for listening, but there are negative consequences when we don't. Think of a time, for example, when someone did not pay attention to you by looking at his or her watch or doing some other activity such as typing on a keyboard. How did you feel? You may have felt put down, unimportant, or offended. In turn, such feelings can erode the quality of interpersonal relationships as well as fuel job dissatisfaction, lower productivity, and poor customer service. Listening is an important skill that can be improved by avoiding the 10 habits of bad listeners while cultivating the 10 good listening habits (see Table 12–2).

In addition, a communication expert suggests that we can all improve our listening skills by adhering to the following three fundamental recommendations:[32]

1. Attending closely to what's being said, not to what you want to say next.

2. Allowing others to finish speaking before taking our turn.

3. Repeating back what you've heard to give the speaker the opportunity to clarify the message.

Self-Assessment Exercise

Active Listening Skills Inventory

The Keys to Effective Listening   **TABLE 12–2**

Keys to Effective Listening	The Bad Listener	The Good Listener
1. Capitalize on thought speed	Tends to daydream	Stays with the speaker, mentally summarizes the speaker, weighs evidence, and listens between the lines
2. Listen for ideas	Listens for facts	Listens for central or overall ideas
3. Find an area of interest	Tunes out dry speakers or subjects	Listens for any useful information
4. Judge content, not delivery	Tunes out dry or monotone speakers	Assesses content by listening to entire message before making judgments
5. Hold your fire	Gets too emotional or worked up by something said by the speaker and enters into an argument	Withholds judgment until comprehension is complete
6. Work at listening	Does not expend energy on listening	Gives the speaker full attention
7. Resist distractions	Is easily distracted	Fights distractions and concentrates on the speaker
8. Hear what is said	Shuts out or denies unfavorable information	Listens to both favorable and unfavorable information
9. Challenge yourself	Resists listening to presentations of difficult subject matter	Treats complex presentations as exercise for the mind
10. Use handouts, overheads, or other visual aids	Does not take notes or pay attention to visual aids	Takes notes as required and uses visual aids to enhance understanding of the presentation

SOURCES: Derived from N Skinner, "Communication Skills," *Selling Power*, July/August 1999, pp 32–34; and G Manning, K Curtis, and S McMillen, *Building the Human Side of Work Community* (Cincinnati, OH: Thomson Executive Press, 1996), pp 127–54.

Women and Men Communicate Differently

Women and men have communicated differently since the dawn of time. Gender-based differences in communication are partly caused by linguistic styles commonly used by women and men. Deborah Tannen, a communication expert, defines **linguistic style** as follows:

> **linguistic style**
> **A person's typical speaking pattern.**

Linguistic style refers to a person's characteristic speaking pattern. It includes such features as directness or indirectness, pacing and pausing, word choice, and the use of such elements as jokes, figures of speech, stories, questions, and apologies. In other words, linguistic style is a set of culturally learned signals by which we not only communicate what we mean but also interpret others' meaning and evaluate one another as people.[33]

Linguistic style not only helps explain communication differences between women and men, but it also influences our perceptions of others' confidence, competence, and abilities. Increased awareness of linguistic styles can thus improve communication accuracy and your communication competence. This section strives to increase your understanding of interpersonal communication between women and men by

Research reveals that men and women possess different communication styles. For example, men are more boastful about their accomplishments whereas women are more modest. How might differences in male and female communication patterns affect how men and women are perceived during group problem-solving meetings?

discussing alternative explanations for differences in linguistic styles, various communication differences between women and men, and recommendations for improving communication between the sexes.

Why Linguistic Styles Vary between Women and Men

Although researchers do not completely agree on the cause of communication differences between women and men, there are two competing explanations that involve the well-worn debate between *nature* and *nurture*. Some researchers believe that interpersonal differences between women and men are due to inherited biological differences between the sexes. More specifically, this perspective, which also is called the "Darwinian perspective" or "evolutionary psychology," attributes gender differences in communication to drives, needs, and conflicts associated with reproductive strategies used by women and men. For example, proponents would say that males communicate more aggressively, interrupt others more than women, and hide their emotions because they have an inherent desire to possess features attractive to females in order to compete with other males for purposes of mate selection. Although males are certainly not competing for mate selection during a business meeting, evolutionary psychologists propose that men cannot turn off the biologically based determinants of their behavior.[34]

In contrast, social role theory is based on the idea that females and males learn ways of speaking as children growing up. Research shows that girls learn conversational skills and habits that focus on rapport and relationships, whereas boys learn skills and habits that focus on status and hierarchies. Accordingly, women come to view communication as a network of connections in which conversations are negotiations for closeness. This orientation leads women to seek and give confirmation and support more so than men. Men, on the other hand, see conversations as negotiations in which people try to achieve and maintain the upper hand. It thus is important for males to protect themselves from others' attempts to put them down or push them around. This perspective increases a male's need to maintain independence and avoid failure.[35]

Gender Differences in Communication

Research demonstrates that women and men communicate differently in a number of ways.[36] Women, for example, are more likely to share credit for success, to ask questions for clarification, to tactfully give feedback by mitigating criticism with praise, and to indirectly tell others what to do. In contrast, men are more likely to boast about themselves, to bluntly give feedback, and to withhold compliments, and are less likely to ask questions and to admit fault or weaknesses.

There are two important issues to keep in mind about these trends. First, the trends identified cannot be generalized to include all women and men. Some men are less likely to boast about their achievements while some women are less likely to share the credit. The point is that there are always exceptions to the rule. Second, your linguistic style influences perceptions about your confidence, competence, and authority. These judgments may, in turn, affect your future job assignments and subsequent promotability.

Improving Communications between the Sexes   Deborah Tannen recommends that everyone needs to become aware of how linguistic styles work and how they influence our perceptions and judgments. She believes that knowledge of linguistic styles helps to ensure that people with valuable insights or ideas get heard. Consider how gender-based linguistic differences affect who gets heard at a meeting:

> Those who are comfortable speaking up in groups, who need little or no silence before raising their hands, or who speak out easily without waiting to be recognized are far more likely to get heard at meetings. Those who refrain from talking until it's clear that the previous speaker is finished, who wait to be recognized, and who are inclined to link their comments to those of others will do fine at a meeting where everyone else is following the same rules but will have a hard time getting heard in a meeting with people whose styles are more like the first pattern. Given the socialization typical of boys and girls, men are more likely to have learned the first style and women the second, making meetings more congenial for men than for women.[37]

Knowledge of these linguistic differences can assist managers in devising methods to ensure that everyone's ideas are heard and given fair credit both in and out of meetings. Furthermore, it is useful to consider the organizational strengths and limitations of your linguistic style. You may want to consider modifying a linguistic characteristic that is a detriment to perceptions of your confidence, competence, and authority. In conclusion, communication between the sexes can be improved by remembering that women and men have different ways of saying the same thing.

Communication in the Computerized Information Age

As discussed in Chapter 1, the use of computers and information technology is dramatically affecting many aspects of organizational behavior. Consider, for example, how Bill Gates, chairman and chief software architect at Microsoft, is using information technology to change the way in which he works.

> On my desk I have three screens, synchronized to form a single desktop. I can drag items from one screen to the next. Once you have that large display area, you'll never go back, because it has a direct impact on productivity. The screen on the left has my list of e-mails. On the center screen is usually the specific e-mail I'm reading and responding to. And my browser is on the right-hand screen. This setup gives me the ability to glance and see what new has come in while I'm working on something, and to bring up a link that's related to an e-mail and look at it while the e-mail is still in front of me. . . . Paper is no longer a big part of my day.[38]

Bill Gates is not the only person using information technology to improve his productivity. A recent study of 2,032 youth by the Kaiser Family Foundation suggests that young people are also multitasking and spending a great deal of time using electronics. Results revealed that "8- to 18-year-olds live media-saturated lives, spending 44.5 hours a week with electronics. The 6.5 hours a day compares with 2.25 hours spent with parents, 1.5 hours spent in physical activity, and just 50 minutes on homework."[39]

You might expect that someone as closely linked to paperless technology as Bill Gates, CEO of Microsoft, would rely almost entirely on electric forms of communication. And you'd be right. Says Gates, "Paper is no longer a big part of my day."

"The webcam and electric prod? Oh, it's just something we're trying out."

Copyright © Ted Goff. Reprinted with permission.

The computerized information age is radically changing communication patterns in both our personal and work lives. For example, recent statistics reveal that 69% of the population in North America uses the Internet. Cross-culturally, this percentage is higher than the percentage of the population using the Internet in Africa (3%), Asia (10%), Europe (36%), Middle East (10%), Latin America/Caribbean (14%), and Oceania/Australia (53%).[40] Interestingly, 30 percent of Internet users go online on any particular day simply to have fun or pass the time.[41] This section explores key components of information technology that influence communication patterns and management within a computerized workplace: Internet/intranet/extranet, electronic mail, handheld devices, blogs, videoconferencing, group support systems, and teleworking.

Internet

A global network of computer networks.

intranet

An organization's private Internet.

extranet

Connects internal employees with selected customers, suppliers, and strategic partners.

Internet/Intranet/Extranet

The Internet, or more simply, the Net, is more than a computer network. It is a network of computer networks. The **Internet** is a global network of independently operating but interconnected computers. The Internet connects everything from supercomputers, to large mainframes contained in businesses, government, and universities, to the personal computers in our homes and offices. An **intranet** is nothing more than an organization's private Internet. Intranets also have *firewalls* that block outside Internet users from accessing internal information. This is done to protect the privacy and confidentiality of company documents. In contrast to the internal focus of an intranet, an **extranet** is an extended intranet in that it connects internal employees with selected customers, suppliers, and other strategic partners. Ford Motor Company, for instance, has an extranet that connects its dealers worldwide. Ford's extranet was set up to help support the sales and servicing of cars and to enhance customer satisfaction.

The primary benefit of the Internet, intranets, and extranets is that they can enhance the ability of employees to find, create, manage, and distribute information. The effectiveness of these systems, however, depends on how organizations set up and manage their intranet/extranet and how employees use the acquired information because information by itself cannot solve or do anything; information is knowledge or a thing. For example, communication effectiveness actually can decrease if a corporate intranet becomes a dumping ground of unorganized information. In this case, employees will find themselves flailing in a sea of information. To date, however, no rigorous research studies have been conducted that directly demonstrate productivity increases from using the Internet, intranets, or extranets. But there are case studies that reveal other organizational benefits. For example, the University of Michigan and the University of Louisville saved $200,000 and $90,000 a year, respectively, by asking employees to enroll for employee benefits on their intranets.[42] United Parcel Service (UPS) also estimated that productivity increased 35% after the implementation of high-speed wireless Internet access via Wi-Fi.[43] Employee training is another online application that has saved companies millions of dollars.[44]

In contrast to these positive case studies, a recent study by Harris Interactive revealed that 51% admitted using the Internet at work from one to five hours a week for personal matters. Another survey of 474 human resource professionals indicated that 43% found that employees were viewing pornography while at work.[45] All told, International Data Corp. estimated personal use of the Internet during work hours contributes to a 30% to 40% decrease in productivity.[46] Organizations are taking these statistics to heart and are attempting to root out cyberslackers by tracking employee behavior with electronic monitoring. A survey of more than 700 companies by the Society for Human Resource Management revealed that almost 75% of those companies monitored their employees' use of the Internet and checked their e-mail.[47]

There is one last aspect of the Internet worth noting—cybercrime. It strikes individuals and organizations alike. For example, Figure 12–3 shows the amount of cybercrime committed for three catgories of illegal behavior. All told, cyber-fraud cost businesses about $1.5 billion in 2005.[48] Interestingly, almost 50% of this criminal activity originates inside an organization. It may occur as the result of employee

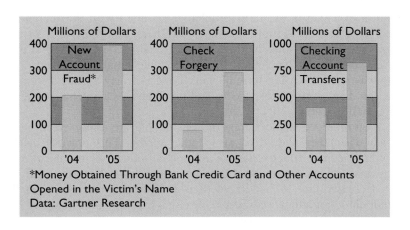

FIGURE 12–3
The Costs of Cybercrime

SOURCE: S E Ante and B Grow, "Meet the Hackers," *BusinessWeek*, May 29, 2006, p. 60.

carelessness, for example, leaving a laptop unsecured or sending confidential, unencrypted information over the Internet. Alternatively, employees can steal trade secrets or sell customer information. Organizations can combat this problem by educating employees about security, classifying data as open or sensitive and confidential, using encryption for sensitive and confidential information, monitoring employee activities, and holding employees accountable for failure to follow rules regarding information security.[49]

Electronic Mail

electronic mail

Uses the Internet/intranet to send computer-generated text and documents.

Electronic mail or e-mail uses the Internet/intranet to send computer-generated text and documents between people. The use of e-mail is on the rise throughout the world. For example, surveys reveal that US employees receive somewhere between 50 to 250 e-mail messages per day.[50] E-mail is becoming a major communication medium because of four key benefits:

1. E-mail reduces the cost of distributing information to a large number of employees.
2. E-mail is a tool for increasing teamwork. It enables employees to quickly send messages to colleagues on the next floor, in another building, or in another country.
3. E-mail reduces the costs and time associated with print duplication and paper distribution. One management expert estimated that these savings can total $9,000 a year per employee.[51]
4. E-mail fosters flexibility. This is particularly true for employees with a portable computer because they can log onto e-mail whenever and wherever they want. Wireless technology and handheld devices enhance the flexibility of e-mail.

In spite of these positive benefits, there are four key drawbacks to consider. First, sending and receiving e-mail can lead to a lot of wasted time and effort, or it can distract employees from completing critical job duties. For example, a national survey of US workers indicated that between 10% and 40% of their e-mail messages were unimportant.[52] Second, people overestimate their ability to effectively communicate via e-mail.[53] Further, people have a tendency to write things in an e-mail that they would not say in person. This can lead to negative interactions and defensiveness.

Information overload is the third problem associated with the increased use of e-mail: People tend to send more messages to others, and there is a lot of "spamming" going on: sending junk mail, bad jokes, chain letters, or irrelevant memos (e.g., the "cc" of e-mail). Nucleus Research estimated that 75% of all e-mail traffic in 2004 was spam.[54] Going through junk e-mail clearly wastes a lot of productivity time for many employees. Skills & Best Practices contains suggestions for managing e-mail overload.

Finally, preliminary evidence suggests that people are using electronic mail to communicate when they should be using other media. This practice can result in reduced communication effectiveness. A four-year study of communication patterns within a university demonstrated that the increased use of electronic mail was associated with decreased face-to-face interactions and with a drop in the overall amount of organizational communication. Employees also expressed a feeling of being less connected and less cohesive as a department as the amount of e-mails increased.[55] This interpersonal "disconnection" may be caused by the trend of replacing everyday face-to-face interactions with electronic messages. It is important to remember that employees' social needs are satisfied through the many different interpersonal interactions that occur at work.

There are three additional issues to consider when using e-mail: (1) E-mail only works when the party you desire to communicate with also uses it. E-mail may not be a viable communication medium in all cases. (2) The speed of getting a response to an e-mail message is dependent on how frequently the receiver examines his or her messages. It is important to consider this issue when picking a communication medium. (3) Many companies do not have policies for using e-mail, which can lead to misuse and potential legal liability. For instance, four female employees working at Chevron filed a suit claiming that they were sexually harassed through e-mail. The company settled for $2.2 million, plus legal fees and court costs. Do not assume that your e-mail messages are private and confidential. Organizations are advised to develop policies regarding the use of e-mail.[56]

Handheld Devices

Handheld devices, which also are referred to as PDAs (personal digital assistants), offer users the portability to do work from any location. They are used by millions of people and were designed to allow users to multitask from any location. For example, PDAs can be used to make and track appointments, do word processing, crunch numbers on a spreadsheet, check out favorite tunes and video clips, receive and send e-mail, organize photos, play games, and complete a variety of other tasks.[57] Manufacturers of these devices claim that the combination of portability and multitasking features enable people to be more efficient and productive. (See Skills & Best Practices.) The question from an OB perspective is whether or not these devices actually lead to higher productivity.

Although many people seem addicted to their handheld devices, some academics are skeptical about their real value. Consider the following comments made by several professors to a reporter from *BusinessWeek*.

> The idea that gadgets always make us more efficient, "is a scam, and illusion," says David Greenfield, director of the Hartford-based Center for Internet Studies. That's because at their heart, gadgets enable multitasking. And a growing body of evidence suggests that multitasking can easily turn into multislacking. It also increases errors, short-circuits attention spans, induces air-traffic-controller-like stress, and elongates the time it takes to accomplish the most basic tasks by up to

Managing Your E-Mail

1. Scan first, read second.

2. Learn to delete without reading. Over time, you will get a sense for low-value messages and you should be able to delete messages from unrecognizable addresses.

3. Group messages by topic. Read the first message in a series and then go to the most recent. This enables you to save time by skipping e-mails between the first and last message.

4. Once steps 1–3 are complete, prioritize your inbox and respond in order of a message's importance.

5. Stop the madness by asking people to stop sending you unimportant messages.

6. Rather than continuing to engage in ping-pong e-mailing, determine if a phone call can get to the heart of the matter.

7. Get off cc lists. Ask to be removed from distribution lists.

8. Only respond to a message when it is absolutely required.

9. Keep messages brief and clear. Use clear subject headings and state the purpose of your e-mail in the first sentence or paragraph.

10. Avoid the "reply to all" feature.

11. If the message concerns a volatile or critical matter, e-mail is probably the wrong medium to use. Consider using the phone.

SOURCE: These recommendations were taken from C Cavanagh, *Managing Your E-Mail: Thinking Outside the Inbox.* Copyright © 2003 John Wiley & Sons, Inc. Reprinted with permission of John Wiley & Sons, Inc.

SKILLS & BEST PRACTICES

Fast-Food Chains Use iPods to Train Employees

Trying to turn out productive workers as efficiently as possible, a few fast-food chains are using iPod video players to train new employees. Pal's Sudden Service, a regional chain with Tennessee and Virginia outlets, started iPod video training in its 20 restaurants in February. "We're looking to expedite the learning process through technology," says Pal's CEO Thom Crosby. Chuck E. Cheese's, the pizza-and-games chain, is a few months into testing the video iPods in one of its Dallas outlets.

Both programs, developed by podTraining, a Flower Mound (Tex.) startup, use short video clips to show new hires how to do their jobs. Unlike video or DVD-based training systems, the iPods can be updated quickly and cheaply by downloading new content. And the portability of the iPod allows training to be done on the job.

SOURCE: Excerpted from "Labor Notes: The Boss Is Watching–So Watch Your iPod," *BusinessWeek*, April 24, 2006, p 16.

50% or more, according to University of Michigan psychology professor David Meyer. . . .

Gadgets also trigger cognitive overload, says Harvard Medical School psychiatry instructor Dr Edward M. Hallowell. . . . All that toggling back and forth "dilutes performance and increases irritability," says Hallowell, causing steady managers to become disorganized and underachievers.[58]

In addition to drawbacks associated with multitasking, the use of handheld devices has produced physical ailments for some users. Consider the experiences of Chris Kwak and Helena Bell. Chris Kwak, a 31-year-old financial planner, spends several hours each day looking at his handheld computer. "He fires off emails, checks stock prices—and recently plowed through the novel *The Da Vinci Code*. But staring at the two-inch screen is taking its toll on Mr. Kwak's eyes: He regularly pops Tylenol to dull the headaches he gets from focusing on the tiny font he has chosen for his device." Twenty-four-year-old Helena Bell "says that even scrolling through an iPod song menu makes her eyes feel sore." She ultimately abandoned her handheld device because of eye strain.[59] Producers of these devices are currently experimenting with alternative ways to alleviate these eye problems.

Given these considerations, we wonder why sales of handheld devices continue to explode. Dr Meyer offers one potential explanation. He notes that the use of PDAs activates our dopamine-reward system, which induces a pleasurable state for approximately 6% of the population. Dr Meyer says that this effect is clinically addictive.[60] Alternatively, people may view these devices as one way to cope with increasing pressures to accomplish more in the face of ever increasing informational demands. In the end, time and additional research will determine the actual value of handheld devices.

Blogs

blog

Online journal in which people comment on any topic.

A **blog** is an online journal in which people write whatever they want about any topic. Blogging is one of the latest Internet trends. Experts estimate that there are around 23.7 million blogs in existence, and 70,000 new ones pop up every day.[61] Current technology also allows people to blog on cell phones. The benefits of blogs include the opportunity for people to discuss issues in a casual format. These discussions serve much like a chat group and thus provide managers with insights from a wide segment of the employee and customer base as well as the general public. Executives like Jonathan Schwartz, president and COO of Sun Microsystems, and Paul Otellini, the new CEO of Intel, are both using blogs at work to discuss issues of importance.[62] Blogs also give people the opportunity to air their opinions, grievances, and creative ideas. Blogs can also be used to obtain feedback. For example, Christopher Barger, a blogger from IBM, reads others other people's blogs to see what people are saying about IBM's products. Other companies with blogs include Microsoft, Hewlett-Packard, Sun Microsystems, General Motors, and Boeing.[63]

Blogs also have pitfalls. One entails the lack of legal and organizational guidelines regarding what can be posted online. For example, flight attendant Ellen Simonetti and Google employee Mark Jen were both fired for information they included on their blogs. Simonetti posted suggestive pictures of herself in uniform, and Jen commented about his employer's finances.[64] Another involves the potential for employees to say unflattering things about their employer and to leak confidential information. Finally, one can waste a lot of time reading silly and unsubstantiated postings. For example, a recent study showed that 25% of employees read blogs at work, losing approximately 9% of their workweek.[65]

We cannot make any overall conclusion regarding blogs because there has not been any research into their effectiveness as a communication, marketing, or managerial tool. Once again, time will tell.

Videoconferencing

Videoconferencing, also known as teleconferencing, uses video and audio links along with computers to enable people in different locations to see, hear, and talk with one another. This enables people from many locations to conduct a meeting without having to travel. Consider the following applications of videoconferencing:

> At Harken Energy Corp., an oil and gas exploration company in Houston, engineers use video capabilities to share seismic graphs and other geological displays and data from offices in Latin America. The Department of Labor uses videoconferencing to impart basic computer, financial, and résumé-writing skills to citizens. The potential uses of the technology seem even brighter, particularly in marketing and community outreach efforts. . . . Video also is a critical component of eGetgoing's virtual therapy offering. "Treatment requires the participants to see the reaction of the counselor in order to create an emotional bond," says [Barry] Karlin, who notes that the one-way streaming video eGetgoing uses contains the benefit of maintaining anonymity among the 10 patients in each single-group session.[66]

Videoconferencing thus can significantly reduce an organization's travel expenses. Many organizations set up special videoconferencing rooms or booths with specially equipped television cameras. More recent equipment enables people to attach small cameras and microphones to their desks or computer monitors. This enables employees to conduct long-distance meetings and training classes without leaving their office or cubicle.

Group Support Systems

Group support systems (GSSs) entail using state-of-the-art computer software and hardware to help people work better together. They enable people to share information without the constraints of time and space. This is accomplished by utilizing computer networks to link people across a room or across the globe. Collaborative applications include messaging and e-mail systems, calendar management, videoconferencing, computer teleconferencing, electronic whiteboards, and the type of computer-aided decision-making systems discussed in Chapter 10.

group support systems (GSSs)

Using computer software and hardware to help people work better together.

GSS applications have demonstrated increased productivity and cost savings. A recent meta-analysis of 48 experiments also revealed that groups using GSSs during brainstorming experienced greater participation and influence quality, a greater quantity of ideas generated, and less domination by individual members than did groups meeting face-to-face.[67]

Organizations that use full-fledged GSSs have the ability to create virtual teams or to operate as a virtual organization. Virtual organizations are discussed in Chapter 15. You may recall from Chapter 9 that a virtual team represents a physically dispersed task group that conducts its business by using the types of information technology currently being discussed. Specifically, virtual teams tend to use Internet/intranet systems, GSSs, and videoconferencing systems. These real-time systems enable people to communicate with anyone at anytime.[68]

It is important to keep in mind that modern-day information technology only enables people to interact virtually; it doesn't guarantee effective communications. Interestingly, there are a whole host of unique communication problems associated with using the information technology needed to operate virtually.[69]

Teleworking

teleworking

Doing work that is generally performed in the office away from the office using different information technologies.

Teleworking, also referred to as telecommuting, is a work practice in which an employee does part of his or her job in a remote location, typically at home, using a variety of information technologies. That said, any employee with a laptop, Internet access, and a phone can work from almost anywhere. Recent years have seen an explosion of telework within virtual call centers in home offices across the country.[70] For example, a recent survey of 350 US and Canadian call centers revealed that 24% of the employees, or 672,000 workers, were working from home.[71] Experts estimate that 41 million people will telework from home at least one day a week by 2008.[72] Telework is more common for jobs involving computer work, writing, and phone work that require concentration and limited interruptions. Proposed benefits of telework include:

1. *Reduction of capital costs.* Sun Microsystems reported saving $50 million in 2002 by letting employees work from home.

2. *Increased flexibility and autonomy for workers.*

3. *Competitive edge in recruitment.* Arthur Andersen, Merrill Lynch, Cisco, and JetBlue used telecommuting to increase their ability to keep and attract qualified personnel.

4. *Increased job satisfaction and lower turnover.* Employees like telecommuting because it helps resolve work–family conflicts. AT&T's telecommuters had less absenteeism than traditional employees.

5. *Increased productivity.* Telecommuting resulted in productivity increases of 25% and 35% for FourGen Software and Continental Traffic Services, respectively.

6. *Tapping nontraditional labor pools* (such as prison inmates and homebound disabled persons).[73]

Although telecommuting represents an attempt to accommodate employee needs and desires, it requires adjustments and is not for everybody. Many people thoroughly enjoy the social camaraderie that exists within an office setting. These individuals probably would not like to telecommute. Others lack the self-motivation needed to work at home. Finally, organizations must be careful to implement telecommuting in a nondiscriminatory manner. Organizations can easily and unknowingly violate one of several antidiscrimination laws.

key terms

aggressive style   307
assertive style   307
blog   318
communication   299
communication competence   305
electronic mail   316

extranet   314
group support systems (GSSs)   319
Internet   314
intranet   314
linguistic style   311
listening   309

noise   302
nonassertive style   307
nonverbal communication   307
teleworking   320

chapter summary

• *Describe the perceptual process model of communication.* Communication is a process of consecutively linked elements. This model of communication depicts receivers as information processors who create the meaning of messages in their own mind. Because receivers' interpretations of messages often differ from those intended by senders, miscommunication is a common occurrence.

• *Describe the process, personal, physical, and semantic barriers to effective communication.* Every element of the perceptual model of communication is a potential process barrier. There are eight personal barriers that commonly influence communication: (a) the ability to effectively communicate, (b) the way people process and interpret information, (c) the level of interpersonal trust between people, (d) the existence of stereotypes and prejudices, (e) the egos of the people communicating, (f) the ability to listen, (g) the natural tendency to evaluate or judge a sender's message, and (h) the inability to listen with understanding. Physical barriers pertain to distance, physical objects, time, and work and office noise. Semantic barriers show up as encoding and decoding errors because these phases of communication involve transmitting and receiving words and symbols. Cultural diversity is a key contributor to semantic barriers.

• *Contrast the communication styles of assertiveness, aggressiveness, and nonassertiveness.* An assertive style is expressive and self-enhancing but does not violate others' basic human rights. In contrast, an aggressive style is expressive and self-enhancing but takes unfair advantage of others. A nonassertive style is characterized by timid and self-denying behavior. An assertive communication style is more effective than either an aggressive or nonassertive style.

• *Discuss the primary sources of nonverbal communication.* There are several identifiable sources of nonverbal communication effectiveness. Body movements and gestures, touch, facial expressions, and eye contact are important nonverbal cues. The interpretation of these nonverbal cues significantly varies across cultures.

• *Review the five dominant listening styles and 10 keys to effective listening.* The five dominant listening styles are appreciative, empathetic, comprehensive, discerning, and evaluative. Good listeners use the following 10 listening habits: (1) capitalize on thought speed by staying with the speaker and listening between the lines, (2) listen for ideas rather than facts, (3) identify areas of interest between the speaker and listener, (4) judge content and not delivery, (5) do not judge until the speaker has completed his or her message, (6) put energy and effort into listening, (7) resist distractions, (8) listen to both favorable and unfavorable information, (9) read or listen to complex material to exercise the mind, and (10) take notes when necessary and use visual aids to enhance understanding.

• *Explain the information technology of Internet/intranet/extranet, e-mail, handheld devices, blogs, videoconferencing, and group support systems, and explain the related use of teleworking.* The Internet is a global network of computer networks. An intranet is an organization's private Internet. It contains a firewall that blocks outside Internet users from accessing private internal information. An extranet connects an organization's internal employees with selected customers, suppliers, and strategic partners. The primary benefit of these "nets" is that they can enhance the ability of employees to find, create, manage, and distribute information. E-mail uses the Internet/intranet/extranet to send computer-generated text and documents between people. Handheld devices, also known as PDAs (personal digital assistants), offer users the portability to do work from any location. They serve as minicomputers and communication devices. A blog is an online journal in which people write whatever they want about any topic. Blogging is the latest Internet trend. Videoconferencing uses video and audio links along with computers to enable people located at different locations to see, hear, and talk with one another. GSSs use state-of-the-art computer software and hardware to help people work better together. Information is shared across time and space by linking people with computer networks. Teleworking involves doing work that is generally performed in the office away from the office using different information technologies.

discussion questions

1. What are the pros and cons of Boeing's use of blogs? Explain.
2. What are some sources of noise that interfere with communication during a class lecture, an encounter with a professor in his or her office, or a movie?
3. Which of the keys to effective listening are most difficult to follow when listening to a class lecture? Explain.
4. Which barrier to effective communication is most difficult to reduce? Explain
5. What are the pros and cons of using PDAs? Discuss.

ethical dilemma

Are Camera Cell Phones Creating Ethical Problems?[74]

Although camera phones have been broadly available for years in the United States, more than 25 million of the devices are out on the streets of Japan. . . . Now that cell phones with little digital cameras have spread throughout Asia, so have new brands of misbehavior. Some people are secretly taking photos up women's skirts and down into bathroom stalls. Others are avoiding buying books by snapping free shots of desired pages.

"The problem with a new technology is that society has yet to come up with a common understanding about appropriate behavior," said Mizuko Ito, an expert on mobile phone culture at Keio University Tokyo.

Samsung Electronics is banning their use in semiconductor and research facilities, hoping to stave off industrial espionage. Samsung, a leading maker of cell phones, is taking a low-tech approach: requiring employees and visitors to stick tape over the handset's camera lens.

Solving the Dilemma

You are the manager of a large bookstore. You have a camera phone as do several of your employees. You have seen customers use their camera phones to take pictures of one another in the store. Yesterday, for the first time, you observed a customer taking photos of 10 pages of material from a cookbook. Although you did not say anything to this customer, you are wondering what should be done in the future. Select one of the following options.

1. Place a sign on the door asking customers to mind their "cell phone manners." This way you don't have to prevent anyone from using their phone; you can rely on common decency.

2. Ask customers to leave their camera cell phones with an employee at the front of the store. The employee will give the customer a claim check and they can retrieve their phones once they finish shopping.

3. Station an employee at the front of the store who places tape over the lens of camera phones as customers come in.

4. Don't do anything. There is nothing wrong with people taking pictures of materials out of a book.

5. Invent other options. Discuss.

If you're looking for additional study materials, be sure to check out the Online Learning Center at

www.mhhe.com/kinickiob3e

for more information and interactivities that correspond to this chapter.

Influence, Power, and Politics: An Organizational Survival Kit

HOW URSULA BURNS GETS RESULTS AT XEROX

Here's what you need to know about Ursula Burns. As Xerox was teetering on the brink of bankruptcy in early 2001, Burns was in charge of one of the crucial parts of the company's turnaround—holding contract talks with its 2,000 unionized workers in Rochester, N.Y.—even as she was exploring the

her living room, where she was recovering from an emergency hysterectomy.

Now Burns, 47, is the president of Business Group Operations, in charge of engineering, product development, manufacturing, the supply chain, global purchasing, and R&D. Whew. That's basically everything except

Ursula Burns is skilled at using influence to get the job done at Xerox Corp.

growth rate of 5%. "We think we execute fairly well, but we aren't excellent," Burns says.

As you can tell, Burns's style is direct; she doesn't spin and there's no spinning her. "If there was a moose in the room, Ursula would be the person to put it on the table," says Quincy Allen, a VP of product development. Says Mulcahy: "She is the ultimate straight-shooter." She is also personable. Everybody who works with her knows that son Malcolm, 17, is now driving, and daughter Melissa, 13, is adept at drawing. They know about her extraordinary past—growing up in a tenement house in Manhattan, where her mother, Olga, ironed shirts and "did whatever the hell she needed to keep us all going," says Burns.

After earning a master's degree in engineering from Columbia, she joined Xerox as a summer intern in 1980. She worked her way through engineering and product development and then up the ladder to senior VP in 2000, just in time to play a big role in helping Mulcahy keep Xerox from going off a cliff. Now she is leading Xerox's drive into color printing, which grew 15% last

outsourcing of their jobs. "Most people would have run for the hills," says CEO Anne Mulcahy. But Burns wouldn't take a pass, even when she had the chance. She negotiated the deal in

sales and service at the $15.7 billion company. The job puts her in the hot seat once again: This time cracking what Mulcahy calls "the hardest part of the equation for us"—achieving a revenue

year and contributes almost a third of revenue. She has nearly completed the company's transition to digital printing. Meanwhile, the headhunters are eyeing her, but she plans to stay at Xerox for "as long as they'll have me." What about becoming a CEO? "I can't let myself get confused by tomorrow," she says. As her mother taught her, "If I keep focused on what I need to do today, the future will take care of itself."[1]

FOR DISCUSSION

How would you assess Ursula Burns's use of power and influence to get the job done at Xerox? Explain. For an interpretation of this case and additional comments, visit our Online Learning Center at

www.mhhe.com/kinickiob3e

Influencing and Persuading Others

How do you get others to carry out your wishes? Do you simply tell them what to do? Or do you prefer a less direct approach, such as promising to return the favor? Whatever approach you use, the crux of the issue is *social influence*. A large measure of interpersonal interaction involves attempts to influence others, including parents, bosses, co-workers, spouses, teachers, friends, and children.

Let's start sharpening your influence skills with a familiarity of the following research insights.

Nine Generic Influence Tactics

A particularly fruitful stream of research, initiated by David Kipnis and his colleagues in 1980, reveals how people influence each other in organizations. The Kipnis methodology involved asking employees how they managed to get either their bosses, co-workers, or subordinates to do what they wanted them to do.[3] Statistical refinements and replications by other researchers over a 13-year period eventually yielded nine influence tactics. The nine tactics, ranked in diminishing order of use in the workplace are as follows:

1. *Rational persuasion.* Trying to convince someone with reason, logic, or facts.

2. *Inspirational appeals.* Trying to build enthusiasm by appealing to others' emotions, ideals, or values.

3. *Consultation.* Getting others to participate in planning, making decisions, and changes.

4. *Ingratiation.* Getting someone in a good mood prior to making a request; being friendly, helpful, and using praise, flattery, or humor. [4]

5. *Personal appeals.* Referring to friendship and loyalty when making a request.

6. *Exchange.* Making express or implied promises and trading favors.

7. *Coalition tactics.* Getting others to support your effort to persuade someone.

8. *Pressure.* Demanding compliance or using intimidation or threats.

9. *Legitimating tactics.* Basing a request on one's authority or right, organizational rules or policies, or express or implied support from superiors.[5]

These approaches can be considered *generic* influence tactics because they characterize social influence in all directions. Researchers have found this ranking to be fairly consistent regardless of whether the direction of influence is downward, upward, or lateral.[6]

Some call the first five influence tactics—rational persuasion, inspirational appeals, consultation, ingratiation, and personal appeals—"soft" tactics because they are friendlier and not as coercive as the last four tactics. Exchange, coalition, pressure, and legitimating tactics accordingly are called "hard" tactics because they involve more overt pressure.

Three Influence Outcomes

According to researchers, an influence attempt has three possible outcomes:

1. *Commitment*: Substantial agreement followed by initiative and persistence in pursuit of common goals.

2. *Compliance*: Reluctant or insincere agreement requiring subsequent prodding to satisfy minimum requirements.

3. *Resistance*: Stalling, unproductive arguing, or outright rejection.[7]

Commitment is the best outcome in the workplace because the target person's intrinsic motivation will energize good performance.[8] A G Lafley, the highly respected CEO of 100,000-employee Procter & Gamble, made commitment the cornerstone of his growth plan after taking charge in 2000:

As CEO of Procter & Gamble, A G Lafley uses persuasive power to win commitment to company goals.

I always talk about this hierarchy of commitment. On the high end it's disciples—people who really believe in what you're doing and in you. And on the low end it's saboteurs. And there's everything in between. So I had to make sure that we got rid of the saboteurs, built a strong cadre of disciples, and moved all fence sitters to the positive side.[9]

The fence sitters required Lafley's best powers of influence and persuasion during a hectic schedule of face-to-face meetings with P&G employees worldwide. Too often in today's hurried workplaces managers must settle for compliance or face resistance because they do not invest themselves in the situation, as Lafley did.

Practical Research Insights

Laboratory and field studies have taught us useful lessons about the relative effectiveness of influence tactics along with other instructive insights:

- Commitment is more likely when people rely on consultation, strong rational persuasion, and inspirational appeals and *do not* rely on pressure and coalition tactics.[10] Interestingly, in one study, managers were not very effective at *downward* influence. They relied most heavily on inspiration (an effective tactic), ingratiation (a moderately effective tactic), and pressure (an ineffective tactic).[11]

- A review of 69 studies suggests ingratiation (making the boss feel good) can slightly improve your performance appraisal results and make your boss like you significantly more.[12]

- Commitment is more likely when the influence attempt involves something *important* and *enjoyable* and is based on a *friendly* relationship.[13]
- Credible (believable and trustworthy) people tend to be the most persuasive.[14]
- In a survey, 214 employed MBA students (55% female) tended to perceive their superiors' "soft" influence tactics as fair and "hard" influence tactics as unfair. *Unfair* influence tactics were associated with greater *resistance* among employees.[15]

How to Do a Better Job of Influencing and Persuading Others

Practical, research-based advice has been offered by Robert B Cialdini, a respected expert at Arizona State University. Based on many years of research by himself and others, Cialdini (pronounced Chal-*dee*-knee) derived the following six principles of influence and persuasion:[16]

1. *Liking.* People tend to like those who like them. Learning about another person's likes and dislikes through informal conversations builds friendship bonds. So do sincere and timely praise, empathy, and recognition.

2. *Reciprocity.* The belief that both good and bad deeds should be repaid in kind is virtually universal. Managers who act unethically and treat employees with contempt can expect the same in return. Worse, those employees, in turn, are likely to treat each other and their customers unethically and with contempt. Managers need to be positive and constructive role models and fair-minded to benefit from the principle of reciprocity (see Skills & Best Practices).

3. *Social proof.* People tend to follow the lead of those most like themselves. Role models and peer pressure are powerful cultural forces in social settings. Managers are advised to build support for workplace changes by first gaining the enthusiastic support of informal leaders who will influence their peers.

4. *Consistency.* People tend to do what they are personally committed to do. A manager who can elicit a verbal commitment from an employee has taken an important step toward influence and persuasion.

5. *Authority.* People tend to defer to and respect credible experts. According to Cialdini, too many managers and professionals take their expertise for granted, as in the case of a hospital where he consulted:

> The physical therapy staffers were frustrated because so many of their stroke patients abandoned their exercise routines as soon as they left the

A Second Chance Can Tap the Power of Reciprocity

Richard Branson, the British founder and chairman of the Virgin Group:

When I was 7 or 8, I took some change from my dad's drawer and went 'round to the sweet shop. The shopkeeper called my dad and said. "We've got your son here; could you come down?" Here I am, with 50 pence, and the shopkeeper says, "I assume your son has taken this, that you didn't give it to him?" My dad says, "How dare you accuse him of stealing!" My dad knew I'd taken it, and I gave it back—but I never stole again.

Years later, when Virgin was about 20 people, the manager of a secondhand music shop tells me that one of our staffers is selling albums that were new from Virgin. It was petty theft. Rather than sacking him, I brought him in and we had a chat. Today he is the head of marketing of one of our companies and one of the best people Virgin has.

SOURCE: Excerpted from R Branson, "When People Screw Up, Give Them a Second Chance," *Business 2.0*, December 2005, p 120.

hospital. No matter how often the staff emphasized the importance of regular home exercise—it is, in fact, crucial to the process of regaining independent function—the message just didn't sink in.

Interviews with some of the patients helped us pinpoint the problem. They were familiar with the background and training of their physicians, but the patients knew little about the credentials of the physical therapists who were urging them to exercise. It was a simple matter to remedy that lack of information: We merely asked the therapy director to display all the awards, diplomas, and certifications of her staff on the walls of the therapy rooms. The result was startling: Exercise compliance jumped 34% and has never dropped since.[17]

6. *Scarcity.* People want items, information, and opportunities that have limited availability. Special opportunities and privileged information are influence builders for managers.

Importantly, Cialdini recommends using these six principles in combination, rather than separately, for maximum impact. Because of major ethical implications, one's goals need to be worthy and actions need to be sincere and genuine when using these six principles.

By demonstrating the rich texture of social influence, the foregoing research evidence and practical advice whet our appetite for learning more about how today's managers can and do reconcile individual and organizational interests. Let us focus on social power.

Social Power and Empowerment

The term *power* evokes mixed and often passionate reactions. To skeptics, Lord Acton's time-honored declaration that "power corrupts and absolute power corrupts absolutely" is truer than ever.[18] However, OB specialists remind us that, like it or not, power is a fact of life in modern organizations. According to one management writer:

> Power must be used because managers must influence those they depend on. Power also is crucial in the development of managers' self-confidence and willingness to support subordinates. From this perspective, power should be accepted as a natural part of any organization. Managers should recognize and develop their own power to coordinate and support the work of subordinates; it is powerlessness, not power, that undermines organizational effectiveness.[19]

social power

Ability to get things done with human, informational, and material resources.

reward power

Obtaining compliance with promised or actual rewards.

coercive power

Obtaining compliance through threatened or actual punishment.

Thus, power is a necessary and generally positive force in organizations.[20] As the term is used here, **social power** is defined as "the ability to marshal the human, informational, and material resources to get something done."[21]

Importantly, the exercise of social power in organizations is not necessarily a downward proposition. Employees can and do exercise power upward and laterally. An example of an upward power play occurred at Alberto-Culver Company, the personal care products firm. Leonard Lavin, founder of the company, was under pressure to revitalize the firm because key employees were departing for more innovative competitors such as Procter & Gamble. Lavin's daughter Carol Bernick, and her husband Howard, both long-time employees, took things into their own hands. As *BusinessWeek* reported:

Even the Bernicks were thinking of jumping ship. Instead, in September 1994, they marched into Lavin's office and presented him with an ultimatum: Either hand over the reins as CEO or run the company without them. It was a huge blow for Lavin, forcing him to face selling his company to outsiders or ceding control to the younger generation. Unwilling to sell, he reluctantly stepped down, though he remains chairman.

How does it feel to push aside your own father and wrest operating control of the company he created? "It isn't an easy thing to do with the founder of any company, whether he's your father or not," says Carol Bernick, 46, now vice-chairman and president of Alberto-Culver North America.[22]

Howard Bernick became CEO, the firm's top-down management style was scrapped in favor of a more open culture, and Lavin reportedly was happy with how things turned out.

Five Bases of Power

A popular classification scheme for social power traces back to the landmark work of John French and Bertram Raven. They proposed that power arises from five different bases: reward power, coercive power, legitimate power, expert power, and referent power.[23] Each involves a different approach to influencing others. Each has advantages and drawbacks.

Reward Power   Managers have **reward power** if they can obtain compliance by promising or granting rewards. Pay-for-performance plans and positive reinforcement programs attempt to exploit reward power.

Coercive Power   Threats of punishment and actual punishment give an individual **coercive power.** Richard M Scrushy, the former head of HealthSouth now facing legal action, reportedly relied heavily on coercive power. According to *BusinessWeek:*

> As he assumed the trappings of wealth, Scrushy became an increasingly imperious leader, say insiders. He publicly berated financial analysts who dared to challenge his forecasts of continued growth. Staffers feared him, too. Scrushy would pop up unannounced at his rehab centers for surprise inspections. Like a drill sergeant, he would run a finger along the tops of a picture frame, then wipe it on the blazer of the center's administrator. Any visible mark meant points deducted—and possible dismissal.[24]

How would you respond to this management style?

How to "Get Elected Boss" after Being Promoted to Management

I was just promoted and will now become the manager of the team I once belonged to. Any advice on how to make a successful transition?

——Tim Purkis, Folsom, Calif.

Yes, start campaigning. The higher-ups have just appointed you boss. Congratulations. Now you need to go out and get elected by your former peers.

The transition from peer to manager is one of the most delicate and complicated organizational situations you will ever experience. For months, or even years, you have been in the trenches with your co-workers as a friend, confidant, and (probably) fellow grouser. . . .

Surely, some of your former peers are cheering your promotion and are eager to fall in line. That will feel good, but don't let their support lead you to do something disastrous—namely, gallop into town with guns blazing. . . .

But here's the rub: You have to campaign without compromising your new authority. That's right. You have to run for office while holding office. It's a critical component in moving from peer to manager, and all effective managers go through it, often several times in their careers.

Getting this transition right is all about timing. Your kinder, gentler election drive can't last forever. Give it three months. Six at most. If you haven't won over the skeptics by then, you never will. In fact, after a certain point, the softer you are, the less effective you will become. And you'll be fighting battles that do nothing but wear you down. Save your energy for bigger things and begin the process of moving out steadfast resisters and bringing in people who accept the changes that you and your core of supporters deem necessary.

SOURCE: Excerpted from J and S Welch, "The Welch Way: How to Get Elected Boss," *BusinessWeek,* May 15, 2006, p 112. Jack Welch is the former CEO of General Electric and his wife, Suzy Welch, is the former editor of *Harvard Business Review.*

How Much Power Do You Have?

INSTRUCTIONS: Score your various bases of power for your current (or former) job, using the following scale:

1 = Strongly disagree   4 = Agree
2 = Disagree   5 = Strongly agree
3 = Slightly agree

Reward Power Score = _____

1. I can reward persons at lower levels. _____
2. My review actions affect the rewards gained at lower levels. _____
3. Based on my decisions, lower level personnel may receive a bonus. _____

Coercive Power Score = _____

1. I can punish employees at lower levels. _____
2. My work is a check on lower level employees. _____
3. My diligence reduces error. _____

Legitimate Power Score = _____

1. My position gives me a great deal of authority. _____
2. The decisions made at my level are of critical importance. _____
3. Employees look to me for guidance. _____

Expert Power Score = _____

1. I am an expert in this job. _____
2. My ability gives me an advantage in this job. _____
3. Given some time, I could improve the methods used on this job. _____

Referent Power Score = _____

1. I attempt to set a good example for other employees. _____
2. My personality allows me to work well in this job. _____
3. My fellow employees look to me as their informal leader. _____

Arbitrary norms for each of the five bases of power are: 3–6 = Weak power base; 7–11 = Moderate power base; 12–15 = Strong power base.

SOURCE: Adapted and excerpted in part from D L Dieterly and B Schneider, "The Effect of Organizational Environment on Perceived Power and Climate: A Laboratory Study.'" *Organizational Behavior and Human Performance*, June, 1974, pp 316–37.

Legitimate Power   This base of power is anchored to one's formal position or authority.[25] Thus, managers who obtain compliance primarily because of their formal authority to make decisions have **legitimate power.** Legitimate power may be expressed either positively or negatively. Positive legitimate power focuses constructively on job performance (see Skills & Best Practices on page 331). Negative legitimate power tends to be threatening and demeaning to those being influenced. Its main purpose is to build the power holder's ego.

legitimate power

Obtaining compliance through formal authority.

Expert Power   Valued knowledge or information gives an individual **expert power** over those who need such knowledge or information. The power of supervisors is enhanced because they know about work assignments and schedules before their employees do. Skillful use of expert power played a key role in the effectiveness of team leaders in a study of three physician medical diagnosis teams.[26] Knowledge *is* power in today's high-tech workplaces. For example, the rigor of complying with the

expert power

Obtaining compliance through one's knowledge or information.

tough Sarbanes-Oxley law, passed in the wake of the Enron, Tyco, and WorldCom scandals, has bolstered the prestige of accountants. The results of a recent survey of 30,000 college students prompted this conclusion: "The fact that an accountant can bring a whole company down or can keep one alive shows how accountants have a lot of power."[27]

Referent Power   Also called charisma, **referent power** comes into play when one's personality becomes the reason for compliance. Role models have referent power over those who identify closely with them.[28]

referent power

Obtaining compliance through charisma or personal attraction.

To further your understanding of these five bases of power, take a moment to complete the questionnaire in the Hands-On Exercise. What is your power profile? Where do you need improvement?

Practical Lessons from Research

Researchers have identified the following relationships between power bases and work outcomes such as job performance, job satisfaction, and turnover:

Test Your Knowledge

Sources of Power

- Expert and referent power had a generally positive effect.
- Reward and legitimate power had a slightly positive effect.
- Coercive power had a slightly negative effect.[29]

A follow-up study involving 251 employed business seniors looked at the relationship between influence styles and bases of power. This was a bottom-up study. In other words, employee perceptions of managerial influence and power were examined. Rational persuasion was found to be a highly acceptable managerial influence tactic. Why? Because employees perceived it to be associated with the three bases of power they viewed positively: legitimate, expert, and referent.[30]

In summary, expert and referent power appear to get the best *combination* of results and favorable reactions from lower-level employees.[31]

Employee Empowerment

An exciting trend in today's organizations centers on giving employees a greater say in the workplace. This trend wears various labels, including "participative management" and "open-book management."[32] Regardless of the label one prefers, it is all about empowerment. One management writer defines **empowerment** in terms of serving the customer:

empowerment

Sharing varying degrees of power with lower-level employees to better serve the customer.

> Empowerment quite simply means granting supervisors or workers permission to give the customer priority over other issues in the operation. In practical terms, it relates to the resources, skill, time and support to become leaders rather than controllers or mindless robots.[33]

Steve Kerr, a pioneer in employee empowerment, explains: "We say empowerment is moving decision making down to the lowest level *where a competent decision can be made*."[34] Of course, it is naive and counterproductive to hand power over to unwilling and/or unprepared employees.

Group Exercise

The Effects of Abusing Power

The concept of empowerment requires some adjustment in traditional thinking (see Skills & Best Practices). First and foremost, power is *not* a zero-sum situation

Hitting the Right Note with Empowerment

The Orpheus Chamber Orchestra is known principally for the musical accomplishments of its 28 members. Based in New York City, the Grammy Award–winning ensemble performs Mozart and Stravinsky to rave reviews around the world. But the group is also famous for a novel approach to management: Unlike most orchestras its size, Orpheus has no conductor.

Its unique conductor-less approach to performance affords the well-known Orpheus Chamber Orchestra many advantages. It also requires members to share responsibilities like staffing and fund-raising.

Orpheus is not a captainless ship. It has a managing director, Ronnie Bauch, who recently spoke to MBA students at Stanford's Graduate School of Business. Bauch explained that Orpheus members share responsibility for many functions (not only keeping time but also fund-raising, staffing, and educational outreach) that most organizations assign to individual leaders. It's a distributed approach to management that at first seems impractical but that—like open-source software programming—turns out to have many advantages.

SOURCE: Excerpted from J Pfeffer, "Why Employees Should Lead Themselves," *Business 2.0,* January/February 2006, p 76.

where one person's gain is another's loss. Social power is unlimited. This requires win–win thinking. Frances Hesselbein, the woman credited with modernizing the Girl Scouts of the USA, put it this way: "The more power you give away, the more you have."[35] Authoritarian managers who view employee empowerment as a threat to their personal power are missing the point because of their win–lose thinking.[36] A good role model of a manager who uses win–win thinking is Motorola executive Greg Brown:

> He boils his philosophy down to three words: listen, learn, lead. It means you need to understand your business down to the nuts and bolts, let your employees know you won't have all the answers, and focus on just a handful of truly crucial things, even though dozens seem just as important.[37]

What is your own philosophy of management, and does it include empowerment?

Making Empowerment Work

We believe empowerment has good promise if managers go about it properly. Empowerment is a sweeping concept with many different definitions. Consequently, researchers use inconsistent measurements, and cause-effect relationships are fuzzy.[38] Managers committed to the idea of employee empowerment need to follow the path of continuous improvement, learning from their successes and failures. Eight years of research with 10 "empowered" companies led consultant W Alan Randolph to formulate the three-pronged empowerment plan in Figure 13–1. Notice how open-book management and active information sharing are needed to build the necessary foundation of trust. Beyond that, clear goals and lots of relevant training are needed. While noting that the empowerment process can take several years to unfold, Randolph offered this perspective:

> While the keys to empowerment may be easy to understand, they are hard to implement. It takes tremendous courage to start sharing sensitive information. It takes true strength to build more structure just at the point when people want more freedom of action. It takes real growth to allow teams to take over the management decision-making process. And above all, it takes perseverance to complete the empowerment process.[39]

Randolph's Empowerment Model | **FIGURE 13-1**

The Empowerment Plan

Share Information
- Share company performance information.
- Help people understand the business.
- Build trust through sharing sensitive information.
- Create self-monitoring possibilities.

Create Autonomy through Structure	**Let Teams Become the Hierarchy**
• Create a clear vision and clarify the little pictures. • Create new decision-making rules that support empowerment. • Clarify goals and roles collaboratively. • Establish new empowering performance management processes. • Use heavy doses of training.	• Provide direction and training for new skills. • Provide encouragement and support for change. • Gradually have managers let go of control. • Work through the leadership vacuum stage. • Acknowledge the fear factor.

**Remember: Empowerment is not magic;
it consists of a few simple steps and a lot of persistence.**

SOURCE: Reprinted from *Organizational Dynamics,* W Alan Randolph, "Navigating the Journey to Empowerment," Spring 1995. Copyright © 1995, with permission from Elsevier.

Organizational Politics and Impression Management

Most students of OB find the study of organizational politics intriguing. Perhaps this topic owes its appeal to the antics of television's corporate villains and contestants on *The Apprentice* stepping on each other to avoid Donald Trump's dreaded words, "You're fired!"[40] As we will see, however, organizational politics includes, but is not limited to, dirty dealing. Organizational politics is an ever-present and sometimes annoying feature of modern work life. "According to 150 executives from large US companies, office politics wastes an average of 20% of their time; that's 10 weeks a year."[41] On the other hand, organizational politics is often a positive force in modern work organizations. Skillful and well-timed politics can help you get your point across, neutralize resistance to a key project, relieve stress, or get a choice job assignment.[42]

We explore this important and interesting area by (1) defining the term *organizational politics,* (2) identifying three levels of political action, (3) discussing eight specific political tactics, (4) considering a related area called *impression management,* and (5) discussing how to curb organizational politics.

Definition and Domain of Organizational Politics

"**Organizational politics** involves intentional acts of influence to enhance or protect the self-interest of individuals or groups."[43] An emphasis on *self-interest* distinguishes this form of social influence.

organizational politics
Intentional enhancement of self-interest.

Managers are endlessly challenged to achieve a workable balance between employees' self-interests and organizational interests, as discussed at the beginning of this chapter. When a proper balance exists, the pursuit of self-interest may serve the organization's interests. Political behavior becomes a negative force when self-interests erode or defeat organizational interests. For example, researchers have documented the political tactic of filtering and distorting information flowing up to the boss. This self-serving practice put the reporting employees in the best possible light.[44]

Political Behavior Triggered by Uncertainty   Political maneuvering is triggered primarily by *uncertainty*. Five common sources of uncertainty within organizations are

1. Unclear objectives.
2. Vague performance measures.
3. Ill-defined decision processes.
4. Strong individual or group competition.[45]
5. Any type of change.

Closely akin to the second factor—vague performance measures—is the problem of *unclear performance–reward linkages* (recall our discussion of expectancy motivation theory in Chapter 7). This is a significant problem, according to the results of a recent survey of 10,000 employees. Regarding the statement, "Employees who do a better job get paid more," 48 percent of the responding managers agreed, whereas only 31 percent of the nonmanagers agreed.[46] Employees tend to resort to political games when they are unsure about what it takes to get ahead. Relative to the fifth factor— any type of change—organization development specialist Anthony Raia noted, "Whatever we attempt to change, the political subsystem becomes active. Vested interests are almost always at stake and the distribution of power is challenged."[47]

We would expect a field sales representative, striving to achieve an assigned quota, to be less political than a management trainee working on a variety of projects. While some management trainees stake their career success on hard work, competence, and a bit of luck, many do not. These people attempt to gain a competitive edge through some combination of the political tactics discussed below. Meanwhile, the salesperson's performance is measured in actual sales, not in terms of being friends with the boss or taking credit for others' work. Thus, the management trainee would tend to be more political than the field salesperson because of greater uncertainty about management's expectations.

Because employees generally experience greater uncertainty during the earlier stages of their careers, are junior employees more political than more senior ones? The answer is yes, according to a survey of 243 employed adults in upstate New York. In fact, one senior employee nearing retirement told the researcher: "I used to play political games when I was younger. Now I just do my job."[48]

Three Levels of Political Action   Although much political maneuvering occurs at the individual level, it also can involve group or collective action. Figure 13–2 illustrates three different levels of political action: the individual level, the coalition level, and the network level.[49] Each level has its distinguishing characteristics. At the individual level, personal self-interests are pursued by the individual. The political aspects of coalitions and networks are not so obvious, however.

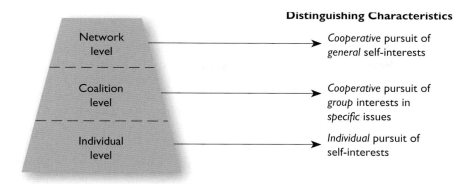

Distinguishing Characteristics

Cooperative pursuit of *general* self-interests

Cooperative pursuit of *group* interests in *specific* issues

Individual pursuit of self-interests

FIGURE 13–2
Levels of Political Action in Organizations

People with a common interest can become a political coalition by fitting the following definition. In an organizational context, a **coalition** is an informal group bound together by the *active* pursuit of a *single* issue. Coalitions may or may not coincide with formal group membership. When the target issue is resolved (a sexually harassing supervisor is fired, for example), the coalition disbands. Experts note that political coalitions have "fuzzy boundaries," meaning they are fluid in membership, flexible in structure, and temporary in duration.[50]

coalition

Temporary groupings of people who actively pursue a single issue.

Coalitions are a potent political force in organizations. During the 1990s, coalitions on the corporate boards of American Express, IBM, and General Motors ousted the heads of those giant companies.

A third level of political action involves networks.[51] Unlike coalitions, which pivot on specific issues, networks are loose associations of individuals seeking social support for their general self-interests. Politically, networks are people oriented, while coalitions are issue oriented. Networks have broader and longer term agendas than do coalitions. For instance, Avon's Hispanic and Latino employees have built a network to enhance the members' career opportunities.

Eight Political Tactics   Anyone who has worked in an organization has first-hand knowledge of blatant politicking. Blaming someone else for your mistake is an obvious political ploy. So are these self-serving games, as reported in *The Wall Street Journal:*

> A former Wall Street analyst, a veteran of several investment banks who knows the value of that most ludicrous of achievements—performing "better than expected"—advises us to list easy goals and just make them sound hard. That way next year you can say you "achieved 100% of goals" last year.
>
> All year long, she would collect kudos as ammo, dumping them into folders she named "Success" and "Yay." The latter was for praise from colleagues. "Getting messages from my boss's boss—or anyone else he respected and was also slightly intimidated by—was even better," she confides.
>
> Brownie points, we all know, come from personally saving a few pennies. "Point out in the review—not in writing!—that the rest of the team stayed at the Four Seasons and flew American," the analyst says. Then, wipe your fingerprints from the knives you stuck in everyone's backs.[52]

But other political tactics are more subtle. Researchers have identified a range of political behavior.

One landmark study, involving in-depth interviews with 87 managers from 30 electronics companies in Southern California, identified eight political tactics. Top-, middle-, and low-level managers were represented about equally in the sample. According to the researchers: "Respondents were asked to describe organizational political tactics and personal characteristics of effective political actors based upon their accumulated experience in *all* organizations in which they had worked."[53] Listed in descending order of occurrence, the eight political tactics that emerged were

1. Attacking or blaming others.
2. Using information as a political tool.
3. Creating a favorable image. (Also known as *impression management.*)[54]
4. Developing a base of support.
5. Praising others (ingratiation).
6. Forming power coalitions with strong allies.
7. Associating with influential people.
8. Creating obligations (reciprocity).

The researchers distinguished between reactive and proactive political tactics. Some of the tactics, such as scapegoating, were *reactive* because the intent was to *defend* one's self-interest. Other tactics, such as developing a base of support, were *proactive* because they sought to *promote* the individual's self-interest.[55]

Impression Management

impression management

Getting others to see us in a certain manner.

"So, with just a few extra lines and a splash of color, our dismal sales become a lovely mountain scene."

Mark Anderson, Andertoons.com. Reprinted with permission.

Impression management is defined as "the process by which people attempt to control or manipulate the reactions of others to images of themselves or their ideas."[56] This encompasses how one talks, behaves, and looks. Most impression management attempts are directed at making a *good* impression on relevant others. But, as we will see, some employees strive to make a *bad* impression. For purposes of conceptual clarity, we will focus on *upward* impression management (trying to impress one's immediate supervisor) because it is most relevant for managers. Still, it is good to remember that *anyone* can be the intended target of impression management. Parents, teachers, peers, employees, and customers are all fair game when it comes to managing the impressions of others.

Good Impressions If you "dress for success," project an upbeat attitude at all times, and avoid offending others, you are engaging in favorable impression management—particularly so if your motive is to improve your chances of getting what you want in life.[57] There are questionable ways to create a good impression, as well. For instance, Stewart Friedman, director of the University of Pennsylvania's Leadership Program, offered this gem:

Last year, I was doing some work with a large bank. The people there told me a story that astounded me: After 7 PM, people would open the door to their office, drape a spare jacket on the back of their chair, lay a set of glasses down on some reading material on their desk—and then go home for the night. The point of this elaborate gesture was to create the illusion that they were just out grabbing dinner and would be returning to burn the midnight oil.[58]

Impression management often strays into unethical territory.

A statistical factor analysis of the influence attempts reported by a sample of 84 bank employees (including 74 women) identified three categories of favorable upward impression management tactics.[59] Favorable upward impression management tactics can be *job-focused* (manipulating information about one's job performance), *supervisor-focused* (praising and doing favors for one's supervisor), and *self-focused* (presenting oneself as a polite and nice person). A moderate amount of upward impression management is a necessity for the average employee today. Too little, and busy managers are liable to overlook some of your valuable contributions when they make job assignment, pay, and promotion decisions. Too much, and you run the risk of being branded a "schmoozer," a "phony," and other unflattering things by your co-workers.[60] Excessive flattery and ingratiation can backfire by embarrassing the target person and damaging one's credibility. Also, the risk of unintended insult is very high when impression management tactics cross gender, racial, ethnic, and cultural lines.[61] International management experts warn:

Impression management would appear to be a low priority for Jim Buckmaster, CEO of craigslist.org. Buckmaster wears casual dress to work, shares an office with company founder Craig Newmark, and takes public transportation to his rented house. His wife picks him up at the ferry landing.

> The impression management tactic is only as effective as its correlation to accepted norms about behavioral presentation. In other words, slapping a Japanese subordinate on the back with a rousing "Good work, Hiro!" will not create the desired impression in Hiro's mind that the expatriate intended. In fact, the behavior will likely create the opposite impression.[62]

Bad Impressions   At first glance, the idea of consciously trying to make a bad impression in the workplace seems absurd.[63] But an interesting new line of impression management research has uncovered both motives and tactics for making oneself look *bad*. In a survey of the work experiences of business students at a large northwestern US university, more than half "reported witnessing a case of someone intentionally looking bad at work."[64] Why? Four motives came out of the study:

(1) *Avoidance:* Employee seeks to avoid additional work, stress, burnout, or an unwanted transfer or promotion. (2) *Obtain concrete rewards:* Employee seeks to obtain a pay raise or a desired transfer, promotion, or demotion. (3) *Exit:* Employee seeks to get laid off, fired, or suspended, and perhaps also to collect unemployment or workers' compensation. (4) *Power:* Employee seeks to control, manipulate, or intimidate others, get revenge, or make someone else look bad.[65]

Within the context of these motives, *unfavorable* upward impression management makes sense.

Five unfavorable upward impression management tactics identified by the researchers are as follows:

- *Decreasing performance*—restricting productivity, making more mistakes than usual, lowering quality, neglecting tasks.

- *Not working to potential*—pretending ignorance, having unused capabilities.
- *Withdrawing*—being tardy, taking excessive breaks, faking illness.
- *Displaying a bad attitude*—complaining, getting upset and angry, acting strangely, not getting along with co-workers.
- *Broadcasting limitations*—letting co-workers know about one's physical problems and mistakes (both verbally and nonverbally).[66]

Recommended ways to manage employees who try to make a bad impression can be found throughout this book. They include more challenging work, greater autonomy, better feedback, supportive leadership, clear and reasonable goals, and a less stressful work setting.[67]

Keeping Organizational Politics in Check

Organizational politics cannot be eliminated. A manager would be naive to expect such an outcome. But political maneuvering can and should be managed to keep it constructive and within reasonable bounds. Harvard's Abraham Zaleznik put the issue this way: "People can focus their attention on only so many things. The more it lands on politics, the less energy—emotional and intellectual—is available to attend to the problems that fall under the heading of real work."[68]

An individual's degree of politicalness is a matter of personal values, ethics, and temperament. People who are either strictly nonpolitical or highly political generally pay a price for their behavior. The former may experience slow promotions and feel left out, while the latter may run the risk of being called self-serving and lose their credibility. People at both ends of the political spectrum may be considered poor team players. A moderate amount of prudent political behavior generally is considered a survival tool in complex organizations. Experts remind us that

> political behavior has earned a bad name only because of its association with politicians. On its own, the use of power and other resources to obtain your objectives is not inherently unethical. It all depends on what the preferred objectives are.[69]

With this perspective in mind, the practical steps in Skills & Best Practices are recommended. Notice the importance of reducing uncertainty through clear performance–reward linkages. Measurable objectives are management's first line of defense against negative expressions of organizational politics. General Electric, number one on *Fortune* magazine's 2006 list of Most Admired Companies, studiously cultivates a no-nonsense culture where political maneuvering and impression management are discouraged. Kevin Sharer, the CEO of bio-tech giant Amgen, who was a GE executive, explains:

> It has . . . set a standard in candor—that is, dealing with reality and rigor in communicating around the company. Everybody has a real chance to know exactly where they are. There is no puffery. That is

---

SKILLS & BEST PRACTICES

How to Keep Organizational Politics within Reasonable Bounds

- Screen out overly political individuals at hiring time.
- Create an open-book management system.
- Make sure every employee knows how the business works and has a personal line of sight to key results with corresponding measureable objectives for individual accountability.
- Have nonfinancial people interpret periodic financial and accounting statements for all employees.
- Establish formal conflict resolution and grievance processes.
- As an ethics filter, do only what you would feel comfortable doing on national television.
- Publicly recognize and reward people who get real results without political games.

SOURCE: Adapted in part from discussion in LB MacGregor Server, "The End of Office Politics as Usual" (New York: American Management Association, 2002), pp 184–99.

buttressed by rigorous, fact-based, honest assessment of the business situation. There isn't an ounce of denial in the place.

In addition, there's a real pride in being part of GE—a common sense of purpose. It's well known but still worth noting that the operations and financial promises are not "we'll give it our best shot" kind of promises. They're really sacrosanct. Finally, GE is aggressive. They think big and they take risks.[70]

key terms

coalition 337

coercive power 330

empowerment 333

expert power 332

impression management 338

legitimate power 332

organizational politics 335

referent power 333

reward power 330

social power 330

chapter summary

- *Name five "soft" and four "hard" influence tactics, and summarize Cialdini's principles of influence and persuasion.* Five soft influence tactics are rational persuasion, inspirational appeals, consultation, ingratiation, and personal appeals. They are more friendly and less coercive than the four hard influence tactics: exchange, coalition tactics, pressure, and legitimating tactics. According to research, soft tactics are better for generating commitment and are perceived as more fair than hard tactics. Cialdini's six principles of influence and persuasion are *liking* (favoring friends), *reciprocity* (belief that one good or bad turn deserves to be repaid in kind), *social proof* (following those similar to oneself), *consistency* (following through on personal commitments), *authority* (deferring to credible and respected experts), and *scarcity* (seeking things of limited availability).

- *Identify and briefly describe French and Raven's five bases of power.* French and Raven's five bases of power are reward power (rewarding compliance), coercive power (punishing noncompliance), legitimate power (relying on formal authority), expert power (providing needed information), and referent power (relying on personal attraction).

- *Define the term* empowerment, *and explain how to make it succeed.* Empowerment involves sharing varying degrees of power and decision-making authority with lower-level employees to better serve the customer. According to Randolph's model, empowerment requires active sharing of key information, structure that encourages autonomy, transfer of control from managers to teams, and persistence. Trust and training also are very important.

- *Define organizational politics, explain what triggers it, and specify the three levels of political action in organizations.* Organizational politics is defined as intentional acts of influence to enhance or protect the self-interests of individuals or groups. Uncertainty triggers most politicking in organizations. Political action occurs at individual, coalition, and network levels. Coalitions are informal, temporary, and single-issue alliances.

- *Distinguish between favorable and unfavorable impression management tactics.* Favorable upward impression management can be job-focused (manipulating information about one's job performance), supervisor-focused (praising or doing favors for the boss), or self-focused (being polite and nice). Unfavorable upward impression management tactics include decreasing performance, not working to potential, withdrawing, displaying a bad attitude, and broadcasting one's limitations.

- *Explain how to manage organizational politics.* Although organizational politics cannot be eliminated, managers can keep it within reasonable bounds. Measurable objectives for personal accountability are key. Participative management also helps, especially in the form of open-book management. Formal conflict resolution and grievance programs are helpful. Overly political people should not be hired, and employees who get results without playing political games should be publicly recognized and rewarded. The "how-would-it-look-on-TV" ethics test can limit political maneuvering.

discussion questions

1. Based on the chapter-opening vignette about Xerox, what would likely happen to a highly political executive reporting to Ursula Burns? Explain.
2. Before reading this chapter, did the term *power* have a negative connotation for you? Do you view it differently now? Explain.
3. In your opinion, how much empowerment is too much in today's workplaces?
4. Why do you think organizational politics is triggered primarily by uncertainty?
5. How much impression management do you see in your classroom or workplace today? Citing specific examples, are those tactics effective?

ethical dilemma

The Carrot-and-Stick Approach to Employee Wellness

It was a sight that drove Jeff Bedard crazy nearly every time he pulled up to his office in Johnson City, Tennessee: a half-dozen employees, huddled outside the plant where they manufactured over-the-counter and prescription skincare products—some of them designed to prevent skin cancer—puffing on cigarettes.

The scene invariably got Bedard, CEO of Crown Laboratories, thinking about his health care bill, which had risen 30 percent a year for the past three years. What's the point of insuring people who are determined to kill themselves, he'd wonder. What's more, Crown's motto is "Creating a healthier world through technology." Every time Bedard saw the cloud of cigarette smoke, he wondered whether the company was living up to the motto.

Last fall, Bedard decided he'd had enough, and he rolled out a tough new wellness program designed to force his 61 employees to live healthier lives. Each worker is required to get an annual onsite health assessment. Based on a number of indicators—including blood pressure, weight, physical activity, and cholesterol levels—the individuals are given a "wellness number" of up to 24.

Those who improve their scores by at least three points a year, or maintain a score of 20 or more, will get a $500 bonus and extra days off. Smoking is now officially against Crown policy—even during off-hours—and nicotine levels are measured in the health assessment. Smokers have until January 2007 to kick the habit. If they don't, they'll have to start paying their own health insurance premiums.[71]

What Is Your Position on This Ethically Charged Workplace Power Play?

1. This is a heavy-handed and unethical abuse of managerial power. Explain.
2. While this is an extreme measure, the end justifies the means. Explain the ethics of this choice.
3. Jeff Bedard is a man of integrity who wants his employees to "walk the company's talk." Explain your ethical position.

4. This is an ethical course of action because everyone wins when the company enjoys lower absenteeism, higher productivity, and lower health insurance costs. Explain.

5. Employees with unhealthy habits really want to be healthier, this program just gives them some needed incentives. Explain your ethical rationale.

6. This is an open invitation to lawsuits of various kinds. It is a good idea whose time has *not* come. Explain.

7. Invent other options. Discuss.

For an interpretation of this situation, visit our Web site, www.mhhe.com/kinickiob3e.

If you're looking for additional study materials, be sure to check out the Online Learning Center at

www.mhhe.com/kinickiob3e

for more information and interactivities that correspond to this chapter.

chapter Fourteen

Leadership

A NEW LEADER IS RIGHTING THE SHIP AT CITIGROUP

Assuming the role of chief executive of the world's largest financial institution in October 2003, didn't come easily to Charles O. Prince III. His natural inclination from day one was to hole up in his office and attend to the company's many pressing matters, just as he had done for almost two decades at Citigroup and its predecessor companies. As general counsel to former company like Citigroup needed more than competence and accountability in the corner office; it needed a charismatic leader. He had no choice but to try filling the bill. "I'm not used to operating in the limelight," he concedes," but the difficulty of the moment demanded it. I had to get out front and say, 'we're going in this direction, follow me.'" . . .

Charles Prince, new CEO of Citigroup, is focusing on acquiring new leadership skills to restore public confidence in the bank after a series of regulatory and public relations problems.

CEO Sanford I. "Sandy" Weill, Prince's preference was to blend into the paneled woodwork of his spacious Park Avenue office.

Today, he is a different man. Prince is stepping out of the long shadow of his legendary former boss and pursuing his own strategy. . . .

Prince, now 56, came to recognize that a sprawling

He took over just as regulatory and public-relations troubles brought on by the collapse of Enron and WorldCom were doing maximum damage to the bank.

One year on the job and billions in legal fines later, Prince had met investors' low expectations, focusing mostly on regulatory matters and failing to become

the commander in chief the bank sorely needed. His main objective at the time: "to keep Citigroup out of the headlines." He was failing there as well. Two big scandals erupted during his tenure: the Japanese private banking fiasco and charges of illegal European bond trading. And last summer the Federal Reserve, in a severe and unprecedented rebuke, banned Citi from making any future acquisitions until it got its house in order. It was a smackdown not only of the company's business practices, but also Weill's strategy of growth by acquisitions.

Looking back, Prince says he felt like he was flying with no navigation. He heard himself emphasizing to employees that he was in charge and that a plan was on its way. "I may not have known what it was going to be," he concedes, "but I knew it was coming."

Prince is making great efforts to change his management style. He has deliberately distanced himself from the qualities that landed him the job in the first place. His initial approach to leadership was to dictate rules and regulations; now he's fashioning himself a big thinker. He's working on his image, calling on CEOs like Michael S. Dell and Johnson & Johnson's William C. Weldon for advice. He has cut ties with key Citi veterans, cultivating what he calls a "new generation" of leaders. And he is turning away from the Weill strategy of being all things to all customers....

In the face of such adversity, Prince is getting out from behind his desk. On Dec. 16 at the annual Citigroup Investor Day, he dispensed with the long-held tradition of department heads making individual presentations. Instead, he emceed the two-hour event himself. "Bad behavior is aberrational," he told the audience, and although "never is a big word . . . the chances of [the company] getting into trouble again are virtually nil." Then he enthusiastically punched the air and declared: "I know where Citigroup is going!" Coming from someone else, a line like that might have been met with snickering. But from the understated Prince, it was reassuring, even inspiring.

"Chuck is trying to introduce a change of culture rather than reinforce a long-held one, and that's . . . difficult," says his friend Weldon. "It's one thing to talk, it's another to go out there and make sure it's reinforced and people understand you're serious. That's what [he] has to do." . . .

Prince may not have had a plan, but he wasn't afraid to act. In his first month, he summoned Thomas W. Jones, chairman and CEO of Global Investment Management & Citigroup Asset Management; Deryck Maughan, vice-chairman and CEO of Citigroup International; and Peter K. Scaturro, CEO of Citigroup Private Bank. He wanted to know why the scandals in Japan had happened and why they hadn't yet met regulators' demands for a clean-up. No one would take responsibility. So Prince fired all three on the spot, a move that would have seemed unimaginable even a few months earlier....

Then, on March 1, 2005, operation charisma began. Prince launched his "five-point plan," which included new standards for training, development, compensation, and annual reviews, all designed to inspire and monitor good behavior. Citi created a slick DVD sent to employees and journalists around the globe. Within two months, Prince personally addressed some 45,000 employees in 11 town hall meetings in 10 countries....

Prince says inertia is his biggest obstacle. "I have to be able to inspire people, to motivate people," he says. "That's my job. It cuts against traditional patterns of doing business, it's new, and it feels awkward at first.". . .

Prince says the key requirement of a strong leader is to accept change.[1]

SOMEONE ONCE OBSERVED THAT a leader is a person who finds out which way the parade is going, jumps in front, and yells "Follow me!" The plain fact is that this approach to leadership has little chance of working in today's rapidly changing world. As illustrated in the chapter's opening vignette, leadership involves more than simply taking charge. Charles O. Prince III not only had to deal with ethical scandals, he also needed to focus on a change-resistant culture and a host of strategic and operational issues. In short, successful leaders are those individuals who can step into a difficult situation and make a noticeable difference. But how much of a difference can leaders make in modern organizations?

OB researchers have discovered that leaders can make a difference. One study, for instance, revealed that leadership was positively associated with net profits from 167 companies over a time span of 20 years.[2] Research also showed that a coach's leadership skills affected the success of his or her team. Specifically, teams in both Major League Baseball and college basketball won more games when players perceived the coach to be an effective leader.[3] Rest assured, leadership make a difference!

After formally defining the term *leadership,* this chapter focuses on the following areas: (1) trait and behavioral approaches to leadership, (2) alternative situational theories of leadership, (3) the full-range model of leadership, and (4) additional perspectives on leadership. Because there are many different leadership theories within each of these areas, it is impossible to discuss them all. This chapter reviews those theories with the most research support.

What Does Leadership Involve?

Disagreement about the definition of leadership stems from the fact that it involves a complex interaction among the leader, the followers, and the situation. For example, some researchers define leadership in terms of personality and physical traits, while others believe leadership is represented by a set of prescribed behaviors. In contrast, other researchers believe that leadership is a temporary role that can be filled by anyone. There is a common thread, however, among the different definitions of leadership. The common thread is social influence.

As the term is used in this chapter, **leadership** is defined as "a social influence process in which the leader seeks the voluntary participation of subordinates in an effort to reach organizational goals."[4] This definition implies that leadership involves more than wielding power and exercising authority and is exhibited on different levels. At the individual level, for example, leadership involves mentoring, coaching, inspiring, and motivating. Leaders build teams, create cohesion, and resolve conflict at the group level. Finally, leaders build culture and create change at the organizational level.[5]

> **leadership**
>
> Influencing employees to voluntarily pursue organizational goals.

There are two components of leadership missing from the above definition: the moral and follower perspectives. Leadership is not a moral concept. History is filled with examples of effective leaders who were killers, corrupt, and morally bankrupt. Barbara Kellerman, a leadership expert, commented on this notion by concluding "Leaders are like the rest of us: trustworthy and deceitful, cowardly and brave, greedy and generous. To assume that all good leaders are good people is to be willfully blind to the reality of the human condition, and it more severely limits our scope for becoming more effective at leadership."[6] The point is that good leaders develop a keen sense of their strengths and weaknesses and build on their positive attributes.[7]

Moreover, research on the follower perspective reveals that people seek, admire, and respect leaders who foster three emotional responses in others. Followers want organizational leaders to create feelings of *significance* (what one does at work is important and meaningful), *community* (a sense of unity encourages people to treat others with respect and dignity and to work together in pursuit of organizational goals), and *excitement* (people are engaged and feel energy at work).[8]

Trait and Behavioral Theories of Leadership

This section examines the two earliest approaches used to explain leadership. Trait theories focused on identifying the personal traits that differentiated leaders from followers. Behavioral theorists examined leadership from a different perspective. They tried to uncover the different kinds of leader behaviors that resulted in higher work group performance. Both approaches to leadership can teach current and future managers valuable lessons about leading.

Trait Theory

Trait theory is the successor to what was called the "great man" theory of leadership. This approach was based on the assumption that leaders such as Abraham Lincoln, Martin Luther King, or Jack Welch were born with some inborn ability to lead. In contrast, trait theorists believed that leadership traits were not innate, but could be developed through experience and learning. A **leader trait** is a physical or personality characteristic that can be used to differentiate leaders from followers.

leader trait

Personal characteristic that differentiates leaders from followers.

Before World War II, hundreds of studies were conducted to pinpoint the traits of successful leaders. Dozens of leadership traits were identified. During the postwar period, however, enthusiasm was replaced by widespread criticism. Researchers simply were unable to uncover a consistent set of traits that accurately predicted which individuals became leaders in organizations.

Contemporary Trait Research   Two OB researchers concluded in 1983 that past trait data may have been incorrectly analyzed. By applying modern statistical techniques to an old database, they demonstrated that the majority of a leader's behavior could be attributed to stable underlying traits.[9] Unfortunately, their methodology did not single out specific traits.

More recently, results from three separate meta-analyses shed light on important leadership traits. The first was conducted in 1986 by Robert Lord and his associates. Based on a reanalysis of past studies, Lord concluded that people have leadership *prototypes* that affect our perceptions of who is and who is not an effective leader. Your **leadership prototype** is a mental representation of the traits and behaviors that you believe are possessed by leaders. We thus tend to perceive that someone is a leader when he or she exhibits traits or behaviors that are consistent with our prototypes.[10]

leadership prototype

Mental representation of the traits and behaviors possessed by leaders.

Lord's research demonstrated that people are perceived as being leaders when they exhibit the traits associated with intelligence, masculinity, and dominance. Another study of 6,052 middle-level managers from 22 European countries revealed that leadership prototypes are culturally based. In other words, leadership prototypes are influenced by national cultural values.[11] Researchers have not yet identified a set of global leadership prototypes.

The next two meta-analyses were completed by Timothy Judge and his colleagues. The first examined the relationship among the Big Five personality traits (see Table 5–2 for a review of these traits) and leadership emergence and effectiveness in 94 studies. Results revealed that extraversion was most consistently and positively related to both leadership emergence and effectiveness. Conscientiousness and openness to experience also were positively correlated with leadership effectiveness.[12] Judge's second meta-analysis involved 151 samples and demonstrated that intelligence was modestly related to leadership effectiveness. Judge concluded that personality is more important than intelligence when selecting leaders.[13]

This conclusion is supported by research that examined emotional and political intelligence. Recall that *emotional intelligence,* which was discussed in Chapter 5, is the ability to manage oneself and one's relationships in mature and constructive ways. Given that leadership is an influence process, it should come as no surprise that emotional intelligence is associated with leadership effectiveness.[14] Political intelligence is a recently proposed leadership trait and represents an offshoot of emotional intelligence. Politically intelligent leaders use power and intimidation to push followers in the pursuit of an inspiring vision and challenging goals. Although these leaders can be insensitive, hard to work with, and demanding, they tend to be effective when faced with stagnant and change-resistant situations.[15] Martha Stewart and Michael Eisner are two such examples. Consider how colleagues described these leaders.

Bishop Katharine Jefferts Schori was recently appointed the first woman bishop in the American Episcopal Church. Among the personal traits that contribute to her leadership ability are her appetite for challenge and risk-taking—she holds a pilot's license, is a skilled mountaineer, and entered the Episcopal priesthood at 40 after a successful career in oceanography. She is also fluent in Spanish. Another trait, her sex, may prove controversial for some, but Jefferts Shori views it as a means "to build a holy community."

> She [Stewart] had the most amazing, well-organized and disciplined mind I've ever known. She grasped things instantly, and she had the ability to direct your attention to the single most important thing you should be thinking about or doing at that particular moment. She could be incredibly impatient and brusque if you were slow on the uptake—but if you could keep up with her, and perform to her standard, it was tremendously satisfying.
>
> What is lost in the stories about Mr. Eisner's arrogance, greed, and insensitivity is the more illuminating tale of how he transformed a faltering animation and amusement park company into one of the world's most successful entertainment companies. When he assumed command in 1984, Disney had a market value of $1.8 billion. Today its market value is $57.1 billion.[16]

Farcus

by David Waisglass
Gordon Coulthart

© 1992 Farcus Cartoons   WAISGLASS/COULTHART

www.farcus.com

"Because I'm the boss, that's why!"

Politically intelligent leaders seem to walk a fine line between using intimidation to achieve organizational goals and humiliation and bullying to make themselves feel good. Future research is needed to examine the long-term effectiveness of leaders with political intelligence.

Gender and Leadership   The increase of women in the workforce has generated much interest in understanding the similarities and differences in female and male leaders. Three separate meta-analyses and a series of studies conducted by consultants across the country uncovered the following differences: (1) Men and women were seen as displaying more task and social leadership, respectively;[17] (2) women used a more democratic or participative style than men, and men used a more autocratic and directive style than women;[18] (3) men and women were equally assertive;[19] and (4) women executives, when rated by their peers, managers, and direct reports, scored higher than their male counterparts on a variety of effectiveness criteria.[20]

Group Exercise

What Is Your Motivation to Lead?

Self-Assessment Exercise

Do You Have What It Takes to Be a Leader?

What Are the Takeaways from Trait Theory?   We can no longer afford to ignore the implications of leadership traits. Traits play a central role in how we perceive leaders, and they ultimately impact leadership effectiveness. What can be learned from the previous research on traits? Integrating across past studies leads to the extended list of positive traits shown in Table 14–1. This list, provides guidance regarding the leadership traits you should attempt to cultivate if you want to assume a leadership role. Personality tests, which were discussed in Chapter 5, and other trait assessments can be used to evaluate your strengths and weaknesses vis-à-vis these traits. Results can then be used to prepare a personal development plan.[21]

There are two organizational applications of trait theory. First, organizations may want to include personality and trait assessments into their selection and promotion processes. It is important to remember that this should only be done with valid measures of leadership traits. Second, management development programs can be used to enhance employees' leadership traits. Hasbro, Inc., for example, sent a targeted group of managers

TABLE 14–1   Key Positive Leadership Traits

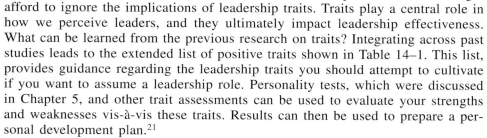

Positive Traits	
Intelligence	Sociability
Self-confidence	Emotional intelligence
Determination	Extraversion
Honesty/integrity	Conscientiousness

to a program that included a combination of 360-degree feedback, trait assessments, executive coaching, classroom training, and problem-solving assignments on real-life projects. Hasbro is very excited and pleased with the results of their leadership development program.[22]

Behavioral Styles Theory

This phase of leadership research began during World War II as part of an effort to develop better military leaders. It was an outgrowth of two events: the seeming inability of trait theory to explain leadership effectiveness and the human relations movement, an outgrowth of the Hawthorne Studies. The thrust of early behavioral leadership theory was to focus on leader behavior, instead of on personality traits. It was believed that leader behavior directly affected work group effectiveness. This led researchers to identify patterns of behavior (called leadership styles) that enabled leaders to effectively influence others.

The Ohio State Studies   Researchers at Ohio State University began by generating a list of behaviors exhibited by leaders. Ultimately, the Ohio State researchers concluded there were only two independent dimensions of leader behavior: consideration and initiating structure. **Consideration** involves leader behavior associated with creating mutual respect or trust and focuses on a concern for group members' needs and desires. **Initiating structure** is leader behavior that organizes and defines what group members should be doing to maximize output. These two dimensions of leader behavior were oriented at right angles to yield four behavioral styles of leadership: low structure–high consideration, high structure–high consideration, low structure–low consideration, and high structure–low consideration.

consideration
Creating mutual respect and trust with followers.

initiating structure
Organizing and defining what group members should be doing.

It initially was hypothesized that a high-structure–high-consideration style would be the one best style of leadership. Through the years, the effectiveness of the high–high style has been tested many times. Overall, results have been mixed and there has been very little research about these leader behaviors until just recently. Findings from a 2004 meta-analysis of 130 studies and more than 20,000 individuals demonstrated that consideration and initiating structure had a moderately strong, significant relationship with leadership outcomes. Results revealed that followers performed more effectively for structuring leaders even though they preferred considerate leaders.[23] All told, results do not support the idea that there is one best style of leadership, but they do confirm the importance of considerate and structuring leader behaviors. Follower satisfaction, motivation, and performance are significantly associated with these two leader behaviors. Future research is needed to incorporate them into more contemporary leadership theories.

University of Michigan Studies   As in the Ohio State studies, this research sought to identify behavioral differences between effective and ineffective leaders. Researchers identified two different styles of leadership: one was employee centered, the other was job centered. These behavioral styles parallel the consideration and initiating-structure styles identified by the Ohio State group.

What Are the Takeaways from Behavioral Styles Theory?   By emphasizing leader *behavior,* something that is learned, the behavioral style approach makes it clear that leaders are made, not born. Given what we know about

Peter Drucker's Tips for Improving Leadership Effectiveness

1. Determine what needs to be done.

2. Determine the right thing to do for the welfare of the entire enterprise or organization.

3. Develop action plans that specify desired results, probable restraints, future revisions, check-in points, and implications for how one should spend his or her time.

4. Take responsibility for decisions.

5. Take responsibility for communicating action plans and give people the information they need to get the job done.

6. Focus on opportunities rather than problems. Do not sweep problems under the rug, and treat change as an opportunity rather than a threat.

7. Run productive meetings. Different types of meetings require different forms of preparation and different results. Prepare accordingly.

8. Think and say "we" rather than "I." Consider the needs and opportunities of the organization before thinking of your own opportunities and needs.

9. Listen first, speak last.

SOURCE: Reprinted by permission of *Harvard Business Review*. These recommendations were derived from P F Drucker, "What Makes an Effective Executive," *Harvard Business Review*, June 2004, pp 58–63. Copyright © 2004 by the Harvard Business School Publishing Corporation; all rights reserved.

situational theories

Propose that leader styles should match the situation at hand.

behavior shaping and model-based training, leader *behaviors* can be systematically improved and developed.[24]

Behavioral styles research also revealed that there is no one best style of leadership. The effectiveness of a particular leadership style depends on the situation at hand. For instance, employees prefer structure over consideration when faced with role ambiguity.[25] Finally, research also reveals that it is important to consider the difference between how frequently and how effectively managers exhibit various leader behaviors. For example, a manager might ineffectively display a lot of considerate leader behaviors. Such a style is likely to frustrate employees and possibly result in lowered job satisfaction and performance. Because the frequency of exhibiting leadership behaviors is secondary in importance to effectiveness, managers are encouraged to concentrate on improving the effective execution of their leader behaviors.[26] Finally, Peter Drucker, an internationally renowned management expert and consultant, recommended a set of nine behaviors (see Skills & Best Practices) managers can focus on to improve their leadership effectiveness. The first two practices provide the knowledge leaders need. The next four help leaders convert knowledge into effective action, and the following two ensure that the whole organization feels responsible and accountable. Drucker refers to the last recommendation as a managerial rule.

Situational Theories

Situational leadership theories grew out of an attempt to explain the inconsistent findings about traits and styles. **Situational theories** propose that the effectiveness of a particular style of leader behavior depends on the situation. As situations change, different styles become appropriate. This directly challenges the idea of one best style of leadership. Let us closely examine three alternative situational theories of leadership that reject the notion of one best leadership style.

Fiedler's Contingency Model

Fred Fiedler, an OB scholar, developed a situational model of leadership. It is the oldest and one of the most widely known models of leadership. Fiedler's model is based on the following assumption:

> The performance of a leader depends on two interrelated factors: (1) the degree to which the situation gives the leader control and influence—that is, the likelihood that [the leader] can successfully accomplish the job; and (2) the leader's basic

motivation—that is, whether [the leader's] self-esteem depends primarily on accomplishing the task or on having close supportive relations with others.[27]

With respect to a leader's basic motivation, Fiedler believes that leaders are either task motivated or relationship motivated. These basic motivations are similar to initiating structure/concern for production and consideration/concern for people.

Fiedler's theory also is based on the premise that leaders have one dominant leadership style that is resistant to change. He suggests that leaders must learn to manipulate or influence the leadership situation in order to create a "match" between their leadership style and the amount of control within the situation at hand. After discussing the components of situational control and the leadership matching process, we review relevant research and managerial implications.[28]

Situational Control   Situational control refers to the amount of control and influence the leader has in her or his immediate work environment. Situational control ranges from high to low. High control implies that the leader's decisions will produce predictable results because the leader has the ability to influence work outcomes. Low control implies that the leader's decisions may not influence work outcomes because the leader has very little influence. There are three dimensions of situational control: leader–member relations, task structure, and position power. These dimensions vary independently, forming eight combinations of situational control (see Figure 14–1).

The three dimensions of situational control are defined as follows:

- *Leader–member relations* reflect the extent to which the leader has the support, loyalty, and trust of the work group.

Representation of Fiedler's Contingency Model   FIGURE 14–1

Situational Control	High Control Situations			Moderate Control Situations				Low Control Situations
Leader–member relations	Good	Good	Good	Good	Poor	Poor	Poor	Poor
Task structure	High	High	Low	Low	High	High	Low	Low
Position power	Strong	Weak	Strong	Weak	Strong	Weak	Strong	Weak
Situation	I	II	III	IV	V	VI	VII	VIII

Optimal Leadership Style	Task-Motivated Leadership	Relationship-Motivated Leadership	Task-Motivated Leadership

SOURCE: Adapted from F E Fiedler, "Situational Control and a Dynamic Theory of Leadership," in *Managerial Control and Organizational Democracy*, eds B King, S Streufert, and F E Fiedler (New York: John Wiley & Sons, 1978), p 114.

- *Task structure* is concerned with the amount of structure contained within tasks performed by the work group.
- *Position power* refers to the degree to which the leader has formal power to reward, punish, or otherwise obtain compliance from employees.

Linking Leadership Motivation and Situational Control   Fiedler's complete contingency model is presented in Figure 14–1. The last row under the Situational Control column shows that there are eight different leadership situations. Each situation represents a unique combination of leader–member relations, task structure, and position power. Situations I, II, and III represent high control situations. Figure 14–1 shows that task-motivated leaders are hypothesized to be most effective in situations of high control. Under conditions of moderate control (situations IV, V, VI, and VII), relationship-motivated leaders are expected to be more effective. Finally, the results orientation of task-motivated leaders is predicted to be more effective under the condition of very low control (situation VIII).

Research and Managerial Implications   Research has provided mixed support for Fiedler's model, suggesting that the model needs theoretical refinement.[29] That said, the major contribution of Fiedler's model is that it prompted others to examine the contingency nature of leadership. This research, in turn, reinforced the notion that there is no one best style of leadership. Leaders are advised to alter their task and relationship orientation to fit the demands of the situation at hand. Consider, for example, the different leadership styles of IBM's current CEO—Sam Palmisano—and former CEO—Lou Gerstner:

> His aw-schucks nature, coupled with Palmisano's ability to chat up just about anyone he meets, makes him approachable for customers and employees. . . . He's constantly on the phone, calling all over the world: "How's your quarter?" "Did we close this deal?" . . . Software chief Steve Mills calls Palmisano an "execution maniac." . . . This single-mindedness about results is a big reason Palmisano was selected by Gerstner to take over IBM two years ago. Says Merrill Lynch security analyst . . . Steve Milunovich: "Sam is the right guy to run IBM right now. He's great externally and a hard-charging Marine internally."
>
> Palmisano's style is a big departure from that of the gruff and intimidating Gerstner. But then Gerstner's role wasn't to be nice; it was to keep IBM from disintegrating. He took over just as it was about to split itself up into 13 distinct, loosely affiliated entities.[30]

Test Your Knowledge
Fiedler's Contingency Model of Leadership

Sam Palmisano and Lou Gerstner used different leadership styles to successfully lead employees within IBM. As suggested by Fiedler, they both were effective because their respective leadership styles were appropriate for the situation at the time.

Path–Goal Theory

Path–goal theory was originally proposed by Robert House in the 1970s.[31] He developed a model that describes how leadership effectiveness is influenced by the interaction between four leadership styles (directive, supportive, participative, and achievement-oriented) and a variety of contingency factors. **Contingency factors** are situational variables that cause one style of leadership to be more effective than another. Path–goal theory has two groups of contingency variables. They are employee characteristics and environmental factors. Five important employee characteristics are locus of control, task

contingency factors

Variables that influence the appropriateness of a leadership style.

ability, need for achievement, experience, and need for clarity. Two relevant environmental factors are task structure (independent versus interdependent tasks) and work group dynamics. In order to gain a better understanding of how these contingency factors influence leadership effectiveness, we illustratively consider locus of control (see Chapter 5), task ability and experience, and task structure.

Employees with an internal locus of control are more likely to prefer participative or achievement-oriented leadership because they believe they have control over the work environment. Such individuals are unlikely to be satisfied with directive leader behaviors that exert additional control over their activities. In contrast, employees with an external locus tend to view the environment as uncontrollable, thereby preferring the structure provided by supportive or directive leadership. An employee with high task ability and experience is less apt to need additional direction and thus would respond negatively to directive leadership. This person is more likely to be motivated and satisfied by participative and achievement-oriented leadership. Oppositely, an inexperienced employee would find achievement-oriented leadership overwhelming as he or she confronts challenges associated with learning a new job. Supportive and directive leadership would be helpful in this situation. Finally, directive and supportive leadership should help employees experiencing role ambiguity. However, directive leadership is likely to frustrate employees working on routine and simple tasks. Supportive leadership is most useful in this context.

There have been about 50 studies testing various predictions derived from House's original model. Results have been mixed, with some studies supporting the theory and others not.[32] House thus proposed a new version of path–goal theory in 1996 based on these results and the accumulation of new knowledge about OB.

A Reformulated Theory   The revised theory is presented in Figure 14–2.[33] There are three key changes in the new theory. First, House now believes that leadership is more complex and involves a greater variety of leader behavior. He thus

A General Representation of House's Revised Path–Goal Theory   FIGURE 14–2

Leader behaviors
- Path–goal clarifying
- Achievement oriented
- Work facilitation
- Supportive
- Interaction facilitation
- Group-oriented decision making
- Representation and networking
- Value based

Employee characteristics
- Locus of control
- Task ability
- Need for achievement
- Experience
- Need for clarity

Environmental factors
- Task structure
- Work group dynamics

Leadership effectiveness
- Employee motivation
- Employee satisfaction
- Employee performance
- Leader acceptance
- Work-unit performance

The leadership style of Jamie Dimon, CEO of J P Morgan Chase, wins admiration from some but can include aggression and rudeness.

identifies eight categories of leadership styles or behavior (see Table 14–2). The need for an expanded list of leader behaviors is supported by current research and descriptions of business leaders.[34] Consider the different leader behaviors exhibited by Jamie Dimon, CEO of J P Morgan Chase.

> Jamie Dimon is not known for his subtlety. . . . He will lash out in meetings with trusted confidants— "That's the dumbest thing I've ever heard"—and expect them to come right back at him. . . . A huge operation "can get arrogant and full of hubris and lose focus, like the Roman Empire," says Dimon. To prevent J.P. Morgan from falling into that trap, he has imposed rigorous pay-for-performance metrics and requires managers to present exhaustive monthly reviews, then grills them on the data for hours at a time. "He jumps into the decision-making process," says Steve Black, co-head of investment banking. . . . While Dimon's rudeness can be offputting, the sheer force of his passion and intensity can be irresistible. . . . He yanked Bank One's sponsorship of the Masters golf tournament because the country club hosting the event doesn't accept women members.[35]

Jamie Dimon exhibits path–goal clarifying behaviors, achievement-oriented behaviors, group-oriented decision-making behaviors, and value-based behaviors. He also seems to rely on intimidation to get people to do what he wants.

The second key change involves the role of intrinsic motivation (discussed in Chapter 6) and empowerment (discussed in Chapter 13) in influencing leadership effectiveness. House places much more emphasis on the need for leaders to foster intrinsic motivation through empowerment. Shared leadership represents the final change in the revised theory. That is, path–goal theory is based on the premise that an employee does not have to be a supervisor or manager to engage in leader behavior. Rather, House believes that leadership is shared among all employees within an organization. More is said about shared leadership in the final section of this chapter.

Research and Managerial Implications   There are not enough direct tests of House's revised path–goal theory using appropriate research methods and statistical procedures to draw overall conclusions. Future research is clearly needed to assess the accuracy of this model. That said, there still are two important managerial implications. First, effective leaders possess and use more than one style of leadership. Managers are encouraged to familiarize themselves with the different categories of leader behavior outlined in path–goal theory and to try new behaviors when the situation calls for them. Second, a small set of employee characteristics (i.e., ability, experience, and need for independence) and environmental factors (task characteristics of autonomy, variety, and significance) are relevant contingency factors.[36] Managers are advised to modify their leadership style to fit these various employee and task characteristics.

Test Your Knowledge

Path–Goal Theory

Categories of Leader Behavior within the Revised **TABLE 14-2**
Path–Goal Theory

Category of Leader Behavior	Description of Leader Behaviors
Path–goal clarifying behaviors	Clarifying employees' performance goals; providing guidance on how employees can complete tasks; clarifying performance standards and expectations; use of positive and negative rewards contingent on performance
Achievement-oriented behaviors	Setting challenging goals; emphasizing excellence; demonstrating confidence in employees' abilities
Work facilitation behaviors	Planning, scheduling, organizing, and coordinating work; providing mentoring, coaching, counseling, and feedback to assist employees in developing their skills; eliminating roadblocks; providing resources; empowering employees to take actions and make decisions
Supportive behaviors	Showing concern for the well-being and needs of employees; being friendly and approachable; treating employees as equals
Interaction facilitation behaviors	Resolving disputes; facilitating communication; encouraging the sharing of minority opinions; emphasizing collaboration and teamwork; encouraging close relationships among employees
Group-oriented decision-making behaviors	Posing problems rather than solutions to the work group; encouraging group members to participate in decision making; providing necessary information to the group for analysis; involving knowledgeable employees in decision making
Representation and networking behaviors	Presenting the work group in a positive light to others; maintaining positive relationships with influential others; participating in organizationwide social functions and ceremonies; doing unconditional favors for others
Value-based behaviors	Establishing a vision, displaying passion for it, and supporting its accomplishment; demonstrating self-confidence; communicating high performance expectations and confidence in others' abilities to meet their goals; giving frequent positive feedback

SOURCE: Descriptions were adapted from R J House, "Path–Goal Theory of Leadership: Lessons, Legacy, and a Reformulated Theory," *Leadership Quarterly*, 1996, pp 323–52.

Hersey and Blanchard's Situational Leadership Theory

Situational leadership theory (SLT) was developed by management writers Paul Hersey and Kenneth Blanchard.[37] According to the theory, effective leader behavior depends on the readiness level of a leader's followers. **Readiness** is defined as the extent to which a follower possesses the ability and willingness to complete a task. Willingness is a combination of confidence, commitment, and motivation.

readiness

Follower's ability and willingness to complete a task.

The SLT model is summarized in Figure 14–3. The appropriate leadership style is found by cross-referencing follower readiness, which varies from low to high, with one of four leadership styles. The four leadership styles represent combinations of task and relationship-oriented leader behaviors (S_1 to S_4). Leaders

FIGURE 14–3   Situational Leadership Model

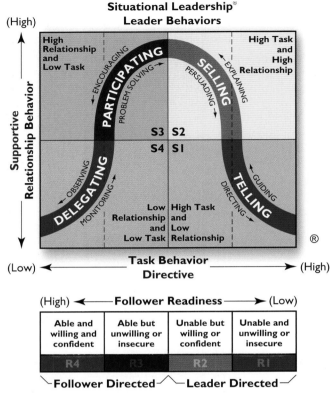

SOURCE: Paul Hersey, *The Management of Organizational Behavior: Utilizing Human Resources,* Center for Leadership Studies, Escondido, CA, 1984. Reprinted with permission. Situational Leadership® is a registered trademark of the Center for Leadership Studies, Inc. Copyright © 2002, Center for Leadership Studies, Inc. All Rights Reserved.

are encouraged to use a "telling style" for followers with low readiness. This style combines high task-oriented leader behaviors, such as providing instructions, with low relationship-oriented behaviors, such as close supervision (see Figure 14–3). As follower readiness increases, leaders are advised to gradually move from a telling, to a selling, to a participating, and, ultimately, to a delegating style.[38]

Although SLT is widely used as a training tool, it is not strongly supported by scientific research. Finally, researchers have concluded that the self-assessment instrument used to measure leadership style and follower readiness is inaccurate and should be used with caution.[39] In summary, managers should exercise discretion when using prescriptions from SLT.

The Full-Range Model of Leadership: From Laissez-Faire to Transformational Leadership

One of the most recent approaches to leadership is referred to as a full-range model of leadership.[40] The authors of this theory, Bernard Bass and Bruce Avolio, proposed that leadership behavior varied along a continuum from laissez-faire leadership (i.e., a general failure to take responsibility for leading) to transactional leadership to transformational leadership. Of course, laissez-faire leadership is a terrible way for any manager to behave and should be avoided. In contrast, transactional and transformational leadership are both positively related to a variety of employee attitudes and behaviors and represent different aspects of being a good leader. Let us consider these two important dimensions of leadership.

Transactional leadership focuses on clarifying employees' role and task requirements and providing followers with positive and negative rewards contingent on performance. Further, transactional leadership encompasses the fundamental managerial activities of setting goals, monitoring progress toward goal achievement, and rewarding and punishing people for their level of goal accomplishment.[41] You can see from this description that transactional leadership is based on using extrinsic motivation (recall our discussion in Chapter 6) to increase employee productivity. Consider how Miller Brewing's CEO, Norman Adami, uses transactional leadership to improve organizational performance.

> **transactional leadership**
>
> Focuses on clarifying employees' roles and providing rewards contingent on performance.

> Adami has made staff far more accountable with a performance system imported from SAB that rewards people for stepping up their game. (South African Breweries [SAB] is Miller's parent company.) The old system didn't challenge employees, says Adami, who once referred to the company as the "Socialist Republic of Miller." For example, in 2002, a year the business was in free-fall, 60% of managers got a four or five rating, the highest possible. Last year [2005] 50% of employees got three on a six-point scale, meaning they met their goals.[42]

In contrast, **transformational leaders** "engender trust, seek to develop leadership in others, exhibit self-sacrifice and serve as moral agents, focusing themselves and followers on objectives that transcend the more immediate needs of the work group."[43] Transformational leaders can produce significant organizational change and results because this form of leadership fosters higher levels of intrinsic motivation, trust, commitment, and loyalty from followers than does transactional leadership. That said, however, it is important to note that transactional leadership is an essential prerequisite to effective leadership, and that the best leaders learn to display both transactional and transformational leadership to various degrees. In support of this proposition, research reveals that transformational leadership leads to superior performance when it "augments" or adds to transactional leadership.[44] Let us return to the example of Norman Adami, CEO of Miller Brewing, to see how he augmented transactional leadership with transformational leadership shortly after taking over as CEO.

> **transformational leadership**
>
> Transforms employees to pursue organizational goals over self-interests.

> Amid declining sales, management upheaval, and an uncertain outlook, Adami got plenty of criticism from staffers when he decided to turn some half-empty offices and storerooms into a bar for Miller's 900 headquarters employees in one of his first moves as CEO in 2003. But Adami considered opening Fred's Pub, named after company founder Frederick J. Miller, an essential step in overhauling a moribund culture. He envisioned the pub as a place where the chief marketing officer could chat with an hourly worker in bottling, or a brand manager could have a casual team meeting. . . . His charm offensive, which includes touches like having flowers sent to his male executives' wives on birthdays, is paired with a demanding, no-BS management style. . . . Adami has instilled his sense of urgency into Miller. He'll often pick up the phone in a meeting to get the latest statistic. And after seeing an AB [Anheuser-Busch] commercial, he hustled to get a response ad launched within a week.[45]

Jason Calcanis (seated to the right of the Netscape logo) is leading the transformation of AOL's Netscape.com Web site into a source for links to news articles contributed by users and amplified by bloggers. He sees himself as a renegade inside AOL, building a new Netscape operation from the ground up. As a result, "We have a smaller, quicker, lighter organization inside a bigger organization," he says.

Adami's leadership has helped turn around Miller Brewing Company. Miller's stock has climbed 190% since Adami became CEO. We now turn our attention to examining the process by which transformational leadership influences followers.

How Does Transformational Leadership Transform Followers?

Transformational leaders transform followers by creating changes in their goals, values, needs, beliefs, and aspirations. They accomplish this transformation by appealing to followers' self-concepts—namely their values and personal identity. Figure 14–4 presents a model of how leaders accomplish this transformation process.

Figure 14–4 shows that transformational leader behavior is first influenced by various individual and organizational characteristics. For example, research reveals that transformational leaders tend to have personalities that are more extraverted, agreeable, and proactive than nontransformational leaders, and female leaders use transformational leadership more than male leaders.[46] Organizational culture also influences the extent to which leaders are transformational. Cultures that are adaptive and flexible rather than rigid

FIGURE 14–4   A Transformational Model of Leadership

Individual and organizational characteristics	Leader behaviors	Effects on followers and work groups	Outcomes
• Traits • Organizational culture	• Inspirational motivation	• Increased intrinsic motivation, achievement orientation, and goal pursuit	• Personal commitment to leader and vision
	• Idealized influence	• Increased identification and trust with the leader	• Self-sacrificial behavior
	• Individualized consideration	• Increased identification and cohesion with work group members	• Organizational commitment
	• Intellectual stimulation	• Increased self-esteem, self-efficacy, and intrinsic interests in goal accomplishment	• Task meaningfulness and satisfaction
		• Increased role modeling of transformational leadership	• Increased individual, group, and organizational performance

SOURCE: Based in part on D A Waldman and F J Yammarino, "CEO Charismatic Leadership: Levels-of-Management and Levels-of-Analysis Effects," *Academy of Management Review*, April 1999, pp 266–85; and B Shamir, R J House, and M B Arthur, "The Motivational Effects of Charismatic Leadership: A Self-Concept Based Theory," *Organization Science*, November 1993, pp 577–94.

and bureaucratic are more likely to create environments that foster the opportunity for transformational leadership to be exhibited.

Transformational leaders engage in four key sets of leader behavior (see Figure 14–4).[47] The first set, referred to as *inspirational motivation,* involves establishing an attractive vision of the future, the use of emotional arguments, and exhibition of optimism and enthusiasm. A vision is "a realistic, credible, attractive future for your organization."[48] According to Burt Nanus, a leadership expert, the "right" vision unleashes human potential because it serves as a beacon of hope and common purpose. It does this by attracting commitment, energizing workers, creating meaning in employees' lives, establishing a standard of excellence, promoting high ideals, and bridging the gap between an organization's present problems and its future goals and aspirations. Anne Mulcahy, Xerox's CEO, understands the importance of using a vision to energize the workforce. She used a vision, which was created by asking a group of her top management team to write a story about how various constituents would describe the company in five years, to gain employees' commitment to needed and difficult organizational change. This process resulted in increased buy-in and support of a host of organizational changes that brought the company back from near bankruptcy.[49]

Idealized influence, the second set of leader behaviors, includes behaviors such as sacrificing for the good of the group, being a role model, and displaying high ethical standards. Through their actions, transformational leaders model the desired values, traits, beliefs, and behaviors needed to realize the vision. The third set, *individualized consideration,* entails behaviors associated with providing support, encouragement, empowerment, and coaching to employees. *Intellectual stimulation,* the fourth set of leadership behaviors, involves behaviors that encourage employees to question the status quo and to seek innovative and creative solutions to organizational problems.

Research and Managerial Implications

Components of the transformational model of leadership have been the most widely researched leadership topic over the last decade. Overall, the relationships outlined in Figure 14–4 generally were supported by previous research. For example, transformational leader behaviors were positively associated with the extent to which employees identified with both their leaders and immediate work groups.[50] Followers of transformational leaders also were found to set goals that were consistent with those of the leader, to be more engaged in their work, to have higher levels of intrinsic motivation, and to have higher levels of group cohesion.[51] With respect to the direct relationship between transformational leadership and work outcomes, a meta-analysis of 49 studies indicated that transformational leadership was positively associated with measures of leadership effectiveness and employees' job satisfaction.[52] At the organizational level, a second meta-analysis demonstrated that transformational leadership was positively correlated with organizational measures of effectiveness.[53]

These results underscore four important managerial implications. First, the best leaders are not just transformational; they are both transactional and transformational. Leaders should attempt to use these two types of leadership while avoiding a "laissez-faire" or "wait-and-see" style.

Second, transformational leadership not only affects individual-level outcomes like job satisfaction, organizational commitment, and performance, but it also

Recommendations for Creating World-Class Leadership Development Programs

1. Develop and automate a formal leadership succession plan.

2. Identify the leadership competencies needed to help the organization achieve its vision and strategic goals.

3. Rollout leadership development programs that fill gaps between current and desired leadership competencies.

4. Hold leaders accountable for developing their direct reports.

5. Hold individuals accountable for establishing and achieving personal leadership development goals.

6. Involve current managers in teaching leadership development programs.

SOURCE: Derived from material presented in J Kornik, "Jack Welch: A Legacy of Leadership," *Training*, May 2006, pp 20–24; D Robb, "Succeeding with Succession," *HR Magazine*, January 2006, pp 89–94; and Pomeroy, "Developing Leaders Is Key to Success," *HR Magazine*, June 2005, pp 20, 24.

influences group dynamics and group-level outcomes. Managers can thus use the four types of transformational leadership shown in Figure 14–4 as a vehicle to improve group dynamics and work-unit outcomes. This is important in today's organizations because most employees do not work in isolation. Rather, people tend to rely on the input and collaboration of others, and many organizations are structured around teams. The key point to remember is that transformational leadership transforms individuals as well as teams and work groups. We encourage you to use this to your advantage.

Third, employees at any level in an organization can be trained to be more transactional and transformational.[54] This reinforces the organizational value of developing and rolling out a combination of transactional and transformational leadership training for all employees. The Skills & Best Practices box entitled "Recommendations for Creating World-Class Leadership Development Problems" contains a list of recommendations that can help organizations to effectively develop leadership talent within their organizations.[55]

Fourth, transformational leaders can be ethical or unethical. Whereas ethical transformational leaders enable employees to enhance their self-concepts, unethical ones select or produce obedient, dependent, and compliant followers. Top management can create and maintain ethical transformational leadership by

1. Creating and enforcing a clearly stated code of ethics.

2. Recruiting, selecting, and promoting people who display ethical behavior.

3. Developing performance expectations around the treatment of employees—these expectations can then be assessed in the performance appraisal process.

4. Training employees to value diversity.

5. Identifying, rewarding, and publicly praising employees who exemplify high moral conduct.[56]

Additional Perspectives on Leadership

This section examines four additional perspectives to leadership: leader–member exchange theory, shared leadership, servant-leadership, and Level 5 leadership. We spend more time discussing leader–member exchange theory because it has been more thoroughly investigated.

Group Exercise

What Kind of Leader Do You Prefer?

The Leader–Member Exchange Model of Leadership

The leader–member exchange (LMX) model of leadership revolves around the development of dyadic relationships between managers and their direct reports. This model is quite different from those previously discussed in that it focuses on the quality of relationships between managers and subordinates as opposed to the behaviors or traits of either leaders or followers. It also is different in that it does not assume that leader behavior is characterized by a stable or average leadership style as does behavioral styles theory and Fiedler's contingency theory. In other words, these models assume a leader treats all employees in about the same way. In contrast, the LMX model is based on the assumption that leaders develop unique one-to-one relationships with each of the people reporting to them. Behavioral scientists call this sort of relationship a *vertical dyad.* The forming of vertical dyads is said to be a naturally occurring process, resulting from the leader's attempt to delegate and assign work roles. As a result of this process, two distinct types of leader–member exchange relationships are expected to evolve.[57]

One type of leader–member exchange is called the **in-group exchange.** In this relationship, leaders and followers develop a partnership characterized by reciprocal influence, mutual trust, respect and liking, and a sense of common fates. In the second type of exchange, referred to as an **out-group exchange,** leaders are characterized as overseers who fail to create a sense of mutual trust, respect, or common fate.[58]

> **in-group exchange**
>
> A partnership characterized by mutual trust, respect, and liking.
>
> **out-group exchange**
>
> A partnership characterized by a lack of mutual trust, respect, and liking.

Research Findings If the leader–member exchange model is correct, there should be a significant relationship between the type of leader–member exchange and job-related outcomes. Research supports this prediction. For example, a positive leader–member exchange was positively associated with job satisfaction, job performance, goal commitment, trust between managers and employees, work climate, and satisfaction with leadership.[59] The type of leader–member exchange also was found to predict not only turnover among nurses and computer analysts, but also career outcomes, such as promotability, salary level, and receipt of bonuses over a seven-year period.[60] Finally, studies also have identified a variety of variables that influence the quality of an LMX. For example, LMX was related to personality similarity and demographic similarity.[61] Further, the quality of an LMX was positively related with the extent to which leaders and followers like each other, the leaders' positive expectations of their subordinates, the frequency of communications between managers and their direct reports, and organizational culture.[62]

Managerial Implications There are three important implications associated with the LMX model of leadership. First, leaders are encouraged to establish high-performance expectations for all of their direct reports because setting high-performance standards fosters high-quality LMXs. Second, because personality and demographic similarity between leaders and followers is associated with higher LMXs, managers need to be careful that they don't create a homogeneous work environment in the spirit of having positive relationships with their direct reports. Our discussion of diversity in Chapter 4 clearly documented that there are many positive benefits of having a diverse workforce. The third implication pertains to those of us who find ourselves in a poor LMX. Before providing advice about what to do in this situation, we would like you to assess the quality of your current leader–member exchange. The Hands-On Exercise contains a measure of leader–member exchange that segments an LMX into four subdimensions: mutual affection, loyalty, contribution to work activities, and professional respect.

What is the overall quality of your LMX? Do you agree with this assessment? Which subdimensions are high and low? If your overall LMX and associated

Assessing Your Leader–Member Exchange

INSTRUCTIONS: For each of the items shown below, use the following scale to circle the answer that best represents how you feel about the relationship between you and your current manager/supervisor. If you are not currently working, complete the survey by thinking about a previous manager. Remember, there are no right or wrong answers. After circling a response for each of the 12 items, use the scoring key to compute scores for the subdimensions within your leader–member exchange.

1 = Strongly disagree
2 = Disagree
3 = Neither agree nor disagree
4 = Agree
5 = Strongly agree

1. I like my supervisor very much as a person. 1 2 3 4 5

2. My supervisor is the kind of person one would like to have as a friend. 1 2 3 4 5

3. My supervisor is a lot of fun to work with. 1 2 3 4 5

4. My supervisor defends my work actions to a superior, even without complete knowledge of the issue in question. 1 2 3 4 5

5. My supervisor would come to my defense if I were "attacked" by others. 1 2 3 4 5

6. My supervisor would defend me to others in the organization if I made an honest mistake. 1 2 3 4 5

7. I do work for my supervisor that goes beyond what is specified in my job description. 1 2 3 4 5

8. I am willing to apply extra efforts, beyond those normally required, to meet my supervisor's work goals. 1 2 3 4 5

9. I do not mind working my hardest for my supervisor. 1 2 3 4 5

10. I am impressed with my supervisor's knowledge of his/her job. 1 2 3 4 5

11. I respect my supervisor's knowledge of and competence on the job. 1 2 3 4 5

12. I admire my supervisor's professional skills. 1 2 3 4 5

SCORING KEY

Mutual affection (add items 1–3) _____

Loyalty (add items 4–6) _____

Contribution to work activities (add items 7–9) _____

Professional respect (add items 10–12) _____

Overall score (add all 12 items) _____

ARBITRARY NORMS

Low mutual affection = 3–9
High mutual affection = 10–15
Low loyalty = 3–9
High loyalty = 10–15
Low contribution to work activities = 3–9
High contribution to work activities = 10–15
Low professional respect = 3–9
High professional respect = 10–15
Low overall leader–member exchange = 12–38
High overall leader–member exchange = 39–60

SOURCE: Reprinted from *Journal of Management*, R C Liden and J M Maslyn, "Multidimensionality of Leader–Member Exchange: An Empirical Assessment through Scale Development," p 56, Vol 24, No 1. Copyright © 1998 by Sage Publications. Reprinted by permission of Sage Publications.

subdimensions are all high, you should be in a very good situation with respect to the relationship between you and your manager. Having a low LMX overall score or a low dimensional score, however, reveals that part of the relationship with your manager may need improvement. A management consultant offers the following tips for improving the quality of leader–member exchanges.[63]

1. Stay focused on your department's goals and remain positive about your ability to accomplish your goals. An unsupportive boss is just another obstacle to be overcome.

2. Do not fall prey to feeling powerless, and empower yourself to get things done.

3. Exercise the power you have by focusing on circumstances you can control and avoid dwelling on circumstances you cannot control.

4. Work on improving your relationship with your manager. Begin by examining the level of trust between the two of you and then try to improve it by frequently and effectively communicating. You can also increase trust by following through on your commitments and achieving your goals.

5. Use an authentic, respectful, and assertive approach to resolve differences with your manager. It also is useful to use a problem-solving approach when disagreements arise.

Self-Assessment Exercise

Assessing Your Leader–Member Exchange

Shared Leadership

A pair of OB scholars noted that "there is some speculation, and some preliminary evidence, to suggest that concentration of leadership in a single chain of command may be less optimal than shared leadership responsibility among two or more individuals in certain task environments."[64] This perspective is quite different from the previous theories and models discussed in this chapter, which assume that leadership is a vertical, downward-flowing process. In contrast, the notion of shared leadership is based on the idea that people need to share information and collaborate to get things done at work. This, in turn, underscores the need for employees to adopt a horizontal process of influence or leadership. **Shared leadership** entails a simultaneous, ongoing, mutual influence process in which individuals share responsibility for leading regardless of formal roles and titles.

shared leadership
Simultaneous, ongoing, mutual influence process in which people share responsibility for leading.

Shared leadership is most likely to be needed when people work in teams, when people are involved in complex projects, and when people are doing knowledge work—work that requires voluntary contributions of intellectual capital by skilled professionals.[65] Marv Levy, the former head coach of the Buffalo Bills football team and a member of the Hall of Fame, is a strong believer in shared leadership. He concluded that a head coach "must be willing and desirous of forming a relationship with others in the organization that results in their working together productively and even enjoyably. A head honcho who thinks he can do it all by himself is fooling no one but himself. Working in concert with the team owner, the general manager, the personnel department, etc., allows everyone the opportunity to maximize his talents."[66]

Researchers are just now beginning to explore the process of shared leadership, and results are promising. For example, shared leadership in teams was positively associated with group cohesion, group citizenship, and group effectiveness.[67] Table 14–3 contains a list of key questions and answers that managers should consider when determining how they can develop shared leadership.

Servant-Leadership

Servant-leadership is more a philosophy of managing than a testable theory. The term *servant-leadership* was coined by Robert Greenleaf in 1970. Greenleaf believes that great leaders act as servants, putting the needs of others, including employees,

servant-leadership

Focuses on increased service to others rather than to oneself.

customers, and community, as their first priority. **Servant-leadership** focuses on increased service to others rather than to oneself.[68] Steve Sanghi, CEO and president of Microchip Technology, Inc., is a good example of a servant-leader. Here is how he described his leadership philosophy to a reporter from *The Arizona Republic:*

> Sanghi describes Microchip's leadership like an upside-down pyramid. "I am at the bottom while all my vice presidents, directors, engineers and sales associates are above me. Work is not done by me—I don't design it, I don't sell it. My job is to ensure that the people who do these jobs are successful. Instead of 'What have you done for me lately?,' we ask, 'How can I help you?' Doing this ensures that we break down barriers. We serve our internal customers (employees) so that external customers are served to the best of our ability."[69]

Sanghi's approach to leadership has helped Microchip Technology to increase its stock price 5,700% from 1990 to 2006.

According to Jim Stuart, co-founder of the leadership circle in Tampa, Florida, "Leadership derives naturally from a commitment to service. You know that you're

TABLE 14–3 Key Questions and Answers to Consider When Developing Shared Leadership

Key Questions	Answers
What task characteristics call for shared leadership?	Tasks that are highly *interdependent.* Tasks that require a great deal of *creativity.* Tasks that are highly *complex.*
What is the role of the leader in developing shared leadership?	*Designing the team,* including clarifying purpose, securing resources, articulating vision, selecting members, and defining team processes. *Managing the boundaries* of the team.
How can organizational systems facilitate the development of shared leadership?	*Training and development systems* can be used to prepare both designated leaders and team members to engage in shared leadership. *Reward systems* can be used to promote and reward shared leadership. *Cultural systems* can be used to articulate and to demonstrate the value of shared leadership.
What vertical and shared leadership behaviors are important to team outcomes?	*Directive leadership* can provide task-focused directions. *Transactional leadership* can provide both personal and material rewards based on key performance metrics. *Transformational leadership* can stimulate commitment to a team vision, emotional engagement, and fulfillment of higher-order needs. *Empowering leadership* can reinforce the importance of self-motivation.
What are the ongoing responsibilities of the vertical leader?	The vertical leader needs to be able to step in and *fill voids* in the team. The vertical leader needs to continue to *emphasize the importance of the shared leadership approach,* given the task characteristics facing the team.

SOURCE: C L Pearce, "The Future of Leadership: Combining Vertical and Shared Leadership to Transform Knowledge Work," *Academy of Management Executive: The Thinking Manager's Source,* February 2004, p 48. Copyright 2004 by Academy of Management. Reproduced with permission of Academy of Management via Copyright Clearance Center.

practicing servant-leadership if your followers become wiser, healthier, more autonomous—and more likely to become servant-leaders themselves."[70] Servant-leadership is not a quick-fix approach to leadership. Rather, it is a long-term, transformational approach to life and work. Table 14–4 presents 10 characteristics possessed by servant-leaders. One can hardly go wrong by trying to adopt these characteristics.

Level 5 Leadership

This model of leadership was not derived from any particular theory or model of leadership. Rather, it was developed from a longitudinal research study attempting to answer the following question: Can a good company become a great company and, if so, how? The study was conducted by a research team headed by Jim Collins, a former university professor who started his own research-based consulting company. He summarized his work in the best seller *Good to Great*.[71]

To answer the research question, Collins identified a set of companies that shifted from good performance to great performance. Great performance was defined as "cumulative stock returns at or below the general stock market for 15 years, punctuated by a transition point, then cumulative returns at least three times the market over the next 15 years."[72] Beginning

Steve Sanghi, CEO of Microchip Techology, Inc., is a servant-leader who sees his role as one of making sure that everyone else in the company is successful. Rather than "What have you done for me lately?" he prefers to ask, "How can I help you?" For more information on Steve Sanghi's leadership models, please visit www.drivingexcellence.biz.

with a sample of 1,435 companies on the *Fortune* 500 from 1965 to 1995, he identified 11 good-to-great companies: Abbot, Circuit City, Fannie Mae, Gillette, Kimberly-Clark, Kroger, Nucor, Philip Morris, Pitney Bowes, Walgreens, and Wells Fargo. His next step was to compare these 11 companies with a targeted set of direct comparison companies. This comparison enabled him to uncover the drivers of good-to-great transformations. One of the key drivers was called Level 5 leadership (see Figure 14–5). In other words, every company that experienced good-to-great performance was led by an individual possessing the characteristics associated with Level 5 leadership. Let us consider this leadership hierarchy.

Figure 14–5 reveals that a Level 5 leader possesses the characteristics of humility and a fearless will to succeed. American president Abraham Lincoln is an example of such an individual. Although he was soft-spoken and shy, he possessed great will to accomplish his goal of uniting his country during the Civil War in the 1860s. This determination resulted in the loss of 250,000 Confederates, 360,000 Union soldiers, and ultimately to a united country. Being humble and determined, however, was not enough for Lincoln to succeed at his quest. Rather, a Level 5 leader must also possess the capabilities associated with the other levels in the hierarchy. Although an individual does not move up the hierarchy in a stair-step fashion, a Level 5 leader must possess the capabilities contained in Levels 1 to 4 before he or she can use the Level 5 characteristics to transform an organization.

TABLE 14–4   Characteristics of the Servant-Leader

Servant-Leadership Characteristics	Description
1. Listening	Servant-leaders focus on listening to identify and clarify the needs and desires of a group.
2. Empathy	Servant-leaders try to empathize with others' feelings and emotions. An individual's good intentions are assumed even when he or she performs poorly.
3. Healing	Servant-leaders strive to make themselves and others whole in the face of failure or suffering.
4. Awareness	Servant-leaders are very self-aware of their strengths and limitations.
5. Persuasion	Servant-leaders rely more on persuasion than positional authority when making decisions and trying to influence others.
6. Conceptualization	Servant-leaders take the time and effort to develop broader based conceptual thinking. Servant-leaders seek an appropriate balance between a short-term, day-to-day focus and a long-term, conceptual orientation.
7. Foresight	Servant-leaders have the ability to foresee future outcomes associated with a current course of action or situation.
8. Stewardship	Servant-leaders assume that they are stewards of the people and resources they manage.
9. Commitment to the growth of people	Servant-leaders are committed to people beyond their immediate work role. They commit to fostering an environment that encourages personal, professional, and spiritual growth.
10. Building community	Servant-leaders strive to create a sense of community both within and outside the work organization.

SOURCE: These characteristics and descriptions were derived from L C Spears, "Introduction: Servant-Leadership and the Greenleaf Legacy," in *Reflections on Leadership: How Robert K Greenleaf's Theory of Servant-Leadership Influenced Today's Top Management Thinkers*, ed L C Spears (New York: John Wiley & Sons, 1995), pp 1–14.

It is important to note the overlap between the capabilities represented in this model and the previous leadership theories discussed in this chapter. For example, Level 1 is consistent with research on trait theory. Trait research tells us that leaders are intelligent, self-confident, determined, honest, sociable, emotionally intelligent, extraverted, and conscientious. Levels 3 and 4 also seem to contain behaviors associated with transactional and transformational leadership. The novel and unexpected component of this theory revolves around the conclusion that good-to-great leaders are not only transactional and transformational, but most importantly, they are humble and fiercely determined.

There are three points to keep in mind about Level 5 leadership. First, Collins notes that there are additional drivers for taking a company from good to great other than being a Level 5 leader.[73] Level 5 leadership enables the implementation of these additional drivers. Second, to date there has not been any additional research testing Collins's conclusions. Future research is clearly needed to confirm the Level 5 hierarchy. Finally, Collins believes that some people will never become Level 5 leaders because their narcissistic and boastful tendencies do not allow them to subdue their own ego and needs for the greater good of others.

FIGURE 14–5
The Level 5
Hierarchy

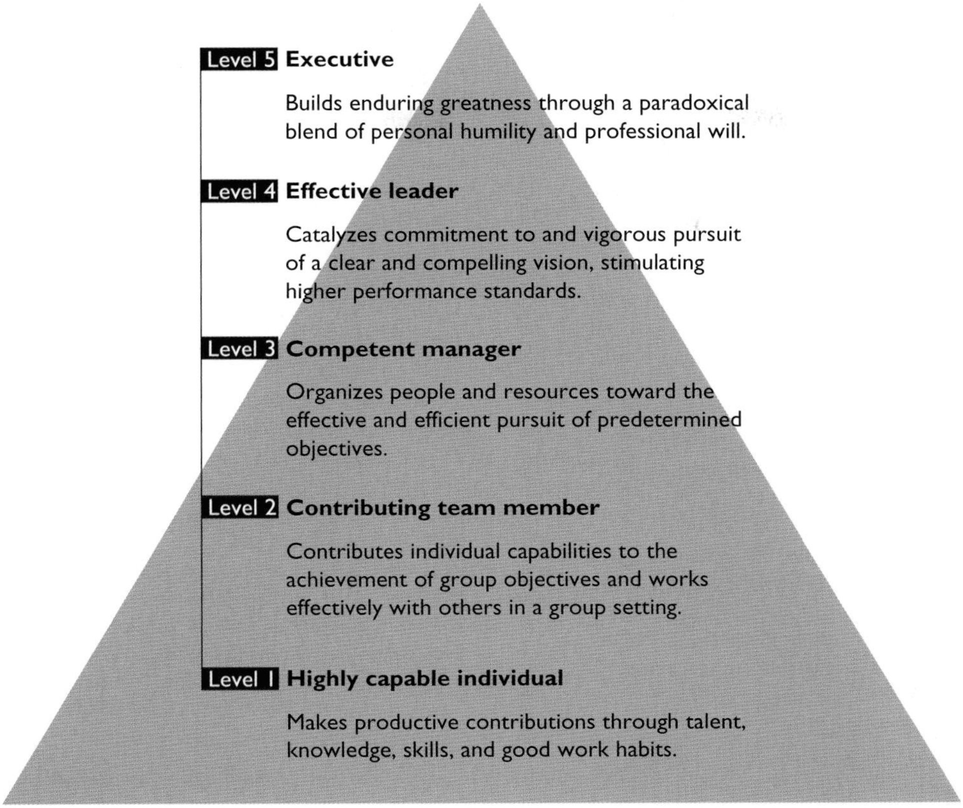

Level 5 Executive

Builds enduring greatness through a paradoxical blend of personal humility and professional will.

Level 4 Effective leader

Catalyzes commitment to and vigorous pursuit of a clear and compelling vision, stimulating higher performance standards.

Level 3 Competent manager

Organizes people and resources toward the effective and efficient pursuit of predetermined objectives.

Level 2 Contributing team member

Contributes individual capabilities to the achievement of group objectives and works effectively with others in a group setting.

Level 1 Highly capable individual

Makes productive contributions through talent, knowledge, skills, and good work habits.

SOURCE: Figure from *Good to Great: Why Some Companies Make the Leap and Others Don't* by J Collins. Copyright © 2001 by J Collins. Reprinted with permission from Jim Collins.

key terms

consideration   351
contingency factors   354
in-group exchange   363
initiating structure   351
leader trait   348

leadership   347
leadership prototype   348
out-group exchange   363
readiness   357
servant-leadership   366

shared leadership   365
situational theories   352
transactional leadership   359
transformational leadership   359

chapter summary

• *Review trait theory, and discuss the takeaways from both the trait and behavioral styles theories of leadership.* Historical leadership research does not support the notion that effective leaders possess traits unique from followers. More recent research shows that effective leaders possess the following traits: intelligence, self-confidence, determination, honesty/integrity, sociability, emotional intelligence, extraversion, and conscientiousness. Research also demonstrates that men and women exhibit different styles of leadership. The takeaways from trait theory are that (a) we can no longer ignore the implications of traits; traits influence leadership effectiveness; (b) organizations may want to include personality and trait assessments into their selection and promotion processes; and (c) management development programs can be used to enhance employees' leadership traits. The takeaways from behavioral styles theory are as follows: (a) leaders are made, not born; (b) there is no one best style of leadership; (c) the effectiveness of a particular style depends on the situation at hand; and (d) managers are encouraged to concentrate on improving the effective execution of their leadership behaviors.

• *Explain, according to Fiedler's contingency model, how leadership style interacts with situational control.* Fiedler believes leader effectiveness depends on an appropriate match between leadership style and situational control. Leaders are either task motivated or relationship motivated. Situation control is composed of leader–member relations, task structure, and position power. Task-motivated leaders are effective under situations of both high and low control. Relationship-motivated leaders are more effective when they have moderate situational control.

• *Discuss House's revised path–goal theory and Hersey and Blanchard's situational leadership theory.* There are three key changes in the revised path–goal theory. Leaders now are viewed as exhibiting eight categories of leader behavior (see Table 14–2) instead of four. In turn, the effectiveness of these styles depends on various employee characteristics and environmental factors. Second, leaders are expected to spend more effort fostering intrinsic motivation through empowerment. Third, leadership is not limited to people in managerial roles. Rather, leadership is shared among all employees within an organization. According to situational leadership theory (SLT), effective leader behavior depends on the readiness level of a leader's followers. As follower readiness increases, leaders are advised to gradually move from a telling to a selling to a participating and, finally, to a delegating style. Research does not support SLT.

• *Describe the difference between transactional and transformational leadership and discuss how transformational leadership transforms followers and work groups.* There is an important difference between transactional and transformational leadership. Transactional leaders focus on clarifying employees' role and task requirements and provide followers with positive and negative rewards contingent on performance. Transformational leaders motivate employees to pursue organizational goals over their own self-interests. Both forms of leadership are important for organizational success. Individual characteristics and organizational culture are key precursors of transformational leadership, which is comprised of four sets of leader behavior. These leader behaviors, in turn, positively affect followers' and work groups' goals, values, beliefs, aspirations, and motivation. These positive effects are then associated with a host of preferred outcomes.

• *Explain the leader–member exchange (LMX) model of leadership and the concept of shared leadership.* The LMX model revolves around the development of dyadic relationships between managers and their direct reports. These leader–member exchanges qualify as either in-group or out-group relationships. Research supports this model of leadership. Shared leadership involves a simultaneous, ongoing, mutual influence process in which individuals share responsibility for leading regardless of formal roles and titles. This type of leadership is most likely to be needed when people work in teams, when people are involved in complex projects, and when people are doing knowledge work.

• *Review the principles of servant-leadership and discuss Level 5 leadership.* Servant-leadership is more a philosophy than a testable theory. It is based on the premise that great leaders act as servants, putting the needs of others, including employees, customers, and community, as their first priority. Level 5 leadership represents a hierarchy of leadership capabilities that are needed to lead companies in transforming from good to great.

discussion questions

1. Citing examples, which different leadership traits and styles were displayed by Charles Prince III?
2. Is everyone cut out to be a leader? Explain.
3. Does it make more sense to change a person's leadership style or the situation? How would Fred Fiedler and Robert House answer this question?
4. Have you ever worked for a transformational leader? Describe how she or he transformed followers.
5. In your view, which leadership theory has the greatest practical application? Why?

ethical dilemma

You are a manager at a call center and are faced with the difficult task of having to lay off a friend who works for the company. This employee has performed wonderfully in the past and you would hate to see him go. Nonetheless, your company lost a contract with a major client and his position is obsolete. You are aware that this employee has been building a house and is 10 days from closing. He has sold his other home and now is living with his in-laws. The employee has come to you and is asking for a favor. He wants you to extend his employment for 10 more days so that he can qualify for the loan for his new home. Unfortunately, you do not have the authority to do so, and you told him you cannot grant this favor. He then told you that the mortgage company will be calling sometime soon to get a verbal confirmation of his employment. This confirmation is an essential prerequisite in order for your friend to obtain the loan for his new home. Because you can't extend his employment, he now is asking for another favor. He wants you to tell the mortgage company that he is still employed.

Solving the Dilemma

As a manager at this call center, what would you do?

1. Tell the mortgage company he is still working for the company. Your friend needs a break and you are confident that he'll find a job in the near future.

2. Refuse to lie. It is unethical to falsify information regarding employment.

3. Simply avoid the mortgage company's phone call.

4. Invent other options. Discuss.

If you're looking for additional study materials, be sure to check out the Online Learning Center at
www.mhhe.com/kinickiob3e
for more information and interactivities that correspond to this chapter.

part
five

Managing Evolving Organizations

Fifteen Designing Effective Organizations

Sixteen Managing Change and Organizational Learning

chapter
fifteen

Designing
Effective
Organizations

LEARNING OBJECTIVES

After reading the material in this chapter, you should be able to:

- Describe the four characteristics common to all organizations.

- Explain the difference between closed and open systems, and contrast the military/mechanical, biological, and cognitive systems metaphors for organizations.

- Describe the four generic organizational effectiveness criteria.

- Explain what the contingency approach to organization design involves.

- Discuss Burns and Stalker's findings regarding mechanistic and organic organizations.

- Describe new-style and old-style organizations, and list three keys to managing geographically dispersed employees in virtual organizations.

THE TWO FACES OF WAL-MART

There is an evil company in Arkansas, some say. It's a discount store—a very, very big discount store—and it will do just about anything to get bigger. You've seen the headlines. Illegal immigrants mopping its floors. Workers locked inside overnight. A big gender discrimination suit. Wages low enough to make other companies' workers go on strike. And we know what it does to weaker suppliers

and competitors. Crushing the dream of the independent proprietor—an ideal as American as Thomas Jefferson—it is the enemy of all that's good and right in our nation.

There is another big discount store in Arkansas, yet this one couldn't be more different from the first. Founded by a folksy entrepreneur whose notions of thrift, industry, and the square deal were pure Ben

Franklin, this company is not a tyrant but a servant. Passing along the gains of its brilliant distribution system to consumers, its farsighted managers have done nothing less than democratize the American dream. Its low prices are spurring productivity and helping win the fight against inflation.

Weirdest part is, both these companies are named Wal-Mart Stores, Inc.

The more America talks about Wal-Mart, it seems, the more polarized its image grows. Its executives are credited with the most expansive of visions and the meanest of intentions; its CEO is presumed to be in league with Lex Luthor and St. Francis of Assisi. It's confusing. Which should we believe in: good Wal-Mart or evil Wal-Mart?

Some of the allegations—and Wal-Mart was sued

more than 6,000 times in 2002—certainly seem damning. Yet there's an important piece of context: Wal-Mart employs 1.4 million people. That's three times as many as the nation's next biggest employer and 56 times as many as the average FORTUNE 500 company. Meaning that all things being equal, a bad event is 5,500% more likely to happen at Wal-Mart than at Borders.

One consistent refrain is that Wal-Mart squeezes its suppliers to death—and you don't have to do much digging to find horror stories. But while Wal-Mart's reputation for penny-pinching is well deserved, so is its reputation for straightforwardness— none of the slotting fees, rebates, or other game playing that many merchants engage in. . . .

Another rap on Wal-Mart—that it stomps competitors to dust through sheer brute force—seems undeniable: Studies have indicated a decline in the life expectancy of local businesses after Wal-Mart moves in. But this morality play is missing some key characters—namely, you and me. The scene where we drop into Wal-Mart to pick up a case of Coke, for instance, has been conveniently cut.

No small omission, since the main reason we can't shop at Ed's Variety Store anymore is that we stopped shopping at Ed's Variety Store.

Evil Wal-Mart's original sin, then, was to open stores that sold things for less. This was a powerful idea but hardly a new one. . . .

Not surprisingly, that's how the people running Good Wal-Mart see their story. They cast their jobs in almost missionary terms—"to lower the world's cost of living"—and in this, they have succeeded spectacularly. One consultancy estimates that Wal-Mart saves consumers $20 billion a year. Its constant push for low prices, meanwhile, puts the heat on suppliers and competitors to offer better deals.

That's a good thing, right? If a company achieves its lower prices by finding better and smarter ways of doing things, then yes, everybody wins. But if it cuts costs by cutting pay and benefits—or by sending production to China—then

not everybody wins. And here's where the story of Good Wal-Mart starts to falter. Just as its Everyday Low Prices benefit shoppers who've never come near a Wal-Mart, there are mounting signs that its Everyday Low Pay (Wal-Mart's full-time hourly employees average $9.76 an hour) is hurting some workers who have never worked there. . . .

Where you stand on Wal-Mart, then, seems to depend on where you sit. If you're a consumer, Wal-Mart is good for you. If you're a wage earner, there's a good chance it's bad. If you're a Wal-Mart shareholder, you want the company to grow. If you're a citizen, you probably don't want it growing in your backyard. So, which one are you?

And that's the point: Chances are, you're more than one. And you may think each role is important. Yet America has elevated one above the rest. . . .

Wal-Mart swore fealty to the consumer and rode its coattails straight to the top.

Now we have more than just a big retailer on our hands, though. We have a servant-king—one powerful enough to place everyone else in servitude to the consumer too. Gazing up at this new order, we wonder if our original choices made so much sense after all. . . .

Now Wal-Mart has been brought face to face with its own contradiction: Its promises of the good life threaten to ring increasingly hollow if it doesn't pay its workers enough to have that good life.

It's important that this debate continue. But in holding the mirror up to Wal-Mart, we would do well to turn it back on ourselves. Sam Walton created Wal-Mart. But we created it, too.[1]

FOR DISCUSSION

Is Wal-Mart an organizational "good guy" or a "bad guy"? Explain. For an interpretation of this case and additional comments, visit our Online Learning Center:

www.mhhe.com/kinickiob3e

VIRTUALLY EVERY ASPECT OF LIFE is affected at least indirectly by some type of organization.[2] We look to organizations to feed, clothe, house, educate, and employ us. Organizations attend to our needs for entertainment, police and fire protection, insurance, recreation, national security, transportation, news and information, legal assistance, and health care. Many of these organizations seek a profit, others do not. Some are extremely large, others are tiny mom-and-pop operations. Despite this mind-boggling diversity, modern organizations have one basic thing in common. They are the primary context for *organizational* behavior. In a manner of speaking, organizations are the chessboard upon which the game of organizational behavior is played. Therefore, present and future managers need a working knowledge of modern organizations to improve their chances of making the right moves when managing people at work.

This chapter explores the effectiveness, design, and future of today's organizations. We begin by defining the term *organization,* discussing important dimensions of organization charts, and examining alternative organizational metaphors. Our attention then turns to criteria for assessing organizational effectiveness. Next, we discuss the contingency approach to designing organizations. We conclude with a profile of new-style organizations, with special attention to Internet-age *virtual* organizations.

Organizations: Definition and Dimensions

As a necessary springboard for this chapter, we need to formally define the term *organization* and clarify the meaning of organization charts.

What Is an Organization?

According to Chester I Barnard's classic definition, an **organization** is "a system of consciously coordinated activities or forces of two or more persons."[3] Embodied in the *conscious coordination* aspect of this definition are four common denominators of all organizations: coordination of effort, a common goal, division of labor, and a hierarchy of authority.[4] Organization theorists refer to these factors as the organization's *structure.*

> **organization**
>
> System of consciously coordinated activities of two or more people.

Coordination of effort is achieved through formulation and enforcement of policies, rules, and regulations. Division of labor occurs when the common goal is pursued by individuals performing different but related tasks. The hierarchy of authority, also called the chain of command, is a control mechanism dedicated to making sure the right people do the right things at the right time.[5] Historically, managers have maintained the integrity of the hierarchy of authority by adhering to the unity of command principle. The **unity of command principle** specifies that each employee should report to only one manager. Otherwise, the argument goes, inefficiency would prevail because of conflicting orders and lack of personal accountability. (Indeed, these are problems in today's more fluid and flexible organizations based on innovations such as cross-functional and self-managed teams.) Managers in the hierarchy of authority also administer rewards and punishments. When operating in concert, the four definitional factors—coordination of effort, a common goal, division of labor, and a hierarchy of authority—enable an *organization* to come to life and function.

Test Your Knowledge

Allocating Authority

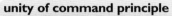

> **unity of command principle**
>
> Each employee should report to a single manager.

Organization Charts

An **organization chart** is a graphic representation of formal authority and division of labor relationships. To the casual observer, the term *organization chart* means the family tree–like pattern of boxes and lines posted on workplace walls. Within each box one usually finds the names and titles of current position holders. To organization theorists, however, organization charts reveal much more. The partial organization chart in Figure 15–1 reveals four basic dimensions of organizational structure: (1) hierarchy of authority (who reports to whom), (2) division of labor, (3) spans of control, and (4) line and staff positions.

Hierarchy of Authority   As Figure 15–1 illustrates, there is an unmistakable hierarchy of authority.[6] Working from bottom to top, the 10 directors report to the two executive directors who report to the president who reports to the chief executive officer. Ultimately, the chief executive officer answers to the hospital's board of directors. The chart in Figure 15–1 shows strict unity of command up and down the line. A formal hierarchy of authority also delineates the official communication network.

FIGURE 15–1   Sample Organization Chart for a Hospital (executive and director levels only)

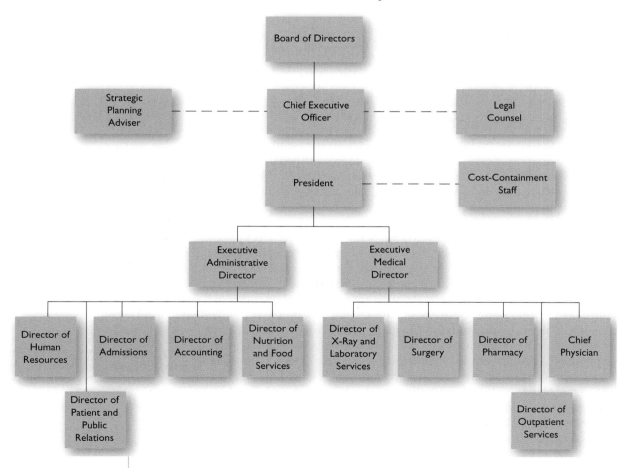

Division of Labor   In addition to showing the chain of command, the sample organization chart indicates extensive division of labor. Immediately below the hospital's president, one executive director is responsible for general administration while another is responsible for medical affairs. Each of these two specialties is further subdivided as indicated by the next layer of positions. At each successively lower level in the organization, jobs become more specialized.

Spans of Control   The **span of control** refers to the number of people reporting directly to a given manager.[7] Spans of control can range from narrow to wide. For example, the president in Figure 15–1 has a narrow span of control of two. (Staff assistants usually are not included in a manager's span of control.) The executive administrative director in Figure 15–1 has a wider span of control of five. Spans of control exceeding 30 can be found in assembly-line operations where machine-paced and repetitive work substitutes for close supervision. Historically, spans of five to six were considered best. Despite years of debate, organization theorists have not arrived at a consensus regarding the ideal span of control.

> **span of control**
> The number of people reporting directly to a given manager.

Generally, the narrower the span of control, the closer the supervision and the higher the administrative costs as a result of a higher manager-to-worker ratio. Recent emphasis on leanness and administrative efficiency dictates spans of control as wide as possible but guarding against inadequate supervision and lack of coordination. Wider spans also complement the trend toward greater worker autonomy and empowerment.

Line and Staff Positions   The organization chart in Figure 15–1 also distinguishes between line and staff positions. Line managers such as the president, the two executive directors, and the various directors occupy formal decision-making positions within the chain of command. Line positions generally are connected by solid lines on organization charts. Dotted lines indicate staff relationships. **Staff personnel** do background research and provide technical advice and recommendations to their **line managers,** who have the authority to make decisions. For example, the cost-containment specialists in the sample organization chart merely advise the president on relevant matters. Apart from supervising the work of their own staff assistants, they have no line authority over other organizational members. Modern trends such as cross-functional teams and reengineering are blurring the distinction between line and staff.

> **staff personnel**
> Provide research, advice, and recommendations to line managers.
>
> **line managers**
> Have authority to make organizational decisions

According to a study of 207 police officers in Israel, line personnel exhibited greater job commitment than did their staff counterparts.[8] This result was anticipated because the line managers' decision-making authority empowered them and gave them comparatively more control over their work situations.

Organizational Metaphors

The complexity of modern organizations makes them somewhat difficult to describe. Consequently, organization theorists have resorted to the use of metaphors.[9] A *metaphor* is a figure of speech that characterizes one object in terms of another object. Good metaphors help us comprehend complicated things by describing them in everyday terms. For example, organizations are often likened to an orchestra. OB scholar Kim Cameron sums up the value of organizational metaphors as

"YOU KNOW, EVER SINCE I STARTED WORKING HERE, I'VE HAD THIS CRAVING FOR CHEESE."

Reprinted by permission of Dave Carpenter from *Harvard Business Review*, April 2004.

closed system

A relatively self-sufficient entity.

open system

Organism that must constantly interact with its environment to survive

follows: "Each time a new metaphor is used, certain aspects of organizational phenomena are uncovered that were not evident with other metaphors. In fact, the usefulness of metaphors lies in their possession of some degree of falsehood so that new images and associations emerge."[10] With the orchestra metaphor, for instance, one could come away with an exaggerated picture of harmony in large and complex organizations. On the other hand, it realistically encourages us to view managers as facilitators rather than absolute dictators.

Early managers and management theorists used military units and machines as metaphors for organizations. These rigid models gave way to more dynamic and realistic metaphors. Today's organizational metaphors require *open-system* thinking.

Needed: Open-System Thinking

A **closed system** is said to be a self-sufficient entity. It is "closed" to the surrounding environment. In contrast, an **open system** depends on constant interaction with the environment for survival. The distinction between closed and open systems is a matter of degree. Because every worldly system is partly closed and partly open, the key question is: How great a role does the environment play in the functioning of the system? For instance, a battery-powered clock is a relatively closed system. Once the battery is inserted, the clock performs its time-keeping function hour after hour until the battery goes dead. The human body, on the other hand, is a highly open system because it requires a constant supply of life-sustaining oxygen from the environment. Nutrients also are imported from the environment. Open systems are capable of self-correction, adaptation, and growth, thanks to characteristics such as homeostasis and feedback control.

The traditional military/mechanical metaphor, discussed next, is a closed system model because it largely ignores environmental influences. It gives the impression that organizations are self-sufficient entities (see Skills & Best Practices). Conversely, the biological and cognitive metaphors emphasize interaction between organizations and their environments. These newer models are based on open-system assumptions. They reveal instructive insights about organizations and how they work. Each of the three metaphorical perspectives offers something useful.

Organizations as Military/ Mechanical Bureaucracies

A major by-product of the Industrial Revolution was the factory system of production. People left their farms and cottage industries to operate steam-powered machines in centralized factories. The social unit of production evolved from the family to formally managed organizations encompassing hundreds or even thousands of people. Managers sought to maximize the economic efficiency of large factories and offices by structuring them according to military principles. At the turn of the 20th century, a German sociologist, Max Weber, formulated what he termed the most rationally efficient form of organization.[11] He patterned his ideal organization after the vaunted Prussian army and called it **bureaucracy.**

Weber's Bureaucracy   According to Weber's theory, the following four factors should make bureaucracies the epitome of efficiency:

1. Division of labor (people become proficient when they perform standardized tasks over and over again).

2. A hierarchy of authority (a formal chain of command ensures coordination and accountability).

3. A framework of rules (carefully formulated and strictly enforced rules ensure predictable behavior).

4. Administrative impersonality (personnel decisions such as hiring and promoting should be based on competence, not favoritism).[12]

How the Term *Bureaucracy* Became a Synonym for Inefficiency   All organizations possess varying degrees of these characteristics. Thus, every organization is a bureaucracy to some extent. In terms of the ideal metaphor, a bureaucracy should run like a well-oiled machine, and its members should perform with the precision of a polished military unit. But practical and ethical problems arise when bureaucratic characteristics become extreme or dysfunctional. For example, extreme expressions of specialization, rule following, and impersonality can cause a bureaucrat to treat a client as a number rather than as a person.[13]

Weber probably would be surprised and dismayed that his model of rational efficiency has become a synonym for inefficiency.[14] Today, bureaucracy stands for being put on hold, waiting in long lines, and getting shuffled from one office to the next. This irony can be explained largely by the fact that organizations with excessive or dysfunctional bureaucratic tendencies become rigid, inflexible, and resistant to environmental demands and influences.[15]

> **bureaucracy**
>
> **Max Weber's idea of the most rationally efficient form of organization.**

SKILLS & BEST PRACTICES

Closed-System Thinking Has Both Hurt and Helped Apple's CEO Steve Jobs

Apple's challengers all face the same problem: Jobs' company will no doubt dominate the digital music market for years to come. That's because Apple has learned its lesson about closed systems.

In the desktop market Apple shrank to a niche player because it designed proprietary hardware and software that were often incompatible with programs that proliferated in the PC universe. Microsoft replicated the basic features of the Macintosh operating system in Windows and licensed it to mass-market PC manufacturers like Dell. Apple ended up with 3.2% of the U.S. desktop market.

With the iPod, Jobs created a closed system with mass appeal.

SOURCE: Excerpted from D Leonard, "The Player," *Fortune,* **March 20, 2006, p 54.**

Organizations as Biological Systems

Drawing upon the field of general systems theory that emerged during the 1950s,[16] organization theorists suggested a more dynamic model for modern organizations. This metaphor likens organizations to the human body. Hence, it has been labeled the *biological model.* In his often-cited organization theory text, *Organizations in Action,* James D Thompson explained the biological model of organizations in the following terms:

> Approached as a natural system, the complex organization is a set of interdependent parts which together make up a whole because each contributes something and

FIGURE 15–2   The Organization as an Open System: The Biological Model

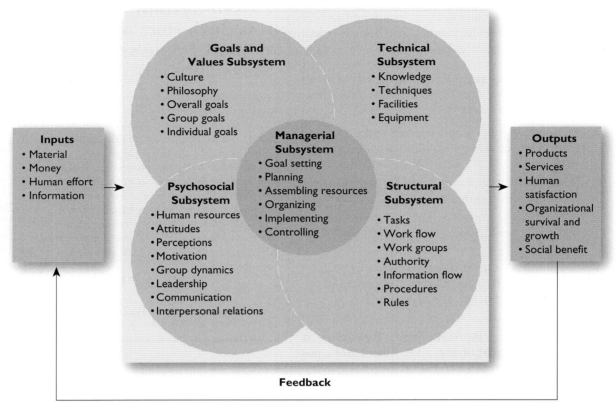

SOURCE: This model is a combination of Figures 5–2 and 5–3 in F E Kast and J E Rosenzweig, *Organization and Management: A Systems and Contingency Approach,* 4th ed (New York: McGraw-Hill, 1986), pp 112, 114. Copyright © 1986 by the McGraw-Hill Companies. Reprinted with permission

receives something from the whole, which in turn is interdependent with some larger environment. Survival of the system is taken to be the goal, and the parts and their relationships presumably are determined through evolutionary processes. . . .

Central to the natural-system approach is the concept of homeostasis, or self-stabilization, which spontaneously, or naturally, governs the necessary relationships among parts and activities and thereby keeps the system viable in the face of disturbances stemming from the environment.[17]

Unlike the traditional military/mechanical theorists who downplayed the environment, advocates of the biological model stress organization–environment interaction. As Figure 15–2 illustrates, the biological model characterizes the organization as an open system that transforms inputs into various outputs. The outer boundary of the organization is permeable. People, information, capital, and goods and services move back and forth across this boundary. Moreover, each of the five organizational subsystems—goals and values, technical, psychosocial, structural, and managerial—is dependent on the others. Feedback about such things as sales and customer satisfaction or dissatisfaction enables the organization to self-adjust and survive despite uncertainty and change.[18] In effect, the organization is alive.

Organizations as Cognitive Systems

A more recent metaphor characterizes organizations in terms of mental functions. According to respected organization theorists Richard Daft and Karl Weick,

> This perspective represents a move away from mechanical and biological metaphors of organizations. Organizations are more than transformation processes or control systems. To survive, organizations must have mechanisms to interpret ambiguous events and to provide meaning and direction for participants. Organizations are meaning systems, and this distinguishes them from lower-level systems. . . .
>
> Almost all outcomes in terms of organization structure and design, whether caused by the environment, technology, or size, depend on the interpretation of problems or opportunities by key decision makers. Once interpretation occurs, the organization can formulate a response.[19]

This interpretation process, as it migrates throughout the organization, leads to organizational *learning* and adaptation.[20]

In fact, the concept of the *learning organization,*[21] discussed in Chapter 16, is popular in management circles these days. Great Harvest Bread Co., based in Dillon, Montana, is an inspiring case in point (the company's nearly 200 retail franchises, where grains for baked goods are fresh ground daily, are located in 34 states):[22]

> While most franchisors dictate everything about their franchisees' operations in order to ensure a predictable experience for customers everywhere, Great Harvest doesn't even require that its franchisees use the same bread recipes. . . . Instead, Great Harvest sets its franchisees free after a one-year apprenticeship to run their stores in the time-honored mom-and-pop way. Be unique, the company tells them; be yourselves, and experiment. . . .
>
> In other words, Great Harvest says to its bakery owners, *Do whatever you want.* Except in one respect, which makes all the difference: Every owner in the chain is encouraged to be part of Great Harvest's "learning community." Those who join (and most have) must share information, financial results, observations, and ideas. If asked questions, they must give answers. They must keep no secrets.[23]

Thus, it takes a cooperative culture, mutual trust, and lots of internal cross communication to fully exploit the organization as a cognitive system (or learning organization).

Striving for Organizational Effectiveness

Assessing organizational effectiveness is an important topic for an array of people, including managers, stockholders, government agencies, and OB specialists. The purpose of this section is to introduce a widely applicable and useful model of organizational effectiveness.

Generic Effectiveness Criteria

A good way to better understand this complex subject is to consider four generic approaches to assessing an organization's effectiveness (see Figure 15–3). These effectiveness criteria apply equally well to large or small and profit or not-for-profit organizations. Moreover, as denoted by the overlapping circles in Figure 15–3, the four effectiveness criteria can be used in various combinations. The key thing to remember is "no single approach to the evaluation of effectiveness is appropriate in all circumstances or for all organization types."[24] What do Coca-Cola and France

One criterion for organizational effectiveness is the respect of your peers. Under **CEO Jeff Immelt, General Electric** has been among *Fortune*'s most admired companies in the United States for several years in a row.

Télécom, for example, have in common, other than being large profit-seeking corporations? Because a multidimensional approach is required, we need to look more closely at each of the four generic effectiveness criteria.

Goal Accomplishment   Goal accomplishment is the most widely used effectiveness criterion for organizations. Key organizational results or outputs are compared with previously stated goals or objectives. Deviations, either plus or minus, require corrective action. This is simply an organizational variation of the personal goal-setting process discussed in Chapter 7.[25] Effectiveness, relative to the criterion of goal accomplishment, is gauged by how well the organization meets or exceeds its goals.[26]

FIGURE 15–3
Four Dimensions of Organizational Effectiveness

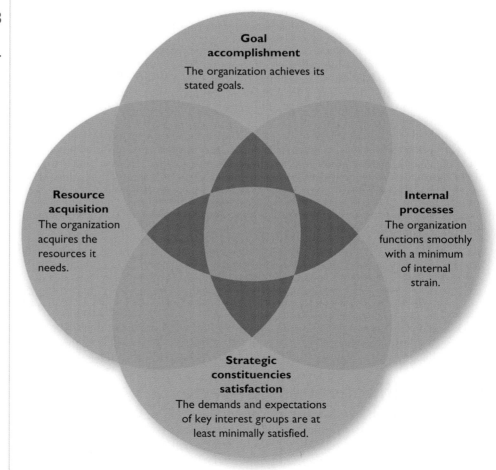

Goal accomplishment
The organization achieves its stated goals.

Resource acquisition
The organization acquires the resources it needs.

Internal processes
The organization functions smoothly with a minimum of internal strain.

Strategic constituencies satisfaction
The demands and expectations of key interest groups are at least minimally satisfied.

SOURCES: Adapted from discussion in K Cameron, "Critical Questions in Assessing Organizational Effectiveness," *Organizational Dynamics,* Autumn 1980, pp 66–80; and K S Cameron, "Effectiveness as Paradox: Consensus and Conflict in Conceptions of Organizational Effectiveness," *Management Science,* May 1986, pp 539–53.

Southwest Airlines is the envy of the beleaguered commercial airline industry because it is consistently effective at turning a profit by satisfying its customers and employees with a low-cost, on-time strategy and a no-layoff policy.

Productivity improvement, involving the relationship between inputs and outputs, is a common organization-level goal.[27] Goals also may be set for organizational efforts such as minority recruiting, pollution prevention, and quality improvement. Given today's competitive pressures and e-commerce revolution, *innovation* and *speed* are very important organizational goals worthy of measurement and monitoring.[28] Toyota gave a powerful indicator of where things are going in this regard. The Japanese automaker announced it could custom-build a car in just five days! A customer's new Toyota would roll off the Ontario, Canada, assembly line just five days after the order was placed. A 30-day lag was the industry standard at the time.[29]

Resource Acquisition   This second criterion relates to inputs rather than outputs. An organization is deemed effective in this regard if it acquires necessary factors of production such as raw materials, labor, capital, and managerial and technical expertise. Charitable organizations such as Habitat for Humanity judge their effectiveness in terms of how much money they raise from private and corporate donations.

Internal Processes   Some refer to this third effectiveness criterion as the "healthy systems" approach. An organization is said to be a healthy system if information flows smoothly and if employee loyalty, commitment, job satisfaction, and trust prevail. Goals may be set for any of these internal processes. Healthy systems, from a behavioral standpoint, tend to have a minimum of dysfunctional conflict and destructive political maneuvering. M Scott Peck, the physician who wrote the highly regarded book, *The Road Less Traveled,* characterizes healthy organizations in ethical terms:

> A healthy organization, Peck says, is one that has a genuine sense of community: It's a place where people are emotionally present with one another, and aren't afraid to talk about fears and disappointments—because that's what allows us to care for one another. It's a place where there is authentic communication, a willingness to be vulnerable, a commitment to speaking frankly and respectfully—and a commitment not to walk away when the going gets tough.[30]

Organizations with healthy internal processes tend to be incubators for creativity and innovation, both of which are very important today[31] (see Skills & Best Practices).

Creativity and Innovation Pay Off on the Bottom Line

So you're one of the 25 Most Innovative Companies in the world, but what about the bottom line? Does innovation really deliver? You bet. More than half of the Top 25 with histories as public companies scored big, with better profit margins and higher stock prices over the past decade.

How big? The innovators achieved median profit margin growth of 3.4% a year since 1995, compared with 0.4% for the median Standard & Poor's Global 1200 company.

Target Stores, Inc.'s operating margin (earnings before interest and taxes as a percentage of revenues) doubled over the 10-year period, reflecting the discount retailer's skill in positioning itself as a hip alternative to Wal-Mart Stores, Inc. with designer brands such as Isaac Mizrahi apparel and Michael Graves housewares. Target's stock performance was half again better than Wal-Mart's, another top innovator.

Starbucks Corp. presses for new ways to sell more than caffeine from its coffee shops. Its operating margin is up to 11.1%, from 9.1% in 2002, a level that had been fairly steady for the previous seven years. Starbucks shares delivered total returns of some 28% a year, nearly three times the S&P 1200's median of 11.1%. Procter & Gamble Co. shifted its product portfolio to higher-margin beauty and health-care businesses. Its operating margins are up to 19.3%, from 12.5%.

SOURCE: Excerpted from D Henry, "Creativity Pays. Here's How Much," *BusinessWeek*, April 24, 2006, p 76.

Strategic Constituencies Satisfaction   Organizations both depend on people and affect the lives of people. Consequently, many consider the satisfaction of key interested parties to be an important criterion of organizational effectiveness.

> A **strategic constituency** is any group of individuals who have some stake in the organization—for example, resource providers, users of the organization's products or services, producers of the organization's output, groups whose cooperation is essential for the organization's survival, or those whose lives are significantly affected by the organization.[32]

Strategic constituencies (or *stakeholders*) generally have competing or conflicting interests.[33] This forces executives to do some strategic juggling to achieve workable balances. In a recent *BusinessWeek* interview, Microsoft's CEO, Steve Ballmer, offered this perspective:

> When you have gone through the kind of experience that we went through with government authorities, it really does cause you to step back and reflect: Who are we, what are we doing? The expectation bar, be it from government, be it from customers, be it from industry partners, is different, and the bar is higher. How do you hit the balance between being forceful and aggressive and still [having the] right level of cooperation [with our industry and] with government? We have worked hard on that theme of responsible leadership.[34]

Mixing Effectiveness Criteria: Practical Guidelines

Experts on the subject recommend a multidimensional approach to assessing the effectiveness of modern organizations. This means no single criterion is appropriate for all stages of the organization's life cycle. Nor will a single criterion satisfy competing stakeholders. Well-managed organizations mix and match effectiveness criteria to fit the unique requirements of the situation.[35] For example, Jamie Dimon, the CEO of J P Morgan Chase, is very goal oriented, an aggressive cost-cutter, and customer focused in his drive to grow the banking giant: "What is growth?" says Dimon, in his trademark staccato style. "It's better service, better products, more hours. Growth to me is every budget review. It's 1,000 small steps."[36]

Managers need to identify and seek input from strategic constituencies. This information, when merged with the organization's stated mission and philosophy, enables management to derive an appropriate *combination* of effectiveness criteria. The following guidelines are helpful in this regard:

- *The goal accomplishment approach* is appropriate when "goals are clear, consensual, time-bounded, measurable."[37]

strategic constituency

Any group of people with a stake in the organization's operation or success.

mechanistic organizations

Rigid, command-and-control bureaucracies.

organic organizations

Fluid and flexible network of multitalented people.

- *The resource acquisition approach* is appropriate when inputs have a traceable effect on results or output. For example, the amount of money the American Red Cross receives through donations dictates the level of services provided.
- *The internal processes approach* is appropriate when organizational performance is strongly influenced by specific processes (e.g., cross-functional teamwork).
- *The strategic constituencies approach* is appropriate when powerful stakeholders can significantly benefit or harm the organization.[38]

The Contingency Approach to Designing Organizations

According to the **contingency approach to organization design,** organizations tend to be more effective when they are structured to fit the demands of the situation.[39] The purpose of this section is to introduce you to the contingency approach to organization design by reviewing a landmark study, drawing a distinction between centralized and decentralized decision making, contrasting new-style and old-style organizations, and discussing today's virtual organizations.

> **contingency approach to organization design**
>
> Creating an effective organization–environment fit.

Test Your Knowledge
Mechanistic vs. Organic Organizations

Mechanistic versus Organic Organizations

A landmark contingency design study was reported by a pair of British behavioral scientists, Tom Burns and G M Stalker. In the course of their research, they drew a very instructive distinction between what they called mechanistic and organic organizations. **Mechanistic organizations** are rigid bureaucracies with strict rules, narrowly defined tasks, and top-down communication. Ironically, it is at the cutting edge of technology that this seemingly out-of-date approach has found a home. In the highly competitive business of Web hosting—running clients' Web sites in high-security facilities humming with Internet servers—speed and reliability are everything. Enter military-style managers who require strict discipline, faithful adherence to thick rule books, and flawless execution. But, as *BusinessWeek* observed, "The regimented atmosphere and military themes . . . may be tough to stomach for skilled workers used to a more free-spirited atmosphere."[40] (For a retail example, refer back to the Home Depot case at the beginning of Chapter 2, which discusses how CEO Robert Nardelli has created a military-style structure and culture.)[41]

Oppositely, **organic organizations** are flexible networks of multitalented individuals who perform a variety of tasks.[42] W L Gore & Associates, for instance, is a highly organic organization because it lacks job descriptions and a formalized hierarchy and deemphasizes titles and status[43] (see Skills & Best Practices).

W L Gore's Organic "Bubble-Up" Structure Enhances Innovation

The invention in the mid-1970s of wonder fabric Gore-Tex . . . put the Delaware-based company on the map. But the successes that have come since that breakthrough—including Glide dental floss and high-end Elixir guitar strings—owe more to the company's grassroots management structure than to high-tech R&D.

Except for a handful of top executives, all 6,800 employees have the same title: associate. From there, upward mobility follows an unusual path. Some associates act as "sponsors" to help pair colleagues' interests to particular projects. If you want to become a "team leader," you don't lobby the higher-ups for a promotion; you form an alliance of people willing to commit to a specific goal, whether it's pitching a product or a new health plan. Beyond the egalitarian appeal, the org structure helps ideas bubble up faster than they might through conventional R&D.

SOURCE: Excerpted from H Collingwood, "Peer-to-Peer Promotion," *Business 2.0,* April 2006, p 86.

SKILLS & BEST PRACTICES

Mechanistic or Organic?

INSTRUCTIONS: Think of your present (or a past) place of employment and rate it on the following eight factors. Calculate a total score and compare it to the scale.

Characteristics

1. Task definition and knowledge required	Narrow, technical	1	2	3	4	5	6	7	Broad; general
2. Linkage between individual's contribution and organization's purpose	Vague or indirect	1	2	3	4	5	6	7	Clear or direct
3. Task flexibility	Rigid; routine	1	2	3	4	5	6	7	Flexible; varied
4. Specification of techniques, obligations, and rights	Specific	1	2	3	4	5	6	7	General
5. Degree of hierarchical control	High	1	2	3	4	5	6	7	Low (self-control emphasized)
6. Primary communication pattern	Top-down	1	2	3	4	5	6	7	Lateral (between peers)
7. Primary decision-making style	Authoritarian	1	2	3	4	5	6	7	Democratic; participative
8. Emphasis on obedience and loyalty	High	1	2	3	4	5	6	7	Low

Total score = _____

Scale

8–24 = Relatively mechanistic
25–39 = Mixed
40–56 = Relatively organic

SOURCE: Adapted from discussion in T Burns and G M Stalker, *The Management of Innovation* (London: Tavistock, 1961), pp 119–25.

A Matter of Degree   Importantly, as illustrated in the Hands-On Exercise, each of the mechanistic-organic characteristics is a matter of degree. Organizations tend to be *relatively* mechanistic or *relatively* organic. Pure types are rare because divisions, departments, or units in the same organization may be more or less mechanistic or organic. From an employee's standpoint, which organization structure would you prefer?

centralized decision making

Top managers make all key decisions.

decentralized decision making

Lower-level managers are empowered to make important decisions.

Different Approaches to Decision Making   Decision making tends to be centralized in mechanistic organizations and decentralized in organic organizations. **Centralized decision making** occurs when key decisions are made by top management. **Decentralized decision making** occurs when important decisions are made by middle- and lower-level managers. Generally, centralized organizations are more tightly controlled while decentralized organizations are more adaptive to changing situations.[44] Each has its appropriate use. For example, home builders Lennar

Corp and D R Horton, Inc, are both successful, but *BusinessWeek* recently described their sharply contrasting structures:

> Lennar has a more button-down, centralized style. . . . In a unique strategy to prevent its homebuilding units from overbuying land to feed construction growth, it has put land acquisition into a separate division that's rewarded for keeping costs low.
> . . . Horton is decentralized. Each of its 77 markets in 26 states is run by a profit-center manager, who decides what to build and where. . . .[45]

KANA, a $60-million software maker, is a relatively organic organization. CEO Michael Fields is a proponent of what he calls "backshoring," or bringing programming jobs back from India to Menlo Park, California, headquarters, so all the firm's designers, project managers, and programmers can work side by side. "If your team isn't closely bonded," says Fields, "you'll see more rewrites, more performances issues, and more delays."

Experts on the subject warn against extremes of centralization or decentralization. The challenge is to achieve a workable balance between the two extremes. A management consultant put it this way:

> The modern organization in transition will recognize the pull of two polarities: a need for greater centralization to create low-cost shared resources; and, a need to improve market responsiveness with greater decentralization. Today's winning organizations are the ones that can handle the paradox and tensions of both pulls. These are the firms that analyze the optimum organizational solution in each particular circumstance, without prejudice for one type of organization over another. The result is, almost invariably, a messy mixture of decentralized units sharing cost-effective centralized resources.[46]

Centralization and decentralization are not an either-or proposition; they are an *and-also* balancing act.

Practical Research Insights   When they classified a sample of actual companies as either mechanistic or organic, Burns and Stalker discovered one type was not superior to the other. Each type had its appropriate place, depending on the environment. When the environment was relatively *stable and certain,* the successful organizations tended to be *mechanistic. Organic* organizations tended to be the successful ones when the environment was *unstable and uncertain.*[47]

In a more recent study of 103 department managers from eight manufacturing firms and two aerospace organizations, managerial skill was found to have a greater impact on a global measure of department effectiveness in organic departments than in mechanistic departments. This led the researchers to recommend the following contingencies for management staffing and training:

> If we have two units, one organic and one mechanistic, and two potential applicants differing in overall managerial ability, we might want to assign the more competent to the organic unit since in that situation there are few structural aids available to the manager in performing required responsibilities. It is also possible that managerial training is especially needed by managers being groomed to take over units that are more organic in structure.[48]

Another interesting finding comes from a study of 42 voluntary church organizations. As the organizations became more mechanistic (more bureaucratic) the intrinsic motivation of their members decreased. Mechanistic organizations apparently undermined the volunteers' sense of freedom and self-determination. Additionally, the

Self-Assessment Exercise

Identify Your Preferred Organization Structure

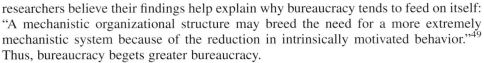

researchers believe their findings help explain why bureaucracy tends to feed on itself: "A mechanistic organizational structure may breed the need for a more extremely mechanistic system because of the reduction in intrinsically motivated behavior."[49] Thus, bureaucracy begets greater bureaucracy.

Most recently, field research in two factories, one mechanistic and the other organic, found expected communication patterns. Command-and-control (downward) communication characterized the mechanistic factory. Consultative or participative (two-way) communication prevailed in the organic factory.[50]

Both Mechanistic and Organic Structures Have Their Places   Although achievement-oriented students of OB typically express a distaste for mechanistic organizations, not all organizations or subunits can or should be organic. For example, McDonald's could not achieve its admired quality and service standards without extremely mechanistic restaurant operations. Imagine the food and service you would get if McDonald's employees used their own favorite ways of doing things and worked at their own pace! On the other hand, mechanistic structure alienates some employees because it erodes their sense of self-control.

New-Style versus Old-Style Organizations

Group Exercise

Designing an Organization

Organization theorists Jay R Galbraith and Edward E Lawler III have called for a "new logic of organizing."[51] They recommend a whole new set of adjectives to describe organizations (see Table 15–1). Traditional pyramid-shaped organizations, conforming to the old-style pattern, tend to be too slow and inflexible today. Leaner, more organic organizations increasingly are needed to accommodate today's strategic balancing act between cost, quality, and speed. These new-style organizations embrace the total quality management (TQM) principles discussed in Chapter 1. This means they are customer focused, dedicated to continuous improvement and learning, and structured around teams. These qualities, along with computerized information technology, hopefully enable big organizations to mimic the speed and flexibility of small organizations.

TABLE 15–1   New-Style versus Old-Style Organizations

New	Old
Dynamic, learning	Stable
Information rich	Information is scarce
Global	Local
Small and large	Large
Product/customer oriented	Functional
Skills oriented	Job oriented
Team oriented	Individual oriented
Involvement oriented	Command/control oriented
Lateral/networked	Hierarchical
Customer oriented	Job requirements oriented

SOURCE: From J R Galbraith and E E Lawler III, "Effective Organizations: Using the New Logic of Organizing," p 298 in *Organizing for the Future: The New Logic for Managing Complex Organizations*, eds J R Galbraith, E E Lawler III, and Associates, 1993. Copyright © 1993 John Wiley & Sons, Inc. Reprinted with permission of John Wiley & Sons, Inc.

The US military used decentralized command during the second war in Iraq. Marine commanders gave colonels unprecedented autonomy as long as they achieved results. Shifting this power down enabled colonels to make decisions within the heat of battle. In relation to business, Jason Santamaria, a former Marine and author of *The Marine Corps Way: Using Maneuver Warfare to Lead a Winning Organization*, says "you want to push the decision making onto the people with interaction in the market." *Inc.*, May 2004, p 24.

Virtual Organizations

Like virtual teams, discussed in Chapter 9, modern information technology allows people in virtual organizations to get something accomplished despite being geographically dispersed.[52] Instead of relying heavily on face-to-face meetings, members of virtual organizations send e-mail and voice-mail messages, exchange project information over the Internet, and convene videoconferences among far-flung participants. In addition, cellular phones and the wireless Internet have made the dream of doing business from the beach a reality. This disconnection between work and location is causing managers to question traditional assumptions about centralized offices and factories. Various configurations have emerged. For example, consider this description of JetBlue Airways Corp:

> Look no further than JetBlue's 700-person reservation center in Salt Lake City. You don't see it? That's because its sales agents all work from their homes. They're linked by an Internet telephone system in which e-mail, chat, Web searches, and phone calls all pour through the same pipes.[53]

A more controversial form of virtual organization involves "offshoring" jobs to lower-wage countries. Sapient, a consulting firm based in Cambridge, Massachusetts, is a case in point:

> About half its 700 employees are in India. Via broadband, employees there and in Cambridge share electronic documents in real time and scribble to each other on virtual white boards.
>
> Broadband makes it possible, says Vice President Alan Wexler. "It's almost as if the work is being done in one physical place."[54]

Yet another form of virtual organization is not a single organization, but rather a *network* of several organizations linked together contractually and electronically.[55] Why own a computer factory when contract-manufacturer Solectron will do the job for you? Why own warehouses and fleets of delivery trucks when UPS and FedEx can provide a complete supply chain? These different types of virtual organization—and the e-leadership lessons listed in Chapter 1—require new thinking about how to interact with and manage people who are out of sight, but not out of mind[56] (see Skills & Best Practices).

Manager's Hot Seat Application

Virtual Workplace: Out of the Office Reply

SKILLS & BEST PRACTICES

How to Manage Geographically Dispersed Employees

*The three keys are **sharing knowledge, building trust, and maintaining connectedness.*** Other steps include:

Hire carefully: People working in remote locations, especially at home, need to be self-starters who are well-organized, self-motivated, and effective communicators.

Communicate regularly: Daily e-mails and weekly phone conversations, at a minimum, help nip problems in the bud, address complaints, and build strong working relationships.

Practice "management by wandering around": Get out of the home office and regularly visit remote employees on their turf to get a first-hand view of what is happening. These visits also afford opportunities for coaching, feedback, and positive reinforcement.

Conduct regular audits: Formal audits ensure compliance with company policies, legal requirements, and ethical standards.

Use technology as a tool, not a weapon: Rely on cost-effective new technologies to enhance productivity. Be sensitive to privacy rights and employee morale when engaging in electronic performance monitoring (e.g., videotaping, monitoring e-mail and Internet use, and counting keystrokes).

Achieve a workable balance between online and live training. Live face-to-face training is expensive, but can build trust and teamwork.

SOURCE: Adapted from J W Janove, "Management by Remote Control," *HR Magazine*, April 2004, pp 119–24.

Gazing into the Crystal Ball   Here is how we envision life in the emerging virtual organizations and organizational networks. Things will be very interesting and profitable for the elite core of entrepreneurs and engineers who hit on the right business formula. Turnover among the financial and information "have nots"—data entry, customer service, and production employees—will be high because of glaring inequities and limited opportunities for personal fulfillment and growth. Telecommuters who work from home will feel liberated and empowered (and sometimes lonely). Commitment, trust, and loyalty could erode badly if managers do not heed this caution by Charles Handy, a British management expert. According to Handy: "A shared commitment still requires personal contact to make the commitment feel real. *Paradoxically, the more virtual an organization becomes the more its people need to meet in person.*"[57] Independent contractors, both individuals and organizations, will participate in many different organizational networks and thus have diluted loyalty to any single one. Substandard working conditions and low pay at some smaller contractors will make them little more than Internet-age sweat shops.[58] Companies living from one contract to another will offer little in the way of job security and benefits. Offshoring of jobs in both the manufacturing and service sectors, despite being a politically charged issue, will continue as long as consumers demand low-cost (and often foreign-sourced) goods and services.[59] Opportunities to start new businesses will be numerous, but prolonged success could prove elusive at Internet speed.[60]

Needed: Self-Starting Team Players   The only certainty about tomorrow's organizations is they will produce a lot of surprises. Only flexible, adaptable people who see problems as opportunities, are self-starters capable of teamwork, and are committed to lifelong learning will be able to handle whatever comes their way.

key terms

bureaucracy 381

centralized decision making 388

closed system 380

contingency approach to organization design 387

decentralized decision making 388

line managers 379

mechanistic organizations 386

open system 380

organic organizations 386

organization 377

organization chart 378

span of control 379

staff personnel 379

strategic constituency 386

unity of command principle 377

chapter summary

- *Describe the four characteristics common to all organizations.* They are coordination of effort (achieved through policies and rules), a common goal (a collective purpose), division of labor (people performing different but related tasks), and a hierarchy of authority (the chain of command).

- *Explain the difference between closed and open systems, and contrast the military/mechanical, biological, and cognitive systems metaphors for organizations.* Closed systems, such as a battery-powered clock, are relatively self-sufficient. Open systems, such as the human body, are highly dependent on the environment for survival. In the past, the military/mechanical metaphor characterized organizations as self-sufficient closed systems. Newer biological and cognitive metaphors view the organization as an open system. The biological metaphor views the organization as a living organism striving to survive in an uncertain environment. In terms of the cognitive metaphor, an organization is like the human mind, capable of interpreting and learning from uncertain and ambiguous situations.

- *Describe the four generic organizational effectiveness criteria.* They are goal accomplishment (satisfying stated objectives), resource acquisition (gathering the necessary productive inputs), internal processes (building and maintaining healthy organizational systems), and strategic constituencies satisfaction (achieving at least minimal satisfaction for all key stakeholders).

- *Explain what the contingency approach to organization design involves.* The contingency approach to organization design calls for fitting the organization to the demands of the situation.

- *Discuss Burns and Stalker's findings regarding mechanistic and organic organizations.* British researchers Burns and Stalker found that mechanistic (bureaucratic, centralized) organizations tended to be effective in stable situations. In unstable situations, organic (flexible, decentralized) organizations were more effective. These findings underscored the need for a contingency approach to organization design.

- *Describe new-style and old-style organizations, and list three keys to managing geographically dispersed employees in virtual organizations.* New-style organizations are characterized as dynamic and learning, information rich, global, small and large, product/customer oriented, skills oriented, team oriented, involvement oriented, lateral/networked, and customer oriented. Old-style organizations are characterized as stable, information is scarce, local, large, functional, job oriented, individual oriented, command/control oriented, hierarchical, and job requirements oriented. The three keys to effectively managing people geographically dispersed throughout a virtual organization are sharing knowledge, building trust, and maintaining connectedness.

discussion questions

1. How would you interpret Wal-Mart's effectiveness in terms of Figure 15–3? Explain.
2. What would an organization chart of your current (or last) place of employment look like? Does the chart you have drawn reveal the hierarchy (chain of command), division of labor, span of control, and line–staff distinctions? Does it reveal anything else? Explain.
3. Why is it appropriate to view modern organizations as open systems?
4. In a nutshell, what does contingency organization design entail?
5. If organic organizations are popular with most employees, why can't all organizations be structured in an organic fashion?

ethical dilemma

Close Supervision or Unethical "Snoopervision"?

If your employees are working outside your line of sight, how do you know they're working at all?

The days when managers could check up on their minions by looking out over rows of desks are over. More and more workers are toiling far away from their bosses' gaze—at home, in hotel rooms or in other remote locations. So, how is a supervisor to know whether they're really laboring at the monthly report and not shopping on eBay or watching Oprah?

Many managers may find comfort in the fact that the very technology that allows employees to work anywhere also enables companies to monitor their actions. In fact, a wealth of high-tech tools make it possible to keep a closer eye on employees than could ever be done when everybody was on the same floor. Some software can monitor whether employees are logged on to their computers, or working in particular applications. Other programs can track each keystroke or block access to undesirable Web sites. Web-connected video cameras can even watch workers at their desks.[61]

How Much Electronic Surveillance in the Workplace Is Too Much?

1. Electronic surveillance signals a distrust in employees, erodes morale, and ultimately hampers productivity. Explain your rationale.

2. Employers sign the paychecks and own the equipment, so they have the right to make sure they are getting their money's worth and their equipment is being used properly. Explain.

3. This sort of "snoopervision" creates a cat-and-mouse game in which "beating the system" becomes more important than productivity. Explain.

4. Electronic surveillance is unnecessary if properly trained and equipped employees are held accountable for meeting challenging but fair performance goals. Explain your rationale.

5. No amount of electronic performance monitoring can make up for poor hiring decisions, inadequate training, a weak performance-reward system, and inept supervision. Explain.

6. Invent other interpretations or options. Discuss.

For an interpretation of this situation, visit our Web site, www.mhhe.com/kinickiob3e.

chapter Sixteen

Managing Change and Organizational Learning

Even the gentle clinking of silverware stopped dead. Andrew S. Grove, the revered former Intel Corp. chief executive and now a senior adviser, had stepped up to the microphone in a hotel ballroom down the street from Intel's Santa Clara (Calif.) headquarters, preparing to respond to a startling presentation by new Chief Marketing Officer Eric B. Kim. All too familiar with Grove's legendary wrath, many of the 300 top managers at the Oct. 20 gathering tensed in their seats as they waited for a tongue-lashing of epic proportions. "No one knew what to think," recalls one attendee.

The reason? Kim's plan, cooked up with new CEO Paul S. Otellini, was a sharp departure from the company Grove had built. Essentially, they were proposing to blow up Intel's brand, the fifth-best-known in the world. As Otellini looked on from a front table, Kim declared that Intel must "clear out the cobwebs" and kill off many Grove-era creations. Intel Inside? Dump it, he said. The Pentium brand?

Stale. The widely recognized dropped "e" in Intel's corporate logo? A relic.

Grove's deep baritone, sharpened by the accent of his native Hungary, pierced the expectant silence. But instead of smiting the Philistines, Intel's patriarch sprinkled holy water on Otellini's plan. He understood

Paul Otellini has taken Intel in new directions after succeeding the near-legendary Andrew Grove in the CEO spot.

that it was no repudiation of him, but rather a recognition that times had changed—and that Intel needed to change with them. "I want to say," he boomed, "that this program strikes me as one of the best manifestations incorporating Intel values of risk-taking, discipline, and

results orientation I have ever seen here. I, for one, fully support it." . . .

The changes go far deeper than the company's brand. Under Grove and successor Craig R. Barrett, Intel thrived by concentrating on the microprocessors that power personal computers. By narrowing the company's focus, the duo buried the competition. They invested billions in hyperproductive plants that could crank out more processors in a day than some rivals did in a year. Meanwhile, they helped give life to the Information Age, with ever-faster, more powerful chips.

Otellini is tossing out the old model. Instead of remaining focused on PCs, he's pushing Intel to play a key technological role in a half-dozen fields, including consumer electronics, wireless communications, and health care. And rather than just microprocessors, he wants Intel to create all kinds of chips, as well as software, and then meld them together into what he calls "platforms." . . .

Why the shift? Stark necessity. PC growth is slowing, even as cell phones and handheld devices compete for the *numero uno* spot in people's lives. Otellini must reinvent Intel—or face a future of creaky maturity. . . .

Intel has tried entering new markets in the past, particularly under Barrett. Yet it always treated them as tangential and never let them detract from the core processor effort. Not anymore. Otellini, who took over as CEO in May, has reorganized the company top to bottom, putting most of its 98,000 employees into new jobs. He created business units for each product area, including mobility and digital health, and scattered the processor experts among them. He has also added 20,000 people in the past year. The result? Intel is poised to launch more new products in 2006 than at any time in its history.

Intel's culture is changing, too. Under the charismatic Grove, who was CEO from 1987 to 1998 and then chairman until 2005, the company was a rough-and-tumble place. Grove's motto was "Only the paranoid survive," and managers frequently engaged in "constructive confrontation," which any outsider would call shouting. Engineers ruled the roost. Grove and Barrett also instituted the practice of doling out cash to PC makers for joint advertising, which Intel rivals have alleged blocks them from some markets.

Otellini is more diplomatic, partly by nature, partly by necessity. The intensely private 55-year-old rarely reveals irritation—and then, with a slight frown. His management mantra: "Praise in public, criticize in private." . . .

The changes have created some angst among employees. In particular, many high-level engineers working on PC products feel they've been stripped of their star status. "The desktop group used to rule the company, and we liked it that way," says one former chip designer, adding that some engineers now feel "directionless." Other employees are simply uncomfortable with the new emphasis on marketing. "There definitely are people who are highly skeptical, who think this is all fluff, all just gloss—that if you make good technology, you don't need the glitz," says Genevieve Bell, an in-house ethnographer who researches how people in emerging markets like China and India use technology. . . .

So Otellini is shaking things up throughout the company. In addition to the reorg, he's making big changes in the way products are developed. While in the past engineers worked on ever-faster chips and then let marketers try to sell them, there are now teams of people with a cross-section of skills. Chip engineers, software developers, marketers, and market specialists all work together to come up with compelling products.

One example of the new approach is Bern Shen. A doctor who practiced internal medicine for 15 years, he joined Intel three months ago to help develop technologies for digital health. He works with Intel's ethnographers to figure out which technologies might help in monitoring the vital signs of the elderly or tracking the diet of people with Alzheimer's. "The fact that they hired me is an indication of the new Intel," he says.[1]

What are the key reasons that Paul Otellini is instituting major change within Intel? Discuss. For an interpretation of this case and additional comments, visit our Online Learning Center at

www.mhhe.com/kinickiob3e

FOR DISCUSSION

PAUL OTELLINI'S EXPERIENCES AT INTEL are not the exception. Increased global competition, startling breakthroughs in information technology, changes in consumer preferences, and calls for greater corporate ethics are forcing companies to change the way they do business. Employees want satisfactory work environments, customers are demanding greater value, and investors want more integrity in financial disclosures. The rate of organizational and societal change is clearly accelerating.

As exemplified by Intel in the opening vignette, organizations must change in order to satisfy customers and shareholders. The Intel case also illustrates a subtle and important aspect about any type of change, whether it be product driven, personal, or organizational. Organizational change is likely to encounter resistance even when it represents an appropriate course of action. Peter Senge, a well-known expert on the topic of organizational change, made the following comment about organizational change during an interview with *Fast Company* magazine:

> When I look at efforts to create change in big companies over the past 10 years, I have to say that there's enough evidence of success to say that change is possible—and enough evidence of failure to say that it isn't likely.[2]

If Senge is correct, then it is all the more important for current and future managers to learn how they can successfully implement organizational change. This final chapter was written to help managers navigate the journey of change.

Specifically, we discuss the forces that create the need for organization change, models of planned change, resistance to change, and creating a learning organization.

Forces of Change

How do organizations know when they should change? What cues should an organization look for? Although there are no clear-cut answers to these questions, the "cues" that signal the need for change are found by monitoring the forces for change.

Organizations encounter many different forces for change. These forces come from external sources outside the organization and from internal sources. This section examines the forces that create the need for change. Awareness of the forces of change can help managers determine when they should consider implementing an organizational change.

External Forces

External forces for change originate outside the organization. Because these forces have global effects, they may cause an organization to question the essence of what business it is in and the process by which products and services are produced. There are four key external forces for change: demographic characteristics, technological advancements, market changes, and social and political pressures. Each is now discussed.

external forces for change

Originate outside the organization.

Test Your Knowledge

Macro-environmental Forces

Demographic Characteristics   Chapter 4 provided a detailed discussion of the demographic changes occurring in the US workforce. We concluded that organizations need to effectively manage diversity if they are to receive maximum contribution and commitment from employees. Consider the implications associated with hiring the 80 million people dubbed the Net or Echo-Boom Generation—people born between 1977 and 1997:

> Employers will have to face the new realities of the Net Generation's culture and values, and what it wants from work if they expect to attract and retain those talents and align them with corporate goals. . . . The new wave of 80 million young people entering the workforce during the next 20 years are technologically equipped and, therefore, armed with the most powerful tools for business. That makes their place in history unique: No previous generation has grown up understanding, using, and expanding on such a pervasive instrument as the PC.[3]

The organizational challenge will be to motivate and utilize this talented pool of employees to its maximum potential.

Under its new CEO Robert Siegel, the venerable clothier Lacoste is responding to market forces. Shifting tastes among US shoppers inspired the company to restore its brand's luxury image with better fabrics, higher prices, more exclusive distribution, and newly designed multiseason fashions like stylish boots and shearling jackets that appeal to a new generation of shoppers. "When you think back to Lacoste 10 years ago," says Seigel, "we never had the young customer that we have now."

Technological Advancements   Both manufacturing and service organizations are increasingly using technology as a means to improve productivity, competitiveness, and customer service while also cutting costs. Microsoft and ExxonMobil are good examples. Microsoft hired Ray Ozzie, a renowned software expert who designed Lotus Notes, to "webify" all of Microsoft's products. To do this, "Microsoft must build a global network of server farms that will cost 'staggering' amounts of money, says Ozzie."[4] Microsoft is pursuing this change strategy in response to technological changes occurring within the global software industry. In contrast to Microsoft, ExxonMobil is already ahead of the game due to its application of technology. "Despite Big Oil's reputation as an old-economy industry, Exxon likes to think of itself as a technology company, pointing to systems like its brand-new Fast Drill Press that have allowed it to reduce the time it takes to drill wells by 35%, saving hundred of millions of dollars annually."[5] There is no question that the development and use of technological advancements is probably one of the biggest forces for change.

Customer and Market Changes   Increasing customer sophistication is requiring organizations to deliver higher value in their products and services. Customers are simply demanding more now than they did in the past. Moreover, customers are more likely to shop elsewhere if they do not get what they want because of lower customer switching costs. Wal-Mart, for example, stays abreast of customer preferences by conducting customer surveys and focus groups. This has enabled Wal-Mart to customize the product mix in its stores to local tastes.[6]

With respect to market changes, service companies are experiencing increased pressure to obtain more productivity because competition is fierce and prices have remained relatively stable.[7] Further, the emergence of a global economy is forcing companies to change the way they do business. US companies have been forging new partnerships and alliances with their suppliers and potential competitors in order to gain advantages in the global marketplace.

Social and Political Pressures These forces are created by social and political events. For example, the collapse of Enron and major accounting scandals at companies like WorldCom, American International Group, and Fannie Mae have created increased focus on the process by which organizations conduct financial reporting. This, in turn, has fueled boards of directors to pay more attention to what CEOs are doing and to exert more power and control into the manner in which organizations are being operated.[8]

Exelon is the largest nuclear power operator in the United States. Under CEO John Rowe, its response to internal forces must include increased capacity and a better safety record.

In general, social and political pressure is exerted through legislative bodies that represent the American populace. Political events also can create substantial change. For example, the war in Iraq created tremendous opportunities for defense contractors and organizations like Halliburton that are involved in rebuilding the country. Although it is difficult for organizations to predict changes in political forces, many organizations hire lobbyists and consultants to help them detect and respond to social and political changes.

Internal Forces

Internal forces for change come from inside the organization. These forces can be subtle, such as low job satisfaction, or can manifest in outward signs, such as low productivity or high turnover and conflict. For example, Exelon, America's largest nuclear power operator, undertook large-scale organizational change because its plants were running at only 47% capacity and safety problems landed the company on the Nuclear Regulatory Commission's watch list.[9] In general, internal forces for change come from both human resource problems and managerial behavior/decisions.

internal forces for change

Originate inside the organization.

Manager's Hot Seat Application

Change: More Pain than Gain

Models of Planned Change

American managers are criticized for emphasizing short-term, quick-fix solutions to organizational problems. When applied to organizational change, this approach is doomed from the start. Quick-fix solutions do not really solve underlying causes of problems and they have little staying power. Researchers and managers alike have thus tried to identify effective ways to manage the change process. This section reviews three models of planned change—Lewin's change model, a systems model of change, and Kotter's eight steps for leading organizational change—and organizational development.

Lewin's Change Model

Most theories of organizational change originated from the landmark work of social psychologist Kurt Lewin. Lewin developed a three-stage model of planned change which explained how to initiate, manage, and stabilize the change process.[10] The three stages are unfreezing, changing, and refreezing.

Unfreezing   The focus of this stage is to create the motivation to change. In so doing, individuals are encouraged to replace old behaviors and attitudes with those desired by management. Managers can begin the unfreezing process by disconfirming the usefulness or appropriateness of employees' present behaviors or attitudes. In other words, employees need to become dissatisfied with the old way of doing things. Managers frequently create the motivation for change by presenting data regarding levels of effectiveness, efficiency, or customer satisfaction. For example, Mark Hurd, CEO of Hewlett-Packard (HP), unfroze the organization about the need to restructure by using information he obtained from corporate customers and HP employees. Customers told Hurd that HP's structure was so confusing that they did not know whom to call for help. HP salespeople complained that they spent only 33 percent of their time with customers because they were required to complete so much administrative paperwork.[11]

benchmarking

Process by which a company compares its performance with that of high-performing organizations.

Benchmarking is another technique that can be used to unfreeze an organization. **Benchmarking** "describes the overall process by which a company compares its performance with that of other companies, then learns how the strongest-performing companies achieve their results."[12] For example, one company for which we consulted discovered through benchmarking that their costs to develop software were twice as high as the best companies in the industry, and the time it took to get a new product to market was four times longer than the benchmarked organizations. These data were ultimately used to unfreeze employees' attitudes and motivate people to change the organization's internal processes in order to remain competitive. Managers also need to devise ways to reduce the barriers to change during this stage.

Changing   Organizational change, whether large or small, is undertaken to improve some process, procedure, product, service, or outcome of interest to management. Because change involves learning and doing things differently, this stage entails providing employees with new information, new behavioral models, new processes or procedures, new equipment, new technology, or new ways of getting the job done. How does management know what to change?

There is no simple answer to this question. Organizational change can be aimed at improvement or growth, or it can focus on solving a problem such as poor customer service or low productivity. Change also can be targeted at different levels in an organization. For example, sending managers to leadership training programs can be a solution to improving individuals' job satisfaction and productivity. In contrast, installing new information technology may be the change required to increase work group productivity and overall corporate profits. The point to keep in mind is that change should be targeted at some type of desired end-result. The systems model of change, which is the next model to be discussed, provides managers with a framework to diagnose the target of change.

Refreezing   Change is stabilized during refreezing by helping employees integrate the changed behavior or attitude into their normal way of doing things. This is accomplished by first giving employees the chance to exhibit the new behaviors or attitudes. Once exhibited, positive reinforcement is used to reinforce the desired change. Additional coaching and modeling also are used at this point to reinforce the stability of the change. Extrinsic rewards, particularly monetary incentives (recall our discussion in Chapter 8), are frequently used to reinforce behavioral change.

A Systems Model of Change

A systems approach takes a "big picture" perspective of organizational change. It is based on the notion that any change, no matter how large or small, has a cascading effect throughout an organization.[13] For example, promoting an individual to a new work group affects the group dynamics in both the old and new groups. Similarly, creating project or work teams may necessitate the need to revamp compensation practices. These examples illustrate that change creates additional change. Today's solutions are tomorrow's problems.

A systems model of change offers managers a framework or model to use for diagnosing *what* to change and for determining *how* to evaluate the success of a change effort. To further your understanding about this model, we first describe its components and then discuss a brief application. The four main components of a systems model of change are inputs, strategic plans, target elements of change, and outputs (see Figure 16–1).

Inputs   All organizational changes should be consistent with an organization's mission, vision, and resulting strategic plan. A **mission statement** represents the "reason" an organization exists, and an organization's *vision* is a long-term goal that describes "what" an organization wants to become. Consider how the difference between mission and vision affects organizational change. Your university probably has a mission to educate people. This mission does not necessarily imply anything about change. It simply defines the university's overall purpose. In contrast, the university may have a vision to be recognized as the "best" university in the country. This vision requires the organization to benchmark itself against other world-class universities and to create plans for achieving the vision. For example, the vision of the W. P. Carey School of Business at Arizona State University is to be among the top 25 business schools in the world. An assessment of an organization's internal strengths and weaknesses against its environmental opportunities and threats (SWOT) is another key input within the systems model. This SWOT analysis is a key component of the strategic planning process.

> **mission statement**
>
> **Summarizes "why" an organization exists.**

Strategic Plans   A **strategic plan** outlines an organization's long-term direction and the actions necessary to achieve planned results. Among other things, strategic plans are based on results from a SWOT analysis. This analysis aids in developing an organizational strategy to attain desired goals such as profits, customer satisfaction, quality, adequate return on investment, and acceptable levels of turnover and employee satisfaction and commitment.

> **strategic plan**
>
> **A long-term plan outlining actions needed to achieve desired results.**

Target Elements of Change   **Target elements of change** are the components of an organization that may be changed. They essentially represent change levers that managers can push and pull to influence various aspects of an organization. The choice of which lever to pull, however, is based on a diagnosis of a problem, or problems, or the actions needed to accomplish a vision or goal: A problem exists when

> **target elements of change**
>
> **Components of an organization that may be changed.**

FIGURE 16–1   A Systems Model of Change

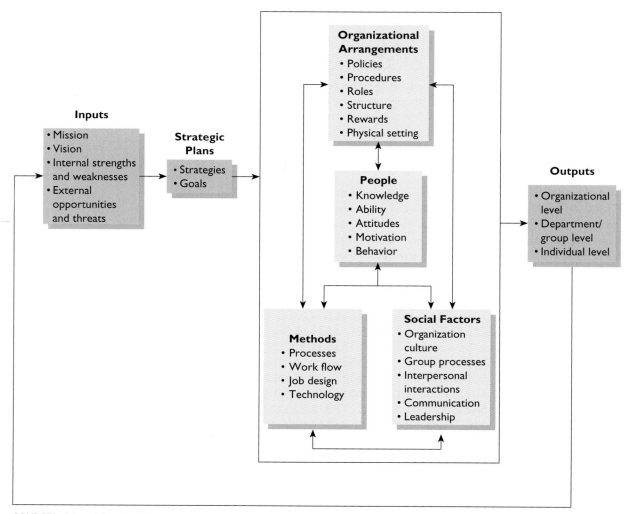

Target Elements of Change

SOURCES: Adapted from D R Fuqua and D J Kurpius, "Conceptual Models in Organizational Consultation," *Journal of Counseling & Development*, July/August 1993, pp 602–18; and D A Nadler and M L Tushman, "Organizational Frame Bending: Principles for Managing Reorientation," *Academy of Management Executive*, August 1989, pp 194–203.

managers are not obtaining the results they desire. The target elements of change are used to diagnose problems and to identify change-related solutions.

As shown in Figure 16–1, there are four targeted elements of change: organizational arrangements, social factors, methods, and people.[14] Each target element of change contains a subset of more detailed organizational features. For instance, the "social factors" component includes consideration of an organization's culture, group processes, interpersonal interactions, communication, and leadership. There are two final issues to keep in mind about the target elements of change shown in Figure 16–1. First, the double-headed arrows connecting each target element of change convey the message that change ripples across an organization. For example, changing a reward system to reinforce team rather than individual performance (an organizational arrangement) is likely to impact organizational culture (a social factor). Second, the "people" component is placed in the center of the target elements of change box because all organizational change ultimately impacts employees. Organizational change is more likely to succeed when managers proactively consider the impact of change on its employees.

Outputs   Outputs represent the desired end-results of a change. Once again, these end-results should be consistent with an organization's strategic plan. Figure 16–1 indicates that change may be directed at the organizational level, department/group level, or individual level. Change efforts are more complicated and difficult to manage when they are targeted at the organizational level. This occurs because organizational-level changes are more likely to affect multiple target elements of change shown in the model.

Applying the Systems Model of Change   There are two different ways to apply the systems model of change. The first is as an aid during the strategic planning process. Once a group of managers has determined its vision and strategic goals, the target elements of change can be considered when developing action plans to support the accomplishment of goals. For example, the management team at J P Morgan Chase & Co. established goals to increase revenue and decrease costs. They decided to cut 12,000 jobs (a people factor), decrease executive perks like country club memberships and first-class airfare (an organizational arrangements factor), and to invest heavily in information technology in order to redesign the work flow (a method factor).[15] The second application involves using the model as a diagnostic framework to determine the causes of an organizational problem and to propose solutions. We highlight this application by considering a consulting project in which we used the model.[16]

We were contacted by the CEO of a software company and asked to figure out why the presidents of three divisions were not collaborating with each other—the problem. It turned out that two of the presidents submitted a proposal for the same $4 million project from a potential customer. Our client did not get the work because the customer was appalled at having received two proposals from the same company; hence the CEO's call to us. We decided to interview employees by using a structured set of questions that pertained to each of the target elements of change. For instance, we asked employees to comment on the extent to which the reward system, organizational culture, work flow, and physical setting contributed to collaboration across divisions. The interviews taught us that the lack of collaboration among the division presidents was due to the reward system (an organizational arrangement), a competitive culture and poor communications (social factors), and poor work flow (a methods factor). Our recommendation was to change the reward systems, restructure the organization, and redesign the work flow.

Kotter's Eight Steps for Leading Organizational Change

John Kotter, an expert in leadership and change management, believes that organizational change typically fails because senior management makes a host of implementation errors. Kotter proposed an eight-step process for leading change (see Table 16–1) based on these errors.[17] Unlike the systems model of change, this

TABLE 16–1   Steps to Leading Organizational Change

Step	Description
1. Establish a sense of urgency	Unfreeze the organization by creating a compelling reason for why change is needed.
2. Create the guiding coalition	Create a cross-functional, cross-level group of people with enough power to lead the change.
3. Develop a vision and strategy	Create a vision and strategic plan to guide the change process.
4. Communicate the change vision	Create and implement a communication strategy that consistently communicates the new vision and strategic plan.
5. Empower broad-based action	Eliminate barriers to change, and use target elements of change to transform the organization. Encourage risk taking and creative problem solving.
6. Generate short-term wins	Plan for and create short-term "wins" or improvements. Recognize and reward people who contribute to the wins.
7. Consolidate gains and produce more change	The guiding coalition uses credibility from short-term wins to create more change. Additional people are brought into the change process as change cascades throughout the organization. Attempts are made to reinvigorate the change process.
8. Anchor new approaches in the culture	Reinforce the changes by highlighting connections between new behaviors and processes and organizational success. Develop methods to ensure leadership development and succession.

SOURCE: The steps were developed by J P Kotter, *Leading Change* (Boston: Harvard Business School Press, 1996).

Communicating change is an important step in all models of organizational change. When US Airways and America West merged their operations, Troy Fernwalt (standing at whiteboard) helped coordinate and explain to colleagues the merging of the two companies' complex corporate Web sites.

model is not diagnostic in orientation. Its application will not help managers to diagnose *what* needs to be changed. Rather, this model is more like Lewin's model of change in that it prescribes *how* managers should sequence or lead the change process.

Kotter's eight steps shown in Table 16–1 subsume Lewin's model of change. The first four steps represent Lewin's "unfreezing" stage. Steps 5, 6, and 7 represent "changing," and step 8 corresponds to "refreezing." The value of Kotter's steps is that they provide specific recommendations about behaviors that managers need to exhibit to successfully lead organizational change. It is important to remember that Kotter's research reveals that it is ineffective to skip steps and that successful organizational change is 70% to 90%

leadership and only 10% to 30% management. Senior managers are thus advised to focus on leading rather than managing change.[18]

Creating Change through Organization Development

Organization development (OD) is different from the previously discussed models of change. OD does not entail a structured sequence as proposed by Lewin and Kotter, but it does possess the same diagnostic focus associated with the systems model of change. That said, OD is much broader in orientation than any of the previously discussed models. Specifically, a pair of experts in this field of study and practice defined **organization development** as follows:

> **organization development**
>
> **A set of techniques or tools that are used to implement organizational change.**

> OD consists of planned efforts to help persons work and live together more effectively, over time, in their organizations. These goals are achieved by applying behavioral science principles, methods, and theories adapted from the fields of psychology, sociology, education, and management.[19]

As you can see from this definition, OD constitutes a set of techniques or interventions that are used to implement "planned" organizational change aimed at increasing "an organization's ability to improve itself as a humane and effective system."[20] OD techniques or interventions apply to each of the change models discussed in this section. For example, OD is used during Lewin's "changing" stage. It also is used to identify and implement targeted elements of change within the systems model of change. Finally, OD might be used during Kotter's steps 1, 3, 5, 6, and 7. In this section, we briefly review the four identifying characteristics of OD and its research and practical implications.[21]

OD Involves Profound Change Change agents using OD generally desire deep and long-lasting improvement. OD consultant Warner Burke, for example, who strives for fundamental *cultural* change, wrote: "By fundamental change, as opposed to fixing a problem or improving a procedure, I mean that some significant aspect of an organization's culture will never be the same."[22]

OD Is Value Loaded Owing to the fact that OD is rooted partially in humanistic psychology, many OD consultants carry certain values or biases into the client organization. They prefer cooperation over conflict, self-control over institutional control, and democratic and participative management over autocratic management. In addition to OD being driven by a consultant's values, OD practitioners now believe that there is a broader "value perspective" that should underlie any organizational change. Specifically, OD should always be customer focused and it should help an organization achieve its vision and strategic goals. This approach implies that organizational interventions should be aimed at helping to satisfy customers' needs and thereby provide enhanced value of an organization's products and services.

OD Is a Diagnosis/Prescription Cycle OD theorists and practitioners have long adhered to a medical model of organization. Like medical doctors, internal and external OD consultants approach the "sick" organization, "diagnose" its ills, "prescribe" and implement an intervention, and "monitor" progress. Table 16–2 presents a list of several different OD interventions that can be used to change individual, group, or organizational behavior as whole.

TABLE 16-2   Some OD Interventions for Implementing Change

- **Survey feedback:** A questionnaire is distributed to employees to ascertain their perceptions and attitudes. The results are then shared with them. The questionnaire may ask about such matters as group cohesion, job satisfaction, and managerial leadership. Once the survey is done, meaningful results can be communicated with employees so that they can then engage in problem solving and constructive changes.

- **Process consultation:** An OD consultant observes the communication process—interpersonal-relations, decision-making, and conflict-handling patterns—occurring in work groups and provides feedback to the members involved. In consulting with employees (particularly managers) about these processes, the change agent hopes to give them the skills to identify and improve group dynamics on their own.

- **Team building:** Work groups are made to become more effective by helping members learn to function as a team. For example, members of a group might be interviewed independently by the OD change agent to establish how they feel about the group, then a meeting may be held away from their usual workplace to discuss the issues. To enhance team cohesiveness, the OD consultant may have members work together on a project such as rock climbing, with the consultant helping with communication and conflict resolution. The objective is for members to see how they can individually contribute to the group's goals and efforts.

- **Intergroup development:** Intergroup development resembles team building in many of its efforts. However, intergroup development attempts to achieve better cohesiveness among several work groups, not just one. During the process, the change agent tries to elicit misperceptions and stereotypes that the groups have for each other so that they can be discussed, leading to better coordination among them.

- **Technostructural activities:** Technostructural activities are interventions concerned with improving the work technology or organizational design with people on the job. An intervention involving a work-technology change might be the introduction of e-mail to improve employee communication. An intervention involving an organizational-design change might be making a company less centralized in its decision making.

SOURCE: A Kinicki and B Williams, *Management: A Practical Introduction,* 2nd ed. (Burr Ridge: IL: McGraw-Hill/Irwin, 2006), p 329.

OD Is Process Oriented   Ideally, OD consultants focus on the form and not the content of behavioral and administrative dealings. For example, product design engineers and market researchers might be coached on how to communicate more effectively with one another without the consultant knowing the technical details of their conversations. In addition to communication, OD specialists focus on other processes, including problem solving, decision making, conflict handling, trust, power sharing, and career development.

OD Research and Practical Implications   Before discussing OD research, it is important to note that many of the topics contained in this book are used during OD interventions. Team building, for example, is commonly used as an OD technique. It is used to improve the functioning of work groups. The point is that

OD research has practical implications for a variety of OB applications previously discussed. OD-related interventions produced the following insights:

- A meta-analysis of 18 studies indicated that employee satisfaction with change was higher when top management was highly committed to the change effort.[23]

- A meta-analysis of 52 studies provided support for the systems model of organizational change. Specifically, varying one target element of change created changes in other target elements. Also, there was a positive relationship between individual behavior change and organizational-level change.[24]

- A meta-analysis of 126 studies demonstrated that multifaceted interventions using more than one OD technique were more effective in changing job attitudes and work attitudes than interventions that relied on only one human-process or technostructural approach.[25]

- A survey of 1,700 firms from China, Japan, the United States, and Europe revealed that (1) US and European firms used OD interventions more frequently than firms from China and Japan and (2) some OD interventions are culture free and some are not.[26]

There are four practical implications derived from this research. First, planned organizational change works. However, management and change agents are advised to rely on multifaceted interventions. As indicated elsewhere in this book, goal setting, feedback, recognition and rewards, training, participation, and challenging job design have good track records relative to improving performance and satisfaction. Second, change programs are more successful when they are geared toward meeting both short-term and long-term results. Managers should not engage in organizational change for the sake of change. Change efforts should produce positive results. Third, organizational change is more likely to succeed when top management is truly committed to the change process and the desired goals of the change program. This is particularly true when organizations pursue large-scale transformation. Finally, the effectiveness of OD interventions is affected by cross-cultural considerations. Managers and OD consultants should not blindly apply an OD intervention that worked in one country to a similar situation in another country.

Understanding and Managing Resistance to Change

We are all creatures of habit. It generally is difficult for people to try new ways of doing things. It is precisely because of this basic human characteristic that most employees do not have enthusiasm for change in the workplace. Rare is the manager who does not have several stories about carefully cultivated changes that died on the vine because of resistance to change. It is important for managers to learn to manage resistance because failed change efforts are costly. Costs include decreased employee loyalty, lowered probability of achieving corporate goals, waste of money and resources, and difficulty in fixing the failed change effort. This section examines employee resistance to change and practical ways of dealing with the problem.

Group Exercise

Overcoming Resistance to Change

Why People Resist Change in the Workplace

No matter how technically or administratively perfect a proposed change may be, people make or break it. Individual and group behavior following an organizational change can take many forms. The extremes range from acceptance to active resistance. **Resistance to change** is an emotional/behavioral response to real or imagined threats to an established work routine. Resistance can be as subtle as passive resignation and as overt as deliberate sabotage. Let us now consider the reasons employees resist change in the first place. Eleven of the leading reasons are listed here:[27]

resistance to change

Emotional/behavioral response to real or imagined work changes.

© 2004 Ted Goff

BECAUSE WE'VE ALWAYS DONE IT THIS WAY, THAT'S WHY.

Copyright © Ted Goff. Reprinted with permission.

1. *An individual's predisposition toward change.* This predisposition is highly personal and deeply ingrained. It is an outgrowth of how one learns to handle change and ambiguity as a child. While some people are distrustful and suspicious of change, others see change as a situation requiring flexibility, patience, and understanding.[28]

2. *Surprise and fear of the unknown.* When innovative or radically different changes are introduced without warning, affected employees become fearful of the implications. Grapevine rumors fill the void created by a lack of official announcements. This is exactly what happened when General Motors announced its negotiated plan to reduce its workforce through a carefully designed attrition program. The reduction in workforce was needed to help GM lower its operating costs.

Almost as soon as yesterday's buyout offer from General Motors Corp. was announced, news—and rumors—began sweeping through the company's truck assembly plant in Pontiac, Mich. "It spread like wildfire," said 52-year-old Larry Walker, a 33-year veteran of the plant, which employs 2,500 hourly workers and makes the GMC Sierra Truck and Chevrolet Silverado. "I talked about it with my buddies all day long. We're all trying to figure out what we should do."[29]

3. *Climate of mistrust.* Trust, as discussed in Chapter 9, involves reciprocal faith in others' intentions and behavior. Mutual mistrust can doom to failure an otherwise well-conceived change. Mistrust encourages secrecy, which begets deeper mistrust. Managers who trust their employees make the change process an open, honest, and participative affair. Employees who, in turn, trust management are more willing to expend extra effort and take chances with something different.

4. *Fear of failure.* Intimidating changes on the job can cause employees to doubt their capabilities. Self-doubt erodes self-confidence and cripples personal growth and development.

5. *Loss of status and/or job security.* Administrative and technological changes that threaten to alter power bases or eliminate jobs generally trigger strong

resistance. For example, most corporate restructuring involves the elimination of managerial jobs. One should not be surprised when middle managers resist restructuring and participative management programs that reduce their authority and status.

6. *Peer pressure.* Someone who is not directly affected by a change may actively resist it to protect the interest of his or her friends and co-workers.

7. *Disruption of cultural traditions and/or group relationships.* Whenever individuals are transferred, promoted, or reassigned, cultural and group dynamics are thrown into disequilibrium.

8. *Personality conflicts.* Just as a friend can get away with telling us something we would resent hearing from an adversary, the personalities of change agents can breed resistance.

9. *Lack of tact and/or poor timing.* Undue resistance can occur because changes are introduced in an insensitive manner or at an awkward time.

10. *Nonreinforcing reward systems.* Individuals resist when they do not foresee positive rewards for changing. For example, an employee is unlikely to support a change effort that is perceived as requiring him or her to work longer with more pressure.

11. *Past success.* Success can breed complacency. It also can foster a stubbornness to change because people come to believe that what worked in the past will work in the future. Coca-Cola's strategic change initiatives were undermined by this form of resistance.

> For too long Coke has stayed stubbornly, defiantly rooted in its past, holding on to the belief that its business model was as good as gold: Make cola concentrate for pennies, then sell it for dollars through a global bottling system to a mass market that still pretty much drank what it saw on TV. When bottled water came along, one director called it a "low-margin road to nowhere." The company was late to the game in sports drinks, energy drinks, and coffee, regarding them as low volume distractions. . . . The irony, says analyst Matthew Reilly of Morningstar, is that until just recently, "Coke wasn't even a player in energy drinks—and it was the original energy drink."[30]

Alternative Strategies for Overcoming Resistance to Change

Before recommending specific approaches to overcome resistance, there are five key conclusions that should be kept in mind. First, an organization must be ready for change. Just as a table must be set before you can eat, so must an organization be ready for change before it can be effective.[31] Second, people are more likely to resist change when they do not agree on the causes of current problems and the need for change. This is a "cognitive" hurdle that must be overcome by increasing employees' commitment to change.[32] **Commitment to change** is defined as a mind-set "that binds an individual to a course of action deemed necessary for the successful implementation of a change initiative."[33] In order to bring this concept to life, we would like you to complete a shortened version of a commitment to change instrument

commitment to change

A mind-set of doing whatever it takes to effectively implement change.

Does Your Commitment to a Change Initiative Predict Your Behavioral Support for the Change?

INSTRUCTIONS: First, think of a time in which a previous or current employer was undergoing a change initiative that required you to learn something new or to discontinue an attitude, behavior, or organizational practice. Next, evaluate your commitment to this change effort by indicating the extent to which you agree with the following survey items. Use the rating scale shown below. Finally, assess your behavioral support for the change.

$$1 = \text{Strongly disagree}$$
$$2 = \text{Disagree}$$
$$3 = \text{Neither agree nor disagree}$$
$$4 = \text{Agree}$$
$$5 = \text{Strongly agree}$$

1. I believe in the value of this change   1——2——3——4——5
2. This change serves an important purpose   1——2——3——4——5
3. This change is a good strategy for the organization   1——2——3——4——5
4. I have no choice but to go along with this change   1——2——3——4——5
5. It would be risky to speak out against this change   1——2——3——4——5
6. It would be too costly for me to resist this change   1——2——3——4——5
7. I feel a sense of duty to work toward this change   1——2——3——4——5
8. It would be irresponsible of me to resist this change   1——2——3——4——5
9. I feel obligated to support this change   1——2——3——4——5

Total score =_____

ARBITRARY NORMS

9–18 = Low commitment
19–35 = Moderate commitment
36–45 = High commitment

BEHAVIORAL SUPPORT FOR THE CHANGE

Overall, I modified my attitudes and behavior in line with what management was trying to accomplish   1——2——3——4——5

SOURCE: Survey items were obtained from L Herscovitch and J P Meyer, "Commitment to Organizational Change: Extension of a Three-Component Model," *Journal of Applied Psychology*, June 2002, p 477.

presented in the Hands-On Exercise. Were you committed to the change? Did this level of commitment affect your behavioral support for what management was trying to accomplish?

Third, organizational change is less successful when top management fails to keep employees informed about the process of change. Fourth, do not assume that people are consciously resisting change. Managers are encouraged to use the systems model of change to identify the obstacles that are affecting the implementation process. Fifth, employees' perceptions or interpretations of a change significantly affect resistance. Employees are less likely to resist when they perceive that the benefits of a change overshadow the personal costs. At a minimum then, managers are advised to (1) provide as much information as possible to employees about the

Six Strategies for Overcoming Resistance to Change   TABLE 16–3

Approach	Commonly Used in Situations	Advantages	Drawbacks
Education + Communication	Where there is a lack of information or inaccurate information and analysis.	Once persuaded, people will often help with the implementation of the change.	Can be very time consuming if lots of people are involved.
Participation + Involvement	Where the initiators do not have all the information they need to design the change and where others have considerable power to resist.	People who participate will be committed to implementing change, and any relevant information they have will be integrated into the change plan.	Can be very time consuming if participators design an inappropriate change.
Facilitation + Support	Where people are resisting because of adjustment problems.	No other approach works as well with adjustment problems.	Can be time consuming, expensive, and still fail.
Negotiation + Agreement	Where someone or some group will clearly lose out in a change and where that group has considerable power to resist.	Sometimes it is a relatively easy way to avoid major resistance.	Can be too expensive in many cases if it alerts others to negotiate for compliance.
Manipulation + Co-optation	Where other tactics will not work or are too expensive.	It can be a relatively quick and inexpensive solution to resistance problems.	Can lead to future problems if people feel manipulated.
Explicit + Implicit coercion	Where speed is essential and where the change initiators possess considerable power.	It is speedy and can overcome any kind of resistance.	Can be risky if it leaves people angry at the initiators.

change, (2) inform employees about the reasons/rationale for the change, (3) conduct meetings to address employees' questions regarding the change, and (4) provide employees the opportunity to discuss how the proposed change might affect them.[34] These recommendations underscore the importance of communicating with employees throughout the process of change.

In addition to communication, employee participation in the change process is another generic approach for reducing resistance. That said, however, organizational change experts have criticized the tendency to treat participation as a cure-all for resistance to change. They prefer a contingency approach because resistance can take many forms and, furthermore, because situational factors vary (see Table 16–3). As seen in Table 16–3, Participation + Involvement does have its place, but it takes time that is not always available. Also as indicated in Table 16–3, each of the other five methods has its situational niche, advantages, and drawbacks. In short, there is no universal strategy for overcoming resistance to change. Managers need a complete repertoire of change strategies.

Creating a Learning Organization

Organizations are finding that yesterday's competitive advantage is becoming the minimum entrance requirement for staying in business. This puts tremendous pressure on organizations to learn how best to improve and stay ahead of competitors. In fact, both researchers and practicing managers agree that an organization's capability to learn is a key strategic weapon. It thus is important for organizations to enhance and nurture their capability to learn.[35]

So what is organizational learning and how do organizations become learning organizations? To help clarify what this process entails, this section begins by defining organizational learning and a learning organization. We then present a model of organizational learning and conclude by reviewing new roles and skills required of leaders to create a learning organization.

Defining Organizational Learning and a Learning Organization

Organizational learning (OL) and a learning organization (LO) are not the same thing. Susan Fisher and Margaret White, experts on organizational change and learning, define organizational learning as follows:

> Organizational learning is a reflective process, played out by members at all levels of the organization, that involves the collection of information from both the external and internal environments. This information is filtered through a collective sensemaking process, which results in shared interpretations that can be used to instigate actions resulting in enduring changes to the organization's behavior and theories in use.[36]

This definition highlights that organizational learning represents a process by which information is gathered and then interpreted through a cognitive, social process. The accumulated information from this interpretative process represents an organization's knowledge base. This knowledge in turn is stored in organizational "memory," which consists of files, records, procedures, policies, and organizational culture. In contrast, learning organizations use organizational knowledge to foster innovation and organizational effectiveness.

Peter Senge, a professor at the Massachusetts Institute of Technology, popularized the term *learning organization* in his best-selling book entitled *The Fifth Discipline.* He described a learning organization as "a group of people working together to collectively enhance their capacities to create results that they truly care about."[37] A practical interpretation of these ideas results in the following definition. A **learning organization** is one that proactively creates, acquires, and transfers knowledge and that changes its behavior on the basis of new knowledge and insights.

By breaking this definition into its three component parts, we can clearly see the characteristics of a learning organization. First, new ideas

learning organization

Proactively creates, acquires, and transfers knowledge throughout the organization.

FIGURE 16–2
Building an
Organization's
Learning
Capability

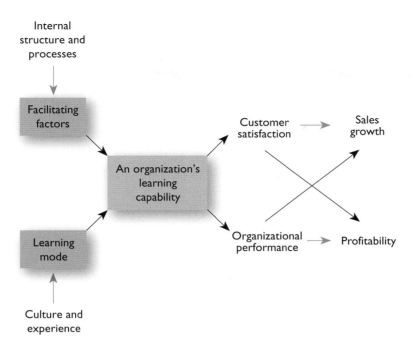

are a prerequisite for learning. Learning organizations actively try to infuse their organizations with new ideas and information. They do this by constantly scanning their external environments, hiring new talent and expertise when needed, and devoting significant resources to train and develop their employees. Second, new knowledge must be transferred throughout the organization. Learning organizations strive to reduce structural, process, and interpersonal barriers to the sharing of information, ideas, and knowledge among organizational members. Finally, behavior must change as a result of new knowledge. Learning organizations are results oriented. They foster an environment in which employees are encouraged to use new behaviors and operational processes to achieve corporate goals.[38]

Building an Organization's Learning Capability

Figure 16–2 presents a model of how organizations build and enhance their learning capability. **Learning capabilities** represent the set of core competencies, which are defined as the special knowledge, skills, and technological know-how that differentiate an organization from its competitors, and processes that enable an organization to adapt to its environment. The general idea underlying Figure 16–2 is that learning capabilities are the fuel for organizational success. Just like gasoline enables a car's engine to perform, learning capabilities equip an organization to foresee and respond to internal and external changes. This capability, in turn, increases the chances of satisfying customers and boosting sales and profitability. Let us now consider the two major contributors to an organization's learning capability: facilitating factors and learning mode.

learning capabilities

The set of core competencies and internal processes that enable an organization to adapt to its environment.

Facilitating Factors *Facilitating factors* represent "the internal structure and processes that affect how easy or hard it is for learning to occur and the amount of

TABLE 16–4   Factors That Facilitate Organizational Learning Capabilities

1. Scanning imperative	Interest in external happenings and in the nature of one's environment. Valuing the processes of awareness and data generation. Curious about what is "out there" as opposed to "in here."
2. Performance gap	Shared perception of a gap between actual and desired state of performance. Disconfirming feedback interrupts a string of successes. Performance shortfalls are seen as opportunities for learning.
3. Concern for measurement	Spend considerable effort in defining and measuring key factors when venturing into new areas; strive for specific, quantifiable measures; discourse over metrics is seen as a learning activity.
4. Experimental mind-set	Support for trying new things; curiosity about how things work; ability to "play" with things. Small failures are encouraged, not punished. See changes in work processes, policies, and structures as a continuous series of graded tryouts.
5. Climate of openness	Accessibility of information; relatively open boundaries. Opportunities to observe others; problems/errors are shared, not hidden; debate and conflict are acceptable.
6. Continuous education	Ongoing commitment to education at all levels; support for development of members.
7. Operational variety	Variety exists in response modes, procedures, systems; significant diversity in personnel. Pluralistic rather than monolithic definition of valued internal capabilities.
8. Multiple advocates	Top-down and bottom-up initiatives are possible; multiple advocates and gatekeepers exist.
9. Involved leadership	Leadership at significant levels articulates vision and is very actively engaged in its actualization; takes ongoing steps to implement vision; "hands-on" involvement in educational and other implementation steps.
10. Systems perspective	Strong focus on how parts of the organization are interdependent; seek optimization of organizational goals at the highest levels; see problems and solutions in terms of systemic relationships.

SOURCE: From B Moingeon and A Edmondson, *Organizational Learning and Competitive Advantage.* Copyright © 1996 by Sage Publications. Reprinted by permission of Sage Publications, Inc.

effective learning that takes place."[39] Table 16–4 contains a list of 10 key facilitating factors. Keep in mind as you read them that these factors can either enable or impede an organization's ability to respond to its environment. Consider, for example, the "scanning imperative" and "concern for measurement" factors. We noted in Chapter 10 that high-performance organizations were five times more likely than low-performing organizations to use analytics when making decisions: Analytics involves a conscientious and explicit process of making decisions on the basis of the best available evidence.[40] The practice of analytics can only be implemented if an organization is scanning its environment for information and measuring the effectiveness of its operations and decisions.[41] It thus appears that an organization's learning capabilities are a key component of using analytics and creating competitive advantage.

Learning Mode **Learning modes** represent the various ways in which organizations attempt to create and maximize their learning. Figure 16–2 shows that learning modes are directly influenced by an organization's culture and experience or past history.[42] The Men's Wearhouse, for example, is highly committed to organizational learning. The company sends all employees on average to 40 hours of training a year. Consider how the organizational culture affects this commitment to training:

> **learning modes**
> The various ways in which organizations attempt to create and maximize their learning.

> "We know that the only constant is change," says Eric Anderson, Men's Wearhouse's director of training. "We have said for a long time that we are in the people business, not the men's clothing business. We happen to sell men's clothing, but by recognizing what is really important—the people—we have a different paradigm than many other businesses. In order of priority, our employees, our customers, our vendors, our communities in which we do business, and our stockholders are our key stakeholders."
>
> Anderson says his challenge has been to create an environment where employees want to bring the best of themselves to work so that the business achieves positive results. "How do you nurture creativity, empowerment, responsibility, trust, and excitement?" he asks. "We try to recognize and nurture the potential in people. Because we are in the people business, training permeates our company culture."[43]

OB researcher Danny Miller reviewed the literature on organizational learning and identified six dominant modes of learning:[44]

1. *Analytic learning.* Learning occurs through systematic gathering of internal and external information. Information tends to be quantitative and analyzed via formal systems. The emphasis is on using deductive logic to numerically analyze objective data.

2. *Synthetic learning.* Synthetic learning is more intuitive and generic than the analytic mode. It emphasizes the synthesis of large amounts of complex information by using systems thinking. That is, employees try to identify interrelationships between issues, problems, and opportunities.

3. *Experimental learning.* This mode is a rational methodological approach that is based on conducting small experiments and monitoring the results.

4. *Interactive learning.* This mode involves learning-by-doing. Rather than using systematic methodological procedures, learning occurs primarily through the exchange of information. Learning is more intuitive and inductive.

5. *Structural learning.* This mode is a methodological approach that is based on the use of organizational routines. Organizational routines represent standardized processes and procedures that specify how to carry out tasks and roles. People learn from routines because they direct attention, institutionalize standards, and create consistent vocabularies.

6. *Institutional learning.* This mode represents an inductive process by which organizations share and model values, beliefs, and practices either from their external environments or from senior executives. Employees learn by observing environmental examples or senior executives. Socialization and mentoring play a significant role in institutional learning.

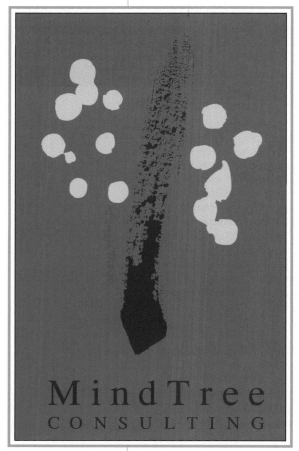

At MindTree Consulting, an engineering firm, learning was built in from the company's founding. Its corporate logo was designed by a child with cerebral palsy, which signifies, according to Chief Operating Officer Subroto Bagchi, that "We believe there is much we can learn from everyone." To "break the engineering mindset," the company invites people from widely diverse backgrounds such as dance, space exploration, and writing to present lectures for its 3,500 employees.

Leadership Is the Foundation of a Learning Organization

Leadership is the key to fostering organizational learning and the creation of a learning organization. The most effective leaders are those who use both transactional and transformational leadership (recall our discussion in Chapter 14) to facilitate organizational learning.[45] To make this happen, however, leaders must adopt new roles and associated activities. Specifically, leaders perform three key functions in building a learning organization: (1) building a commitment to learning, (2) working to generate ideas with impact, and (3) working to generalize ideas with impact.[46]

Building a Commitment to Learning
Leaders need to instill an intellectual and emotional commitment to learning. Thomas Tierney, former CEO of Bain & Company, proposes that leaders foster this commitment by building a culture that promotes the concept of "teacher-learners." His concept is based on the idea that organizational learning and innovation are enhanced when employees behave like both teachers and learners.[47] Of course, leaders also need to invest the financial resources needed to create a learning infrastructure.

Working to Generate Ideas with Impact
Ideas with impact are those that add value to one or more of an organization's three key stakeholders: employees, customers, and shareholders. Experts suggest the following ways to generate ideas with impact:

- Implement continuous improvement programs.
- Increase employee competence through training, or buy talent from outside the organization.
- Experiment with new ideas, processes, and structural arrangements.
- Go outside the organization to identify world-class ideas and processes.
- Instill systems thinking throughout the organization.

Working to Generalize Ideas with Impact   Leaders must make a concerted effort to reduce interpersonal, group, and organizational barriers to learning. This can be done by creating a learning infrastructure.[48] This is a large-scale effort that includes the following activities:

- Measuring and rewarding learning.
- Increasing open and honest dialogue among organizational members.

- Reducing conflict.
- Increasing horizontal and vertical communication.
- Promoting teamwork.
- Rewarding risk taking and innovation.
- Reducing the fear of failure.
- Increasing the sharing of successes, failures, and best practices across organizational members.
- Reducing stressors and frustration.
- Reducing internal competition.
- Increasing cooperation and collaboration.
- Creating a psychologically safe and comforting environment.[49]

Unlearning the Organization

In addition to implementing the ideas discussed earlier, organizations must concurrently unlearn organizational practices and paradigms that made them successful. Quite simply, traditional organizations and the associated organizational behaviors they created have outlived their usefulness. Management must seriously question and challenge the ways of thinking that worked in the past if they want to create a learning organization.[50] For example, the old management paradigm of planning, organizing, and control might be replaced with one of vision, values, and empowerment. The time has come for management and employees to think as owners, not as "us" and "them" adversaries.

key terms

benchmarking   402
commitment to change   411
external forces for change   399
internal forces for change   401

learning capabilities   415
learning modes   417
learning organization   414
mission statement   403

organization development   407
resistance to change   410
strategic plan   403
target elements of change   403

chapter summary

- *Discuss the external and internal forces that create the need for organizational change.* Organizations encounter both external and internal forces for change. There are four key external forces for change: demographic characteristics, technological advancements, customer and market changes, and social and political pressures. Internal forces for change come from both human resource problems and managerial behavior/decisions.

- *Describe Lewin's change model and the systems model of change.* Lewin developed a three-stage model of planned change that explained how to initiate, manage, and stabilize the change process. The three stages were *unfreezing*, which entails creating the motivation to change, *changing*, and stabilizing change through *refreezing*. A systems model of change takes a big picture perspective of change. It focuses on the interaction among the key components of change. The three main components of change are inputs, target elements of change, and outputs. The target elements of change represent the components of an organization that may be changed. They include organizing arrangements, social factors, methods, goals, and people.

- *Discuss Kotter's eight steps for leading organizational change.* John Kotter believes that organizational change fails for one or more of eight common errors. He proposed eight steps that organizations should follow to overcome these errors. The eight steps are as follows: (a) establish a sense of urgency, (b) create the guiding coalition, (c) develop a vision and strategy, (d) communicate the change vision, (e) empower broad-based action, (f) generate short-term wins, (g) consolidate gains and produce more change, and (h) anchor new approaches in the culture.

- *Discuss the 11 reasons employees resist change.* Resistance to change is an emotional/behavioral response to real or imagined threats to an established work routine. Eleven reasons employees resist change are (a) an individual's predisposition toward change, (b) surprise and fear of the unknown, (c) climate of mistrust, (d) fear of failure, (e) loss of status and/or job security, (f) peer pressure, (g) disruption of cultural traditions and/or group

relationships, (h) personality conflicts, (i) lack of tact and/or poor timing, (j) nonreinforcing reward systems, and (k) past success.

- *Identify alternative strategies for overcoming resistance to change.* Organizations must be ready for change. Assuming an organization is ready for change, the alternative strategies for overcoming resistance to change are education + communication, participation + involvement, facilitation + support, negotiation + agreement, manipulation + co-operation, and explicit + implict coercion. Each has its situational appropriateness and advantages and drawbacks.

- *Discuss the process organizations use to build their learning capabilities.* Learning capabilities represent the set of core competencies and processes that enable an organization to adapt to its environment. Learning capabilities are directly affected by organizational facilitating factors and learning modes. Facilitating factors constitute the internal structure and processes that either encourage or impede learning within an organization. Learning modes represent the various ways by which organizations attempt to create and maximize their learning. Researchers believe that there is some type of optimal matching between the facilitating factors and learning modes that affects learning capability.

discussion questions

1. Which of the external and internal forces for changes are influencing Intel's strategy? Explain.
2. How would you respond to a manager who made the following statement? "Unfreezing is not important; employees will follow my directives."
3. Have you ever gone through a major organizational change at work? If yes, what type of organizational development intervention was used? Was it effective? Explain.

4. Which source of resistance to change do you think is the most common? Which is the most difficult for management to deal with?
5. How would you assess the extent to which an organization is truly a learning organization? Discuss different alternative methods.

ethical dilemma

What Is More Important? Your Manager's Advice or Your Customer's Needs?

You are a broker for a trusted brokerage firm. Part of your job is to offer advice to clients concerning their mutual funds. A client's mutual fund was not performing very well and she was losing money. As her broker, you advised her to sell. Your client was happy but you were called into your boss's office where he questioned your advice. He informs you that your brokerage firm receives hefty incentives from that mutual fund company in exchange for favoring its funds. Your boss tells you that the practice is known as "revenue sharing"—mutual fund companies give brokers a cut of their management fees to get them to sell their products. He also tells you that the mutual fund company pays for cruises and other lavish vacations for brokers who meet sales goals and since you just advised your client to sell, you probably won't be on that list.

Solving the Dilemma

As a broker for this firm what should you do?

1. If it is the firm's policy that you recommend certain mutual funds over others, then this is the policy you will follow from here on out. Besides, you want a chance to win a cruise or some other lavish vacation.

2. Even though you might receive certain perks for recommending a specific mutual fund over others, your client sees you as an objective advisor and you will continue to base your decisions on her best interests rather than a managerial edict or incentives.

3. Because it is the firm's policy to recommend certain mutual funds over others, you will follow this practice. However, you make sure you advise your clients that you are paid an incentive if they purchase a specific mutual fund.

4. Invent other options. Discuss.

(Source: This case was based on material contained in L Johannes and J Hechinger, "Conflicting Interests: Why a Brokerage Giant Pushes Some Mediocre Mutual Funds," *The Wall Street Journal*, January 9, 2004, pp A1, A5.)

Chapter 1

1. From N Byrnes, "The Art of Motivation," *BusinessWeek,* May 1, 2006, pp 57–58.

2. As quoted in D Reed, "Kelly Must Build on Success," *USA Today,* August 16, 2004, p 4B. Also see "The Best Advice I Ever Got: Herb Kelleher, Founder and Chairman of Southwest Airlines," *Fortune,* March 21, 2005, pp 116, 118; D Kirkpatrick, "Star Power: Kevin Johnson, Microsoft," *Fortune,* February 6, 2006, p 58; and "Larry Johnston: CEO of Albertson's," *Fortune,* March 6, 2006, p 104.

3. Data from "Fortune 1,000 Ranked Within Industries," *Fortune,* April 17, 2006, p F-45.

4. J Pfeffer and J F Veiga, "Putting People First for Organizational Success," *Academy of Management Executive,* May 1999, p 37.

5. Adapted from ibid. Also see J K Harter, F L Schmidt, and T L Hayes, "Business-Unit-Level Relationship Between Employee Satisfaction, Employee Engagement, and Business Outcomes: A Meta-Analysis," *Journal of Applied Psychology,* April 2002, pp 268–79. Also see J Pfeffer, "Producing Sustainable Competitive Advantage Through the Effective Management of People," *Academy of Management Executive,* November 2005, pp 95–106; J Pfeffer and R I Sutton, "Evidence-Based Management," *Harvard Business Review,* January 2006, pp 62–74; J Pfeffer and R I Sutton, *Hard Facts, Dangerous Half-Truths & Total Nonsense* (Boston: Harvard Business School Press, 2006); and J McGregor, "Forget Going with Your Gut," *BusinessWeek,* March 20, 2006, p 112.

6. See J Pfeffer, "The Myth of the Disposable Worker," *Business 2.0,* October 2005, p 78; W F Cascio, "Strategies for Responsible Restructuring," *Academy of Management Executive,* November 2005, pp 39–50; and M Conlin, "The Shortsighted Solution," *BusinessWeek,* April 10, 2006, p 110.

7. Data from Pfeffer and Veiga, "Putting People First for Organizational Success," p 47.

8. S Zuboff, "From Subject to Citizen," *Fast Company,* May 2004, p 104. Also see "The Stat," *BusinessWeek,* March 28, 2005, p 14; "Quitting Time: Top 10 Reasons People Leave Their Jobs," *Training,* January 2006, p 8; and J Durett, "Why Am I Here?" *Training,* April 2006, p 13.

9. For inspiring discussion and examples, see S Clifford, "Jim Sinegal: Because Who Knew a Big-Box Chain Could Have a Generous Soul?" *Inc.,* April 2005, p 88; C T Sullivan, "A Stake in the Business," *Harvard Business Review,"* September 2005, pp 57–64; and D Brady, "Best Ideas: Employees Who March to Their Own Music," *BusinessWeek,* December 19, 2005, p 81.

10. R Levering and M Moskowitz, "2004 Special Report: The 100 Best Companies to Work For," *Fortune,* January 12, 2004, p 76. See G Colvin, "The 100 Best Companies to Work For: 2006," *Fortune,* January 23, 2006, pp 71–113.

11. See I S Fulmer, B Gerhart, and K S Scott, "Are the 100 Best Better? An Empirical Investigation of the Relationship Between Being a 'Great Place to Work' and Firm Performance," *Personnel Psychology,* Winter 2003, pp 965–93.

12. H Mintzberg, "The Manager's Job: Folklore and Fact," *Harvard Business Review,* July–August 1975, p 61. Also see M M Clark, "NLRB General Counsel's Office Issues Liberal Criteria for Defining 'Supervisor,'" *HR Magazine,* February 2004, p 30.

13. See, for example, H Mintzberg, "Managerial Work: Analysis from Observation," *Management Science,* October 1971, pp B97–B110; and F Luthans, "Successful vs. Effective Real Managers," *Academy of Management Executive,* May 1988, pp 127–32. For an instructive critique of the structured observation method, see M J Martinko and W L Gardner, "Beyond Structured Observation: Methodological Issues and New Directions," *Academy of Management Review,* October 1985, pp 676–95. Also see N Fondas, "A Behavioral Job Description for Managers," *Organizational Dynamics,* Summer 1992, pp 47–58.

14. See L B Kurke and H E Aldrich, "Mintzberg Was Right! A Replication and Extension of *The Nature of Managerial Work,*" *Management Science,* August 1983, pp 975–84.

15. For example, see J Gosling and H Mintzberg, "The Five Minds of a Manager," *Harvard Business Review,* November 2003, pp 54–63; G Yukl and R Lepsinger, "Why Integrating the Leading and Managing Roles Is Essential for Organizational Effectiveness," *Organizational Dynamics,* no. 4, 2005, pp 361–75; A I Kraut, P R Pedigo, D D McKenna, and M D Dunnette, "The Role of the Manager: What's Really Important in Different Management Jobs," *Academy of Management Executive,* November 2005, pp 122–29; G Hamel, "The Why, What, and How of Management Innovation," *Harvard Business Review,* February 2006, pp 72–84; K R Brousseau, M J Driver, G Hourihan, and R Larsson, "The Seasoned Executive's Decision-Making Style," *Harvard Business Review,* February 2006, pp 111–21; "Secrets of Greatness: How I Work," *Fortune,* March 20, 2006, pp 66–85; and J Jenkins, "Getting Up to Full Speed," *HR Magazine,* April 2006, pp 117–20.

16. Validation studies can be found in E Van Velsor and J B Leslie, *Feedback to Managers, Volume II: A Review and Comparison of Sixteen Multi-Rater Feedback Instruments* (Greensboro, NC: Center for Creative Leadership, 1991); F Shipper, "A Study of the Psychometric Properties of the Managerial Skill Scales of the Survey of Management Practices," *Educational and Psychological Measurement,* June 1995, pp 468–79; and C L Wilson, *How and Why Effective Managers Balance Their Skills: Technical, Teambuilding, Drive* (Columbia, MD: Rockatech Multimedia Publishing, 2003).

17. For example, see J Sandberg, "Understanding Competence at Work," *Harvard Business Review,* March 2001, pp 24–28; and D Bartram, "The Great Eight Competencies: A Criterion-Centric Approach to Validation," *Journal of Applied Psychology,* November 2005, pp 1185–203.

18. See F Shipper, "Mastery and Frequency of Managerial Behaviors Relative to Sub-Unit Effectiveness," *Human Relations,* April 1991, pp 371–88.

19. Ibid; and Wilson, *How and Why Effective Managers Balance Their Skills.*

20. Data from F Shipper, "A Study of Managerial Skills of Women and Men and Their Impact on Employees' Attitudes and Career Success in a Nontraditional Organization," paper presented at the Academy of Management Meeting, August 1994, Dallas, Texas. The same outcome for on-the-job studies is reported in A H Eagly and B T Johnson, "Gender and Leadership Style: A Meta-Analysis," *Psychological Bulletin,* September 1990, pp 233–56.

21. For instance, see J B Rosener, "Ways Women Lead," *Harvard Business Review,* November–December 1990, pp 119–25; C Lee, "The Feminization of Management," *Training,* November 1994, pp 25–31; and A Fels, "Do Women Lack Ambition?" *Harvard Business Review,* April 2004, pp 50–60.

22. See T W Malone, *The Future of Work: How the New Order of Business Will Shape Your Organization, Your Management Style, and Your Life* (Boston: Harvard Business School Press, 2004); and P Aburdene, *Megatrends 2010: The Rise of Conscious Capitalism* (Charlottesville, VA: Hampton Roads Publishing Co., 2005).

23. Essential sources on reengineering are M Hammer and J Champy, *Reengineering the Corporation: A Manifesto for Business Revolution* (New York: HarperCollins, 1993); and J Champy, *Reengineering Management: The Mandate for New Leadership* (New York: HarperCollins, 1995). Also see "Anything Worth Doing Is Worth Doing from Scratch," *Inc.,* May 18, 1999 (20th Anniversary Issue), pp 51–52.

24. See J Weber, "'Mosh Pits' of Creativity," *BusinessWeek,* November 7, 2005, pp 98–100; R D Hof, "Collaboration: Teamwork, Supercharged," *BusinessWeek,* November 21, 2005, pp 90–94; P Kaihla, "Google: Office Graffiti," *Business 2.0,* April 2006, p 90; and M A Prospero, "Top Scalpel," *Fast Company,* April 2006, p 31.

25. See C L Pearce and C C Manz, "The New Silver Bullets of Leadership: The Importance of Self- and Shared Leadership in Knowledge Work," *Organizational Dynamics,* no. 2, 2005, pp 130–40; F Vogelstein, "Star Power: Greg Brown, Motorola," *Fortune,* February 6, 2006, p 57; and R E Boyatzis, M L Smith, and N Blaize, "Developing Sustainable Leaders Through Coaching and Compassion," *Academy of Management Learning and Education,* March 2006, pp 8–24.

26 See K Carnes, D Cottrell, and M C Layton, *Management Insights: Discovering the Truths to Management Success* (Dallas: CornerStone Leadership Institute, 2004).

27 For details, see J B Miner, "The Rated Importance, Scientific Validity, and Practical Usefulness of Organizational Behavior Theories: A Quantitative Review," *Academy of Management Learning and Education,* September 2003, pp 250–68.

28 B S Lawrence, "Historical Perspective: Using the Past to Study the Present," *Academy of Management Review,* April 1984, p 307. Also see H Rubin, "Past Track to the Future," *Fast Company,* May 2001, pp 166–73.

29 Evidence indicating that the original conclusions of the famous Hawthorne studies were unjustified may be found in R G Greenwood, A A Bolton, and R A Greenwood, "Hawthorne a Half Century Later: Relay Assembly Participants Remember," *Journal of Management,* Fall–Winter 1983, pp 217–31; and R H Franke and J D Kaul, "The Hawthorne Experiments: First Statistical Interpretation," *American Sociological Review,* October 1978, pp 623–43. For a positive interpretation of the Hawthorne studies, see J A Sonnenfeld, "Shedding Light on the Hawthorne Studies," *Journal of Occupational Behaviour,* April 1985, pp 111–30.

30 See M Parker Follett, *Freedom and Coordination* (London: Management Publications Trust, 1949).

31 See D McGregor, *The Human Side of Enterprise* (New York: McGraw-Hill, 1960). Also see D Jacobs, "Book Review Essay: Douglas McGregor—The Human Side of Enterprise in Peril," *Academy of Management Review,* April 2004, pp 293–96.

32 J Hall, "Americans Know How to Be Productive If Managers Will Let Them," *Organizational Dynamics,* Winter 1994, p 38.

33 For an interesting historical perspective on the behavioral sciences, see J Adler, "Freud in Our Midst," *Newsweek,* March 27, 2006, pp 42–49.

34 See, for example, R Zemke, "TQM: Fatally Flawed or Simply Unfocused?" *Training,* October 1992, p 8; and D Dickson, R C Ford, and B Laval, "The Top Ten Excuses for Bad Service (and How to Avoid Needing Them)," *Organizational Dynamics,* no. 2, 2005, pp 168–84.

35 L Wah, "The Almighty Customer," *Management Review,* February 1999, p 17.

36 Data from "AMA Global Survey on Key Business Issues," *Management Review,* December 1998, p 30. Also see "1999 Annual Survey: Corporate Concerns," *Management Review,* March 1999, pp 55–56.

37 Instructive background articles on TQM are R Zemke, "A Bluffer's Guide to TQM," *Training,* April 1993, pp 48–55; R R Gehani, "Quality Value-Chain: A Meta-Synthesis of Frontiers of Quality Movement," *Academy of Management Executive,* May 1993, pp 29–42; P Mears, "How to Stop Talking About, and Begin Progress Toward, Total Quality Management," *Business Horizons,* May–June 1993, pp 11–14; and the Total Quality Special Issue of *Academy of Management Review,* July 1994.

38 M Sashkin and K J Kiser, *Putting Total Quality Management to Work* (San Francisco: Berrett-Koehler, 1993), p 39.

39 R J Schonberger, "Total Quality Management Cuts a Broad Swath—Through Manufacturing and Beyond," *Organizational Dynamics,* Spring 1992, p 18. Other quality-related articles include H Liao and A Chuang, "A Multilevel Investigation of Factors Influencing Employee Service Performance and Customer Outcomes," *Academy of Management Journal,* February 2004, pp 41–58; L Heuring, "Six Sigma in Sight," *HR Magazine,* March 2004, pp 76–80; N Brodsky, "You're Fired!" *Inc.,* May 2004, pp 51–52; and D McDonald, "Roll Out the Blue Carpet," *Business 2.0,* May 2004, pp 53–54.

40 Deming's landmark work is W E Deming, *Out of the Crisis* (Cambridge, MA: MIT, 1986).

41 See M Trumbull, "What Is Total Quality Management?" *The Christian Science Monitor,* May 3, 1993, p 12; and J Hillkirk, "World-Famous Quality Expert Dead at 93," *USA Today,* December 21, 1993, pp 1B–2B.

42 Based on discussion in M Walton, *Deming Management at Work* (New York: Putnam/Perigee, 1990).

43 Ibid., p 20.

44 Adapted from D E Bowen and E E Lawler III, "Total Quality-Oriented Human Resources Management," *Organizational Dynamics,* Spring 1992, pp 29–41. Also see L Selden and I C MacMillan, "Manage Customer-Centric Innovation—Systematically," *Harvard Business Review,* April 2006, pp 108–16.

45 J Tayman, "The Enormous Engine That Could," *Business 2.0,* April 2005, p 122. Also see Y Kageyama, "Toyota Spreads Quality Globally," *The Arizona Republic,* April 16, 2006, p D5.

46 As quoted in P LaBarre, "The Industrialized Revolution," *Fast Company,* November 2003, pp 116, 118.

47 See J M Ivancevich, T N Duening, and W Lidwell, "Bridging the Manager-Organizational Scientist Collaboration Gap," *Organizational Dynamics,* no. 2, 2005, pp 103–17; E W Ford, W J Duncan, A G Bedeian, P M Ginter, M D Rousculp, and A M Adams, "Mitigating Risks, Visible Hands, Inevitable Disasters, and Soft Variables: Management Research That Matters to Managers," *Academy of Management Executive,* November 2005, pp 24–38; and J M Bartunek, S L Rynes, and R D Ireland, "What Makes Management Research Interesting, and Why Does It Matter?" *Academy of Management Journal,* February 2006, pp 9–15.

48 B E Becker, M A Huselid, and D Ulrich, *The HR Scorecard: Linking People, Strategy, and Performance* (Boston: Harvard Business School Press, 2001), p 4. Also see J McGregor, "The World's Most Innovative Companies," *BusinessWeek,* April 24, 2006, pp 63–74.

49 See L Bassi and D McMurrer, "How's Your Return on People?" *Harvard Business Review,* March 2004, p 18; B Hall, "Here Comes Human Capital Management," *Training,* March 2004, pp 16–17; "Employers Say Measuring Is Vital But Still Don't Do It," *HR Magazine,* April 2004, p 18; R J Grossman, "Developing Talent," *HR Magazine,* January 2006, pp 40–46; J Schlosser, "Infosys U.," *Fortune,* March 20, 2006, pp 41–42; M Bolch, "Bearing Fruit," *HR Magazine,* March 2006, pp 56–60; and E Woyke, "The Boss is Watching—So Watch Your iPod," *BusinessWeek,* April 24, 2006, p 16.

50 For details, see www.intel.com; select "Education" under the heading "About Intel." Also see C R Barrett, "A Corporate Science Project," *BusinessWeek,* December 19, 2005, p 108; and "Utah Student Wins Science Talent Search," *USA Today,* March 15, 2006, p 4D.

51 Data from "The 100 Best Companies to Work For," *Fortune,* February 4, 2002, p 84. For updates on Intel, see C Edwards, "Inside Intel," *BusinessWeek,* January 9, 2006, pp 46–54; and M Kessler, "Intel Plans to Carve Costs Within 90 Days," *USA Today,* April 28, 2006, p 8B.

52 See L Bassi and D McMurrer, "Developing Measurement Systems for Managing in the Knowledge Era," *Organizational Dynamics,* no. 2, 2005, pp 185–196.

53 Inspired by P S Adler and S Kwon, "Social Capital: Prospects for a New Concept," *Academy of Management Review,* January 2002, pp 17–40. Also see "Social Capitalists: The Top 20 Groups That Are Changing the World," *Fast Company,* January 2004, pp 45–57; J Hempel, "A Corporate Peace Corps Catches on," *BusinessWeek,* January 31, 2005, p 14; G Morse, "When Stability Breeds Instability," *Harvard Business Review,* December 2005, p 32; and E de Nijs, "GRACE at Work," *Training and Development,* March 2006, pp 47–49.

54 L Prusak and D Cohen, "How to Invest in Social Capital," *Harvard Business Review,* June 2001, p 93.

55 Data from "What Makes a Job OK," *USA Today,* May 15, 2002, p 1B.

56 L D Tyson, "Good Works—With a Business Plan," *BusinessWeek,* May 3, 2004, p 32.

57 M E P Seligman and M Csikszentmihalyi, "Positive Psychology: An Introduction," *American Psychologist,* January 2000, p 5. Also see the other 15 articles in the January 2000 issue of *American Psychologist;* M Elias, "There's a Recipe for Resilience," *USA Today,* June 29, 2005, pp 1D-2D; B L Fredrickson and M F Losada, "Positive Affect and the Complex Dynamics of Human Flourishing," *American Psychologist,* October 2005, pp 678–86; and S Jayson, "Unhappiness Has Risen in the Past Decade," *USA Today,* January 9, 2006, p 7D.

58 See F Luthans, K W Luthans, and B C Luthans, "Positive Psychological Capital: Beyond Human and Social Capital," *Business Horizons,* January–February 2004, pp 45–50.

59 F Luthans, "The Need for and Meaning of Positive Organizational Behavior," *Journal of Organizational Behavior,* September 2002, p 698. Also see T A Wright, "Positive Organizational Behavior: An Idea Whose Time Has Truly Come," *Journal of Organizational Behavior,* June 2003, pp 437–42; S Fineman, "On Being Positive: Concerns and Counterpoints," *Academy of Management Review,* April 2006, pp 270–91; and L M Roberts, "Shifting the Lens on Organizational Life: The Added Value of Positive Scholarship," *Academy of Management Review,* April 2006, pp 292–305.

[60] See A Marsh, "The Art of Work," *Fast Company,* August 2005, pp 76–79; and S J Peterson and B K Spiker, "Establishing the Positive Contributory Value of Older Workers: A Positive Psychology Perspective," *Organizational Dynamics,* no. 2, 2005, pp 153–67.

[61] "The 100 Best Companies to Work For: and the Winners Are," *Fortune,* January 23, 2006, p 90.

[62] Ibid., p 96.

[63] See S Baker, "Wiser About the Web," *BusinessWeek,* March 27, 2006, pp 54–58; S Levy and B Stone, "The New Wisdom of the Web," *Newsweek,* April 3, 2006, pp 46–53; and A Lashinsky, "The Boom Is Back," *Fortune,* May 1, 2006, pp 70–87.

[64] M J Mandel and R D Hof, "Rethinking the Internet," *BusinessWeek,* March 26, 2001, p 118. Also see G T Lumpkin and G G Dess, "E-Business Strategies and Internet Business Models: How the Internet Adds Value," *Organizational Dynamics,* no. 2, 2004, pp. 161–73; and T J Mullaney, "E-Biz Strikes Again!" *BusinessWeek,* May 10, 2004, pp. 80–82.

[65] A Bernasek, "Buried in Tech," *Fortune,* April 16, 2001, p. 52.

[66] T J Mullaney and A Weintraub, "The Digital Hospital," *BusinessWeek,* March 28, 2005, p 77.

[67] See M A Tucker, "E-Learning Evolves," *HR Magazine,* October 2005, pp 74–78; S Boehle, "Putting the 'Learning' Back in E-Learning," *Training,* January 2006, pp 30–34; B West, "Online, It's All About Design," *Training,* March 2006, p 76; and J Gordon, "Seven Revelations About E-Learning," *Training,* April 2006, pp 28–31.

[68] J Merritt, "You Mean Cheating Is Wrong?" *BusinessWeek,* December 9, 2002, p 8. Also see R M Henig, "Looking for the Lie," *The New York Times Magazine,* February 5, 2006, pp 46–53, 76, 80, 83; H Oh, "Biz Majors Get an F for Honesty," *BusinessWeek,* February 6, 2006, p 14; and "USA Today Snapshots: Top Items Employees Pilfer," *USA Today,* March 29, 2006, p 1B.

Ethics Learning Module

[1] Excerpted from Y Dreazen, "Contractor Admits Bribing a U.S. Official in Iraq," *The Wall Street Journal,* April 19, 2006, p B1.

[2] This example was discussed in D Vergano, "Study: Medical Experts Tied to Drugmakers," *The Arizona Republic,* April 20, 2006, p A18.

[3] For a related discussion, see D J Moberg, "Ethics Blind Spots in Organizations: How Systematic Errors in Person Perception Undermine Moral Agency," *Organization Studies,* 2006, pp 413–28; and C J Fombrun, "Corporate Governance," *Corporate Reputation Review,* Winter 2006, pp 267–71.

[4] Support for these statistics can be found at the Johnson Institute Reports, "The Hidden Costs of Unethical Behavior," 2004, www.josephsoninstitute.org.

[5] See "Reporting Unethical Behavior," *The Arizona Republic,* March 4, 2006, p D3.

[6] Results can be found in "Class Notes: Biz Majors Get an F for Honesty," *BusinessWeek,* February 6, 2006, p 14.

[7] See S J Reynolds, "Moral Awareness and Ethical Predispositions: Investigating the Role of Individual Differences in the Recognition of Moral Issues," *Journal of Applied Psychology,* January 2006, pp 233–43; and C Gilligan, "In a Different Voice: Women's Conceptions of Self and Morality," *Harvard Educational Review,* November 1977, pp 481–517.

[8] The following discussion is based on A J Daboub, A M A Rasheed, R L Priem, and D A Gray, "Top Management Team Characteristics and Corporate Illegal Activity," *Academy of Management Review,* January 1995, pp 138–70.

[9] L Simpson, "Taking the High Road," *Training,* January 2002, p 38.

[10] Supportive results are discussed in B E Litzky, K A Eddleston, and D L Kidder, "The Good, the Bad, and the Misguided: How Managers Inadvertently Encourage Deviant Behaviors," *Academy of Management Perspectives,* February 2006, pp 91–102.

[11] Excerpted from Mark Gimein, "What Did Joe Know?" *Fortune,* May 12, 2003, pp 122, 124.

[12] These statistics, and counterfeiting in general, are discussed in F Balfour, "The Global Counterfeit Business Is Out of Control, Targeting Everything from Computer Chips to Life-Saving Medicines. It's So Bad That Even China May Need to Crack Down," *BusinessWeek,* February 7, 2005, pp 54–64. Also see L Paine, R Deshpandé, J D Margolis, and

K E Bettcher, "Up to Code: Does Your Company's Conduct Meet World-Class Standards?" *Harvard Business Review,* December 2005, pp 122–33.

[13] Results can be found in T Jackson, "Cultural Values and Management Ethics: A 10-Nation Study," *Human Relations,* October 2001, pp 1267–1302.

[14] The following discussion is based on A J Daboub, A M A Rasheed, R L Priem, and D A Gray, "Top Management Team Characteristics and Corporate Illegal Activity," *Academy of Management Review,* January 1995, pp 138–70.

[15] This discussion is based on Constance E Bagley, "The Ethical Leader's Decision Tree," *Harvard Business Review,* February 2003, pp 18–19.

[16] For a thorough discussion of this issue, see Schultz and Francis, "Financial Surgery: How Cuts in Retiree Benefits Fatten Companies' Bottom Lines."

[17] T Gutner, "Blowing Whistles—and Being Ignored," *BusinessWeek,* March 18, 2002, p 107.

[18] A discussion of moral character is provided by E M Hartman, "Can We Teach Character: An Aristotelian Answer," *Academy of Management Learning & Education,* March 2006, pp 68–81.

[19] Results are presented in Gutner, "Blowing Whistles—and Being Ignored."

[20] C Gilligan and J Attanucci, "Two Moral Orientations: Gender Differences and Similarities," *Merril-Palmer Quarterly,* July 1988, pp 224–25.

[21] Results can be found in S Jaffee and J Hyde, "Gender Differences in Moral Orientation: A Meta-Analysis," *Psychological Bulletin,* September 2000, pp 703–26.

[22] Ibid., p 719.

[23] See Ch. 6 in K Hodgson, *A Rock and a Hard Place: How to Make Ethical Business Decisions When the Choices Are Tough* (New York: AMACOM, 1992), pp 66–77.

[24] Excerpted from G Colvin, "The 100 Best Companies to Work for 2006," *Fortune,* January 23, 2006, pp 89, 96.

[25] Adapted from W E Stead, D L Worrell, and J Garner Stead, "An Integrative Model for Understanding and Managing Ethical Behavior in Business Organizations," *Journal of Business Ethics,* March 1990, pp 233–42.

[26] Excerpted from B Mclean and P Elkind, "No More Mr. Nice Guy," *Fortune,* May 15, 2006, p 74.

[27] See J McGregor, "The Workplace: Background Checks That Never End," *BusinessWeek,* March 20, 2006, p 40; and M Conlin, "You Are What You Post," *BusinessWeek,* March 27, 2006, pp 52–53.

[28] The relationship between internal communication and ethics was supported by A Dortok, "A Managerial Look at the Interaction between Internal Communication and Corporate Reputation," *Corporate Reputation Review,* Winter 2006, pp 322–38.

[29] Guidelines for ethics training is discussed by D Zielinski, "The Right Direction: Can Ethics Training Save Your Company?" *Training,* June 2005, pp 26–32.

[30] Excerpted from J Weber, "The New Ethics Enforcers," *BusinessWeek,* February 13, 2006, p 76.

[31] These scenarios were excerpted from L M Dawson, "Women and Men, Morality, and Ethics," *Business Horizons,* July–August 1995, pp 62, 65.

[32] Comparative norms were obtained from Dawson, "Women and Men, Morality and Ethics." Scenario 1: would sell (28% males, 57% females); would not sell (66% males, 28% females); unsure (6% males, 15% females). Scenario 2: would consult (84% males, 32% females); would not consult (12% males, 62% females); unsure (4% males, 6% females).

[33] The following trends were taken from Dawson, "Women and Men, Morality and Ethics." Women were likely to primarily respect feelings, ask "Who will be hurt?", avoid being judgmental, search for compromise, seek solutions that minimize hurt, rely on communication, believe in contextual relativism, be guided by emotion, and challenge authority. Men were likely to primarily respect rights, ask "Who is right?", value decisiveness, make unambiguous decisions, seek solutions that are objectively fair, rely on rules, believe in blind impartiality, be guided by logic, and accept authority.

Chapter 2

[1] Excerpted from B Grow, "Renovating Home Depot," *BusinessWeek,* March 6, 2006, pp 50, 52–53, 56, 58.

[2] E H Schein, "Culture: The Missing Concept in Organization Studies," *Administrative Science Quarterly,* June 1996, p 236.

[3] This figure and related discussion are based on C Ostroff, A Kinicki, and M Tamkins, "Organizational Culture and Climate," in *Handbook of Psychology,* vol. 12, eds W C Borman, D R Ilgen, and R J Klimoski (New York: Wiley & Sons, 2003), pp 565–93.

[4] This discussion is based on E H Schein, *Organizational Culture and Leadership,* 2nd ed (San Francisco: Jossey-Bass, 1992), pp 16–48.

[5] Excerpted from E Byron, "'Call Me Mike!'" *The Wall Street Journal,* March 27, 2006, p B1.

[6] S H Schwartz, "Universals in the Content and Structure of Values: Theoretical Advances and Empirical Tests in 20 Countries," in *Advances in Experimental Social Psychology,* ed M P Zanna (New York: Academic Press, 1992), p 4.

[7] P Babcock, "Is Your Company Two-Faced?" *HR Magazine,* January 2004, p 43.

[8] Results can be found in S Clarke, "Perceptions of Organizational Safety: Implications for the Development of Safety Culture," *Journal of Organizational Behavior,* March 1999, pp 185–98.

[9] "Time to Take Action," *Training,* September 2004, p18. Also see L Lee, "It's Dell vs. The Dell Way," *BusinessWeek,* March 6, 2006, pp 61–62.

[10] A description of Google's innovative culture is discussed by J Larson, "Maintaining Culture of Innovation," *The Arizona Republic,* April 13, 2006, pp D1, D3.

[11] Adapted from L Smircich, "Concepts of Culture and Organizational Analysis," *Administrative Science Quarterly,* September 1983, pp 339–58.

[12] Statistics and data contained in the Southwest Airlines example can be found in the Southwest Airlines Fact Sheet, updated March 28, 2006, www.southwest.com. Also see "Southwest Airlines New Release: Southwest Airlines Rapid Rewards Named Program of the Year at Frequent Flyer Awards Ceremony," May 4, 2006, www.southwest.com.

[13] K D Godsey, "Slow Climb to New Heights," *Success,* October 1996, p 21.

[14] Southwest's mission statement can be found in "Customer Service Commitment," May 2006, www.southwest.com.

[15] See Ostroff, Kinicki, and Tamkins, "Organizational Culture and Climate."

[16] The validity of these cultural types was summarized and supported by R A Cooke and J L Szumal, "Using the Organizational Culture Inventory to Understand the Operating Cultures of Organizations," in *Handbook of Organizational Culture and Climate,* eds N M Ashkanasy, C P M Wilderom, and M F Peterson (Thousand Oaks, CA: Sage Publications, 2000), pp 147–62.

[17] B Bremner and G Edmondson, "Japan: A Tale of Two Mergers," *BusinessWeek,* May 10, 2004, p 42.

[18] N D Schwartz, ". . . Is Also a Big Target," *Fortune,* April 17, 2006, p 80.

[19] Subcultures were examined by G Hofstede, "Identifying Organizational Subcultures: An Empirical Approach," *Journal of Management Studies,* January 1998, pp 1–12.

[20] Results can be found in R Cooke and J Szumal, "Measuring Normative Beliefs and Shared Behavioral Expectations in Organizations: The Reliability and Validity of the Organizational Culture Inventory," *Psychological Reports,* June 1993, pp 1299–330. Also see B Erdogan, R C Liden, and M L Kraimer, "Justice and Leader-member Exchange: The Moderating Role of Organizational Culture," *Academy of Management Journal,* April 2006, pp 395–406.

[21] Supportive results can be found in C Ostroff, Y Shin, and A Kinicki, "Multiple Perspectives of Congruence: Relationships between Value Congruence and Employee Attitudes," *Journal of Organizational Behavior,* September 2005, pp 591–623; and A L Kristof-Brown, R D Zimmerman, and E C Johnson, "Consequences of Individuals' Fit At Work: A Meta-Analysis of Person-Job, Person-Organization, Person-Group, and Person-Supervision Fit," *Personnel Psychology,* Summer 2005, pp 281–342.

[22] See C Wilderom, U Glunk, and R Maslowski, "Organizational Culture as a Predictor of Organizational Performance," in *Handbook of Organizational Culture & Climate,* eds N Ashkanasy, C Wilderom, and M Peterson (Thousand Oaks, CA: Sage, 2000), pp 193–210.

[23] Results can be found in J P Kotter and J L Heskett, *Corporate Culture and Performance* (New York: The Free Press, 1992). Also see G L Neilson, B A Pasternack, and K E Van Nuys, "The Passive-Aggressive Organization," *Harvard Business Review,* October 2005, pp 82–95.

[24] The success rate of mergers is discussed in M J Epstein, "The Drivers of Success in Post-Merger Integration," *Organizational Dynamics,* May 2004, pp 174–89. A practical application of culture change associated with a merger can be found in S Young, S Silver, and L Abboud, "Alcatel, Lucent Combine to Form Paris-Based Titan," *The Wall Street Journal,* April 3, 2006, pp A1, A12.

[25] Practical examples of culture change can be found in R Charan, "Home Depot's Blueprint for Culture Change," *Harvard Business Review,* April 2006, pp 60–70; M D Hovanesian, "Rewiring Chuck Prince," *BusinessWeek,* February 20, 2006, pp 75–78; and M Weinstein, "Out of the Blue," *Training,* April 2006, pp 22–27.

[26] D-A Durbin, "Ford Cuts Part of Culture Shift," *The Arizona Republic,* January 24, 2005, p D3.

[27] The mechanisms were based on material contained in E H Schein, "The Role of the Founder in Creating Organizational Culture," *Organizational Dynamics,* Summer 1983, pp 13–28.

[28] See N Byrnes, "The Art of Motivation," *BusinessWeek,* May 1, 2006, pp 57–62.

[29] S Holmes, "Cleaning Up Boeing," *BusinessWeek,* March 13, 2006, p 66.

[30] Ibid, p 68. Also see J McGregor, "The Structure to Measure Performance," *BusinessWeek,* January 9, 2006, pp 26–28.

[31] The effective use of storytelling is discussed by S Denning, "Effective Storytelling: Strategic Business Narrative Techniques," *Strategy & Leadership,* 2006, pp 42–48.

[32] S Tully, "Taking a Shot at the Title of World's Most Important Banker," *Fortune,* April 3, 2006, p 58. Also see D Brady, "GE: When Execs Outperform the Stock," *BusinessWeek,* April 17, 2006, pp 74–76.

[33] A good example is provided by B Hindo, "Making the Elephant Dance," *BusinessWeek,* May 1, 2006, pp 88–90.

[34] Practical examples can be found in P Dvorak, "A Firm's Culture Can Get Lost in Translation," *The Wall Street Journal,* April 3, 2006, pp B1, B3; and B E Litzky, K A Eddleston, and D L Kidder, "The Good, the Bad, and the Misguided: How Managers Inadvertently Encourage Deviant Behaviors," *Academy of Management Perspectives,* February 2006, pp 91–102.

[35] J Van Maanen, "Breaking In: Socialization to Work," in *Handbook of Work, Organization, and Society,* ed R Dubin (Chicago: Rand-McNally, 1976), p 67.

[36] This example was described in J Stearns, "Sedona Company Wants Happy Employees," *Arizona Republic,* April 10, 2005, p D2.

[37] Onboarding programs are discussed by D Moscato, "Using Technology to Get Employees on Board," *HR Magazine,* March 2005, pp 107–09.

[38] S J Wells, "Diving In," *HR Magazine,* March 2005, p. 56.

[39] Reprinted by permission of *Harvard Business Review.* From "No Ordinary Boot Camp" by N M Tichy, April 2001. Copyright © 2001 by the Harvard Business School Publishing Corporation; all rights reserved.

[40] See J Durett, "Training 101," *Training,* March 2006, pp 70–71; and K Gustafson, "A Better Welcome Mat," *Training,* June 2005, pp 34–41.

[41] See D Cable and C Parsons, "Socialization Tactics and Person-Organization Fit," *Personnel Psychology,* Spring 2001, pp 1–23.

[42] R Levering and M Moskowitz, "The 100 Best Companies to Work For: And the Winners Are …" *Fortune,* January 23, 2006, p 94.

[43] See A M Saks and B E Ashforth, "Proactive Socialization and Behavioral Self-Management," *Journal of Vocational Behavior,* June 1996, pp 301–23.

[44] For a thorough review of research on the socialization of diverse employees with disabilities see A Colella, "Organizational Socialization of Newcomers with Disabilities: A Framework for Future Research," in *Research in Personnel and Human Resources Management,* ed G R Ferris (Greenwich, CT: JAI Press, 1996), pp 351–417.

[45] This definition is based on the network perspective of mentoring proposed by M Higgins and K Kram, "Reconceptualizing Mentoring at Work: A Development Network Perspective," *Academy of Management Review,* April 2001, pp 264–88.

[46] Supportive results can be found in Monica L Forret and Thomas W Dougherty, "Networking Behaviors and Career Outcomes: Differences for Men and Women?" *Journal of Organizational Behavior,* May 2004, pp 419–37; and T W H Ng, L T Eby, K L Sorensen, and D C Feldman, "Predictors of Objective and Subjective Career Success: A Meta-Analysis," *Personnel Psychology,* Summer 2005, pp 367–408.

[47] Career functions are discussed in detail in K Kram, *Mentoring of Work: Developmental Relationships in Organizational Life* (Glenview, IL: Scott, Foresman, 1985).

[48] Excerpted from Kris Maher, "The Jungle: Focus on Retirement, Pay and Getting Ahead," *The Wall Street Journal,* February 24, 2004, p B8.

[49] This discussion is based on Higgins and Kram, "Reconceptualizing Mentoring at Work." Developmental networks are also discussed by B Uzzi and S Dunlap, "How to Build Your Network," *Harvard Business Review,* December 2005, pp 53–60.

[50] See T D Allen, L T Eby, and E Lentz, "The Relationship between Formal Mentoring Program Characteristics and Perceived Program Effectiveness," *Personnel Psychology,* Spring 2006, pp 125–53; and J Ewing, "Making Those Connections Work," *BusinessWeek,* March 13, 2006, p 91.

[51] Results can be found in "Leadership Needs Development," *Training,* February 2006, p 7. Also see J S Lublin, "New Chiefs Ask Former Bosses: 'Now What?'" *The Wall Street Journal,* January 30, 2006, p B3.

[52] Excerpted from "Best Practice: Mentoring—Blue Cross and Blue Shield of North Carolina," *Training,* March 2004, p 62.

[53] K Brown and J Weil, "How Andersen's Embrace of Consulting Altered the Culture of the Auditing Firm," *The Wall Street Journal,* Eastern Edition, March 12, 2002, pp C1, C16. Copyright 2002 by Dow Jones & Co. Inc. Reproduced with permission of Dow Jones & Co. Inc. via Copyright Clearance Center.

Chapter 3

[1] Excerpted from S Coyle, "Training Day in Afghanistan," *Training,* April 2006, pp 50–52.

[2] R Levering and M Moskowitz, "2004 Special Report: The 100 Best Companies to Work For," *Fortune,* January 12, 2004, p 70. Also see J Fox, "Rockin' in the Flat World," *Fortune,* September 19, 2005, pp 154–164.

[3] G Barrett, "Made in America? Not Likely," *USA Today,* December 15, 2003, p 1B. Also see Palmer, "U.S. Trade Gap Falls More Than Expected in November," *USA Today,* January 13, 2006, p 8B; and F Balfour, "One Foot in China," *BusinessWeek,* May 1, 2006, pp 44–45.

[4] P Coy, "The Future of Work," *BusinessWeek,* March 22, 2004, p 52 (emphasis added). Also see P Engardio, "The Future of Outsourcing," *BusinessWeek,* January 30, 2006, pp 50–58; and M Kripalani, "Five Off-shore Practices That Pay Off," *BusinessWeek,* January 30, 2006, pp 60–61.

[5] B De Lollis, "Marriott CEO Blasts Congress Over Immigrant Bill," *USA Today,* April 12, 2006, p 4B.

[6] H Maurer, "More Asian Auto Plants," *BusinessWeek,* March 27, 2006, p 30. Also see D Welch and D Foust, "The Good News About America's Auto Industry," *BusinessWeek,* February 13, 2006, pp 32–35.

[7] Also see D Nilsen, B Kowske, and K Anthony, "Managing Globally," *HR Magazine,* August 2005, pp 111–115; and A Taylor III, "How I Work," *Fortune,* March 20, 2006, pp 66, 68.

[8] See Y Kashima, "Conceptions of Culture and Person for Psychology," *Journal of Cross-Cultural Psychology,* January 2000, pp 14–32; and the cultural dimensions in Table 1 of G T Chao and H Moon, "The Cultural Mosaic: A Metatheory for Understanding the Complexity of Culture," *Journal of Applied Psychology,* November 2005, pp 1128–140.

[9] "How Cultures Collide," *Psychology Today,* July 1976, p 69. Also see E T Hall, *The Hidden Dimension* (Garden City, NY: Doubleday, 1966).

[10] F Trompenaars and C Hampden-Turner, *Riding the Waves of Culture: Understanding Cultural Diversity in Global Business,* 2nd ed (New York: McGraw-Hill, 1998), pp 6–7.

[11] See M Mendenhall, "A Painless Approach to Integrating 'International' into OB, HRM, and Management Courses," *Organizational Behavior Teaching Review,* no. 3 (1988–89), pp 23–27.

[12] See C L Sharma, "Ethnicity, National Integration, and Education in the Union of Soviet Socialist Republics," *The Journal of East and West Studies,* October 1989, pp 75–93; and R Brady and P Galuszka, "Shattered Dreams," *BusinessWeek,* February 11, 1991, pp 38–42.

[13] J Main, "How to Go Global—And Why," *Fortune,* August 28, 1989, p 73.

[14] An excellent contrast between French and American values can be found in C Gouttefarde, "American Values in the French Workplace," *Business Horizons,* March–April 1996, pp 60–69.

[15] See M R Testa, S L Mueller, and A S Thomas, "Cultural Fit and Job Satisfaction in a Global Service Environment," *Management International Review,* April 2003, pp 129–148; R E Nelson and S Gopalan, "Do Organizational Cultures Replicate National Cultures? Isomorphism, Rejection and Reciprocal Opposition in the Corporate Values of Three Countries," *Organization Studies,* September 2003, pp 1115–51; P B Smith, "Nations, Cultures, and Individuals," *Journal of*

Cross-Cultural Psychology, January 2004, pp 6–12; and G P Zachary, "Plugging into Africa," *Business 2.0,* November 2005, pp 134–44.

[16] W D Marbach, "Quality: What Motivates American Workers?" *BusinessWeek,* April 12, 1993, p 93.

[17] See G A Sumner, *Folkways* (New York: Ginn, 1906). Also see J G Weber, "The Nature of Ethnocentric Attribution Bias: Ingroup Protection or Enhancement?" *Journal of Experimental Social Psychology,* September 1994, pp 482–504.

[18] E Thomas, J Barry, and C Caryl, "A War in the Dark," *Newsweek,* November 10, 2003, p 30. Also see "The Right Way to Fight a War That Was a Mistake," *USA Today,* March 22, 2006, p 11A.

[19] D A Heenan and H V Perlmutter, *Multinational Organization Development* (Reading, MA: Addison-Wesley, 1979), p 17.

[20] Data from R Kopp, "International Human Resource Policies and Practices in Japanese, European, and United States Multinationals," *Human Resource Management,* Winter 1994, pp 581–99.

[21] See D Doke, "Shipping Diversity Abroad," *HR Magazine,* November 2003, pp 58–64; M B Marklein, "Foreign Student Enrollment on the Decline, Study Finds," *USA Today,* November 14, 2005, p 7D; M B Marklein, "USA Losing Its Advantage Drawing Foreign Students," *USA Today,* January 6, 2006, p 10A; and "Foreigners Returning to U.S. Grad Schools," *USA Today,* March 23, 2006, p 6D.

[22] Data from B Hagerty, "Trainers Help Expatriate Employees Build Bridges to Different Cultures," *The Wall Street Journal,* June 14, 1993, pp B1, B3.

[23] C M Farkas and P De Backer, "There Are Only Five Ways to Lead," *Fortune,* January 15, 1996, p 111.

[24] For related research, see G S Van Der Vegt, E Van De Vliert, and X Huang, "Location-Level Links Between Diversity and Innovative Climate Depend on National Power Distance," *Academy of Management Journal,* December 2005, pp 1171–182.

[25] For complete details, see G Hofstede, *Culture's Consequences: International Differences in Work-Related Values,* abridged ed (Newbury Park, CA: Sage Publications, 1984); G Hofstede, "The Interaction between National and Organizational Value Systems," *Journal of Management Studies,* July 1985, pp 347–57; and G Hofstede, "Management Scientists Are Human," *Management Science,* January 1994, pp 4–13. Also see M H Hoppe, "Introduction: Geert Hofstede's *Culture's Consequences: International Differences in Work-Related Values,*" *Academy of Management Executive,* February 2004, pp 73–74; M H Hoppe, "An Interview with Geert Hofstede," *Academy of Management Executive,* February 2004, pp 75–79; J W Bing, "Hofstede's Consequences: The Impact of His Work on Consulting and Business Practices," *Academy of Management Executive,* February 2004, pp 80–87; and H C Triandis, "The Many Dimensions of Culture," *Academy of Management Executive,* February 2004, pp 88–93.

[26] A similar conclusion is presented in the following replication of Hofstede's work: A Merritt, "Culture in the Cockpit: Do Hofstede's Dimensions Replicate?" *Journal of Cross-Cultural Psychology,* May 2000, pp 283–301. Another extension of Hofstede's work can be found in S M Lee and S J Peterson, "Culture, Entrepreneurial Orientation, and Global Competitiveness," *Journal of World Business,* Winter 2000, pp 401–16.

[27] J S Osland and A Bird, "Beyond Sophisticated Stereotyping: Cultural Sensemaking in Context," *Academy of Management Executive,* February 2000, p 67.

[28] "Fujio Mitarai: Canon," *BusinessWeek,* January 14, 2002, p 55.

[29] P C Earley and E Mosakowski, "Cultural Intelligence," *Harvard Business Review,* October 2004, p 140. Also see P C Earley and E Mosakowski, "Toward Culture Intelligence: Turning Cultural Differences into a Workplace Advantage." *Academy of Management Executive,* August 2004, pp 151–57; and I Alon and J M Higgins, "Global Leadership Success Through Emotional and Cultural Intelligences," *Business Horizons,* November–December 2005, pp 501–512.

[30] For background, see Javidan and House, "Cultural Acumen for the Global Manager," pp 289–305; the entire Spring 2002 issue of *Journal of World Business;* and R J House, P J Hanges, M Javidan, P W Dorfman, and V Gupta, eds, *Culture, Leadership, and Organizations: The GLOBE Study of 62 Societies* (Thousand Oaks, CA: Sage, 2004).

[31] R House, M Javidan, P Hanges, and P Dorfman, "Understanding Cultures and Implicit Leadership Theories across the Globe: An Introduction to Project GLOBE," *Journal of World Business,* Spring 2002, p 4.

³² See J C Kennedy, "Leadership in Malaysia: Traditional Values, International Outlook," *Academy of Management Executive,* August 2002, pp 15–26; M Javidan and A Dastmalchian, "Culture and Leadership in Iran: The Land of Individual Achievers, Strong Family Ties, and Powerful Elite," *Academy of Management Executive,* November 2003, pp 127–42; and M Javidan, G K Stahl, F Brodbeck, and C P M Wilderom, "Cross-Border Transfer of Knowledge: Cultural Lessons from Project GLOBE," *Academy of Management Executive,* May 2005, pp 59–76.

³³ Adapted from the list in House, Javidan, Hanges, and Dorfman, "Understanding Cultures and Implicit Leadership Theories across the Globe," pp 5–6.

³⁴ M Irvine, "Young Workers Saving to Retire," *The Arizona Republic,* December 28, 2003, p D5.

³⁵ Data from Trompenaars and Hampden-Turner, *Riding the Waves of Culture: Understanding Cultural Diversity in Global Business,* Ch 5. For relevant research evidence, see J Allik and A Realo, "Individualism-Collectivism and Social Capital," *Journal of Cross-Cultural Psychology,* January 2004, pp 29–49; A K Lalwani, S Shavitt, and T Johnson, "What Is the Relation Between Cultural Orientation and Socially Desirable Responding?" *Journal of Personality and Social Psychology,* January 2006, pp 165–78; C Robert, W C Lee, and K Chan, "An Empirical Analysis of Measurement Equivalence with the INDCOL Measure of Individualism and Collectivism: Implications for Valid Cross-Cultural Inference," *Personnel Psychology,* Spring 2006, pp 65–99; and W McEwen, X Fang, C Zhang, and R Burkholder, "Inside the Mind of the Chinese Consumer," *Harvard Business Review,* March 2006, pp 68–76.

³⁶ S Jayson, "American Families Are Envied, Disdained," *USA Today,* April 3, 2006, p 6D.

³⁷ See J A Vandello and D Cohen, "Patterns of Individualism and Collectivism across the United States," *Journal of Personality and Social Psychology,* August 1999, pp 279–92.

³⁸ As quoted in E E Schultz, "Scudder Brings Lessons to Navajo, Gets Some of Its Own," *The Wall Street Journal,* April 29, 1999, p C12.

³⁹ Trompenaars and Hampden-Turner, *Riding the Waves of Culture: Understanding Cultural Diversity in Global Business,* p 56. The importance of "relationships" in Eastern and Western cultures is explored in S H Ang, "The Power of Money: A Cross-Cultural Analysis of Business-Related Beliefs," *Journal of World Business,* Spring 2000, pp 43–60.

⁴⁰ See M Munter, "Cross-Cultural Communication for Managers," *Business Horizons,* May–June 1993, pp 69–78.

⁴¹ I Adler, "Between the Lines," *Business Mexico,* October 2000, p 24.

⁴² See C Saunders, C Van Slyke, and D R Vogel, "My Time or Yours? Managing Time Visions in Global Virtual Teams," *Academy of Management Executive,* February 2004, pp 19–31.

⁴³ D J Lynch, "Building Explosion in China Pumps Up Exports from USA," *USA Today,* April 20, 2006, p 2B.

⁴⁴ R W Moore, "Time, Culture, and Comparative Management: A Review and Future Direction," in *Advances in International Comparative Management,* vol. 5, ed S B Prasad (Greenwich, CT: JAI Press, 1990), pp 7–8.

⁴⁵ See A C Bluedorn, C F Kaufman, and P M Lane, "How Many Things Do You Like to Do at Once? An Introduction to Monochronic and Polychronic Time," *Academy of Management Executive,* November 1992, pp 17–26.

⁴⁶ "Multitasking" term drawn from S McCartney, "The Breaking Point: Multitasking Technology Can Raise Stress and Cripple Productivity," *The Arizona Republic,* May 21, 1995, p D10.

⁴⁷ See M Archer, "Too Busy to Read This Book? Then You Really Need To," *USA Today,* April 17, 2006, p 10B.

⁴⁸ O Port, "You May Have To Reset This Watch—In a Million Years," *BusinessWeek,* August 30, 1993, p 65.

⁴⁹ See M Toda and K Morimoto, "Ramadan Fasting—Effect on Healthy Muslims," *Social Behavior and Personality,* no. 1, 2004, pp 13–18.

⁵⁰ See T Scandura and P Dorfman, "Leadership Research in an International and Cross-Cultural Context," *The Leadership Quarterly,* April 2004, pp 277–307; M Javidan and N Lynton, "The Changing Face of the Chinese Leadership," *Harvard Business Review,* December 2005, pp 28, 30; and M Javidan, P W Dorfman, M S de Luque, and R J House, "In the Eye of the Beholder: Cross Cultural Lessons in Leadership from Project GLOBE," *Academy of Management Perspectives,* February 2006, pp 67–90.

⁵¹ J Guyon, "David Whitwam," *Fortune,* July 26, 2004, p 174.

⁵² M Vande Berg, "Siemens: Betting That Big Is Once Again Beautiful," *Milken Institute Review,* Second Quarter 2002, p 47.

⁵³ J S Black and H B Gregersen, "The Right Way to Manage Expats," *Harvard Business Review,* March–April 1999, p 53. A more optimistic picture is presented in R L Tung, "American Expatriates Abroad: From Neophytes to Cosmopolitans," *Journal of World Business,* Summer 1998, pp 125–44.

⁵⁴ Data from G S Insch and J D Daniels, "Causes and Consequences of Declining Early Departures from Foreign Assignments," *Business Horizons,* November–December 2002, pp 39–48. Also see J P Shay and S A Baack, "Expatriate Assignment, Adjustment and Effectiveness: An Empirical Examination of the Big Picture," *Journal of International Business Studies,* May 2004, pp 216–32; and A E M Van Vianen, I E De Pater, A L Kristof-Brown, and E C Johnson, "Fitting In: Surface- and Deep-Level Cultural Differences and Expatriates' Adjustment," *Academy of Management Journal,* October 2004, pp 697–709.

⁵⁵ S Dallas, "Rule No. 1: Don't Diss the Locals," *BusinessWeek,* May 15, 1995, p 8. Also see S M Toh and A S DeNisi, "A Local Perspective to Expatriate Success," *Academy of Management Executive,* February 2005, pp 132–46.

⁵⁶ P Capell, "Employers Seek to Trim Pay for US Expatriates," April 16, 2005, www.careerjournal.com. Also see E Krell, "Evaluating Returns on Expatriates," *HR Magazine,* March 2005, pp 60–65; and S P Nurney, "The Long and Short of It," *HR Magazine,* March 2005, pp 91–94.

⁵⁷ These insights come from Tung, "American Expatriates Abroad: From Neophytes to Cosmopolitans"; P M Caligiuri and W F Cascio, "*Can We Send Her There?* Maximizing the Success of Western Women on Global Assignments," *Journal of World Business,* Winter 1998, pp 394–416; T L Speer, "Gender Barriers Crumbling, Traveling Business Women Report," *USA Today,* March 16, 1999, p 5E; G Koretz, "A Woman's Place Is . . . ," *BusinessWeek,* September 13, 1999, p 28; and L K Stroh, A Varma, and S J Valy-Durbin, "Why Are Women Left at Home: Are They Unwilling to Go on International Assignments?" *Journal of World Business,* Fall 2000, pp 241–55. Also see S Bates, "Are Women Better for International Assignments?" *HR Magazine,* December 2003, p 16.

⁵⁸ An excellent reference book on this topic is J S Black, H B Gregersen, and M E Mendenhall, *Global Assignments: Successfully Expatriating and Repatriating International Managers* (San Francisco: Jossey-Bass, 1992). Also see M B Hess and P Linderman, *The Expert Expatriate: Your Guide to Successful Relocation Abroad* (Yarmouth, Maine: Intercultural Press, 2002); and E Gundling, *Working GlobeSmart: 12 People Skills for Doing Business across Borders* (Palo Alto, CA: Davies-Black Publishing, 2003).

⁵⁹ See J Carter, "Globe Trotters," *Training,* August 2005, pp 22–28; M A Shaffer, D A Harrison, H Gregersen, J S Black, and L A Ferzandi, "You Can Take It With You: Individual Differences and Expatriate Effectiveness," *Journal of Applied Psychology,* January 2006, pp 109–125; and Y Gong and J Fan, "Longitudinal Examination of the Role of Goal Orientation in Cross-Cultural Adjustment," *Journal of Applied Psychology,* January 2006, pp 176–184.

⁶⁰ See K Roberts, E E Kossek, and C Ozeki, "Managing the Global Workforce: Challenges and Strategies," *Academy of Management Executive,* November 1998, pp 93–106.

⁶¹ J S Lublin, "Younger Managers Learn Global Skills," *The Wall Street Journal,* March 31, 1992, p B1.

⁶² See P C Earley, "Intercultural Training for Managers: A Comparison of Documentary and Interpersonal Methods," *Academy of Management Journal,* December 1987, pp 685–98; and J S Black and M Mendenhall, "Cross-Cultural Training Effectiveness: A Review and a Theoretical Framework for Future Research," *Academy of Management Review,* January 1990, pp 113–36. Also see M R Hammer and J N Martin, "The Effects of Cross-Cultural Training on American Managers in a Japanese-American Joint Venture," *Journal of Applied Communication Research,* May 1992, pp 161–81; and J K Harrison, "Individual and Combined Effects of Behavior Modeling and the Cultural Assimilator in Cross-Cultural Management Training," *Journal of Applied Psychology,* December 1992, pp 952–62.

⁶³ See K Tyler, "I Say Potato, You Say *Patata,*" *HR Magazine,* January 2004, pp 85–87; D J Lynch, "U.S. Firms Becoming Tongue-tied," *USA Today,* February 9, 2006, p 6B; J Ewing, "Going Global for an MBA," *BusinessWeek,* March 13, 2006, pp 88–90; D Belluomini, "Translation by

Machine: A Bridge Across the Multicultural Gap," *The Futurist,* March–April 2006, 56–59; P Engardio, "Making Bangalore Sound Like Boston," *BusinessWeek,* April 10, 2006, p 48; and R Yu, "To Make Speaking Easier, E-translation Devices Talk for Visitors," *USA Today,* April 26, 2006, p 7E.

[64] Data from "USA Today Snapshots: Learning the Lingo," *USA Today,* January 26, 2006, p 1A. Also see L Lavelle, "China's B-School Boom," *BusinessWeek,* January 9, 2006, pp 40–43.

[65] See D Stamps, "Welcome to America: Watch Out for Culture Shock," *Training,* November 1996, pp 22–30; L Glanz, R Williams, and L Hoeksema, "Sensemaking in Expatriation—A Theoretical Basis," *Thunderbird International Business Review,* January–February 2001, pp 101–19; E Marx, *Breaking Through Culture Shock: What You Need to Succeed in International Business* (London: Nicholas Brealey Publishing, 2001); G K Stahl and P Caligiuri, "The Effectiveness of Expatriate Coping Strategies: The Moderating Role of Cultural Distance, Position Level, and Time on the International Assignment," *Journal of Applied Psychology,* July 2005, pp 603–15; and R Takeuchi, M Wang, and S V Marinova, "Antecedents and Consequences of Psychological Workplace Strain During Expatriation: A Cross-Sectional and Longitudinal Investigation," *Personnel Psychology,* Winter 2005, pp 925–48.

[66] S Armour, "For Chao, It's a Labor of Love As She Initiates Big Changes," *USA Today,* August 29, 2003, p 2B. Also see R Hampson, "After 3 Years, Somalis Struggle to Adjust to USA," *USA Today,* March 22, 2006, pp 1A–2A.

[67] S Tully, "The Modular Corporation," *Fortune,* February 8, 1993, pp 108, 112.

[68] See H H Nguyen, L A Messe, and G E Stollak, "Toward a More Complex Understanding of Acculturation and Adjustment," *Journal of Cross-Cultural Psychology,* January 1999, pp 5–31.

[69] K L Miller, "How a Team of Buckeyes Helped Honda Save a Bundle," *BusinessWeek,* September 13, 1993, p 68.

[70] For more, see S Overman, "Mentors Without Borders," *HR Magazine,* March 2004, pp 83–86; and E Krell, "Budding Relationships," *HR Magazine,* June 2005, pp 114–18.

[71] B Newman, "For Ira Caplan, Re-Entry Has Been Strange," *The Wall Street Journal,* December 12, 1995, p A12.

[72] See Black, Gregersen, and Mendenhall, *Global Assignments: Successfully Expatriating and Repatriating International Managers,* p 227. Also see H B Gregersen, "Commitments to a Parent Company and a Local Work Unit During Repatriation," *Personnel Psychology,* Spring 1992, pp 29–54; and H B Gregersen and J S Black, "Multiple Commitments upon Repatriation: The Japanese Experience," *Journal of Management,* no. 2, 1996, pp 209–29.

[73] Ibid., pp 226–27.

[74] See L K Stroh, H B Gregersen, and J S Black, "Closing the Gap: Expectations versus Reality among Repatriates," *Journal of World Business,* Summer 1998, pp 111–24; and K Tyler, "Retaining Repatriates," *HR Magazine,* March 2006, pp 97–102.

[75] Excerpted from M V Gratchev, "Making the Most of Cultural Differences," *Harvard Business Review,* October 2001, pp 28, 30.

Chapter 4

[1] Excerpted from R L Kuhn, "A Problem of Perception: Why China and the U.S. Aren't on the Same Page," *BusinessWeek,* April 24, 2006, p 33.

[2] C Palmeri, *BusinessWeek,* February 6, 2006, p 53.

[3] Research on object perception is thoroughly discussed by L J Rips, S Blok, and G Newman, "Tracing the Identity of Objects," *Psychological Review,* January 2006, pp 1–30.

[4] The negativity bias was examined by N Kyle Smith, J T Larsen, T L Chartrand, and J T Cacioppo, "Being Bad Isn't Always Good: Affective Context Moderates the Attention Bias Toward Negative Information," *Journal of Personality and Social Psychology,* February 2006, pp 210–20.

[5] E Rosch, C B Mervis, W D Gray, D M Johnson, and P Boyes-Braem, "Basic Objects in Natural Categories," *Cognitive Psychology,* July 1976, p 383.

[6] The use of stereotypes is discussed by D C Molden and C S Dweck, "Finding 'Meaning' In Psychology," *American Psychologist,* April 2006, pp 192–203

[7] C M Judd and B Park, "Definition and Assessment of Accuracy in Social Stereotypes," *Psychological Review,* January 1993, p 110.

[8] Results can be found in "Accounting and Race: A Long Way to Go," *Training,* April 2006, p 15.

[9] Results are reported in C Daniels, "Young, Gifted, Black—and Out of Here," *Fortune,* May 3, 2004, p 48.

[10] Results can be found in J L Berdahl and C Moore, "Workplace Harassment: Double Jeopardy for Minority Women," *Journal of Applied Psychology,* March 2006, pp 426–36.

[11] This discussion is based on material presented in G V Bodenhausen, C N Macrae, and J W Sherman, "On the Dialectics of Discrimination," in *Dual-Process Theories in Social Psychology,* eds S Chaiken and Y Trope (New York: Guilford Press, 1999) pp 271–90.

[12] For a thorough discussion about the structure and organization of memory, see L R Squire, B Knowlton, and G Musen, "The Structure and Organization of Memory," in *Annual Review of Psychology,* eds L W Porter and M R Rosenzweig (Palo Alto, CA: Annual Reviews Inc., 1993), vol. 44, pp 453–95.

[13] Various training approaches are discussed by P Babcock, "Detecting Hidden Bias," *HR Magazine,* February 2006, pp 51–55.

[14] Results can be found in C M Marlowe, S L Schneider, and C E Nelson, "Gender and Attractiveness Biases in Hiring Decisions: Are More Experienced Managers Less Biased?" *Journal of Applied Psychology,* February 1996, pp 11–21.

[15] Details of this study can be found in C K Stevens, "Antecedents of Interview Interactions, Interviewers' Ratings, and Applicants' Reactions," *Personnel Psychology,* Spring 1998, pp 55–85.

[16] See R C Mayer and J H Davis, "The Effect of the Performance Appraisal System on Trust for Management: A Field Quasi-Experiment," *Journal of Applied Psychology,* February 1999, pp 123–36.

[17] Results can be found in W H Bommer, J L Johnson, G A Rich, P M Podsakoff, and S B Mackenzie, "On the Interchangeability of Objective and Subjective Measures of Employee Performance: A Meta-Analysis," *Personnel Psychology,* Autumn 1995, pp 587–605.

[18] The effectiveness of rater training was supported by D V Day and L M Sulsky, "Effects of Frame-of-Reference Training and Information Configuration on Memory Organization and Rating Accuracy," *Journal of Applied Psychology,* February 1995, pp 158–67.

[19] Results can be found in J S Phillips and R G Lord, "Schematic Information Processing and Perceptions of Leadership in Problem-Solving Groups," *Journal of Applied Psychology,* August 1982, pp 486–92.

[20] See S Begley, "All in Your Head? Yes, and Scientists Are Figuring Out Why," *The Wall Street Journal,* March 17, 2006, p B1.

[21] See E C Baig, "Survey Offers a 'Sneak Peek' Into Net Surfers' Brains," *USA Today,* March 27, 2006, p 4B; and L Winerman, "Screening Surveyed," *Monitor on Psychology,* January 2006, pp 28–29.

[22] Kelley's model is discussed in detail in H H Kelley, "The Processes of Causal Attribution," *American Psychologist,* February 1973, pp 107–28.

[23] For examples, see J Susskind, K Maurer, V Thakkar, D L Hamilton, and J W Sherman, "Perceiving Individuals and Groups: Expectancies, Dispositional Inferences, and Causal Attributions," *Journal of Personality and Social Psychology,* February 1999, pp 181–91. Also see K White, D R Lehman, K J Hemphill, and D R Mandel, "Causal Attributions, Perceived Control, and Psychological Adjustment: A Study of Chronic Fatigue Syndrome," *Journal of Applied Social Psychology,* 2006, pp 75–99.

[24] Results from these studies can be found in D A Hofmann and A Stetzer, "The Role of Safety Climate and Communication in Accident Interpretation: Implications for Learning from Negative Events," *Academy of Management Journal,* December 1998, pp 644–57; and I Choi, R E Nisbett, and A Norenzayan, "Causal Attribution across Cultures: Variation and Universality," *Psychological Bulletin,* January 1999, pp 47–63.

[25] L Woellert, "The-Reporter-Did-It Defense," *BusinessWeek,* May 8, 2006, p 34.

[26] Details may be found in S E Moss and M J Martinko, "The Effects of Performance Attributions and Outcome Dependence on Leader Feedback Behavior Following Poor Subordinate Performance," *Journal of Organizational Behavior,* May 1998, pp 259–74; and E C Pence, W C Pendelton, G H Dobbins, and J A Sgro, "Effects of Causal Explanations and Sex Variables on Recommendations for Corrective Actions Following Employee Failure," *Organizational Behavior and Human Performance,* April 1982, pp 227–40.

[27] See D Konst, R Vonk, and R V D Vlist, "Inferences about Causes and Consequences of Behavior of Leaders and Subordinates," *Journal of Organizational Behavior,* March 1999, pp 261–71.

[28] See J Silvester, F Patterson, E Ferguson, "Comparing Two Attributional Models of Job Performance in Retail Sales: A Field Study," *Journal of Occupational and Organizational Psychology,* March 2003, pp 115–32.

[29] The following discussion is based on L Gardenswartz and A Rowe, *Diverse Teams at Work* (New York: McGraw-Hill, 1994), pp 31–57.

[30] H Collingwood, "Who Handles a Diverse Work Force Best?" *Working Women,* February 1996, p 25.

[31] Excerpted from "Workforce Optimas Awards 2003," *Workforce,* March 2003, p 47.

[32] F J Crosby, A Iyer, S Clayton, and R A Downing, "Affirmative Action: Psychological Data and the Policy Debates," *American Psychologist,* February 2003, p 94.

[33] See L Anderson Snyder, J N Cleveland, and G C Thornton III, "Support for Affirmative Action Initiatives among Diverse Groups: The Role of Ethnic Identity," *Journal of Applied Social Psychology,* 2006, pp 527–51; and C Lausanne Renfro, A Duran, W G Stephan, and D L Clason, "The Role of Threat in Attitudes Toward Affirmative Action and Its Beneficiaries," *Journal of Applied Social Psychology,* 2006, pp 41–74.

[34] See Crosby, Iyer, Clayton, and Downing, "Affirmative Action: Psychological Data and the Policy Debates," pp 93–115.

[35] "Jury Awards $1.7M to Woman Spanked on Job," http:www.usatoday.com/news/nation/2006-04-28-spanking-trial_x.htm, accessed April 28, 2006; and "Woman Spanked at Work Awarded $1.7 Million," http://abcnews.go.com/GMA/LegalCenter/story?id=19356349&page=1&CMP=OTC-RSSF, accessed May 16, 2006.

[36] A M Morrison, *The New Leaders: Guidelines on Leadership Diversity in America* (San Francisco: Jossey-Bass, 1992), p 78.

[37] See the related discussion by S M Colarelli, J L Spranger, and M A R Hechanova, "Women, Power, and Sex Composition in Small Groups: An Evolutionary Perspective," *Journal of Organizational Behavior,* March 2006, pp 163–84; and P L Perrewé and D L Nelson, "Gender and Career Success: The Facilitative Role of Political Skill," *Organizational Dynamics,* December 2004, pp 366–78.

[38] See "Women in the Labor Force in 2004," *U.S. Department of Labor Women's Bureau,* www.dol.gov/wb/factsheets/Qf-laborforce-04.htm, accessed May 11, 2006; and "Women in the Labor Force: A Databook Updated and Available on the Internet," *News: Bureau of Labor Statistics,* http:www.bls.gov/cps/, accessed May 13, 2006.

[39] Results can be found in K S Lyness and D E Thompson, "Above the Glass Ceiling: A Comparison of Matched Samples of Female and Male Executives," *Journal of Applied Psychology,* June 1997, pp 359–75.

[40] This study was conducted by K S Lyness and M K Judiesch, "Are Women More Likely to Be Hired or Promoted into Management Positions?" *Journal of Vocational Behavior,* February 1999, pp 158–73.

[41] See "Women CEO's for Fortune 500 Companies," http://money.cnn.com/magazines/fortune/fortune500/womenceos/, accessed May 11, 2006; and J Jones, "Female CEOs Struggle in '04' but over Two Years. They're Topping Firms Led by Men," *USA Today,* January 4, 2005, retrieved March 29, 2005, from www.usatoday.com/educate/college/careers/hottopic35.htm, January 4, 2005.

[42] Here are the ranks for each career strategy: Strategy 1 = 12; Strategy 2 = 6; Strategy 3 = 5; Strategy 4 = 11; Strategy 5 = 9; Strategy 6 = 3; Strategy 7 = 10; Strategy 8 = 1; Strategy 9 = 7; Strategy 10 = 8; Strategy 11 = 4; Strategy 12 = 2; and Strategy 13 = 13.

[43] Details of this study can be found in B R Ragins, B Townsend, and M Mattis, "Gender Gap in the Executive Suite: CEOs and Female Executives Report on Breaking the Glass Ceiling," *Academy of Management Executive,* February 1998, pp 28–42. Also see K R Browne, "Evolved Sex Differences and Occupational Segregation," *Journal of Organizational Behavior,* March 2006, pp 143–62.

[44] For details regarding these statistics, see G C Armas, "Almost Half of US Likely to be Minorities by 2050," *Arizona Republic,* March 18, 2004, p A5.

[45] These statistics were obtained from "Race-Based Charges FY 1992–FY 2005," The U.S. Equal Employment Opportunity Commission, www.eeoc.gov/stats/race.html, last revised January 27, 2006.

[46] See "Table 1: Income and Earnings Summary Measures by Selected Characteristics: 2003–2004," U.S. Census Bureau, www.census.gov/prod/2005pubs/p60-229.pdf, 2004.

[47] For a review of this research, see L Roberson and C J Block, "Racioethnicity and Job Performance: A Review and Critique of Theoretical Perspectives on the Causes of Group Differences," in *Research in Organizational Behavior,* vol 23, eds B M Staw and R I Sutton (New York: JAI Press, 2001), pp 247–326.

[48] See "USA Statistics in Brief—Law, Education, Communications, Transportation, Housing," http://www.census.gov, last revised March 16, 2004.

[49] See D Dooley and J Prause, "Underemployment and Alcohol Misuse in the National Longitudinal Survey of Youth," *Journal of Studies on Alcohol,* November 1998, pp 669–80; and D C Feldman, "The Nature, Antecedents and Consequences of Underemployment," *Journal of Management,* 1966, pp 385–407.

[50] See U.S. Census Bureau, "B2004. Median Earning in the Past 12 Months by Sex by Educational Attainment for the Population 25 Years and Over," http://factfinder.census.gov/servlet/DTTable?_bm=y&geo_id=01000US&-ds_name=ACS_2004_EST, 2004.

[51] See "High School Dropout Rates," *Child Trends DataBank,* http://www.childtrendsdatabank.org/indicators/1HighSchoolDroupout.cfm, 2004.

[52] "Facts on Literacy," *National Literacy Facts,* August 27, 1998, www.svs.net/wpei/Litfacts.htm.

[53] See H London, "The Workforce, Education, and the Nation's Future," www.hudson.org/american_outlook/articles_sm98/london.htm, Summer 1998.

[54] International age and wage issues are discussed by D Roberts, "How Rising Wages Are Changing the Game in China," *BusinessWeek,* March 27, 2006, pp 32–35; and H Karoui, "World Security Network Newsletter," 2006, newsletter@worldsecuritynetwork.net, accessed April 5.

[55] An example is provided by "'Emergent' Workers Make Up One-Third of Workforce," *HR Magazine,* January 2006, p 16; also see D R Avery and P F McKay, "Target Practice: An Organizational Impression Management Approach to Attracting Minority and Female Job Applicants," *Personnel Psychology,* Spring 2006, pp 1578–187.

[56] See R Levering and M Moskowitz, "The 100 Best Companies to Work For," *Fortune,* January 24, 2005, p 76.

[57] Details of this program can be found in S A Hewlett and C Buck Luce, "Off-Ramps and On-Ramps: Keeping Talented Women on the Road to Success," *Harvard Business Review,* March 2005, pp 43–54.

[58] S Armour, "Welcome Mat Rolls Out for Hispanic Workers: Corporate America Cultivates Talent as Ethnic Population Booms," *USA Today,* April 12, 2001, pp 1B, 2B.

[59] See the related discussion in N Byrnes, "Get' Em While They're Young," *BusinessWeek,* May 22, 2006, pp 86–87; and R J Stevens, "Social Engineering," *The Wall Street Journal,* April 19, 2006, p A12.

[60] Training and educational solutions are discussed by K Merriman, "Employers Warm Up to Online Education," *HR Magazine,* January 2006, pp 79–82; and D S Onley, "Internship Program Dividends," *HR Magazine,* January 2006, pp 85–87.

[61] Approaches for handling elder care are discussed by T F Shea, "Help with Elder Care," *HR Magazine,* September 2003, pp 113–14, 116, 118.

[62] Managerial issues and solutions for an aging workforce are discussed by J W Hedge, W C Borman, and S E Lammelein, *The Aging Workforce: Realities, Myths, and Implications for Organizations,* 2006, Washington, DC: American Psychological Association.

[63] These barriers were taken from discussions in Loden, *Implementing Diversity;* E E Spragins, "Benchmark: The Diverse Work Force," *Inc.,* January 1993, p 33; and Morrison, *The New Leaders: Guidelines on Leadership Diversity in America.*

[64] See the related discussion in A Fisher, "The Sky's the Limit," *Fortune,* May 1, 2006, pp 124B–124H.

[65] For complete details and results from this study, see A M Morrison, *The New Leaders: Guidelines on Leadership Diversity in America* (San Francisco: Jossey-Bass, 1992).

[66] Excerpted from "The Diversity Factor," *Fortune,* October 13, 2003, p S4.

[67] Excerpted from R Koonce, "Redefining Diversity," *Training & Development,* December 2001, pp 24, 26.

[68] Excerpted from J Leopold, "En-Ruse? Workers at Enron Say They Posed as Busy Traders to Impress Visiting Analysts," *The Wall Street Journal,* February 17, 2002, p C1.

Chapter 5

[1] Excerpted from N Byrnes, "Making It Work by Not Doing It All," *BusinessWeek,* March 20, 2006, pp 84–85. Other inspiring women executives are profiled in B Morris, "Star Power: Ursula Burns, Xerox," *Fortune,* February 6, 2006, p 57; and D Foust, "A Sister Act That's Wowing Them," *BusinessWeek,* March 13, 2006, pp 84, 86.

[2] D Seligman, "The Trouble with Buyouts," *Fortune,* November 30, 1992, p 125. For related reading, see P Falcone, "Preserving Restless Top Performers," *HR Magazine,* March 2006, pp 117–22.

[3] Data from "Nearly 1 in 7 Workers Foreign Born," *USA Today,* April 17, 2006, p 1B.

[4] See G A Odums, "A New Year's Resolution: Optimize Older Workers," *Training and Development,* January 2006, pp 34–36; P Babcock, "Detecting Hidden Bias," *HR Magazine,* February 2006, pp 50–55; J A Segal, "Time Is on Their Side," *HR Magazine,* February 2006, pp 129–33; A Fisher, "The Sky's the Limit," *Fortune,* May 1, 2006, pp 124B–124H; S Kehrli and T Sopp, "Managing Generation Y," *HR Magazine,* May 2006, pp 113–19; and M Orey, "White Men Can't Help It: Courts Have Been Buying the Idea That They Have Innate Biases," *BusinessWeek,* May 15, 2006, pp 54, 57.

[5] Data from "If We Could Do It Over Again," *USA Today,* February 19, 2001, p 4D.

[6] See D S Vogt and C R Colvin, "Assessment of Accurate Self-Knowledge," *Journal of Personality Assessment,* June 2005, pp 239–51; L M Roberts, J E Dutton, G M Spreitzer, E D Heaphy, and R E Quinn, "Composing the Reflected Best-Self Portrait: Building Pathways for Becoming Extraordinary in Work Organizations," *Academy of Management Review,* October 2005, pp 712–36; S Srivastava and J S Beer, "How Self-Evaluations Relate to Being Liked by Others: Integrating Sociometer and Attachment Perspectives," *Journal of Personality and Social Psychology,* December 2005, pp 966–77; N Haslam, P Bain, L Douge, M Lee, and B Bastian, "More Human Than You: Attributing Humanness to Self and Others," *Journal of Personality and Social Psychology,* December 2005, pp 937–50; G D Bromgard, D Trafimow, and I K Bromgard, "Valence of Self-Cognitions: The Positivity of Individual Self-Statements," *The Journal of Social Psychology,* no. 1, 2006, pp 85–94; and S P Forrest III and T O Peterson, "It's Called Andragogy," *Academy of Management Learning and Education,* March 2006, pp 113–22.

[7] V Gecas, "The Self-Concept," in *Annual Review of Sociology,* eds R H Turner and J F Short, Jr. (Palo Alto, CA: Annual Reviews Inc., 1982), vol. 8, p 3.

[8] L Festinger, *A Theory of Cognitive Dissonance* (Stanford, CA: Stanford University Press, 1957), p 3. Also see T Lombardo, "Thinking Ahead: The Value of Future Consciousness," *The Futurist,* January/February 2006, pp 45–50.

[9] A Canadian versus Japanese comparison of self-concept can be found in J D Campbell, P D Trapnell, S J Heine, I M Katz, L F Lavallee, and D R Lehman, "Self-Concept Clarity: Measurement, Personality Correlates, and Cultural Boundaries," *Journal of Personality and Social Psychology,* January 1996, pp 141–56. Also see R W Tafarodi, C Lo, S Yamaguchi, W W S Lee, and H Katsura, "The Inner Self in Three Countries," *Journal of Cross-Cultural Psychology,* January 2004, pp 97–117.

[10] See D C Barnlund, "Public and Private Self in Communicating with Japan," *Business Horizons,* March/April 1989, pp 32–40; and the section on "Doing Business with Japan" in P R Harris and R T Moran, *Managing Cultural Differences,* 4th ed (Houston: Gulf Publishing, 1996), pp 267–76.

[11] As quoted in A Deutschman, "What I Know Now," *Fast Company,* September 2005, p 96. Also see M G Pratt, K W Rockmann, and J B Kaufmann, "Constructing Professional Identity: The Role of Work and Identity Learning Cycles in the Customization of Identity among Medical Residents," *Academy of Management Journal,* April 2006, pp 235–62.

[12] Based in part on a definition found in Gecas, "The Self-Concept." Also see N Branden, *Self-Esteem at Work: How Confident People Make Powerful Companies* (San Francisco: Jossey-Bass, 1998).

[13] H W Marsh, "Positive and Negative Global Self-Esteem: A Substantively Meaningful Distinction or Artifacts?" *Journal of Personality and Social Psychology,* April 1996, p 819.

[14] Ibid.

[15] See P Borghesi, "I Was Out of a Job—And an Identity," *Newsweek,* January 30, 2006, p 13.

[16] E Diener and M Diener, "Cross-Cultural Correlates of Life Satisfaction and Self-Esteem," *Journal of Personality and Social Psychology,* April 1995, p 662. For cross-cultural evidence of a similar psychological process for self-esteem, see T M Singelis, M H Bond, W F Sharkey, and C S Y Lai, "Unpackaging Culture's Influence on Self-Esteem and Embarrassability," *Journal of Cross-Cultural Psychology,* May 1999, pp 315–41. Also see Z Stambor, "People Rate Their Self-Esteem High across Cultures," *Monitor on Psychology,* December 2005, p 13.

[17] See C Kobayashi and J D Brown, "Self-Esteem and Self-Enhancement in Japan and America," *Journal of Cross-Cultural Psychology,* September 2003, pp 567–80.

[18] Based on data in F L Smoll, R E Smith, N P Barnett, and J J Everett, "Enhancement of Children's Self-Esteem through Social Support Training for Youth Sports Coaches," *Journal of Applied Psychology,* August 1993, pp 602–10.

[19] W J McGuire and C V McGuire, "Enhancing Self-Esteem by Directed-Thinking Tasks: Cognitive and Affective Positivity Asymmetries," *Journal of Personality and Social Psychology,* June 1996, p 1124.

[20] S Begley, "Real Self-Esteem Builds on Achievement, Not Praise for Slackers," *The Wall Street Journal,* April 18, 2003, p B1. Also see A Dijksterhuis, "I Like Myself But I Don't Know Why: Enhancing Implicit Self-Esteem by Subliminal Evaluative Conditioning," *Journal of Personality and Social Psychology,* February 2004, pp 345–55; and J V Wood, S A Heimpel, I R Newby-Clark, and M Ross, "Snatching Defeat from the Jaws of Victory: Self-Esteem Differences in the Experience and Anticipation of Success," *Journal of Personality and Social Psychology,* November 2005, pp 764–80.

[21] M E Gist, "Self-Efficacy: Implications for Organizational Behavior and Human Resource Management," *Academy of Management Review,* July 1987, p 472. Also see A Bandura, "Self-Efficacy: Toward a Unifying Theory of Behavioral Change," *Psychological Review,* March 1977, pp 191–215; M E Gist and T R Mitchell, "Self-Efficacy: A Theoretical Analysis of Its Determinants and Malleability," *Academy of Management Review,* April 1992, pp 183–211; and T J Maurer and K D Andrews, "Traditional, Likert, and Simplified Measures of Self-Efficacy," *Educational and Psychological Measurement,* December 2000, pp 965–73.

[22] C Brennan, "Tiger Loses Favorite Driver," *USA Today,* May 4, 2006, p 3C.

[23] Based on D H Lindsley, D A Brass, and J B Thomas, "Efficacy-Performance Spirals: A Multilevel Perspective," *Academy of Management Review,* July 1995, pp 645–78.

[24] See, for example, V Gecas, "The Social Psychology of Self-Efficacy," in *Annual Review of Sociology,* eds W R Scott and J Blake (Palo Alto, CA: Annual Reviews, Inc., 1989), vol. 15, pp 291–316; C K Stevens, A G Bavetta, and M E Gist, "Gender Differences in the Acquisition of Salary Negotiation Skills: The Role of Goals, Self-Efficacy, and Perceived Control," *Journal of Applied Psychology,* October 1993, pp 723–35; and D Eden and Y Zuk, "Seasickness as a Self-Fulfilling Prophecy: Raising Self-Efficacy to Boost Performance at Sea," *Journal of Applied Psychology,* October 1995, pp 628–35.

[25] For more on learned helplessness, see Gecas, "The Social Psychology of Self-Efficacy"; M J Martinko and W L Gardner, "Learned Helplessness: An Alternative Explanation for Performance Deficits," *Academy of Management Review,* April 1982, pp 195–204; and C R Campbell and M J Martinko, "An Integrative Attributional Perspective of Empowerment and Learned Helplessness: A Multimethod Field Study," *Journal of Management,* no. 2, 1998, pp 173–200. Also see A Dickerson and M A Taylor, "Self-Limiting Behavior in Women: Self-Esteem and Self-Efficacy as Predictors," *Group & Organization Management,* June 2000, pp 191–210.

[26] For an update on Bandura, see D Smith, "The Theory Heard 'Round the World," *Monitor on Psychology,* October 2002, pp 30–32.

[27] Research on this connection is reported in R B Rubin, M M Martin, S S Bruning, and D E Powers, "Test of a Self-Efficacy Model of Interpersonal Communication Competence," *Communication Quarterly,* Spring 1993, pp 210–20.

[28] Excerpted from T Petzinger Jr, "Bob Schmonsees Has a Tool for Better Sales, and It Ignores Excuses," *The Wall Street Journal,* March 26, 1999, p B1. Also see H Zhao, S E Seibert, and G E Hills, "The Mediating Role of Self-Efficacy in the Development of Entrepreneurial Intentions," *Journal of Applied Psychology,* November 2005, pp 1265–272.

29 Data from A D Stajkovic and F Luthans, "Self-Efficacy and Work-Related Performance: A Meta-Analysis," *Psychological Bulletin,* September 1998, pp 240–61.

30 Based in part on discussion in Gecas, "The Social Psychology of Self-Efficacy."

31 See S K Parker, "Enhancing Role Breadth Self-Efficacy: The Roles of Job Enrichment and Other Organizational Interventions," *Journal of Applied Psychology,* December 1998, pp 835–52.

32 The positive relationship between self-efficacy and readiness for retraining is documented in L A Hill and J Elias, "Retraining Midcareer Managers: Career History and Self-Efficacy Beliefs," *Human Resource Management,* Summer 1990, pp 197–217. Also see A M Saks, "Longitudinal Field Investigation of the Moderating and Mediating Effects of Self-Efficacy on the Relationship between Training and Newcomer Adjustment," *Journal of Applied Psychology,* April 1995, pp 211–25.

33 See A D Stajkovic and Fred Luthans, "Social Cognitive Theory and Self-Efficacy: Going beyond Traditional Motivational and Behavioral Approaches," *Organizational Dynamics,* Spring 1998, pp 62–74.

34 See P C Earley and T R Lituchy, "Delineating Goal and Efficacy Effects: A Test of Three Models," *Journal of Applied Psychology,* February 1991, pp 81–98.

35 See P Tierney and S M Farmer, "Creative Self-Efficacy: Its Potential Antecedents and Relationship to Creative Performance," *Academy of Management Journal,* December 2002, pp 1137–48.

36 See W S Silver, T R Mitchell, and M E Gist, "Response to Successful and Unsuccessful Performance: The Moderating Effect of Self-Efficacy on the Relationship between Performance and Attributions," *Organizational Behavior and Human Decision Processes,* June 1995, pp 286–99; R Zemke, "The Corporate Coach," *Training,* December 1996, pp 24–28; and J P Masciarelli, "Less Lonely at the Top," *Management Review,* April 1999, pp 58–61.

37 For a comprehensive update, see S W Gangestad and M Snyder, "Self-Monitoring: Appraisal and Reappraisal," *Psychological Bulletin,* July 2000, pp 530–55.

38 M Snyder and S Gangestad, "On the Nature of Self-Monitoring: Matters of Assessment, Matters of Validity," *Journal of Personality and Social Psychology,* July 1986, p 125.

39 Data from M Kilduff and D V Day, "Do Chameleons Get Ahead? The Effects of Self-Monitoring on Managerial Careers," *Academy of Management Journal,* August 1994, pp 1047–60.

40 Data from D B Turban and T W Dougherty, "Role of Protege Personality in Receipt of Mentoring and Career Success," *Academy of Management Journal,* June 1994, pp 688–702.

41 See F Luthans, "Successful vs. Effective Managers," *Academy of Management Executive,* May 1988, pp 127–32. Also see I M Jawahar and J Mattsson, "Sexism and Beautyism Effects in Selection as a Function of Self-Monitoring Level of Decision Maker," *Journal of Applied Psychology,* May 2005, pp 563–73; M R Barrick, L Parks, and M K Mount, "Self-Monitoring as a Moderator of the Relationships between Personality Traits and Performance," *Personnel Psychology,* Autumn 2005, pp 745–67; and K G DeMarree, S C Wheeler, and R E Petty, "Priming a New Identity: Self-Monitoring Moderates the Effects of Nonself Primes on Self-Judgments and Behavior," *Journal of Personality and Social Psychology,* November 2005, pp 657–71.

42 See A Bandura, *Social Learning Theory* (Englewood Cliffs, NJ: Prentice Hall, 1977). A further refinement is reported in A D Stajkovic and F Luthans, "Social Cognitive Theory and Self-Efficacy: Going Beyond Traditional Motivational and Behavioral Approaches," *Organizational Dynamics,* Spring 1998, pp 62–74. Also see M Uhl-Bien and G B Graen, "Individual Self-Management: Analysis of Professionals' Self-Managing Activities in Functional and Cross-Functional Work Teams," *Academy of Management Journal,* June 1998, pp 340–50.

43 Bandura, *Social Learning Theory,* p 13.

44 For related research, see M Castaneda, T A Kolenko, and R J Aldag, "Self-Management Perceptions and Practices: A Structural Equations Analysis," *Journal of Organizational Behavior,* January 1999, pp 101–20. An alternative model is discussed in K M Sheldon, D B Turban, K G Brown, M R Barrick, and T M Judge, "Applying Self-Determination Theory to Organizational Research," in *Research in Personnel and*

Human Resources Management, vol 22, eds J J Martocchio and G R Ferris (New York: Elsevier, 2003), pp 357–93.

45 "Career Self-Management," *Industry Week,* September 5, 1994, p 36.

46 See L Nash and H Stevenson, "Success That Lasts," *Harvard Business Review,* February 2004, pp 102–9.

47 S R Covey, *The 7 Habits of Highly Effective People* (New York: Simon & Schuster, 1989), p 42. Also see S R Covey, *The 8th Habit: From Effectiveness to Greatness* (NY: Free Press, 2004); and S Covey, "Power to the People," *Training,* April 2006, p 64.

48 "Labor Letter: A Special News Report on People and Their Jobs in Offices, Fields, and Factories," *The Wall Street Journal,* October 15, 1985, p 1.

49 J Chatzky, "The 4 Steps to Setting Goals & 6 Keys to Achieving Them," *Money,* November 2003, pp 111, 113. Also see C L Porath and T S Bateman, "Self-Regulation: From Goal Orientation to Job Performance," *Journal of Applied Psychology,* January 2006, pp 185–92; J Pfeffer, "Why Employees Should Lead Themselves," *Business 2.0,* January/February 2006, p 76; and N Hellmich. "Dieters Are Setting Ambitious Goals," *USA Today,* April 26, 2006, p 1A.

50 R McGarvey, "Rehearsing for Success," *Executive Female,* January/February 1990, p 36.

51 See W P Anthony, R H Bennett, III, E N Maddox, and W J Wheatley, "Picturing the Future: Using Mental Imagery to Enrich Strategic Environmental Assessment," *Academy of Management Executive,* May 1993, pp 43–56.

52 D S Looney, "Mental Toughness Wins Out," *The Christian Science Monitor,* July 31, 1998, p B4.

53 For excellent tips on self-management, see C P Neck, "Managing Your Mind," *Internal Auditor,* June 1996, pp 60–63.

54 C Zastrow, *Talk to Yourself: Using the Power of Self-Talk* (Englewood Cliffs, NJ: Prentice Hall, 1979), p 60. Also see C C Manz and C P Neck, "Inner Leadership: Creating Productive Thought Patterns," *Academy of Management Executive,* August 1991, pp 87–95; C P Neck and R F Ashcraft, "Inner Leadership: Mental Strategies for Nonprofit Staff Members," *Nonprofit World,* May–June 2000, pp 27–30; and T C Brown, "The Effect of Verbal Self-Guidance Training on Collective Efficacy and Team Performance," *Personnel Psychology,* Winter 2003, pp 935–64.

55 E Franz, "Private Pep Talk," *Selling Power,* May 1996, p 81. Also see B Blades, "7 Strategies to Successful Selling," *Training,* April 2006, p 17; J Mandell, "Saying No Can Be a Positive," *USA Today,* April 24, 2006, p 9D; and A Danigelis, "Like, Um, You Know: Verbal Tics May Be Holding You Back. How to Identify Them and Overcome Them. Totally," *Fast Company,* May 2006, p 99.

56 Drawn from discussion in A Bandura, "Self-Reinforcement: Theoretical and Methodological Considerations," *Behaviorism,* Fall 1976, pp 135–55.

57 R Kreitner and F Luthans, "A Social Learning Approach to Behavioral Management: Radical Behaviorists 'Mellowing Out,' " *Organizational Dynamics,* Autumn 1984, p 63.

58 See K Painter, "We Are Who We Are, or Are We?" *USA Today,* October 3, 2002, p 9; S Begley, "In the Brave Guppy and Hyper Octopus, Clues to Personality," *The Wall Street Journal,* October 10, 2003, p B1; and S Kuchinskas, "A Match Made in Hormones," *Business 2.0,* January/February 2006, p 24.

59 The landmark report is J M Digman, "Personality Structure: Emergence of the Five-Factor Model," *Annual Review of Psychology,* vol. 41, 1990, pp 417–40. Also see M K Mount, M R Barrick, S M Scullen, and J Rounds, "Higher-Order Dimensions of the Big Five Personality Traits and the Big Six Vocational Interest Types," *Personnel Psychology,* Summer 2005, pp 447–78; P Warr, D Bartram, and A Brown, "Big Five Validity: Aggregation Method Matters," *Journal of Occupational and Organizational Psychology,* September 2005, pp 377–86; and A B Bakker, K I Van Der Zee, K A Lewig, and M F. Dollard, "The Relationship between the Big Five Personality Factors and Burnout: A Study among Volunteer Counselors," *The Journal of Social Psychology,* February 2006, pp 31–50.

60 For more on personality measurement and assessment, see C H Van Iddekinge, P H Raymark, and P L Roth, "Assessing Personality with a Structured Employment Interview: Construct-Related Validity and Susceptibility to Response Inflation," *Journal of Applied Psychology,* May 2005, pp 536–52; P Barrett, "What If There Were No Psychometrics? Constructs, Complexity, and Measurement," *Journal of*

Personality Assessment, October 2005, pp 134–40; E D Heggestad, M Morrison, C L Reeve, and R A McCloy, "Forced-Choice Assessments of Personality for Selection: Evaluating Issues of Normative Assessment and Faking Resistance," *Journal of Applied Psychology,* January 2006, pp 9–24; S Stark, O S Chernyshenko, F Drasgow, and B A Williams, "Examining Assumptions about Item Responding in Personality Assessment: Should Ideal Point Methods Be Considered for Scale Development and Scoring?" *Journal of Applied Psychology,* January 2006, pp 25–39; and J R Matthews and L H Matthews, "Personality Assessment Training: View from a Licensing Board," *Journal of Personality Assessment,* February 2006, pp 46–50.

⁶¹ Data from S V Paunonen et al., "The Structure of Personality in Six Cultures," *Journal of Cross-Cultural Psychology,* May 1996, pp 339–53. Also see C Ward, C Leong, and M Low, "Personality and Sojourner Adjustment: An Exploration of the Big Five and the Cultural Fit Proposition," *Journal of Cross-Cultural Psychology,* March 2004, pp 137–51.

⁶² J Allik and R R McCrae, "Toward a Geography of Personality Traits: Patterns of Profiles across 36 Cultures," *Journal of Cross-Cultural Psychology,* January 2004, p 13.

⁶³ See M R Barrick and M K Mount, "The Big Five Personality Dimensions and Job Performance: A Meta-Analysis," *Personnel Psychology,* Spring 1991, pp 1–26. Also see R P Tett, D N Jackson, and M Rothstein, "Personality Measures as Predictors of Job Performance: A Meta-Analytic Review," *Personnel Psychology,* Winter 1991, pp 703–42; and S E Seibert and M L Kraimer, "The Five-Factor Model of Personality and Career Success," *Journal of Vocational Behavior,* February 2001, pp 1–21.

⁶⁴ Barrick and Mount, "The Big Five Personality Dimensions and Job Performance: A Meta-Analysis," p 18. Also see J E Kurtz and S B Tiegreen, "Matters of Conscience and Conscientiousness: The Place of Ego Development in the Five-Factor Model," *Journal of Personality Assessment,* December 2005, pp 312–17; and N M Dudley, K A Orvis, J E Lebiecki, and J M Cortina, "A Meta-Analytic Investigation of Conscientiousness in the Prediction of Job Performance: Examining the Intercorrelations and the Incremental Validity of Narrow Traits" *Journal of Applied Psychology,* January 2006, pp 40–57.

⁶⁵ For details, see S Clarke and I T Robertson, "A Meta-Analytic Review of the Big Five Personality Factors and Accident Involvement in Occupational and Non-Occupational Settings," *Journal of Occupational and Organizational Psychology,* September 2005, pp 355–76.

⁶⁶ Barrick and Mount, "The Big Five Personality Dimensions and Job Performance: A Meta-Analysis," p 21. Also see D M Tokar, A R Fischer, and L M Subich, "Personality and Vocational Behavior: A Selective Review of the Literature, 1993–1997," *Journal of Vocational Behavior,* October 1998, pp 115–53; and K C Wooten, T A Timmerman, and R Folger, "The Use of Personality and the Five-Factor Model to Predict New Business Ventures: From Outplacement to Start-up," *Journal of Vocational Behavior,* February 1999, pp 82–101.

⁶⁷ For details, see L A Witt and G R Ferris, "Social Skill as Moderator of the Conscientiousness-Performance Relationship: Convergent Results across Four Studies," *Journal of Applied Psychology,* October 2003, pp 809–20. Also see H Liao and A Chuang, "A Multilevel Investigation of Factors Influencing Employee Service Performance and Customer Outcomes," *Academy of Management Journal,* February 2004, pp 41–58.

⁶⁸ Lead researcher William Fleeson, as quoted in M Dittmann, "Acting Extraverted Spurs Positive Feelings, Study Finds," *Monitor on Psychology,* April 2003, p 17. Also see L D Smillie, G B Yeo, A F Furnham, and C J Jackson, "Benefits of All Work and No Play: The Relationship between Neuroticism and Performance as a Function of Resource Allocation," *Journal of Applied Psychology,* January 2006, pp 139–55.

⁶⁹ J M Crant, "Proactive Behavior in Organizations," *Journal of Management,* no. 3, 2000, p 439.

⁷⁰ Ibid., pp 439–41. Also see J A Thompson, "Proactive Personality and Job Performance: A Social Capital Perspective," *Journal of Applied Psychology,* September 2005, pp 1011–017; and B Erdogan and T N Bauer, "Enhancing Career Benefits of Employee Proactive Personality: The Role of Fit with Jobs and Organizations," *Personnel Psychology,* Winter 2005, pp 859–91.

⁷¹ For inspiration, see P Burrows, "HP's Ultimate Team Player," *BusinessWeek,* January 30, 2006, pp 76–78; B Hagenbaugh and S Kirchhoff, "From BET to Hotels to Banking, Johnson Keeps Moving

Forward," *USA Today,* April 12, 2006, pp 1B–2B; and P B Gray, "Business Class," *Fortune,* April 17, 2006, pp 336B–336H.

⁷² See S B Gustafson and M D Mumford, "Personal Style and Person-Environment Fit: A Pattern Approach," *Journal of Vocational Behavior,* April 1995, pp 163–88; and T M Glomb and E T Walsh, "Can Opposites Attract? Personality Heterogeneity in Supervisor-Subordinate Dyads as a Predictor of Subordinate Outcomes," *Journal of Applied Psychology,* July 2005, pp 749–57.

⁷³ For an instructive update, see J B Rotter, "Internal versus External Control of Reinforcement: A Case History of a Variable," *American Psychologist,* April 1990, pp 489–93. A critical review of locus of control and a call for a meta-analysis can be found in R W Renn and R J Vandenberg, "Differences in Employee Attitudes and Behaviors Based on Rotter's (1966) Internal-External Locus of Control: Are They All Valid?" *Human Relations,* November 1991, pp 1161–77.

⁷⁴ For an overall review of research on locus of control, see P E Spector, "Behavior in Organizations as a Function of Employee's Locus of Control," *Psychological Bulletin,* May 1982, pp 482–97; the relationship between locus of control and performance and satisfaction is examined in D R Norris and R E Niebuhr, "Attributional Influences on the Job Performance–Job Satisfaction Relationship," *Academy of Management Journal,* June 1984, pp 424–31; salary differences between internals and externals were examined by P C Nystrom, "Managers' Salaries and Their Beliefs about Reinforcement Control," *Journal of Social Psychology,* August 1983, pp 291–92. Also see S S K Lam and J Schaubroeck, "The Role of Locus of Control in Reactions to Being Promoted and to Being Passed Over: A Quasi Experiment," *Academy of Management Journal,* February 2000, pp 66–78.

⁷⁵ Robert Solomon, as quoted in D Vera and A Rodriguez-Lopez, "Strategic Virtues: Humility as a Source of Competitive Advantage," *Organizational Dynamics,* no. 4, 2004, pp 394–95.

⁷⁶ Ibid., p 395.

⁷⁷ As quoted in "Believe in Something Bigger Than Yourself," *Business 2.0,* December 2005, p 126. Also see "Never, Ever Forget That You Are a Servant," *Business 2.0,* December 2005, p 122; A Park, "Taming the Alpha Exec," *Fast Company,* May 2006, pp 86–90; J Janove, "A 'Sorry' Strategy," *HR Magazine,* March 2006, pp 127–32; and B Kellerman, "When Should a Leader Apologize and When Not?" *Harvard Business Review,* April 2006, pp 72–81.

⁷⁸ M Fishbein and I Ajzen, *Belief, Attitude, Intention and Behavior: An Introduction to Theory and Research* (Reading, MA: Addison-Wesley Publishing, 1975), p 6. For more, see D Andrich and I M Styles, "The Structural Relationship between Attitude and Behavior Statements from the Unfolding Perspective," *Psychological Methods,* December 1998, pp 454–69; A P Brief, *Attitudes in and around Organizations* (Thousand Oaks, CA: Sage Publications, 1998); and "Tips to Pick the Best Employee," *BusinessWeek,* March 1, 1999, p 24.

⁷⁹ See B M Staw and J Ross, "Stability in the Midst of Change: A Dispositional Approach to Job Attitudes," *Journal of Applied Psychology,* August 1985, pp 469–80. Also see J Schaubroeck, D C Ganster, and B Kemmerer, "Does Trait Affect Promote Job Attitude Stability?" *Journal of Organizational Behavior,* March 1996, pp 191–96.

⁸⁰ Data from P S Visser and J A Krosnick, "Development of Attitude Strength over the Life Cycle: Surge and Decline," *Journal of Personality and Social Psychology,* December 1998, pp 1389–410.

⁸¹ For interesting reading on intelligence, see J R Flynn, "Searching for Justice: The Discovery of IQ Gains over Time," *American Psychologist,* January 1999, pp 5–20; and E Benson, "Intelligent Intelligence Testing," *Monitor on Psychology,* February 2003, pp 48–54.

⁸² For an excellent update on intelligence, including definitional distinctions and a historical perspective of the IQ controversy, see R A Weinberg, "Intelligence and IQ," *American Psychologist,* February 1989, pp 98–104. Genetics and intelligence are discussed in R Plomin and F M Spinath, "Intelligence: Genetics, Genes, and Genomics," *Journal of Personality and Social Psychology,* January 2004, pp 112–29.

⁸³ Ibid. Also see M Elias, "Mom's IQ, Not Family Size, Key to Kids' Smarts," *USA Today,* June 12, 2000, p 1D; and R Sapolsky, "Score One for Nature—or Is It Nurture?" *USA Today,* June 21, 2000, p 17A.

⁸⁴ S L Wilk, L Burris Desmarais, and P R Sackett, "Gravitation to Jobs Commensurate with Ability: Longitudinal and Cross-Sectional Tests," *Journal of Applied Psychology,* February 1995, p 79. Also see J Menkes,

"Hiring for Smarts," *Harvard Business Review,* November 2005, pp 100–09.

[85] B Azar, "People Are Becoming Smarter—Why?" *APA Monitor,* June 1996, p 20. Also see " 'Average' Intelligence Higher than It Used to Be," *USA Today,* February 18, 1997, p 6D.

[86] See D Lubinski, "Introduction to the Special Section on Cognitive Abilities: 100 Years after Spearman's (1904) 'General Intelligence,' Objectively Determined and Measured," *Journal of Personality and Social Psychology,* January 2004, pp 96–111.

[87] See F L Schmidt and J E Hunter, "Employment Testing: Old Theories and New Research Findings," *American Psychologist,* October 1981, p 1128; and N R Kuncel, S A Hezlett, and D S Ones, "Academic Performance, Career Potential, Creativity, and Job Performance: Can One Construct Predict Them All?" *Journal of Personality and Social Psychology,* January 2004, pp 148–61. A brief overview of the foregoing study can be found in M Greer, "General Cognition Also Makes the Difference on the Job, Study Finds," *Monitor on Psychology,* April 2004, p 12. Also see F L Schmidt and J Hunter, "General Mental Ability in the World of Work: Occupational Attainment and Job Performance," *Journal of Personality and Social Psychology,* January 2004, pp 162–73; and R L Cardy and T T Selvarajan, "Competencies: Alternative Frameworks for Competitive Advantage," *Business Horizons,* May/June 2006, pp 235–45.

[88] A Reinhardt, "I've Left a Few Dead Bodies," *Business Week,* January 31, 2000, p 69. Also see K Tyler, "Helping Employees Cope with Grief," *HR Magazine,* September 2003, pp 54–58; L W Andrews, "Aftershocks of War," *HR Magazine,* April 2004, pp 64–70; C Tkaczyk, "Stanley O'Neal: Merrill Lynch CEO Since 2003," *Fortune,* December 12, 2005, p 130; R M Kramer, "The Great Intimidators," *Harvard Business Review,* February 2006, pp 88–96; and S Bing, "The Upside of Anger," *Fortune,* March 20, 2006, p 186.

[89] Quoted in B Schlender, "Why Andy Grove Can't Stop," *Fortune,* July 10, 1995, p 91. Also see A Grove, "Only the Paranoid Survive (Now More Than Ever)," *Business 2.0,* December 2005, p 114.

[90] D Lieberman, "Fear of Failing Drives Diller," *USA Today,* February 10, 1999, p 3B.

[91] R S Lazarus, *Emotion and Adaptation* (New York: Oxford University Press, 1991), p 6. Also see, J A Russell and L F Barrett, "Core Affect, Prototypical Emotional Episodes, and Other Things Called *Emotion:* Dissecting the Elephant," *Journal of Personality and Social Psychology,* May 1999, pp 805–19; S Fineman, *Understanding Emotion at Work* (Thousand Oaks, CA: Sage, 2003); D DeSteno, R E Petty, D D Rucker, D T Wegener, and J Braverman, "Discrete Emotions and Persuasion: The Role of Emotion-Induced Expectancies," *Journal of Personality and Social Psychology,* January 2004, pp 43–56; L A King, J A Hicks, J L Krull, and A K Del Gaiso, "Positive Affect and the Experience of Meaning in Life," *Journal of Personality and Social Psychology,* January 2006, pp 179–96; and G Morse, "Decisions and Desire," *Harvard Business Review,* January 2006, pp 42–51.

[92] Based on discussion in R D Arvey, G L Renz, and T W Watson, "Emotionality and Job Performance: Implications for Personnel Selection," in *Research in Personnel and Human Resources Management,* vol. 16, ed G R Ferris (Stamford, CT: JAI Press, 1998), pp 103–47. Also see L A King, "Ambivalence over Emotional Expression and Reading Emotions," *Journal of Personality and Social Psychology,* March 1998, pp 753–62; and J L Tsai and Y Chentsova-Dutton, "Variation among European Americans in Emotional Facial Expression," *Journal of Cross-Cultural Psychology,* November 2003, pp 650–57.

[93] Data from S D Pugh, "Service with a Smile: Emotional Contagion in the Service Encounter," *Academy of Management Journal,* October 2001, pp 1018–27.

[94] Drawn from P Totterdell, S Kellett, K Teuchmann, and R B Briner, "Evidence of Mood Linkage in Work Groups," *Journal of Personality and Social Psychology,* June 1998, pp 1504–15. Also see C D Fisher, "Mood and Emotions while Working: Missing Pieces of Job Satisfaction," *Journal of Organizational Behavior,* March 2000, pp 185–202; K M Lewis, "When Leaders Display Emotion: How Followers Respond to Negative Emotional Expression of Male and Female Leaders," *Journal of Organizational Behavior,* March 2000, pp 221–34; and A Singh-Manoux and C Finkenauer, "Cultural Variations in Social Sharing of Emotions: An Intercultural Perspective," *Journal of Cross-Cultural Psychology,* November 2001, pp 647–61.

[95] As quoted in D Jones, "Music Director Works to Blend Strengths," *USA Today,* October 27, 2003, p 6B.

[96] N M Ashkanasy and C S Daus, "Emotion in the Workplace: The New Challenge for Managers," *Academy of Management Executive,* February 2002, p 79. Also see A A Grandey, "When 'The Show Must Go On': Surface Acting and Deep Acting as Determinants of Emotional Exhaustion and Peer-Rated Service Delivery," *Academy of Management Journal,* February 2003, pp 86–96; C M Brotheridge and R T Lee, "Development and Validation of the Emotional Labour Scale," *Journal of Occupational and Organizational Psychology,* September 2003, pp 365–79; Y Guerrier and A Adib, "Work at Leisure and Leisure at Work: A Study of the Emotional Labour of Tour Reps," *Human Relations,* November 2003, pp 1399–417; A A Grandey, G M Fisk, and D D Steiner, "Must 'Service With a Smile' Be Stressful? The Moderating Role of Personal Control for American and French Employees," *Journal of Applied Psychology,* September 2005, pp 893–904; R H Gosserand and J M Diefendorff, "Emotional Display Rules and Emotional Labor: The Moderating Role of Commitment," *Journal of Applied Psychology,* November 2005, pp 1256–264; S Burling, "Stress Study Shows Ills of Call-Center Workers," *The Arizona Republic,* December 10, 2005, p D3; and P O'Connell, "Taking the Measure of Mood," *Harvard Business Review,* March 2006, pp 25–26.

[97] Data from A M Kring and A H Gordon, "Sex Differences in Emotions: Expression, Experience, and Physiology," *Journal of Personality and Social Psychology,* March 1998, pp 686–703.

[98] D Goleman, *Emotional Intelligence* (New York: Bantam Books, 1995), p 34. For more, see M Dittmann, "How 'Emotional Intelligence' Emerged," *Monitor on Psychology,* October 2003, p 64; M M Tugade and B L Fredrickson, "Resilient Individuals Use Positive Emotions to Bounce Back from Negative Emotional Experiences," *Journal of Personality and Social Psychology,* February 2004, pp 320–33; I Goldenberg, K Matheson, and J Mantler, "The Assessment of Emotional Intelligence: A Comparison of Performance-Based and Self-Report Methodologies," *Journal of Personality Assessment,* February 2006, pp 33–45; and J E Barbuto Jr. and M E Burbach, "The Emotional Intelligence of Transformational Leaders: A Field Study of Elected Officials," *The Journal of Social Psychology,* February 2006, pp 51-64.

[99] See the box titled "Get Happy Carefully" on p 49 of D Goleman, R Boyatzis, and A McKee, "Primal Leadership: The Hidden Driver of Great Performance," *Harvard Business Review,* Special Issue: Breakthrough Leadership, December 2001, pp 43–51.

[100] J S Lublin, "Surviving the Pressure with a Ready Plan or, Literally, a Script," *The Wall Street Journal,* March 2, 2004, p B1.

[101] M N Martinez, "The Smarts That Count," *HR Magazine,* November 1997, pp 72–78.

[102] "What's Your EQ at Work?" *Fortune,* October 26, 1998, p 298.

[103] Based on M Davies, L Stankov, and R D Roberts, "Emotional Intelligence: In Search of an Elusive Construct," *Journal of Personality and Social Psychology,* October 1998, pp 989–1015; and K A Barchard, "Does Emotional Intelligence Assist in the Prediction of Academic Success?" *Educational and Psychological Measurement,* October 2003, pp 840–58. Also see B P Chapman and B Hayslip, Jr., "Incremental Validity of a Measure of Emotional Intelligence," *Journal of Personality Assessment,* October 2005, pp 154–69.

[104] A Fisher, "Success Secret: A High Emotional IQ," *Fortune,* October 26, 1998, p 294. Also see Daniel Goleman, "Never Stop Learning," *Harvard Business Review,* Special Issue: Inside the Mind of the Leader," January 2004, pp 28–29.

[105] Excerpted from J Macht, "To Get Ahead, Get Mad," *Business 2.0,* May 2002, p 94. © Time, Inc. All rights reserved.

Chapter 6

[1] Excerpted from Z Stambor, "Employees: A Company's Best Asset," *Monitor on Psychology,* March 2006, pp 28–30.

[2] T R Mitchell, "Motivation: New Direction for Theory, Research, and Practice," *Academy of Management Review,* January 1982, p 81.

[3] This discussion is based on T R Mitchell and D Daniels, "Motivation," in *Handbook of Psychology,* vol 12, eds W C Borman, D R Ilgen, and R J Klimoski (Hoboken, NJ: John Wiley & Sons, Inc., 2003), pp 225–54.

[4] R Simmons, "Designing High-Performance Jobs," *Harvard Business Review,* July–August 2005, p 56.

[5] See J Mehring, "What's Lifting Productivity," *BusinessWeek,* May 24, 2004, p 32.

[6] For a complete description of Maslow's theory, see A H Maslow, "A Theory of Human Motivation," *Psychological Review,* July 1943, pp 370–96. For an update on this theory, see B Cooke, A J Mils, and E S Kelley, "Situating Maslow in Cold War America: A Recontextualization of Management Theory," *Group & Organization Management,* April 2005, pp 129–52.

[7] "Baird Named to *Fortune's* '100 Best Companies to Work For,' for Third Consecutive Year," http:www.rwbaird.com/news/currentnews/ fraNewsRelease029.aspx?Seg=1919, accessed January 9, 2006.

[8] R Levering and M Moskowitz, "The 100 Best Companies to Work For: And the Winners Are . . ." *Fortune,* January 23, 2006, p 96.

[9] H A Murray, *Explorations in Personality* (New York: John Wiley & Sons, 1938), p 164.

[10] See K G Shaver, "The Entrepreneurial Personality Myth," *Business and Economic Review,* April/June 1995, pp 20–23.

[11] See the following series of research reports: D K McNeese-Smith, "The Relationship between Managerial Motivation, Leadership, Nurse Outcomes and Patient Satisfaction," *Journal of Organizational Behavior,* March 1999, pp 243–59; A M Harrell and M J Stahl, "A Behavioral Decision Theory Approach for Measuring McClelland's Trichotomy of Needs," *Journal of Applied Psychology,* April 1981, pp 242–47; and M J Stahl, "Achievement, Power and Managerial Motivation: Selecting Managerial Talent with the Job Choice Exercise," *Personnel Psychology,* Winter 1983, pp 775–89.

[12] Evidence for the validity of motivation training can be found in H Heckhausen and S Krug, "Motive Modification," in *Motivation and Society,* ed A J Stewart (San Francisco: Jossey-Bass, 1982). Also see S Hamm, "A Red Flag in the Brain Game," *BusinessWeek,* May 1, 2006, pp 32–35.

[13] Results can be found in D B Turban and T L Keon, "Organizational Attractiveness: An Interactionist Perspective," *Journal of Applied Psychology,* April 1993, pp 184–93.

[14] Supportive results can be found in R Eisenberger, J R Jones, F Stinglhamber, L Shanock, and A T Randall, "Flow Experiences at Work: For High Need Achievers Alone?" *Journal of Organizational Behavior,* November 2005, pp 755–75.

[15] J L Bowditch and A F Buono, *A Primer on Organizational Behavior* (New York: John Wiley & Sons, 1985), p 210.

[16] This framework was proposed by M A Campion and P W Thayer, "Development and Field Evaluation of an Interdisciplinary Measure of Job Design," *Journal of Applied Psychology,* February 1985, pp 29–43.

[17] Supportive results can be found in S K Parker, "Longitudinal Effects of Lean Production on Employee Outcomes and the Mediating Role of Work Characteristics," *Journal of Applied Psychology,* August 2003, pp 620–34.

[18] This type of program was developed and tested by M A Campion and C L McClelland, "Follow-Up and Extension of the Interdisciplinary Costs and Benefits of Enlarged Jobs," *Journal of Applied Psychology,* June 1993, pp 339–51.

[19] Excerpted from R J Grossman, "Putting HR in Rotation," *HR Magazine,* March 2003, p 53.

[20] See F Herzberg, B Mausner, and B B Snyderman, *The Motivation to Work* (New York: John Wiley & Sons, 1959).

[21] J Mero, "You Do What?" *Fortune,* April 3, 2006, p 33. Another example is provided by J Mero, "You Do What?" *Fortune,* May 1, 2006, p 33.

[22] F Herzberg, "One More Time: How Do You Motivate Employees?" *Harvard Business Review,* January/February 1968, p 56.

[23] For a thorough review of research on Herzberg's theory, see C C Pinder, *Work Motivation: Theory, Issues, and Applications* (Glenview, IL: Scott, Foresman, 1984).

[24] J R Hackman, G R Oldham, R Janson, and K Purdy, "A New Strategy for Job Enrichment," *California Management Review,* Summer 1975, p 58.

[25] Definitions of the job characteristics were adapted from J R Hackman and G R Oldham, "Motivation through the Design of Work: Test of a Theory," *Organizational Behavior and Human Performance,* August 1976, pp 250–79.

[26] A review of this research can be found in M L Ambrose and C T Kulik, "Old Friends, New Faces: Motivation Research in the 1990s," *Journal of Management,* 1999, pp 231–92.

[27] These examples were obtained from R Levering and M Moskowitz, "The 100 Best Companies to Work For: And the Winners Are . . ." *Fortune,* January 23, 2006, pp 100, 106.

[28] Supportive results can be found in R F Piccolo and J A Colquitt, "Transformational Leadership and Job Behaviors: The Mediating Role of Core Job Characteristics," *Academy of Management Journal,* April 2006, pp 327–40; and S Ohly, S Sonnentag, and F Pluntke, "Routinization, Work Characteristics and Their Relationships with Creative and Proactive Behaviors," *Journal of Organizational Behavior,* May 2006, pp 257–79.

[29] The turnover meta-analysis was conducted by R W Griffeth, P W Hom, and S Gaertner, "A Meta-Analysis of Antecedents and Correlates of Employee Turnover: Update, Moderator Tests, and Research Implications for the Next Millennium," *Journal of Management,* 2000, pp 463–88. Absenteeism results are discussed in Y Fried and G R Ferris, "The Validity of the Job Characteristics Model: A Review and Meta-Analysis," *Personnel Psychology,* Summer 1987, pp 287–322.

[30] Results can be found in M R Kelley, "New Process Technology, Job Design, and Work Organization: A Contingency Model," *American Sociological Review,* April 1990, pp 191–208.

[31] Productivity studies are reviewed in R E Kopelman, *Managing Productivity in Organizations* (New York: McGraw-Hill, 1986).

[32] A thorough discussion of reengineering and associated outcomes can be found in J Champy, *Reengineering Management: The Mandate for New Leadership* (New York: HarperBusiness, 1995).

[33] See S Sonnentag and F R H Zijlstra, "Job Characteristics and Off-Job Activities as Predictors of Need for Recovery, Well-Being, and Fatigue," *Journal of Applied Psychology,* March 2006, pp 330–50; and D Moyer, "Best with Rest," *Harvard Business Review,* March 2006, p 152.

[34] S Armour, "Young Tech Workers Face Crippling Injuries," *USA Today,* February 9, 2001, p 2B.

[35] This description was taken from J R Edwards, J A Scully, and M D Brtek, "The Nature and Outcome of Work: A Replication and Extension of Interdisciplinary Work-Design Research," *Journal of Applied Psychology,* December 2000, pp 860–68.

[36] These descriptions were excerpted from J Prichard, "Reinventing the Office," *Arizona Republic,* January 16, 2002, p D1.

[37] "NINDS Repetitive Motion Disorders Information Page," http://www.ninds.nih.gov/disorders/repetitive_motion/repetitive_ motion.htm, last updated February 7, 2006.

[38] See "Repetitive Motion Results in Longest Work Absences," Bureau of Labor Statistics, http://www.bls.gov/opub/ted/2004/ mar/wk5/art02.htm, last updated March 30, 2005.

[39] Definitions of engagement and results from the survey can be found in "Dilbert Is Right, Says Gallup Study," *Gallup Management Journal,* http:// gmj.gallup.com/content/defajult.asp?ci=22381, accessed April 13, 2006.

[40] See A Gopal, "Worker Disengagement Continues to Cost Singapore," *Gallup Management Journal,* http://gmj.gallup.com/content/ defajult.asp?ci=22720, accessed May 11, 2006.

[41] The definition and discussion of intrinsic motivation were drawn from R M Ryan and E L Deci, "Intrinsic and Extrinsic Motivations: Classic Definitions and New Directions," *Contemporary Educational Psychology,* January 2000, pp 54–67.

[42] The definition and discussion of extrinsic motivation were drawn from ibid.

[43] See K W Thomas, E Jansen, and W G Tymon, Jr, "Navigating in the Realm of Theory: An Empowering View of Construct Development," in *Research in Organizational Change and Development,* vol. 10, eds W A Pasmore and R W Woodman (Greenwich, CT: JAI Press, 1997), pp 1–30.

[44] See E L Deci and R M Ryan, "The 'What' and 'Why' of Goal Pursuits: Human Needs and Self-Determination of Behavior," *Psychological Inquiry,* December 2000, pp 227–68.

[45] Thomas, *Intrinsic Motivation at Work,* p 44.

[46] Results are presented in J Barbian, "In the Battle to Attract Talent, Companies Are Finding New Ways to Keep Employees Smiling," *Training,* January 2001, pp 93–96.

[47] Thomas, *Intrinsic Motivation at Work,* p 44.

[48] See "The 100 Best Companies to Work For," p 100.

[49] Thomas, *Intrinsic Motivation at Work,* p 44.

[50] Thomas, *Intrinsic Motivation at Work,* p 44.

[51] Preliminary supportive results can be found in B Kuvaas, "Work Performance, Affective Commitment, and Work Motivation: The Roles of

Pay Administration and Pay Level," *Journal of Organizational Behavior,* May 2006, pp 365–85; and N W Van Yperen and M Hagedoorn, "Do High Job Demands Increase Intrinsic Motivation or Fatigue or Both? The Role of Job Control and Job Social Support," *Academy of Management Journal,* June 2003, pp 339–48.

[52] Results can be found in "Why am I Here?" *Training,* April 2006, p 13.

[53] See the related discussion in N C Nelson, "Valuing Employees," *HR Magazine,* February 2006, pp 117–22; and H Dolezalek, "Working Smart," *Training,* April 2006, pp 40–44.

[54] C Taylor, "On-the-Spot Incentives," *HR Magazine,* May 2004, p 82.

[55] For norms on this survey, see D J Weiss, R V Dawis, G W England, and L H Lofquist, *Manual for the Minnesota Satisfaction Questionnaire* (Minneapolis: Industrial Relations Center, University of Minnesota, 1967).

[56] Results are reported in M Boyle, "Happiness Index: Nothing Is Rotten in Denmark," *Fortune,* February 19, 2001, p 242.

[57] For a review of these models, see A P Brief, *Attitudes In and Around Organizations* (Thousand Oaks, CA: Sage Publications, 1998).

[58] See A R Karr, "Work Week: A Special News Report about Life on the Job—And Trends Taking Shape There," *The Wall Street Journal,* June 29, 1999, p A1. Also see D P Donnelly and J J Quirin, "An Extension of Lee and Mitchell's Unfolding Model of Voluntary Turnover," *Journal of Organizational Behavior,* February 2006, pp 59–77.

[59] For a review of need satisfaction models, see E F Stone, "A Critical Analysis of Social Information Processing Models of Job Perceptions and Job Attitudes," in *Job Satisfaction: How People Feel about Their Jobs and How It Affects Their Performance,* eds C J Cranny, P Cain Smith, and E F Stone (New York: Lexington Books, 1992), pp 21–52.

[60] See J P Wanous, T D Poland, S L Premack, and K S Davis, "The Effects of Met Expectations on Newcomer Attitudes and Behaviors: A Review and Meta-Analysis," *Journal of Applied Psychology,* June 1992, pp 288–97.

[61] A complete description of this model is provided by E A Locke, "Job Satisfaction," in *Social Psychology and Organizational Behavior,* eds M Gruneberg and T Wall (New York: John Wiley & Sons, 1984).

[62] For a test of the value fulfillment value, see W A Hochwarter, P L Perrewé, G R Ferris, and R A Brymer, "Job Satisfaction and Performance: The Moderating Effects of Value Attainment and Affective Disposition," *Journal of Vocational Behavior,* April 1999, pp 296–313.

[63] Results can be found in J Cohen-Charash and P E Spector, "The Role of Justice in Organizations: A Meta-Analysis." *Organizational Behavior and Human Decision Processes,* November 2001, pp 278–321.

[64] A thorough discussion of this model is provided by C L Hulin, and T A Judge, "Job Attitudes," in *Handbook of Psychology,* vol 12, eds W C Borman, D R Ilgen, and R J Klimoski (Hoboken, NJ: John Wiley & Sons, Inc., 2003), pp 255–76. Also see R Ilies, R D Arvey, T J Bouchard, "Darwinism, Behavioral Genetics, and Organizational Behavior: A Review and Agenda for Future Research," *Journal of Organizational Behavior,* March 2006, pp 121–41.

[65] Supportive results can be found in R Ilies and T A Judge, "On the Heritability of Job Satisfaction: The Mediating Role of Personality," *Journal of Applied Psychology,* August 2003, pp 750–59; and B M Staw and J Ross, "Stability in the Midst of Change: A Dispositional Approach to Job Attitudes," *Journal of Applied Psychology,* August 1985, pp 69–80.

[66] See R D Arvey, T J Bouchard, Jr, N L Segal, and L M Abraham, "Job Satisfaction: Environmental and Genetic Components," *Journal of Applied Psychology,* April 1989, pp 187–92.

[67] See C Dormann and D Zapf, "Job Satisfaction: A Meta-Analysis of Stabilities," *Journal of Organizational Behavior,* August 2001, pp 483–504.

[68] Results can be found in A J Kinicki, F M McKee-Ryan, C A Schriesheim, and K P Carson, "Assessing the Construct Validity of the Job Descriptive Index (JDI): A Review and Analysis," *Journal of Applied Psychology,* February 2002, pp 14–32.

[69] See S P Brown, "A Meta-Analysis and Review of Organizational Research on Job Involvement," *Psychological Bulletin,* September 1996, pp 235–55.

[70] Results can be found in A Cooper-Hakim and C Viswesvaran, "The Construct of Work Commitment: Testing an Integrative Framework," *Psychological Bulletin,* March 2005, pp 241–59.

[71] D W Organ, "The Motivational Basis of Organizational Citizenship Behavior," in *Research in Organizational Behavior,* eds B M Staw and L L Cummings (Greenwich, CT: JAI Press, 1990), p 46.

[72] Results can be found in J A LePine, A Erez, and D E Johnson, "The Nature and Dimensionality of Organizational Citizenship Behavior: A Critical Review and Meta-Analysis," *Journal of Applied Psychology,* February 2002, pp 52–65.

[73] Supportive results can be found in B J Tepper, M K Duffy, J Hoobler, and M D Ensley, "Moderators of the Relationship between Coworkers' Organizational Citizenship Behavior and Fellow Employees' Attitudes," *Journal of Applied Psychology,* June 2004, pp 455–65.

[74] See S C Payne and S S Webber, "Effects of Service Provider Attitudes and Employment Status on Citizenship Behaviors and Customers' Attitudes and Loyalty Behavior," *Journal of Applied Psychology,* March 2006, pp 365–78; and D C Bachrach, B C Powell, E Bendoly, and R G Richey, "Organizational Citizenship Behavior and Performance Evaluations: Exploring the Impact of Task Interdependence," *Journal of Applied Psychology,* January 2006, pp 193–201.

[75] Results can be found in D J Koys, "The Effects of Employee Satisfaction, Organizational Citizenship Behavior, and Turnover on Organizational Effectiveness: A Unit-Level, Longitudinal Study," *Personnel Psychology,* Spring 2001, pp 101–14.

[76] Results are reported in "Sick Day or Just Sick and Tired?" *Training,* December 2005, p 8.

[77] See R D Hackett, "Work Attitudes and Employee Absenteeism: A Synthesis of the Literature," *Journal of Occupational Psychology,* 1989, pp 235–48.

[78] Results can be found in P W Hom and A J Kinicki, "Toward a Greater Understanding of How Dissatisfaction Drives Employee Turnover," *Academy of Management Journal,* October 2001, pp 975–87.

[79] Y Lermusiaux, "Calculating the High Cost of Employee Turnover," www.ilogos.com/en/expertviews/articles/strategic/ 200331007_YL.html, accessed April 15, 2005, p 1. The various costs of employee turnover are also discussed by W G Bliss, "Cost of Employee Turnover," www.isquare.com/turnover.cfm, accessed April 15, 2005.

[80] See Lermusiaux, "Calculating the High Cost of Employee Turnover." An automated program for calculating the cost of turnover can be found at "Calculate Your Turnover Costs," www.keepemployees.com/turnovercalc.htm, accessed April 15, 2005.

[81] Results can be found in R W Griffeth, P W Hom, and S Gaertner, "A Meta-Analysis of Antecedents and Correlates of Employee Turnover: Update, Moderator Tests, and Research Implications for the Next Millennium," *Journal of Management,* 2000, pp 463–88.

[82] Results can be found in M A Blegen, "Nurses' Job Satisfaction: A Meta-Analysis of Related Variables," *Nursing Research,* January/February 1993, pp 36–41.

[83] The various models are discussed in T A Judge, C J Thoresen, J E Bono, and G K Patton, "The Job Satisfaction–Job Performance Relationship: A Qualitative and Quantitative Review," *Psychological Bulletin,* May 2001, pp 376–407.

[84] Results can be found in ibid.

[85] One example is provided by D J Schleicher, J D Watt, and G J Greguras, "Reexamining the Job Satisfaction–Performance Relationship: The Complexity of Attitudes," *Journal of Applied Psychology,* February 2004, pp 165–77.

[86] These issues are discussed by C Ostroff, "The Relationship between Satisfaction, Attitudes, and Performance: An Organizational Level Analysis," *Journal of Applied Psychology,* December 1992, pp 963–74.

[87] Results can be found in J K Harter, F L Schmidt, and T L Hayes, "Business-Unit-Level Relationship between Employee Satisfaction, Employee Engagement, and Business Outcomes: A Meta-Analysis," *Journal of Applied Psychology,* April 2002, pp 268–79.

[88] K W Smola and C D Sutton, "Generational Differences: Revisiting Generational Work Values for the New Millennium," *Journal of Organizational Behavior,* June 2002, p 379.

[89] S Lacy, "Just Don't Call It Retirement," *BusinessWeek,* March 6, 2006, pp 66, 68.

[90] P L Perrewé and W A Hochwarter, "Can We Really Have It All? The Attainment of Work and Family Values," *Current Directions in Psychological Science,* February 2001, p 31.

[91] See Levering and Moskowitz, "The 100 Best Companies to Work For: And the Winners Are . . .," pp 89–108; and M Arndt, "Nice Work If You Can Get It," *BusinessWeek,* January 9, 2006, pp 56–57.

[92] An integrated approach is discussed by J H Greenhaus and G N Powell, "When Work and Family Are Allies: A Theory of Work-Family Enrichment," *Academy of Management Review,* January 2006, pp 72–92.
[93] R Rapoport, L Bailyn, J K Fletcher, and B H Pruitt, *Beyond Work–Family Balance: Advancing Gender Equity and Workplace Performance* (San Francisco: Jossey-Bass, 2002), p 36.

Chapter 7

[1] Excerpted from R Tomsho, "More Districts Pay Teachers for Performance," *The Wall Street Journal,* March 23, 2006, pp B1, B6. Copyright © 2006 by Dow Jones & Company, Inc. Reproduced with permission of Dow Jones & Company, Inc. via Copyright Clearance Center.
[2] See L Festinger, *A Theory of Cognitive Dissonance* (Stanford, CA: Stanford University Press, 1957).
[3] See B S Bell, D Wiechmann, and A M Ryan, "Consequences of Organizational Justice Expectations in a Selection System," *Journal of Applied Psychology,* March 2006, pp 455–66; and S J Deery, R D Iverson, and J T Walsh, "Toward a Better Understanding of Psychological Contract Breach: A Study of Customer Service Employees," *Journal of Applied Psychology,* January 2006, pp 166–75.
[4] Inputs and outputs are discussed by J S Adams, "Toward an Understanding of Inequity," *Journal of Abnormal and Social Psychology,* November 1963, pp 422–36.
[5] The generalizability of the equity norm was examined by L K Scheer, N A Kumar, and J-B E M Steenkamp, "Reactions to Perceived Inequity in U.S. and Dutch Interorganizational Relationships," *Academy of Management Journal,* June 2003, pp 303–16.
[6] CEO pay information can be found in "Executive Pay Watch," http://www.aflcio.org/corporatewatch/paywatch, accessed May 22, 2006; and "Facts & Figures: CEO Pay," http://www.epinet.org, accessed May 22, 2006.
[7] M N Bing and S M Burroughs, "The Predictive and Interactive Effects of Equity Sensitivity in Teamwork-Oriented Organizations," *Journal of Organizational Behavior,* May 2001, p 271.
[8] Types of equity sensitivity are discussed by ibid., pp 271–90; and K S Sauley and A G Bedeian, "Equity Sensitivity: Construction of a Measure and Examination of Its Psychometric Properties," *Journal of Management,* 2000, pp 885–910.
[9] These examples are discussed in D Brady, "Executive Pay: No Hair Shirts, but Still . . ." *BusinessWeek,* May 1, 2006, p 36; and S Hamm, "SAP Dangles a Big, Fat Carrot," *BusinessWeek,* May 22, 2006, pp 67–68.
[10] For a thorough review of organizational justice theory and research, see R Cropanzano, D E Rupp, C J Mohler, and M Schminke, "Three Roads to Organizational Justice," in *Research in Personnel and Human Resources Management,* vol. 20, eds G R Ferris (New York: JAI Press, 2001), pp 269–329.
[11] J A Colquitt, D E Conlon, M J Wesson, C O L H Porter, and K Y Ng, "Justice at the Millennium: A Meta-Analytic Review of 25 Years of Organizational Justice Research," *Journal of Applied Psychology,* June 2001, p 426.
[12] E Tahmincioglu, "Electronic Workplace Vulnerable to Revenge," *Arizona Republic,* August 6, 2001, p D1.
[13] Results can be found in C Spitzmüller, D M Glenn, C D Barr, S G Rogelberg, and P Daniel, "'If You Treat Me Right, I Reciprocate': Examining the Role of Exchange in Organizational Survey Response," *Journal of Organizational Behavior,* February 2006, pp 19–35; and J Greenberg, "Losing Sleep Over Organizational Injustice: Attenuating Insomniac Reactions to Underpayment Inequity with Supervisory Training in Interactional Justice," *Journal of Applied Psychology,* January 2006, pp 58–69.
[14] Supportive results can be found in R Loi, N Hang-Yue, and S Foley, "Linking Employees' Justice Perceptions to Organizational Commitment and Intention to Leave: The Mediating Role of Perceived Organizational Support," *Journal of Occupational and Organizational Psychology,* March 2006, pp 101–20; M Ambrose and R Cropanzano, "A Longitudinal Analysis of Organizational Fairness: An Examination of Reactions to Tenure and Promotion Decisions," *Journal of Applied Psychology,* April 2003, pp 266–75; and S J Farmer, T A Beehr, and K G Love, "Becoming an Undercover Police Officer: A Note on Fairness

Perceptions, Behavior, and Attitudes," *Journal of Organizational Behavior,* June 2003, pp 373–87.
[15] See J Brockner, "Why It's So Hard to Be Fair," *Harvard Business Review,* March 2006, pp 122–29.
[16] See Korsgaard, Roberson, and Rymph, "What Motivates Fairness? The Role of Subordinate Assertive Behavior on Managers' Interactional Fairness."
[17] The role of equity in organizational change is thoroughly discussed by A T Cobb, R Folger, and K Wooten, "The Role Justice Plays in Organizational Change," *Public Administration Quarterly,* Summer 1995, pp 135–51.
[18] Group level effects of justice were examined by S E Naumann and N Bennett, "A Case for Procedural Justice Climate: Development and Test of a Multilevel Model," *Academy of Management Journal,* October 2000, pp 881–89.
[19] See W R Boswell and J B Olson-Buchanan, "Experiencing Mistreatment at Work: The Role of Grievance Filing, Nature of Mistreatment, and Employee Withdrawal," *Academy of Management Journal,* February 2004, pp 129–39. Also see S Silver, "Revenge of the Retirees May Cut Pay at Lucent," *The Wall Street Journal,* February 15, 2006, pp C1, C3.
[20] The relationship between justice perceptions and leadership was examined by B Erdogan and R C Liden, "Collectivism As a Moderator of Responses to Organizational Justice: Implications for Leader-member Exchange and Ingratiation," *Journal of Organizational Behavior,* February 2006, pp 1–17; and B J Tepper, M K Duffy, C A Henle, and L Schurer Lambert, "Procedural Injustice, Victim Precipitation, and Abusive Supervision," *Personnel Psychology,* Spring 2006, pp 101–23.
[21] Results can be found in M G Ehrhart, "Leadership and Procedural Justic Climate as Antecedents of Unit-Level Organizational Citizenship Behavior," *Personnel Psychology,* Spring 2004, pp 61–94.
[22] For a complete discussion of Vroom's theory, see V H Vroom, *Work and Motivation* (New York: John Wiley & Sons, 1964).
[23] See J Chowdhury, 'The Motivational Impact of Sales Quotas on Effort," *Journal of Marketing Research,* February 1993, pp 28–41; and C C Pinder, *Work Motivation* (Glenview, IL: Scott, Foresman, 1984), ch 7.
[24] Excerpted from L Lavelle and D Brady, "The Gravy Train May Be Drying Up," *BusinessWeek,* April 5, 2004, pp 52–53. Also see D Brady, "GE: When Execs Outperform the Stock," *BusinessWeek,* April 17, 2006, pp 74–75.
[25] Excerpted from "Federal Express's Fred Smith," *Inc.,* October 1986, p 38.
[26] Results can be found in W van Eerde and H Thierry, "Vroom's Expectancy Models and Work-Related Criteria: A Meta-Analysis," *Journal of Applied Psychology,* October 1996, pp 575–86.
[27] See J P Wanous, T L Keon, and J C Latack, "Expectancy Theory and Occupational/Organizational Choices: A Review and Test," *Organizational Behavior and Human Performance,* August 1983, pp 66–86.
[28] See the discussion in T R Mitchell and D Daniels, "Motivation," in *Handbook of Psychology,* vol. 12, eds W C Borman, D R Ilgen, and R J Klimoski (Hoboken, NJ: John Wiley & Sons, Inc., 2003), pp 225–54.
[29] This issue is discussed by S J Dubner, "The Freaky Side of Business," *Training,* February 2006, pp 8–9.
[30] See D R Spitzer, "Power Rewards: Rewards That Really Motivate," *Management Review,* May 1996, pp 45–50; and A Kohn, *Punished by Rewards: The Trouble with Gold Stars, Incentive Plans, A's, Praise, and Other Bribes* (Boston: Houghton Mifflin, 1993).
[31] Result can be found in G D Jenkins, Jr, A Mitra, N Gupta, and J D Shaw, "Are Financial Incentives Related to Performance? A Meta-Analytic Review of Empirical Research," *Journal of Applied Psychology,* October 1998, pp 777–87.
[32] See S Bates, "Top Pay for Best Performance," *HR Magazine,* January 2003, pp 31–38.
[33] See R Levering and M Moskowitz, "The 100 Best Companies to Work For: And the Winners Are . . . " *Fortune,* January 23, 2006, p 92.
[34] Results are presented in "Performance Anxiety: When Performance Management Doesn't Work," *Training,* January 2006, p 9.
[35] See J McGregor, "Would You Recommend Us?" *BusinessWeek,* January 30, 2006, pp 94–95.
[36] R Charan, "Conquering a Culture of Indecision," *Harvard Business Review,* April 2001, pp 75–82.
[37] E A Locke, K N Shaw, L M Saari, and G P Latham, "Goal Setting and Task Performance: 1969–1980," *Psychological Bulletin,* July 1981, p 126.

[38] Results from both studies can be found in R Rodgers and J E Hunter, "Impact of Management by Objectives on Organizational Productivity," *Journal of Applied Psychology,* April 1991, pp 322–36; and R Rodgers, JE Hunter, and D L Rogers, "Influence of Top Management Commitment on Management Program Success," *Journal of Applied Psychology,* February 1993, pp 151–55.

[39] The following discussion is based on E A Locke and G P Latham, "Building a Practically Useful Theory of Goal Setting and Task Motivation," *American Psychologist,* September 2002, pp 705–17.

[40] See A Barrett, "Cracking the Whip at Wyeth," *BusinessWeek,* February 6, 2006, pp 70–71.

[41] Annika Sorenstam's biography can be found at www.lpga.com/, accessed May 2006.

[42] J Davis, "For Now, Sorenstam Feels She Still Has Peaks to Scale," *Arizona Republic,* March 18, 2004, p C14.

[43] Results can be found in P M Wright, "Operationalization of Goal Difficulty as a Moderator of the Goal Difficulty–Performance Relationship," *Journal of Applied Psychology,* June 1990, pp 227–34.

[44] See Locke, Shaw, Saari, and Latham, "Goal Setting and Task Performance: 1969–1980"; and A J Mento, R P Steel, and R J Karren, "A Meta-Analytic Study of the Effects of Goal Setting on Task Performance: 1966–1984," *Organizational Behavior and Human Decision Processes,* February 1987, pp 52–83.

[45] Results from the meta-analysis can be found in R E Wood, A J Mento, and E A Locke, "Task Complexity as a Moderator of Goal Effects: A Meta-Analysis," *Journal of Applied Psychology,* August 1987, pp 416–25.

[46] See Locke and Latham, "Building a Practically Useful Theory of Goal Setting and Task Motivation."

[47] See R P DeShon and R A Alexander, "Goal Setting Effects on Implicit and Explicit Learning of Complex Tasks," *Organizational Behavior and Human Decision Processes,* January 1996, pp 18–36.

[48] Supportive results can be found in K L Langeland, C M Johnson, and T C Mawhinney, "Improving Staff Performance in a Community Mental Health Setting: Job Analysis, Training, Goal Setting, Feedback, and Years of Data," *Journal of Organizational Behavior Management,* 1998, pp 21–43; and L A Wilk, "The Effects of Feedback and Goal Setting on the Productivity and Satisfaction of University Admissions Staff," *Journal of Organizational Behavior Management,* 1998, pp 45–68.

[49] See Locke and Latham, "Building a Practically Useful Theory of Goal Setting and Task Motivation."

[50] See ibid.

[51] See J J Donovan and D J Radosevich, "The Moderating Role of Goal Commitment on the Goal Difficulty-Performance Relationship: A Meta-Analytic Review and Critical Reanalysis," *Journal of Applied Psychology,* April 1998, pp 308–15.

[52] See the related discussion in T P Flannery, D A Hofrichter, and P E Platten, *People, Performance, & Pay* (New York: The Free Press, 1996). Also see D C Kayes, "The Destructive Pursuit of Idealized Goals," *Organizational Dynamics,* November 2005, pp 391–401.

[53] See F M Moussa, "Determinants, Process, and Consequences of Personal Goals and Performance," *Journal of Management,* 2000, pp 1259–85; and P M Wright, J M George, S R Farnsworth, and G C McMahan, "Productivity and Extra-Role Behavior: The Effects of Goals and Incentives on Spontaneous Helping," *Journal of Applied Psychology,* June 1993, pp 374–81.

[54] Results are presented in "Coming Up Short? Join the Club," *Training,* April 2006, p 14.

[55] See J A Colquitt and M J Simmering, "Conscientiousness, Goal Orientation, and Motivation to Learn during the Learning Process: A Longitudinal Study," *Journal of Applied Psychology,* August 1998, pp 654–65.

[56] C L Porath and T S Bateman, "Self-Regulation: From Goal Orientation to Job Performance," *Journal of Applied Psychology,* January 2006, pp 185–86.

[57] Ibid., pp 185–92; Y Gong and J Fan, "Longitudinal Examination of the Role of Goal Orientation in Cross-Cultural Adjustment," *Journal of Applied Psychology,* January 2006, pp 176–84; and R P DeShon and J Z Gillespie, "A Motivated Action Theory Account of Goal Orientation," *Journal of Applied Psychology,* November 2005, pp 1096–127.

[58] See DeShon and Gillespie, "A Motivated Action Theory Account of Goal Orientation."

[59] Results are shown in "Coming Up Short? Join the Club," *Training,* April 2006, p 14.

[60] T R Mitchell, "Motivation: New Directions for Theory, Research, and Practice," *Academy of Management Review,* January 1982, p 81.

[61] See the related discussion in J Welch and S Welch, "Ideas the Welch Way: How Healthy Is Your Company?" *BusinessWeek,* May 8, 2006, p 126.

[62] G Colvin, "What Makes GE Great?" *Fortune,* March 6, 2006, p 96.

[63] Results are reported in "Study: HR Exec Don't Trust Employee Evaluations," *Training,* April 2006, p 11.

[64] "HMO Clerks Who Pare Doctor Visits Rewarded," *Arizona Republic,* May 18, 2002, p A10.

[65] See I Appleby, "HMO to Pay Bonuses for Good Care," *USA Today,* July11, 2001, p 3B.

[66] This issue is discussed in E White, "The Best vs. the Rest," *The Wall Street Journal,* January 30, 2006, pp B1, B3.

[67] See the related discussion in C Hymowitz, "In the Lead: Rewarding Competitors Over Collaborators No Longer Makes Sense," *The Wall Street Journal,* February 13, 2006, p B1.

[68] Nucor is discussed in N Byrnes, "The Art of Motivation," *BusinessWeek,* May 1, 2006, pp 57–62.

[69] Excerpted from C Bellamy, "Teacher Resigns as School Backs Plagiarizing Kids," *Arizona Republic,* February 10, 2002, p A21.

Chapter 8

[1] Excerpted from S Hamm, "Motivating the Troops," *BusinessWeek,* November 21, 2005, pp 88, 90. Also see S E Ante, "Giving the Boss the Big Picture: A 'Dashboard' Pulls Up Everything the CEO Needs to Run the Show," *BusinessWeek,* February 13, 2006, pp 48–51.

[2] Data from S Bates, "Performance Appraisals: Some Improvement Needed," *HR Magazine,* April 2003, p 12. For related reading, see M A Huselid, R W Beatty, and B E Becker, "A Players or A Positions?" *Harvard Business Review,* December 2005, pp 110–17; D Zielinski, "Best and Brightest," *Training,* January 2006, pp 11–16; and B Morris, "The GE Mystique," *Fortune,* March 6, 2006, pp 98–104.

[3] See G P Latham, J Almost, S Mann, and C Moore, "New Developments in Performance Management," *Organizational Dynamics,* no. 1, 2005, pp 77–87; and D Grote, "Driving True Development," *Training,* July 2005, pp 24–29.

[4] For example, see "Views Differ on Performance Reviews," *USA Today,* September 10, 2003, p 1B. Also see D D Van Fleet, T O Peterson, and E W Van Fleet, "Closing the Performance Feedback Gap with Expert Systems," *Academy of Management Executive,* August 2005, pp 38–53.

[5] As quoted in C Fishman, "Fred Smith," *Fast Company,* June 2001, pp 64, 66.

[6] Data from M Hequet, "Giving Feedback," *Training,* September 1994, pp 72–77.

[7] C Bell and R Zemke, "On–Target Feedback," *Training,* June 1992, p 36.

[8] Both the definition of feedback and the functions of feedback are based on discussion in D R Ilgen, C D Fisher, and M S Taylor, "Consequences of Individual Feedback on Behavior in Organizations," *Journal of Applied Psychology,* August 1979, pp 349–71; and R E Kopelman, *Managing Productivity in Organizations: A Practical People-Oriented Perspective* (New York: McGraw-Hill, 1986), p 175. Also see S E Moss and J I Sanchez, "Are Your Employees Avoiding You? Managerial Strategies for Closing the Feedback Gap," *Academy of Management Executive,* February 2004, pp 32–44; and M Goldsmith, "Leave It at the Stream," *Fast Company,* May 2004, p 103.

[9] See P C Earley, G B Northcraft, C Lee, and T R Lituchy, "Impact of Process and Outcome Feedback on the Relation of Goal Setting to Task Performance," *Academy of Management Journal,* March 1990, pp 87–105. Also see D Rohn, J Austin, and S M Lutrey, "Using Feedback and Performance Accountability to Decrease Cash Register Shortages," *Journal of Organizational Behavior Management,* no 1, 2002, pp 33–46.

[10] Based on C C Rosen, P E Levy, and R J Hall, "Placing Perceptions of Politics in the Context of the Feedback Environment, Employee Attitudes, and Job Performance," *Journal of Applied Psychology,* January 2006, pp 211–20.

[11] For relevant research, see J S Goodman, "The Interactive Effects of Task and External Feedback on Practice Performance and Learning,"

Organizational Behavior and Human Decision Processes,
December 1998, pp 223–52.

[12] See J M Jackman and M H Strober, "Fear of Feedback," *Harvard Business Review,* April 2003, pp 101–7.

[13] See B D Bannister, "Performance Outcome Feedback and Attributional Feedback: Interactive Effects on Recipient Responses," *Journal of Applied Psychology,* May 1986, pp 203–10.

[14] For complete details, see P M Podsakoff and J-L Farh, "Effects of Feedback Sign and Credibility on Goal Setting and Task Performance," *Organizational Behavior and Human Decision Processes,* August 1989, pp 45–67. Also see S J Ashford and A S Tsui, "Self-Regulation for Managerial Effectiveness: The Role of Active Feedback Seeking," *Academy of Management Journal,* June 1991, pp 251–80.

[15] See "How to Take the Venom Out of Vitriol," *Training,* June 2000, p 28.

[16] W S Silver, T R Mitchell, and M E Gist, "Responses to Successful and Unsuccessful Performance: The Moderating Effect of Self-Efficacy on the Relationship between Performance and Attributions," *Organizational Behavior and Human Decision Processes,* June 1995, p 297. Also see T A Louie, "Decision Makers' Hindsight Bias after Receiving Favorable and Unfavorable Feedback," *Journal of Applied Psychology,* February 1999, pp 29–41.

[17] See T J DeLong and V Vijayaraghavan, "Let's Hear It for B Players," *Harvard Business Review,* June 2003, pp 96–102.

[18] See A Rossett and G Marino, "If Coaching is Good, Then E-Coaching is . . .," *Training and Development,* November 2005, pp 46–53.

[19] See D A Waldman, "Does Working with an Executive Coach Enhance the Value of Multisource Performance Feedback?" *Academy of Management Executive,* August 2003, pp 146–48; M Weinstein, "Interpersonal Effectiveness Training: Beyond the Water Cooler," *Training,* April 2006, p 10; and A S Wellner, "Do You Need a Coach?" *Inc.,* April 2006, pp 86–97.

[20] M Weinstein, "Study: HR Execs Don't Trust Employee Evaluations," *Training,* April 2006, p 11.

[21] See M R Edwards, A J Ewen, and W A Verdini, "Fair Performance Management and Pay Practices for Diverse Work Forces: The Promise of Multisource Assessment," *ACA Journal,* Spring 1995, pp 50–63.

[22] See G D Huet-Cox, T M Nielsen, and E Sundstrom, "Get the Most from 360-Degree Feedback: Put It on the Internet," *HR Magazine,* May 1999, pp 92–103.

[23] This list is based in part on discussion in H J Bernardin, "Subordinate Appraisal: A Valuable Source of Information about Managers," *Human Resource Management,* Fall 1986, pp 421–39.

[24] For a complete list, see "Companies Where Employees Rate Executives," *Fortune,* December 27, 1993, p 128. Also see J A Byrne, "Do You Make the Grade?" *Fast Company,* May 2004, p 101.

[25] Data from D Antonioni, "The Effects of Feedback Accountability on Upward Appraisal Ratings," *Personnel Psychology,* Summer 1994, pp 349–56.

[26] See L Atwater, P Roush, and A Fischthal, "The Influence of Upward Feedback on Self- and Follower Ratings of Leadership," *Personnel Psychology,* Spring 1995, pp 35–59.

[27] Data from J W Smither, M London, N L Vasilopoulos, R R Reilly, R E Millsap, and N Salvemini, "An Examination of the Effects of an Upward Feedback Program over Time," *Personnel Psychology,* Spring 1995, pp 1–34.

[28] C Hymowitz, "Managers See Feedback from Their Staffers as the Most Valuable," *The Wall Street Journal,* November 11, 2003, p. B1. Other recent 360-degree feedback examples may be found in A Jung, "Seek Frank Feedback," *Harvard Business Review,* Special Issue: Inside the Mind of the Leader, January 2004, pp 31–32; the first question-and-answer pairing in "Ask *Inc.*: Do I Deserve a Raise?" *Inc.,* February 2004, p 38; "Best Practices: Executive Coaching; Wachovia," *Training,* March 2004, p 61; M Goldsmith, "To Help Others Develop, Start with Yourself," *Fast Company,* March 2004, p 100; and C Tkaczyk, "Hank Paulson: Goldman Sachs CEO Since 1998," *Fortune,* December 12, 2005, pp 131–32.

[29] Data from J L Seglin, "Reviewing Your Boss," *Fortune,* June 11, 2001, p 248. For a comprehensive overview of 360-degree feedback, see W W Tornow and M London, *Maximizing the Value of 360-Degree Feedback* (San Francisco: Jossey-Bass, 1998). Also see G Toegel and J A Conger, "360-Degree Assessment: Time for Reinvention," *Academy*

of Management Learning and Education, September 2003, pp 297–311.

[30] See S Haworth, "The Dark Side of Multi-Rater Assessments," *HR Magazine,* May 1998, pp 106–14; and D A Waldman, L E Atwater, and D Antonioni, "Has 360 Degree Feedback Gone Amok?" *Academy of Management Executive,* May 1998, pp 86–94.

[31] See M M Harris and J Schaubroeck, "A Meta-Analysis of Self-Supervisor, Self-Peer, and Peer-Supervisor Ratings," *Personnel Psychology,* Spring 1988, pp 43–62; and J Lane and P Herriot, "Self-Ratings, Supervisor Ratings, Positions and Performance," *Journal of Occupational Psychology,* March 1990, pp 77–88.

[32] Fisher Hazucha, S A Hezlett, and R J Schneider, "The Impact of 360-Degree Feedback on Managerial Skills Development," *Human Resource Management,* Summer/Fall 1993, p 42. Also see M K Mount, T A Judge, S E Scullen, M R Sytsma, and S A Hezlett, "Trait, Rater and Level Effects in 360-Degree Performance Ratings," *Personnel Psychology,* Autumn 1998, pp 557–76.

[33] F Luthans and S J Peterson, "360-Degree Feedback with Systematic Coaching: Empirical Analysis Suggests a Winning Combination," *Human Resource Management,* Fall 2003, p 243.

[34] See D E Coates, "Don't Tie 360 Feedback to Pay," *Training,* September 1998, pp 68–78.

[35] Adapted from C Bell and R Zemke, "On-Target Feedback," *Training,* June 1992, pp 36–44. A model feedback program at Saint Luke's Hospital of Kansas City is presented in D Jones, "Baldrige Award Honors Record 7 Quality Winners," *USA Today,* November 26, 2003, p 6B. Tips on giving feedback can be found in S Godin, "How to Give Feedback," *Fast Company,* March 2004, p 103.

[36] See J Kerr and J W Slocum, Jr., "Managing Corporate Culture through Reward Systems," *Academy of Management Executive,* November 2005, pp 130–38; S Ladika, "Decompressing Pay," *HR Magazine,* December 2005, pp 79–82; and J Brockner, "Why It's So Hard to Be Fair," *Harvard Business Review,* March 2006, pp 122–29.

[37] See J and S Welch, "Keeping Your People Pumped," *Business Week,* March 27, 2006, p 122.

[38] For example, see B Nelson, *1001 Ways to Reward Employees,* 2nd ed (NY: Workman Publishing, 2005); M J Conyon, "Executive Compensation and Incentives," *Academy of Management Perspectives,* February 2006, pp 25–44; J Larson, "Stock Grants Taking Place of Options," *The Arizona Republic,* February 24, 2006, pp D1–D2; S S Carty, "Chrysler Pegs Premiums to Salary Level," *USA Today,* March 16, 2006, p 4B; and P Babcock, "Options to Stock Options," *HR Magazine,* April 2006, pp 103–06.

[39] W J Wiatrowski, "Family-Related Benefits in the Workplace," *Monthly Labor Review,* March 1990, p 28. Also see J A Byrne, "How to Lead Now: Getting Extraordinary Performance When You Can't Pay for It," *Fast Company,* August 2003, pp 62–70; and S J Wells, "Merging Compensation Strategies," *HR Magazine,* May 2004, pp 66–78.

[40] For complete discussions, see A P Brief and R J Aldag, "The Intrinsic-Extrinsic Dichotomy: Toward Conceptual Clarity," *Academy of Management Review,* July 1977, pp 496–500; E L Deci, *Intrinsic Motivation* (New York: Plenum Press, 1975), ch 2; and E L Deci, R Koestner, and R M Ryan, "A Meta-Analytic Review of Experiments Examining the Effects of Extrinsic Rewards on Intrinsic Motivation," *Psychological Bulletin,* November 1999, pp 627–68.

[41] L Cauley, "BellSouth Rings Up Wins in Big Easy," *USA Today,* November 9, 2005, p 3B.

[42] M Von Glinow, "Reward Strategies for Attracting, Evaluating, and Retaining Professionals," *Human Resource Management,* Summer 1985, p 193.

[43] A Markels and J S Lublin, "Longevity-Reward Programs Get Short Shrift," *The Wall Street Journal,* April 27, 1995, p B1.

[44] Six reward system objectives are discussed in E E Lawler III, "The New Pay: A Strategic Approach," *Compensation & Benefits Review,* July/August 1995, pp 14–22. Also see S C Currall, A J Towler, T A Judge, and L Kohn, "Pay Satisfaction and Organizational Outcomes," *Personnel Psychology,* Autumn 2005, pp 613–40; and D Brady, "GE: When Execs Outperform the Stock," *BusinessWeek,* April 17, 2006, pp 74–75.

[45] See D Cadrain, "Put Success in Sight," *HR Magazine,* May 2003, pp 84–92; J Kiska, "Customer Satisfaction Pays Off," *HR Magazine,*

February 2004, 87–93; and C Taylor, "On-the-Spot Incentives," *HR Magazine,* May 2004, pp 80–84.

[46] For both sides of the "Does money motivate?" debate, see N Gupta and J D Shaw, "Let the Evidence Speak: Financial Incentives *Are* Effective!!" *Compensation & Benefits Review,* March/April 1998, pp 26, 28–32; A Kohn, "Challenging Behaviorist Dogma: Myths about Money and Motivation," *Compensation & Benefits Review;* March/April 1998, pp 27, 33–37; and B Ettorre, "Is Salary a Motivator?" *Management Review,* January 1999, p 8. Also see W J Duncan, "Stock Ownership and Work Motivation," *Organizational Dynamics,* Summer 2001, pp 1–11; and J Pfeffer, "Sins of Commission," *Business 2.0,* May 2004, p 56.

[47] Data from D Kiley, "Crafty Basket Makers Cut Downtime, Waste," *USA Today,* May 10, 2001, p 3B.

[48] See M V Copeland, "The Shrink Shrinker," *Business 2.0,* April 2006, p 86; P Kaihla, "The Anti-Star System," *Business 2.0,* April 2006, p 87; and "Coke Links Directors' Pay, Performance," *USA Today,* April 6, 2006, p 1B.

[49] Data from N J Perry, "Here Come Richer, Riskier Pay Plans," *Fortune,* December 19, 1998, p 51. Also see W Zellner, "Trickle-Down Is Trickling Down at Work," *BusinessWeek,* March 18, 1996, p 34.

[50] Data from M Bloom and G T Milkovich, "Relationships among Risk, Incentive Pay, and Organizational Performance," *Academy of Management Journal,* June 1998, pp 283–97.

[51] For details, see G D Jenkins, Jr, N Gupta, A Mitra, and J D Shaw, "Are Financial Incentives Related to Performance? A Meta-Analytic Review of Empirical Research," *Journal of Applied Psychology,* October 1998, pp 777–87. Also see S J Peterson and F Luthans, "The Impact of Financial and Nonfinancial Incentives on Business-Unit Outcomes Over Time," *Journal of Applied Psychology,* January 2006, pp 156–65.

[52] See M J Mandel, "Those Fat Bonuses Don't Seem to Boost Performance," *BusinessWeek,* January 8, 1990, p 26; J Pfeffer, "The Pay-for-Performance Fallacy," *Business 2.0,* July 2005, p 64; and L A Bebchuk and J M Fried, "Pay without Performance: Overview of the Issues," *Academy of Management Perspectives,* February 2006, pp 5–24.

[53] Based on discussion in R Ricklefs, "Whither the Payoff on Sales Commissions?" *The Wall Street Journal,* June 6, 1990, p BI.

[54] G Koretz, "Bad Marks for Pay-by-Results," *BusinessWeek,* September 4, 1995, p 28. Also see L King, "School Systems Argue the Merits of Teacher 'Bonuses' Tied to Test Scores," *USA Today,* March 21, 2006, p 8D.

[55] D R Spitzer, "Power Rewards: Rewards That Really Motivate," *Management Review,* May 1996, p 47. Also see S Kerr, "An Academy Classic: On the Folly of Rewarding A, while Hoping for B," *Academy of Management Executive,* February 1995, pp 7–14.

[56] List adapted from discussion in Spitzer, "Power Rewards: Rewards That Really Motivate," pp 45–50. Also see R Eisenberger and J Cameron, "Detrimental Effects of Reward: Reality or Myth?" *American Psychologist,* November 1996, pp 1153–66; and "What Has Undermined Your Trust in Companies?" *USA Today,* February 10, 2004, p 1B.

[57] See J B Arthur and C L Huntley, "Ramping Up the Organizational Learning Curve: Assessing the Impact of Deliberate Learning on Organizational Performance Under Gainsharing," *Academy of Management Journal,* December 2005, pp 1159–170; M Weinstein, "Performance Anxiety: When Performance Management Doesn't Work," *Training,* January 2006, p 9; and M D Johnson, J R Hollenbeck, S E Humphrey, D R Ilgen, D Jundt, and C J Meyer, "Cutthroat Cooperation: Asymmetrical Adaptation to Changes in Team Reward Structures," *Academy of Management Journal,* February 2006, pp 103–19.

[58] See B E Litzky, K A Eddleston, and D L Kidder, "The Good, the Bad, and the Misguided: How Managers Inadvertently Encourage Deviant Behaviors," *Academy of Management Perspectives,* February 2006, pp 91–103.

[59] For a recent unconventional perspective, see R J DeGrandpre, "A Science of Meaning? Can Behaviorism Bring Meaning to Psychological Science?" *American Psychologist,* July 2000, pp 721–38.

[60] See E L Thorndike, *Educational Psychology: The Psychology of Learning,* vol. II (New York: Columbia University Teachers College, 1913).

[61] Discussion of an early behaviorist who influenced Skinner's work can be found in P J Kreshel, "John B Watson at J Walter Thompson: The

Legitimation of 'Science' in Advertising," *Journal of Advertising,* no. 2, 1990, pp 49–59. Recent discussions involving behaviorism include M R Ruiz, "B F Skinner's Radical Behaviorism: Historical Misconstructions and Grounds for Feminist Reconstructions," *Psychology of Women Quarterly,* June 1995, pp 161–79; J A Nevin, "Behavioral Economics and Behavioral Momentum," *Journal of the Experimental Analysis of Behavior,* November 1995, pp 385–95; and H Rachlin, "Can We Leave Cognition to Cognitive Psychologists? Comments on an Article by George Loewenstein," *Organizational Behavior and Human Decision Processes,* March 1996, pp 296–99.

[62] For more recent discussion, see J W Donahoe, "The Unconventional Wisdom of B F Skinner: The Analysis-Interpretation Distinction," *Journal of the Experimental Analysis of Behavior,* September 1993, pp 453–56.

[63] See B F Skinner, *The Behavior of Organisms* (New York: Appleton-Century-Crofts, 1938).

[64] For modern approaches to respondent behavior, see B Azar, "Classical Conditioning Could Link Disorders and Brain Dysfunction, Researchers Suggest," *APA Monitor,* March 1999, p 17.

[65] For interesting discussions of Skinner and one of his students, see M B Gilbert and T F Gilbert, "What Skinner Gave Us," *Training,* September 1991, pp 42–48; and "HRD Pioneer Gilbert Leaves a Pervasive Legacy," *Training,* January 1996, p 14.

[66] See F Luthans and R Kreitner, *Organizational Behavior Modification and Beyond: An Operant and Social Learning Approach* (Glenview, IL: Scott, Foresman, 1985), pp 49–56.

[67] See K Blanchard and S Johnson, *The One Minute Manager* (New York: Berkley Books, 1981); K Blanchard and R Lorber, *Putting the One Minute Manager to Work* (New York: Berkley Books, 1984); and K Maney, "For a Price, Would You Let Car Insurer Tag Along for the Ride?" *USA Today,* August 3, 2005, p 3B.

[68] Adapted from R Levering and M Moskowitz, "2004 Special Report: The 100 Best Companies to Work For," *Fortune,* January 12, 2004, p 68. Another interesting positive reinforcement example can be found in J McCuan, "The Ultimate Sales Incentive," *Inc.,* May 2004, p 32.

[69] Ways to deal with tardiness are discussed in D DeLonzor, "Running Late," *HR Magazine,* November 2005, pp 109–12.

[70] Research on punishment is reported in B P Niehoff, R J Paul, and J F S Bunch, "The Social Effects of Punishment Events: The Influence of Violator Past Performance Record and Severity of the Punishment on Observers' Justice Perceptions and Attitudes," *Journal of Organizational Behavior,* November 1998, pp 589–602.

[71] See C B Ferster and B F Skinner, *Schedules of Reinforcement* (New York: Appleton-Century-Crofts, 1957).

[72] See L M Saari and G P Latham, "Employee Reactions to Continuous and Variable Ratio Reinforcement Schedules Involving a Monetary Incentive," *Journal of Applied Psychology,* August 1982, pp 506–8.

[73] P Brinkley-Rogers and R Collier, "Along the Colorado, the Money's Flowing," *Arizona Republic,* March 4, 1990, p A12.

[74] The topic of managerial credibility is covered in J M Kouzes and B Z Posner, *Credibility* (San Francisco: Jossey-Bass, 1993).

[75] An on-the-job example of behavior shaping can be found in J Case, "Are Your Meetings Like This?" *Inc.,* March 2003, p 79.

[76] Data from K L Alexander, "Continental Airlines Soars to New Heights," *USA Today,* January 23, 1996, p 4B. Also see J Huey, "Outlaw Flyboy CEOs," *Fortune,* November 13, 2000, pp 237–50.

[77] Data from R Levering and M Moskowitz, "100 Best Companies to Work For," *Fortune,* January 20, 2003, p 136.

[78] L Gerdes, "You Have 20 Minutes to Surf. Go." *BusinessWeek,* December 26, 2005, p 16.

Chapter 9

[1] M A Prospero, "Top Scalpel," *Fast Company,* April 2006, p 31. Copyright © 2006 by Mansueto Ventures LLC. Reproduced with permission of Mansueto Ventures LLC via Copyright Clearance Center.

[2] E Van Velsor and J Brittain Leslie, "Why Executives Derail: Perspectives across Time and Cultures," *Academy of Management Executive,* November 1995, p 62.

[3] Ibid., p 63.

⁴ Also see A L Kristof-Brown, R D Zimmerman, and E C Johnson, "Consequences of Individuals' Fit at Work: A Meta-Analysis of Person-Job, Person-Organization, Person-Group, and Person-Supervisor Fit," *Personnel Psychology,* Summer 2005, pp 281–342; F J Flynn, "Identity Orientations and Forms of Social Exchange in Organizations," *Academy of Management Review,* October 2005, pp 737–50; and J E Perry-Smith, "Social Yet Creative: The Role of Social Relationships in Facilitating Individual Creativity," *Academy of Management Journal,* February 2006, pp 85–101.

⁵ For interesting cases in point, see W C Symonds, "Campus Revolutionary," *BusinessWeek,* February 27, 2006, pp 64–70; and J Ewing, "Making Those Connections Work," *BusinessWeek,* March 13, 2006, p 91.

⁶ See R Mirchandani, "Postmodernism and Sociology: From the Epistemological to the Empirical," *Sociological Theory,* March 2005, pp 86–115.

⁷ This definition is based in part on one found in D Horton Smith, "A Parsimonious Definition of 'Group': Toward Conceptual Clarity and Scientific Utility," *Sociological Inquiry,* Spring 1967, pp 141–67. Also see W B Swann, Jr; J T Polzer; D C Seyle; and S J Ko, "Finding Value in Diversity: Verification of Personal and Social Self-Views in Diverse Groups," *Academy of Management Review,* January 2004, pp 9–27.

⁸ E H Schein, *Organizational Psychology,* 3rd ed (Englewood Cliffs, NJ: Prentice Hall, 1980), p 145. For more, see L R Weingart, "How Did They Do That? The Ways and Means of Studying Group Process," in *Research in Organizational Behavior,* vol. 19, eds L L Cummings and B M Staw (Greenwich, CT: JAI Press, 1997), pp 189–239.

⁹ See R Cross, N Nohria, and A Parker, "Six Myths about Informal Networks—and How to Overcome Them," *MIT Sloan Management Review,* Spring 2002, pp 67–75; C Shirky, "Watching the Patterns Emerge," *Harvard Business Review,* February 2004, pp 34–35; P Chattopadhyay, M Tluchowska, and E George, "Identifying the Ingroup: A Closer Look at the Influence of Demographic Dissimilarity on Employee Social Identity," *Academy of Management Review,* April 2004, pp 180–202; S Allen, "Water Cooler Wisdom," *Training,* August 2005, pp 30–34; and E Watters, "The Organization Woman," *Business 2.0,* April 2006, pp 106–10.

¹⁰ Data from "Co-workers Support Each Other," *USA Today,* May 28, 2003, p 1B.

¹¹ Excerpted from S Armour, "Company 'Alumni' Groups Keep Word Out after Workers Go," *USA Today,* August 30, 2005, p 4B.

¹² See J Janove, "FOB: Friend of Boss," *HR Magazine,* June 2005, pp 153–56.

¹³ See Schein, *Organizational Psychology,* pp 149–53.

¹⁴ J Castro, "Mazda U," *Time,* October 20, 1986, p 65.

¹⁵ For an instructive overview of five different theories of group development, see J P Wanous, A E Reichers, and S D Malik, "Organizational Socialization and Group Development: Toward an Integrative Perspective," *Academy of Management Review,* October 1984, pp 670–83. Also see L R Offermann and R K Spiros, "The Science and Practice of Team Development: Improving the Link," *Academy of Management Journal,* April 2001, pp 376–92; and A Chang, P Bordia, and J Duck, "Punctuated Equilibrium and Linear Progression: Toward a New Understanding of Group Development," *Academy of Management Journal,* February 2003, pp 106–17.

¹⁶ See B W Tuckman, "Developmental Sequence in Small Groups," *Psychological Bulletin,* June 1965, pp 384–99; and B W Tuckman and M A C Jensen, "Stages of Small-Group Development Revisited," *Group & Organization Studies,* December 1977, pp 419–27. An instructive adaptation of the Tuckman model can be found in J Holpp, "If Empowerment Is So Good, Why Does It Hurt?" *Training,* March 1995, p 56.

¹⁷ See T Postmes, R Spears, A T Lee, and R J Novak, "Individuality and Social Influence in Groups: Inductive and Deductive Routes to Group Identity," *Journal of Personality and Social Psychology,* November 2005, pp 747–63.

¹⁸ J McGregor, "Forget Going with Your Gut," *BusinessWeek,* March 20, 2006, p 112.

¹⁹ A useful resource book is T Ursiny, *The Coward's Guide to Conflict: Empowering Solutions for Those Who Would Rather Run than Fight*

(Naperville, IL: Sourcebooks, 2003). Also see J Li and D C Hambrick, "Factional Groups: A New Vantage on Demographic Faultlines, Conflict, and Disintegration in Work Teams," *Academy of Management Journal,* October 2005, pp 794–813; and M D Johnson, J R Hollenbeck, S E Humphrey, D R Ilgen, D Jundt, and C J Meyer, "Cutthroat Cooperation: Asymmetrical Adaptation to Changes in Team Reward Structures," *Academy of Management Journal,* February 2006, pp 103–19.

²⁰ For related research, see M Van Vugt and C M Hart, "Social Identity as Social Glue: The Origins of Group Loyalty," *Journal of Personality and Social Psychology,* April 2004, pp 585–98.

²¹ See C M Mason and M A Griffin, "Group Task Satisfaction: The Group's Shared Attitude to Its Task and Work Environment," *Group and Organization Management,* December 2005, pp 625–52.

²² G Graen, "Role-Making Processes within Complex Organizations," in *Handbook of Industrial and Organizational Psychology,* ed M D Dunnette (Chicago: Rand McNally, 1976), p 1201. Also see S D Dobrev and W P Barnett, "Organizational Roles and Transition to Entrepreneurship," *Academy of Management Journal,* June 2005, pp 433–49; M A Eys, A V Carron, M R Beauchamp, and S R Brays, "Athletes' Perceptions of the Sources of Role Ambiguity," *Small Group Research,* August 2005, pp 383–403; and T Schellens, H Van Keer, and M Valcke, "The Impact of Role Assignment on Knowledge Construction in Asynchronous Discussion Groups: A Multilevel Analysis," *Small Group Research,* December 2005, pp 704–45.

²³ See K D Benne and P Sheats, "Functional Roles of Group Members," *Journal of Social Issues,* Spring 1948, pp 41–49.

²⁴ See H J Klein and P W Mulvey, "Two Investigations of the Relationships among Group Goals, Goal Commitment, Cohesion, and Performance," *Organizational Behavior and Human Decision Processes,* January 1995, pp 44–53; D F Crown and J G Rosse, "Yours, Mine, and Ours: Facilitating Group Productivity through the Integration of Individual and Group Goals," *Organizational Behavior and Human Decision Processes,* November 1995, pp 138–50; and D Knight, C C Durham, and E A Locke, "The Relationship of Team Goals, Incentives, and Efficacy to Strategic Risk, Tactical Implementation, and Performance," *Academy of Management Journal,* April 2001, pp 326–38.

²⁵ A Zander, "The Value of Belonging to a Group in Japan," *Small Group Behavior,* February 1983, pp 7–8. Also see E Gundling, *Working GlobeSmart: 12 People Skills for Doing Business across Borders* (Palo Alto, CA: Davies-Black Publishing, 2003).

²⁶ R R Blake and J Srygley Mouton, "Don't Let Group Norms Stifle Creativity," *Personnel,* August 1985, p 28.

²⁷ See D Kahneman, "Reference Points, Anchors, Norms, and Mixed Feelings," *Organizational Behavior and Human Decision Processes,* March 1992, pp 296–312; and J M Marques, D Abrams, D Paez, and C Martinez-Taboada, "The Role of Categorization and In-Group Norms in Judgments of Groups and Their Members," *Journal of Personality and Social Psychology,* October 1998, pp 976–88.

²⁸ A Dunkin, "Pepsi's Marketing Magic: Why Nobody Does It Better," *BusinessWeek,* February 10, 1986, p 52.

²⁹ See J Pfeffer, "Bring Back Shame," *Business 2.0,* September 2003, p 80.

³⁰ P Sellers, "Gap's New Guy Upstairs," *Fortune,* April 14, 2003, p 112.

³¹ D C Feldman, "The Development and Enforcement of Group Norms," *Academy of Management Review,* January 1984, pp 50–52.

³² Ibid.

³³ "Top 10 Leadership Tips from Jeff Immelt," *Fast Company,* April 2004, p 96.

³⁴ J Pfeffer and J F Veiga, "Putting People First for Organizational Success," *Academy of Management Executive,* May 1999, p 41.

³⁵ See N Enbar, "What Do Women Want? Ask 'Em," *Business Week,* March 29, 1999, p 8; and M Hickins, "Duh! Gen Xers Are Cool with Teamwork," *Management Review,* March 1999, p 7. For related reading, see L Gerdes, "Why Put Real Work Off Till Tomorrow?" *BusinessWeek,* May 8, 2006, p 92.

³⁶ Quote and data from D Jones, "Optimism Puts Rose-Colored Tint in Glasses of Top Execs," *USA Today,* December 16, 2005, p 2B.

³⁷ J R Katzenbach and D K Smith, *The Wisdom of Teams: Creating the High-Performance Organization* (New York: HarperBusiness, 1999), p 45.

³⁸ Condensed and adapted from ibid., p 214. Also see B Beersma, J R Hollenbeck, S E Humphrey, H Moon, D Conlon, and D R Ilgen,

"Cooperation, Competition, and Team Performance: Toward a Contingency Approach," *Academy of Management Journal,* October 2003, pp 572–90; L L Gilson, J E Mathieu, C E Shalley, and T M Ruddy, "Creativity and Standardization: Complementary or Conflicting Drivers of Team Effectiveness?" *Academy of Management Journal,* June 2005, pp 521–31; B Fischer and A Boynton, "Virtuoso Teams," *Harvard Business Review,* July/August 2005, pp 116–23; R D Hof, "Teamwork Supercharged," *BusinessWeek,* November 21, 2005, pp 90–94; J E Mathieu, L L Gibson, and T M Ruddy, "Empowerment and Team Effectiveness: An Empirical Test of an Integrated Model," *Journal of Applied Psychology,* January 2006, pp 97–108; P Balkundi and W A Harrison, "Ties, Leaders, and Time in Teams: Strong Inference about Network Structure's Effects on Team Viability and Performance," *Academy of Management Journal,* February 2006, pp 49–68; and J M Howell and C M Shea, "Effects of Champion Behavior, Team Potency, and External Communication Activities on Predicting Team Performance," *Group and Organization Management,* April 2006, pp 180–211.

³⁹ See M P Hillmann, P Dongier, R P Murgallis, M Khosh, E K Allen, and R Evernham, "When Failure Isn't an Option," *Harvard Business Review,* July/August 2005, pp 41–50.

⁴⁰ J R Katzenbach and D K Smith, "The Discipline of Teams," *Harvard Business Review,* March/April 1993, p 112.

⁴¹ "A Team's-Eye View of Teams," *Training,* November 1995, p 16.

⁴² P Burrows, "Cisco's Comeback," *BusinessWeek,* November 24, 2003, p 124. For material related to teamwork skills, see F P Morgenson, M H Reider, and M A Campion, "Selecting Individuals in Team Settings: The Importance of Social Skills, Personality Characteristics, and Teamwork Knowledge," *Personnel Psychology,* Autumn 2005, pp 583–611; A P J Ellis, B S Bell, R E Ployhart, J R Hollenbeck, and D R Ilgen, "An Evaluation of Generic Teamwork Skills Training with Action Teams: Effects on Cognitive and Skills-Based Outcomes," *Personnel Psychology,* Autumn 2005, pp 641–72; L Conley, "Credit Where Credit Is Due," *Fast Company,* November 2005, pp 99–101; H Minssen, "Challenges of Teamwork in Production: Demands of Communication," *Organization Studies,* no. 1, 2006, pp 103–24; B Erdogan, R C Liden, and M L Kraimer, "Justice and Leader-Member Exchange: The Moderating Role of Organizational Culture," *Academy of Management Journal,* April 2006, pp 395–406; and P Kaihla, "Office Graffiti," *Business 2.0,* April 2006, p 90.

⁴³ See, for example, P Suciu, "Listen Up, Soldiers," *Newsweek,* July 11, 2005, p 70; J Alsever, "Hello Muddah, Hello Faddah . . . What Executives Learn at Summer Camp," *Fast Company,* September 2005, p 30; and S Datta, "Cooking Up a Better Team," *Business 2.0,* May 2006, p 143.

⁴⁴ Excerpted from S Max, "Seagate's Morale-athon," *BusinessWeek,* April 3, 2006, p 110–12.

⁴⁵ See D McDonald, "Why We All Hate Offsites," *Business 2.0,* May 2006, pp 79–80.

⁴⁶ E Nordwall, "Moneyline," *USA Today,* February 16, 2006, p 1B.

⁴⁷ M Adams, "United Execs' Stock Could Zoom in Value," *USA Today,* January 30, 2006, p 1B. Also see E Thornton, "Fat Merger Payouts for CEOs," *BusinessWeek,* December 12, 2005, pp 34–37; A Borrus, "Not Your Ordinary Gold Watch," *BusinessWeek,* February 6, 2006, p 40; and W E Gillis and J G Combs, "How Much Is Too Much? Board of Director Responses to Shareholder Concerns About CEO Stock Options," *Academy of Management Perspectives,* May 2006, pp 70–72.

⁴⁸ S Zuboff, "From Subject to Citizen," *Fast Company,* May 2004, p 104. Also see "Minorities Distrust Companies," *USA Today,* January 14, 2004, p 1B; and "Little Faith in Top Executives," *USA Today,* April 5, 2004, p 1B.

⁴⁹ L Prusak and D Cohen, "How to Invest in Social Capital," *Harvard Business Review,* June 2001, p 90. Also see V U Druskat and S B Wolff, "Building the Emotional Intelligence of Groups," *Harvard Business Review,* March 2001, pp 80–90.

⁵⁰ See D M Rousseau, S B Sitkin, R S Burt, and C Camerer, "Not So Different After All: A Cross-Discipline View of Trust," *Academy of Management Review,* July 1998, pp 393–404; and A C Wicks, S L Berman, and T M Jones, "The Structure of Optimal Trust: Moral and Strategic Implications," *Academy of Management Review,* January 1999, pp 99–116.

⁵¹ J D Lewis and A Weigert, "Trust as a Social Reality," *Social Forces,* June 1985, p 971. Trust is examined as an *indirect* factor in K T Dirks, "The Effects of Interpersonal Trust on Work Group Performance," *Journal of Applied Psychology,* June 1999, pp 445–55. Also see J B Cunningham and J MacGregor, "Trust and the Design of Work: Complementary Constructs in Satisfaction and Performance," *Human Relations,* December 2000, pp 1575–88.

⁵² Adapted from C Johnson-George and W C Swap, "Measurement of Specific Interpersonal Trust: Construction and Validation of a Scale to Assess Trust in a Specific Other," *Journal of Personality and Social Psychology,* December 1982, pp 1306–17; and D J McAllister, "Affect- and Cognition-Based Trust as Foundations for Interpersonal Cooperation in Organizations," *Academy of Management Journal,* February 1995, pp 24–59.

⁵³ See R Zemke, "Little Lies," *Training,* February 2004, p 8.

⁵⁴ For support, see G M Spreitzer and A K Mishra, "Giving Up Control without Losing Control: Trust and Its Substitutes' Effects on Managers' Involving Employees in Decision Making," *Group & Organization Management,* June 1999, pp 155–87. Also see G Johnson, "11 Keys to Leadership," *Training,* January 2004, p 18.

⁵⁵ Adapted from F Bartolomé, "Nobody Trusts the Boss Completely—Now What?" *Harvard Business Review,* March/April 1989, pp 135–42. For more on building trust, see R Galford and A S Drapeau, "The Enemies of Trust," *Harvard Business Review,* February 2003, pp 88–95; L C Abrams, R Cross, E Lesser, and D Z Levin, "Nurturing Interpersonal Trust in Knowledge-Sharing Networks," *Academy of Management Executive,* November 2003, pp 64–77; C Huxham and S Vangen, "Doing Things Collaboratively: Realizing the Advantage or Succumbing to Inertia?" *Organizational Dynamics,* no 2, 2004, pp 190–201; S A Joni, "The Geography of Trust," *Harvard Business Review,* March 2004, pp 82–88; P Evans and B Wolf, "Collaboration Rules," *Harvard Business Review,* July/August 2005, pp 96–104; and R Goffee and G Jones, "Managing Authenticity: The Paradox of Great Leadership," *Harvard Business Review,* December 2005, pp 86–94.

⁵⁶ Data from C Joinson, "Teams at Work," *HR Magazine,* May 1999, pp 30–36.

⁵⁷ B Dumaine, "Who Needs a Boss?" *Fortune,* May 7, 1990, p 52. Also see D Vredenburgh and I Y He, "Leadership Lessons from a Conductorless Orchestra," *Business Horizons,* September/October 2003, pp 19–24; and C A O'Reilly III and M L Tushman, "The Ambidextrous Organization," *Harvard Business Review,* April 2004, pp 74–81.

⁵⁸ Adapted from Table 1 in V U Druskat and J V Wheeler, "Managing from the Boundary: The Effective Leadership of Self-Managing Work Teams," *Academy of Management Journal,* August 2003, pp 435–57.

⁵⁹ See A E Randal and K S Jaussi, "Functional Background Identity, Diversity, and Individual Performance in Cross-Functional Teams," *Academy of Management Journal,* December 2003, pp 763–74; and G S Van Der Vegt and J S Bunderson, "Learning and Performance in Multidisciplinary Teams: The Importance of Collective Team Identification," *Academy of Management Journal,* June 2005, pp 532–47.

⁶⁰ Excerpted from "Fast Talk," *Fast Company,* February 2004, p 50. For cross-functional teams in action, see B Nussbaum, "How to Build Innovative Companies: Get Creative!" *BusinessWeek,* August 1, 2005, pp 61–68; C Edwards, "Inside Intel," *BusinessWeek,* January 9, 2006, pp 46–54; "How to Break Out of Commodity Hell," *BusinessWeek,* March 27, 2006, p 76; and B Finn, "Outside-In R&D," *Business 2.0,* April 2006, p 85.

⁶¹ For example, see J Merritt, "How to Rebuild a B-School," *BusinessWeek,* March 29, 2004, pp 90–91.

⁶² See "1996 Industry Report: What Self-Managing Teams Manage," *Training,* October 1996, p 69.

⁶³ See L L Thompson, *Making the Team: A Guide for Managers* (Upper Saddle River, NJ: Prentice Hall, 2000).

⁶⁴ See P S Goodman, R Devadas, and T L Griffith Hughson, "Groups and Productivity: Analyzing the Effectiveness of Self-Managing Teams," in *Productivity in Organizations,* eds J P Campbell, R J Campbell and Associates (San Francisco: Jossey-Bass, 1988), pp 295–327. Also see R C Liden, S J Wayne, and M L Kraimer "Managing Individual Performance in Work Groups," *Human Resource Management,* Spring 2001, pp 63–72; R Batt, "Who Benefits from

Teams? Comparing Workers, Supervisors, and Managers," *Industrial Relations,* January 2004, pp 183–209; F P Morgeson, "The External Leadership of Self-Managing Teams: Intervening in the Context of Novel and Disruptive Events," *Journal of Applied Psychology,* May 2005, pp 497–508; and S Kauffeld, "Self-Directed Work Groups and Team Competence," *Journal of Occupational and Organizational Psychology,* March 2006, pp 1–21.

⁶⁵ Drawn from H van Mierlo, C G Rutte, M A Kompier, and H A C M Doorewaard, "Self-Managing Teamwork and Psychological Well-Being: Review of a Multilevel Research Domain," *Group and Organization Management,* April 2005, pp 211–35.

⁶⁶ For more, see W F Cascio, "Managing a Virtual Workplace," *Academy of Management Executive,* August 2000, pp 81–90; and the collection of articles on E-leadership and virtual teams in *Organizational Dynamics,* no 4, 2003.

⁶⁷ Excerpted from M Conlin, "The Easiest Commute of All," *BusinessWeek,* December 12, 2005, pp 78–79. Also see J T Arnold, "Making the Leap," *HR Magazine,* May 2006, pp 80–86.

⁶⁸ See A M Townsend, S M DeMarie, and A R Hendrickson, "Virtual Teams: Technology and the Workplace of the Future," *Academy of Management Executive,* August 1998, pp 17–29.

⁶⁹ See C Saunders, C Van Slyke, and D R Vogel, "My Time or Yours? Managing Time Visions in Global Virtual Teams," *Academy of Management Executive,* February 2004, pp 19–31.

⁷⁰ Excerpted from K Naughton, "Styling with Digital Clay," *Newsweek,* April 28, 2003, pp 46–47. For a large-scale example, see S E Ante, "Collaboration: IBM," *BusinessWeek,* November 24, 2003, p 84.

⁷¹ Based on P Bordia, N DiFonzo, and A Chang, "Rumor as Group Problem Solving: Development Patterns in Informal Computer-Mediated Groups," *Small Group Research,* February 1999, pp 8–28.

⁷² See K A Graetz, E S Boyle, C E Kimble, P Thompson, and J L Garloch, "Information Sharing in Face-to-Face, Teleconferencing, and Electronic Chat Groups," *Small Group Research,* December 1998, pp 714–43.

⁷³ Based on F Niederman and R J Volkema, "The Effects of Facilitator Characteristics on Meeting Preparation, Set Up, and Implementation," *Small Group Research,* June 1999, pp 330–60.

⁷⁴ Based on J J Sosik, B J Avolio, and S S Kahai, "Inspiring Group Creativity: Comparing Anonymous and Identified Electronic Brainstorming," *Small Group Research,* February 1998, pp 3–31. For practical advice on brainstorming, see C Caggiano, "The Right Way to Brainstorm," *Inc.,* July 1999, p 94. Also see A M Hardin, M A Fuller, and J S Valacich, "Measuring Group Efficacy in Virtual Teams: New Questions in an Old Debate," *Small Group Research,* February 2006, pp 65–85.

⁷⁵ See B L Kirkman, B Rosen, C B Gibson, P E Tesluk, and S O McPherson, "Five Challenges to Virtual Team Success: Lessons from Sabre, Inc.," *Academy of Management Executive,* August 2002, pp 67–79; P J Hinds and D E Bailey, "Out of Sight, Out of Sync: Understanding Conflict in Distributed Teams," *Organization Science,* November– December 2003, pp 615–32; and Y Shin, "Conflict Resolution in Virtual Teams," *Organizational Dynamics,* November 2005, pp 331–45.

⁷⁶ See E Kelley, "Keys to Effective Virtual Global Teams," *Academy of Management Executive,* May 2001, pp 132–33.

⁷⁷ Practical perspectives are offered in "Virtual Teams that Work," *HR Magazine,* July 2003, p 121; D D Davis, "The Tao of Leadership in Virtual Teams," *Organizational Dynamics,* no 1, 2004, pp 47–62; A Majchrzak, A Malhotra, J Stamps, and J Lipnack, "Can Absence Make a Team Grow Stronger?" *Harvard Business Review,* May 2004, pp 131–37; and J Gordon, "Do Your Virtual Teams Deliver Only Virtual Performance?" *Training,* June 2005, pp 20–26.

⁷⁸ For a comprehensive update on groupthink, see the entire February/March 1998 issue of *Organizational Behavior and Human Decision Processes* (12 articles).

⁷⁹ I L Janis, *Groupthink,* 2nd ed (Boston: Houghton Mifflin, 1982), p 9. Alternative models are discussed in K Granstrom and D Stiwne, "A Bipolar Model of Groupthink: An Expansion of Janis's Concept," *Small Group Research,* February 1998, pp 32–56; A R Flippen, "Understanding Groupthink from a Self-Regulatory Perspective," *Small Group Research,* April 1999, pp 139–65; and M Harvey, M M Novicevic, M R Buckley, and J R B Halbesleben, "The Abilene Paradox after Thirty Years:

A Global Perspective," *Organizational Dynamics,* no 2, 2004, pp 215–26.

⁸⁰ Ibid. For an alternative model, see R J Aldag and S Riggs Fuller, "Beyond Fiasco: A Reappraisal of the Groupthink Phenomenon and a New Model of Group Decision Processes," *Psychological Bulletin,* May 1993, pp 533–52. Also see A A Mohamed and F A Wiebe, "Toward a Process Theory of Groupthink," *Small Group Research,* August 1996, pp 416–30.

⁸¹ Adapted from Janis, *Groupthink,* pp 174–75. Also see J M Wellen and M Neale, "Deviance, Self-Typicality, and Group Cohesion: The Corrosive Effects of the Bad Apples on the Barrel," *Small Group Research,* April 2006, pp 165–86.

⁸² L Baum, "The Job Nobody Wants," *BusinessWeek,* September 8, 1986, p 60. Also see L Perlow and S Williams, "Is Silence Killing Your Company?" *Harvard Business Review,* May 2003, pp 52–58; W F Cascio, "Board Governance: A Social Systems Perspective," *Academy of Management Executive,* February 2004, pp 97–100; L Letendre, "The Dynamics of the Boardroom," *Academy of Management Executive,* February 2004, pp 101–4; W Schiano and J W Weiss, "Y2K All Over Again: How Groupthink Permeates IS and Compromises Security," *Business Horizons,* March/April 2006, pp 115–25; and N Fick, "General Dissent: When Less Isn't More," *USA Today,* April 25, 2006, p 13A.

⁸³ D D Henningsen, M L M Henningsen, J Eden, and M G Cruz, "Examining the Symptoms of Groupthink and Retrospective Sensemaking," *Small Group Research,* February 2006, pp 36–64.

⁸⁴ Based on discussion in B Latane, K Williams, and S Harkins, "Many Hands Make Light the Work: The Causes and Consequences of Social Loafing," *Journal of Personality and Social Psychology,* June 1979, pp 822–32; and D A Kravitz and B Martin, "Ringelmann Rediscovered: The Original Article," *Journal of Personality and Social Psychology,* May 1986, pp 936–41.

⁸⁵ See S J Karau and K D Williams, "Social Loafing: Meta-Analytic Review and Theoretical Integration," *Journal of Personality and Social Psychology,* October 1993, pp 681–706; and L Thompson, "Improving the Creativity of Organizational Work Groups," *Academy of Management Executive,* February 2003, pp 96–109.

⁸⁶ See S J Zaccaro, "Social Loafing: The Role of Task Attractiveness," *Personality and Social Psychology Bulletin,* March 1984, pp 99–106; J M Jackson and K D Williams, "Social Loafing on Difficult Tasks: Working Collectively Can Improve Performance," *Journal of Personality and Social Psychology,* October 1985, pp 937–42; and J M George, "Extrinsic and Intrinsic Origins of Perceived Social Loafing in Organizations," *Academy of Management Journal,* March 1992, pp 191–202.

⁸⁷ For complete details, see K Williams, S Harkins, and B Latane, "Identifiability as a Deterrent to Social Loafing: Two Cheering Experiments," *Journal of Personality and Social Psychology,* February 1981, pp 303–11.

⁸⁸ See J M Jackson and S G Harkins, "Equity in Effort: An Explanation of the Social Loafing Effect," *Journal of Personality and Social Psychology,* November 1985, pp 1199–1206.

⁸⁹ Both studies are reported in S G Harkins and K Szymanski, "Social Loafing and Group Evaluation," *Journal of Personality and Social Psychology,* June 1989, pp 934–41. Also see R Hoigaard, R Safvenbom, and F E Tonnessen, "The Relationship between Group Cohesion, Group Norms, and Perceived Social Loafing in Soccer Teams," *Small Group Research,* June 2006, pp 217–32.

⁹⁰ Data from J A Wagner III, "Studies of Individualism-Collectivism: Effects on Cooperation in Groups," *Academy of Management Journal,* February 1995, pp 152–72. Also see P W Mulvey and H J Klein, "The Impact of Perceived Loafing and Collective Efficacy on Group Goal Processes and Group Performance," *Organizational Behavior and Human Decision Processes,* April 1998, pp 62–87; P W Mulvey, L Bowes-Sperry, and H J Klein, "The Effects of Perceived Loafing and Defensive Impression Management on Group Effectiveness," *Small Group Research,* June 1998, pp 394–415; and H Goren, R Kurzban, and A Rapoport, "Social Loafing vs. Social Enhancement: Public Goods Provisioning in Real-Time with Irrevocable Commitments," *Organizational Behavior and Human Decision Processes,* March 2003, pp 277–90.

⁹¹ See S G Scott and W O Einstein, "Strategic Performance Appraisal in Team-Based Organizations: One Size Does Not Fit All," *Academy of Management Executive,* May 2001, pp 107–16.

92 B T Thornton, "Sexual Harassment, I: Discouraging It in the Work Place," *Personnel,* April 1986, p 18. Also see T O McCarthy, "Sexual Conduct: Equal Abuse Unequal Harm," *HR Magazine,* January 2005, pp 93–94.

93 Excerpted from J A Segal, "Dangerous Liaisons," *HR Magazine,* December 2005, pp 104–108. Copyright © 2005 by Society for Human Resource Management (SHRM). Reproduced with permission of Society for Human Resource Management (SHRM) via Copyright Clearance Center. Also see "Workers Split on Office Romance," *USA Today,* February 2006, p 1B; C Woodyard, "Toyota to Review Conduct Policies," *USA Today,* May 10, 2006, p 3B; and M Orey, "Trouble at Toyota," *BusinessWeek,* May 22, 2006, pp 46–48.

Chapter 10

1 Excerpted from P A Salz, "High Performance: Intelligent Use of Information Is a Powerful Corporate Tool," *The Wall Street Journal,* April 27, 2006, p A10. Copyright © 2006 by Dow Jones & Company, Inc. Reproduced with permission of Dow Jones & Company, Inc. via Copyright Clearance Center.

2 T A Stewart, "Did You Ever Have to Make Up Your Mind?" *Harvard Business Review,* January 2006, p 12.

3 Results are presented in Salz, "High Performance: Intelligent Use of Information Is a Powerful Corporate Tool." Also see T H Davenport, "Competing on Analytics," *Harvard Business Review,* January 2006, pp 99–108; and J Pfeffer and R I Sutton, "Evidence-Based Management," *Harvard Business Review,* January 2006, pp 63–74.

4 A thorough discussion of the rational model can be found in M H Bazerman, *Judgment in Managerial Decision Making* (Hoboken, NJ: John Wiley & Sons, 2006).

5 Excerpted from "Contented Employees Mean Satisfied Customers at Baptist Health Care," *Training,* January 2005, p 11.

6 Results can be found in J P Bymes, D C Miller, and W D Schafer, "Gender Differences in Risk Taking: A Meta-Analysis," *Psychological Bulletin,* May 1999, pp 367–83. Also see R A Lowe and A A Ziedonis, "Overoptimism and the Performance of Entrepreneurial Firms," *Management Science,* February 2006, pp 173–86.

7 H A Simon, "Rational Decision Making in Business Organizations," *American Economic Review,* September 1979, p 510.

8 For a complete discussion of bounded rationality, see H A Simon, *Administrative Behavior,* 2nd ed (New York: Free Press, 1957). Also see M H Bazerman and D Chugh, "Decisions without Blinders," *Harvard Business Review,* January 2006, pp 88–97.

9 See T DeAngelis, "Too Many Choices?" *Monitor on Psychology,* June 2004, pp 56–57. Also see J S Hammond, R L Keeney, and H Raiffa, "The Hidden Traps in Decision Making," *Harvard Business Review,* January 2006, pp 118–26.

10 D W De Long and P Seemann, "Confronting Conceptual Confusion and Conflict in Knowledge Management," *Organizational Dynamics,* Summer 2000, p 33.

11 C Stoll, "Writing the Book on Knowledge Management," *American Society of Association Executives,* April 2004, pp 56–58, 60, 62–63. Also see M Trottman, "Choices in Stormy Weather: How Airline Employees Make Hundreds of Decisions to Cancel or Reroute Flights," *The Wall Street Journal,* February 14, 2006, pp B1, B2.

12 These statistics can be found in P Babcock, "Shedding Light on Knowledge Management," *HR Magazine,* May 2004, pp 47–50.

13 R Lubit, "Tacit Knowledge and Knowledge Management: The Keys to Sustainable Competitive Advantage," *Organizational Dynamics,* 2001, p 166.

14 The role of intuition in decision making is discussed by C C Miller and R D Ireland, "Intuition in Strategic Decision Making: Friend or Foe in the Fast-Paced 21st Century," *Academy of Management Executive,* February 2005, pp 19–30.

15 See R D Hof, "The Power of Us," *BusinessWeek,* June 20, 2005, pp 74–81. Also see M Overfelt, "Wireless Grapes," *Fortune,* March 6, 2006, pp 158B–158D.

16 R Cross, A Parker, L Prusak, and S P Borgatti, "Knowing What We Know: Supporting Knowledge Creation and Sharing in Social Networks," *Organizational Dynamics,* Fall 2001, p 109.

17 Ibid.

18 This definition was derived from A J Rowe and R O Mason, *Managing with Style: A Guide to Understanding, Assessing and Improving Decision Making* (San Francisco: Jossey-Bass, 1987).

19 The discussion of styles was based on material contained in ibid.

20 Excerpted from B Gimbel, "Keeping Planes Apart," *Fortune,* June 27, 2005, p 112.

21 B Bremner and D Roberts, "A Billion Tough Sells," *BusinessWeek,* March 20, 2006, p 44.

22 J Useem, "How the Marine Corps Trains Leaders," *Fortune,* June 27, 2005, p 108.

23 Norms were obtained from Rowe and Mason, *Managing with Style: A Guide to Understanding, Assessing and Improving Decision Making.*

24 See ibid.; and M J Dollinger and W Danis, "Preferred Decision-Making Styles: A Cross-Cultural Comparison," *Psychological Reports,* 1998, pp 755–61.

25 L Kopeikina, "The Elements of a Clear Decision," *MIT Sloan Management Review,* Winter 2006, p 19. Also see G Morse, "Decisions and Desire," *Harvard Business Review,* January 2006, pp 42–51.

26 A thorough discussion of escalation situations can be found in B M Staw and J Ross, "Behavior in Escalation Situations: Antecedents, Prototypes, and Solutions," in *Research in Organizational Behavior,* vol. 9, eds L L Cummings and B M Staw (Greenwich, CT: JAI Press, 1987), pp 39–78.

27 Ibid.

28 Supportive results can be found in J R Schmidt and R J Calantone, "Escalation of Commitment During New Product Development," *Journal of the Academy of Marketing Sciences,* 2002, pp 103–18.

29 See D A Hantula and J L D Bragger, "The Effects of Feedback Equivocality on Escalation of Commitment: An Empirical Investigation of Decision Dilemma Theory," *Journal of Applied Social Psychology,* February 1999, pp 424–44.

30 Results can be found in C R Greer and G K Stephens, "Escalation of Commitment: A Comparison of Differences between Mexican and U.S. Decision Makers," *Journal of Management,* 2001, pp 51–78.

31 This issue is discussed by S Hamm, "Innovation: The View from the Top," *BusinessWeek,* April 3, 2006, pp 52–54; M Weinstein, "Innovate or Die Trying," *Training,* May 2006, pp 40–44; and F Vogelstein, "Mastering the Art of Disruption," *Fortune,* February 6, 2006, pp 23–24.

32 This definition was based on R J Sternberg, "What Is the Common Thread of Creativity?" *American Psychologist,* April 2001, pp 360–62.

33 R Langreth and Z Moukheiber, "Medical Merlins," *Forbes,* June 2003, p 115.

34 S Holmes, "Just Plain Genius," *BusinessWeek,* April 17, 2006, p 20.

35 Results can be found in E Tahmincioglu, "Gifts that Gall," *Workforce Management,* April 2004, p 45.

36 Details of this study can be found in M Basadur, "Managing Creativity: A Japanese Model," *Academy of Management Executive,* May 1992, pp 29–42.

37 See P Loewe and J Dominiquini, "Overcoming the Barriers to Effective Innovation," *Strategy & Leadership,* 2006, pp 24–31; and J S Lublin, "Nurturing Innovation," *The Wall Street Journal,* March 20, 2006, pp B1, B3.

38 R Levering and M Moskowitz, "The 100 Best Companies to Work For: And the Winners Are . . ." *Fortune,* January 23, 2006, p 89.

39 Results can be found in C K W De Dreu and M A West, "Minority Dissent and Team Innovation: The Importance of Participation in Decision Making," *Journal of Applied Psychology,* December 2001, pp 1191–201.

40 These recommendations were derived from R Y Hirokawa, "Group Communication and Decision-Making Performance: A Continued Test of the Functional Perspective," *Human Communication Research,* October 1988, pp 487–515.

41 See the related discussion in B B Baltes, M W Dickson, M P Sherman, C C Bauer, and J S LaGanke, "Computer-Mediated Communication and Group Decision Making: A Meta-Analysis," *Organizational Behavior and Human Decision Processes,* January 2002, pp 156–79. Also see P Rogers and M Blenko, "What Has the D?" *Harvard Business Review,* January 2006, pp 53–61.

42 These guidelines were derived from G P Huber, *Managerial Decision Making* (Glenview, IL: Scott, Foresman, 1980), p 149.

[43] G W Hill, "Group versus Individual Performance: Are N + 1 Heads Better than One?" *Psychological Bulletin,* May 1982, p 535.

[44] See T Connolly and L Ordóñez, "Judgment and Decision Making," in *Handbook of Psychology,* vol. 12, eds W C Borman, D R Ilgen, and R J Klimoski (Hoboken, NJ: John Wiley & Sons, 2003), pp 493–518. Also see S Dingfelder, "Groups May Find More Elegant Solutions than Individuals," *Monitor on Psychology,* May 2006, p 15.

[45] For a review of this research, see M J Handel and D I Levine, "Editors' Introduction: The Effects of New Work Practices on Workers," *Industrial Relations,* January 2004, pp 1–43; and J A Wagner III, C R Leana, E A Locke, and D M Schweiger, "Cognitive and Motivational Frameworks in US Research on Participation: A Meta-Analysis of Primary Effects," *Journal of Organizational Behavior,* 1997, pp 49–65.

[46] S Carey, "The Thrifty Get Thriftier," *The Wall Street Journal,* May 10, 2004, p R7.

[47] G M Parker, *Team Players and Teamwork: The New Competitive Business Strategy* (San Francisco: Jossey-Bass, 1990).

[48] The effect of group dynamics on brainstorming is discussed by P B Paulus and H-C Yang, "Idea Generation in Groups: A Basis for Creativity in Organizations," *Organizational Behavior and Human Decision Processes,* May 2000, pp 76–87.

[49] These recommendations were obtained from Parker, *Team Players and Teamwork: The New Competitive Business Strategy.*

[50] See A F Osborn, *Applied Imagination: Principles and Procedures of Creative Thinking,* 3rd ed (New York: Scribners, 1979).

[51] See W H Cooper, R Brent Gallupe, S Pollard, and J Cadsby, "Some Liberating Effects of Anonymous Electronic Brainstorming," *Small Group Research,* April 1998, pp 147–78.

[52] These recommendations and descriptions were derived from B Nussbaum, "The Power of Design," *BusinessWeek,* May 17, 2004, pp 88–94.

[53] The NGT procedure is discussed by L Thompson, "Improving the Creativity of Organizational Work Groups," *Academy of Management Executive,* February 2003, pp 96–109.

[54] See ibid.

[55] See N C Dalkey, D L Rourke, R Lewis, and D Snyder, *Studies in the Quality of Life: Delphi and Decision Making* (Lexington, MA: Lexington Books: D C Heath and Co., 1972).

[56] An application of the Delphi technique can be found in K D Joshi, "A Formal Knowledge Management Ontology: Conduct, Activities, Resources, and Influences," *Journal of the American Society for Information Science and Technology,* May 2004, p 593.

[57] A thorough description of computer-aided decision-making systems is provided by M C Er and A C Ng, "The Anonymity and Proximity Factors in Group Decision Support Systems," *Decision Support Systems,* May 1995, pp 75–83.

[58] M Weinstein, "So Happy Together," *Training,* May 2006, p 38.

[59] Supportive results can be found in S S Lam and J Schaubroeck, "Improving Group Decisions by Better Polling Information: A Comparative Advantage of Group Decision Support Systems," *Journal of Applied Psychology,* August 2000, pp 565–73; and I Benbasat and J Lim, "Information Technology Support for Debiasing Group Judgments: An Empirical Evaluation," *Organizational Behavior and Human Decision Processes,* September 2000, pp 167–83.

[60] Results can be found in Baltes, Dickson, Sherman, Bauer, and LaGanke, "Computer-Mediated Communication and Group Decision Making."

[61] Excerpted from J Kelley, "Westwood Students Get OK for Eagle Feathers," *The Mesa Republic,* May 25, 2006, p 15.

Chapter 11

[1] Excerpted from J Greene and M France, "Culture Wars Hit Corporate America," *BusinessWeek,* May 23, 2005, pp 90–93.

[2] D Tjosvold, *Learning to Manage Conflict: Getting People to Work Together Productively* (New York: Lexington Books, 1993), p xi.

[3] Ibid., pp xi–xii. High-tech change is discussed in B Stone, "Big Bucks, Big Thinker," *Newsweek,* May 22, 2006, p 46.

[4] See M Conlin, "Good Divorce, Good Business," *BusinessWeek,* October 31, 2005, pp 90–91.

[5] J A Wall, Jr, and R Robert Callister, "Conflict and Its Management," *Journal of Management,* no. 3, 1995, p 517.

[6] Ibid., p 544.

[7] See O Jones, "Scientific Management, Culture and Control: A First-Hand Account of Taylorism in Practice," *Human Relations,* May 2000, pp 631–53.

[8] See A Fisher, "How to Prevent Violence at Work," *Fortune,* February 21, 2005, p 42; and K Gurchick, "Study: Domestic Violence Spills Over into Workplace," *HR Magazine,* March 2005, pp 32, 38.

[9] See S Alper, D Tjosvold, and K S Law, "Interdependence and Controversy in Group Decision Making: Antecedents to Effective Self-Managing Teams," *Organizational Behavior and Human Decision Processes,* April 1998, pp 33–52.

[10] S P Robbins, "'Conflict Management' and 'Conflict Resolution' Are Not Synonymous Terms," *California Management Review,* Winter 1978, p 70.

[11] Cooperative conflict is discussed in Tjosvold, *Learning to Manage Conflict: Getting People to Work Together Productively.* Also see A C Amason, "Distinguishing the Effects of Functional and Dysfunctional Conflict on Strategic Decision Making: Resolving a Paradox for Top Management Teams," *Academy of Management Journal,* February 1996, pp 123–48; D E Warren, "Constructive and Destructive Deviance in Organizations," *Academy of Management Review,* October 2003, pp 622–32; H Johnson, "The Next Management Revolution," *Inc.,* July 2004, pp 78–83; A Hanft, "The Joy of Conflict," *Inc.,* August 2005, p 112; and J Pfeffer, "The Courage to Rise Above," *Business 2.0,* May 2006, p 86.

[12] K Brooker, "Can Anyone Replace Herb?" *Fortune,* April 17, 2000, p 190.

[13] K Brooker, "I Built This Company, I Can Save It," *Fortune,* April 30, 2001, p 102. Also see L Stack, "Employees Behaving Badly," *HR Magazine,* October 2003, pp 111–16.

[14] Adapted in part from discussion in A C Filley, *Interpersonal Conflict Resolution* (Glenview, IL: Scott, Foresman, 1975), pp 9–12; and B Fortado, "The Accumulation of Grievance Conflict," *Journal of Management Inquiry,* December 1992, pp 288–303. Also see D Tjosvold and M Poon, "Dealing with Scarce Resources: Open-Minded Interaction for Resolving Budget Conflicts," *Group & Organization Management,* September 1998, pp 237–55.

[15] Excerpted from T Ursiny, *The Coward's Guide to Conflict: Empowering Solutions for Those Who Would Rather Run than Fight* (Naperville, IL: Sourcebooks, 2003), p 27.

[16] Adapted from discussion in Tjosvold, *Learning to Manage Conflict: Getting People to Work Together Productively,* pp 12–13.

[17] L Gardenswartz and A Rowe, *Diverse Teams at Work: Capitalizing on the Power of Diversity* (New York: McGraw-Hill, 1994), p 32.

[18] Data from "Do I Have It?" *BusinessWeek,* July 7, 2003, p 14.

[19] S Armour, "Music Hath Charms for Some Workers—Others It Really Annoys," *USA Today,* March 24, 2006, p 1B.

[20] See O Barker, "Whatever Happened to Thank-You Notes?" *USA Today,* December 27, 2005, pp 1A–2A; and S Jayson, "Are Social Norms Steadily Unraveling?" *USA Today,* April 13, 2006, p 4D.

[21] See L M Andersson and C M Pearson, "Tit for Tat? The Spiraling Effect of Incivility in the Workplace," *Academy of Management Review,* July 1999, pp 452–71; J Pfeffer, "How to Turn On the Charm," *Business 2.0,* June 2004, p 76; and S Lim and L M Cortina, "Interpersonal Mistreatment in the Workplace: The Interface and Impact of General Incivility and Sexual Harassment," *Journal of Applied Psychology,* May 2005, pp 483–96.

[22] Data from M Weinstein, "Racism, Sexism, Ageism: Workplace Not Getting Any Friendlier," *Training,* May 2006, p 11.

[23] See D L Coutu, "In Praise of Boundaries: A Conversation with Miss Manners," *Harvard Business Review,* December 2003, pp 41–45; R Kurtz, "Is Etiquette a Core Value?" *Inc.,* May 2004, p 22; and K Gurchiek, "Office Etiquette Breaches: Dial It Down," *HR Magazine,* May 2006, p 36.

[24] Data from D Stamps, "Yes, Your Boss Is Crazy," *Training,* July 1998, pp 35–39. Also see K Tyler, "Mind Matters," *HR Magazine,* August 2003, pp 54–62; J Britt, "Cutting Mental Health Benefits May Not Be Cost-Effective," *HR Magazine,* August 2003, p 10; C Arnst, "Attention Deficit: Not Just Kid Stuff," *BusinessWeek,* October 27, 2003, pp 84, 86; M Elias, "Mental Illness: Surprising, Disturbing Findings," *USA Today,*

June 7, 2005, p 8D; and A Deutschman, "Is Your Boss a Psychopath?" *Fast Company,* July 2005, pp 45–51.

25 For more, see L W Andrews, "Hiring People with Intellectual Disabilities," *HR Magazine,* July 2005, pp 74–77; L M Franze and M B Burns, "Risky Business: Err on the Side of Safety When Balancing Job Qualification Standards with ADA Compliance," *HR Magazine,* November 2005, pp 119–25; F Jossi, "High-Tech Enables Employee," *HR Magazine,* February 2006, pp 109–15; and A Smith, "ADA Accommodation Is Not One-Stop Shopping," *HR Magazine,* May 2006, p 34.

26 See N W Janove, "Sexual Harassment and the Three Big Surprises," *HR Magazine,* November 2001, pp 123–30; and M M Clark, "Failure to Cure Harassment Can Be 'Continuing Violation,'" *HR Magazine,* February 2003, p 106.

27 See D Smith, "Hostility Associated with Immune Function," *Monitor on Psychology,* March 2003, p 47; "The Walking Time Bomb," *Inc.,* December 2003, p 52; and D L Coutu, "Losing It," *Harvard Business Review,* April 2004, pp 37–42; and K Gurchiek, "Domestic Abuse: Serious Hidden Workplace Problem," *HR Magazine,* March 2006, p 38.

28 For practical advice, see N Nicholson, "How to Motivate Your Problem People," *Harvard Business Review,* Special Issue: Motivating People, January 2003, pp 56–65; and M Archer, "How to Work With Annoying People," *USA Today,* March 20, 2006, p 4B.

29 Drawn from J C McCune, "The Change Makers," *Management Review,* May 1999, pp 16–22.

30 Based on discussion in G Labianca, D J Brass, and B Gray, "Social Networks and Perceptions of Intergroup Conflict: The Role of Negative Relationships and Third Parties," *Academy of Management Journal,* February 1998, pp 55–67. Also see C Gómez, B L Kirkman, and D L Shapiro, "The Impact of Collectivism and In-Group/Out-Group Membership on the Evaluation Generosity of Team Members," *Academy of Management Journal,* December 2000, pp 1097–106; and K A Jehn and E A Mannix, "The Dynamic Nature of Conflict: A Longitudinal Study of Intragroup Conflict and Group Performance," *Academy of Management Journal,* April 2001, pp 238–51.

31 See J Barbian, "Racism Shrugged," *Training,* February 2003, p 68; R J Eidelson and J I Eidelson, "Dangerous Ideas: Five Beliefs That Propel Groups toward Conflict," *American Psychologist,* March 2003, pp 182–92; T M Glomb and H Liao, "Interpersonal Aggression in Work Groups: Social Influence, Reciprocal, and Individual Effects," *Academy of Management Journal,* August 2003, pp 486–96; and S Kehrli and T Sopp, "Managing Generation Y," *HR Magazine,* May 2006, pp 113–19.

32 Labianca, Brass, and Gray, "Social Networks and Perceptions of Intergroup Conflict: The Role of Negative Relationships and Third Parties," p 63 (emphasis added). Also see J Li and D C Hambrick, "Factional Groups: A New Vantage on Demographic Faultlines, Conflict, and Disintegration in Work Teams," *Academy of Management Journal,* October 2005, pp 794–813.

33 For example, see S C Wright, A Aron, T McLaughlin-Volpe, and S A Ropp, "The Extended Contact Effect: Knowledge of Cross-Group Friendships and Prejudice," *Journal of Personality and Social Psychology,* July 1997, pp 73–90.

34 See C D Batson, M P Polycarpou, E Harmon-Jones, H J Imhoff, E C Mitchener, L L Bednar, T R Klein, and L Highberger, "Empathy and Attitudes: Can Feeling for a Member of a Stigmatized Group Improve Feelings toward the Group?" *Journal of Personality and Social Psychology,* January 1997, pp 105–18.

35 For more, see N J Adler, *International Dimensions of Organizational Behavior,* 4th ed (Cincinnati: South-Western, 2002); P Engardio, "The Future of Outsourcing," *BusinessWeek,* January 30, 2006, pp 50–58; F Balfour, "One Foot in China," *BusinessWeek,* May 1, 2006, pp 44–45; E Iwata, "Immigrants Courted as Good Customers," *USA Today,* May 11, 2006, p 3B; L Buchanan, "The Thinking Man's Outsourcing," *Inc.,* May 2006, pp 31–33; B Helm, "Life on the Web's Factory Floor," *BusinessWeek,* May 22, 2006, pp 70–71; B Einhorn, "The Hunt for Chinese Talent," *BusinessWeek,* May 22, 2006, p 104; and R Buderi, "The Talent Magnet," *Fast Company,* June 2006, pp 80–84.

36 "Negotiating South of the Border," *Harvard Management Communication Letter,* August 1999, p 12.

37 Reprinted from A Rosenbaum, "Testing Cultural Waters," *Management Review,* July/August 1999, p 43. Copyright 1999 American Management Association. Reproduced with permission of American Management Association via Copyright Clearance Center.

38 See R L Tung, "American Expatriates Abroad: From Neophytes to Cosmopolitans," *Journal of World Business,* Summer 1998, pp 125–44.

39 See H M Guttman, "Conflict Management as a Core Leadership Competency," *Training,* November 2005, pp 34–39.

40 R A Cosier and C R Schwenk, "Agreement and Thinking Alike: Ingredients for Poor Decisions," *Academy of Management Executive,* February 1990, p 71. Also see J P Kotter, "Kill Complacency," *Fortune,* August 5, 1996, pp 168–70; and S Caudron, "Keeping Team Conflict Alive," *Training & Development,* September 1998, pp 48–52.

41 For example, see "Facilitators as Devil's Advocates," *Training,* September 1993, p 10. Also see K L Woodward, "Sainthood for a Pope?" *Newsweek,* June 21, 1999, p 65.

42 Good background reading on devil's advocacy can be found in C R Schwenk, "Devil's Advocacy in Managerial Decision Making," *Journal of Management Studies,* April 1984, pp 153–68. Also see G Colvin, "The Wisdom of Dumb Questions," *Fortune,* June 27, 2005, p 157; "Consider Extreme Opinions in Decision-Making," *HR Magazine,* March 2006, p 20; and the critique of devil's advocacy in T Kelley and J Littman, *The Ten Faces of Innovation* (NY: Currency Doubleday, 2005), pp 2–3.

43 See G Katzenstein, "The Debate on Structured Debate: Toward a Unified Theory," *Organizational Behavior and Human Decision Processes,* June 1996, pp 316–32.

44 W Kiechel III, "How to Escape the Echo Chamber," *Fortune,* June 18, 1990, p 130.

45 See D M Schweiger, W R Sandberg, and P L Rechner, "Experiential Effects of Dialectical Inquiry, Devil's Advocacy, and Consensus Approaches to Strategic Decision Making," *Academy of Management Journal,* December 1989, pp 745–72.

46 See J S Valacich and C Schwenk, "Devil's Advocacy and Dialectical Inquiry Effects on Face-to-Face and Computer-Mediated Group Decision Making," *Organizational Behavior and Human Decision Processes,* August 1995, pp 158–73.

47 As quoted in D Jones, "CEOs Need X-Ray Vision in Transition," *USA Today,* April 23, 2001, p 4B. For an update, see K Maney, "EMC Chief Tucci Has Twice Led Turnarounds," *USA Today,* September 26, 2005, p 2B.

48 Based on C K W De Dreu and M A West, "Minority Dissent and Team Innovation: The Importance of Participation in Decision Making," *Journal of Applied Psychology,* December 2001, pp 1191–201.

49 A statistical validation for this model can be found in M A Rahim and N R Magner, "Confirmatory Factor Analysis of the Styles of Handling Interpersonal Conflict: First-Order Factor Model and Its Invariance across Groups," *Journal of Applied Psychology,* February 1995, pp 122–32.

50 M A Rahim, "A Strategy for Managing Conflict in Complex Organizations," *Human Relations,* January 1985, p 84.

51 See R Rubin, "Study: Bullies and Their Victims Tend to Be More Violent," *USA Today,* April 15, 2003, p 9D; D Salin, "Ways of Explaining Workplace Bullying: A Review of Enabling, Motivating and Precipitating Structures and Processes in the Work Environment," *Human Relations,* October 2003, pp 1213–32; K Gurchiek, "Bullying: It's Not Just on the Playground," *HR Magazine,* June 2005, p 40; L W Andrews, "When It's Time For Anger Management," *HR Magazine,* June 2005, pp 131–35; and K Hannon, "You Can Take That Bully Down, Gently," *USA Today,* July 5, 2005, p 4B.

52 For more on managing conflict, see G Roper, "Managing Employee Relations," *HR Magazine,* May 2005, pp 101–04; Y Shin, "Conflict Resolution in Virtual Teams," *Organizational Dynamics,* no. 4, 2005, pp 331–45; and M DuPraw, "Cut the Conflict with Consensus Building," *Training,* May 2006, p 20.

53 See J Rasley, "The Revolution You Won't See on TV," *Newsweek,* November 25, 2002, p 13; and C Bendersky, "Organizational Dispute Resolution Systems: A Complementarities Model," *Academy of Management Review,* October 2003, pp 643–56.

54 See M Bordwin, "Do-It-Yourself Justice," *Management Review,* January 1999, pp 56–58.

55 B Morrow and L M Bernardi, "Resolving Workplace Disputes," *Canadian Manager,* Spring 1999, p 17.

⁵⁶ Adapted from discussion in K O Wilburn, "Employment Disputes: Solving Them Out of Court," *Management Review,* March 1998, pp 17–21; and Morrow and Bernardi, "Resolving Workplace Disputes," pp 17–19, 27. Also see L Ioannou, "Can't We Get Along?" *Fortune,* December 7, 1998, p 244[E]; and D Weimer and S A Forest, "Forced into Arbitration? Not Any More," *BusinessWeek,* March 16, 1998, pp 66–68.
⁵⁷ For more, see M M Clark, "A Jury of Their Peers," *HR Magazine,* January 2004, pp 54–59.
⁵⁸ Wilburn, "Employment Disputes: Solving Them Out of Court," p 19.
⁵⁹ For more, see S Armour, "Arbitration's Rise Raises Fairness Issue," *USA Today,* June 12, 2001, pp 1B–2B; and G Weiss and D Serchuk, "Walled Off from Justice?" *BusinessWeek,* March 22, 2004, pp 90–92. Also see J Janove, "In Defense of Litigation," *HR Magazine,* May 2006, pp 125–29.
⁶⁰ Based on a definition in M A Neale and M H Bazerman, "Negotiating Rationally: The Power and Impact of the Negotiator's Frame," *Academy of Management Executive,* August 1992, pp 42–51. Also see M J Gelfand, V S Major, J L Raver, L H Nishii, and K O'Brien, "Negotiating Relationally: The Dynamics of the Relational Self in Negotiations," *Academy of Management Review,* April 2006, pp 427–51.
⁶¹ See, for example, J K Sebenius, "Six Habits of Merely Effective Negotiators," *Harvard Business Review,* April 2001, pp 87–95; R Walker, "Take It or Leave It: The *Only* Guide to Negotiating You Will *Ever* Need," *Inc.,* August 2003, pp 74–82; B Rosenstein, "Successful Negotiating Depends on Respect For Others, Yourself," *USA Today,* October 10, 2005, p 6B; and R Grover, "The Prime (Time) of Nancy Tellem," *BusinessWeek,* May 29, 2006, pp 50–51.
⁶² M H Bazerman and M A Neale, *Negotiating Rationally* (New York: The Free Press, 1992), p 16. Also see J F Brett, G B Northcraft, and R L Pinkley, "Stairways to Heaven: An Interlocking Self-Regulation Model of Negotiation," *Academy of Management Review,* July 1999, pp 435–51; G Cullinan, J Le Roux, and R Weddigen, "When to Walk Away from a Deal," *Harvard Business Review,* April 2004, pp 96–104; G A van Kleef, C K W De Dreu, and A S R Manstead, "The Interpersonal Effects of Anger and Happiness in Negotiations, " *Journal of Personality and Social Psychology,* January 2004, pp 57–76; and P H Kim, R L Pinkley, and A R Fragale, "Power Dynamics in Negotiation," *Academy of Management Review,* October 2005, pp 799–822.
⁶³ Good win–win negotiation strategies can be found in R R Reck and B G Long, *The Win–Win Negotiator: How to Negotiate Favorable Agreements That Last* (New York: Pocket Books, 1987); R Fisher and W Ury, *Getting to YES: Negotiating Agreement without Giving In* (Boston: Houghton Mifflin, 1981); and R Fisher and D Ertel, *Getting Ready to Negotiate: The Getting to YES Workbook* (New York: Penguin Books, 1995).
⁶⁴ Adapted from K Albrecht and S Albrecht, "Added Value Negotiating," *Training,* April 1993, pp 26–29. For an interesting look at Donald Trump's negotiating style, see "The Trophy Life," *Fortune,* April 19, 2004, pp 70–83.
⁶⁵ L Babcock, S Laschever, M Gelfand, and D Small, "Nice Girls Don't Ask," *Harvard Business Review,* October 2003, p 14. Also see L A Barron, "Ask and You Shall Receive? Gender Differences in Negotiators' Beliefs about Requests for a Higher Salary," *Human Relations,* June 2003, pp 635–62; L D Tyson, "New Clues to the Pay and Leadership Gap," *BusinessWeek,* October 27, 2003, p 36; D Kersten, "Women Need to Learn the Art of the Deal," *USA Today,* November 17, 2003, p 7B; A Fels, "Do Women Lack Ambition?" *Harvard Business Review,* April 2004, pp 50–60; B Brophy, "Bargaining for Bigger Bucks: A Step-by-Step Guide to Negotiating Your Salary," *Business 2.0,* May 2004, p 107; and H R Bowles, L Babcock, and K L McGinn, "Constraints and Triggers: Situational Mechanics of Gender in Negotiation," *Journal of Personality and Social Psychology,* December 2005, pp 951–65.
⁶⁶ Excerpted from S Hamm, "Less Ego, More Success," *BusinessWeek,* July 23, 2001, p 59; for an update, see S Hamm, "A Software Visionary Bows Out," *BusinessWeek,* March 31, 2003, p 61.

Chapter 12

¹ Excerpted from S Holmes, "Into the Wild Blog Yonder," *BusinessWeek,* May 22, 2006, pp 84, 86.
² C Hymowitz, "In the Lead: What Adecco Can Do to Improve Its Image after Bad News Bungle," *The Wall Street Journal,* January 20, 2004, p B1.
³ Results are summarized in "Why Am I Here," *Training,* April 2006, p 13. Also see J Robison, "An HCA Hospital's Miracle Workers," *Gallup Management Journal,* January 12, 2006, http://gmj.gallup.com/content/default.asp?ci=20707.
⁴ J L Bowditch and A F Buono, *A Primer on Organizational Behavior,* 4th ed (New York: John Wiley & Sons, 1997), p 120.
⁵ M Orey, "Lawyer's Firing Signals Turmoil in Legal Circles," *The Wall Street Journal,* May 21, 2001, p B1. Also see "The Good News About Bad News," *Training,* April 2006, pp 10–11.
⁶ For a detailed discussion about selecting an appropriate medium, see B Barry and I Smithey-Fulmer, "The Medium and the Message: The Adaptive Use of Communication Media in Dyadic Influence," *Academy of Management Review,* April 2004, pp 272–92.
⁷ C Hymowitz, "Diebold's New Chief Shows How to Lead After a Sudden Rise," *The Wall Street Journal,* May 8, 2006, p B1.
⁸ Quotes taken from S Greenhouse and M Barbaro, "Wal-Mart's Leader Shows Sides Online," *The Arizona Republic,* February 19, 2006, p D4.
⁹ Excerpted from J Sandberg, "Cookies, Gossip, Cubes: It's a Wonder Any Work Gets Done at the Office," *The Wall Street Journal,* April 28, 2004, p B1.
¹⁰ Communication noise is discussed by J Sandberg, "Office Minstrels Drive the Rest of Us Nuts but Are Hard to Silence," *The Wall Street Journal,* February 14, 2006, p B1.
¹¹ An approach to overcome this barrier is discussed in "Exit-Interview Software Ideal for Employees Who Just Don't Click," *Training,* February 2006, p 6.
¹² The preceding barriers are discussed by J P Scully, "People: The Imperfect Communicators," *Quality Progress,* April 1995, pp 37–39.
¹³ For a thorough discussion of these barriers, see C R Rogers and F J Roethlisberger, "Barriers and Gateways to Communication," *Harvard Business Review,* July/August 1952, pp 46–52.
¹⁴ Ibid., p 47.
¹⁵ The use of jargon and acronyms is discussed by C Hymowitz, "Mind Your Language: To Do Business Today, Consider Delayering," *The Wall Street Journal,* March 27, 2006, p B1.
¹⁶ J Sandberg, "In the Workplace, Every Bleeping Word Can Show Your Rank," *The Wall Street Journal,* March 21, 2006, p B1.
¹⁷ Results can be found in J D Johnson, W A Donohue, C K Atkin, and S Johnson, "Communication, Involvement, and Perceived Innovativeness," *Group & Organization Management,* March 2001, pp 24–52; and B Davenport Sypher and T E Zorn, Jr, "Communication-Related Abilities and Upward Mobility: A Longitudinal Investigation," *Human Communication Research,* Spring 1986, pp 420–31.
¹⁸ The measurement of communication competence is discussed by J M Schirmer, L Mauksch, F Lang, M K Marvel, K Zoppi, R E Epstein, D Brock, and M Pryzbylski, "Assessing Communication Competence: A Review of Current Tools," *Family Medicine,* March 2005, pp 184–192.
¹⁹ 1. *False.* Clients always take precedence, and people with the greatest authority or importance should be introduced first.
2. *False.* You should introduce yourself. Say something like "My name is _____. I don't believe we've met."
3. *False.* It's OK to admit you can't remember. Say something like "My mind just went blank, your name is?" Or offer your name and wait for the other person to respond with his or hers.
4. *False.* Business etiquette has become gender neutral.
5. *a. Host.* This enables him or her to lead their guest to the meeting place.
6. *False.* Not only is it rude to invade public areas with your conversation, but you never know who might hear details of your business transaction or personal life.
7. *b. 3 feet.* Closer than this is an invasion of personal space. Farther away forces people to raise their voices. Because communication varies from country to country, you should also inform yourself about cultural differences.
8. *True.* An exception to this would be if your company holds an event at the beach or the pool.
9. *False.* Just wave your hand over it when asked, or say "No thank you."
10. *True.* The person who initiated the call should redial if the connection is broken.

11. *True.* If you must use a speakerphone, you should inform all parties who's present.

12. *True.* You should record a greeting such as "I'm out of the office today, March 12. If you need help, please dial _____ at extension . . ."

20 See F Timmins and C McCabe, "How Assertive Are Nurses in the Workplace? A Preliminary Pilot Study," *Journal of Nursing Management,* January 2005, pp 61–67.

21 J A Waters, "Managerial Assertiveness," *Business Horizons,* September/October 1982, p 25.

22 Ibid., p 27.

23 This statistic was provided by A Fisher, "How Can I Survive a Phone Interview?" *Fortune,* April 19, 2004, p 54.

24 Problems with body language analysis are discussed by A Pihulyk, "Communicate with Clarity: The Key to Understanding and Influencing Others," *The Canadian Manager,* Summer 2003, pp 12–13.

25 Related research is summarized by J A Hall, "Male and Female Nonverbal Behavior," in *Multichannel Integrations of Nonverbal Behavior,* eds A W Siegman and S Feldstein (Hillsdale, NJ: Lawrence Erlbaum, 1985), pp 195–226.

26 See R E Axtell, *Gestures: The Do's and Taboos of Body Language around the World* (New York: John Wiley & Sons, 1991).

27 See J A Russell, "Facial Expressions of Emotion: What Lies Beyond Minimal Universality?" *Psychological Bulletin,* November 1995, pp 379–91.

28 Norms for cross-cultural eye contact are discussed by C Engholm, *When Business East Meets Business West: The Guide to Practice and Protocol in the Pacific Rim* (New York: John Wiley & Sons, 1991).

29 See D Knight, "Perks Keeping Workers out of Revolving Door," *The Wall Street Journal,* April 30, 2005, p D3; and G Rooper, "Managing Employee Relations," *HR Magazine,* May 2005, pp 101–104.

30 The discussion of listening styles is based on "5 Listening Styles," http://www.crossroadsinstitute.org/listyle.html, June 19, 2004; and "Listening and Thinking: What's Your Style," http://www.pediatricservices.com/prof/prof-10.htm, last modified August 10, 2002.

31 See the related discussion in J Condrill, "What Is Your Listening Style?" *AuthorsDen,* July 7, 2005, http://www.authorsden.com/visit/viewarticle.asp?id=18707; and D A Nadler, "Confessions of a Trusted Counselor," *Harvard Business Review,* September 2005, pp 68–77.

32 These recommendations were excerpted from J Jay, "On Communicating Well," *HR Magazine,* January 2005, pp 87–88.

33 D Tannen, "The Power of Talk: Who Gets Heard and Why," *Harvard Business Review,* September/October 1995, p 139.

34 For a thorough review of the evolutionary explanation of sex differences in communication, see A H Eagly and W Wood, "The Origins of Sex Differences in Human Behavior," *American Psychologist,* June 1999, pp 408–23.

35 See D Tannen, "The Power of Talk: Who Gets Heard and Why," in *Negotiation: Readings, Exercises, and Cases,* 3rd ed, eds R J Lewicki and D M Saunders (Boston, MA: Irwin/McGraw-Hill, 1999), pp 160–73; and D Tannen, *You Just Don't Understand: Women and Men in Conversation* (New York: Ballantine Books, 1990).

36 See M Dainton and E D Zelley, *Applying Communication Theory for Professional Life: A Practical Introduction* (Thousand Oaks, CA: Sage, 2005); and C Dreifus, "Author Applies Tools of Linguistics to Mend Mother-Daughter Divide," *New York Times,* February 14, 2006, http://www.nytimes.com/2006/02/14/science/14conv.html?ex=1297573200&en=181770cea.

37 Tannen, "The Power of Talk: Who Gets Heard and Why," pp 147–48.

38 B Gates, "How I Work: 'Paper Isn't a Big Part of My Day'," *Fortune,* April 17, 2006, pp 45–46.

39 These statistics were obtained from "Kids' Lives 'Saturated' by Media, Study Says," *Arizona Republic,* March 10, 2005, p A7.

40 These statistics were obtained from "Internet World Statistics—The Big Picture: World Internet Users and Population Stats," March 31, 2006, http://www.internetworldstats.com/stats.htm, accessed June 1, 2006. Also see R O Crockett, "Why the Web Is Hitting a Wall," *BusinessWeek,* March 20, 2006, pp 90–92.

41 This result was presented in "On Any Given Day, About 40 Million Internet Users Go Online Just For Fun," *The Pew Charitable Trusts,*

February 2006, http://www.pewtrusts.org/ideas/ideas_item.cfm?content_item_id=3254&content_type_id=8.

42 These examples were discussed in D Caterinicchia, "University HR's Self-Service Solution," *HR Magazine,* February 2005, pp 105–9.

43 This statistic was reported in H Green, S Rosenbush, R O Crockett, and S Holmes, "Wi-Fi Means Business," *BusinessWeek,* April 28, 2003, pp 86–92.

44 Online training is discussed by L Bealko, "Running Effective Online Trainings," January 12, 2006, *Techsoup,* http://www.techsoup.org/howto/articles/training/page4245.cfm.

45 See M E Medland, "Time Squeeze," *HR Magazine,* November 2004, pp 66–70; and "X-Rated," *Training,* p 10.

46 See D Buss, "Spies Like Us," *Training,* December 2001, pp 44–48.

47 Results of the survey are presented in "Electronic Monitoring," www.nolo.com/lawcenter/ency/article.cfm/ObjectID/C1066E74-A5CA-4EE3-Acd2, June 20, 2004.

48 See B Grow, "The Mind Games Cybercrooks Play," *BusinessWeek,* April 17, 2006, pp 54, 58; and S E Ante and B Grow, "Meet the Hackers," *BusinessWeek,* May 29, 2006, pp 58–63.

49 Information security is discussed by M Tott, "The Dangers Within," *The Wall Street Journal,* February 13, 2006, pp R1, R4; and B Einhorn and B Elgin, "The Great Firewall of China," *BusinessWeek,* January 23, 2006, pp 32–34.

50 See "Making E-Mail Work Again—ClearContext 2005 E-mail Usage Survey Analysis," posted April 5, 2005, http://blog.clearcontext.com/2005/04/ making_email_wo.html, accessed May 6, 2005.

51 See B Hemphill, "File, Act, or Toss?" *Training & Development,* February 2001, pp 38–41.

52 See "Making E-Mail Work Again."

53 Results can be found in L Winerman, "E-Mails and Egos," *Monitor on Psychology,* February 2006, pp 16–17; and J Kruger, N Epley, J Parker, and Z-W Ng, "Egocentrism Over E-Mail: Can We Communicate As Well As We Think?" *Journal of Applied Psychology,* December 2005, pp 925–36.

54 This statistic was reported in E Chambers, "Web Watch: The Lid on Spam Is Still Loose," *BusinessWeek,* February 7, 2005, p 10.

55 Results can be found in M S Thompson and M S Feldman, "Electronic Mail and Organizational Communication: Does Saying 'Hi' Really Matter?" *Organization Science,* November/December 1998, pp 685–98.

56 See the related discussion in A Pomeroy, "Business 'Fast and Loose' with E-Mail, IMs—Study," *HR Magazine,* November 2004, pp 32, 34.

57 See descriptions in "Labor Notes: The Boss Is Watching—So Watch Your iPod," *BusinessWeek,* April 24, 2006, p 16; and "Podcast Popularity Grows," *Training,* April 2006, p 14.

58 Excerpted from M Conlin, "Take a Vacation from Your BlackBerry," *BusinessWeek,* December 20, 2004, p 56.

59 Excerpted from J Spencer, "The BlackBerry Squint: Growing PDA Use Hurts Eyes," *The Wall Street Journal,* April 25, 2006, p D1.

60 See Conlin, "Take a Vacation from Your BlackBerry."

61 These statistics were reported in J M Alterio, "IBM Taps into Blogosphere," *The Arizona Republic,* January 21, 2006, p D3.

62 Cell phone blogging is discussed by "The Son Rises at Qualcomm," *Fortune,* April 18, 2005, p 45. Also see D Kirkpatrick, "Sun Microsystems: It's Hard to Manage if You Don't Blog," *Fortune,* October 4, 2004, p 46; and A Lashinsky, *"Is This the Right Man for Intel?"* Fortune, April 18, 2005, pp 110–20.

63 See Alterio, "IBM Taps Into Blogosphere."

64 This example is discussed in "Firms Taking Action against Worker Blogs," *MSNBC News,* posted March 7, 2005, www.msnbc.msn.com/id/7116338, accessed March 7, 2005.

65 See J Gordon, "Straight Talk: Wasting Time on the Company Dime," *Training,* May 2006, p 6.

66 E Krell, "Videoconferencing Gets the Call," *Training,* December 2001, p 38.

67 Results can be found in S A Rains, "Leveling the Organizational Playing Field—Virtually: A Meta-Analysis of Experimental Research Assessing the Impact of Group Support System Use on Member Influence Behaviors," *Communication Research,* April 2005, pp 193–234.

68 See J Forster, "Virtual Call Centers Cyberagents on Rise," *The Arizona Republic,* March 4, 2006, p D3.

[69] Challenges associated with virtual operations are discussed by S O'Mahony and S R Barley, "Do Digital Telecommunications Affect Work and Organization? The State of Our Knowledge," in *Research in Organizational Behavior,* vol. 21, eds R I Sutton and B M Staw (Stamford, CT: JAI Press, 1999), pp 125–61.

[70] See M Naylor, "There's No Workforce Like Home," *BusinessWeek* Online, May 2, 2006, http://www.businessweek.com/print/technology/content/may2006/tc20060502_763202.htm.

[71] These statistics are reported in S Shellenbarger, "Outsourcing Jobs to the Den: Call Centers Tap People Who Want to Work at Home," *The Wall Street Journal,* January 12, 2006, p D1.

[72] See A Donoghue, "2010: The Year of the Techie," *ZDNet UK News,* May 13, 2006, http://news.zdnet.co.uk/business/o,39020645,39269493,00.htm.

[73] Supporting evidence can be found in B Hemphill, "Telecommuting Productively," *Occupational Health & Safety,* March 2004, pp 16, 18; R Konrad, "Sun's 'iWork' Shuns Desks for Flexibility," *Arizona Republic,* May 28, 2003, p D4; and C Hymowitz, "Remote Managers Find Ways to Narrow the Distance Gap," *The Wall Street Journal,* April 6, 1999, p B1.

[74] Excerpted from Yuri Kageyama, "Cellphones with Cameras Creating Trouble: Concerns Include Voyeurism," *Arizona Republic,* July 10, 2003, pp A18.

Chapter 13

[1] B Morris, "Star Power: Ursula Burns, Xerox," *Fortune,* February 6, 2006, p 57. Copyright © 2006 Time Inc. All rights reserved.

[2] See A Hanft, "Every Business Needs a Nanny," *Inc.,* March 2006, p 128.

[3] See D Kipnis, S M Schmidt, and J Wilkinson, "Intraorganizational Influence Tactics: Explorations in Getting One's Way," *Journal of Applied Psychology,* August 1980, pp 440–52. Also see C A Schriesheim and T R Hinkin, "Influence Tactics Used by Subordinates: A Theoretical and Empirical Analysis and Refinement of the Kipnis, Schmidt, and Wilkinson Subscales," *Journal of Applied Psychology,* June 1990, pp 246–57; and G Yukl and C M Falbe, "Influence Tactics and Objectives in Upward, Downward, and Lateral Influence Attempts," *Journal of Applied Psychology,* April 1990, pp 132–40.

[4] For more on humor, see C D Cooper, "Just Joking Around? Employee Humor Expression as an Ingratiatory Behavior," *Academy of Management Review,* October 2005, pp 765–76.

[5] Based on Table 1 in G Yukl, C M Falbe, and J Y Youn, "Patterns of Influence Behavior for Managers," *Group & Organization Management,* March 1993, pp 5–28. An additional influence tactic is presented in B P Davis and E S Knowles, "A Disrupt-then-Reframe Technique of Social Influence," *Journal of Personality and Social Psychology,* February 1999, pp 192–99. Also see Table 1 in P P Fu, T K Peng, J C Kennedy, and G Yukl, "Examining the Preferences of Influence Tactics in Chinese Societies: A Comparison of Chinese Managers in Hong Kong, Taiwan and Mainland China," *Organizational Dynamics,* no. 1, 2004, pp 32–46; and S Mellor, L A Barclay, C A Bulger, and L M Kath, "Augmenting the Effect of Verbal Persuasion on Self-Efficacy to Serve as a Steward: Gender Similarity in a Union Environment," *Journal of Occupational and Organizational Psychology,* March 2006, pp 121–29.

[6] For related reading, see K D Elsbach, "How to Pitch a Brilliant Idea," *Harvard Business Review,* September 2003, pp 117–23; "Daddy Dearest," *Inc.,* January 2004, p 46; K Hannon, "Working for the I-Boss," *USA Today,* March 1, 2004, p 5B; J Battelle, "The Net of Influence," *Business 2.0,* March 2004, p 70; B Barry and I S Fulmer, "The Medium and the Message: The Adaptive Use of Communication Media in Dyadic Influence," *Academy of Management Review,* April 2004, pp 272–92; D Jones, "Study Says Flirtatious Women Get Fewer Raises, Promotions," *USA Today,* August 5, 2005, p 6B; and C Bartz, "If You Think You Can't, You're Right," *Business 2.0,* December 2005, p 118.

[7] Based on discussion in G Yukl, H Kim, and C M Falbe, "Antecedents of Influence Outcomes," *Journal of Applied Psychology,* June 1996, pp 309–17.

[8] See R E Boyatzis, M L Smith, and N Blaize, "Developing Sustainable Leaders Through Coaching and Compassion," *Academy of Management Learning and Education,* March 2006, pp 8–24.

[9] C Tkaczyk, "Follow These Leaders," *Fortune,* December 12, 2005, p 125.

[10] Data from Yukl, Kim, and Falbe, "Antecedents of Influence Outcomes."

[11] Data from G Yukl and J B Tracey, "Consequences of Influence Tactics Used with Subordinates, Peers, and the Boss," *Journal of Applied Psychology,* August 1992, pp 525–35. Also see C M Falbe and G Yukl, "Consequences for Managers of Using Single Influence Tactics and Combinations of Tactics," *Academy of Management Journal,* August 1992, pp 638–52.

[12] Data from R A Gordon, "Impact of Ingratiation on Judgments and Evaluations: A Meta-Analytic Investigation," *Journal of Personality and Social Psychology,* July 1996, pp 54–70. Also see S J Wayne, R C Liden, and R T Sparrowe, "Developing Leader-Member Exchanges," *American Behavioral Scientist,* March 1994, pp 697–714; A Oldenburg, "These Days, Hostile Is Fitting for Takeovers Only," *USA Today,* July 22, 1996, pp 8B, 10B; and J H Dulebohn and G R Ferris, "The Role of Influence Tactics in Perceptions of Performance Evaluations' Fairness," *Academy of Management Journal,* June 1999, pp 288–303.

[13] Data from Yukl, Kim, and Falbe, "Antecedents of Influence Outcomes."

[14] Based on C Pornpitakpan, "The Persuasiveness of Source Credibility: A Critical Review of Five Decades' Evidence," *Journal of Applied Social Psychology,* February 2004, pp 243–81.

[15] Data from B J Tepper, R J Eisenbach, S L Kirby, and P W Potter, "Test of a Justice-Based Model of Subordinates' Resistance to Downward Influence Attempts," *Group & Organization Management,* June 1998, pp 144–60. Also see H G Enns and D B McFarlin, "When Executives Influence Peers: Does Function Matter?" *Human Resource Management,* Summer 2003, pp 125–42.

[16] Adapted from R B Cialdini, "Harnessing the Science of Persuasion," *Harvard Business Review,* October 2001, pp 72–79. Also see C Decker, "The 5 Paths to Persuasion," *Fast Company,* July 2004, p 92; D A Garvin and M A Roberto, "Change through Persuasion," *Harvard Business Review,* February 2005, pp 104–12; J Pfeffer, "Executive-in-Chief," *Business 2.0,* March 2005, p 62; I Mount, "The Great Persuader," *Inc.,* March 2005, pp 92–97; and J Pfeffer, "Breaking through Excuses," *Business 2.0,* May 2005, p 76.

[17] Cialdini, "Harnessing the Science of Persuasion," p 77. Also see K M Douglas and R M Sutton, "Right about Others, Wrong about Ourselves? Actual and Perceived Self–Other Differences in Resistance to Persuasion," *British Journal of Social Psychology,* December 2004, pp 585–603.

[18] See A Pomeroy, "Ethical Leaders Needed," *HR Magazine,* July 2005, p 16; A Pomeroy, "The Ethics Squeeze," *HR Magazine,* March 2006, pp 48–55; R A Caro, "Lessons in Power: Lyndon Johnson Revealed," *Harvard Business Review,* April 2006, pp 47–52; Editor, "Heights of Arrogance," *USA Today,* April 5, 2006, p 11A; and M Hosenball and E Thomas, "Hold the Phone: Big Brother Knows Whom You Call. Is That Legal, and Will It Help Catch the Bad Guys?" *Newsweek,* May 22, 2006, pp 22–32.

[19] D Tjosvold, "The Dynamics of Positive Power," *Training and Development Journal,* June 1984, p 72. Also see T A Stewart, "Get with the New Power Game," *Fortune,* January 13, 1997, pp 58–62.

[20] See J Welch and S Welch, "Tough Guys Finish First," *BusinessWeek,* April 24, 2006, p 112; and W B Werther, "From Manager to Executive," *Organizational Dynamics,* no. 2, 2006, pp 196–204.

[21] M W McCall, Jr, *Power, Influence, and Authority: The Hazards of Carrying a Sword,* Technical Report No. 10 (Greensboro, NC: Center for Creative Leadership, 1978), p 5. For an excellent overview of power, see E P Hollander and L R Offermann, "Power and Leadership in Organizations," *American Psychologist,* February 1990, pp 179–89.

[22] D Weimer, "Daughter Knows Best," *BusinessWeek,* April 19, 1999, pp 132, 134.

[23] See J R P French and B Raven, "The Bases of Social Power," in *Studies in Social Power,* ed D Cartwright (Ann Arbor: University of Michigan Press, 1959), pp 150–67. Also see C M Fiol, E J O'Connor, and H Aguinis, "All for One and One for All? The Development and Transfer of Power across Organizational Levels," *Academy of Management Review,* April 2001, pp 224–42.

[24] Excerpted from C Haddad, "Too Good to Be True," *BusinessWeek,* April 14, 2003, p 71. Also see C Dickey, "The Demise of the Don," *Newsweek,* April 24, 2006, p 40.

25 See S M Farmer and H Aguinis, "Accounting for Subordinate Perceptions of Supervisor Power: An Identity-Dependence Model," *Journal of Applied Psychology,* November 2005, pp 1069–83.

26 Data from J R Larson, Jr, C Christensen, A S Abbott, and T M Franz, "Diagnosing Groups: Charting the Flow of Information in Medical Decision-Making Teams," *Journal of Personality and Social Psychology,* August 1996, pp 315–30.

27 L Gerdes, "Revenge of the Bean Counters," *BusinessWeek,* October 10, 2005, p 16. Also see S Wagner and L Dittmar, "The Unexpected Benefits of Sarbanes-Oxley," *Harvard Business Review,* April 2006, pp 133–40; and J McGregor, "CFOs Sing the SarbOx Blues," *BusinessWeek,* May 29, 2006, p 11.

28 See D Jones, "Meeting a CEO's Spouse Can Affect Job, in a Good Way, or Bad," *USA Today,* August 29, 2005, pp 1B–2B; and D A Nadler, "Confessions of a Trusted Counselor," *Harvard Business Review,* September 2005, pp 68–77.

29 P M Podsakoff and C A Schriesheim, "Field Studies of French and Raven's Bases of Power: Critique, Reanalysis, and Suggestions for Future Research," *Psychological Bulletin,* May 1985, p 388. Also see M A Rahim and G F Buntzman, "Supervisory Power Bases, Styles of Handling Conflict with Subordinates, and Subordinate Compliance and Satisfaction," *Journal of Psychology,* March 1989, pp 195–210; D Tjosvold, "Power and Social Context in Superior-Subordinate Interaction," *Organizational Behavior and Human Decision Processes,* June 1985, pp 281–93; and C A Schriesheim, T R Hinkin, and P M Podsakoff, "Can Ipsative and Single-Item Measures Produce Erroneous Results in Field Studies of French and Raven's (1950) Five Bases of Power? An Empirical Investigation," *Journal of Applied Psychology,* February 1991, pp 106–14.

30 See T R Hinkin and C A Schriesheim, "Relationships between Subordinate Perceptions and Supervisor Influence Tactics and Attributed Bases of Supervisory Power," *Human Relations,* March 1990, pp 221–37. Also see D J Brass and M E Burkhardt, "Potential Power and Power Use: An Investigation of Structure and Behavior," *Academy of Management Journal,* June 1993, pp 441–70; and K W Mossholder, N Bennett, E R Kemery, and M A Wesolowski, "Relationships between Bases of Power and Work Reactions: The Mediational Role of Procedural Justice," *Journal of Management,* no. 4, 1998, pp 533–52.

31 See J A Clair, R DuFresne, N Jackson, and J Ladge, "Being the Bearer of Bad News: Challenges Facing Downsizing Agents in Organizations," *Organizational Dynamics,* no. 2, 2006, pp 131–44.

32 See C L Pearce and C C Manz, "The New Silver Bullets of Leadership: The Importance of Self- and Shared Leadership in Knowledge Work," *Organizational Dynamics,* no. 2, 2005, pp 130–40; R Adler, "Putting Sport into Organizations: The Role of the Accountant," *Business Horizons,* January/February 2006, pp 31–39; and H Dolezalek, "Working Smart," *Training,* April 2006, pp 40–44.

33 J Macdonald, "The Dreaded 'E Word,'" *Training,* September 1998, p 19. Also see R C Liden and S Arad, "A Power Perspective of Empowerment and Work Groups: Implications for Human Resources Management Research," in *Research in Personnel and Human Resources Management,* vol. 14, ed G R Ferris (Greenwich, CT: JAI Press, 1996), pp 205–51.

34 R M Hodgetts, "A Conversation with Steve Kerr," *Organizational Dynamics,* Spring 1996, p 71. See L Holp, "If Empowerment Is So Good, Why Does It Hurt?" *Training,* March 1995, pp 52–57; Liden and Arad, "A Power Perspective of Empowerment and Work Groups: Implications for Human Resources Management Research"; and G M Spreitzer, "Social Structural Characteristics of Psychological Empowerment," *Academy of Management Journal,* April 1996, pp 483–504.

35 L Shaper Walters, "A Leader Redefines Management," *The Christian Science Monitor,* September 22, 1992, p 14.

36 See S Zuboff, "Ranking Ourselves to Death," *Fast Company,* November 2004, p 125; and "Managing a Micromanager," *Inc.,* April 2005, p 50.

37 F Vogelstein, "Star Power: Greg Brown, Motorola," *Fortune,* February 6, 2006, p 57.

38 For recent research, see S H Wagner, C P Parker, and N D Christiansen, "Employees That Think and Act Like Owners: Effects of Ownership Beliefs and Behaviors on Organizational Effectiveness," *Personnel Psychology,* Winter 2003, pp 847–71; D J Leach, T D Wall, and P R Jackson, "The Effect of Empowerment on Job Knowledge: An Empirical Test Involving Operators of Complex Technology," *Journal of Occupational and Organizational Psychology,* March 2003, pp 27–52; P T Coleman, "Implicit Theories of Organizational Power and Priming Effects on Managerial Power-Sharing Decisions: An Experimental Study," *Journal of Applied Social Psychology,* February 2004, pp 297–321; B L Kirkman, B Rosen, P E Tesluk, and C B Gibson, "The Impact of Team Empowerment on Virtual Team Performance: The Moderating Role of Face-to-Face Interaction," *Academy of Management Journal,* April 2004, pp 175–92; and M Ahearne, J Mathieu, and A Rapp, "To Empower or Not to Empower Your Sales Force? An Empirical Examination of the Influence of Leadership Empowerment Behavior on Customer Satisfaction and Performance," *Journal of Applied Psychology,* September 2005, pp 945–55.

39 W A Randolph, "Navigating the Journey to Empowerment," *Organizational Dynamics,* Spring 1995, p 31.

40 See D Jones, "It's Nothing Personal? On 'Apprentice,' It's All Personal," *USA Today,* March 26, 2004, p 6B; and D Jones and B Keveney, "10 Lessons of *The Apprentice,*" *USA Today,* April 15, 2004, pp 1A–5A. Also see R Grover, "A Sizzling Family Food Fight," *BusinessWeek,* February 27, 2006, p 10; and "Quiz: Am I a Total Jerk?" *Fast Company,* May 2006, p 33.

41 C Pasternak, "Corporate Politics May Not Be a Waste of Time," *HR Magazine,* September 1994, p 18.

42 See J Sandberg, "From the Front Lines: Bosses Muster Staffs for Border Skirmishes," *The Wall Street Journal,* February 18, 2004, p B1; K Hannon, "Change the Way You Play: Small Things You Can Do to Get Ahead," *USA Today,* March 15, 2004, p 6B; G R Ferris, S L Davidson, and P L Perrewe, *Political Skill at Work* (Palo Also, CA: Davies-Black, 2005); and G Ferris, S Davidson, and P Perrewe, "Developing Political Skill at Work," *Training,* November 2005, pp 40–45.

43 R W Allen, D L Madison, L W Porter, P A Renwick, and B T Mayes, "Organizational Politics: Tactics and Characteristics of Its Actors," *California Management Review,* Fall 1979, p 77. Also see K M Kacmar and G R Ferris, "Politics at Work: Sharpening the Focus of Political Behavior in Organizations," *Business Horizons,* July/August 1993, pp 70–74. A comprehensive overview can be found in K M Kacmar and R A Baron, "Organizational Politics: The State of the Field, Links to Related Processes, and an Agenda for Future Research," in *Research in Personnel and Human Resources Management,* vol. 17, ed G R Ferris (Stamford, CT: JAI Press, 1999), pp 1–39.

44 See P M Fandt and G R Ferris, "The Management of Information and Impressions: When Employees Behave Opportunistically," *Organizational Behavior and Human Decision Processes,* February 1990, pp 140–58; L R Offermann, "When Followers Become Toxic," *Harvard Business Review,* Special Issue: Inside the Mind of the Leader, January 2004, pp 54–60; and K J Sulkowicz, "Worse than Enemies: The CEO's Destructive Confidant," *Harvard Business Review,* February 2004, pp 64–71.

45 First four based on discussion in D R Beeman and T W Sharkey, "The Use and Abuse of Corporate Politics," *Business Horizons,* March–April 1987, pp 26–30.

46 Quote and data from "The Big Picture: Reasons for Raises," *BusinessWeek,* May 29, 2006, p 11.

47 A Raia, "Power, Politics, and the Human Resource Professional," *Human Resource Planning,* no. 4, 1985, p 203.

48 A J DuBrin, "Career Maturity, Organizational Rank, and Political Behavioral Tendencies: A Correlational Analysis of Organizational Politics and Career Experience," *Psychological Reports,* October 1988, p 535.

49 This three-level distinction comes from A T Cobb, "Political Diagnosis: Applications in Organizational Development," *Academy of Management Review,* July 1986, pp 482–96. Also see L J Stybel and M Peabody, "Friend, Foe, Ally, Adversary . . . or Something Else?" *MIT Sloan Management Review,* Summer 2005, pp 13–16.

50 An excellent historical and theoretical perspective of coalitions can be found in W B Stevenson, J L Pearce, and L W Porter, "The Concept of 'Coalition' in Organization Theory and Research," *Academy of Management Review,* April 1985, pp 256–68. Also see A Kleiner, "Are You In with the In Crowd?" *Harvard Business Review,* July 2003, pp 86–92.

51 See B Uzzi and S Dunlap, "How to Build Your Network," *Harvard Business Review,* December 2005, pp 53–60.

52 J Sandberg, "Better Than Great—and Other Tall Tales of Self-Evaluations," *The Wall Street Journal,* March 12, 2003, p B1. Also see

J Sandberg, "Sabotage 101: The Sinister Art of Back-Stabbing," *The Wall Street Journal,* February 11, 2004, p B1.

[53] Allen, Madison, Porter, Renwick, and Mayes, "Organizational Politics: Tactics and Characteristics of Its Actors," p 77.

[54] See W L Gardner III, "Lessons in Organizational Dramaturgy: The Art of Impression Management," *Organizational Dynamics,* Summer 1992, pp 33–46.

[55] See G Brown, T B Lawrence, and S L Robinson, "Territoriality in Organizations," *Academy of Management Review,* July 2005, pp 577–94.

[56] A Rao, S M Schmidt, and L H Murray, "Upward Impression Management: Goals, Influence Strategies, and Consequences," *Human Relations,* February 1995, p 147. Also see M C Andrews and K M Kacmar, "Impression Management by Association: Construction and Validation of a Scale," *Journal of Vocational Behavior,* February 2001, pp 142–61; P F Hewlin, "And the Award for Best Actor Goes to . . . : Facades of Conformity in Organizational Settings," *Academy of Management Review,* October 2003, pp 633–42; and D Rosato, "The 'Oh, S#&%!' Moment," *Money,* February 2006, pp 126–30.

[57] See Z I Barsness, K A Diekmann, and M L Seidel, "Motivation and Opportunity: The Role of Remote Work, Demographic Dissimilarity, and Social Network Centrality in Impression Management," *Academy of Management Journal,* June 2005, pp 401–19; L M Roberts, "Changing Faces: Professional Image Construction in Diverse Organizational Settings," *Academy of Management Review,* October 2005, pp 685–711; L A McFarland, G Yun, C M Harold, L Viera Jr., and L G Moore, "An Examination of Impression Management Use and Effectiveness Across Assessment Center Exercises: The Role of Competency Demands," *Personnel Psychology,* Winter 2005, pp 949–80; and D R Avery and P F McKay, "Target Practice: An Organizational Impression Management Approach to Attracting Minority and Female Job Applicants," *Personnel Psychology,* Spring 2006, pp 157–87.

[58] S Friedman, "What Do You Really Care About? What Are You Most Interested In?" *Fast Company,* March 1999, p 90. Also see B M DePaulo and D A Kashy, "Everyday Lies in Close and Casual Relationships," *Journal of Personality and Social Psychology,* January 1998, pp 63–79.

[59] See S J Wayne and G R Ferris, "Influence Tactics, Affect, and Exchange Quality in Supervisor-Subordinate Interactions: A Laboratory Experiment and Field Study," *Journal of Applied Psychology,* October 1990, pp 487–99. For another version, see Table 1 (p 246) in S J Wayne and R C Liden, "Effects of Impression Management on Performance Ratings: A Longitudinal Study," *Academy of Management Journal,* February 1995, pp 232–60.

[60] See R Vonk, "The Slime Effect: Suspicion and Dislike of Likeable Behavior toward Superiors," *Journal of Personality and Social Psychology,* April 1998, pp 849–64; and M Wells, "How to Schmooze Like the Best of Them," *USA Today,* May 18, 1999, p 14E.

[61] See P Rosenfeld, R A Giacalone, and C A Riordan, "Impression Management Theory and Diversity: Lessons for Organizational Behavior," *American Behavioral Scientist,* March 1994, pp 601–4; R A Giacalone and J W Beard, "Impression Management, Diversity, and International Management," *American Behavioral Scientist,* March 1994, pp 621–36; and A Montagliani and R A Giacalone, "Impression Management and Cross-Cultural Adaptation," *Journal of Social Psychology,* October 1998, pp 598–608.

[62] M E Mendenhall and C Wiley, "Strangers in a Strange Land: The Relationship between Expatriate Adjustment and Impression Management," *American Behavioral Scientist,* March 1994, pp 605–20. Also see J Kurman, "Why Is Self-Enhancement Low in Certain Collectivist Cultures? An Investigation of Two Competing Explanations," *Journal of Cross-Cultural Psychology,* September 2003, pp 496–510.

[63] For a humorous discussion of making a bad impression, see P Hellman, "Looking BAD," *Management Review,* January 2000, p 64.

[64] T E Becker and S L Martin, "Trying to Look Bad at Work: Methods and Motives for Managing Poor Impressions in Organizations," *Academy of Management Journal,* February 1995, p 191.

[65] Ibid., p 181. Also see S L Grover, "The Truth, the Whole Truth, and Nothing But the Truth: The Causes and Management of Workplace Lying," *Academy of Management Executive,* May 2005, pp 148–57.

[66] Adapted from ibid., pp 180–81.

[67] Based on discussion in ibid., pp 192–93. Also see K J Harris and K M Kacmar, "Easing the Strain: The Buffer Role of Supervisors in the Perceptions of Politics-Strain Relationship," *Journal of Occupational and Organizational Psychology,* September 2005, pp 337–54; and R Goffee and G Jones, "Managing Authenticity: The Paradox of Great Leadership," *Harvard Business Review,* December 2005, pp 86–94.

[68] A Zaleznik, "Real Work," *Harvard Business Review* January/February 1989, p 60.

[69] C M Koen, Jr, and S M Crow, "Human Relations and Political Skills," *HR Focus,* December 1995, p 11.

[70] As quoted in B Morris, "The GE Mystique," *Fortune,* March 6, 2006, p 98. Also see the first Q&A in Jack Welch and Suzy Welch, "Knowing When to Fold 'Em," *BusinessWeek,* February 27, 2006, p 102; and the second Q&A in Jack Welch and Suzy Welch, "Is China for Everyone?" *BusinessWeek,* May 22, 2006, p 108. For recent research on the positive impact of feedback, see C C Rosen, P E Levy, and R J Hall, "Placing Perceptions of Politics in the Context of the Feedback Environment, Employee Attitudes, and Job Performance," *Journal of Applied Psychology,* January 2006, pp 211–20.

[71] Excerpted from D Gill, "Get Healthy . . . or Else," *Inc.,* April 2006, pp 35–37. Copyright © 2006 by Mansueto Ventures LLC. Reproduced with permission of Mansueto Ventures LLC via Copyright Clearance Center.

Chapter 14

[1] Excerpted from M D Hovanesian, "Rewiring Chuck Prince," *BusinessWeek,* February 20, 2006, pp 75–78.

[2] See S Lieberson and J F O'Connor, "Leadership and Organizational Performance: A Study of Large Corporations," *American Sociological Review,* April 1972, pp 117–30.

[3] Results can be found in K T Dirks, "Trust in Leadership and Team Performance: Evidence from NCAA Basketball," *Journal of Applied Psychology,* December 2000, pp 1004–12; and D Jacobs and L Singell, "Leadership and Organizational Performance: Isolating Links between Managers and Collective Success," *Social Science Research,* June 1993, pp 165–89.

[4] C A Schriesheim, J M Tolliver, and O C Behling, "Leadership Theory: Some Implications for Managers," *MSU Business Topics,* Summer 1978, p 35.

[5] The different levels of leadership are thoroughly discussed by F J Yammarino, F Dansereau, and C J Kennedy, "A Multiple-Level Multidimensional Approach to Leadership: Viewing Leadership through an Elephant's Eye," *Organizational Dynamics,* 2001, pp 149–62.

[6] B Kellerman, "Leadership Warts and All," *Harvard Business Review,* January 2004, p 45.

[7] See S Covey, "Why Is It Always About You?" *Training,* May 2006, p 64.

[8] See R Goffee and G Jones, "Followership: It's Personal, Too," *Harvard Business Review,* December 2001, p 148. The role of followers is also discussed in J M Howell and B Shamir, "The Role of Followers in the Charismatic Leadership Process: Relationships and Their Consequences," *Academy of Management Review,* January 2005, pp 96–112.

[9] See D A Kenny and S J Zaccaro, "An Estimate of Variance Due to Traits in Leadership," *Journal of Applied Psychology,* November 1983, pp 678–85.

[10] See J S Phillips and R G Lord, "Schematic Information Processing and Perceptions of Leadership in Problem-Solving Groups," *Journal of Applied Psychology,* August 1982, pp 486–92.

[11] Results from this study can be found in F C Brodbeck et al., "Cultural Variation of Leadership Prototypes across 22 European Countries," *Journal of Occupational and Organizational Psychology,* March 2000, pp 1–29. Also see M Javidan, P W Dorfman, M S de Lugue, and R J House, "In the Eye of the Beholder: Cross Cultural Lesson in Leadership from Project Globe," *Academy of Management Perspectives,* February 2006, pp 67–90.

[12] Results can be found in T A Judge, J E Bono, R Ilies, & M W Gerhardt, "Personality and Leadership: A Qualitative and Quantitative Review," *Journal of Applied Psychology,* August 2002, pp 765–80.

[13] See T A Judge, A E Colbert, and R Ilies, "Intelligence and Leadership: A Quantitative Review and Test of Theoretical Propositions," *Journal of Applied Psychology,* June 2004, pp 542–52.

[14] Supportive results can be found in S Xavier, "Are You at the Top of Your Game? Checklist for Effective Leaders," *Journal of Business Strategy*, 2005, pp 35–42.

[15] Political intelligence is discussed by R M Kramer, "The Great Intimidators," *Harvard Business Review*, February 2006, pp 88–96. An example can be found in J Ball, "The New Act at Exxon," *The Wall Street Journal*, March 8, 2006, pp B1, B2.

[16] Kramer, "The Great Intimidators," pp 95–96.

[17] Gender and the emergence of leaders was examined by A H Eagly and S J Karau, "Gender and the Emergence of Leaders: A Meta-Analysis," *Journal of Personality and Social Psychology*, May 1991, pp 685–710; and R K Shelly and P T Munroe, "Do Women Engage in Less Task Behavior than Men?" *Sociological Perspectives*, Spring 1999, pp 49–67.

[18] See A H Eagly, S J Karau, and B T Johnson, "Gender and Leadership Style among School Principals: A Meta-Analysis," *Educational Administration Quarterly*, February 1992, pp 76–102.

[19] Supportive findings are contained in J M Twenge, "Changes in Women's Assertiveness in Response to Status and Roles: A Cross-Temporal Meta-Analysis, 1931–1993," *Journal of Personality and Social Psychology*, July 2001, pp 133–45.

[20] For a summary of this research, see R Sharpe, "As Leaders, Women Rule," *BusinessWeek*, November 20, 2000, pp 74–84. Also see C Casaburi, "Avon, the New, and Glass Ceilings," *BusinessWeek*, February 6, 2006, p 104.

[21] The process of preparing a development plan is discussed by L Morgan, G Spreitzer, J Dutton, R Quinn, E Heaphy, and B Barker, "How to Play to Your Strengths," *Harvard Business Review*, January 2005, pp 75–80.

[22] Details on Hasbro's program can be found in A Pomeroy, "Head of the Class," *HR Magazine*, January 2005, pp 54–58. Leadership development is also discussed by J Durett, "GE Hones Its Leaders at Crotonville," *Training*, May 2006, pp 25–27; and K Lamoureux, "Wanted: Better Leaders," *Training*, May 2006, p 16

[23] Results can be found in T A Judge, R F Piccolo, and R Ilies, "The Forgotten Ones? The Validity of Consideration and Initiating Structure in Leadership Research," *Journal of Applied Psychology*, February 2004, pp 36–51.

[24] For corporate examples of leadership development see J Sandberg, "Trying to Tease Out My Leadership Talent in One Easy Seminar," *The Wall Street Journal*, March 28, 2006, p B1; J Sandberg, "The Sensitive Me Won't Be Leading Corporate America," *The Wall Street Journal*, April 11, 2006, p B1; and S Max, "Seagate's Morale-athon," *BusinessWeek*, April 3, 2006, p 110–12.

[25] See B M Bass, *Bass & Stogdill's Handbook of Leadership: Theory, Research, and Managerial Applications*, 3rd ed (New York: The Free Press, 1990), chs 20–25.

[26] The relationships between the frequency and mastery of leader behavior and various outcomes were investigated by F Shipper and C S White, "Mastery, Frequency, and Interaction of Managerial Behaviors Relative to Subunit Effectiveness," *Human Relations*, January 1999, pp 49–66.

[27] F E Fiedler, "Job Engineering for Effective Leadership: A New Approach," *Management Review*, September 1977, p 29.

[28] For more on this theory, see F E Fiedler, "A Contingency Model of Leadership Effectiveness," in *Advances in Experimental Social Psychology*, vol. 1, ed L Berkowitz (New York: Academic Press, 1964); F E Fiedler, *A Theory of Leadership Effectiveness* (New York: McGraw-Hill, 1967).

[29] See L H Peters, D D Hartke, and J T Pohlmann, "Fiedler's Contingency Theory of Leadership: An Application of the Meta-Analyses Procedures of Schmidt and Hunter," *Psychological Bulletin*, March 1985, pp 274–85; and C A Schriesheim, B J Tepper, and L A Tetrault, "Least Preferred Co-Worker Score, Situational Control, and Leadership Effectiveness: A Meta-Analysis of Contingency Model Performance Predictions," *Journal of Applied Psychology*, August 1994, pp 561–73.

[30] Excerpted from D Kirkpatrick, "Inside Sam's $100 Billion Growth Machine," *Fortune*, June 14, 2004, pp 86, 88. Also see B Groyberg, A N McLean, and N Nohria, "Are Leaders Portable?" *Harvard Business Review*, May 2006, pp 92–100.

[31] For more detail on this theory, see R J House, "A Path–Goal Theory of Leader Effectiveness," *Administrative Science Quarterly*, September 1971, pp 321–38.

[32] This research is summarized by R J House, "Path–Goal Theory of Leadership: Lessons, Legacy, and a Reformulated Theory," *Leadership Quarterly*, Autumn 1996, pp 323–52.

[33] See ibid.

[34] Examples can be found in K Brokker, "The Pepsi Machine," *Fortune*, February 6, 2006, pp 68–72; B Morris, "Star Power: Ursula Burns," *Fortune*, February 6, 2006, p 57; and P Burrows, "HP's Ultimate Team Player," *BusinessWeek*, January 30, 2006, pp 76–78.

[35] Excerpted from S Tully, "The Contender in This Corner: Jamie Dimon," *Fortune*, April 3, 2006, pp 56, 58.

[36] Results can be found in P M Podsakoff, S B MacKenzie, M Ahearne, and W H Bommer, "Searching for a Needle in a Haystack: Trying to Identify the Illusive Moderators of Leadership Behaviors," *Journal of Management*, 1995, pp 422–70. Also see S Yun, S Faraj, and H P Sims Jr, "Contingent Leadership and Effectiveness of Trauma Resuscitation Teams," *Journal of Applied Psychology*, November 2005, pp 1288–296.

[37] A thorough discussion of this theory is provided by P Hersey and K H Blanchard, *Management of Organizational Behavior: Utilizing Human Resources*, 5th ed (Englewood Cliffs, NJ: Prentice Hall, 1988).

[38] A comparison of the original theory and its latent version is provided by P Hersey and K H Blanchard, "Great Ideas Revisited," *Training & Development*, January 1996, pp 42–47.

[39] See D C Lueder, "Don't Be Misled by LEAD," *Journal of Applied Behavioral Science*, May 1985, pp 143–54; and C L Graeff, "The Situational Leadership Theory: A Critical View," *Academy of Management Review*, April 1983, pp 285–91.

[40] For a complete description of this theory see B J Bass and B J Avolio, *Revised Manual for the Multi-Factor Leadership Questionnaire* (Palo Alto, CA: Mindgarden, 1997).

[41] A definition and description of transactional leadership is provided by J Antonakis and R J House, "The Full-Range Leadership Theory: The Way Forward," in *Transformational and Charismatic Leadership: The Road Ahead*, eds B J Avolio and F J Yammarino (New York: JAI Press, 2002), pp 3–34.

[42] A Carter, "It's Norman Time," *BusinessWeek*, May 29, 2006, p 68.

[43] U R Dumdum, K B Lowe, and B J Avolio, "A Meta-Analysis of Transformational and Transactional Leadership Correlates of Effectiveness and Satisfaction: An Update and Extension," in *Transformational and Charismatic Leadership: The Road Ahead*, eds B J Avolio and F J Yammarino (New York: JAI Press, 2002), p 38.

[44] Supportive research is summarized by J Antonakis and R J House, "The Full-Range Leadership Theory: The Way Forward."

[45] Carter, "It's Norman Time," *BusinessWeek*, pp 65, 67.

[46] Supportive results can be found in R S Rubin, D C Munz, and W H Bommer, "Leading from Within: The Effects of Emotion Recognition and Personality on Transformational Leadership Behavior," *Academy of Management Journal*, October 2005, pp 845–58; and T A Judge and J E Bono, "Five-Factor Model of Personality and Transformational Leadership," *Journal of Applied Psychology*, October 2000, pp 751–65.

[47] These definitions are derived from R Kark, B Shamir, and C Chen, "The Two Faces of Transformational Leadership: Empowerment and Dependency," *Journal of Applied Psychology*, April 2003, pp 246–55. Also see A E Rafferty and M A Griffin, "Refining Individualized Consideration: Distinguishing Developmental Leadership and Supportive Leadership," *Journal of Occupational and Organizational Psychology*, March 2006, pp 37–61.

[48] B Nanus, *Visionary Leadership* (San Francisco: Jossey-Bass, 1992), p 8.

[49] W H Bulkeley, "Back from the Brink: Mulcahy Leads a Renaissance at Xerox by Emphasizing Color, Customers, and Costs," *The Wall Street Journal*, April 24, 2006, pp B1, B3.

[50] See R Kark, B Shamir, and G Chen, "The Two Faces of Transformational Leadership," *Journal of Applied Psychology*, April 2003, pp 246–55.

[51] Supportive results can be found in W H Bommer, G A Rich, and R S Rubin, "Changing Attitudes about Change: Longitudinal Effects of Transformational Leader Behavior on Employee Cynicism about Organizational Change," *Journal of Organizational Behavior*, November 2005, pp 733–53; B M Bass, B J Avolio, D I Jung, and Y Berson,

"Predicting Unit Performance by Assessing Transformational and Transactional Leadership," *Journal of Applied Psychology,* April 2003, pp 207–18; and J E Bono and T A Judge, "Self-Concordance at Work: Toward Understanding the Motivational Effects of Transformational Leaders," *Academy of Management Journal,* October 2003, pp 554–71.

⁵² Results can be found in U R Dumdum, K B Lowe, and B J Avolio, "A Meta-Analysis of Transformational and Transactional Leadership Correlates of Effectiveness and Satisfaction: An Update and Extension." Also see R T Keller, "Transformational Leadership, Initiating Structure, and Substitutes for Leadership: A Longitudinal Study of Research and Development Project Team Performance," *Journal of Applied Psychology,* January 2006, pp 202–10.

⁵³ See K B Lowe, K G Kroeck, and N Sivasubramaniam, "Effectiveness Correlates of Transformational and Transactional Leadership: A Meta-Analytic Review of the MLQ Literature," *Leadership Quarterly,* 1996, pp 385–425. Also see B R Agle, N J Nagarajan, J A Sonnenfeld, and D Srinivasan, "Does CEO Charisma Matter? An Empirical Analysis of the Relationship among Organizational Performance, Environmental Uncertainty, and Top Management Team Perceptions of CEO Charisma," *Academy of Management Journal,* February 2006, pp 161–74.

⁵⁴ See A J Towler, "Effects of Charismatic Influence Training on Attitudes, Behavior, and Performance," *Personnel Psychology,* Summer 2003, pp 363–81; and L A DeChurch and M A Marks, "Leadership in Multiteam Systems," *Journal of Applied Psychology,* March 2006, pp 311–29.

⁵⁵ Further suggestions and details are discussed in M Weinstein, "Out of the Blue," *Training,* April 2006, pp 22–27; D Robb, "Succeeding with Succession," *HR Magazine,* January 2006, pp 89–94.

⁵⁶ These recommendations were derived from J M Howell and B J Avolio, "The Ethics of Charismatic Leadership: Submission or Liberation," *The Executive,* May 1992, pp 43–54.

⁵⁷ See F Dansereau, Jr, G Graen, and W Haga, "A Vertical Dyad Linkage Approach to Leadership within Formal Organizations," *Organizational Behavior and Human Performance,* February 1975, pp 46–78; and R M Dienesch and R C Liden, "Leader–Member Exchange Model of Leadership: A Critique and Further Development," *Academy of Management Review,* July 1986, pp 618–34.

⁵⁸ These descriptions were taken from D Duchon, S G Green, and T D Taber, "Vertical Dyad Linkage: A Longitudinal Assessment of Antecedents, Measures, and Consequences," *Journal of Applied Psychology,* February 1986, pp 56–60.

⁵⁹ Supportive results can be found in T N Bauer, B Erodgan, R C Liden, and S J Wayne, "A Longitudinal Study of the Moderating Role of Extraversion: Leader-Member Exchange, Performance, and Turnover During New Executive Development," *Journal of Applied Psychology,* March 2006, pp 298–310; C A Schriesheim, S L Castro, and F J Yammarino, "Investigating Contingencies: An Examination of the Impact of Span of Supervision and Upward Controllingness on Leader–Member Exchange Using Traditional and Multivariate within— and between—Entities Analysis," *Journal of Applied Psychology,* October 2000, pp 659–77; and C Cogliser and C A Schriesheim, "Exploring Work Unit Context and Leader-Member Exchange: A Multi-Level Perspective," *Journal of Organizational Behavior,* August 2000, pp 487–511.

⁶⁰ A turnover study was conducted by G B Graen, R C Liden, and W Hoel, "Role of Leadership in the Employee Withdrawal Process," *Journal of Applied Psychology,* December 1982, pp 868–72. The career progress study was conducted by M Wakabayashi and G B Graen, "The Japanese Career Progress Study: A 7-Year Follow-Up," *Journal of Applied Psychology,* November 1984, pp 603–14.

⁶¹ See D O Adebayo and I B Udegbe, "Gender in the Boss-Subordinate Relationship: A Nigerian Study," *Journal of Organizational Behavior,* June 2004, pp 515–25.

⁶² Supportive results can be found in B Erdogan, R C Liden, and M L Kraimer, "Justice and Leader-Member Exchange: The Moderating Role of Organizational Culture," *Academy of Management Journal,* April 2006, pp 395–406; and K M Kacmar, L A Witt, S Zivnuska, and S M Gully, "The Interactive-Effect of Leader–Member Exchange and Communication Frequency on Performance Ratings," *Journal of Applied Psychology,* August 2003, pp 764–72.

⁶³ These recommendations were derived from G C Mage, "Leading Despite Your Boss," *HR Magazine,* September 2003, pp 139–44.

⁶⁴ R J House and R N Aditya, "The Social Scientific Study of Leadership: Quo Vadis?" *Journal of Management,* 1997, p 457.

⁶⁵ A thorough discussion of shared leadership is provided by C L Pearce, "The Future of Leadership: Combining Vertical and Shared Leadership to Transform Knowledge Work," *Academy of Management Executive,* February 2004, pp 47–57.

⁶⁶ M Levy, "Coaching Success Boils Down to Three Traits," *USA Today,* November 2, 2005, p 6C.

⁶⁷ This research is summarized in B J Avolio, J J Soskik, D I Jung, and Y Berson, "Leadership Models, Methods, and Applications," in *Handbook of Psychology,* eds W C Borman, D R Ilgen, R J Klimoski (Hobohen, NJ: John Wiley & Sons, 2003), vol 12, pp 277–307.

⁶⁸ An overall summary of servant-leadership is provided by L C Spears, *Reflections on Leadership: How Robert K Greenleaf's Theory of Servant-Leadership Influenced Today's Top Management Thinkers* (New York: John Wiley & Sons, 1995).

⁶⁹ Excerpted from H Kim and S Bannan, "The Best Business Leaders," *The Arizona Republic,* March 16, 2006, p D3.

⁷⁰ J Stuart, *Fast Company,* September 1999, p 114.

⁷¹ See J Collins, *Good to Great* (New York: Harper Business, 2001).

⁷² J Collins, "Level 5 Leadership," *Harvard Business Review,* p 68.

⁷³ See J Collins, *Good to Great.*

Chapter 15

¹ Excerpted from J Useem, "Should We Admire Wal-Mart?" *Fortune,* March 8, 2004, pp 118, 120. Also see M Maier, "How to Beat Wal-Mart," *Business 2.0,* May 2005, pp 108–114; J Welch and S Welch, "What's Right About Wal-Mart," *BusinessWeek,* May 1, 2006, p 112; J Elliott, "Wal-Mart Must Wait," *Fortune,* May 29, 2006, pp 37–40.

² See K H Hammonds, "We, Incorporated," *Fast Company,* July 2004, pp 87–89.

³ C I Barnard, *The Functions of the Executive* (Cambridge, MA: Harvard University Press, 1938), p 73.

⁴ Drawn from E H Schein, *Organizational Psychology,* 3rd ed (Englewood Cliffs, NJ: Prentice Hall, 1980), pp 12–15.

⁵ For related reading, see N Bennett and S A Miles, "Second in Command: The Misunderstood Role of the Chief Operating Officer," *Harvard Business Review,* May 2006, pp 71–78.

⁶ For an interesting historical perspective of hierarchy, see P Miller and T O'Leary, "Hierarchies and American Ideals, 1900–1940," *Academy of Management Review,* April 1989, pp 250–65. Also see H J Leavitt, "Why Hierarchies Thrive," *Harvard Business Review,* March 2003, pp 96–102.

⁷ For an excellent overview of the span of control concept, see D D Van Fleet and A G Bedeian, "A History of the Span of Management," *Academy of Management Review,* July 1977, pp 356–72. Also see E E Lawler III and J R Galbraith, "New Roles for the Staff: Strategic Support and Service," in *Organizing for the Future: The New Logic for Managing Complex Organizations,* eds J R Galbraith, E E Lawler III, and Associates (San Francisco: Jossey-Bass, 1993), pp 65–83.

⁸ M Koslowsky, "Staff/Line Distinctions in Job and Organizational Commitment," *Journal of Occupational Psychology,* June 1990, pp 167–73.

⁹ For an illustrative management-related metaphor, see J E Beatty, "Grades as Money and the Role of the Market Metaphor in Management Education," *Academy of Management Learning and Education,* June 2004, pp 187–96. Also see C Oswick and P Jones, "Beyond Correspondence? Metaphor in Organization Theory," *Academy of Management Review,* April 2006, pp 483–85; and J Cornelissen, "Metaphor in Organization Theory: Progress and the Past," *Academy of Management Review,* April 2006, pp 485–88.

¹⁰ K S Cameron, "Effectiveness as Paradox: Consensus and Conflict in Conceptions of Organizational Effectiveness," *Management Science,* May 1986, pp 540–41. Also see S Sackmann, "The Role of Metaphors in Organization Transformation," *Human Relations,* June 1989, pp 463–84; and H Tsoukas, "The Missing Link: A Transformational View of Metaphors in Organizational Science," *Academy of Management Review,* July 1991, pp 566–85.

[11] See W R Scott, "The Mandate Is Still Being Honored: In Defense of Weber's Disciples," *Administrative Science Quarterly,* March 1996, pp 163–71. Also see D Jones, "Military a Model for Execs," *USA Today,* June 9, 2004, p 4B.

[12] Based on M Weber, *The Theory of Social and Economic Organization,* translated by A M Henderson and T Parsons (New York: Oxford University Press, 1947). An instructive analysis of the mistranslation of Weber's work may be found in R M Weiss, "Weber on Bureaucracy: Management Consultant or Political Theorist?" *Academy of Management Review,* April 1983, pp 242–48.

[13] For a critical appraisal of bureaucracy, see R P Hummel, *The Bureaucratic Experience,* 3rd ed (New York: St. Martin's Press, 1987). The positive side of bureaucracy is presented in C T Goodsell, *The Case for Bureaucracy: A Public Administration Polemic* (Chatham, NJ: Chatham House Publishers, 1983).

[14] See G Pinchot and E Pinchot, "Beyond Bureaucracy," *Business Ethics,* March–April 1994, pp 26–29; and O Harari, "Let the Computers Be the Bureaucrats," *Management Review,* September 1996, pp 57–60.

[15] For examples of what managers are doing to counteract bureaucratic tendencies, see B Dumaine, "The Bureaucracy Busters, " *Fortune,* June 17, 1991, pp 36–50; and C J Cantoni, "Eliminating Bureaucracy— Roots and All," *Management Review,* December 1993, pp 30–33.

[16] A management-oriented discussion of general systems theory—an interdisciplinary attempt to integrate the various fragmented sciences— may be found in K E Boulding, "General Systems Theory—The Skeleton of Science," *Management Science,* April 1956, pp 197–208.

[17] J D Thompson, *Organizations in Action* (New York: McGraw-Hill, 1967), pp 6–7. Also see A C Bluedorn, "The Thompson Interdependence Demonstration," *Journal of Management Education,* November 1993, pp 505–9.

[18] For interesting updates on the biological systems metaphor, see A M Webber, "How Business Is a Lot Like Life," *Fast Company,* April 2001, pp 130–36; E Bonabeau and C Meyer, "Swarm Intelligence: A Whole New Way to Think about Business," *Harvard Business Review,* May 2001, pp 106–14; and R Adner, "Match Your Innovation Strategy to Your Innovation Ecosystem," *Harvard Business Review,* April 2006, pp 98–107.

[19] R L Daft and K E Weick, "Toward a Model of Organizations as Interpretation Systems," *Academy of Management Review,* April 1984, p 293. Also see J Reingold, "My (Long) Day at the Top," *Fast Company,* June 2006, pp 64–66.

[20] See M Crossan, "Altering Theories of Learning and Action: An Interview with Chris Argyris," *Academy of Management Executive,* May 2003, pp 40–46; D Gray, "Wanted: Chief Ignorance Officer," *Harvard Business Review,* November 2003, pp 22, 24; and G T M Hult, D J Ketchen, Jr, and S F Slater, "Information Processing, Knowledge Development, and Strategic Supply Chain Performance," *Academy of Management Journal,* April 2004, pp 241–253.

[21] For good background reading, see the entire Autumn 1998 issue of *Organizational Dynamics;* D Lei, J W Slocum, and R A Pitts, "Designing Organizations for Competitive Advantage: The Power of Unlearning and Learning," *Organizational Dynamics,* Winter 1999, pp 24–38; L Baird, P Holland, and S Deacon, "Learning from Action: Imbedding More Learning into the Performance Fast Enough to Make a Difference," *Organizational Dynamics,* Spring 1999, pp 19–32; "Leading-Edge Learning: Two Views," *Training & Development,* March 1999, pp 40–42; and A M Webber, "Learning for a Change," *Fast Company,* May 1999, pp 178–88.

[22] Data from www.greatharvest.com, May 29, 2006.

[23] Excerpted from M Hopkins, "Zen and the Art of the Self-Managing Company," *Inc.,* November 2000, pp 56, 58.

[24] K Cameron, "Critical Questions in Assessing Organizational Effectiveness," *Organizational Dynamics,* Autumn 1980, p 70. Also see T D Wall, J Michie, M Patterson, S J Wood, M Sheehan, C W Clegg, and M West, "On the Validity of Subjective Measures of Company Performance," *Personnel Psychology,* Spring 2004, pp 95–118; W F Joyce, "What Really Works: Building the 4 + 2 Organization," *Organizational Dynamics,* no. 2, 2005, pp 118–29; and J Kirby, "Toward a Theory of High Performance," *Harvard Business Review,* July–August 2005, pp 30–39.

[25] See G H Seijts, G P Latham, K Tasa, and B W Latham, "Goal Setting and Goal Orientation: An Integration of Two Different yet Related Literatures," *Academy of Management Journal,* April 2004, pp 227–39.

[26] For discussion of a very goal-oriented company, see "What Makes GE Great?" *Fortune,* March 6, 2006, pp 90–96.

[27] See, for example, R O Brinkerhoff and D E Dressler, *Productivity Measurement: A Guide for Managers and Evaluators* (Newbury Park, CA: Sage Publications, 1990); and D Jones and B Hansen, "Productivity Gains Roll at Their Fastest Clip in 31 Years," *USA Today,* June 14, 2004, pp 1B–2B.

[28] See S Baker, "Wiser about the Web," *BusinessWeek,* March 27, 2006, pp 54–58; S Levy and B Stone, "The New Wisdom of the Web," *Newsweek,* April 3, 2006, pp 46–53; and A Lashinsky, "The Boom Is Back," *Fortune,* May 1, 2006, pp 70–87.

[29] Data from M Maynard, "Toyota Promises Custom Order in 5 Days," *USA Today,* August 6, 1999, p 1B.

[30] "Interview: M Scott Peck," *Business Ethics,* March/April 1994, p 17. Also see C B Gibson and J Birkinshaw, "The Antecedents, Consequences, and Mediating Role of Organizational Ambidexterity," *Academy of Management Journal,* April 2004, pp 209–26.

[31] See P Puranam, H Singh, and M Zollo, "Organizing for Innovation: Managing the Coordination-Autonomy Dilemma in Technology Acquisitions," *Academy of Management Journal,* April 2006, pp 263–80; R E Herzlinger, "Why Innovation in Health Care Is So Hard," *Harvard Business Review,* May 2006, pp 58–66; and D L Laurie, Y L Doz, and C P Sheer, "Creating New Growth Platforms," *Harvard Business Review,* May 2006, pp 80–90.

[32] Cameron, "Critical Questions in Assessing Organizational Effectiveness," p 67. Also see W Buxton, "Growth from Top to Bottom," *Management Review,* July/August 1999, p 11.

[33] See R K Mitchell, B R Agle, and D J Wood, "Toward a Theory of Stakeholder Identification and Salience: Defining the Principle of Who and What Really Counts," *Academy of Management Review,* October 1997, pp 853–96; T J Rowley and M Moldoveanu, "When Will Stakeholder Groups Act? An Interest- and Identity-Based Model of Stakeholder Group Mobilization," *Academy of Management Review,* April 2003, pp 204–19; G Kassinis and N Vafeas, "Stakeholder Pressures and Environmental Performance," *Academy of Management Journal,* February 2006, pp 145–59; and N A Gardberg and C J Fombrun, "Corporate Citizenship: Creating Intangible Assets across Institutional Environments," *Academy of Management Review,* April 2006, pp 329–46.

[34] S B Shepard, "Steve Ballmer on Microsoft's Future," *BusinessWeek,* December 1, 2003, p 72. See J Greene, "A Rendezvous with Microsoft's Deep Throat," *BusinessWeek,* September 26, 2005, p 104; and D Kirkpatrick, "Microsoft's New Brain," *Fortune,* May 1, 2006, pp 56–68.

[35] See J Welch and S Welch, "How Healthy Is Your Company?" *BusinessWeek,* May 8, 2006, p 126.

[36] M Der Hovanesian, "Dimon's Grand Design," *BusinessWeek,* March 28, 2005, p 98.

[37] K S Cameron, "Effectiveness as Paradox: Consensus and Conflict in Conceptions of Organizational Effectiveness," *Management Science,* May 1986, p 542.

[38] Alternative effectiveness criteria are discussed in ibid.; A G Bedeian, "Organization Theory: Current Controversies, Issues, and Directions," in *International Review of Industrial and Organizational Psychology,* eds C L Cooper and I T Robertson (New York: John Wiley & Sons, 1987), pp 1–33; and M Keeley, "Impartiality and Participant-Interest Theories of Organizational Effectiveness," *Administrative Science Quarterly,* March 1984, pp 1–25.

[39] For updates, see M Goold and A Campbell, "Do You Have a Well-Designed Organization?" *Harvard Business Review,* March 2002, pp 117–24; and J A A Sillince, "A Contingency Theory of Rhetorical Congruence," *Academy of Management Review,* July 2005, pp 608–21.

[40] B Elgin, "Running the Tightest Ships on the Net," *BusinessWeek,* January 29, 2001, p 126.

[41] For the complete article, see B Grow, "Renovating Home Depot," *BusinessWeek,* March 6, 2006, pp 50–58.

[42] See D A Morand, "The Role of Behavioral Formality and Informality in the Enactment of Bureaucratic versus Organic Organizations," *Academy of Management Review,* October 1995, pp 831–72.

[43] See F Shipper and C C Manz, "Employee Self-Management without Formally Designated Teams: An Alternative Road to Empowerment,"

Organizational Dynamics, Winter 1992, pp 48–61; and A Deutschman, "The Fabric of Creativity," *Fast Company,* December 2004, pp 54–62.

⁴⁴ See G P Huber, C C Miller, and W H Glick, "Developing More Encompassing Theories about Organizations: The Centralization-Effectiveness Relationship as an Example," *Organization Science,* no. 1, 1990, pp 11–40; and C Handy, "Balancing Corporate Power: A New Federalist Paper," *Harvard Business Review,* November/December 1992, pp 59–72. Also see A Slywotzky and D Nadler, "The Strategy Is the Structure," *Harvard Business Review,* February 2004, p 16; and N Gull, "Managing on the Front Lines," *Inc.,* May 2004, p 24.

⁴⁵ Excerpted from P Coy, "More Than One Way to Build a Home," *BusinessWeek,* April 3, 2006, p 74.

⁴⁶ P Kaestle, "A New Rationale for Organizational Structure," *Planning Review,* July/August 1990, p 22. For examples, see N McKinstry, "Changing Direction," *Fortune,* November 14, 2005, p 153; A A King, M J Lenox, and A Terlaak, "The Strategic Use of Decentralized Institutions: Exploring Certification with the ISO 14001 Management Standard," *Academy of Management Journal,* December 2005, pp 1091-1106; and A Barrett, "J&J: Reinventing How It Invents," *BusinessWeek,* April 17, 2006, pp 60–61.

⁴⁷ Details of this study can be found in T Burns and G M Stalker, *The Management of Innovation* (London: Tavistock, 1961). Also see W D Sine, H Mitsuhashi, and D A Kirsch, "Revisiting Burns and Stalker: Formal Structure and New Venture Performance in Emerging Economic Sectors," *Academy of Management Journal,* February 2006, pp 121–32; and N Nohria, "Survival of the Adaptive," *Harvard Business Review,* May 2006, p 23.

⁴⁸ D J Gillen and S J Carroll, "Relationship of Managerial Ability to Unit Effectiveness in More Organic versus More Mechanistic Departments," *Journal of Management Studies,* November 1985, pp 674–75.

⁴⁹ J D Sherman and H L Smith, "The Influence of Organizational Structure on Intrinsic versus Extrinsic Motivation," *Academy of Management Journal,* December 1984, p 883.

⁵⁰ See J A Courtright, G T Fairhurst, and L E Rogers, "Interaction Patterns in Organic and Mechanistic Systems," *Academy of Management Journal,* December 1989, pp 773–802.

⁵¹ See J R Galbraith and E E Lawler III, "Effective Organizations: Using the New Logic of Organizing," in J R Galbraith, E E Lawler III, and Associates, eds, *Organizing for the Future: The New Logic for Managing Complex Organizations* (San Francisco: Jossey-Bass, 1993), pp 285–99.

⁵² See Y Shin, "A Person-Environment Fit Model for Virtual Organizations," *Journal of Management,* no. 5, 2004, pp 725–43; D Roth, "The Amazing Rise of the Do-It-Yourself Economy," *Fortune,* May 30, 2005, pp 43, 46; M V Copeland and A Tilin, "The New Instant Companies," *Business 2.0,* June 2005, pp 82–94; J Des Jardins, "The Wisdom of Crowds," *Fast Company,* December 2005, pp 35–36; D Brady, "Geography Is So Twentieth Century," *BusinessWeek,* December 19, 2005, pp 74–75; and R D Hof, "It's Not All Fun and Games," *BusinessWeek,* May 1, 2006, pp 76–77.

⁵³ "David Neeleman, JetBlue," *BusinessWeek,* September 29, 2003, p 124.

⁵⁴ J Hopkins, "Other Nations Zip by USA in High-Speed Net Race," *USA Today,* January 19, 2004, p 2B. See P Engardio, "The Future of Outsourcing," *BusinessWeek,* January 30, 2006, pp 50–58; L Buchanan, "The Thinking Man's Outsourcing," *Inc.,* May 2006, pp 31–33; and B Helm, "Life on the Web's Factory Floor," *BusinessWeek,* May 22, 2006, pp 70–71.

⁵⁵ For interesting reading, see A Kamenetz, "The Network Unbound," *Fast Company,* June 2006, pp 68–73.

⁵⁶ See B J Avolio and S S Kahai, "Adding the 'E' to E-Leadership: How It May Impact Your Leadership," *Organizational Dynamics,* no 4, 2003, pp 325–38; and S Parise and A Casher, "Alliance Portfolios: Designing and Managing Your Network of Business-Partner Relationships," *Academy of Management Executive,* November 2003, pp 25–39. A good update on trust is R Zemke, "The Confidence Crisis," *Training,* June 2004, pp 22–30.

⁵⁷ C Handy, *The Hungry Spirit: Beyond Capitalism—A Quest for Purpose in the Modern World* (New York: Broadway Books, 1998), p 186. (Emphasis added.)

⁵⁸ See B Lessard and S Baldwin, *NetSlaves: True Tales of Working the Web* (New York: McGraw-Hill, 2000).

⁵⁹ See M Arndt, "Trade Winds: Made in Wherever," *BusinessWeek,* May 31, 2004, p 14; J E Garten, "Offshoring: You Ain't Seen Nothin' Yet,"

Business Week, June 21, 2004, p 28; and S Hamm, "Services," *BusinessWeek,* June 21, 2004, pp 82–83.

⁶⁰ See A R Winger, "Face-to-Face Communication: Is It Really Necessary in a Digitizing World?" *Business Horizons,* May/June 2005, pp 247–53; and D Ernst and J Bamford, "Your Alliances Are Too Stable," *Harvard Business Review,* June 2005, pp 133–41.

⁶¹ Excerpted from R Richmond, "It's 10 A.M.: Do You Know Where Your Workers Are?" *The Wall Street Journal,* Eastern Edition, January 12, 2004, pp R1, R4. Copyright © 2006 by Dow Jones & Co. Inc. Reproduced with permission of Dow Jones & Co. Inc. via Copyright Clearance Center.

Chapter 16

¹ Excerpted from C Edwards, "Inside Intel," *BusinessWeek,* January 9, 2006, pp 47–50.

² A M Webber, "Learning for a Change," *Fast Company,* May 1999, p 180.

³ Excerpted from M L Alch, "Get Ready for the Net Generation," *Training & Development,* February 2000, pp 32, 34.

⁴ D Kirkpatrick, "Microsoft's New Brain," *Fortune,* May 1, 2006, p 59.

⁵ N D Schwartz, ". . . Is Also a Big Target," *Fortune,* April 17, 2006, p 87.

⁶ See J Mero and M Boyle, "Star Power: Eduardo Castro-Wright," *Fortune,* February 6, 2006, p 58.

⁷ Productivity in the service industry is discussed by S Hamm, S E Ante, A Reinhardt, and M Kripalani, "Services," *BusinessWeek,* June 21, 2004, pp 82–83.

⁸ For an example, see M Langley, "Driving Force: Newest Director Shakes Up GM with Calls for Radical Change," *The Wall Street Journal,* March 20, 2006, pp A1, A15.

⁹ This example is discussed in C Daniels, "Meet Mr. Nuke," *Fortune,* May 15, 2006, p 140–46.

¹⁰ For a thorough discussion of the model, see K Lewin, *Field Theory in Social Science* (New York: Harper & Row, 1951).

¹¹ This example was derived from P-W Tam, "System Reboot: Hurd's Big Challenge at HP: Overhauling Corporate Sales," *The Wall Street Journal,* April 3, 2006, pp A1, A3; and A Lashinsky, "The Hurd Way," *Fortune,* April 17, 2006, pp 92–102.

¹² C Goldwasser, "Benchmarking: People Make the Process," *Management Review,* June 1995, p 40.

¹³ See T A Stewart, "Architects of Change," *Harvard Business Review,* April 2006, p 10.

¹⁴ A thorough discussion of the target elements of change can be found in M Beer and B Spector, "Organizational Diagnosis: Its Role in Organizational Learning," *Journal of Counseling & Development,* July/August 1993, pp 642–50.

¹⁵ Details of this example can be found in S Tully, "The Contender: In This Corner Jamie Dimon," *Fortune,* April 3, 2006, pp 54–66; and M D Hovanesian, "Dimon's Grand Design," *BusinessWeek,* March 28, 2005, pp 96–99.

¹⁶ Organizational diagnosis is discussed by S E Ante, "The Science of Desire," *BusinessWeek,* June 5, 2006, pp 98–106.

¹⁷ These errors are discussed by J P Kotter, "Leading Change: The Eight Steps to Transformation," in *The Leader's Change Handbook,* eds J A Conger, G M Spreitzer, and E E Lawler III (San Francisco: Jossey-Bass, 1999), pp 87–99.

¹⁸ F Ostroff, "Change Management in Government," *Harvard Business Review,* May 2006, pp 141–47.

¹⁹ P G Hanson and B Lubin, "Answers to Questions Frequently Asked about Organization Development," in *The Emerging Practice of Organization Development,* ed W Sikes, A Drexter, and J Grant (Alexandria, VA: NTL Institute, 1989), p 16.

²⁰ Different stage-based models of OD are discussed by R A Gallagher, "What Is OD?" www.orgdct.com/what_is_od.htm, accessed May 12, 2005.

²¹ The stages of OD are discussed by R Cacioppe and M Edwards, "Seeking the Holy Grail of Organizational Development: A Synthesis of Integral Theory, Spiral Dynamics, Corporate Transformation and Action Inquiry," *Leadership and Organization Development Journal,* no. 2, 2005, pp 86–105.

²² W W Burke, *Organization Development: A Normative View* (Reading, MA: Addison-Wesley, 1987), p 9.

23 See R Rodgers, J E Hunter, and D L Rogers, "Influence of Top Management Commitment on Management Program Success," *Journal of Applied Psychology,* February 1993, pp 151–55.

24 Results can be found in P J Robertson, D R Roberts, and J I Porras, "Dynamics of Planned Organizational Change: Assessing Empirical Support for a Theoretical Model," *Academy of Management Journal,* June 1993, pp 619–34.

25 Results from the meta-analysis can be found in G A Neuman, J E Edwards, and N S Raju, "Organizational Development Interventions: A Meta-Analysis of Their Effects on Satisfaction and Other Attitudes," *Personnel Psychology,* Autumn 1989, pp 461–90.

26 Results can be found in C-M Lau and H-Y Ngo, "Organization Development and Firm Performance: A Comparison of Multinational and Local Firms," *Journal of International Business Studies,* First Quarter 2001, pp 95–114.

27 Adapted in part from B W Armentrout, "Have Your Plans for Change Had a Change of Plan?" *HRFOCUS,* January 1996, p 19; and A S Judson, *Changing Behavior in Organizations: Minimizing Resistance to Change* (Cambridge, MA: Blackwell, 1991).

28 An individual's predisposition to change was investigated by C R Wanberg and J T Banas, "Predictors and Outcomes of Openness to Changes in a Reorganizing Workplace," *Journal of Applied Psychology,* February 2000, pp 132–42.

29 G Chon, K Maher, and C Dade, "On Plant Assembly Lines and At Kitchen Tables, Worry About the Future," *The Wall Street Journal,* March 23, 2006, p A1. Also see "GM, The UAW and Delphi Reach Agreement on Accelerated Attrition Program," *GM Media Online,* March 22, 2006, http://media.gm.com/servlet/GatewayServlet?target=http://image. emerald. gm.com/gmnews/

30 B Morris, "Coke Gets a Jolt," *Fortune,* May 15, 2006, pp 77–78.

31 Readiness for change is discussed by S R Madsen, "Wellness in the Workplace: Preparing Employees for Change," *Organization Development Journal,* Spring 2003, pp 46–56.

32 See D B Fedor, S Caldwell, and D M Herold, "The Effects of Organizational Changes on Employee Commitment: A Multilevel Investigation," *Personnel Psychology,* Spring 2006, pp 1–29.

33 L Herscovitch and J P Meyer, "Commitment to Organizational Change: Extension of a Three-Component Model," *Journal of Applied Psychology,* June 2003, p 475.

34 See R Charan, "Home Depot's Blueprint for Culture Change," *Harvard Business Review,* April 2006, pp 61–70.

35 See K L Turner and M V Makhija, "The Role of Organizational Controls in Managing Knowledge," *Academy of Management Review,* January 2006, pp 197–217.

36 S Reynolds Fisher and M A White, "Downsizing in a Learning Organization: Are There Hidden Costs?" *Academy of Management Review,* January 2000, p 245.

37 R M Fulmer and J B Keys, "A Conversation with Peter Senge: New Development in Organizational Learning," *Organizational Dynamics,* Autumn 1998, p 35.

38 A results-oriented approach to learning is discussed by M Crossan, "Alternating Theories of Learning and Action: An Interview with Chris Argyris," *Academy of Management Executive,* May 2003, pp 40–46.

39 A J DiBella, E C Nevis, and J M Gould, "Organizational Learning Style as a Core Capability," in *Organizational Learning and Competitive Advantage,* eds B Moingeon and A Edmondson (Thousand Oaks, CA: Sage, 1996), pp 41–42.

40 Results can be found in P A Salz, "High Performance: Intelligent Use of Information Is a Powerful Corporate Tool," *The Wall Street Journal,* April 27, 2006, p A10.

41 For more information on analytics see T H Davenport, "Competing on Analytics," *Harvard Business Review,* January 2006, pp 99–108; and J Pfeffer and R I Sutton, "Evidence-Based Management," *Harvard Business Review,* January 2006, pp 63–74.

42 The impact of organizational culture on organizational learning was demonstrated by A Jashapara, "Cognition, Culture and Competition: An Empirical Test of the Learning Organization," *The Learning Organization,* 2003, pp 31–50.

43 Excerpted from V D Infante, "Men's Wearhouse: Tailored for Any Change That Retail Brings," *Workforce,* March 2001, p 48.

44 This discussion and definitions are based on D Miller, "A Preliminary Typology of Organizational Learning: Synthesizing the Literature," *Journal of Management,* 1996, pp 485–505.

45 The role of leadership in organizational learning is thoroughly discussed by D Vera and M Crossan, "Strategic Leadership and Organizational Learning," *Academy of Management Review,* April 2004, pp 222–40.

46 This discussion is based in part on D Ulrich, T Jick, and M Von Glinow, "High-Impact Learning: Building and Diffusing Learning Capability," *Organizational Dynamics,* Autumn 1993, pp 52–66.

47 See J W Lorsch and T J Tierney, *Aligning the Stars: Organizing Professionals to Win* (Boston, MA: Harvard Business School Press, 2002).

48 The creation of learning infrastructure is discussed by C R James, "Designing Learning Organizations," *Organizational Dynamics,* 2003, pp 46–61.

49 See J B Quinn, "Leveraging Intellect," *Academy of Management Executive,* November 2005, pp 78–94; and M T Hansen, M L Mors, and B Lovås, "Knowledge Sharing in Organizations: Multiple Networks, Multiple Phases," *Academy of Management Journal,* October 2005, pp 776–93.

50 See the related discussion in D Lei, J W Slocum, and R A Pitts, "Designing Organizations for Competitive Advantage: The Power of Unlearning and Learning," *Organizational Dynamics,* Winter 1999, pp 24–38.

PHOTO CREDITS

PART ONE
Page 1   © Photodisc Imaging/ Getty Images

Chapter 1
Page 3   AP/Wide World Photos
Page 10   Property of AT&T Archives. Reprinted with permission of AT&T
Page 16   © Joe Raedle/Getty Images
Page 17   AP/Wide World Photos
Page 20   © Robert Wright Photography

Ethics Learning Module
Page 25   AP/Wide World Photos
Page 26   © Stuart Ramson/Getty Images
Page 27   © Keith Meyers/ The New York Times
Page 28   AP/Wide World Photos
Page 32   © Mark Wilson/Getty Images

Chapter 2
Page 39   © Najlah Feanny/ Corbis
Page 43   Daniel Acker/Bloomberg News/Landov
Page 45   Courtesy of Southwest Airlines
Page 49   © Lynsey Addario/ Corbis
Page 52   AP/Wide World Photos

Chapter 3
Page 63   Photo courtesy of Service Winners International
Page 68   Jonathan Ernst/ Reuters
Page 71   © David Butow/ Redux Pictures
Page 72   Photo courtesy of InfiniTec Pte. Ltd.
Page 82   Jim Watson/AFP/Getty Images

PART TWO
Page 87   © Photodisc/Getty Images

Chapter 4
Page 89   © Kevin Lamarque/Reuters/ Corbis
Page 93   © Ed Alcock/The New York Times
Page 98   © Ryan McVay/Getty Images
Page 103 Shannon Stapleton/Reuters/ Landov
Page 105 Evan Agostini/Getty Images

Chapter 5
Page 117 © Forest McMullen, Courtesy of Xerox
Page 120 © Brian Park
Page 132 © Copyright 2006. USA Today. Reprinted with permission
Page 136 Kevin P. Casey/The New York Times
Page 138 Spencer Platt/Getty Images

Chapter 6
Page 145 Courtesy of IBM
Page 150 © John Van Hasselt/ Corbis
Page 153 © Michael Lewis
Page 156 Courtesy of Kinesis Corporation: www. kinesis.com
Page 158 Yuri Kadobnov/AFP /Getty Images
Page 169 Phil Marino/The New York Times

Chapter 7
Page 173 Photodisc/Getty Images
Page 178 AP/Wide World Photos
Page 184 John Zich/Bloomberg News/Landov
Page 187 PRNews Foto/Cutter & Buck Inc./AP/Wide World Photos
Page 190 AP/Wide World Photos

Chapter 8
Page 199 Courtesy of UMB Financial Corp.
Page 203 Courtesy of oDesk
Page 209 AP/Wide World Photos
Page 213 Courtesy of Robert Kreitner
Page 215 PhotoLink/Getty Images

PART THREE
Page 221 © Photodisc/Getty Images

Chapter 9
Page 223 LifeWings Partners LLC
Page 226 AP/Wide World Photos
Page 229 © Scott Thode/ Fortune Magazine
Page 234 Courtesy of Seagate
Page 238 AP/Wide World Photos

Chapter 10
Page 247 Photo provided by Cemex
Page 251 Mike Segar/Reuters/ Landov
Page 255 © Donald C. Johnson/Corbis
Page 258 © Greg Miller
Page 265 Keith Brofsky/Getty Images

Chapter 11
Page 273 Brian Smale Photography
Page 277 Steve Cole/Getty Images
Page 278 © Copyright 2006, USA Today. Reprinted with permission.
Page 283 © Namas Bhojani
Page 287 Photo courtesy of IRS

PART FOUR
Page 295 Nick Koudis/Getty Images

Chapter 12
Page 297 Larry W. Smith/Getty Images
Page 301 PhotoDisc/Getty Images
Page 304 AP/Wide World Photos

Page 312 John A. Rizzo/Getty Images
Page 314 Nacho Doce/Reuters/ Landov

Chapter 13
Page 325 Courtesy of Xerox
Page 328 AP/Wide World Photos
Page 329 AP/Wide World Photos
Page 334 Ken Nahoum/Edge Films/Courtesy of Orpheus Chamber Orchestra
Page 339 Yunghi Kim/Contact Press Images

Chapter 14
Page 345 © Zack Seckler/Corbis
Page 349 Ethan Miller/Getty Images
Page 356 Henry Ray Abrams/ Reuters/Landov
Page 360 Ozier Muhammad/ The New York Times
Page 367 Photo by Brian Fiske, Courtesy of Microchip Technology, Inc.

PART FIVE
Page 373 © RF/Corbis

Chapter 15
Page 375 Tim Boyle/Getty Images
Page 384 © Erik Freeland/ Corbis Saba
Page 385 Courtesy of SWA
Page 389 © Gabriela Hasbun
Page 391 Photo courtesy of U.S. Army, photo by Staff Sgt. Charles B. Johnson

Chapter 16
Page 397 AP/Wide World Photos
Page 400 The McGraw-Hill Companies, Inc./Lars A. Niki, photographer
Page 401 © Najlah Feanny/ Corbis
Page 406 © Jeff Topping/ The New York Times
Page 418 © Mind Tree Consulting

ability Stable characteristic responsible for a person's maximum physical or mental performance.

accountability practices Focus on treating diverse employees fairly.

added-value negotiation (AVN) Cooperatively developing multiple-deal packages while building a long-term relationship.

affirmative action Focuses on achieving equality of opportunity in an organization.

aggressive style Expressive and self-enhancing, but takes unfair advantage of others.

aided-analytic Using tools to make decisions.

alternative dispute resolution Avoiding costly lawsuits by resolving conflicts informally or through mediation or arbitration.

analytics A conscientious and explicit process of making decisions on the basis of the best available evidence.

anticipatory socialization Occurs before an individual joins an organization, and involves the information people learn about different careers, occupations, professions, and organizations.

assertive style Expressive and self-enhancing, but does not take advantage of others.

attention Being consciously aware of something or someone.

attitude Learned predisposition toward a given object.

availability heuristic Tendency to base decisions on information readily available in memory.

benchmarking Process by which a company compares its performance with that of high-performing organizations.

blog Online journal in which people comment on any topic.

bounded rationality Constraints that restrict decision making.

brainstorming Process to generate a quantity of ideas.

bureaucracy Max Weber's idea of the most rationally efficient form of organization.

care perspective Involves compassion and an ideal of attention and response to need.

case study In-depth study of a single person, group, or organization.

causal attributions Suspected or inferred causes of behavior.

centralized decision making Top managers make all key decisions.

change and acquisition Requires employees to master tasks and roles and to adjust to work group values and norms.

charismatic leadership Transforms employees to pursue organizational goals over self-interests.

closed system A relatively self-sufficient entity.

coalition Temporary groupings of people who actively pursue a single issue.

coercive power Obtaining compliance through threatened or actual punishment.

cognitions A person's knowledge, opinions, or beliefs.

cognitive categories Mental depositories for storing information.

collaborative computing Using computer software and hardware to help people work better together.

collectivist culture Personal goals less important than community goals and interests.

commitment to change A mind-set of doing whatever it takes to effectively implement change.

communication Interpersonal exchange of information and understanding.

communication competence Ability to effectively use communication behaviors in a given context.

conflict One party perceives its interests are being opposed or set back by another party.

consensus Presenting opinions and gaining agreement to support a decision.

consideration Creating mutual respect and trust with followers.

contingency approach Using management tools and techniques in a situationally appropriate manner; avoiding the one-best-way mentality.

contingency approach to organization design Creating an effective organization–environment fit.

contingency factors Variables that influence the appropriateness of a leadership style.

continuous reinforcement Reinforcing every instance of a behavior.

core job dimensions Job characteristics found to various degrees in all jobs.

creativity Process of developing something new or unique.

cross-cultural training Structured experiences to help people adjust to a new culture/country.

cross-functionalism Team made up of technical specialists from different areas.

cultural intelligence The ability to interpret ambiguous cross-cultural situations accurately.

culture shock Anxiety and doubt caused by an overload of new expectations and cues.

decentralized decision making Lower-level managers are empowered to make important decisions.

decision making Identifying and choosing solutions that lead to a desired end result.

decision-making style A combination of how individuals perceive and respond to information.

Delphi technique Process to generate ideas from physically dispersed experts.

development practices Focus on preparing diverse employees for greater responsibility and advancement.

developmental relationship strength The quality of relationships among people in a network.

devil's advocacy Assigning someone the role of critic.

dialectic method Fostering a debate of opposing viewpoints to better understand an issue.

distributive justice The perceived fairness of how resources and rewards are distributed.

diversity The host of individual differences that make people different from and similar to each other.

diversity of developmental relationships The variety of people in a network used for developmental assistance.

dysfunctional conflict Threatens organization's interests.

e-business Running the *entire* business via the Internet.

electronic mail Uses the Internet/intranet to send computer-generated text and documents.

emotional intelligence Ability to manage oneself and interact with others in mature and constructive ways.

emotions Complex human reactions to personal achievements and setbacks that may be felt and displayed.

empowerment Sharing varying degrees of power with lower-level employees to better serve the customer.

enacted values The values and norms that are exhibited by employees.

encounter phase Employees learn what the organization is really like and reconcile unmet expectations.

equity sensitivity An individual's tolerance for negative and positive equity.

equity theory Holds that motivation is a function of fairness in social exchanges.

escalation of commitment   Sticking to an ineffective course of action too long.

espoused values   The stated values and norms that are preferred by an organization.

ethics   Study of moral issues and choices.

ethnocentrism   Belief that one's native country, culture, language, and behavior are superior.

expatriate   Anyone living or working in a foreign country.

expectancy   Belief that effort leads to a specific level of performance.

expectancy theory   Holds that people are motivated to behave in ways that produce valued outcomes.

expert power   Obtaining compliance through one's knowledge or information.

explicit knowledge   Information that can be easily put into words and shared with others.

external factors   Environmental characteristics that cause behavior.

external forces for change   Originate outside the organization.

external locus of control   Attributing outcomes to circumstances beyond one's control.

extinction   Making behavior occur less often by ignoring or not reinforcing it.

extranet   Connects internal employees with selected customers, suppliers, and strategic partners.

extrinsic motivation   Motivation caused by the desire to attain specific outcomes.

extrinsic rewards   Financial, material, or social rewards from the environment.

feedback   Objective information about performance.

field study   Examination of variables in real-life settings.

formal group   Formed by the organization.

functional conflict   Serves organization's interests.

fundamental attribution bias   Ignoring environmental factors that affect behavior.

glass ceiling   Invisible barrier blocking women and minorities from top management positions.

goal   What an individual is trying to accomplish.

goal commitment   Amount of commitment to achieving a goal.

goal difficulty   The amount of effort required to meet a goal.

goal specificity   Quantifiability of a goal.

group   Two or more freely interacting people with shared norms and goals and a common identity.

group cohesiveness   A "we feeling" binding group members together.

group support systems (GSSs)   Using computer software and hardware to help people work better together.

groupthink   Janis's term for a cohesive in-group's unwillingness to realistically view alternatives.

high-context cultures   Primary meaning derived from nonverbal situational cues.

human capital   The productive potential of one's knowledge and actions.

humility   Considering the contributions of others and good fortune when gauging one's success.

hygiene factors   Job characteristics associated with job dissatisfaction.

impression management   Getting others to see us in a certain manner.

individualistic culture   Primary emphasis on personal freedom and choice.

informal group   Formed by friends.

in-group exchange   A partnership characterized by mutual trust, respect, and liking.

initiating structure   Organizing and defining what group members should be doing.

instrumentality   A performance → outcome perception.

intelligence   Capacity for constructive thinking, reasoning, problem solving.

interactional justice   The perceived fairness of the decision maker's behavior in the process of decision making.

intermittent reinforcement   Reinforcing some but not all instances of behavior.

internal factors   Personal characteristics that cause behavior.

internal forces for change   Originate inside the organization.

internal locus of control   Attributing outcomes to one's own actions.

internal motivation   Motivation caused by positive internal feelings.

Internet   The global system of networked computers.

intranet   An organization's private Internet.

intrinsic motivation   Motivation caused by positive internal feelings.

intrinsic rewards   Self-granted, psychic rewards.

job design   Changing the content and/or process of a specific job to increase job satisfaction and performance.

job enlargement   Putting more variety into a job.

job enrichment   Building achievement, recognition, stimulating work, responsibility, and advancement into a job.

job rotation   Moving employees from one specialized job to another.

job satisfaction   An affective or emotional response to one's job.

judgmental heuristics   Rules of thumb or shortcuts that people use to reduce information-processing demands.

justice perspective   Based on the ideal of reciprocal rights and driven by rules and regulations.

knowledge management (KM)   Implementing systems and practices that increase the sharing of knowledge and information throughout an organization.

laboratory study   Manipulation and measurement of variables in contrived situations.

law of effect   Behavior with favorable consequences is repeated; behavior with unfavorable consequences disappears.

leadership   Influencing employees to voluntarily pursue organizational goals.

leadership prototype   Mental representation of the traits and behaviors possessed by leaders.

leader trait   Personal characteristics that differentiate leaders from followers.

learned helplessness   Debilitating lack of faith in one's ability to control the situation.

learning capabilities   The set of core competencies and internal processes that enable an organization to adapt to its environment.

learning modes   The various ways in which organizations attempt to create and maximize their learning.

learning organization   Proactively creates, acquires, and transfers knowledge throughout the organization.

legitimate power   Obtaining compliance through formal authority.

line managers   Have authority to make organizational decisions.

linguistic style   A person's typical speaking pattern.

listening   Actively decoding and interpreting verbal messages.

low-context cultures   Primary meaning derived from written and spoken words.

maintenance roles   Relationship-building group behavior.

management   Process of working with and through others to achieve organizational objectives efficiently and ethically.

management by objectives   Management system incorporating participation in decision making, goal setting, and feedback.

managing diversity   Creating organizational changes that enable all people to perform up to their maximum potential.

mechanistic organizations   Rigid, command-and-control bureaucracies.

mentoring   Process of forming and maintaining developmental relationships between a mentor and a junior person.

meta-analysis   Pools the results of many studies through statistical procedure.

met expectations   The extent to which one receives what he or she expects from a job.

mission statement   Summarizes "why" an organization exists.

monochronic time   Preference for doing one thing at a time because time is limited, precisely segmented, and schedule driven.

motivation   Psychological processes that arouse and direct goal-directed behavior.

motivators   Job characteristics associated with job satisfaction.

need for achievement   Desire to accomplish something difficult.

need for affiliation   Desire to spend time in social relationships and activities.

need for power   Desire to influence, coach, teach, or encourage others to achieve.

needs   Physiological or psychological deficiencies that arouse behavior.

negative inequity   Comparison in which another person receives greater outcomes for similar inputs.

negative reinforcement   Making behavior occur more often by contingently withdrawing something negative.

negotiation   Give-and-take process between conflicting interdependent parties.

noise   Interference with the transmission and understanding of a message.

nominal group technique   Process to generate ideas and evaluate solutions.

nonanalytic   Using preformulated rules to make decisions.

nonassertive style   Timid and self-denying behavior.

nonverbal communication   Messages sent outside of the written or spoken word.

norm   Shared attitudes, opinions, feelings, or actions that guide social behavior.

normative beliefs   Thoughts and beliefs about expected behavior and modes of conduct.

onboarding   Programs aimed at helping employees integrate, assimilate, and transition to new jobs.

open system   Organism that must constantly interact with its environment to survive.

operant behavior   Skinner's term for learned, consequence-shaped behavior.

optimizing   Choosing the best possible solution.

organic organizations   Fluid and flexible network of multitalented people.

organization   System of consciously coordinated activities of two or more people.

organizational behavior   Interdisciplinary field dedicated to better understanding and managing people at work.

organizational citizenship behaviors (OCBs)   Employee behaviors that exceed work-role requirements.

organizational culture   Shared values and beliefs that underlie a company's identity.

organizational politics   Intentional enhancement of self-interest.

organizational socialization   Process by which employees learn an organization's values, norms, and required behaviors.

organization-based self-esteem   An organization member's self-perceived value.

organization chart   Boxes-and-lines illustration showing chain of formal authority and division of labor.

organization development   A set of techniques or tools that are used to implement organizational change.

ostracism   Rejection by other group members.

out-group exchange   A partnership characterized by a lack of mutual trust, respect, and liking.

participative management   Involving employees in various forms of decision making.

pay for performance   Monetary incentives tied to one's results or accomplishments.

perception   Process of interpreting one's environment.

personality   Stable physical and mental characteristics responsible for a person's identity.

personality conflict   Interpersonal opposition driven by personal dislike or disagreement.

polychronic time   Preference for doing more than one thing at a time because time is flexible and multidimensional.

positive inequity   Comparison in which another person receives lesser outcomes for similar inputs.

positive organizational behavior (POB)   The study and improvement of employees' positive attributes and capabilities.

positive reinforcement   Making behavior occur more often by contingently presenting something positive.

proactive personality   Action-oriented person who shows initiative and perseveres to change things.

problem   Gap between an actual and desired situation.

procedural justice   The perceived fairness of the process and procedures used to make allocation decisions.

process-style listeners   Like to discuss issues in detail.

programmed conflict   Encourages different opinions without protecting management's personal feelings.

punishment   Making behavior occur less often by contingently presenting something negative or withdrawing something positive.

rational model   Logical four-step approach to decision making.

readiness   Follower's ability and willingness to complete a task.

reasons-style listeners   Interested in hearing the rationale behind a message.

recruitment practices   Attempts to attract qualified, diverse employees at all levels.

referent power   Obtaining compliance through charisma or personal attraction.

repetitive motion disorders (RMDs)   Muscular disorder caused by repeated motions.

representativeness heuristic   Tendency to assess the likelihood of an event occurring based on impressions about similar occurrences.

resistance to change   Emotional/behavioral response to real or imagined work changes.

respondent behavior   Skinner's term for unlearned stimulus–response reflexes.

results-style listeners   Interested in hearing the bottom line or result of a message.

reward power   Obtaining compliance with promised or actual rewards.

roles   Expected behaviors for a given position.

sample survey   Questionnaire responses from a sample of people.

satisficing   Choosing a solution that meets a minimum standard of acceptance.

schema   Mental picture of an event or object.

self-concept   Person's self-perception as a physical, social, spiritual being.

self-efficacy   Belief in one's ability to do a task.

self-esteem   One's overall self-evaluation.

self-managed teams   Groups of employees granted administrative oversight for their work.

self-monitoring   Observing one's own behavior and adapting it to the situation.

self-serving bias   Taking more personal responsibility for success than failure.

self-talk   Evaluating thoughts about oneself.

sense of choice   The ability to use judgment and freedom when completing tasks.

sense of competence Feelings of accomplishment associated with doing high-quality work.

sense of meaningfulness The task purpose is important and meaningful.

sense of progress Feeling that one is accomplishing something important.

servant-leadership Focuses on increased service to others rather than to oneself.

shaping Reinforcing closer and closer approximations to a target behavior.

shared leadership Simultaneous, ongoing, mutual influence process in which people share responsibility for leading.

situational theories Propose that leader styles should match the situation at hand.

social capital The productive potential of strong, trusting, and cooperative relationships.

social loafing Decrease in individual effort as group size increases.

social power Ability to get things done with human, informational, and material resources.

societal culture Socially derived, taken-for-granted assumptions about how to think and act.

span of control The number of people reporting directly to a given manager.

spillover model Describes the reciprocal relationship between job and life satisfaction.

staff personnel Provide research, advice, and recommendations to line managers.

stereotype Beliefs about the characteristics of a group.

strategic constituency Any group of people with a stake in the organization's operation or success.

strategic plan A long-term plan outlining actions needed to achieve planned results.

substitutes for leadership Situational variables that can substitute for, neutralize, or enhance the effects of leadership.

tacit knowledge Information gained through experience that is difficult to express and formalize.

target elements of change Components of an organization that may be changed.

task roles Task-oriented group behavior.

team Small group with complementary skills who hold themselves mutually accountable for common purpose, goals, and approach.

team building Experiential learning aimed at better internal functioning of groups.

teleworking Doing work that is generally performed in the office away from the office using different information technologies.

theory Y McGregor's modern and positive assumptions about employees being responsible and creative.

360-degree feedback Comparison of anonymous feedback from one's superior, subordinates, and peers with self-perceptions.

total quality management An organizational culture dedicated to training, continuous improvement, and customer satisfaction.

transactional leadership Focuses on interpersonal interactions between managers and employees.

transformational leadership Transforms employees to pursue organizational goals over self-interests.

trust Reciprocal faith in others' intentions and behavior.

unaided-analytic Analysis is limited to processing information in one's mind.

underemployment The result of taking a job that requires less education, training, or skills than possessed by a worker.

unity of command principle Each employee should report to a single manager.

upward feedback Employees evaluate their boss.

valence The value of a reward or outcome.

value attainment The extent to which a job allows fulfillment of one's work values.

values Enduring belief in a mode of conduct or end-state.

virtual team Information technology allows group members in different locations to conduct business.

withdrawal cognitions Overall thoughts and feelings about quitting a job.

A

Abbot, 367
Abbott, A S, 449
Abboud, L, 425
ABC Carpet and Home, 27
Abraham, L M, 435
Abrams, D, 440
Abrams, L C, 441
Aburdene, P, 422
Accenture Institute for High
      Performance Business, 247
Adami, Norman, 359–360
Adams, A M, 423
Adams, J Stacey, 175, 436
Adams, M, 441
Adebayo, D O, 452
Adecco SA, 299
Adib, A, 433
Aditya, R N, 452
Adler, J, 423, 427
Adler, N J, 445
Adler, P S, 423
Adler, R, 449
Adner, R, 453
Agilent Technologies, 108
Agle, B R, 452, 453
Agree Systems, 98
Aguinis, H, 448, 449
Ahearne, M, 449, 451
Airbus, 298
Ajzen, I, 432
Alarm One, Inc., 104
Albaugh, James F, 297–298, 299
Alberto-Culver Company, 330
Albrecht, K, 446
Albrecht, S, 446
Alcatel, 425
Alch, M L, 454
Alcoa, 253
Alcon, 71
Aldag, R J, 431, 438, 442
Aldrich, H E, 422
Alexander, K L, 439
Alexander, R A, 437
Allen, E K, 441
Allen, Quincy, 325
Allen, R W, 449, 450
Allen, S, 440
Allen, T D, 426
Allgyer, Robert, 61
Allik, J, 427, 432
Almost, J, 437
Alon, I, 426
Alper, S, 444

Alsever, J, 441
Alteon WebSystems, 137
Alterio, J M, 447
Amason, A C, 444
Amazon.com, 3
Ambrose, M L, 434, 436
America West, 406
American Express, 138, 337
American International Group, 401
Amgen, 340
Anderson, Eric, 417
Anderson, Jim, 194
Anderson Snyder, L, 429
Andersson, L, 280, 444
Andrews, K D, 430
Andrews, L, 433, 445
Andrews, M C, 450
Andrich, D, 432
Ang, S H, 427
Anheuser-Busch Companies, 247, 249,
      286, 359
Ante, S E, 315, 437, 442, 447, 454
Anthony, K, 426
Anthony, W P, 431
Antonakis, J, 451
Antonioni, D, 438
AOL, 360
Apple, 182, 381
Appleby, I, 437
Applegate Farms, 20
Arad, S, 449
Archer, M, 427, 445
Argyris, Chris, 453, 455
Armas, G C, 429
Armentrout, B W, 455
Armour, S, 428, 429, 434, 440, 444, 446
Arndt, M, 166, 435, 454
Arnold, J T, 442
Arnst, C, 445
Aron, A, 445
Arthur, J B, 439
Arthur, M B, 360
Arthur Andersen, 61, 320
ARUP Laboratories, 145, 147
Arvey, R D, 433, 435
Ashcraft, R F, 431
Ashford, S J, 438
Ashforth, B E, 54, 425
Ashkanasy, N M, 425, 433
AT&T, 206, 276, 320
Atkin, C K, 446
Attanucci, J, 424
Atwater, L, 438
Austin, J, 437
Autodesk, 168

Avaya, 206
Avery, D R, 429, 450
Avolio, Bruce J, 358, 442, 451, 452, 454
Avon, 337, 451
Axtell, R E, 447
Azar, B, 433, 439

B

Baack, S A, 427
Babcock, L, 446
Babcock, P, 425, 428, 430, 438, 443
Bachrach, D C, 435
Baer, Jennifer, 223
Bagchi, Subroto, 418
Bagley, Constance E, 29, 424
Baig, E C, 98, 428
Bailey, D E, 442
Bailyn, L, 436
Bain, P, 430
Bain & Company, 418
Baird, L, 453
Baker, S, 424, 453
Bakker, A B, 431
Baldwin, S, 454
Balfour, F, 424, 426, 445
Balkundi, P, 441
Ball, J, 451
Ballmer, Steven A, 273–274, 386, 453
Baltes, B B, 443, 444
Bamford, J, 454
Banas, J T, 455
Bandura, Albert, 122–123, 127, 129, 130,
     430, 431
Bank One, 50, 356
Bannan, S, 452
Bannister, B D, 438
Baptist Health Care Hospital, 213, 249–250
Barbaro, M, 446
Barbian, J, 434, 445
Barbuto, J E, Jr., 433
Barchard, K A, 433
Barclay, L A , 448
Barger, Christopher, 318
Barker, B, 451
Barker, O, 444
Barley, S R, 448
Barnard, Chester I, 377, 452
Barnett, N P, 430
Barnett, W P, 440
Barnlund, D C, 430
Baron, R A, 449
Barr, C D, 436
Barrett, A, 437 454
Barrett, Craig R, 397–398

Barrett, G, 426
Barrett, L F, 433
Barrett, P, 431
Barrick, M R, 131, 431, 432
Barron, L A, 446
Barry, B, 446, 448
Barry, J, 426
Barsness, Z I, 450
Bartolomé, Fernanado, 235, 441
Bartram, D, 422, 431
Bartunek, J M, 423
Bartz, Carol, 168, 448
Basadur, M, 443
Baseler, Randy, 297, 299
Bass, B J, 451
Bass, B M, 451
Bass, Bernard, 358
Bassi, L, 15, 423
Bastian, B, 430
Bateman, Thomas S, 132, 431, 437
Bates, S, 427, 436, 437
Batson, D C, 282, 445
Batt, R, 441
Battelle, J, 448
Bauch, Ronnie, 334
Bauer, C C, 443, 444
Bauer, T N, 432, 452
Baum, L, 442
Bavetta, A G, 430
Bazerman, M H, 443, 446
Bealko, L, 447
Beard, J W, 450
Beatty, J E, 452
Beatty, R W, 437
Beauchamp, M R, 440
Bebchuk, L A, 439
Becker, B E, 423, 437, 450
Bedard, Jeff, 342
Bedeian, A G, 423, 436, 452, 453
Bednar, L L, 445
Beehr, T A, 436
Beeman, D R, 449
Beer, J S, 430
Beer, M, 454
Beersma, B, 440
Begley, S, 428, 430, 431
Behling, O C, 450
Bell, B S, 436, 441
Bell, Chip, 202, 437, 438
Bell, Genevieve, 72, 398
Bell, Helena, 318
Bellamy, C, 437
BellSouth, 209
Belluomini, D, 427
Benbasat, I, 444
Benchimol, Claude, 67
Bendersky, C, 445
Bendoly, E, 435
Benne, K D, 230, 440
Bennet, R H, III, 431

Bennett, N, 436, 449, 452
Benson, E, 432
Berdahl, J L, 428
Berg, Matt, 70
Berkowitz, L, 451
Berman, S L, 441
Bernardi, L M, 445, 446
Bernardin, H J, 438
Bernasek, A, 424
Bernick, Carol and Howard, 330–331
Berson, Y, 451, 452
Bettcher, K E, 424
Bing, J W, 426
Bing, M N, 436
Bing, S, 433
Bird, A, 426
Birkinshaw, J, 453
Black, J S, 427, 428
Black, Sandra, 148
Black, Steve, 356
Blades, B, 431
Blaize, N, 422, 448
Blake, J, 430
Blake, R R, 440
Blanchard, Kenneth, 357, 439, 451
Blank, Arthur, 39
Blau, G, 280
Blegen, M A, 435
Blenko, M, 443
Bliss, W G, 435
Block, C J, 429
Blok, S, 428
Bloom, M, 439
Bloom, Phillip, 24
Bloomberg, 43
Blue Cross and Blue Shield of North Carolina, 59
Bluedorn, A C, 427, 453
Bodenhausen, G V, 428
Boehle, S, 424
Boeing, 50, 260, 297–298, 318, 425
Bolch, M, 423
Bolton, A A, 423
Bommer, W H, 428, 451
Bonabeau, E, 453
Bond, M H, 430
Bono, J E, 435, 450, 451, 452
Borders Books and Music, 375
Bordia, P, 440, 442
Bordwin, M, 445
Borgatti, S P, 443
Borghesi, P, 430
Borman, W C, 148, 425, 429, 433, 435, 436, 444, 452
Borrus, A, 441
Bostrom, Sue, 233
Boswell, W R, 436
Bouchard, T J, 435
Boulding, K E, 453
Bowditch, J L, 434, 446

Bowen, D E, 423
Bowen, Stuart, 24
Bowes-Sperry, L, 442
Bowles, H R, 446
Boyatzis, R E, 140, 422, 433, 448
Boyd, Eric, 274
Boyes-Braem, P, 428
Boyle, E S, 442
Boyle, M, 435, 454
Boynton, A, 441
BP, 46
Bradbury, Jim, 76
Brady, D, 178, 422, 425, 436, 438, 454
Brady, G, 438
Brady, R, 426
Bragger, J L D, 443
Branden, Nathaniel, 120, 430
Branson, Richard, 329
Brass, D A, 430
Brass, D J, 282, 445, 449
Braverman, J, 433
Brays, S R, 440
Breaugh, J A, 237
Bremner, B, 425, 443
Brennan, C, 430
Brent Gallupe, R, 444
Brett, J F, 446
Brief, A P, 432, 435, 438
Briner, R B, 433
Brinkerhoff, R O, 453
Brinkley-Rogers, P, 439
Bristol-Myers Squibb, 53
Britt, J, 444
Brittain Leslie, J, 439
Brobeck, Phleger & Harrison, 301
Brock, D, 446
Brockner, J, 436, 438
Brodbeck, F C, 78, 427, 450
Brodsky, N, 423
Brody, M, 306
Brokker, K, 451
Bromgard, G D, 430
Bromgard, I K, 430
Brooker, K, 444
Brophy, B, 290, 446
Brotheridge, C M, 433
Brousseau, K R, 422
Brown, A, 431
Brown, Greg, 334, 422, 450
Brown, J D, 430
Brown, K, 99, 426, 431
Brown, S P, 435
Brown, T C, 431
Browne, K R, 429
Bruning, S S, 430
Brymer, R A, 435
Brynes, N, 425
Buchanan, L, 445, 454
Buckley, M R, 442
Buckmaster, Jim, 339

Buderi, R, 445
Bulger, C A, 448
Bulkeley, W H, 451
Bunch, J F S, 439
Bunderson, J S, 441
Buntzman, G F, 449
Buono, A F, 434, 446
Burbach, M E, 433
Burger King, 92
Burke, Warner, 407, 454
Burkhardt, Michael, 12, 449
Burkholder, R, 427
Burling, S, 433
Burman, W C, 41
Burns, M B, 445
Burns, Tom, 387–389, 454
Burns, Ursula, 325–326, 430, 451
Burris Desmarais, L, 432
Burroughs, S M, 436
Burrows, P, 432, 441, 451
Burt, R S, 441
Buss, D, 447
Buxton, W, 453
Bymes, J P, 443
Byrne, J A, 438
Byrnes, N, 422, 429, 430, 437
Byron, D L, 298
Byron, E, 425

C

Cable, D, 55, 425
Cacioppe, R, 454
Cacioppo, J T, 428
Cadbury Schweppes, 153
Cadrain, D, 438
Cadsby, J, 444
Caggiano, C, 442
Cain Smith, P, 435
Calantone, R J, 443
Calcanis, Jason, 360
Caldwell, S, 455
Caliguri, P, 427, 428
Callister, R Robert, 444
CallMiner, 133
Calpine, 234
Camerer, C, 441
Cameron, J, 439
Cameron, Kim, 379, 384, 452, 453
Campbell, A, 453
Campbell, C R, 430
Campbell, J D, 430
Campbell, J P, 441
Campion, M A, 434, 441
Canon, 71, 283, 426
Cantoni, C J, 453
Capell, P, 427
Caplan, Ira, 83, 428
Cardy, R L, 433
Carey, S, 444

Carnes, K, 423
Caro, R A, 448
Carpenter, Dave, 380
Carroll, S J, 454
Carron, A V, 440
Carson, K P, 435
Carter, A, 451
Carter, J, 427
Cartwright, D, 448
Carty, S S, 438
Caryl, C, 426
Casaburi, C, 451
Cascio, W F, 422, 427, 442
Case, J, 439
Casher, A, 454
Castaneda, Maureen, 30, 431
Castro, J, 440
Castro, S L, 452
Castro-Wright, Eduardo, 454
Caterinicchia, D, 447
Caudron, S, 445
Cauley, L, 438
Cavanagh, C, 317
Cavanaugh, William, III, 112
Cemex S A, 247–248, 249
Cendant Mobility, 79
Center for Internet Studies, 317
Chaiken, S, 428
Chambers, E, 447
Chambers, John, 56, 233
Champy, J, 422, 434
Chan, K, 427
Chang, A, 440, 442
Chao, Elaine, 82
Chao, G T, 426
Chapman, B P, 433
Charan, R, 425, 436, 455
Chartrand, T L, 428
Chattopadhyay, P, 440
Chatzky, Jean, 129, 431
Chen, G, 233, 451
Chenault, Kenneth I, 138
Chentsova-Dutton, Y, 433
Chernyshenko, O S, 432
Chevron, 46, 108, 317
Choi, I, 428
Chon, G, 455
Chowdhury, J, 436
Christensen, Clayton, 13, 449
Christiansen, N D, 449
Chrysler, 439
Chuang, A, 423, 432
Chubb Group, 57
Chuck E. Cheese's, 318
Chugh, D, 443
Cialdini, Robert B, 329–330, 448
Circuit City, 367
Cisco Systems, 56, 122, 320
Citigroup, 345–346
Clair, J A, 449

Clark, M M, 422, 445, 446
Clarke, S, 425, 432
Clason, D L, 429
Clayton, S, 429
Clegg, C W, 453
Cleveland, J N, 429
Clifford, S, 422
CMP Media, 169
Coates, D E, 438
Cobb, A T, 436, 449
Coca-Cola, 383, 411
Cogliser, C, 452
Cohen, D, 423, 427, 441
Cohen, Sasha, 158
Cohen-Charash, J, 435
Colarelli, S M, 429
Colbert, A E, 450
Cole, Paulette, 27
Colella, A, 425
Coleman, P T, 449
Collier, R, 439
Collingwood, H, 387, 429
Collins, Jim, 367–369, 452
Colquitt, J A, 434, 436, 437
Colvin, C R, 430
Colvin, G, 422, 424, 437, 445
Combs, J G, 441
Comporium Group, 145
Computer Associates (CA) International
    Inc., 34
Conger, J A, 438, 454
Conley, L, 441
Conlin, M, 422, 424, 442, 444, 447
Conlon, D, 436, 440
Connolly, T, 444
Continental Airlines, 217, 440
Continental Traffic Services, 320
Conyon, M J, 438
Cooke, B, 434
Cooke, R A, 47, 425
Cooper, C, 448, 453
Cooper, W H, 444
Cooper-Hakim, A, 435
Copeland, M V, 12, 439, 454
Cornelissen, J, 452
Cortina, J M, 432
Cortina, L M, 444
Cosier, R A, 285, 445
Cottrell, D, 423
Coulthart, Gordon, 48, 350
Courtright, J A, 454
Coutu, D L, 444, 445
Covey, Stephen R, 128, 431, 450
Coy, P, 426, 454
Coyle, Steve, 63–64, 426
Coyne, Kara Pernice, 98
Craigslist, 339
Cranny, C J, 435
Crant, J Michael, 132–133, 432
Crockett, R O, 447

Cropanzano, R, 436
Crosby, F J, 429
Crosby, Thom, 318
Cross, R, 440, 441, 443
Crossan, M, 453, 455
Crow, S M, 450
Crown, D F, 440
Crown Laboratories, 342
Cruz, M G, 442
Csikszentmihalyi, M, 423
CSM Worldwide, 65
Cullinan, G, 446
Cullum, Leo, 135
Cummings, L L, 435, 440, 443
Cunningham, J B, 441
Cunningham, Laurie, 173
Currall, S C, 438
Curtis, K, 311
Customer Growth Partners Inc., 39

D

D R Horton, Inc., 389
D'Alessandro, David F, 141
Daboub, A J, 27, 424
Dade, C, 455
Daft, Richard L, 383, 453
DaimlerChrysler, 13, 46
Dainton, M, 447
Dalkey, N C, 444
Dallas, S, 427
Daniel, P, 436
Daniels, C, 428, 454
Daniels, D, 148, 433, 436
Daniels, J D, 427
Danigelis, A, 431
Danis, W, 443
Dansereau, F, 450, 452
Dastmalchian, A, 427
Datta, S, 441
Daus, C S, 433
Davenport, T H, 443, 455
Davenport Sypher, B, 446
Davidson, S, 449
Davies, M, 433
Davis, B P, 448
Davis, D D, 442
Davis, J, 428, 437
Davis, K S, 435
Dawis, R V, 162, 435
Dawson, L M, 424
Day, D V, 428, 431
DBA Public Relations, 279
Deacon, S, 453
DeAngelis, T, 443
De Backer, P, 426
DeChurch, L A, 452
Deci, Edward L, 158, 434, 438
Decker, Ann, 229
Decker, C, 448

De Dreu, C K W, 262, 443, 445, 446
Deeman, D R, 450
Deery, S J, 436
DeGrandpre, R J, 439
de Janasz, Suzanne C, 59
Del Gaiso, A K, 433
Dell, Michael S, 250, 345
Dell Computers, 250, 381, 425
De Lollis, B, 426
De Long, D W, 443
DeLong, T J, 438
DeLonzor, D, 439
Delta Airlines, 4
de Luque, M S, 427, 450
DeMarie, S M, 442
DeMarree, K G, 431
Deming, W Edwards, 12–13, 423
de Nijs, E, 423
DeNisi, A S, 427
Denning, S, 425
De Pater, I E, 427
DePaulo, B M, 450
DeShon, R P, 437
Deshpandé, R, 424
deSilva, Peter J, 199
Des Jardins, J, 454
Dess, G G, 424
DeSteno, D, 433
Deutschman, A, 430, 445, 454
Devadas, R, 441
DiBella, A J, 455
Dickerson, A, 430
Dickey, C, 448
Dickman, K A, 450
Dickson, D, 423
Dickson, M W, 443, 444
Diebold, 302
Diefendorff, J M, 433
Diener, E, 430
Diener, M, 430
Dienesch, R M, 452
Dieterly, D L, 332
DiFonzo, N, 442
Digman, J M, 431
Dijksterhuis, A, 430
Diller, Barry, 137
DiMicco, Daniel R, 4
Dimon, Jamie, 50, 356, 386, 455
Dingfelder, S, 444
Dirks, K T, 441, 450
Dittmann, M, 432, 433
Dittmar, L, 449
Dobbins, G H, 428
Dobrev, S D, 440
Doke, D, 426
Dolezalek, H, 435, 449
Dollard, M F, 431
Dollinger, M J, 443
Dominiquini, J, 260, 443

Dominquez, Robert, 229
Donahoe, J W, 439
Donahue, L M, 233
Dongier, P, 441
Donnelly, D P, 435
Donoghue, A, 448
Donohue, W A, 446
Donovan, J J, 437
Donovan, M A, 180
Dooley, D, 429
Doorewaard, H A C M, 442
Dorfman, P W, 78, 426, 427, 450
Dormann, C, 435
Dortok, A, 424
Douge, L, 430
Dougherty, Thomas W, 425, 431
Douglas, K M, 448
Downing, R A, 429
Doz, Y L, 453
Draimer, M L, 425
Drapeau, A S, 441
Drasgow, F, 180, 432
Dreazen, Y, 424
Dreifus, C, 447
Dressler, D E, 453
Drew, R, 76
Drexter, A, 454
Driver, M J, 422
Drucker, Peter F, 352
Druskat, V U, 441
Dubin, R, 425
Dubner, S J, 436
DuBrin, A J, 449
Duchon, D, 452
Duck, J, 440
Dudley, N M, 432
Duening, T N, 423
Duffy, M K, 435, 436
DuFresne, R, 449
Dulebohn, J H, 448
Dumaine, B, 441, 453
Dumdum, U R, 451, 452
Duncan, W J, 423, 439
Dunkin, A, 440
Dunlap, S, 426, 449
Dunnette, M D, 137, 422, 440
DuPraw, M, 445
Duran, A, 429
Durbin, D-A, 425
Durett, J, 422, 425, 451
Durham, C C, 440
Dutton, J, 430, 451
Dvorak, P, 425
Dweck, C S, 428

E

Eagly, A H, 422, 447, 451
Earley, P C, 426, 427, 431, 437
eBay, 3, 203

Ebbers, Bernard, 26
Eby, L T, 425, 426
Eddleston, K A, 424, 425, 439
Eden, D, 430
Eden, J, 442
Edmondson, A, 416, 455
Edmondson, G, 425
Edwards, C, 423, 441, 454
Edwards, J E, 455
Edwards, M, 438, 454
eGetgoing, 319
Ehrhart, M G, 436
Eidelson, J I, 445
Eidelson, R J, 445
Einhorn, B, 445, 447
Einstein, W O, 442
Eisenbach, R J, 448
Eisenberger, R, 434, 439
Eisner, Michael, 349
Elgin, B, 447, 453
Elias, J, 431
Elias, M, 423, 432, 444
Elkind, P, 424
Ellenthal, Andy, 290
Elliott, J, 452
Ellis, P J, 441
Elsbach, K D, 97, 448
EMC, 250, 278, 286
Enbar, N, 440
Engardio, P, 426, 428, 445, 454
Engholm, C, 447
England, G W, 162, 435
Enns, H G, 448
Enron, 30, 32, 33–34, 91, 100–101, 114,
      333, 345, 401, 430
Ensley, M D, 435
Epley, N, 447
Epstein, M J, 425
Epstein, R E, 446
Er, M C, 444
Erdogan, B, 425, 432, 436, 441, 452
Erez, A, 435
Ernst, D, 454
Ernst & Young, 108–109, 226
Ertel, D, 446
Ettorre, B, 439
Evans, P, 441
Everett, J J, 430
Evernham, R, 441
Ewen, A J, 438
Ewing, J, 426, 427, 440
Exelon, 401
ExxonMobil, 46, 92, 400
Eye, M A, 440

F

Fairhurst, G T, 454
Falbe, C M, 448
Falcone, P, 430

Fallon, Gayle, 174
Fan, J, 427, 437
Fandt, P M, 449
Fang, X, 427
Fannie Mae, 112, 193, 367, 401
Faraj, S, 451
Farh, J-L, 438
Farkas, C M, 426
Farmer, S J, 436
Farmer, S M, 431, 449
Farnsworth, S R, 437
Fastow, Andrew S, 101
Federal Express, 183, 202, 223, 391, 437
Fedor, D B, 455
Feldman, Daniel C, 51, 52, 425, 429, 440
Feldman, M S, 447
Feldstein, S, 447
Fels, A, 422, 446
Fenn, D, 20
Fenwick, Lex, 43
Ferguson, E, 429
Ferrara, Napoleone, 259
Ferris, G R, 425, 432, 433, 435, 448, 449,
      450
Ferster, C B, 439
Ferzandi, L A, 427
Festinger, Leon, 175, 430, 436
Fiber, Jason, 258
Fick, N, 442
Fidelity Investments, 199
Fiedler, Fred E, 352–354, 363, 451
Fields, Mark, 48–49
Fields, Michael, 389
Filley, A C, 444
Fineman, S, 423, 433
Finkenauer, C, 433
Finn, B, 441
Finn, David, 26
Fiol, C M, 448
Fischer, A R, 432
Fischer, B, 441
Fischthal, A, 438
Fishbein, M, 432
Fisher, A, 429, 430, 433, 444, 447
Fisher, C D, 433, 437
Fisher, R, 446
Fisher, Susan, 414
Fishman, C, 437
Fisk, G M, 433
Flannery, T P, 437
Fleeson, William, 432
Fletcher, J K, 436
Flippen, A R, 442
Florida, Richard, 239
Flotek Industries, 911
Fluntke, F, 434
Flynn, F J, 440
Flynn, J R, 432
Foler, R, 436
Foley, S, 436

Folger, F, 432
Follett, Mary Parker, 10
Fombrun, C J, 424, 453
Fondas, N, 422
Ford, E W, 423
Ford, R C, 423
Ford Motor Co., 4, 48, 315, 425
Forest, S A, 446
Forrest, S P, III, 430
Forrester Research, 199, 297
Forret, Monica L, 425
Forster, J, 447
Fortado, B, 444
FourGen Software, 320
Fouse, Jackie, 71
Foust, D, 426, 430
Fragale, A R, 446
France, M, 444
France Télécom, 383–384
Franke, R H, 423
Franz, E, 431
Franz, T M, 449
Franze, L M, 445
Frederickson, B L, 423, 433
French, John, 331, 448, 449
Frenwalt, Troy, 406
Fried, J M, 439
Friedman, Stewart, 338, 450
Fu, P P, 448
Fuller, M A, 442
Fulmer, I S, 422, 448
Fulmer, R M, 455
Fuqua, D R, 404
Furnham, A F, 432

G

Gaertner, S, 434, 435
Galbraith, Jay R, 390, 452, 454
Galford, R, 441
Gallagher, R A, 454
Gallino, Jeff, 33
Galuszka, P, 426
Gangestad, S, 126, 431
Ganster, D C, 432
Gap Inc., 231
Garcia, Ann, 304–305
Garcia, Kim, 114
Gardberg, N A, 453
Gardenswartz, Lee, 102, 429, 444
Gardner, W L, 422, 430, 450
Garloch, J L, 442
Garner Stead, J, 424
Garten, J E, 454
Garvin, D A, 448
Gates, Bill, 273, 313–314, 447
Gateway, 276–277
Gecas, Vikton, 119, 430, 431
Geekcorps, 70
Gehani, R R, 423

Gelfand, M J, 446
Genentech, 259
General Electric, 67, 151–152, 182, 185,
  193, 232, 331, 340–341, 384
General Mills, 206, 236
General Motors, 4, 297, 318, 337, 410
George, E, 440
George, J M, 437, 442
Gerdes, L, 439, 440, 449
Gerhardt, M W, 450
Gerhart, B, 422
Gernster, Louis, 173, 354
Giacalone, R A, 450
Gibson, C B, 442, 449, 453
Gilbert, M B, 439
Gilbert, T F, 439
Gile, Keith, 199
Gill, D, 450
Gillen, D J, 454
Gillespie, J Z, 437
Gillette, 69–70, 367
Gillette, Walt, 260
Gilligan, Carol, 31, 424
Gillis, W E, 441
Gilson, L L , 441
Gimbel, B, 443
Gimein, Mark, 424
Ginter, P M, 423
Gist, M E, 430, 431, 438
Givner, Howard, 235
Glanz, L, 428
Glenn, D M, 436
Glick, W H, 454
Glocom, 283
Glomb, T M, 432, 445
Glunk, U, 425
Godin, S, 438
Godsey, K D, 425
Goff, Ted, 18, 96, 151, 183, 314,
  410
Goffee, R, 441, 450
Goldenberg, I, 433
Goldman Sachs, 438
Goldsmith, M, 437, 438
Goldwasser, C, 454
Goleman, Daniel, 140–141, 433
Gómez, C, 445
Gomez, Spector, 53
Gong, Y, 427, 437
Goodman, J S, 437
Goodman, P S, 441
Goodsell, C T, 453
Google, 44, 203, 319, 422, 425
Goold, M, 453
Gopal, A, 434
Gopalan, S, 426
Gordon, A H, 433
Gordon, J, 424, 442, 447
Gordon, R A, 448
Goren, H, 442

Gosling, J, 422
Gosserand, R H, 433
Gott, N, 17
Gould, J M, 455
Gouttefarde, C, 426
Graeff, C L, 451
Graen, G B, 431, 440, 452
Graetz, K A, 442
Grandey, A A, 433
Granite Construction, 215
Granstrom, K, 442
Grant, J, 454
Gratchev, M V, 428
Gray, B, 282, 445
Gray, D A, 27, 424, 453
Gray, P B, 432
Gray, W D, 428
Great Harvest Bread Co., 383
Great River Health Systems,
  145–146, 147
Green, H, 447
Green, S G, 452
Greenberg, J, 436
Greene, J, 444, 453
Greenfield, 317
Greenhaus, J H, 436
Greenhouse, S, 446
Greenleaf, Robert K, 365, 368, 452
Greenwood, R A, 423
Greenwood, R G, 423
Greer, C R, 443
Greer, M, 433
Gregersen, H B, 427, 428
Greguras, G J, 435
Greyhound, 46
Griffeth, R W, 434, 435
Griffin, M A, 440, 451
Griffith Hughson, T L, 441
Grossman, R J, 423, 434
Grote, D, 437
Grove, Andrew S, 137, 397, 433
Grover, R, 446, 449
Grover, S L, 450
Grow, B, 315, 424, 447, 453
Groyberg B, 451
Gruneberg, M, 435
Guerrier, Y, 433
Guidant Corp., 43
Guitar Center, 190
Gully, S M, 452
Gundling, E, 427, 440
Gupta, N, 436, 439
Gupta, V, 78, 426
Gurchick, K, 444, 445
Gustafson, K, 425
Gustafson, S B, 432
Gutierrez, Carlos, 135
Gutner, T, 424
Guttman, H M, 445
Guyon, J, 427

H

Habitat for Humanity, 385
Hackett, R D, 435
Hackman, J Richard, 154–155, 434
Haddad, C, 448
Haga, W, 452
Hagedorn, M, 435
Hagenbaugh, B, 432
Hagerty, B, 426
Halbesleben, J R B, 442
Hall, Edward T, 66, 426
Hall, J, 423, 447
Hall, R J, 437, 450
Halliburton, 401
Hallowell, Edward M, 318
Hambrick, D C, 440, 445
Hamel, G, 422
Hamilton, D L, 428
Hamm, S, 434, 436, 437, 443, 446, 454
Hammer, M, 422, 427
Hammond, J S, 443
Hammonds, K H, 452
Hampden-Turner, Charles, 66, 74, 75, 426,
  427
Hampson, R, 428
Handel, M J, 444
Handy, Charles, 392, 454
Hanft, A, 444, 448
Hanges, P J, 78, 426, 427
Hang-Yue, H, 436
Hannon, K, 445, 448, 449
Hansen, B, 453
Hansen, M T, 455
Hanson, P G, 454
Hantula, D A, 443
Harari, O, 453
Harden, Steve, 223–224
Hardin, A M, 442
Harken Energy Corp., 319
Harkins, S, 442
Harley-Davidson, 94
Harmon-Jones, E, 445
Harold, C M, 450
Harrell, A M, 434
Harris, K J, 450
Harris, M M, 438
Harris, P R, 430
Harris Interactive, 315
Harrison, Debra, 24, 427
Harrison, J K, 427
Harrison, W A, 441
Hart, C M, 440
Hart, Les, 3
Harter, J K, 422, 435
Hartke, D D, 451
Hartman, E M, 424
Harvey, M, 442
Haslam, N, 430
Hauser, Jacqui, 79

Haworth, S, 438
Hayes, T L, 422, 435
Hayslip, B, Jr., 433
Hazucha, Fisher, 438
He, I Y, 441
HealthSouth, 331
Heaphy, E, 430, 451
Hechanova, M A R, 429
Heckhausen, H, 434
Hedge, J W, 429
Heenan, D A, 426
Heggestad, E D, 432
Heider, Fritz, 99
Heine, S J, 430
Hellman, P, 450
Hellmich, N, 431
Helm, B, 445, 454
Hempel, J, 423
Hempel, S A, 430
Hemphill, B, 447, 448
Hemphill, K J, 428
Henderson, A M, 453
Hendrickson, A R, 442
Heneman, Robert, 184
Henig, R M, 424
Henle, C A, 436
Hennequin, Denis, 93
Henningsen, D D, 442
Henningsen, M L M, 442
Henry, D, 386
Hequet, M, 437
Herman Miller, 280
Herold, D M, 204, 455
Herriot, P, 438
Herscovitch, L, 412, 455
Hersey, Paul, 357–358, 451
Herzberg, Frederick, 152–153, 434
Herzlinger, R E, 453
Hesket, J L, 425
Hess, M B, 427
Hesselbein, Frances, 334
Heuring, L, 423
Hewlett, S A, 109, 429
Hewlett-Packard, 226, 318, 402
Hewlin, P F, 450
Hezlett, S A, 433, 438
Hickins, M, 440
Hicks, J A, 433
Higgins, J M, 426
Higgins, M, 58, 425, 426
Highberger, L, 445
Hill, G W, 444
Hill, L A, 431
Hillkirk, J, 423
Hillmann, M P, 441
Hills, G E, 430
Hindo, B, 425
Hinds, P J, 442
Hinkin, T R, 448, 449
Hirokawa, R Y, 443

Hirsch, Jennifer, 75
Hochwarter, Wayne A, 168, 435
Hodgetts, R M, 449
Hodgson, Kent, 32, 424
Hoeksema, L, 428
Hoel, W, 452
Hof, R D, 422, 424, 441, 443, 454
Hoffman, Mike, 286
Hofmann, D A, 428
Hofrichter, D A, 437
Hofstede, Geert, 70, 74, 425, 426
Hoigaard, R, 442
Holland, P, 453
Hollander, Dory, 141
Hollander, E P, 448
Hollenbeck, J R, 439, 440, 441
Hollingsworth, A T, 217
Holmes, S, 425, 443, 446, 447
Holpp, L, 440, 449
Hom, P W, 434, 435
Home Depot, 39–40, 41, 273, 387, 425, 455
Honda, 83
Hoobler, J, 435
Hopkins, J, 454
Hopkins, M, 453
Hoppe, M H, 426
Horbury, Peter, 239
Horton Smith, D, 440
Hosenball, M, 448
Hourihan, G, 422
House, Robert J, 71, 74, 78, 354–357, 360, 426, 427, 450, 451, 452
Hovanesian, M D, 425, 450, 453, 454
Howell, J M, 441, 450, 452
Hoyer, D Tanguay, 217
Hu Jintao, 89
Huang, Z, 426
Huber, G P, 443, 454
Huet-Cox, G D, 438
Huey, J, 439
Hulin, C L, 435
Hullender, Greg, 274
Hult, G T M, 453
Hummel, R P, 453
Humphrey, S E, 439, 440
Hunter, J E, 433, 437, 455
Huntley, C L, 439
Hurd, Mark, 402
Huselid, M A, 423, 437
Hutcherson, Ken, 274
Huxham, C, 441
Hyde, J, 424
Hymowitz, C, 437, 438, 446, 448

IBM, 17, 30, 70, 117, 145–146, 147, 156, 173, 182, 254, 318, 337, 354, 442
Ilgen, D R, 41, 148, 425, 433, 435, 436, 437, 439, 440, 441, 444, 452

Ilies, R, 435, 450, 451
Imhoff, H J, 445
Immelt, Jeffrey R, 182, 232, 384, 440
Infante, V D, 455
Infosys Technologies, 49
In-Q-Tel, 133
Insch, G S, 427
Intel, 15, 51, 72, 137, 156, 318, 397–399, 423, 442
International Data Corp., 315
International Executive Service Corps, 70
Intuit, 18
Ioannou, L, 446
Ireland, R D, 423, 443
Irvine, M, 427
Ito, Mizuko, 322
Ivancevich, J M, 423
Iverson, F Kenneth, 3–4
Iverson, R D, 436
Iwata, E, 445
Iyer, A, 429

J

Jackman, J M, 438
Jackson, C J, 432
Jackson, D N, 432
Jackson, J M, 442
Jackson, N, 449
Jackson, P R, 449
Jackson, T, 31, 424
Jacobs, D, 423, 450
Jacobson, D, 210
Jaffee, S, 424
Jamba Juice, 185
James, C R, 455
Janis, Irving L, 240–241, 285, 442
Janove, J, 392, 432, 440, 446
Janove, N W, 445
Jansen, E, 434
Janson, R, 434
Jashapara, A, 455
Jaussi, K S, 441
Javidan, M, 74, 78, 426, 427, 450
Jawahar, I M, 431
Jay, J, 447
Jayson, S, 423, 427, 444
JCPenney Co., 42
Jefferts Schori, Katharine, 349
Jehn, K A, 445
Jen, Mark, 319
Jenkins, G D Jr., 436, 439
Jenkins, J, 422
Jensen, M A C, 440
JetBlue Airways, 98, 320, 391, 454
Jett, Diana, 83
Jick, T, 455
Jobs, Steve, 182, 381
John Potter Global, 200
Johnson, B T, 422, 451

Johnson, C M, 437
Johnson, Craig R, 39
Johnson, D E, 435
Johnson, D M, 428
Johnson, E C, 425, 427, 440
Johnson, G, 163, 441
Johnson, H, 444
Johnson, J D, 446
Johnson, J L, 428
Johnson, Kevin, 422
Johnson, Keyin, 53
Johnson, M D, 439, 440
Johnson, Robert Louis, 132
Johnson, S, 439, 446
Johnson, T, 427
Johnson & Johnson, 345
Johnson-George, C, 441
Johnston, Larry, 422
Joinson, C, 441
Jones, Christopher, 73
Jones, D, 429, 433, 438, 440, 445, 448, 449,
      453
Jones, G, 441, 450
Jones, J R, 434
Jones, O, 444
Jones, P, 452
Jones, T M, 441
Jones, Thomas W, 346
Joni, S A, 441
Joshi, K D, 444
Jossi, F, 445
Joyce, W F, 453
J.P. Morgan Chase, 50, 356, 386, 405
Judd, C M, 428
Judge, T A, 435, 438, 450, 451, 452
Judge, T M, 431
Judge, Timothy, 349
Judiesch, M K, 429
Judson, A S, 455
Jundt, D, 439, 440
Jung, A, 438
Jung, D I, 451, 452
Junghans, 77

K

Kacmar, K M, 449, 450, 452
Kaestle, P, 454
Kagermann, Henning, 293
Kageyama, Yuri, 423, 448
Kahai, S S, 442, 454
Kahneman, D, 440
Kaihla, P, 286, 422, 439, 441
Kaiser Permanente, 193–194
KANA, 389
Kanawha Scales & Systems, 76
Karatz, Bruce, 251
Karau, S J, 442, 451
Kark, R, 451
Karlin, Barry, 319

Karoui, H, 429
Karr, A R, 435
Karren, R J, 437
Kashima, Y, 426
Kashy, D A, 450
Kassinis, G, 453
Kast, F E, 382
Kath, L M, 448
Katsura, H, 430
Katz, I M, 430
Katzenbach, Jon R, 232–233, 440, 441
Katzenstein, G, 445
Kauffeld, S, 442
Kaufman, Barbara, 50
Kaufman, C F, 427
Kaufmann, J B, 430
Kaul, J D, 423
Kayes, D C, 80, 437
KB Home, 251
Kearns, David, 112
Keat, Dalwi Lee Wei, 63
Keeley, M, 453
Keeney, R L, 443
Kehrli, S, 430, 445
Kelleher, Herb, 44–45, 422
Keller, R T, 452
Kellerman, Barbara, 347, 432, 450
Kellett, S, 433
Kelley, E, 434, 442
Kelley, H H, 99–100, 428
Kelley, J, 444
Kelley, M R, 434
Kelley, T, 445
Kellogg Company, 135
Kelly, Gary, 5
Kelly, Terry, 119
Kemery, E R, 449
Kemmerer, B, 432
Kemna, Wolfgang, 293
Kennedy, J C, 427, 448, 450
Kenny, D A, 450
Keon, T L, 434, 436
Kepcher, Carolyn, 105
Kerr, J, 438
Kerr, Steve, 333, 439, 449
Kersten, D, 446
Kessler, M, 423
Ketchen, D J, Jr., 453
Keveney, B, 449
Keys, J B, 455
Khosh, M, 441
Kidder, D L, 424, 425, 439
Kiechel, W, III, 445
Kiefer, Jesse, 153
Kiley, D, 439
Kim, Eric B, 397
Kim, H, 448, 452
Kim, P H, 446
Kimberly-Clark, 367

Kimble, C E, 442
Kimley-Horn & Associates, 185
King, A A, 454
King, B, 353
King, L, 433, 439
Kinicki, A, 41, 92, 191, 408, 425,
      435
Kipnis, David, 327, 448
Kirby, J, 453
Kirby, S L, 448
Kirchhoff, S, 432
Kirkman, B L, 442, 445, 449
Kirkpatrick, D, 422, 447, 451, 453,
      454
Kirsch, D A, 454
Kiser, K J, 423
Kiska, J, 438
Klein, H J, 440, 442
Klein, T R, 445
Kleiner, A, 449
Klimoski, R J, 41, 148, 233, 425, 433, 435,
      436, 444, 452
Kmart, 108
Knight, D, 440, 447
Knowles, E S, 448
Knowlton, B, 428
Ko, S J, 440
Kobayashi, C, 430
Koen, C M, Jr., 450
Koertzen, Jeff, 273
Koestner, R, 438
Kohn, A, 436, 439
Kohn, L, 438
Kolenko, T A, 431
Kompier, M A, 442
Konrad, R, 448
Konst, D, 429
Koonce, R, 429
Kopeikina, L, 443
Kopelman, R E, 434, 437
Kopp, R, 426
Koretz, G, 427, 439
Kornik, J, 362
Koslowsky, M, 452
Kossek, E E, 427
Kotter, John P, 405–406, 407, 413, 425,
      445, 454
Kouzes, J M, 439
Kowske, B, 426
Koys, D J, 435
Kraft Foods, 273
Kraimer, M L, 425, 432, 441, 452
Kram, Kathy, 57, 58, 425, 426
Kramer, R M, 433, 451
Kraut, A I, 422
Kravitz, D A, 442
Kreitner, Robert, 92, 213, 216, 262, 431,
      439
Krell, E, 427, 428, 447
Kreshel, P J, 439

Kring, A M, 433
Kripalani, M, 426, 454
Kristof-Brown, A L, 425, 427, 440
Kroeck, K G, 452
Kroes, Neelie, 274
Kroger, 367
Krosnick, J A, 432
Krug, S, 434
Kruger, J, 447
Krull, J L, 433
Kuchinskas, S, 431
Kuhn, R L, 428
Kulik, C T, 434
Kumar, N A, 436
Kuncel, N R, 433
Kurke, L B, 422
Kurman, J, 450
Kurpius, D J, 404
Kurtz, R, 444
Kurzban, R, 442
Kushner, D, 70
Kuvaas, B, 434
Kwak, Chris, 318
Kwon, S K, 423
Kyle Smith, N, 428

L

LaBarre, P, 423
Labianca, G, 282, 445
Lacoste, 400
LaCoursiere, Cliff, 133
Lacy, S, 435
Ladge, J, 449
Ladika, S, 438
Lafley, A G, 328
LaGanke, J S, 443, 444
Lai, S C Y, 430
Lalwani, A K, 427
Lam, S S K, 432, 444
Lammelein, S E, 429
Lamoureux, K, 451
Lane, J, 438
Lane, P M, 427
Lang, F, 446
Langeland, K L, 437
Langley, M, 454
Langreth, R, 443
Larsen, J T, 428
Larson, J, 439, 448
Larsson, R, 422
Laschever, S, 446
Lashinsky, A, 424, 447, 453, 454
LaSusa, Kimberly, 169
LaSusa, Thomas, 169
Latack, J C, 436
Latane, B, 442
Latham, B W, 453
Latham, Gary P, 188, 192, 436, 437, 439, 453
Lau, C-M, 455

Laurie, D L, 453
Lausanne Renfro, C, 429
Laval, B, 423
Lavallee, L F, 430
Lavelle, L, 428, 436
Lavin, Leonard, 330–331
Law, K S, 444
Lawler, Edward E, III, 390, 423, 438, 452, 454
Lawrence, B S, 423
Lawrence, T B, 450
Lay, Ken, 33–34, 100–101
Layton, M C, 423
Lazarus, Richard S, 138–139, 433
Leach, D J, 449
Leana, C R, 444
Leavitt, H J, 452
Lebiecki, J E, 432
Lee, A T, 440
Lee, C, 128, 437
Lee, L, 425
Lee, M, 430
Lee, P A, 69
Lee, R T, 433
Lee, S M, 426
Lee, W C, 427
Lee, W W S, 430
Lehman, D R, 428, 430
Lei, D, 453, 455
Leise, Larry, 17
Lennar Corp., 388–389
Lenox, M J, 454
Lentz, E, 426
Leonard, D, 381
Leong, C, 432
Leopold, J, 429
LePine, J A, 435
Lepsinger, R, 422
Lermusiaux, Y, 435
Le Roux, J, 446
Leslie, J B, 422
Lessard, B, 454
Lesser, E, 441
Letendre, L, 442
Levering, R, 422, 425, 426, 429, 434, 435, 436, 439, 443
Levin, D Z, 441
Levine, D I, 444
Levy, Marv, 365, 452
Levy, P E, 437, 450
Levy, S, 424, 453
Lewicki, R J, 447
Lewig, K A, 431
Lewin, Kurt, 402, 406, 407, 454
Lewis, J D, 441
Lewis, K M, 433
Lewis, R, 444
LG Electronics, 72
Li, Charlene, 297
Li, J, 440, 445

Liao, H, 423, 432, 445
Liden, R C, 364, 425, 436, 441, 448, 449, 450, 452
Lidwell, W, 423
Lieberman, D, 433
Lieberson, S, 450
LifeWings, 223–224
Lim, J, 444
Lim, S, 444
Linderman, P, 427
Lindsley, D H, 430
Lipnack, J, 442
Littman, J, 445
Lituchy, T R, 431, 437
Litzky, B E, 424, 425, 439
Lo, C, 430
Lo, Selina Y, 137
Locke, Edwin A, 186, 188, 192, 435, 436, 437, 440, 444
Lockheed Martin, 108, 163
Loden, Marilyn, 102
Loewe, P, 260, 443
Loewenstein, George, 439
Lofquist, L H, 162, 435
Loi, R, 436
Lombardo, T, 430
London, H, 429
London, M, 438
Long, B G, 446
Longaberger's, 210
Looney, D S, 431
Lord, Robert G, 348, 428, 450
Lorsch, J W, 455
Losada, M F, 423
Louie, T A, 438
Louis, Jude, 63
Lovås, B, 455
Love, K G, 436
Low, M, 432
Lowe, K B, 451, 452
Lowe, R A, 443
Lubin, B, 454
Lubinski, D, 433
Lubit, R, 443
Lublin, J S, 426, 427, 433, 438
Luce, C Buck, 109, 429
Lucent, 425
Lueder, D C, 451
Luerich, Susan, 17
Lumpkin, G T, 424
Luthans, B C, 423
Luthans, Fred, 18–19, 216, 422, 423, 431, 438, 439
Luthans, K W, 423
Lutrey, S M, 437
Lynch, D J, 427
Lynch, Lisa, 148
Lyne, Susan, 177–178
Lyness, K S, 429
Lynton, N, 427

M

Maazel, Lorin, 139
McAllister, D J, 441
McCabe, C, 447
McCabe, Donald, 196
McCall, M W, Jr., 448
McCarthy, T O, 443
McCartney, S, 427
McClelland, C L, 434
McClelland, David, 149–150
McCloy, R A, 432
McCrae, R R, 432
McCuan, J, 439
McCune, J C, 445
McDonald, D, 423, 441
Macdonald, J, 449
McDonald, Malcolm, 3
McDonald's, 92, 93, 166, 297, 390
McDonnell, Stephen, 20
McEwen, W, 427
McFarland, L A, 450
McFarlin, D B, 448
McGarvey, R, 431
McGinn, K L, 446
McGowan, Bruce, 215
McGregor, Douglas, 10, 11, 423
McGregor, J, 422, 423, 424, 425, 436, 440, 449
MacGregor Server, L B, 340
McGuire, C V, 430
McGuire, W J, 430
Macht, J, 433
McKay, P F, 429, 450
McKee, A, 140, 433
McKee, Lori, 57
McKee-Ryan, F M, 435
McKenna, D D, 422
MacKenzie, S B, 428, 451
McKinsey & Company, 232
McKinstry, N, 454
McLaughlin-Volpe, T, 445
McLean, A N, 451
McMahan, G C, 437
MacMillan, I C, 423
McMillen, S, 311
McMurrer, D, 15, 423
McNeese-Smith, D K, 434
McNerney, Jim, 50
McPherson, S O, 442
Macrae, C N, 428
Maddox, E N, 431
Madison, D L, 449, 450
Madsen, S R, 455
Mage, G C, 452
Magner, N R, 445
Maher, Kris, 425, 455
Mahurin, Steve, 40
Maier, M, 452
Main, J, 426

Majchrzak, A, 442
Major, V S, 446
Makhija, M V, 455
Malhotra, A, 442
Malik, S D, 440
Malone, T W, 422
Mandel, D R, 428
Mandel, M J, 424, 439
Mandell, J, 431
Maney, K, 439, 445
Mann, S, 437
Manning, G, 311
Mannix, E A, 445
Manstead, A S R, 446
Mantler, J, 433
Manz, C C, 422, 431, 449, 453
Marbach, W D, 426
Marcus, Bernie, 39
Margolis, J D, 424
Marino, G, 438
Marinova, S V, 428
Markels, A, 438
Marklein, M B, 426
Marks, M A, 452
Marksberry, Penny, 114
Marlowe, C M, 428
Marques, J M, 440
Marriott, 65, 426
Marsh, A, 424
Marsh, H W, 430
Martha Stewart Living Omnimedia, Inc., 177–178
Martin, B, 442
Martin, J N, 427
Martin, M M, 430
Martin, S L, 450
Martinez, M N, 433
Martinez-Taboada, C, 440
Martinko, M J, 422, 428, 430
Marvel, M K, 446
Marx, E, 428
Maschiarelli, J P, 431
Maslow, Abraham, 17, 149, 227, 434
Maslowski, R, 425
Maslyn, J M, 364
Mason, C M, 440
Mason, R O, 254, 443
Matheson, K, 433
Mathieu, J E, 441, 449
Matsushita-Kotobuki Electronics (MKE), 82
Matthews, J R, 432
Matthews, L H, 432
Mattis, M, 106, 429
Mattsson, J, 431
Mauer, T J, 430
Maughan, Deryck, 346
Mauksch, L, 447
Maurer, H, 426
Maurer, K, 428
Mausner, B, 434

Mawhinney, T C, 437
Max, S, 441, 451
Mayer, R C, 428
Mayes, B T, 449, 450
Maynard, M, 453
Mayo, Elton, 10
Mazda, 226–227
Mears, P, 423
Medland, M E, 447
Mehring, J, 434
Meier, Lisa Bromiley, 91
Mellor, S, 448
Melrose, Ken, 286
Mendenhall, M E, 426, 427, 428, 450
Menkes, J, 432
Men's Wearhouse, 417, 455
Mento, A J, 437
Mercedes, 65
Mercer Human Resources Consulting, 166
Mero, J, 434, 454
Merrill Lynch, 320, 354, 433
Merriman, K, 429
Merritt, A, 426
Merritt, J, 424, 441
Mervis, C B, 428
Messe, L A, 428
MetLife, 109
Mewton, Lenore, 290
Meyer, C J, 439, 440, 453
Meyer, David, 318
Meyer, J P, 412, 455
Miami Children's Hospital, 267
Michie, J, 453
Microchip Technology, Inc., 366–367
Microsoft, 51, 273–274, 318, 381, 386, 400, 422, 454
Miles, S A, 452
Milkovich, G T, 439
Miller, C C, 443, 454
Miller, Danny, 417, 443, 455
Miller, Frederick J, 359
Miller, K L, 428
Miller, P, 452
Miller Brewing, 359–360
Mills, Steve, 354
Millsap, R E, 438
Mils, A J, 434
Milunovich, Steve, 354
MindTree Consulting, 418
Miner, J B, 423
Minssen, H, 441
Mintzberg, Henry, 6–7, 422
Mirabile, Hector, 68
Mirchandani, R, 440
Mirza, Sahid, 283
Mishra, A K, 441
Mitarai, Fujio, 71, 426
Mitchell, R K, 453
Mitchell, Terrence R, 147, 148, 192, 430, 431, 433, 436, 437, 438

Mitchener, E C, 445
Mitra, A, 436, 439
Mitsubishi, 46
Mitsuhashi, H, 454
Mittelstaedt, Robert, 50
Moberg, D J, 424
Mohamed, A A, 442
Mohler, C J, 436
Moingeon, B, 416, 455
Molden, D C, 428
Moldveanu, M, 453
Montagliani, A, 450
Moon, H, 426, 440
Moore, C, 428, 437
Moore, L G, 450
Moore, R W, 427
Moran, R T, 430
Morand, D A, 453
Morgan, L, 451
Morgeson, F P, 442
Morimoto, K, 427
Morningstar, 411
Morris, B, 430, 437, 448, 450, 451, 455
Morrison, Ann M, 104, 110, 111, 429
Morrison, M, 432
Morrow, B, 445, 446
Mors, M L, 455
Morse, G, 423, 433, 443
Mosakowski, E, 426
Moscato, D, 425
Moskowitz, M, 422, 425, 426, 429, 434, 435, 436, 439, 443
Moss, S E, 428, 437
Mossholder, K W, 449
Motorola, 206, 238, 334, 423
Moukheibert, Z, 443
Mount, I, 448
Mount, M K, 131, 431, 432, 438
Moussa, F M, 437
Moyer, D, 434
MSP Resources, 235
Mudd, Dan, 192
Mueller, S L, 426
Mulcahy, Anne, 325, 361
Mullaney, T J, 424
Mulvey, P W, 440, 442
Mumford, M B, 432
Munroe, P T, 451
Munson, J L, 180
Munter, M, 427
Munz, D C, 451
Murgallis, R P, 441
Murphy, Dave, 75
Murray, Ed, 274
Murray, H A, 434
Murray, L H, 450
Murthy, Narayana, 49
Musen, G, 428
Myerson, Bernard S, 117

N

Naccio, Joe, 26–27
Nadler, D A, 404, 449, 454
Nagarajan, N J, 452
Nanus, Burt, 361, 451
Nardelli, Robert L, 39–40, 387
Nash, L, 431
Naughton, K, 442
Naumann, S E, 436
Naylor, M, 448
NBC, 11
Neale, M, 442, 446
Neck, C P, 431
Neeleman, David, 454
Neilson, G L, 425
Nelson, B, 438
Nelson, C E, 428
Nelson, D L, 429
Nelson, N C, 435
Nelson, R E, 426
Nesbitt, Nik, 26
Nestlé, 71
Netscape, 360
Neuman, G A, 455
Nevin, J A, 439
Nevis, E C, 455
Newby-Clark, I R, 430
Newman, B, 428
Newman, G, 428
Newman, Robert, 229
Newmark, Craig, 339
Ng, A C, 444
Ng, K Y, 436
Ng, T W H, 425
Ng, Z-W, 447
Ngo, H-Y, 455
Nguyen, H H, 428
Nicholson, N, 445
Niebuhr, R E, 432
Niederman, F, 442
Niehoff, B P, 439
Nielsen, T M, 438
Nilsen, D, 426
Ninestar, 283
Nisbet, R E, 428
Nishii, L H, 446
Nohria, N, 440, 451, 454
Nokia, 65
Nordstrom's, 159
Nordwall, E, 441
Norenzayan, A, 428
Norris, D R, 432
Nortel Networks, 65
Northcraft, G B, 437, 446
Northwest Airlines, 264–265
Northwest Community Hospital, 155
Northwestern Mutual, 5, 129
Noureddin, Loubna, 267

Novak, R J, 440
Novicevic, M M, 442
Nucleus Research, 316
Nucor, 3–4, 49, 194, 367, 437
Nunes, F, 247
Nurney, S P, 427
Nussbaum, B, 441, 444
Nystrom, P C, 432

O

O'Brien, K, 446
O'Brien, L, 250
O'Connell, P, 433
O'Connor, E J, 448
O'Connor, J F, 450
Odden, Allan, 173
oDesk, 203
Odums, G A, 430
Offermann, L R, 440, 448, 449
Oh, H, 424
Oldenburg, A, 448
Oldham, Greg R, 154–155, 434
O'Leary, T, 452
Olson, Nina, 287
Olson-Buchanan, J B, 436
O'Mahony, S, 448
O'Neal, Stanley, 433
Ones, D S, 433
Onley, D S, 429
Ordóñez, L, 444
O'Reilly, C A, III, 441
Orey, M, 430, 443, 446
Organ, D W, 435
Orlando, Janet, 104
Orpheus Chamber Orchestra, 334
Orvis, K A, 432
Osborn, A F, 265, 444
Osland, J S, 426
Ostroff, C, 41, 425, 435
Ostroff, F, 454
Oswick, C, 452
Otellini, Paul, 318, 397–399
Overfelt, M, 443
Overman, S, 428
Ozeki, C, 427
Ozzie, Ray, 400

P

Pace, Peter, 256
Paez, D, 440
Paine, L, 424
Paint the Town Red, 235
Painter, K, 431
Pal's Sudden Service, 318
Palmeri, C, 428
Palmieri, Victor H, 240
Palmisano, Samuel J, 182, 354

Palo Alto Research Center, 237
Parise, S, 454
Park, A, 432
Park, B, 428
Parker, A, 440, 443
Parker, C P, 449
Parker, G M, 444
Parker, J, 447
Parker, K, 431
Parker, S K, 434
Parker Follett, M, 423
Parks, L, 431
Parsons, C, 55, 204, 425
Parsons, T, 453
Pasmore, W A, 434
Pasternack, B A, 425
Pasternak, C, 449
Patterson, F, 429
Patterson, M, 453
Patton, G K, 435
Paul, R J, 439
Paulson, Hank, 438
Paulus, P B, 444
Paunonen, S V, 432
Payne, S C, 435
Peabody, M, 449
Pearce, C L, 366, 422, 449, 452
Pearce, J L, 449
Pearson, C M, 444
Pecchia, Joy, 235
Peck, Kelly, 229
Peck, M Scott, 385, 453
Pedigo, P R, 422
Pelton, Christine, 196
Pence, E C, 428
Pendelton, W C, 428
Peng, T K, 448
PepsiCo, 51, 81, 108, 231, 451
Perlmutter, H V, 426
Perlow, L, 442
Perrewé, Pamela L, 168, 429, 435,
    449
Perry, N J, 439
Perry-Smith, J E, 440
Peters, L H, 451
Peters, Susan, 152
Peterson, M F, 425
Peterson, S J, 424, 426, 438, 439
Peterson, T O, 430, 437
Petty, R E, 431, 433
Petzinger, T, Jr., 430
Pfeffer, Jeffrey, 5, 334, 422, 431, 439, 440,
    443, 444, 445, 448, 455
Pfizer, 108
Pharmacia, 185
Philips, 65
Phillip Morris, 367
Phillips, J S, 428, 450
Piccolo, R F, 434, 451
Pihulyk, A, 447

Pinchot, E, 453
Pinchot, G, 453
Pinder, C C, 434, 436
Pink, D H, 134
Pinkley, R L, 446
Pitney Bowes, 367
Pitts, R A, 453, 455
Plante & Moran, 18
Platten, P E, 437
Plattner, Hasso, 177, 293
Plomin, R, 432
Ployhart, R E, 441
Podsakoff, P M, 428, 438, 449,
    451
podTraining, 318
Pohlmann, J T, 451
PointRoll, 290
Poland, T D, 435
Pollard, S, 444
Polycarpou, M P, 445
PolyGram, 69
Polzer, J T, 440
Pomeroy, Ann, 362, 447, 448, 451
Poon, M, 444
Pope, Charles, 234
Porath, C L, 437
Pornpitakpan, C, 448
Porras, J I, 455
Port, O, 427
Porter, C O L H, 436
Porter, L W, 428, 449
Posner, B Z, 439
Postmes, T, 440
Potter, John, 200
Potter, P W, 448
Powell, B C, 435
Powell, G N, 436
Powers, D E, 430
Prasad, S B, 427
Pratt, M G, 430
Prause, J, 429
Premack, S L, 435
Pressler, Paul, 231
PricewaterhouseCoopers, 108
Prichard, J, 434
Priem, D A, 27
Priem, R L, 424
Prince, Charles O, III, 345–347
Principal Financial Group, 155
Procter & Gamble, 206, 253, 328,
    330
Progress Energy, 112
Prospero, M A, 422, 439
Pruitt, B H, 436
Prusak, L, 423, 441, 443
Pryzbylski, M, 446
Pugh, S D, 433
Puranam, P, 453
Purdy, K, 434
Purkis, Tim, 331

Q
Qualcomm, 65, 447
Quantum, 82
Quinn, J B, 455
Quinn, R, 430, 451
Quirin, J J, 435
Qwest, 26–27

R
Rachlin, H, 439
Radosevich, D J, 437
Rafferty, A E, 451
Ragins, B R, 106, 429
Rahim, M Afzalur, 287, 445,
    449
Raia, Anthony, 336, 449
Raiffa, H, 443
Rains, S A, 447
Raju, N S, 455
Rand Corporation, 267
Randal, A E, 441
Randall, A T, 434
Randolph, W Alan, 334–335, 449
Rao, A, 450
Rapaport, A, 442
Rapoport, R, 436
Rapp, A, 449
Rasheed, A M A, 27, 424
Rasley, J, 445
Raven, Bertram, 331, 448, 449
Raver, J L, 446
Raymark, P H, 431
Realo, A, 427
Rechner, P L, 445
Reck, R R, 446
Reed, D, 422
Reeve, C L, 432
Reichers, A E, 440
Reider, M H, 441
Reilly, Matthew, 411
Reilly, R, 438
Reingold, J, 453
Reinhardt, A, 433, 454
Renn, R W, 432
Rensvold, R B, 204
Renwick, P A, 449, 450
Renz, G L, 433
Reynolds Fisher, S, 455
Reynolds, S J, 424
Rich, G A, 428, 451
Richey, R G, 435
Richmond, R, 454
Ricklefs, R, 439
Riddle, Helen, 269
Riggs Fuller, S, 442
Rinaldi, Paul, 255
Riordan, C A, 450
Rips, L J, 428

Robb, D, 362
Robbins, S P, 444
Roberson, L, 429
Robert, C, 427
Robert W Baird & Co., 149
Roberto, M A, 448
Roberts, D, 429, 443, 455
Roberts, Karlene, 224, 427
Roberts, L M, 423, 430, 450
Roberts, R D, 433
Robertson, I T, 432, 453
Robertson, P J, 455
Robinson, S L, 450
Robison, J, 446
Rockmann, K W, 430
Rodgers, R, 437, 455
Rodriquez-Lopez, A, 432
Roethlisberger, F J, 446
Rogelberg, S G, 436
Rogers, Carl, 17, 304, 446
Rogers, D L, 437, 455
Rogers, L E, 454
Rogers, P, 443
Rohn, R, 437
Rollins, Kevin, 250
Roper, G, 445
Ropp, S A, 445
Rosato, D, 450
Rosch, E, 428
Rosen, B, 442, 449
Rosen, C C, 437, 450
Rosenbaum, A, 445
Rosenbush, S, 447
Rosener, Judy B, 102, 422
Rosenfeld, P, 450
Rosenstein, B, 446
Rosenzweig, J E, 382
Rosenzweig, M R, 428
Ross, Jerry, 258–259, 432, 435, 443
Ross, M, 430
Rosse, J G, 440
Rossett, A, 438
Roth, D, 454
Roth, P L, 431
Rothstein, M, 432
Rotter, Julian B, 133, 432
Rounds, J, 431
Rourke, D L, 444
Rousculp, M D, 423
Roush, P, 438
Rousseau, D M, 441
Rowe, Alan J, 254, 257, 443
Rowe, Anita, 102, 429, 444
Rowe, John, 401
Rowley, T J, 453
Royal Dutch Shell, 46, 92
Rubes, Linda, 229
Rubin, H, 423
Rubin, R, 445
Rubin, R B, 430

Rubin, R S, 451
Rucker, D D, 433
Rudder Finn, 26
Ruddy, T M, 441
Ruffolo, Robert, 186
Rupp, D E, 436
Russell, J A, 433, 447
Rutte, C G, 442
Ryan, A M, 436
Ryan, Richard M, 158, 434, 438
Rynes, S L, 423

S

Saari, L M, 436, 437, 439
Sackett, P R, 432
Sackmann, S, 452
Safvenbom, R, 442
Saks, A M, 425, 431
Salin, D, 446
Salvemini, N, 438
Salz, P A, 443, 455
Samsung Electronics, 322
Sanchez, J I, 437
Sanchez, William, 68
Sandberg, J, 422, 446, 449, 450, 451
Sandberg, W R, 445
Sanghi, Steve, 366–367
Santamaria, Jason, 391
SAP, 177, 293, 436
Sapient, 391
Sapolsky, R, 432
Sashkin, M, 423
Sauley, K S, 436
Saunders, C, 427, 442
Saunders, D M, 447
SBC Communications, Inc., 182
Scandura, T, 427
Scaturro, Peter K, 346
Schaefer, Amy, 210
Schafer, W D, 443
Schaubroeck, J, 432, 438, 444
Scheer, L K, 436
Schein, Edgar H, 49, 225, 227, 424, 440, 452
Schellens, T, 440
Schiano, W, 442
Schirmer, J M, 446
Schleicher, D J, 435
Schlender, B, 433
Schlesinger, L A, 413
Schlosser, J, 423
Schmidt, F L, 422, 433, 435
Schmidt, J R, 443
Schmidt, S M, 448, 450
Schminke, M, 436
Schmonsees, Bob, 124, 430
Schneider, B, 332
Schneider, R J, 438
Schneider, S L, 428

Schonberger, Richard J, 12, 423
Schonfeld, E, 133
Schriesheim, C A, 435, 448, 449, 450, 451, 452
Schultz, Howard, 304
Schurer Lambert, L, 436
Schuster, Judith, 130
Schwartz, Jonathan, 318
Schwartz, N D, 425, 454
Schwartz, S H, 425
Schweiger, D M, 444, 445
Schwenk, C R, 285, 445
Scoble, Robert, 273
Scott, H Lee, Jr., 302
Scott, K S, 422
Scott, S G, 442
Scott, W R, 430, 453
Scrushy, Richard M, 331
Scullen, S, 431, 438
Scully, J P, 446
Seagate Technology, 234
Sears, 98, 184
Sebenius, J K, 446
Sedona Center, 51, 53
Seeman, P, 443
Segal, J A, 430, 443
Segal, N L, 435
Seglin, J L, 438
Seibert, S E, 430, 432
Seidel, M L, 450
Seijts, G H, 453
Selden, L, 423
Seligman, D, 430
Seligman, M E P, 423
Sellers, P, 440
Selvarajan, T T, 433
Senge, Peter, 399, 414
Serchuk, D, 446
Service-Winners International, 63
Seyle, D C, 440
Sgro, J A, 428
Shaffer, M A, 427
Shalley, C E, 441
Shamir, B, 360, 450, 451
Shanock, L, 434
Shaper Walters, L, 449
Shapiro, D L, 445
Sharer, Kevin, 340
Sharkey, T W, 449
Sharkey, W F, 430
Sharma, C L, 426
Sharpe, R, 451
Shaver, K G, 434
Shavitt, S, 427
Shaw, J D, 436, 439
Shaw, K N, 436, 437
Shay, J P, 427
Shea, C M, 441
Shea, T F, 429
Sheats, P, 230, 440

Shebesta, Nancy Talbot, 209
Sheehan, M, 453
Sheer, C P, 453
Sheldon, K M, 431
Shellenbarger, S, 448
Shelly, R K, 451
Shen, Bern, 398
Shepard, S B, 453
Sherman, J D, 454
Sherman, J W, 428
Sherman, M P, 443, 444
Shin, Y, 425, 442, 445, 454
Shipper, F, 7, 422, 451, 453
Shirkey, C, 440
Short, J F, Jr., 430
Shultz, E E, 427
Siegel, Robert, 400
Siegman, A W, 447
Siemens, 78
Sikes, W, 454
Sillince, J A A, 453
Silver, S, 425, 436
Silver, W S, 431, 438
Silvester, J, 429
Simmering, M J, 437
Simmons, R, 434
Simon, Herbert A, 251, 443
Simonetti, Ellen, 319
Simpson, L, 424
Sims, H P Jr., 451
Sine, W D, 454
Sinegal, Jim, 422
Singelis, T M, 430
Singell, L, 450
Singh, H, 453
Singh-Manoux, A, 433
Sitkin, S B, 441
Sivasubramaniam, N, 452
Skilling, Jeff, 33–34
Skinner, B F, 212–213, 214, 439
Skinner, N, 311
Slater, S F, 453
Slocum, J W, 438, 453, 455
Slywotzky, A, 454
Small, D, 446
Smalley, Kim, 83
Smilie, L D, 432
Smircich, L, 45, 425
Smith, A, 445
Smith, Douglas K, 232–233, 430, 440, 441, 445
Smith, Frederick W, 183, 202, 437, 438
Smith, H L, 454
Smith, M L, 422, 448
Smith, P B, 426
Smith, R E, 430
Smither, J W, 438
Smithey-Fulmer, I, 446
Smola, K W, 435
Smoll, F L, 430

Snow, Tower, 301
Snyder, D, 444
Snyder, M, 126, 431
Snyderman, B B, 434
Solectron, 391
Solmon, Lewis, 174
Solomon, Robert, 432
Sonnenfeld, J A, 423, 452
Sonnentag, S, 434
Sopp, T, 430, 445
Sorensen, K L, 425
Sorenstam, Annika, 187, 437
Sosik, J J, 442, 452
South African Breweries (SAB), 359
Southwest Airlines, 5, 12, 30, 44–46, 50, 232, 260, 276–277, 385, 422, 425
Sparrowe, R T, 448
Spearman, Charles, 136
Spears, L C, 368, 452
Spears, R, 440
Spector, B, 454
Spector, P E, 432, 435
Speer, T L, 427
Spencer, J, 447
Spiker, B K, 424
Spinath, F M, 432
Spiros, R K, 440
Spitzer, D R, 436, 439
Spitzmüller, C, 436
Spragins, E E, 429
Spranger, J L, 429
Spreitzer, G M, 430, 441, 449, 451, 454
Squire, R L, 428
Srinivasan, D, 452
Srivastava, S, 430
Srygley Mouton, J, 440
Stack, L, 444
Stahl, G K, 427, 428
Stahl, M J, 434
Stajkovic, A D, 431
Stalker, G M, 387–389, 454
Stambor, Z, 430, 433
Stamps, D, 428, 444
Stamps, J, 442
Stankov, L, 433
Starbucks, 3, 304, 386
Stark, S, 432
Staw, Barry M, 258–259, 429, 432, 435, 440, 443, 448
Stead, W E, 424
Stearns, J, 53, 425
Steel, R P, 437
Steelcase, 156
Steenkamp, J-B E M, 436
Stefik, Mark, 237
Stein, Robert, 24
Steiner, D D, 433
Stephan, W G, 429
Stephens, G K, 443
Sternberg, R J, 443

Stetzer, A, 428
Stevens, C K, 428, 430
Stevens, R J, 429
Stevenson, H, 431
Stevenson, W B, 449
Stewart, A J, 434
Stewart, Martha, 349
Stewart, Thomas A, 249, 250, 443, 448, 454
Stinglhamber, F, 434
Stiwne, D, 442
Stokes, Pat, 286
Stoll, C, 443
Stollak, G E, 428
Stone, B, 424, 444, 453
Stone, E F, 435
Streufert, S, 353
Strober, M H, 438
Stroh, L K, 427, 428
Stuart, Jim, 366, 452
Stybel, L J, 449
Styles, I M, 432
Subich, L M, 432
Suciu, P, 441
Sulkowitz, K J, 449
Sullivan, C T, 422
Sullivan, Sherry E, 59
Sulsky, L M, 428
Sumner, G A, 426
Sun Microsystems, 318, 320, 448
Sundstrom, E, 438
Susskind, J, 428
Sutton, C D, 435
Sutton, R I, 422, 429, 443, 448, 455
Sutton, R M, 448
Swann, W B, Jr., 440
Swap, W C, 441
Swartout, Kathy, 136
Swidarski, Thomas, 302
Swissair, 71
Symonds, W C, 440
Sytsma, M R, 438
Szumal, J L, 47, 425
Szymanski, K, 442

T

Tabei, Junko, 150
Taber, T D, 452
Tafarodi, R W, 430
Tahmincioglu, E, 436, 443
Takeuchi, R, 428
Tam, P-W, 454
Tamkins, M, 41, 425
Tannen, Deborah, 311, 313, 447
Target, 16, 386
Tasa, K, 453
Taylor, A, III, 426
Taylor, C, 435, 439
Taylor, Frederick, 151, 186, 275
Taylor, John, 137

Taylor, M A, 430
Taylor, M S, 437
Tayman, J, 423
Teaching Commission, 173
Telecom Development Company, 63
Tepper, B J, 435, 436, 448
Terlaak, A, 454
Tesluk, P E, 442, 449
Testa, M R, 426
Tett, R P, 432
Teuchmann, K, 433
Texas Instruments, 226
Thakkar, V, 428
Thayer, P W, 434
Thierry, H, 436
ThinkEngine Network, 133
Thomas, A S, 426
Thomas, E, 426, 448
Thomas, J B, 430
Thomas, Kenneth, 158–159, 161, 434
Thompson, D E, 429
Thompson, J A, 432
Thompson, James D, 381, 453
Thompson, L, 441, 442, 444
Thompson, M S, 447
Thompson, P, 442
Thoresen, C J, 435
Thorndike, Edward L, 212, 439
Thornton, B T, 443
Thornton, E, 441
Thornton, G C, III, 429
3M, 85
Tichy, N M, 425
Tiedens, Larissa, 143
Tiegreen, S B, 432
Tierney, P, 431
Tierney, Thomas J, 418, 455
Tilin, A, 454
Timken Co., 209
Timmerman, T A, 432
Timmins, F, 447
Tjosvold, Dean, 275, 278, 444, 448, 449
Tkaczyk, C, 433, 438, 448
Tluchowska, M, 440
Toda, M, 427
Toegel, G, 438
Toh, S M, 427
Tokar, D M, 432
Tolliver, J M, 450
Tomsho, R, 436
Tonnessen, F E, 442
Tornow, W W, 438
Toro, 286
Tott, M, 447
Totterdell, P, 433
Towler, A J, 438, 452
Townsend, A M, 442
Townsend, B, 106, 429
Toyota, 385, 423, 443, 453
Tracey, J B, 448

Trader Joe's, 20
Trafimow, D, 430
Trapnell, P D, 430
Triandis, H C, 426
Trilogy, 53–54
Trompenaars, Fons, 66, 74, 75, 426, 427
Trope, Y, 428
Trottman, M, 443
Trout, Gil, 199
True Value Co., 40
Trumble, Bryson, 3
Trumbull, M, 423
Tsai, J L, 69, 433
Tsoukas, H, 452
Tsui, A S, 438
Tucci, Joseph M, 278, 286
Tucker, M A, 424
Tuckman, Bruce W, 227, 233, 440
Tugade, M M, 433
Tully, S, 425, 428, 451, 454
Tung, Rosalie L, 284, 445
Turban, D B, 431, 434
Turner, K L, 455
Turner, R H, 430
Tushman, M L, 404, 441
Twenge, J M, 451
Tyco, 333
Tyler, K, 427, 428, 433, 444
Tymon, W G, Jr., 434
Tyson, Laura D'Andrea, 16, 423, 446

U

Udegbe, I B, 452
Uhl-Bien, M, 431
Ulrich, D, 423, 455
UMB Financial Corp., 199–200
Underwood, R, 235
United Airlines, 234, 301
United Parcel Service (UPS), 315, 391
Urban Outfitters, 209
Urban Trust Bank, 132
Ursiny, Ted, 277, 440, 444
Ury, W, 446
US Airways, 406
Useem, J, 443, 452
Uzzi, B, 426, 449

V

Vafeas, N, 453
Valacich, J S, 442, 445
Valcke, M, 440
Valy-Durbin, S J, 427
Vande Berg, M, 427
Vandebroek, Sophie, 117–118
Vandello, J A, 427
Vandenberg, R J, 432
Van Der Vegt, G S, 426, 441
Van Der Zee, K I, 431

Van De Vliert, E, 426
van Eerde, W, 436
Van Fleet, D D, 437, 452
Van Fleet, E W, 437
Vangen, S, 441
Van Iddekinge, C H, 431
Van Keer, H, 440
van Kleef, G A, 446
Van Maanen, J, 425
van Mierlo, H, 442
Van Nuys, K E, 425
Van Slyke, C, 427, 442
Van Velsor, E, 422, 439
Van Vianen, A E M, 427
Van Vugt, M, 440
Van Yperen, N W, 435
Varma, A, 427
Vasilopoulos, N L, 438
Veiga, J F, 422, 440
Velasco, Samuel, 229
Vera, D, 432, 455
Verdini, W A, 438
Vergano, D, 424
Verizon Communications, 4
Versant, Inc., 145–146, 147
Viera, L, Jr., 450
Vijayaraghavan, V, 438
Virgin Group, 329
Visser, P S, 432
Viswesvaran, C, 435
Vlist, R V D, 429
Vogel, D R, 427, 442
Vogelstein, F, 422, 443, 449
Vogt, D S, 430
Volkema, Michael, 280
Volkema, R J, 442
Volvo, 239
Von Glinow, M, 438, 455
Vonk, R, 429, 450
Vredenburgh, D, 441
Vroom, Victor H, 181–183, 436, 437

W

W L Gore & Associates, 120, 260, 387
Wagner, J A, III, 442, 444
Wagner, S, 449
Wah, L, 423
Waisglass, David, 48, 350
Waitt, Ted, 276–277
Wakabayashi, M, 452
Waldman, D A, 360, 438
Walgreens, 367
Walker, Larry, 410
Walker, R, 446
Wall, J A, Jr., 444
Wall, T D, 449, 453
Wall, T, 435
Wallick, Del, 209

Wal-Mart, 49, 147-148, 302, 375–376, 386, 400, 446, 452
Walsh, E T, 432
Walsh, J T, 436
Walt Disney, 297, 349
Walton, Sam, 49, 376
Walton, W, 423
Wanberg, C R, 455
Wang, Christine, 82
Wang, M, 428
Wanous, J P, 435, 436, 440
Ward, C, 432
Warner Music Group, 258
Warr, P, 431
Warren, D E, 444
Waste Management Inc., 61
Waters, E, 440
Waters, J A, 308, 447
Watkins, Bill, 234
Watkins, Sherron, 30, 32
Watson, John B, 439
Watson, T W, 433
Watt, J D, 435
Wayne, S J, 441, 448, 450, 452
Webber, A M, 453, 454
Webber, S S, 435
Weber, J, 238, 422, 424, 426
Weber, Max, 381, 453
Weddigen, R, 446
Wegener, D T, 433
Weick, Karl E, 383, 453
Weidemann, Sue, 302
Weigert, A, 441
Weil, J, 426
Weill, Sanford I, 345–346
Weimer, D, 446, 448
Weinberg, R A, 432
Weingart, L R, 440
Weinstein, M, 425, 438, 439, 443, 444, 452
Weintraub, A, 424
Weiss, D J, 162, 435
Weiss, G, 446
Weiss, J W, 442
Weiss, R M, 453
Weissman, Adam, 279
Weitzen, Jeff, 276–277
Welch, D, 426
Welch, Jack, 205, 331, 362, 437, 438, 448, 450, 452, 453
Welch, Suzy, 205, 331, 437, 438, 448, 450, 452, 453
Weldon, William C, 345
Wellen, J M, 442
Wellner, A S, 438
Wells, M, 450
Wells, S J, 185, 425, 438
Wells Fargo, 367

Wen Jiabao, 89
Werther, W B, 448
Wesolowski, M A, 449
Wesson, M J, 436
West, B, 424
West, M A, 262, 443, 445, 453
Western Electric, 9
Wexler, Alan, 391
Wheatley, W J, 431
Wheeler, J V, 441
Wheeler, Michael, 24
Wheeler, S C, 431
Whirlpool, 77
Whitacre, Edward E, Jr., 182
White, C S, 451
White, E, 437
White, K, 428
White, Margaret, 414, 455
Whitefield, Lydia, 206
Whiting, Vicki, 59
Whitsett, D A, 152
Whitwam, Dale, 77
Whole Foods Market, 20, 210, 226
Wiatrowski, W J, 438
Wicks, A C, 441
Wiebe, F A, 442
Wiechmann, D, 436
Wilburn, K O, 446
Wild Oats, 20
Wilderom, C P M, 425, 427
Wildmon, Donald E, 274
Wiley, C, 450
Wilk, L A, 437
Wilk, S L, 432
Wilkinson, J, 448
Williams, B, 408, 432
Williams, K, 442
Williams, R, 428
Williams, S, 442
Williams-Sonoma, Inc., 42, 44
Wilson, C L, 7, 422
Winerman, L, 428, 447
Winger, A R, 454
Winslow, E K, 152
Wiseman, Richard, 134
Witt, L A, 432, 452
Woellert, L, 428
Wolf, B, 441
Wood, D J, 453
Wood, J V, 430
Wood, R, 123, 437
Wood, S J, 453
Wood, W, 447
Woodman, R W, 434
Woodring, Kim, 130
Woods, Earl, 122
Woods, Tiger, 122, 187
Woodward, K L, 445

Woodyard, C, 443
Woolley, Theresa, 196
Wooten, K, 432, 436
WorldCom, 26, 333, 345, 401
Worrell, D L, 424
Woyke, E, 423
Wright, P M, 437
Wright, S C, 282, 445
Wright, T A, 423
Wyeth, 186

X

Xavier, S, 451
Xerox, 112, 117–118, 325–326, 361, 430

Y

Yahoo, 226
Yamaguchi, S, 430
Yamazaki, Y, 80
Yammarino, F J, 360, 450, 451, 452
Yang, H-C, 444
Yeo, G B, 432
Ying, Y-W, 69
Youn, J Y, 448
Young, S, 425
Yu, R, 428
Yukl, G, 422, 448
Yun, G, 450
Yun, S, 451

Z

Zaccaro, S J, 442, 450
Zacharay, G P, 426
Zalenik, Abraham, 340, 450
Zander, A, 440
Zapf, D, 435
Zastrow, C, 431
Zelley, E D, 447
Zellner, W, 439
Zemke, Ron, 202, 423, 431, 437, 438, 441, 454
Zhang, C, 427
Zhang Guangming, 255
Zhao, H, 430
Ziedonis, A A, 443
Zielinski, D, 424, 437
Zijlstra, F R H, 434
Zimmerman, R D, 425, 440
Zivnuska, S, 452
Zollo, M, 453
Zoppi, K, 446
Zorn, T E, Jr., 446
Zuboff, S, 422, 441, 449
Zuk, Y, 430

A

Accountability practices, 111
Affirmative action, 104
Aggressive style, 307
Alternative dispute resolution (ADR), 288
Analytics, 249
Anticipatory socialization, 51
Assertive style, 307
Attention, 92
Attitude, 135
Availability heuristic, 252

B

Benchmarking, 402
Blog, 318
Bounded rationality, 251
Brainstorming, 265
Bureaucracy, 381

C

Care perspective, 32
Causal attributions, 98
Centralized decision making, 388
Change
    forces of change, 399–401
    Kotter's eight steps, 405–407
    learning organizations, 414–419
    Lewin's change model, 402–403
    organization development, 407–409
    resistance to change, 410–414
    systems model, 403–405
Change and acquisition, 53
Closed system, 380
Coalition, 337
Coercive power, 330–331
Cognitions, 119
Cognitive categories, 92–93
Collectivist culture, 74
Commitment to change, 411
Communication
    active listening, 309–311
    barriers to effective, 303–305
    blogs, 318–319
    defined, 299
    electronic mail, 316–317
    group support systems, 319–320
    handheld devices, 317–318
    Internet/intranet/extranet, 314–316
    interpersonal communication, 305–309
    linguistic style, 311–313
    perceptual process model, 300–303
    teleworking, 320
    videoconferencing, 319

Communication competence, 305
Conflict
    cross-cultural conflict, 282–284
    defined, 275
    intergroup conflict, 280–282
    managing conflict, 284–289
    modern view, 275–278
    negotiating, 289–291
    personality conflict, 278–280
Consensus, 265
Consideration, 351
Contingency approach, 13
Contingency approach to organization
        design, 387
Contingency factors, 354
Continuous reinforcement, 215
Core job dimensions, 154
Creativity, 259
Cross-cultural training, 81
Cross-functionalism, 237
Cultural intelligence, 71
Culture shock, 81

D

Decentralized decision making, 388
Decision making
    creativity, 259–261
    defined, 249
    escalation of commitment,
        256–259
    group decision making,
        261–264
    group problem-solving techniques,
        265–268
    knowledge management, 252–254
    models, 249–252
    participative management, 264–265
    styles, 254–256
Decision-making style, 254
Delphi technique, 267
Development practices, 112
Developmental relationship strength, 57
Devil's advocacy, 285
Dialectic method, 286
Distributive justice, 178–179
Diversity
    affirmative action, 103–104
    defined, 101
    increasing in the workforce, 105–109
    layers of diversity, 102–103
    managing diversity, 104–105,
        110–112
Diversity of developmental relationships, 57
Dysfunctional conflict, 276

E

E-business, 18
85–15 rule, 12
Electronic mail, 316
Emotional intelligence, 140–141
Emotions, 138
Empowerment, 333
Enacted values, 43
Encounter phase, 52–53
Equity sensitivity, 176
Equity theory
    defined, 175
    individual–organization exchange
        relationship, 175–176
    negative and positive inequity, 176
    organizational justice, 178–179
    perceived inequity, 176–177
    practical lessons, 179–180
Escalation of commitment, 256
Espoused values, 42
Ethics
    decision tree, 29–30
    defined, 25
    gender variations, 30–32
    general moral principles, 32–33
    model of ethical behavior, 25–29
    organizational influences, 26–28, 33–34
Ethnocentrism, 68
Expatriate, 79
Expectancy, 181
Expectancy theory, 181
Expert power, 332
Explicit knowledge, 253
External factors, 99
External forces for change, 399
External locus of control, 135
Extinction, 214
Extranet, 314
Extrinsic rewards, 209

F

Feedback
    behavioral outcomes, 204–205
    defined, 202
    failure of, 207
    providing effective, 201–202
    recipient's perspective, 203–204
    three sources, 203
    two functions, 202–203
    upward and 360-degree feedback,
        205–207
Formal group, 226
Functional conflict, 276
Fundamental attribution bias, 100

G

Glass ceiling, 105
Global mangers
    cross-cultural competency, 70–71
    cultural perceptions of time, 76–77
    ethnocentrism, 68–69
    foreign assignments, 78–83
    GLOBE project, 71–74, 77–78
    high-context vs. low-context cultures,
        75–76
    Hofstede study, 70
    individualism vs. collectivism, 74–75
    societal and organizational cultures,
        66–67
GLOBE project, 71–74, 77–78
Goal, 186
Goal commitment, 189
Goal difficulty, 187
Goal setting
    defined, 186
    insights from research, 187–190
    motivational mechanisms, 186–187
    practical applications, 190–192
Goal specificity, 187
Group, 225
Group cohesiveness, 229
Group support systems (GSSs), 319
Groups and teamwork
    developing teamwork competencies, 233
    formal and informal groups, 226–227
    group development process, 227–229
    group member roles, 229–231
    groupthink, 240–241
    norms, 231–232
    self-managed teams, 236–238
    social loafing, 241
    team building, 234
    trust, 234–236
    virtual teams, 238–240
Groupthink, 240

H

Hawthorne legacy, 9
High-context cultures, 75
Human capital, 15
Humility, 134–135
Hygiene factors, 153

I

Impression management, 338
Improving performance
    feedback; *see* Feedback
    organizational reward systems, 208–212
    positive reinforcement, 212–217
Individual differences
    attitudes, 135
    emotions, 138–141
    intelligence and cognitive abilities, 136–137

Individual differences—*Cont.*
    locus of control, 133–135
    personality, 131–133
    self-concept, 119–120
    self-efficacy, 121–124
    self-esteem, 120–121
    self-management, 127–131
    self-monitoring, 125–126
Individualistic culture, 74
Influence, 327–330
Informal group, 226
In-group exchange, 363
Initiating structure, 351
Instrumentality, 182
Intelligence, 136
Interactional justice, 178–179
Intermittent reinforcement, 215
Internal factors, 99
Internal forces for change, 401
Internal locus of control, 133
Internet, 314
Interpersonal communication,
    305–309
Intranet, 314
Intrinsic motivation, 154
Intrinsic rewards, 209

J

Job design
    biological and perceptual-motor
        approaches, 156–157
    defined, 150
    job characteristics model, 154–156
    job enlargement, 151
    job enrichment, 152–153
    job rotation, 151–152
    mechanistic approach, 151
Job enlargement, 151
Job enrichment, 152–153
Job rotation, 151–152
Job satisfaction
    causes, 162–164
    correlates and consequences, 164–167
    defined, 162
Judgmental heuristics, 251
Justice perspective, 31

K

Knowledge management (KM), 253

L

Law of effect, 212
Leader trait, 348
Leadership
    behavioral styles theory, 351–352
    defined, 347
    Fiedler's contingency model, 352–354
    full-range model, 358–362

Leadership—*Cont.*
    Hersey and Blanchard's situational
        leadership theory, 357–358
    leader–member exchange model, 362–365
    level 5 leadership, 367–369
    path–goal theory, 354–357
    servant-leadership, 365–367
    shared leadership, 365
    trait theory, 348–351
Leadership prototypes, 348
Learned helplessness, 121
Learning capabilities, 415
Learning modes, 417
Learning organization
    building learning capabilities, 415–417
    defined, 414
    leadership, 418–419
Legitimate power, 332
Line managers, 379
Linguistic style, 311
Listening, 309
Low-context cultures, 75

M

Maintenance roles, 229
Management, 6
Management by objectives (MBO), 186
Managers, 7–8; *see also* Global managers
Managing diversity, 104
McGregor's Theory X and Y; *see* Theory X;
    Theory Y
Mechanistic organizations, 386
Mentoring, 56–59
Met expectations, 163
Mission statement, 403
Monochronic time, 77
Motivation
    defined, 147
    equity theory, 175–180
    expectancy theory, 181–185
    goal setting; *see* Goal setting
    implementing theories, 192–194
    intrinsic motivation, 157–161
    job design; *see* Job design
    job performance model, 147–148
    job satisfaction; *see* Job satisfaction
    need theories, 149–150
    work–family conflict, 167–169
Motivators, 152

N

Need for achievement, 149
Need for affiliation, 150
Need for power, 150
Needs, 149
Negative inequity, 176
Negative reinforcement, 213
Negotiation, 289
Noise, 302

Nominal group technique, 266
Nonassertive style, 307
Nonverbal communication, 307
Norm, 231
Normative beliefs, 46

O

Onboarding, 52–53
Open system, 380
Operant behavior, 212–213
Optimizing, 251
Organic organizations, 386
Organization
    defined, 377
    learning organizations, 414–419
    mechanistic vs. organic, 387–390
    new style vs. old style, 390
    organization charts, 378–379
    organizational effectiveness, 383–387
    organizational metaphors, 379–383
    virtual organizations, 391–392
Organization chart, 378
Organization development, 407
Organizational behavior (OB)
    contingency approach to management,
        13–14
    defined, 8
    human relations movement, 9–11
    human and social capital, 14–16
    Internet and e-business, 18–19
    positive organizational behavior, 16–18
    total quality management movement,
        11–13
Organizational citizenship behaviors
    (OCBs), 165
Organizational culture
    defined, 41
    embedding culture, 49–51
    four functions, 44–46
    layers, 42–44
    mentoring, 56–59
    outcomes, 48–49
    types, 46–48
Organizational effectiveness, 383–387
Organizational politics
    definition and domain, 335–338
    employee empowerment,
        333–335
    impression management, 338–340
    influence, 327–330
    keeping in check, 340–341
    power, 330–333
Organizational reward systems, 208–211
Organizational socialization
    defined, 51
    socialization research, 54–56
    three-phase model, 51–54
Ostracism, 231
Out-group exchange, 363

P

Participative management, 264
Pay for performance, 210
Perception
    causal attributions, 98–101
    defined, 91
    managerial implications, 96–98
    social information model,
        91–96
Performance; *see* Improving performance
Personality
    attitudes, 135
    big five personality dimensions,
        131–133
    defined, 131
    intelligence and cognitive abilities,
        136–137
    locus of control, 133–135
Personality conflict, 279
Politics; *see* Organizational politics
Polychronic time, 77
Positive inequity, 176
Positive organizational behavior (POB), 18
Positive reinforcement
    cognitive consequences, 213–214
    defined, 213
    schedules of reinforcement, 214–217
    shaping behavior, 217
    Skinner's operant conditioning model,
        212–213
    Thorndike's law of effect, 212
Proactive personality, 132
Problem, 249
Procedural justice, 178–179
Programmed conflict, 284
Project GLOBE, 71–74, 77–78
Punishment, 214

R

Rational model, 249
Readiness, 357
Recruitment practices, 112
Referent power, 333
Repetitive motion disorders (RMDs), 157
Representativeness heuristic, 252
Resistance to change, 410
Respondent behavior, 212–213
Reward power, 330–331
Rewards, 208–211
Roles, 229

S

Satisficing, 252
Schema, 92–93
Self-concept, 119
Self-efficacy, 121–124
Self-esteem, 120
Self-managed teams, 236

Self-management, 127–131
Self-monitoring, 125
Self-serving bias, 100
Self-talk, 130
Sense of choice, 159
Sense of competence, 159
Sense of meaningfulness, 159
Sense of progress, 159
Servant-leadership, 366
Shaping, 217
Shared leadership, 365
Situational theories, 352
Social capital, 16
Social loafing, 241
Social perception; *see* Perception
Social power, 330
Socialization; *see* Organizational
    socialization
Societal culture, 66
Span of control, 379
Staff personnel, 379
Stereotype, 93
Strategic constituency, 386
Strategic plan, 403

T

Tacit knowledge, 253
Target elements of change, 403
Task roles, 229
Team, 232
Team building, 234
Teamwork; *see* Groups and teamwork
Teleworking, 320
Theory X, 10, 11
Theory Y, 10, 11
360–degree feedback, 206
Total quality management
    (TQM), 12
Transactional leadership, 359
Transformational leadership,
    359
Trust, 235

U

Underemployment, 105
Unity of command principle, 377
Upward feedback, 206

V

Valence, 182
Value attainment, 163
Values, 42
Virtual team, 239

W

Withdrawal cognitions, 166